9 92540

HEALTH IN ELEMENTARY SCHOOLS

HEALTH IN ELEMENTARY SCHOOLS

Harold J. Cornacchia, Ed.D.

Emeritus Professor of Health Education, San Francisco State University,
San Francisco, California

Larry K. Olsen, Dr.P.H.

Associate Professor, Health Science, Arizona State University,
Tempe, Arizona

Carl J. Nickerson, Ed.D.

Supervisor, Health Education, State Office of Public Instruction,
Olympia, Washington

SIXTH EDITION

WITH 66 ILLUSTRATIONS

TIMES MIRROR/MOSBY
COLLEGE PUBLISHING

ST. LOUIS • TORONTO • SANTA CLARA   1984

Editor: **Nancy Roberson**
Assistant editor: **Kathy Spengel**
Manuscript editor: **Timothy O'Brien**
Design: **Nancy Steinmeyer**
Production: **Kathleen L. Teal**

SIXTH EDITION

Copyright © 1984 by Times Mirror/Mosby College Publishing
A division of The C.V. Mosby Company
11830 Westline Industrial Drive
St. Louis, Missouri 63146

Previous editions copyrighted 1962, 1966, 1970, 1974, 1979

Printed in the United States of America

Library of Congress Cataloging in Publication Data

Cornacchia, Harold J.
  Health in elementary schools.

  Bibliography: p.
  Includes index.
  1. School hygiene. 2. Health education (Elementary)
I. Olsen, Larry K. II. Nickerson, Carl J. III. Title.
LB3405.C58 1983   372.3'7   82-24000
ISBN 0-8016-1076-1

AC/VH/VH 9 8 7 6 5 4 3   02/B/245

PREFACE

Numerous health problems continue to exist in the United States despite the control maintained over such communicable diseases as smallpox, diphtheria, and poliomyelitis through immunizations and improvements in sanitation, housing, and nutrition. Heart disease, high blood pressure, cancer, accidental injuries, stress, sexually transmitted diseases, and misuse and abuse of alcohol, tobacco, and other drugs, among others, are common today. Although elementary school–age children generally are in good health, there are numerous health conditions such as respiratory and gastrointestinal disturbances, vision and hearing problems, emotional difficulties, child neglect and abuse, suicide, drug abuse, teenage pregnancies, and overweight that need to be identified by school personnel, with information and guidance provided for pupils and parents. These conditions are more prevalent among poor and disadvantaged students.

It is presently believed that many of the conditions found among children and adults can be *prevented* or at least be reduced in incidence and severity through the avoidance of *risk factors* and through *life-style modifications*. Since many of the adult conditions are dependent on the habit patterns established in the early years of life, programs in schools that provide health education, health services, and a healthful environment will aid in the establishment of the practices of healthful living and contribute to pupil well-being when conducted in cooperation with the home and the community.

Awareness on the part of parents and the community concerning the need for health education and school health generally has increased in recent years. It is universally recognized today that individuals must assume more responsibility for their own health and that health care involves not only physiological considerations but psychological, sociological, and spiritual emphases as well. Health education is needed because of the high cost of illness and medical care, the health misconceptions that exist among people, the millions and perhaps billions of dollars spent on useless, unnecessary, and frequently harmful products and services in the health marketplace, the media and peer and adult influences on people's behavior, and the vast amount of confusing health information disseminated by individuals, the press, and radio and television.

Health education programs are now supported and sponsored by the American School Health Association, the Association for the Advancement of Health Education, the American Public Health Association, the American Association of School Administrators, the National Association of State Boards of Education, the American Medical Association, the American Academy of Pediatrics, and the National Congress of Parents and Teachers. The federal government has established the Center for Health Promotion and Education in the Centers for Disease Control, Public Health Service, Department of Health and Human Services. In the private sector the National Center for Health Education has been functioning for over 5 years. Approximately 89% of the states have requirements that make provision for health education.

Unfortunately less than 25% of the 1,500 elementary school districts in the United States have health education programs, and so-called comprehensive programs are considerably fewer in number. The legal provisions in states frequently are so loosely written that numerous programs are limited to one or more health topics such as nutrition, drugs, or safety. The term *comprehensive* has been subject to a variety of interpretations, and its meaning as defined in this text has not been implemented to any great extent in U.S. schools. Several problems related to the lack of school finances and the public's demand for a return to teaching the basic subjects have compounded difficulty of developing health instruction programs despite the increased awareness of need and the progress made in the number of programs introduced in recent years.

The writers of this text firmly believe that:

1. Good health is essential to learning.
2. The prevention approach to health and the need for self-care must be started in the early years of life.
3. Schools can play an important role in the promotion and maintenance of the well-being of its students.
4. Health education can be introduced into schools despite present problems.

It follows therefore that teachers—especially at the elementary level—need to understand the nature and purpose of school health programs and must learn their role in such programs. To this end this book has been organized to deal mainly with *health* education—curriculum, learning applied to health education, methods and techniques of teaching, instructional aids, evaluation—and with *health services*, the *healthful school environment*, and *coordination* of the program.

While the book is designed primarily for prospective and in-service teachers, it should also be of interest and value to school health coordinators, curriculum coordinators, principals, superintendents, school board members, and health specialists now serving or working with elementary schools. Public health workers should find the book helpful in clarifying certain problems of educational organization, objectives, curriculum development, supervision, and teaching methods and materials as they relate to the elementary school health program.

The book has three broad purposes: (1) it seeks to help elementary school teachers and school personnel recognize more clearly their responsibilities and their many opportunities for protecting and improving the health of their pupils; (2) it provides the information that teachers want and need to improve their contribution to the health service program in raising the level of healthful school living in those elementary schools in which they serve; and (3) it is concerned with developing understanding and skill in curriculum development, teaching methods, and source materials that will help classroom teachers make a major contribution to the improvement of health in youngsters by doing a better job of health education.

Every effort has been made to present the latest and best in research, practice, and pioneer thinking in school health in light of what is feasible and practical in elementary schools throughout the nation. We have attempted to provide a synthesis of fundamental principles that are generally accepted by professionals and that we in our many years of experience indicate are best for elementary schools. The book has been divided into six parts.

Part One identifies the nature and the purpose of the elementary school health program and the classroom teacher's role in health instruction, health services, and healthful environment.

Part Two covers healthful school living with emphasis on the physical and emotional aspects of the elementary school environment. Attention is focused on the emotional climate in the classroom.

Part Three emphasizes the importance of school health services, including health appraisals, disease control, follow-up and guidance, and emergencies and first aid in protecting and improving the health of pupils.

Part Four highlights the status of health education in the United States today and the administrative problems involved in the implementation of programs. It includes principles of organization, illustrative units useful in teaching, and examples of a variety of popular health instruction programs.

Part Five identifies the principles of learning involved in behavior modification, useful methods of teaching, over 1,200 teacher-tested techniques categorized into 17 health areas by three grade level groups, and instructional aids and sources for health instruction.

Part Six provides understanding of evaluation with practical suggestions for teacher use in the classroom.

The Appendixes provide a handy communicable disease summary for teachers, compulsory immunization laws by state, a sample of health education fiction and nonfiction books, sources of free and low-cost sponsored instructional aids for health teaching, and several evaluation instruments.

Throughout the book we have pointed up the importance of cooperative effort on the part of teachers, parents, community health agencies, physicians, nurses, dentists, and others concerned with child health and safety. These mutually favorable relationships are essential in translating good elementary school health program theory into actual practice. We believe that the health of children calls for the highest possible level of partnership between the school, the home, and the community.

The sixth edition of the text has been completely revised, reorganized, and updated to provide greater clarity and sequence of information as well as to remove redundancies. Two new chapters, "Emotional Climate and the Teacher" (Chapter 4) and "Health Education Approaches" (Chapter 10) have been added. The former includes some material from the old mental health chapter, which has been eliminated. The latter contains examples of some of the popular health instruction programs found in U.S. schools. The former school safety chapter has been condensed and changed in title to "Emergency Care Procedures" under Health Services to eliminate repetitive material. Safety education information is contained in Chapters 9, 11, 12, and 13. Chapter 14, "Evaluation," has been rewritten for greater classroom teacher use.

It has been our task to design a text that not only identifies the known principles and practices for health in elementary schools but also to make them operational and functional for school personnel use. It remains for teachers, administrators, and other concerned persons to implement these measures in schools throughout the country.

If we help bring about just one favorable change in the health program of one elementary school, if we lead one classroom teacher to recognize the powerful potential influence he or she has for child health, if we provoke one principal to take a critical look at school health, if we but touch the conscience of one superintendent or school board member, if we pique the curiosity of a health department or a voluntary agency, or—above all—if we in some way indirectly enrich the life of an elementary school boy or girl, this will be the reward that we seek.

Finally, we are grateful to all those people and organizations who have helped us to make this sixth edition of *Health in Elementary Schools* a better book. We are especially indebted to those classroom teachers, our friends in the profession, and our students who offered stimulating and useful suggestions.

Harold J. Cornacchia
Larry K. Olsen
Carl J. Nickerson

CONTENTS

PART ONE

The elementary school health program

1

SCHOOL HEALTH

Its nature and purpose

The health of the American people has never been better. American children today are healthier than ever before.

Julius B. Richmond, M.D.,
Former Surgeon General of
the United States*

Since 1900 the death rate in America has been reduced as a result of medical control over such diseases as tuberculosis, diphtheria, poliomyelitis, and gastroenteritis. Infant, child, and maternal mortality have decreased, and the expected life span of individuals has increased by almost 3 years. Improvements in sanitation, housing, nutrition, and immunization have resulted in control over typhoid fever, smallpox, plague, and other diseases. Progress is evident in the control of heart disease, some cancers, and other chronic conditions. Despite these advances, many health and safety problems among young people, especially the poor, still exist in the United States. Acute illnesses result in an average loss per school year of 4.9 days for each American child. Numerous children are not completely immunized. Accidents are a major cause of death. Child abuse and neglect are of

major concern. Students are experiencing learning difficulties related to such problems as hyperkinesis and dyslexia. Pupils are exposed to a variety of risk factors that lead to adult diseases and conditions. Infants, school-age children, adolescents, adults, and elderly adults are all affected by these risk factors.

The need for preventive actions and services to promote and preserve the health of individuals has now been recognized. A Harris* poll conducted in 1978 revealed that more than 50% of Americans were more concerned with the preventive aspects of health than they were a few years before. Attention to life-styles and behavior together with control of environmental factors can reduce the need for medical and hospital care according to Julius B. Richmond, M.D., former Surgeon General of the United States. Dr. Richmond indicated the Public

---

*U.S. Department of Health, Education, and Welfare, Public Health Service: Healthy people—the Surgeon General's report on health promotion and disease prevention 1979, Washington, D.C., 1979, Superintendent of Documents.

*U.S. Department of Health and Human Services, Office of Health Research, Statistics and Technology: Health United States 1980, Washington, D.C., 1980, Superintendent of Documents.

Health Service reviewed its priorities for the expenditure of funds in America and decided that the improvement of the health status of citizens could be achieved predominantly through preventive actions rather than through the treatment of disease.

In 1979 the Surgeon General's *Report* stated that good health could be preserved and ill health prevented through the following:

1. Improved and increased use of screening, diagnostic, and treatment services
2. Provision for immunizations
3. Control of high blood pressure
4. Identification of groups of individuals with high risk of cancer
5. Reduction of serum cholesterol levels in the blood
6. Fluoridation of community water supplies
7. Avoidance of the misuse of alcohol and other drugs
8. Reduction of stress factors
9. Improvement of nutrition including its relation to obesity
10. Early identification of cardiovascular disease and cancer
11. Increased exercise and fitness

The *Report* claimed that premature deaths could be reduced through:

1. Control of toxic and infectious agents
2. Emphasis on occupational health and safety
3. Reduction of accidental injuries
4. Reduction or elimination of such risk factors as cigarette smoking, poor dietary habits including the consumption of high-fat foods and excess salt and sugar, untreated high blood pressure, misuse of alcohol and other drugs, severe emotional stress, accidents, and sexual promiscuity

Authorities agree that the best time for building the foundations for better health is early in life. It follows then that one of society's largest—and potentially most influential—organizations offers vast opportunities for raising the level of health of the individual, the family, and the community. Obviously, we speak here of the 115,000 elementary schools dotting the cities, suburbs, towns, and countryside of America. We think too of the almost limitless ways in which elementary teachers and school administrators—with the help of health specialists *and* the support of parents and the community—can favorably affect the health of 45 million boys and girls in schools across the land. This is through enlightened *health teaching* and provision for *health services* and a *healthful school environment*. Fig. 1-1 outlines the main activities of the entire school health program.

But our schools are in trouble. Teachers, prospective teachers, educational administrators, legislators, parents, education faculty in colleges and universities, taxpayers, and the news media have all become increasingly concerned about our schools. As problems continue to mount, cluttering the road to quality education for all children, it is clear that bold measures must be taken if we are to give more than lip service to repeated statements of lofty objectives and high ideals for America's schools.

Our schools and our society are beset with the harsh reality of economic, political, and other social problems that affect the quality of life. The question of tax sources for the equitable and adequate support of our schools has become a critical one. Piled atop the money problems are the tangled issues of busing, lowered enrollments and school closings, collective negotiations between teachers and school boards, health and safety conditions for pupils and teachers, conflicts in administrative and learning theories, "accountability" procedures for both pupils and teachers, and recently, public concern over the quality of education and the call for a return to the basic subjects in education.

However, since this is a book about elementary schools and their health programs, we cannot properly analyze all those forces that tend to shape our culture and our schools. Nevertheless, the need for *preventive* health care has never been more critical, and its advocacy is increasing substantially each year. Authorities now realize that it is not only necessary but also economically more feasible and desirable to reduce the incidence of health problems. The

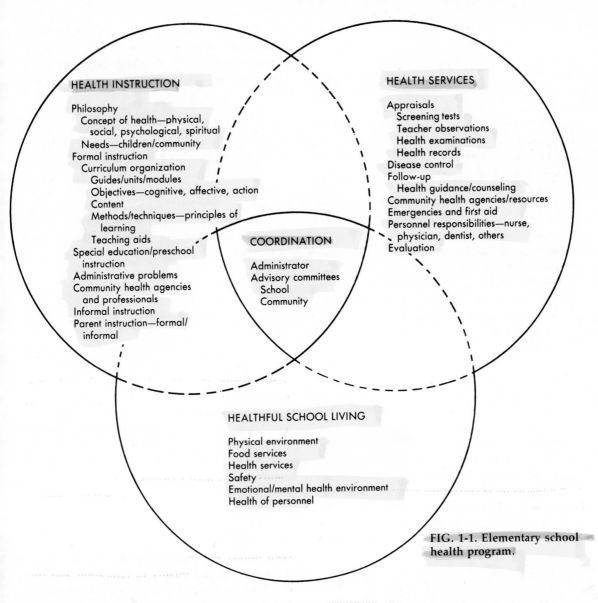

HEALTH INSTRUCTION

Philosophy
  Concept of health—physical,
    social, psychological, spiritual
  Needs—children/community
Formal instruction
  Curriculum organization
    Guides/units/modules
    Objectives—cognitive, affective, action
    Content
    Methods/techniques—principles of
      learning
    Teaching aids
  Special education/preschool
    instruction
  Administrative problems
  Community health agencies
    and professionals
  Informal instruction
  Parent instruction—formal/
    informal

HEALTH SERVICES

Appraisals
  Screening tests
  Teacher observations
  Health examinations
  Health records
Disease control
Follow-up
  Health guidance/counseling
Community health agencies/resources
Emergencies and first aid
Personnel responsibilities—nurse,
  physician, dentist, others
Evaluation

COORDINATION

Administrator
Advisory committees
School
Community

HEALTHFUL SCHOOL LIVING

Physical environment
Food services
Health services
Safety
Emotional/mental health environment
Health of personnel

FIG. 1-1. Elementary school
health program.

schools have a vital role to play in such action.

Yet, school health does not exist in a vacuum. The school health program is part of the life-blood of America's better schools, and like all aspects of good schools, it is sensitive to significant thinking and events in the community in which it thrives. In a very real sense the school reflects the character of its community—local, state, and national. Health instruction must be closely related to day-to-day problems of health and safety; school health services depend in large measure on the community's health resources; and the healthful school environment is in itself part of the community.

It is the basic thesis of education that the thinking and the behavior of people can be changed for the better. We assume with the confidence that grows out of research and experience that good teaching in a favorable setting will raise the quality of living for pupils. By enriching the lives of millions of children, elementary education cannot help but contribute to forming a better society.

This "better society" and "the good life" have challenged humans for thousands of years. Along with the family, the church and temple, and the community in general, schools have continuously sought to help people live better individually and in groups. Although there have been shifts in philosophy from time to time, the ultimate purpose of our schools has remained constant. From the log cabin of colonial times to the ultramodern structures of contemporary suburbia, the nation's schools have always been concerned with helping boys and girls to live better lives.

Teachers and elementary school personnel in the United States are in a unique position to contribute significantly to the preventive concept of health. They can help preserve and promote the well-being of students through the provision of services, programs, and activities that will have great influence on pupil behavior and life-styles.

The curriculum in America's elementary schools must include substantially more than the three Rs despite the present trend to return to so-called basic education. Reading, writing, spelling, arithmetic, social studies, and science need not be neglected with the inclusion of health education. Although health should be included as a separate subject area, it can also be integrated easily into all instructional areas. Teachers, with the help of parents, family members, and the community, must aid students to learn how to live in and make adjustments to the society in which they find themselves. Health is basic to the basics. Without good health, pupils will have difficulty learning to read, write, add, and perform the necessary activities for learning.

WHAT IS SCHOOL HEALTH?

A multiphasic differential program of health as illustrated in Fig. 1-1 is needed to adequately care for the variety of students and health and safety problems found in schools. This program must be one that includes *health instruction, health services, healthful school living,* and *coordination.* The instructional component should be both formal and informal in nature, for both students and parents. The health services should attempt to identify pupils with problems and provide counseling and guidance to obtain corrections where possible and to make adjustments in school programs where necessary. Policies and procedures to prevent the spread of communicable diseases and to take care of children who may be injured or become ill while at school need to be established. The environment should include a physical plant that is healthful and safe, is staffed by well-adjusted employees, and offers an atmosphere of friendliness and comfort conducive to learning. No program of this nature can function effectively without coordination.

An understanding of school health is more easily gained through familiarity with the terminology that follows:

school health The physiological, psychological, sociological, and spiritual aspects of health as they relate to the school setting.

school health program The school procedures and activities designed to protect and promote the well-being of students and school personnel. They include these four categorical phases: health education/instruction, health services, healthful school living/healthful school environment, and coordination.

healthful school environment The phase, sometimes referred to as healthful school living, that relates to those activities that provide a safe and healthful school atmosphere. It includes the physical plant—lighting, heating, ventilation, food services, health services unit, and health of school personnel—as well as the emotional climate in the school.

health education A broad term referring to both formal and informal learning about health that will enable individuals to make intelligent, informed decisions affecting their personal, family, and community well-being. It may take place in school, outside school, and through the media.

health instruction The formal program that takes

place in the school. It includes a program of planned activities in a classroom setting that offers understandings and attempts to develop attitudes and practices of healthful living that will enable children to reach high levels of wellness. The formal program is one that is planned, sequential, and includes all grades in a school or school district. It is now considered to be a *comprehensive school health education* program. It should be based on sound principles of curriculum development and include all subject areas necessary to satisfy student health needs and interests. The subject areas must (1) be repeated at several grade levels to ensure reinforcement of learning, and (2) increase in depth of content, progressing from simple to complex concepts as pupils move upward in grade.

coordination Those activities usually carried out by a school administrator in cooperation with school and/or community health committees or councils. They include the administration and supervision of the school health program with specific responsibilities to integrate the various phases with health instruction, to develop curriculum, to provide inservice teacher and staff training, to prepare policies and procedures, to communicate with community agencies and organizations, and to perform many tasks.

WHY SCHOOL HEALTH?

The health of children and their learning are reciprocally related. Young people must be healthy to obtain optimal benefit from their elementary school experiences. Educational experiences must be provided that will enable pupils to live in a healthful manner.

Students who are frequently absent because of illness, need glasses, are emotionally disturbed, are malnourished or undernourished, are always tired, are "battered"—children with a wide variety of health problems—are simply not able to learn most efficiently and effectively, even with the best teaching. The American Academy of Pediatrics* identifies these factors that contribute to underachievement in pupils: chronic and frequently recurring physical prob-

---

*American Academy of Pediatrics: School health: a guide for health professionals, Evanston, Ill., 1981, The Academy.

lems, specific sensory defects (vision, hearing, speech); neurologic and neuromuscular problems (brain defects, epilepsy); psychological problems (passive-aggressive behavior, fears, anxieties); and mental retardation.

Although parents have the primary responsibility for the health of their children, schools must offer supportive and complementary programs to help counsel pupils and parents. The role of the school is primarily to educate. Schools are expected to provide education to help students live in and adjust to society. Since society places high value on human life and health, schools have a responsibility and an opportunity to help protect and promote the health of pupils and to aid in the prevention of ill health.

WHAT IS PREVENTION?

Prevention has multiple meanings. Literally, to prevent is to keep something from happening. Prevention includes the protection and promotion of health. It involves primary, secondary, and tertiary aspects. Schools generally provide for primary and secondary preventive assistance.

Primary prevention refers to action taken to interfere with something happening or a procedure to stop something before it starts. Specifically, it is an attempt through education and other procedures to help students refrain from the use of or reduce the misuse of drugs, obtain immunizations, and generally make intelligent decisions in regard to their health. This type of prevention may take place in the school or in the community. Within the school the education may be formal or informal in nature and may be provided for students, parents, school personnel, and others.

Secondary prevention relates to procedures taken after an illness or abnormal condition has occurred so that it does not get worse or become more advanced. It includes early detection of conditions and the use of follow-up procedures to obtain the necessary treatment or adjustments. For example, a teacher who observes a student with a suspicious skin rash sends the child to the school nurse. The nurse concludes that the problem needs medical attention and telephones the child's parent, advising that the student be examined by a physician. The school health program usually provides counseling and guidance that may include referral of children to community resources.

Tertiary prevention is an extension of secondary prevention in which action is taken to interrupt the development of more serious conditions. It refers to treatment and rehabilitation services rendered by physicians, psychiatrists, and other professionals to save lives, restore pupils to high levels of wellness, and prevent serious personality damage. This service is generally not a function of schools and usually takes place outside the school setting. For example, a child with diabetes, epilepsy, heart disease, or hyperkinesis is in need of medical assistance. Communication between the school, parents, and physicians is needed for appropriate adjustments to be made in the school setting.

Role of the school in prevention

The role of the school in preventive health is identified in the total school health program (Fig. 1-1).

Schools have both a legal and a moral responsibility to provide a safe, sanitary, and healthful environment for pupils and school personnel. An atmosphere conducive to learning is one that is friendly and comfortable, offers a curriculum that motivates and meets the needs of students, minimizes stress situations, and includes well-adjusted, competent teachers.

The central purpose of the school health program is to help children learn to be responsible for their own health. Students should be able to acquire scientific understandings and attitudes through the health instruction program that will enable them to act intelligently. The health habits established in these formative years greatly influence the quality of life that emerges in adulthood. Young people in ele-

mentary schools can be exposed to many useful health experiences and activities, since they legally must attend school for approximately 6 hours daily, 180 days yearly, for 8 or more years.

Children attend school with a variety of illnesses and conditions such as communicable diseases, speech impediments, and dental problems that are in need of identification and/or possible correction. The school health services program should provide nurses, physicians, dentists, and other professionals who can assist with these problems to protect other students, to counsel and guide pupils and parents, and to recommend adjustments in school programs for more effective learning.

WHAT ARE THE HEALTH PROBLEMS OF CHILDREN?

Despite the apparent good health of many children in the United States, there continues to be a variety of health and safety problems, especially among the poor, that have a draining effect on the energies, stamina, and capabilities of young people. These problems are of such magnitude and diversity that the quality of education will be affected for students in those schools that fail to give them attention and do not provide a health program of the nature described in this text.

According to the American Academy of Pediatrics* the most common health problems in children 3 to 5 years of age are acute infectious diseases (respiratory illnesses and gastrointestinal disorders), accidents, emotional disorders, dental caries, sensory defects (vision, hearing), and iron deficiency. Cancers are the leading cause of death in children aged 1 to 7, with 3,214 deaths occurring yearly.

Early elementary school–age pupils have the next-to-lowest mortality and serious morbidity of any age group. Most physical illness in this age group is the result of accidental trauma and

---

*American Academy of Pediatrics: School health: a guide for professionals, Evanston, Ill., 1981, The Academy.

respiratory illness, usually of infectious origin. These students also have a variety of problems such as hearing, vision, and speech defects, dental caries, mental retardation, and emotional and educational problems.

What are the death rates of children and adults?

The average expected lifespan at birth for all white Americans is 73.3 years (males, 70.2 years; females, 77.8 years), and for nonwhite Americans it is 69.3 years (males, 65 years; females, 73.6 years).

The 15 leading causes of death in 1978 are listed in Table 1-1. Over 1.25 million people die annually from heart disease, cancer, and cerebrovascular diseases and accidents. These conditions may be prevented or reduced in incidence in elementary school children if they receive attention, and good life-style habits are developed.

The death rates, estimated numbers of deaths, and percentages of deaths from selected causes for young people aged 5 to 14 years are shown in Table 1-2. The rates and numbers are exceedingly low in comparison to other age groups when one considers there are over 45 million children of elementary school age in the United States. Accidents are the leading cause of death, while cancer heads the list among the diseases and conditions.

What are the safety hazards for pupils?

Accidents are the leading cause of death and disability among children and adolescents. Mo-

TABLE 1-1. Death rates and estimated numbers of deaths for the 15 leading causes of death: United States, 1978

Rank	Cause of death	Death rate (per 100,000 population)	Percentage of total deaths	Estimated numbers of deaths*
	All causes	883.4	100.0	1,899,310
1	Diseases of heart	334.3	37.8	718,745
2	Malignant neoplasms, including neoplasms of lymphatic and hematopoietic tissues	181.9	20.6	391,085
3	Cerebrovascular diseases	80.5	9.1	173,075
4	Accidents	48.4	5.5	104,060
	Motor vehicle accidents	24.0	—	
	All other accidents	24.4	—	
5	Influenza and pneumonia	26.7	3.0	57,405
6	Diabetes mellitus	15.5	1.8	33,325
7	Cirrhosis of liver	13.8	1.6	29,670
8	Arteriosclerosis	13.3	1.5	28,595
9	Suicide	12.5	1.4	26,875
10	Certain causes of mortality in early infancy	10.1	1.1	21,715
11	Bronchitis, emphysema, and asthma	10.0	1.1	21,500
12	Homicide	9.4	1.1	20,210
13	Congenital anomalies	5.9	0.7	12,685
14	Nephritis and nephrosis	4.1	0.5	8,515
15	Septicemia	3.6	0.4	7,740
	All other causes	113.5	12.8	244,025

From U.S. Department of Health, Education, and Welfare, Public Health Service, National Center for Health Statistics: Vital health statistics, 1978, Washington, D.C., 1980, Superintendent of Documents.
*Based on 215 million population.

TABLE 1-2. Death rates and estimated numbers and percentages for selected causes for children and youth 5 to 14 years of age: United States, 1978

Causes	Death rate (per 100,000 population)	Estimated numbers of deaths*	Percentage
All	33.9	72,885	100
Accidents and violence	18.9	40,635	56
Motor vehicle accidents	8.8	18,920	26
All other accidents	8.4	18,060	25
Suicide	0.4	860	1
Homicide	1.3	2,795	4
Diseases and conditions	11.4	24,510	34
Malignant neoplasms	4.2	9,030	13
Leukemia	2.0	4,300	6
Brain and other parts of nervous system	1.0	2,150	3
Congenital anomalies	1.8	3,870	5
Diseases of heart	1.0	2,150	3
Influenza and pneumonia	1.4	3,010	4
Others	3.6	7,740	10

From U.S. Department of Health, Education, and Welfare, Public Health Service: Vital statistics of the United States for the data years 1976-78, vol. II, Washington, D.C., 1979, Superintendent of Documents.
*Based on 215 million population.

TABLE 1-3. Ranking of top 10 consumer products associated with injuries to children and youths treated in hospital emergency rooms and estimated number of such product-related injuries per 100,000 children and youths under 15 years of age, according to age and product: United States, 1979-80

Rank	Age			
	0 to 4 Years		5 to 14 Years	
	Product	Injuries per 100,000 population	Product	Injuries per 100,000 population
1	Tables (all types)	666.3	Bicycles and accessories	876.7
2	Stairs (including folding), steps, ramps, and landings	470.4	Football, activity and related equipment	424.6
3	Chairs, sofas, and sofa beds	441.4	Baseball, activity and related equipment	330.4
4	Beds (excluding water beds)	392.6	Playground equipment	287.1
5	Playground equipment	318.0	Ice and roller skating and skating not specified (excluding ice hockey)	267.7
6	Bicycles and accessories	262.8	Basketball, activity and related equipment	237.9
7	Desks, cabinets, shelves, racks, and footlockers	180.4	Stairs (including folding) steps, ramps, and landings	215.3
8	Nails, carpet tacks, screws, and thumb tacks	112.0	Nails, carpet tacks, screws and thumb tacks	180.8
9	Bathtub and nonglass shower structures	107.7	Glass doors, windows, and panels	103.6
10	Glass doors, windows, and panels	103.2	Fences, nonelectric or unspecified	101.7

From National Electronic Injury Surveillance System: NEISS data highlights, vol. 4, no. 1, U.S. Consumer Product Safety Commission. Washington, Jan./Mar. 1980; adapted from U.S. Department of Health and Human Services, Public Health Service: Better health for our children—a national strategy, vol. III: a statistical profile, Washington, D.C., 1981, Superintendent of Documents.
NOTE: Data are based on reporting by a sample of hospital emergency rooms.

TABLE 1-4. Student accident* rates and school days lost from school per injury for students in grades K through 12, according to grade, sex, and location and activity: United States, 1977-78 School Year

Sex, location, and activity	Total†	Grades					Days lost per injury
		Kindergarten‡	1 to 3	4 to 6	7 to 9	10 to 12	
Boys		*Accidents per 100,000 student days*					*Days*
All school jurisdictions	9.39	6.29	5.82	8.96	12.12	12.26	1.09
Shops and labs	0.64	0.00	0.00	0.06	1.05	1.56	0.64
Building—general grounds	1.86	2.01	1.32	1.77	2.67	1.72	0.91
Unorganized activities	1.94	2.80	3.01	3.90	0.88	0.20	1.04
Other	0.37	0.30	0.38	0.40	0.39	0.34	1.31
Physical education	2.92	0.47	0.81	2.33	4.93	4.36	1.19
Sports							
Intramural sports	0.12	0.00	0.00	0.05	0.21	0.27	1.12
Interscholastic sports	1.15	0.00	0.00	0.07	1.51	3.40	1.15
Special activities	0.05	0.04	0.03	0.07	0.07	0.05	0.85
Travel to school							
Motor vehicle	0.18	0.37	0.11	0.11	0.21	0.26	1.98
Nonmotor vehicle	0.16	0.30	0.16	0.20	0.20	0.10	1.59
Girls							
All school jurisdictions	5.48	4.01	4.16	6.04	7.85	4.65	1.13
Shops and labs	0.14	0.00	0.00	0.04	0.32	0.19	0.62
Building—general grounds	1.23	0.99	0.89	1.08	1.85	1.18	1.02
Unorganized activities	1.19	1.97	2.24	2.33	0.28	0.09	1.20
Other	0.22	0.22	0.20	0.25	0.21	0.23	1.64
Physical education	2.14	0.34	0.64	2.08	4.25	2.05	1.05
Sports							
Intramural sports	0.04	0.00	0.00	0.02	0.11	0.04	0.81
Interscholastic sports	0.23	0.00	0.00	0.02	0.44	0.51	1.10
Special activities	0.05	0.09	0.03	0.06	0.07	0.05	1.43
Travel to school							
Motor vehicle	0.16	0.22	0.09	0.07	0.20	0.27	1.98
Nonmotor vehicle	0.08	0.18	0.07	0.09	0.12	0.04	1.18

From National Safety Council: Accident facts, 1979 edition, Chicago, 1979; reprinted from U.S. Department of Health and Human Services, Public Health Service: Better health for our children—a national strategy, vol. III: a statistical profile, Washington, D.C., 1981, Superintendent of Documents.
*Accidents are those causing (1) the loss of one-half day or more of school time, (2) the loss of one-half day or more of activity during nonschool time, and/or (3) any property damage as a result of a school jurisdictional accident.
†Total includes other accidents not shown as a separate category.
‡Kindergarten rates adjusted for one-half day.
NOTE: Data are based on reporting by schools.

tor vehicle accidents alone account for 20% of all child deaths each year. Drownings account for about 8.5% and fire about 6% of the deaths. Other common accidental deaths and injuries are caused by burns, falls, and misuse of household products and various other forms of substance abuse. One half of childhood injuries occur in the home from fires, scalds, falls, poisonings, and unsafe and improperly used products. The leading causes of injuries to preschool and elementary school–age children who were treated in hospital emergency rooms are shown in Table 1-3. Recreational activity injuries rank high for the group aged 5 to 14. Bicycle and football injuries are most common. The accident rates and school days lost through school-related injuries for pupils in grades K through 12 are provided in Table 1-4. Motor vehicle injuries cause the most days lost per injury for both boys and girls.

What are the physical illnesses and conditions?

Illnesses. Respiratory and gastrointestinal illnesses are the most common. Streptococcal in-

TABLE 1-5. Common health problems contributing to short-term disability and school absenteeism in elementary school–age children*

Rank	Condition
1	*Respiratory conditions:* including the common cold, sore throat, earache, bronchitis, influenza, asthma, and related conditions
2	*Infectious diseases:* including—despite readily available vaccines—measles, chickenpox, German measles, and mumps; skin infections; venereal diseases among upper grade students
3	*Digestive disorders:* including viral and bacterial intestinal infections, food allergy, constipation, and appendicitis

*Adapted from data from Current estimates from the health interview survey; United States, 1976, Vital Health Statistics 119(10): Nov. 1977.

fection ("strep sore throat") has occurred two to three times in young people by the age of 10 years. Acute rheumatic fever, a serious complication of sore throat, may lead to permanent heart disease. Approximately 61% of school days missed by children are because of acute illnesses, primarily respiratory conditions. The common health problems contributing to short-term disability and school absenteeism of elementary pupils are identified in Table 1-5. Although the incidence of measles, rubella, mumps, pertussis, diphtheria, and poliomyelitis has dropped markedly since 1950, it is estimated that one third of preschool and school-age children in the U.S. are incompletely immunized.* Approximately one third of 12- to 17-year-olds have skin disorders in need of medical attention. About 8 out of every 1,000 children born in the United States each year have one or more congenital heart defects. The incidence of gonorrhea in children under 15 years of age in 1978 was 23.5 per 100,000 population. It continues to increase in incidence along with syphilis and other sexually transmitted diseases.

The two most common dental diseases are caries and periodontal disease. The incidence increases as children get older. Decay probably affects more children than any other health problem with the exception of respiratory infections and injuries. Dental caries have been on the decline because of the use of fluorides and dietary habit changes.* It is estimated that 37% of children 5 to 17 years of age are presently caries free. The average incidence of caries is three to six per child. Many pupils have gingivitis.

Conditions. Approximately 1 child in 20 aged 3 to 5 has a vision problem. About 20% of school-age pupils have visual acuity problems, and another 5% to 7% have some form of eye disease. It is estimated that 10% of students have hearing difficulties, with 3% of these caused by middle-ear infections. One percent of pupils are epileptic, and an additional 1% have major speech disorders.

What are the emotional problems?

It is estimated that 10% of pupils (4 to 5 million) have emotional problems requiring psychiatric help. An additional 2% to 3% have seriously psychotic or prepsychotic conditions. In a class of 30 children, a teacher may expect to recognize emotional difficulties in 3 children and possibly be able to identify 1 child in need of psychiatric assistance. Educational failure, or the "failure syndrome," is one of the underlying stress factors related to depression, acting-out in school, truancy, and maladjustments. Stress has a significant correlation to a variety of illnesses, including depression, asthma, and diabetes. It is also related to skin rashes, children's streptococcal infections, accidents, suicide, and substance abuse.

*Better health for our children—a national strategy, vol. III: a statistical profile, Washington, D.C., 1981, Superintendent of Documents.

*Children's dental caries decreased dramatically, The Nation's Health, Feb. 1982.

What are the social and life-style–related problems?

Child neglect and abuse. The types of child neglect and abuse include physical and emotional neglect and physical and sexual abuse. Neglect refers to lack of adequate nutrition, clothing, and shelter, and failure of parents and caretakers to provide an emotionally stable environment. Physical abuse causes bodily harm to children and is manifested by bruises, welts, abrasions, lacerations, and burns. Sexual abuse includes incest, sodomy, and rape. It is estimated that 1 million young people are victims of child neglect and abuse yearly. Some authorities have placed the numbers at 200,000 to 4 million. Probably 50% of cases involve children 6 years or older. Approximately 2,000 to 5,000 children die annually at the hands of parents and caretakers. It is believed that 60% of battered pupils who are returned home are battered again. Child neglect is apparently more common than direct physical abuse.

Suicide. Approximately 25,000 suicides and 500,000 attempts occur each year, of which 6.6% are committed by 15- to 19-year-olds. The exact number is difficult to determine because suicide is attributed to motor vehicle crashes, drug overdose, falls, firearms, and firearm accidents. Suicide is the most common cause of death in the group aged 10 to 19 years. The rate is increasing among teenagers, and there are 60,000 attempts annually by those under 20 years of age. Boys attempt suicide three times more often than girls.

Cigarette smoking. Of the 430,000 cancer deaths in 1981, 30% were from cigarette smoking. Of these deaths, 90,000 were caused by lung cancer. Smokers have a higher risk of cancer of the larynx, oral cavity, esophagus, and stomach. Smoking is the major cause of emphysema and chronic bronchitis. Although cigarette smoking among young people aged 12 to 17 declined somewhat in 1979, 22% of these individuals used cigarettes regularly. Surveys indicate that 10% of 12- to 13-year-olds, 22% of 14- to 15-year-olds, and 35% of 16- to 17-year-olds smoke on a regular basis. Probably three fourths

of all students have tried cigarettes by their senior year in high school. Girls' rate of smoking was almost as high as boys'. There is evidence that smoking has been tried by children 7 years old and, in some instances, has been tried by younger children.

Alcohol. Alcohol in beverages is the primary drug of choice in the United States and has been tried by 70% of all adolescents and 95% of all young adults. Studies completed on students in grades 7 through 8 and 10 through 12 indicate that 28% were abstainers and 10% were heavy drinkers in the former group, and 25% were abstainers and 15% were heavy drinkers in the latter group. The National Institute on Alcohol Abuse and Alcoholics stated that 10% of 14- to 17-year-olds are problem drinkers.[*] The American Academy of Pediatrics[†] stated there are 500,000 child and adolescent alcoholics. Although the extent of involvement is not known, there is evidence that fourth-grade children are being introduced to and trying alcoholic beverages. Early drinking behavior is a predictor of drinking habits later in life.

Other drugs. Although the drug problem appears to have leveled off and is not rising in terms of extent of use, it continues as a major health problem for young people. We live in a drug-oriented society. We take drugs to wake up, to go to sleep, to keep alert, to escape from reality, to relax, to ease pain, and for many other reasons. People use, misuse, and abuse legal as well as illegal drugs. A recent survey of the extent of drug use by percentages among 12- to 17-year-olds revealed the following:

Legal drugs
Opiates (cough syrups, painkillers)—6%
Stimulants—5%
Tranquilizers—4%
Sedatives—3%

---

[*] National Institute on Alcohol Abuse and Alcoholics: Focus on the Fourth Special Report to the U.S. Congress on Alcohol and Health: patterns of alcohol consumption, Alcohol World **5:** Spring 1981.

[†] American Academy of Pediatrics: School health: a guide for health professionals, 1981, Evanston, Ill., Committee on School Health.

Illegal drugs
Marijuana—28%
Inhalants (glue, gasoline, etc.)—9%
Hallucinogens (LSD)—5%
Cocaine—4%
Heroin—1%

Nutrition. Nutrition is generally good among school-age children but the most prevalent problems are overeating causing obesity and overweight, anorexia nervosa (willful self-starvation) in teenage girls, and poor food choices. The obese 1- to 11-year-olds apparently are more sedentary than the thin children. The problem may be one of adjustment and is a precursor to adolescent and adult obesity. Poor food choices resulted in low intakes of the minerals calcium and copper and the vitamins A, C, and riboflavin.

Exercise and fitness. It is estimated that 50% or more of school-age children do not participate in daily physical education programs. Sedentary living is one of the factors that increase the probability of cardiovascular disease. Although there are no substantial data available that clearly identify the effect of exercise and fitness in reducing the risks of recurring illness, exercise can help in the control of weight and in stress reduction through relaxation. It can help to increase the efficiency of the heart and blood vessels and may aid digestion.

Sexual activity. About 12 million of the 29 million young people between the ages of 13 and 19 years have had sexual intercourse. At 13 to 14 years of age, 18% are boys and 6% are girls. Eight in 10 males and 7 in 10 females report having had sexual intercourse in their teens.*

In 1978 there were 1.1 million teenage pregnancies and 847,000 were unintentional. There were 30,000 pregnancies and 10,000 live births among young people under 15 years old and 500,000 live births among adolescents 15 to 17 years old. A variety of problems complicate

---

*The Alan Guttmacher Institute: Teenage pregnancy: the problem hasn't gone away, New York, 1981, The Institute.

pregnancies in young mothers and they include low birth weight, increased infant mortality, toxemia, anemia, prolonged pregnancy, and mental retardation of the child among others.

What factors are related to school underachievement?

The American Academy of Pediatrics identified a variety of external and internal factors that affect school underachievement of students.

External factors. External factors include (1) improper educational management—curriculum, motivation, resources, class size, and school design; (2) family problems—marital discord, anxiety, and depression; (3) unrealistic parental expectations; and (4) lack of motivation—lack of home support, socially and financially successful parents, and peer pressure.

Internal factors. Internal factors include (1) chronic and recurring physical problems—cerebral palsy and heart problems; (2) sensory defects—defects in vision or hearing; (3) handicapping neurologic and neuromuscular problems—defects of brain, epilepsy, and dysphasia; (4) psychiatric and psychosocial problems; and (5) mental retardation.

Who are the children with special educational needs?

There are approximately 8 million children with special educational needs, as indicated in Table 1-6. The largest group is the learning disabled, including children with such conditions as minimal brain dysfunction, dyslexia, and hyperkinesis among others.

What are the special problems of the poor?

Children from low-income families, and especially families with little income and only one parent, are generally in poorer health than those from high-income families. A study com-

TABLE 1-6. Handicapped children receiving special education and related services as reported by state agencies under P.L. 94-142 and P.L. 89-313—school year 1979-80

Type of handicap	P.L. 94-142					P.L. 89-313				Combined		
	3-5 yr	6-17 yr	18-21 yr	Total	% Popu-lation	State	Local	Total	% Popu-lation	Total	% Popu-lation	% Handi-capped
Mentally retarded	18,012	687,182	63,646	768,840	1.57	91,264	21,635	112,899	0.23	881,739	1.80	21.8
Hard of hearing	3,274	32,556	1,636	37,466	0.07	3,112	805	3,917	0.00	41,383	0.08	1.0
Deaf	2,315	15,746	1,053	19,114	0.03	21,499	876	22,375	0.04	41,489	0.08	1.0
Speech impaired	158,128	1,016,095	5,939	1,180,162	2.41	6,753	2,058	8,811	0.01	1,188,973	2.43	29.4
Visually handi-capped	1,838	19,088	1,733	22,659	0.04	9,396	621	10,017	0.02	32,676	0.06	0.8
Emotion-ally dis-turbed	8,172	277,181	10,458	295,811	0.60	30,509	4,679	35,188	0.07	330,999	0.67	8.2
Orthope-dically impaired	7,207	45,013	3,927	56,147	0.11	8,334	1,762	10,096	0.02	66,243	0.13	1.6
Other health impaired	5,989	92,637	3,781	102,407	0.20	3,216	664	3,880	0.00	106,287	0.21	2.6
Learning disabled	18,882	1,218,166	28,824	1,265,872	2.59	12,402	3,121	15,523	0.03	1,281,395	2.62	31.7
Deaf-blind	232	1,246	97	1,575	0.00	837	166	1,003	0.00	2,578	0.00	0.0
Multihand-icapped	7,766	41,258	3,434	52,458	0.10	6,994	2,471	9,465	0.01	61,923	0.12	1.5
Total	231,815	3,446,168	124,528	3,802,511	7.78	194,316	38,858	233,174	0.47	4,035,685	8.25	100.0

From the Office of the Secretary of Education, Assistant Secretary for Special Education and Rehabilitative Services. The counts were taken on October 1, 1979, for P.L. 89-313 and December 1, 1979, for P.L. 94-142. The percentages listed next to each total column are percentages of school-age population ages 5 through 17 years old in that state or in the nation for the national summary. The last column indicates what percentage the number in each handicapping condition is of the total number reported as handicapped. From American Academy of Pediatrics: School health: a guide for health professionals, Evanston, Ill., 1981, The Academy.

pleted several years ago revealed that of young people under 17 years of age, 70% from high-income families were in excellent health while only 41% of children from low-income families were in excellent health.

In recent years increasing attention has been accorded the unusually high rate of illness among the poor and such minority groups as black Americans, Mexican Americans, and native Americans. Poverty and ignorance are the common contributory causes of these higher disease rates. Poor diet, inadequate medical and dental care, unhealthful housing, health misconceptions and superstitions, high incidence of child abuse and neglect, and lack of adequate childhood immunizations are major reasons for the generally subpar health of minority families.

Some of the health problems of minority groups are based on genetic variances (such as sickle cell anemia in blacks and Tay-Sachs disease in Jewish and other groups of Middle East origin), whereas others appear to be related to life-style and environment (such as alcoholism among Irish Americans, accidents among native Americans, and high blood pressure among black Americans). Migrant and seasonal farmworkers and their children, most of whom are black or Chicano, suffer severely under the burden of poverty, poor housing, inadequate diets, discrimination, occupational accidents, emotional problems, and exposure to agricultural pesticides. Among native Americans these conditions are prevalent: tuberculosis, high death rates, dental decay, alcoholism, drug abuse, diabetes, accidents, and a variety of emotional problems.

WHAT IS GOOD HEALTH FOR PUPILS?

The elementary school health program seeks to protect and improve children's health. The achievement of this goal mandates that teachers and school personnel understand the concept of health, the factors that influence pupil health, and how to tell if pupils are healthy.

What is health?

Health includes a multiplicity of phenomena and therefore cannot be simply nor easily defined. Comprehension of the variety of components that comprise health is essential to understanding its nature and its importance in the school health program.

Health is a condition of the organism that may be represented on a continuum from so-called good health to so-called bad health, or from "wellness" to "illness," with many variations in between. People desire to find themselves at the positive end of the health scale and not at the negative end. Where any person fits on the continuum at any given time depends on these factors:

1. *Health is personal.* Each person is born with a specific constitution or physical body that is provided through the genetic structure inherited from parents. Individuals are the same in many ways—number of arms, legs, and eyes—and different in many ways—size, shape, color of skin and eyes. Some children may be tall, obese, have only one kidney, have allergies, or perhaps minimal brain damage. Some pupils have susceptibil-

ities to certain diseases and conditions. Thus health is individual and variable in nature.

2. *Health is a frequently changing phenomenon.* It is the result of the interaction of the individual (genetic heredity) with many factors and experiences in the environment.

3. *Health is dependent on self-actualization.* It necessitates internalization by the individual. Each person must make a decision whether or not to promote and preserve his or her own health.

4. *Health is a means to an end.* Health is necessary for effective learning and living. A child with poor health may have difficulty learning to read, doing arithmetic, or speaking and may have trouble later in life, such as when trying to obtain a job.

Health is a complex phenomenon that includes a composite of the physiological, psychological, sociological, and spiritual interrelated components of the modified concept of health shown in Fig. 1-2. These components have special significance in helping students make *intelligent decisions* as to the environmental health factors and experiences they face in society. These components must receive greater consideration in teaching to achieve more effective health education.

The isosceles triangle in Fig. 1-2 shows that physiological aspects form the base of the triangle and are fundamental to all learning. Students need to understand the structure and function of the human organism and the nature of good and ill health and diseases and conditions. However, this is of less importance in health instruction than the psychological and sociological aspects represented by the longer, vertical sides of the triangle. The diagram also indicates that emotional and physical needs are reciprocally related to people—friends, relatives, and others—and to the environment found in the social arena. These interrelating factors influence the structure and function of the human body (see dotted lines in Fig. 1-2). Unfortunately, these components are not often stressed in health instruction.

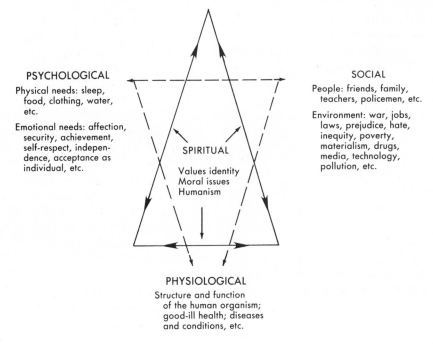

FIG. 1-2. A modified concept of health. *(Health is a complex phenomenon. Adapted from Cornacchia, H.J., Smith, D.E., and Bentel, D.J.: Drugs in the classroom: a conceptual model for school programs, ed. 2, St. Louis, 1978, The C.V. Mosby Co.)*

By way of illustration, a pupil may start to smoke cigarettes to satisfy an emotional need for acceptance or affection as well as to satisfy a desire to be part of a school peer group or to enter into adulthood. Cigarettes are manufactured, made readily available to the public, and widely advertised as an acceptable form of social behavior. Thus the psychological need promotes the demand on the part of the manufacturers to satisfy the need and, reciprocally, the need is satisfied by the availability of the cigarettes and the encouragement of their use. There would be considerably less lung cancer, bronchitis, and emphysema if students could be directed toward alternative ways of satisfying their psychologic needs. Pupils need assistance in this regard as well as help in learning how to cope with societal pressures.

Probably the most important influence on health behavior, yet the one most frequently overlooked or omitted in the classroom, is the spiritual aspect. People's motivations toward health are dependent on their values, their recognition of moral issues in society, and their concern for the welfare of others (humanism). These are the driving forces of human behavior. They provide direction and establish the purposes or meanings of life. They help people determine their life goals. If individuals value their health, they will attempt to satisfy their emotional and physical needs through behavior other than cigarette smoking. They will learn to cope with the environmental and peer influences previously identified. They will conclude that it is unfair to smoke cigarettes in the presence of other people. They will understand that advertising and pressures to sell cigarettes involve moral issues in need of analysis and understanding.

Unfortunately, few health education curricula

in schools have been designed to use the total-person concept of health described in this section. The holistic approach to health is being widely advocated and promoted. There is need to prepare instructional programs that help students understand their own health motivation factors and make them aware of the influence of the environment in which they live on these motivations. In addition, programs must help pupils with the development of values, comprehension of moral issues, and understandings of their effect on people. Such emphasis will enable children to *learn to make intelligent health decisions* and *learn to cope*; it will help them make adjustments to the social climate in which they live. Health instruction programs designed to include the total health concept will have more of an effect on the students' lives.

The concept of health described in this chapter, which includes the physiological, psychological, sociological, and spiritual aspects of health has been used in the development of the illustrative units found in Chapter 9. The extent to which emphasis of these components should be made at various grade levels is also identified in Chapter 9.

WHAT FACTORS INFLUENCE PUPIL HEALTH?

A child's health is determined by three basic factors: *heredity, environment*, and *behavior*. Each boy and girl, as an individual personality, is a product of these fundamental forces.

Pupils differ in many ways. Some are tall and slender, others are short and stocky, some are just plain big, others are tiny, and the rest are distributed in between. Some are fair skinned with blue eyes; others are olive skinned with brown eyes. Some have blond hair, some brown, some black, and a few red. Differences in their facial features are readily apparent, even to the casual observer. As a teacher you find that some learn quickly, others slowly; some show rapid rates of physical growth while others lag behind, at least temporarily. Some

learn motor skills easily and quickly; others seem never able to quite "get the hang of it" when a new physical skill is taught. All these and more are evidence of biological traits transmitted from parents to children. All these are proof of the miracle of heredity.

It is *heredity* that establishes a child's health endowment fund. What is passed on to the child by the genes and their constituent deoxyribonucleic acid (DNA) and ribonucleic acid (RNA) molecules from the parents, grandparents, and more distant ancestors has much to do with the child's capacity for good health. Heredity also plays a part in the predisposition to some mental disorders, infectious diseases, and chronic conditions such as cancer, heart disease, diabetes, hemophilia, and sickle-cell anemia. All experienced teachers have seen the pupil with a strong constitution. This is the boy or girl who is alert, vigorous, seemingly indefatigable, and relatively free from illness. Similarly, teachers are familiar with the opposite—the weak, sickly child who seems always to be perched precariously on the figurative fence dividing health and illness. Often both children are exposed to essentially the same environment and follow much the same daily routine. In the absence of other explanations, such as previous illness or impairment, these health variances must be considered as being significantly influenced by heredity.

Environment has a direct bearing on the health of pupils. Boys and girls must interact with and adjust to an environment that is physical, biological, and social. *Physical* factors, such as weather and climate, housing, soil, water and food supply, medicines, radiation, clean or polluted air, recreational facilities, automobiles, hospitals, school buildings and sites, and many more physical things around us can affect health for better or worse. *Biological* influences include germs, plants, animals, and other people. These, too, may be helpful or harmful to health. For example, a pupil may catch a cold from a parent. At the same time that parent provides shelter, food, clothing, medical care, and other necessities that serve to maintain and improve the child's health. Some "friendly" germs in the intestinal tract manufacture certain vitamins that help prevent deficiencies; other germs are capable of causing disease and death. *Social* or *cultural environment* comprises all the interactions between and among people. These complex human relationships influence and are themselves influenced by patterns of culture at a given time and place. Hence, boys and girls are constantly exposed to the beliefs, attitudes, ideals, values, and customs of family, neighborhood, school, church, and the general community (local, state, national, and world) in which they live. In terms of nationwide values there remains little doubt of the influence of vigorous and persuasive advertising through television and other mass media on the thinking of both children and adults. These cultural forces can directly or indirectly, for better or worse, affect the physical, mental, or emotional health of elementary school pupils.

To a far greater extent than either heredity or environment, *behavior*, or *life-style*, is generally the most influential factor in pupil health. Behavior is the result of the interaction of the psychological, social, and spiritual factors previously discussed. Young people in elementary schools are at impressionable ages, and teachers and schools can have a great impact on their life-styles. With proper guidance and motivation, children can make corrections in their behavior or learn to make adjustments to hereditary limitations and environmental factors. An effective health instruction program can guide pupils toward life-styles that will enable them to live in a healthful manner. It is the fundamental purpose of this text to help teachers and school personnel assist students in elementary schools achieve high levels of wellness.

HOW CAN YOU TELL IF PUPILS ARE IN GOOD HEALTH?

The classroom teacher is not qualified to diagnose illness or make a clinical assessment of pupil health. However, some specific characteristics distinguish healthy children from those who are not healthy. Actually, these attributes help spell out a definition of good health. To be able to enumerate, albeit roughly and incompletely, the more basic telltale clues of good health is to be better prepared to recognize and promote buoyant health among your pupils. These behaviors should be looked for in the healthy child:

1. Is able to carry out routine learning activities in school and in homework assignments without undue fatigue or emotional upset
2. Is able to participate regularly in physical education and other physical activities in the school curriculum
3. Demonstrates skill in games and basic body movements appropriate to his age, sex, body type, and motor learning experiences
4. Shows progressive gains in weight and height without unusually wide deviations
5. Has enough energy to do the things that most children of his age and sex want to do
6. Has smooth and clear skin, without discoloration, eruptions, or excessive dryness or oiliness
7. Has a good appetite
8. Has no more frequent illnesses or accidents than are typical of his or her age and sex group
9. Is interested in and enthusiastic about most activities that are popular with classmates
10. Has confidence in own abilities yet enjoys working and playing with others
11. Is able to control emotions about as well as most of the other children in class

WHERE DO WE STAND NOW?

A great deal of progress has been made in the development and expansion of health instruction programs. Little or no progress has been made to improve health services programs, and the growth of the environmental and coordination of the school health program has remained static or regressed somewhat.

The professional organizations that have helped nurture the growth of school health in the United States include the American School Health Association, the American Public Health Association, and the Association for the Advancement of Health Education. The American Medical Association, The American Academy of Pediatricians, and the National Congress of Parents and Teachers are among other groups that have been supportive over the years.

It should be noted that at the federal level there is the Center for Health Promotion and Education in the Center for Disease Control, in the Public Health Service, within the Department of Health and Human Services. The Center for Health Promotion and Education, formerly the Bureau of Health Education, has supported school health education and provided funds for the development of demonstration and model programs. Until it was eliminated by recent budget cuts, there was also an Office of Comprehensive School Health Education within the Department of Education. There is also the Office of Health Information and Health Promotion, Physical Fitness and Sports Medicine, Public Health Service, Department of Health and Human Services. These offices have all cooperated in efforts to advance school health.

In the private sector, the National Center for Health Education is an organization supported by funds from industry and other sources that promote health education. The National Congress of Parents and Teachers has for many years conducted a program of support for health education, especially comprehensive health education. Several other major curriculum projects are now under way. They have received financial support from several foundations and other sources.

Health education in schools has perhaps made its greatest progress in the last 20 years. According to Castile and others* in a report prepared for the American School Health Associa-

---

*Castile, A., Allensworth, D.D., and Noak, M.: School health in America: survey of state school health programs, Atlanta, 1981, U.S. Department of Health and Human Services and the American School Health Association.

tion and the U.S. Department of Health and Human Services:

1. Eighty percent of the states require some kind of health instruction.
2. Forty-nine states employ a person responsible for health education. This may not be an individual who is a health educator and it may be someone with multiple responsibilities.
3. Twenty-five state laws require elementary teachers to take coursework in health education while preparing to become teachers. Many colleges and universities in the United States require and/or offer courses in addition to state mandates.
4. Thirty-three states have a curriculum or planning guide that is available to school districts.

Despite the tremendous efforts in support of school health education programs in recent years, they are not universally found in elementary schools in the United States. It is estimated that fewer than 25% of the nation's schools provide health instruction programs. Many of these are not comprehensive in nature, and often they are not evaluated in terms of their impact on students. State laws requiring health programs, despite their apparent prevalency, are often written in such general terms that schools can comply with the requirements without providing instructional programs such as those outlined in this text.

With the exception of some large districts, the health services programs found in schools may not be recognizable as such because they are fragmented, uncoordinated, and poorly planned in many instances; there may be little or no administrative leadership. In a number of schools and school districts, some of the services may be provided by local health departments. At best a nurse or some administrator may have the responsibility for the supervision and conduct of such programs. In many districts there may be no nurses or only part-time nurses in schools. Large districts may have specific departments with physicians, nurses, and other health professionals.

In recent years federal legislation has helped to provide some measure of improvement in health services programs. In 1967 Congress approved a program that required states to provide early and periodic screening, diagnosis, and treatment (EPSDT) as a mandatory Medicaid service to improve the health of children from low-income families through preventive health services. It included identification and preventive care for vision problems, hearing problems and dental problems, among others. The program has been under the supervision of local and state health departments but it necessitated school involvement and coordination. In 1975 Congress passed the Education for All Handicapped Children Act, which required that "free appropriate public education" be available to all handicapped children from ages 3 to 21 years regardless of their disabilities and their ability to pay for services. The law requires that provision be made for school health services, speech therapy, medical services, psychological and parent counseling, and other types of programs.

The patterns of organization for health services vary widely in America's schools. Many schools hire their own nurses and other professionals to conduct programs, some have all services provided by local health departments, and a few schools and school districts coordinate their own activities.

School districts in general are attentive to the physical plant including food services, health services, and to a lesser extent, the health of school personnel. The emotional climate may receive consideration to a greater or lesser degree but this depends on the nature of the school services rendered and the individual efforts of teachers and personnel.

Coordination of the phases of the school health program outlined here does not exist except in some large school districts. In those few districts that have administrative personnel to oversee programs, these individuals may be called supervisors, coordinators, consultants, or directors. In some districts, physicians or other health professionals may serve in this capacity.

School health advisory committees can render useful and important aid but such committees are few in number except possibly in large districts. The same probably holds true for community health committees. It should be noted that without administrative supervision, health services or health instruction programs will be hard pressed to develop and if in operation will slowly disappear.

Despite the progress and advances that have been made in school health, health education continues to receive low priority for curriculum inclusion by school superintendents and school board members. Additional awareness programs for such individuals with pressures exerted by parents and community health organizations and professionals must be initiated. Finances and resources for health instruction are greatly limited.

Perhaps the state of school health programs is best described by these remarks of former Secretary of Health, Education, and Welfare Joseph A. Califano when he addressed the American School Health Association annual meeting in Minneapolis, Minnesota, in 1977:

> Improved school health programs will be a key element in the comprehensive national child health policy which I will ask the Public Health Service to develop for the Department. . . . I recognize that interest in improving school health programs has been spotty over the years. . . . I believe that the time has come again to forge ahead in expanding and improving these programs.

The school health program outlined in this text may be considered as a conceptual model of the ideal program. It illustrates the pattern for school health that should exist in America's schools. It identifies the specific components and their organization that if implemented will enable children to achieve high levels of wellness. It will contribute to quality education and aid young people to grow into worthwhile and productive adults.

The health program described here has emerged as a result of a thorough review of the scientific literature and numerous school health programs, consultation with many school health authorities, discussions with a variety of health professionals, and the authors' years of experiences with schools. We have served in numerous capacities in elementary schools at local and state levels as teachers and administrators. We have participated in professional organizations, conducted many in-service teacher-training activities, and been active in health education projects at local, state, and national levels.

IN SUMMARY WE BELIEVE

School health programs are necessary to protect and promote the health of America's elementary school children.

School health programs will continue to expand and become more readily available in elementary schools despite present difficulties.

School health programs will emerge as people become aware of their need and take action to provide for this need.

School health with emphasis on health instruction in elementary schools requires that teachers and administrators be more assertive in the promotion of their need.

School health programs need the involvement of parents, professional health personnel, and other community representatives in development, implementation, and financial support.

School health and health instruction programs for classrooms, schools, and school districts can be prepared by teachers and administrators through the use of the information found in this textbook.

QUESTIONS FOR DISCUSSION

1. How can good health be preserved and ill health prevented according to one former U.S. Surgeon General?
2. What is the nature of the school health program? Identify its components and interrelations.
3. Why do schools have a responsibility to provide for a school health program?
4. What is the meaning of the preventive health concept? Provide illustrations. What is the role of the school?
5. What are 10 important health problems of children? Identify their extent in elementary pupils.
6. What are five of the social and life-style–related health problems of elementary pupils of which teachers must be aware?
7. What are five student health problems in need of special education?
8. Name the special health problems of the poor, and indicate their significance for health education.
9. What is the concept of health described in the text, and how can it be applied to the health instruction program?
10. What is the modified concept of health illustrated in the text? Give examples of its application to health education.
11. What factors influence the health of pupils?
12. How can a teacher tell whether children are in good health?
13. What is the status of school health programs in the United States today?

SELECTED REFERENCES

American Academy of Pediatrics: School health: a guide for health professionals, Evanston, Ill., 1981, The Academy.

American Alliance for Health, Physical Education, and Recreation: Suggested school health policies. Report of the Joint Committee on Health Problems in Education of the National Education Association and the American Medical Association, Washington, D.C., 1966, The Alliance.

American Alliance for Health, Physical Education, and Recreation: Why health education in your school? Report of the Joint Committee on Health Problems in Education of the National Education Association and the American Medical Association, Washington, D.C., 1974, The Alliance.

Cornacchia, H.J., Smith, D.E., and Bentel, D.J.: Drugs in the classroom: a conceptual model for school programs, ed. 2, St. Louis, 1978, The C.V. Mosby Co.

DiAngelis, A.T., and others: Dental needs in children of Mexican-American migrant workers, Journal of School Health 51: Aug., 1981.

Dupont, R.I., and others, (editors): Handbook on drug abuse, Washington, D.C., 1979, National Institute on Drug Abuse.

Hanlon, J.J., and Pickett, G.E.: Public health: administration and practice, ed. 7, St. Louis, 1979, The C.V. Mosby Co.

Lee, P.R.: A new perspective on health, health planning, and health policy, Journal of Allied Health, Winter, 1977.

Miller, C.A.: Health care of children and youth in America, American Journal of Public Health 65:April, 1975.

National Safety Council: Accident facts, Chicago, 1981, The Council.

Read, D.A., Simon, S.B., and Goodman, J.B.: Health education: the search for values, Englewood Cliffs, N.J., 1977, Prentice-Hall, Inc.

Teenage pregnancy: the problem that hasn't gone away, New York, 1981, Guttmacher Institute.

13th annual Gallup poll of the public's attitudes toward the public schools, Phi Delta Kappan 63:Sept., 1981.

U.S. Department of Health and Human Services, Public Health Service: Better health for our children: a national strategy, Vols. I-III, Washington, D.C., 1981, Superintendent of Documents.

U.S. Department of Health and Human Services, Public Health Service, Alcohol, Drug Abuse, and Mental Health Administration: Fourth special report to the U.S. Congress on alcohol and health, Washington, D.C., 1981, Superintendent of Documents.

U.S. Department of Health and Human Services, Public Health Service, Center for Disease Control, Center for Health Promotion and Education: Focal points, May/June, 1981.

U.S. Department of Health and Human Services, Public Health Service, National Center for Health Statistics: Health in United States chartbook, Washington, D.C., 1980, Superintendent of Documents.

U.S. Department of Health and Human Services, Public Health Service, Office of Disease Prevention and Health Promotion: Prevention '80, Washington, D.C., 1981, Superintendent of Documents.

U.S. Department of Health and Human Services, Public Health Service, Office of Health Research, Statistics and Technology: Health United States 1980, Washington, D.C., 1980, Superintendent of Documents.

U.S. Department of Health and Human Services, Public Health Service, Office of Secretary for Health and Surgeon General: Healthy people: the Surgeon General's report on health promotion and disease prevention, Washington, D.C., 1979, Superintendent of Documents.

Warshofsky, F.: The control of life: the twenty-first century, New York, 1969, The Viking Press.

2

THE TEACHER'S ROLE IN SCHOOL HEALTH

The elementary classroom teacher has a unique role in the early development of the child. The teacher is one of the most influential factors in the life of that young person. The teacher has contact with children during their most formative and sensitive years—a precious time when what they know, what they think, and what they do can be significantly affected. Often the teacher sees and communicates with a child for more hours each day than do the parents. This reality becomes increasingly important in light of Department of Labor reports showing that over half of the mothers of school-age children hold regular jobs.

What teachers do with this combined opportunity and responsibility depends on whether they are ready, willing, and able to assume a prominent role in school health, especially classroom health instruction.

To better understand the ways that teachers can contribute to children's health and safety, let us reexamine three basic aspects of the total elementary school health program: health education, health services, and healthful school living (see Fig. 1-1).

Health instruction, through formally planned and sequentially arranged activities and informal counseling and guidance, is designed to promote health knowledge (cognitive), attitudes (affective), and practices (action) that contribute to the highest levels of individual, family, and community health.

Health services include activities that identify the health problems of children and seek corrections and adjustments of school programs to ensure the greatest learning. The purpose of the school health services program is to protect, maintain, and improve the health of children. This involves nurses, physicians, dentists, and others. Teachers must be prepared to deal with common childhood problems such as colds, stomachaches, fevers, sore throats, toothaches, headaches, and allergies.

A healthful school environment includes the physical aspects and the emotional climate of the school setting. The school must be free of hazards and offer a safe, comfortable, warm atmosphere with stable teachers to enable children to learn most effectively.

It is important to understand that the three phases of the school health program are not mutually exclusive but interrelated when implemented. There are opportunities for both formal and informal instruction through health services as well as through the environmental phase. The formal health instruction program provides the greatest responsibility and opportunity for the teacher. Yet, informally, individual health problems can frequently be given attention through counseling and guidance.

In the area of health services, teachers must be able to recognize signs and symptoms of student health problems, refer pupils to health personnel, and assist with screening programs. The teacher may also use service activities as teachable moments to provide informal instruction.

In the area of healthful school living, teachers must assume some responsibility for the proper lighting, heating, and ventilation of the classroom and offer assurance that pupils are free of exposure to hazardous conditions through the provision of safe environment and practices. The emotional climate is a part of the school environment that includes teacher health, fairness in dealing with pupils, consideration for individual differences, creation of a friendly classroom setting, and avoidance of bias and prejudice. All these factors affect children's health. Teachers should provide opportunities for students to learn self-reliance and responsibility for their own health as well as that of others.

The elementary classroom teacher has often been called a "specialized generalist," "a jack-of-all trades," in recognition of the diversity of talents necessary to be a good teacher. Few people in the entire field of education, or in any of the other professions for that matter, need the diversity of competencies required of the good elementary school teacher. Summarily, that person must be a grammarian, mathematician, psychologist, space-age scientist, nutritionist, editor, art and drama critic, geographer, health educator, sociologist, physical educator, agriculture expert, historian, recreation leader, zoologist, anthropologist, safety specialist, chemist, economist, nurse, counselor, and more.

WHAT COMPETENCIES DOES THE ELEMENTARY TEACHER NEED?

It would be unrealistic to expect each classroom teacher to be a health education specialist. However, the teacher must have an understanding of the nature and process of health education as well as the total school health program for an effective instructional program. In 1974 a committee of the California School Health Association identified these competencies and indicated the elementary school teacher should be able to*:

1. Identify and make provisions for the health needs of children and youth from various socioeconomic and cultural levels.

2. As health needs are identified, refer the child to aid through appropriate channels.

3. Describe the effect of the social environment in the mental-emotional and physical well-being of children and youth.

4. Describe the role of the teacher in providing for a safe and healthful school environment.

5. Provide for the growth and development characteristics of children and youth in the teaching-learning situation (see Chapter 5).

6. State factors that influence or determine health behavior and incorporate such factors in planning for health instruction.

7. Plan and organize activities that facilitate physical, emotional, and social development of children and youth.

8. Promote the physical and emotional health of children and youth through varied experiences in the school and community setting.

9. Identify a variety of community health resources that serve children and youth as well as other family members.

10. Explain the role of the family and the community in health education.

11. Communicate health needs of the child to parents without belittling or being critical.

---

*Ad Hoc Committee of the California School Health Association. Suggested competencies for health science teaching majors, May 1974 (mimeographed).

12. Use community health agencies in planning and implementing the curriculum.

13. Identify socioeconomic and cultural conditions in the community that affect the health of the individual.

14. Identify criteria for determining the content of health instruction.

15. Demonstrate a command of the fundamental concepts related to:

Drug use and misuse
Family health
Nutrition
Diseases and disorders
Environmental health hazards
Mental-emotional health
Community health resources
Consumer health
Oral health, vision, and hearing
Exercise, rest, and posture

16. Apply the fundamental concepts relative to sociology, psychology, human anatomy, and physiology in teaching about health.

17. Select important concepts to be taught relative to health problem areas.

18. Write behavioral objectives relative to health concepts being emphasized.

19. Effectively evaluate the progress students make toward achieving behavioral objectives.

20. Develop inquiry skills relative to the modification of health behavior.

21. Interrelate health concepts among health problem areas.

22. Develop strategies for making health decisions that can favorably modify health behavior.

In addition to specific competencies (see pp. 27-28) the teacher as a health educator should (1) realize that health education requires the use of a different approach, (2) understand the controversial nature of some health topics, (3) appreciate the special need for the consideration of individual pupil differences, (4) be familiar with a variety of sources of current scientific health information (also see Chapter 13), (5) be able to identify health problems to include in the instructional program (see Chapters 1, 5, and 9), and (6) plan for the orderly conduct of formal educational experiences and use teachable moments for health instruction (see Chapters 8 through 12).

Health teaching is different

Although in many ways health teaching is much like all other teaching, it does differ in certain crucial respects. In the first place, although much of the content in health education is basic to the complete physical, mental, and social development of the child, motivation is often difficult. The normal, healthy child is largely unconcerned about his or her health and safety. In fact, if public apathy toward the value of auto seat belts and the serious danger of cigarette smoking is any criterion, one may conclude that many youths and adults demonstrate a rather perverse antagonism toward established facts of safe and healthful living. Quite possibly this is because the essential knowledge and favorable attitudes and practices needed to combat this apathy were not developed a decade or more ago when these people were in elementary school. In any event, the classroom teacher faces special challenges in the influential motivation of pupils in health education. At the same time fear psychology, vague exhortation, and the possibility of developing an unhealthy overconcern for health among pupils must be avoided. The balance is often a most delicate one.

Second, health teaching is inextricably bound up in our cultural and social patterns of thinking and doing. Perhaps no other area of learning in the elementary school depends so heavily on positively influencing attitudes and behavior. A person's actions are rooted in feelings, and feelings are colored by experiences and understandings. Even though children may come to school without any preconceived notions regarding reading or arithmetic, they often already have begun to develop some false ideas, poor attitudes, and harmful practices in health

COMPETENCIES

General

The teacher understands and appreciates:

1. The meaning of health as a multidimensional state of well-being that includes physical, psychological, social, and spiritual aspects.
2. That health of individuals is influenced by the reciprocal interaction of the growing and developing organism and environmental factors and is necessary for optimal functioning as productive members of society.
3. The significance of children's and youth's health problems on learning.
4. The importance and the need for the school health program in today's society.
5. The nature of the total school health program.
6. The role of the teacher in each of the school health program components—services, environment, and instruction.
7. The need for basic scientific information about a variety of health content areas, including dental health; drugs (alcohol, tobacco, and other drugs); care of eyes, ears, and feet; exercise, fitness, rest, and fatigue; prevention and control of diseases and disorders (communicable and chronic); safety and first aid; family health; consumer health; community health; environmental health; nutrition; mental health; anatomy; physiology.

Health instruction

The teacher:

1. Can identify and use a variety of techniques and procedures to determine the health needs and interests of pupils.
2. Is able to organize the health instruction program for the grade being taught around the needs and interests of students and can develop effective teaching units.
3. Is able to stress the development of attitudes and behaviors for healthful living based on scientific health information.
4. Can distinguish between the various patterns of health instruction and attempts to use the direct approach in teaching whenever possible.
5. Realizes that health education must receive time in the school program along with other subject areas.
6. Possesses current scientific information about a variety of health content areas.
7. Can use a variety of stimulating and motivating teaching techniques derived from fundamental principles of learning.
8. Is able to identify and use "teachable moments" or incidents that occur in the classroom, in the school, or in the community.
9. Uses a variety of teaching aids in the instructional program and is familiar with their sources.
10. Is familiar with the sources of scientific information and the procedures necessary to keep up to date with current health information.
11. Is able to provide a variety of alternative solutions to health problems to enable students to make wiser decisions.
12. Can integrate health into other phases of the curriculum, such as social science, science, and language arts.
13. Uses a variety of evaluative procedures periodically to (a) assess the effectiveness of the program on students and (b) determine the quality and usefulness of teaching aids and materials.

Continued.

COMPETENCIES—cont'd

Health services

The teacher:

1. Is familiar with the characteristics of the healthy child and can recognize signs and symptoms of unhealthy conditions; refers problems to the school nurse or other appropriate school personnel.
2. Is familiar with the variety of health appraisal procedures used in schools and uses them to enrich the health instruction program.
3. Acquires limited skill in counseling and guiding students and parents regarding student health problems.
4. Understands the value and purposes of teacher-nurse conferences.
5. Is familiar with the variety of health personnel found in schools, their functions, responsibilities, and usefulness to the teacher.
6. Is able to use information contained on health records.
7. Can identify and follow the policies and procedures in schools in regard to such matters as emergency care, accidents, disease control, and referrals, exclusions, and readmittance of pupils.
8. Can administer immediate care when accidents or illnesses to pupils occur or can act promptly to obtain sources of help within the school.
9. Is able to adjust the school program to the individual health needs of students.
10. Is able to relate the health services program to the health instruction program.

Healthful school living

The teacher:

1. Is familiar with the standards for hygiene, sanitation, and safety needed in schools to provide a safe and healthful environment.
2. Is familiar with the physical and emotional needs of students and adjusts classroom activities to help students satisfy these needs whenever possible.
3. Understands the nature and importance of the food services program and is able to relate it to the instructional program.
4. Is able to recognize hazardous conditions on the playground, in the classroom, and elsewhere in the school and takes appropriate action to eliminate or correct such conditions.
5. Is cognizant of the effect of teacher health, personality, biases, and prejudices on student health and learning and is concerned with the humane treatment of pupils.
6. Integrates healthful environmental aspects into the health instruction program.

Coordination

The teacher:

1. Understands the need for school and community health councils or committees and is willing to participate as a member if requested to do so.
2. Realizes the importance of and need for a coordinator, consultant, or a person with administrative responsibility being in charge of the school health program.

and safety. Altering these unsound patterns of thinking and behaving is frequently difficult because of the rigidity of family and community culture and its powerful influence on the child.

Third, health information is constantly changing. What was unknown yesterday will be commonplace tomorrow; what was true last year is false this year; what was an apparently insurmountable problem a decade ago is now relegated to the museum of scientific antiques. Moreover, health science is not a simple listing of pure "blacks and whites." Whereas some concepts are clearly and unalterably established by research, others are supported in varying degrees of authenticity given current scientific evidence. The classroom teacher, therefore, must prepare pupils for scientific change without developing a negative skepticism. The teacher must lead children to understand the scientific method so that, using this understanding, they may weigh the facts at hand and make choices and decisions that will favorably affect health. This idea of decision making is critical, for unlike most other subject matter areas health and safety demand that children be participants, not merely spectators.

Health teaching can be controversial

Some of the topics in health education may occasionally provoke emotional reactions among pupils, parents, and other concerned persons or groups in the community. Such areas of instruction include sex education, sexually transmitted disease, fluoridation, tobacco, alcohol, and other drugs, the choice of a health advisor, and medical care plans.

Of course, sex education and tobacco and alcohol instruction have certain moral and religious implications. Yet, the evidence clearly indicates that despite the hue and cry of small vocal groups, the majority of parents and religious leaders generally favor school instruction in these areas. Fluoridation of public water

supplies has been associated with emotionally tinged publicity in some communities; despite the fact that every responsible scientific organization has endorsed fluoridation as safe and effective in reducing tooth decay, there is still occasional criticism of this topic. Members of some healing professions may take exception to the generalization that medical diagnosis and treatment are best performed by licensed doctors of medicine and osteopathy. Some persons may urge that an ultraliberal view of medical care, barely short of socialized medicine, be presented in class. Those who oppose this tend to question any approach to medical care that suggests anything other than the traditional fee-for-service agreement between patient and physician.

Because health education is so intimately related to the cultural patterns of any community, teachers can expect that now and then some objections will arise. Neither teachers nor administrators should be intimidated by sporadic criticism of this kind. However, to be sure of standing on firm ground in these provocative areas, the classroom teacher should do the following:

1. Maintain a scientific, unbiased approach.
2. Avoid getting involved in partisan politics or personalities.
3. Follow course and unit outlines recommended or approved by local school officials.
4. Seek the help of resource people and groups in the community (for example, local medical and dental societies, the PTA representative, religious leaders, and public health officials) in preparing units of study.
5. Wherever possible, use materials that have been prepared by such reputable groups and organizations as the American Alliance for Health, Physical Education, Recreation, and Dance; American Medical Association; American School Health Association; U.S. Public Health Service; National Education Association; National Council on Alcoholism; American Red Cross; local or state health departments; American Social Health As-

sociation; and other recognized scientific groups.

6. Use resources that are up to date and scientifically sound (detailed criteria are discussed in Chapter 13).

7. Maintain adequate records of pupil activities, questions, interests, and problems.

Many "modern" teaching techniques such as values clarification and behavior modification, though controversial, may be effectively used in a well-planned health instruction program. However, there are numerous pitfalls to avoid if the program is to be a positive learning experience for children. Some of the pitfalls to avoid include the following:

1. Using extrinsic rewards—especially "unhealthy" rewards (e.g., candy) for a child who demonstrates positive health behavior

2. Inserting personal bias into instruction

3. Using students as examples of poor health practices or of health problems

4. Creating a "clean plate" club

5. Overuse of fear tactics or overly graphic portrayals of disease entities or health problems

6. Conducting competition between students on health practices such as grooming or posture

7. Overly emphasizing perfect attendance at school

8. Pushing personal values or interests as fact

9. Setting forth unrealistic standards in terms of health knowledge and practices for children

10. Ridiculing a child's home situation or using it as an example of a poor health practice or environment

Teacher-pupil planning of units and participation by parents and other citizens in curriculum study and development are procedures that help assure public understanding and acceptance of what is taught in the schools. Increasingly closer ties among school, home, and community tend to lessen substantially the possibility of any misunderstandings regarding teaching concepts in controversial areas.

Sources of current scientific information

Many elementary education professional preparation programs require that persons enrolled take a course in personal health, first aid, or school health programs for successful completion of the degree. Other programs require more than a single course. Still others require no health-related courses for their elementary education majors. The reason given for including few or no health courses in the professional preparation programs is the crowded curriculum of elementary education majors. Clearly, a single course is minimal preparation for health teaching, but those who take this single course may be looked to as a source for some health information. All this aside, it is important for teachers to keep abreast of new trends and developments in the constantly changing health field with respect to content, methods and materials, and other aspects of the elementary school health program. Unfortunately, the sources of reliable and new information and the methods used to assess such information present problems not readily or easily resolved. There are no simple or definitive ways to discover with certainty whether material contained in publications is truthful and accurate. There are several reasons for this difficulty: (1) data are limited or inconclusive regarding the cause, treatment, or cure of many conditions such as arthritis, cancer, and obesity; (2) published research data are frequently in conflict; and (3) a number of so-called authorities, including scientists, nutritionists, physicians, and others who may disseminate health information may have been motivated to disseminate inaccurate information for purely profit-related reasons—information clearly not in the best interest of the health consumer. Further, the elementary teacher does not usually have access to basic medical literature for the purpose of double checking the information contained in varied publications. Therefore it is important that teachers attempt to determine the validity of health information they read. These guidelines should be helpful in the evaluation of publications and other printed materials*:

1. What is the purpose of the printed material; is it produced to sell products, make money, or present factual information to the reader?
2. Is it presented in an educational or scientific manner, or does it use exaggerated claims and make misleading and inaccurate statements?
3. Is the author qualified by way of educational background and professional experience? It must be kept in mind that even though the author may be qualified, the information may be inaccurate.
4. Are the data based on appropriate research and experience of experts in the health field or on the opinions of a few individuals?
5. Are the research data acceptable by medical, dental, public health, and other authorities and organizations?
6. What evidence exists to support or refute conflicting claims about health information? Has the claimant generalized from a particular incident or from broad research?

Specifically, here are some of the things teachers may do to obtain current health information:

1. Keep up with new developments in school health by regularly reading one or more professional journals, such as the *Journal of School Health* (American School Health Association), *Health Education* (American Alliance for Health, Physical Education, Recreation, and Dance), the *American Journal of Public Health* (American Public Health Association), and *Health Values* (Charles B. Slack, Inc.). These journals provide abstracts of the latest and best research and information in school health and safety.

2. Keep in touch with the progress in the health sciences taking place by reviewing such publications as *Nutrition Today* (Nutrition Today Society), *FDA Consumer* (Federal Food and Drug Administration), *Consumer Reports* (Consumers Union), and other such magazines.

3. Read the health and medicine sections of *Time, Newsweek,* and *U.S. News and World Report* as well as local newspapers and popular magazines for new developments announced in the health sciences.

4. Use current basic college health texts on the health sciences as references.

5. Obtain up-to-date health pamphlets from government agencies (National Clearinghouses for Alcohol Information, Drug Information, and Smoking and Health), professional associations (American Medical Association and American Dental Association), voluntary health organizations (Lung, Cancer, and Heart), and business firms.

6. Elect health education courses in the college program for certification or advanced degrees and, whenever possible, attend school health workshops, institutes, conferences, and conventions.

7. Make full use of the teacher's manual that publishers provide to accompany elementary health texts and readers.

8. Attend national, regional, or state meetings of health-related organizations whenever possible.

9. Join a professional health-related organization such as the American School Health Association, the Association for the Advancement of Health Education, or the American Public Health Association.

Providing for individual differences

Providing for individual differences including cultural and ethnic differences is something we talk about a great deal in education. Doing much about it becomes increasingly difficult. Overcrowded schools and oversized classes make individual guidance of pupil learning more a theoretical goal than an accomplished fact.

There are numerous ways teachers can learn more about their pupils. Of course, school rec-

*Adapted from Cornacchia, H., and Barrett S.: Consumer health, ed. 2, St. Louis, 1980, The C.V. Mosby Co.

ords furnish significant information on a child's intellectual capacity, status, and progress. Often these records also contain data on a pupil's social and emotional development. Well-kept cumulative health records should provide information on illnesses, injuries, major surgical operations, allergies, health examination findings, dental health, physical growth, and teacher observations from previous years. These, combined with notes and recommendations of school nurse and physician, can be most helpful to the teacher in understanding the health status of each child and the implications such status may have for learning.

Intellectually, one must realize that it is not physically possible for a teacher to meet every need of every student within a given classroom. When a teacher must deal with anywhere from 20 to 30 or more students in a classroom and considerably more than that throughout the school day, the chance is quite good that the teacher will come into contact with one or more students with whom it will be difficult to establish rapport. When this occurs, the teacher would be well advised to examine his or her personal biases to determine if they might be a barrier to the rapport. In like manner, the teacher will have a profound effect on the lives of many other students with whom rapport has been established.

Beyond the variances in the health and growth of pupils, there are important differences that relate to each child's environment. Most important of these is the home background. Economic conditions, cultural level, parental attitude toward the school, social position, marital status, value systems, leisure time activities, occupation of the head of the household, and racial or ethnic origins of parents—all these, and more tend to leave their mark on the child. Children's purposes, interests, and values will tend to align themselves with those of their parents. Thus, while one child comes from a home where meals are carefully planned and medical and dental care readily available, another may leave a home where a full stomach is

the only measure of good nutrition, where breakfast is not served, or where the physician or dentist is seen only for the most extreme conditions, if at all. Surely the needs and interests of these two pupils are different in many respects.

In the same classroom there are pupils whose neighborhoods vary widely. While some live in the town or city, others may be transported to school from outlying rural areas; some enjoy a pleasant suburban neighborhood, while others live in the shadow of factories, railroad yards, commercial sections, or in the ghettos. Home, family, and neighborhood influences will shape the kinds of out-of-school experiences a pupil has. Travel, work, and recreation also play a part in contributing to differences among children.

Attempting to adapt teaching-learning situations and experiences to fit the needs, concerns, and abilities of children, the teacher must also bear in mind that children mature at different rates. What is appealing and important to one fifth grader is, at the moment, beyond the understanding and interest of a classmate. Children grow and mature according to a general pattern, yet each child sets his or her own unique schedule. This is a most important concept for teachers to recognize.

Finally, teachers should remember that effective learning also takes place in many situations. A balance between individual guidance and small and large group learning activities must be maintained. The very nature of these human differences often provides the raw materials with which a good teacher can actually mold a superior setting for health education. Although there is much more likeness than unlikeness among children at the same age and sex, the areas of variance constitute both a stimulating challenge and a rich opportunity for alert teachers to achieve effectiveness in two fundamental functions of good teaching: (1) providing learning experiences suited to individual purposes, needs, concerns, and interests and (2) providing opportunities for pupil sharing of diversified experiences relating to safe and healthful living.

Teachers must choose

Perhaps the most significant function of the classroom teacher is deciding how much time and emphasis to give to various health and safety topics. In general, the teacher designs the curriculum in those districts where such decisions have not been specifically made. Even with textbooks, courses of study, teaching units, and lesson plans as guides, the classroom teacher usually has considerable latitude in selecting content at a given grade level. Moreover, the teacher may have to decide just how much emphasis to place on subtopics within a broad unit. More detailed information is provided in Chapters 8 and 9.

It is important that teachers remember that their primary responsibility and function is to teach, but they also have a role in the elementary school's health services program. The purpose of school health services is to appraise, promote, protect, maintain, and improve the health of the school-age child and school personnel. This broad purpose is achieved through the combined, coordinated efforts of teachers, administrators, school nurses, physicians, dentists, other related health care specialists, and parents. Procedures used to accomplish this purpose may include health examinations, daily observations of pupils, vision and hearing screening, use of health records, dental inspections, disease control, emergency care, health conferences, and often psychological counseling.

THE TEACHER AS COUNSELOR AND GUIDANCE WORKER

The classroom teacher assumes the role of counselor and guidance worker mainly in connection with the health services program. The teacher is in a unique position to observe deviances within the student population. The teacher spends a great deal of time with the child and thus is able to see patterns develop within each child. When a deviation from the normal pattern for a given child occurs, the teacher can refer the child to appropriate sources of care.

Once the child has been referred, the conscientious teacher will follow the progress of the child to be sure that the condition for which the child was referred is alleviated. In some cases, all that will be needed is to move the child's desk to enable that student to see or hear more easily. In other cases, major alterations may be required. Regardless of what needs to be done, the teacher must maintain contact with the school nurse, the parents, and often the referral source if the school health services component is to reach its full potential.

Another way the teacher serves as counselor and guidance worker is through the informal education approach, which provides information, counseling, and guidance that is nondirective, voluntary, and usually has little if any structure. The teacher must be constantly alert for that child who, through some means, expresses a need for help.

Naturally, any informal counseling is intended to supplement and complement the formal program. If the school health services program is to be most effective, both formal and informal opportunities for counseling must be available to the student. An excellent means of informal counseling involves the use of peer groups that can serve as referral sources for students. By informally discussing the various problems that come to the teacher's attention within the classroom setting, the teacher is enhancing the total school health services program.

THE TEACHER'S ROLE IN THE HEALTHFUL SCHOOL ENVIRONMENT

For approximately 9 months of every year, the school is a part of the daily environment of the elementary-school child. It is the responsibility of school personnel to ensure that the environment to which the child is exposed is safe and free of undue hazards. However, provision of safe buildings is insufficient to promote a positive healthful school environment. The general mental and emotional environment of the school, including the classroom environment, has a significant impact on how the child both perceives and feels about the various school-related activities of which he or she is a part. As such, people are a critical component of the total environment of the school and the teacher is a central figure in the total realm of school personnel.*

Although guided by general school policies, the teacher exercises direct control over the immediate classroom environment. What is done in the classroom can be a positive or negative force in overall student achievement. Exposure to a positive, healthful environment in school becomes a model for the child in later years. Thus it is the responsibility of the teacher to do whatever is possible to enhance the positive aspects of the environment and eliminate the negative aspects.

There are numerous physical aspects of the classroom environment that fall under the direct supervision of the teacher. Such things as the arrangement of the desks, tables, or chairs, calling the custodian to replace burned out lights, and controlling room temperature and ventilation all contribute to the total classroom environment. (These subjects will be discussed further in Chapter 3.)

Although the physical environment sets a basic stage for the classroom, it is the students and teacher who set the emotional tone. Regardless of the physical attractiveness or suitability of the classroom as a setting for learning, the interaction of those occupying that setting determines the social environment.

The teacher is in a position to set a positive emotional tone in the classroom through inter-

actions with the students. The elementary teacher who understands the basic growth and development characteristics of children and their varied needs and interests, is empathetic yet firm in dealing with various classroom problems, and can help students understand and use their potential is more likely to promote a positive mental health atmosphere than one who does not possess these attributes. It is important to maintain an adult objectivity while at the same time trying to see things as children see them. This takes a great deal of effort on the part of the teacher, but both teacher and students will benefit a great deal if the teacher strives to reach this goal (see Chapters 3 and 4).

HEALTH OF SCHOOL PERSONNEL

The health of school personnel is not frequently considered to be a part of the total school health program. However, if one considers the amount of contact these persons have with school-age children, it is important to know such things as whether they have a communicable disease or if they are physically unable to perform the multitude of duties required.

Teachers seldom have much of a chance to be completely alone during the school day. Teaching is very demanding, and it is not uncommon for teachers to have inadequate sleep, not find the time for proper exercise, and feel great stress associated with their responsibilities.

The teacher is a role model for the child. As stated in the beginning of this chapter, the teacher exerts a great influence over the child. Thus if the teacher is ill, many additional untoward features may manifest themselves. If the teacher does not feel well, it is quite likely this will show in his or her disposition or in the way classroom problems are handled. How can students gain from the teacher who is chronically tired, is grossly obese, has poor personal hygiene, and constantly complains about one or more problems, physical, mental, or social?

---

*From Anderson, C.L., and Creswell, W.H., Jr.: School health practice, ed. 7, St. Louis, 1980, The C.V. Mosby Co.

BENEFITS DERIVED FROM HEALTH
STANDARDS FOR SCHOOL PERSONNEL*

Benefits for children

- Increased quality of learning experiences when the staff is well.
- Lessening of stress in classrooms and other school areas.
- Greater continuity in the learning experience resulting from fewer absences of teachers and other school staff.
- Lessened exposure to communicable disease.
- Decreased risk of accidents (as from fitness of bus drivers).
- Increased awareness and value of health when employees are good role models.

Benefits for school employees

- Early detection of conditions that can be corrected or minimized.
- Assistance in locating health resources when needed.
- Financial assistance (as for health leaves, like sickness disability insurance).
- Placement in positions and/or assigned tasks based upon consideration of the individual's health status.
- Realization that one's health behavior does relate to his/her fitness and job competency.
- Assistance in coping with stressful situations.

Benefits for the community

- Increased cost-effectiveness when staff members have fewer absences.
- Greater competence of personnel when they are well.
- Improved emotional climate in the schools.
- Increased understanding of how teacher and labor negotiations relate to health issues.
- Established and written health policies are available.
- Reduced incidence of communicable diseases.
- Assured compliance with federal regulations for hiring and placement of handicapped persons.

---

*From Doster, M., and others: Health of school personnel: report of the American Public Health Association, Education and Services School Health Section, Washington, D.C., 1980, The Association.

Health standards for school personnel

When a child is legally mandated to attend school for at least 10 years, it is only right that parents would expect that their child not be exposed to undue health hazards. Thus having health standards for school personnel benefits children, the school personnel themselves, and the community at large.

The School Health Education and Services Section (formerly the School Health Section) of the American Public Health Association summarized the varied benefits to be derived from having health standards for school personnel. These benefits are presented in the box above.

COORDINATION OF THE SCHOOL HEALTH PROGRAM

For a school health program to be effective, coordination of all major aspects of the program is necessary. In some cases, one individual is given primary responsibility for this administrative function. Thus the likelihood of efficient use of various school resources and facilities is enhanced, since the linkage between the instructional, service, and environmental aspects of the program can be brought more clearly into focus.

The teacher and the health coordinator

In an ideal situation, each school district or system should have a coordinator or supervisor for the district's school health program. Unfortunately, few districts have employed such a person. In those instances where employment of a health coordinator is possible, the person employed should be a professionally trained school health educator who works with all of the professional and ancillary school staff, including administrators, to assure that a well-developed school health program is operating within the district. In those cases where a coordinator is not hired, the classroom teacher may have to assume the role of coordinator for a given building.

Numerous functions have been attributed to the health coordinator but a summary of those most commonly found include the following*:

To organize and supervise the school health program

To coordinate the activities of such a program with those in the community—health departments, civic and professional organizations, parents, police safety programs, physicians, dentists, private and voluntary health agencies, and school and community health councils

To help teach in the instructional program

To maintain a continuous evaluation program

To plan for in-service education

To help develop an articulated health and safety curriculum

To counsel individual students following referral

To serve on the community health council

---

*Adapted from Schaller, W.: The school health program, ed. 5, New York, 1981, W.B. Saunders Co. and Anderson, C., and Creswell, W.: School health practice, ed. 7, St. Louis, 1980, The C.V. Mosby Co.

To chair the school health council

To establish procedures for purchasing and distributing instructional material

To furnish the staff with information about the total school health program

To help prepare policies and procedures for school health services

To develop a plan for keeping health records

To provide procedures for student referral

To prepare and interpret emergency care procedures for faculty and staff

To provide leadership in the promotion of healthful school living

In-service education. The provision of in-service education programs for teachers is a responsibility of central administration but is often coordinated by the health coordinator. The in-service program provides one way teachers can keep up to date on health matters that affect the school-age child. A good program of in-service education can help boost teacher morale and keep the school health program dynamic.

Individual guidance. Through planned conferences and informal talks the supervisor can help teachers analyze and solve the problems that relate to their own classroom situations and teaching. Much of this is concerned with evaluation of the teaching-learning process. The conference may be based on classroom observation by the coordinator. Such observation is concerned with helping the teacher do a better job, *not* with personal criticism of the teacher.

Refer to Chapter 6 for detailed information on guidance and informal education.

Communication. To bring helpful information and ideas to teachers is one of the chief functions of the school health coordinator. Elementary classroom teachers cannot possibly keep up with all the important literature in school health, thus the coordinator has a major function to keep the staff aware of new developments in the field.

Research and curriculum development. An important but often overlooked function of the health coordinator is that of stimulating and guiding teachers in research projects. Of course, most teachers cannot be expected to carry out extensive investigations in addition to their normal teaching load. Yet, with help and guidance from the supervisor, significant problems can be selected and delineated for worthwhile study in an elementary school. Important data can often be collected within the framework of routine classroom activities. Policy and procedures based on objective evidence offer far more likelihood of success than those predicated on empirical opinion. By having teachers directly involved in policy making, it is more likely that the policy will be understood and accepted than if the policy were externally developed.

The teacher and the administrator

Technically speaking, education is a function of the state. The Tenth Amendment to the Constitution of the United States clearly places on each state the responsibility for the education of its children and youths. The Supreme Court has interpreted this part of the Constitution as meaning that final authority for education resides with state government. In general, however, local school districts hold the power to almost completely control the educational policies and programs in their schools. This situation works well when the school district is strong and well financed but poorly in those districts where population and money are insufficient to provide adequate schools and educational services.

Even good local school districts cannot provide certain services that make for better schools. These include distribution of state school funds, professional preparation of teachers, and certification of teachers. Then, too, there is a legal provision in almost all of our 50 states that requires that certain aspects of health instruction—notably alcohol, tobacco, and drugs—be included in the curriculum (see Chapter 10). However, most of these are antiquated statutes couched in heavy, stilted terms. Actually, they serve mainly as echoes from the past, reminding us of the bygone era of "blood and bone" health teaching with its emphasis on moralizing and preaching.

The majority of states now require that pupils be immunized against diphtheria, whooping cough (pertussis), tetanus (lockjaw), polio, measles, and German measles. The smallpox vaccination is no longer generally required, since the disease has been officially deemed as having been eradicated.

Since the state health department is the supreme power in matters of public health, the school is legally bound to conform to certain standards of sanitation and communicable disease control. Yet, few of these legal powers are actually brought to bear on a local school system. Most states promote school health programs by providing consultative service and guidance through school health specialists in departments of education and departments of public health at the state level.

Administrators and school board members who understand the problems and appreciate the values of school health and health education are essential to an effective program. Experience with health programs in elementary schools has shown with vivid clarity that the success of any such program is basically dependent on the attitude of school administrators and school board members. When administrators favor and support a sound health program, it is more likely to be initiated and carried out successfully. Fortunately, in recent years the leading professional societies of administrators have recommended that school health programs be established for all schools. However, teachers may need to encourage administrators to take active leadership in providing effective school health programs.

At the superintendent level this leadership often takes shape through stimulation of school evaluations by professional groups and citizens' advisory committees. Specific suggestions for evaluation of the school health program are discussed in Appendix H in some detail.

As the official leader in an individual elementary school, the principal has much influence on the health program. Through concern for a sound program, provision of released time for conferences, establishment of in-service programs on health-related topics, encouragement of teachers, efforts to secure textbooks and other learning materials, and consistent interest in the many activities of the school health program, the principal helps classroom teachers assume their responsible roles in school health.

The teacher and the school nurse

With the lack of coordinators in the schools, the school nurse may commonly be the individual who promotes and coordinates the program. The classroom teacher should make every effort to work closely with the school nurse in matters of pupil health. Although some school nurses are employed directly by the school and others are employed by local or state health departments, it is a fundamental school staff function of the teacher to offer full cooperation to the nurse serving the school.

There are numerous areas in which the teacher and nurse can be of great help to each other. The nurse can help the teacher by letting the teacher know the signs and symptoms of various health problems, by establishing referral mechanisms, by assisting with the instructional program through securing speakers and material aids, by working with the teacher in terms of health guidance (see Chapter 6), and by aiding the returning student to readjust to the classroom. The teacher can help the nurse through the daily observation of children, through assisting in screening, and through referring suspected health problems, including suspected child abuse or neglect. Child abuse is not always physically manifested. In fact, mental abuse may be more devastating to the child in the long run. A child who is "beaten" mentally may become disconsolate, dispirited, and withdrawn. In any case, the basic procedure for reporting any suspected health problem should be part of the written policies and procedures of the school district. The administration should acquaint all employees with these materials.

Once a child has been referred, the teacher is not free of responsibility. It is important that the teacher follow up the referral to see that something is done. Naturally this could and should be done in conjunction with other school personnel. It is usually rather easy to determine if something has been done, since the teacher will have daily contact with the referred child. Further, the teacher can exert some control over the situation through rearrangement of the classroom environment, including seating, and through altering the daily classroom schedule.

The teacher can aid the school nurse through assisting with screening procedures (see Chapter 5). The most common measures include growth and development, vision, hearing, and possibly postural defects (primarily scoliosis). Some schools may offer mental health screening. It must be remembered that these procedures are not diagnostic tools. They are used merely to determine whether a potential problem exists. The teacher should be familiar with various mental health screening measures and know how to explain the results to the parents.

The teacher will be able to do some health counseling using the screening procedures as objective evidence. This should be coordinated with the school nurse. Often this counseling occurs on a less formal basis throughout the progress of the average school day.

Screening tests also afford the opportunity for incidental instruction. As the tests are being administered, the teacher has an opportunity to do incidental health teaching on topics directly related to the screening process. Such questions as "Why should this screening be done?" "What might be detected?" and "Will this hurt?" all provide excellent instructional potential.

To assure close rapport between the teacher and the nurse, teacher-nurse conferences are necessary. Unfortunately, it is often difficult to find the time in the already crowded school day to schedule such meetings, but with the help of the school principal, this problem should not be difficult to resolve. These conferences may be formal or informal, depending on the topics to be considered. Further information concerning the nature of teacher-nurse conferences is presented in Chapter 5.

THE TEACHER AS A LINK WITH THE COMMUNITY IN SCHOOL HEALTH

As the school and the community join more closely in their efforts to improve education, many reciprocal advantages accrue. Opportunities that will benefit the school health program are abundantly evident. The teacher has many occasions to work with resource people in the community and should capitalize on these opportunities.

Community organizations and people who are capable of providing cooperative assistance include the following:

Medical societies and individual physicians
Dental societies, individual dentists, and dental hygienists
Local and state health departments
Local and state voluntary health agencies
Parent-teacher associations
Police and fire departments
Community health and safety councils
Child guidance clinics, individual psychiatrists and clinical psychologists
Red Cross
Service clubs
Departments of education
Departments of welfare
Youth councils
Boy Scouts and Girl Scouts
YMCA, YWCA, YMHA, CYO, 4-H Clubs, Future Farmers of America, and other youth organizations

These organizations often have speakers' bureaus or will provide other resource materials to the classroom teacher. For example, the fire department may be willing to present demonstrations of home fire safety hazards or assist the teacher in teaching children techniques of artificial resuscitation. Other voluntary agencies

may provide pamphlets, slides, or movie films for classroom use. All the teacher has to do is ask for the material.

The new teacher would be well advised to consult with the school nurse and other experienced teachers in the school to learn quickly the resources available in a given area.

SCHOOL HEALTH COUNCILS

One of the best ways to fully coordinate the personnel resources of the community is through the school health council. Membership of the school health council can include representatives from the following groups:

Teachers
Pupils
Parents
Medical society
Dental society
Health department
Voluntary health agencies
Food service and custodial staffs
School administrators (principal and school health coordinator)
School nurses and physicians

Of course membership of the council will vary, depending on the size of the school and the nature of the community. However, even in small rural elementary schools, council membership can include the principal or a delegated representative, parents, pupils, classroom teachers, and custodians. In some communities an advisory health council is established for all schools in the area; in others each school has its own council. Regardless of the size or makeup of the school health council, it has three basic functions: (1) to identify health and safety problems of pupils and school personnel, (2) to study these problems, and (3) to make recommendations to the school administration for solution of the problems. It is important to understand that the council is an advisory body; it is not responsible for taking direct action. The council may, however, conduct evaluation studies, propose changes in the policies for the instructional, services, or environmental program, or propose the need for a total curriculum revision. The school health council is also a good forum to receive input from parents and interested citizens on matters related to school health policies and practices.

COMMUNITY HEALTH COUNCILS

The community health council is the community counterpart to the school health council. It has the potential of linking the school health program and the community health program. This council becomes a community voice for the airing of health problems seen by the various groups within the community. By having a close, cooperative link with the community, the school health program can become more responsive to the needs of that community. Membership on the community health council may include representatives from the following:

School health council
Voluntary health agencies
Medical and dental organizations
Private industry
Civic or community service clubs
Religious organizations
Educational organizations
Parent-teacher groups
Youth organizations
Police and fire departments

In cities where the community health council has been successfully established, the school health program has been used as a focal point for community health services. Such things as sickle cell screening, school safety (especially crosswalks in the vicinity of the school), drug education referral centers, and many other health problems can be coordinated between the school and the community health programs.

THE TEACHER AS A MEMBER OF THE SCHOOL STAFF IN HEALTH MATTERS

As has been discussed, teachers do many things with and for pupils beyond the routine classroom learning activities. The teacher's role as counselor in the various health services, and several ways in which a teacher provides a link between school and community has been presented. In many of these activities the teacher also serves as a member of the school staff.

However, in the role of staff member, the elementary classroom teacher also has the responsibility for taking part in committee work and other organized efforts aimed at improvement of the school health program. The teacher may also serve on committees concerned with textbook selection, curriculum development, civil defense, special events planning, safety patrol, school clubs, building and grounds, audiovisual aids, and food service. The work of certain committees, particularly the health council and the proper concern of all teachers, frequently relates to the safety and health of the school environment.

THE TEACHER AS A MEMBER OF THE PROFESSION IN SCHOOL HEALTH

A good teacher tries constantly to improve health instruction by using better methods and by keeping abreast of new developments in a variety of fields, including school health. As has been suggested earlier, many teachers will conduct surveys and experiments in connection with their health teaching or other school health work. This, too, is the mark of a professional person. Objective conferences with the health coordinator about teaching methods and materials also help the teacher improve approaches in the classroom.

Through membership in national and state educational associations the elementary teacher takes part in the profession to a fuller extent. National and state societies generally make provision for school health concerns through member associations, divisions, or sections. Organizations specifically concerned with school health include the American Alliance for Health, Physical Education, Recreation, and Dance, the

American School Health Association, the American Public Health Association (School Health Education and Services Section), and regional and state branches of such groups.

All in all, the life of elementary school classroom teachers is a diversified one in regard to school health. As has been discussed they must live up to a reputation as "specialized generalists" if they are to make contributions in the three basic phases of the health program. Although many teachers-to-be approach their first position with some trepidation, all the evidence and experience indicate that the majority of classroom teachers can and do make substantial contributions to school health and health education. All they need is a bit of confidence and an understanding of the fundamental concepts of health instruction, health services, and healthful school living. The raw material is America's richest resource; the product is a healthier nation.

QUESTIONS FOR DISCUSSION

1. The text lists five basic areas of competency for the elementary teacher. Do you feel it is realistic to expect that elementary teachers possess all these qualities? Why or why not?
2. What are three characteristics of health teaching that distinguish it from other phases of the elementary school curriculum?
3. What factors do you think led to making certain topics controversial areas of discussion? How might you, as a teacher, deal with these controversial areas in the classroom?
4. How might teachers keep abreast of new trends and developments in the elementary school health program?
5. What are three ways the teacher may provide for individual differences within the classroom?
6. How might the formulation of a school health council enhance the overall school health program?
7. How would you go about organizing a school health council?
8. What is the role of the community health council in the school health program?
9. What are some of the ways teachers can find out about the individual differences in health status among pupils?
10. What are the basic objectives of elementary school health education?
11. What are the fundamental purposes of the health services program in elementary schools?
12. What are the basic purposes and makeup or membership of the typical school health council?
13. How and why should teachers work closely with school nurses?
14. What are four ways in which the school health coordinator can help classroom teachers?

SELECTED REFERENCES

American Association of School Administrators: Curriculum handbook for school executives, Washington, D.C., 1973, The Association.

American Public Health Association: Health of school personnel, report of the School Health Education and Services Section, Washington, D.C., 1980, The Association.

Anderson, C., and Cresswell, W.: The school health program, ed. 7, St. Louis, 1980, The C.V. Mosby Co.

Association for Supervision and Curriculum Development: Perceiving, behaving, becoming; a new focus in education (yearbook), Washington, D.C., 1962, National Education Association.

Berman, L.: New priorities in the classroom, Columbus, Ohio, 1968, Charles E. Merrill Publishing Co.

Bruner, J.: Towards a theory of instruction, Cambridge, Mass., 1966, Harvard University Press.

Charles, C.M.: Individualizing instruction, ed. 2, St. Louis, 1980, The C.V. Mosby Co.

Cornacchia, H., and Barrett, S.: Consumer health, ed. 2, St. Louis, 1980, The C.V. Mosby Co.

Denver Public Schools: The health interests of children, Denver, 1954, Denver Public Schools.

Joint Committee on Health Education Terminology: New definitions, New York, 1973, Society for Public Health Education.

Joint Committee on Health Problems in Education: Why health education in your school? Washington, D.C. and Chicago, 1974, National Education Association and the American Medical Association.

Levy, M.R., Greene, W.H., and Jenne, F.H.: Competency-based professional preparation, School Health Review, July/Aug. 1972.

Ludwig, D.J.: Teacher preparation in health education, School Health Review, Sept./Oct. 1972.

McCormack, P.: Report card grades teachers, Boston Herald American, June 13, 1976.

National Commission on Community Health Services: Health is a community affair, Cambridge, Mass., 1966, Harvard University Press.

Oberteuffer, D., Harrelson, O., and Pollock, M.B.: School health education, New York, 1972, Harper & Row, Publishers, Inc.

Read, D.A., and Greene, W.H.: Creative teaching in health, New York, 1980, Macmillan, Inc.

Read, D.A., Simon, S.B., and Goodman, J.B.: Health education: the search for values, Englewood Cliffs, N.J., 1977, Prentice-Hall, Inc.

Schaller, W.: The school health program, ed. 5, New York, 1981, W.B. Saunders Co.

Sliepcevich, E.M.: School health education study; a summary report, Washington, D.C., 1964, School Health Education (also health education; a conceptual approach to curriculum design, St. Paul, Minn., 1967, 3M Education Press).

Staton, W.M.: Monday morning at the movies, School Health Review, Jan./Feb. 1975.

Valente, C., and Lumb, K.: Organization and function of a school health council, The Journal of School Health, **51**:466-468, Sept. 1981.

Valett, R.E.: Humanistic education: developing the total person, St. Louis, 1977, The C.V. Mosby Co.

Walker, J.E., and Shea, T.M.: Behavior modification: a practical approach for education, ed. 2, St. Louis, 1980, The C.V. Mosby Co.

Willgoose, C.E.: Health education in the elementary school, ed. 5, Philadelphia, 1979, W.B. Saunders Co.

PART TWO

Healthful school living

3

HEALTHFUL SCHOOL ENVIRONMENT

Physical aspects

When we by law require children to spend so many of their formative years in our schools, we assume a legal and ethical responsibility to provide safe and healthful buildings, equipment, facilities, and services.

Even though this obligation is accepted and the concept understood in our educational literature and professional pronouncements, tens of thousands of American schools fail to meet minimal health and safety standards for students. Many schools are considered by experts to be firetraps; others maintain overcrowded classrooms, some are hotbeds of violence; still others carry tenured teachers who are emotionally unstable; many are not meeting the emotional needs of students; many have questionable water and sewerage systems; most are operating unsafe school buses; and few provide a sanitary, nutritious food service.

A physically and emotionally healthful school environment is essential to the highest quality of education in our schools. The quality of life cannot be enriched for students who are forced to strive to learn and grow in schools that fail to provide a pleasant, conducive atmosphere.

WHAT IS A HEALTHFUL SCHOOL ENVIRONMENT?

Healthful school living . . . embraces all efforts to provide at school physical, emotional, and social conditions which are beneficial to the health and safety of pupils. It includes the provision of a safe and healthful physical environment, the organization of a healthful school day, and the establishment of interpersonal relationships favorable to mental health.*

Clearly this definition dispels the idea that healthful school living is confined to the mere provisions of a safe and sanitary environment in which learning can occur. The overriding purpose for providing a healthful school environment is to establish a climate for children that enables them to feel good about being in school and that enhances opportunities for learning.

*Joint Committee on Health Problems in Education of the National Education Association and the American Medical Association: Healthful school environment, Washington, D.C., 1969, The Associations.

HOW DO SCHOOL SITE AND BUILDINGS AFFECT STUDENT HEALTH?

Some specific physical components of healthful school living include site and building construction, internal organization such as thermal control, lighting, and acoustics, water supply, sanitation, food services, school bus safety, and fire prevention and protection.

School site and construction

The construction of facilities in which learning is to occur has been a major concern for many decades. In 1829 Alcott wrote an "Essay on the Construction of Schoolhouses,"* which emphasized the impact of the environment on the education process. Ever since that time, many rules, regulations, and standards have been promulgated to help assure that the school physical plant is safe, sanitary, free of unnecessary hazards, and conducive to maximizing the potential for learning. The critical factor is to plan ahead and not operate on a crisis basis. The mere construction of a new building is no assurance that it contributes favorably to the educational experience of the child. A facility poorly planned in terms of location, internal space, color, internal and external traffic patterns, and many other environmental considerations too numerous to mention here may in fact detract from overall learning.

The selection of a site involves such considerations as the following:

Accessibility for local traffic

Distance from busy or noisy streets

External odor and noise factors (airports, railway stations, dumps, industrial areas)

Adequate space (playgrounds, athletic fields)

Freedom from unnecessary hazards (open holes, water hazards)

Adequate drainage

---

*Means, R.: A history of health education in the United States, Philadelphia, 1962, Lea & Febiger.

Hookups to community water and sewage lines

Amenability to esthetic landscaping

Adequate pupil population within a rather limited radius (often considered one-half mile or less in large cities)

Numerous innovations in school construction occurred in the early 1960s. Too often these facilities were based on an architectural idea rather than the effective use of the facility as an institution of learning. These new ideas in construction frequently did not adequately facilitate learning. Unfortunately, little research that demonstrates what would be best in school facilities has taken place. Now, however, much more consideration has been given the interiors of the building than before. Modular construction, open classrooms, learning wings, and central resource libraries as well as the more traditional single-level or multilevel self-contained classroom may be found in new construction.

Internal organization. It is important that the architect give consideration to the needs of the child and provide lowered drinking fountains, toilets, sinks, light switches, and chalkboards and storage space for coats, hats, lunches, and other items. Of special concern are the needs of the handicapped who might attend the school. Additionally, classrooms large enough to permit activities of children, areas that can be used in quiet study or activity, and overall internal classroom flexibility such as mobile walls must be planned. The well-being of the faculty and staff must also be provided for with a teacher's lounge and separate restroom facilities that are both functional and appealing in appearance. Some newer constructions contain two lounges, one for smokers and one for nonsmokers.

THERMAL CONTROL. The teacher frequently neglects to make adequate provisions for heating, ventilation, and air conditioning. Elementary school children have a higher metabolic rate than adult teachers and tend to be able to stay warm in seeming cold conditions. Since the human body radiates heat, the teacher can avoid adjusting the room temperature upward by wearing a sweater or long-sleeve shirt, blouse, or jacket in the classroom.

A classroom that is too cold for children can have an impact on their learning. The general recommendation for classroom temperature is between 65° to 70° Fahrenheit, depending on the age of the students and the type of activity that takes place.

The flow of air in a classroom must receive primary attention. If the school is not equipped with air conditioning equipment, the teacher should open windows or doors or secure a fan to assure adequate air movement.

LIGHTING. Footcandles of illumination at the work surface and in halls were commonly the determining factor for number, location, and intensity of lights located in schools. Today, the role of color, the use of natural as opposed to artificial lighting, the reflection and glare of light, and the type activity to be performed in the room are factors of greater importance.

The teacher should be aware that glare is a very annoying problem in the classroom setting. Speaking to the class while standing in front of unshaded windows so that the sun is shining brightly into the eyes of students is certainly not in their best interests. Further, if there is a great deal of activity outside the window where the teacher is standing, the child's attention will more easily be distracted. The prudent and judicious use of window shades as well as teacher movement can greatly reduce the problem of glare and outside movement. Glare can be further reduced by the proper placement of student desks or tables and the use of color. Children should not directly face windows or other sources of illumination. Teachers should use bulletin board materials that have a dull, non-reflecting surface rather than a shiny or highly reflective finish. If the bulletin boards are portable, they should be placed in an area of the classroom where the glare is at a minimum.

ACOUSTICS. For the most part, the teacher will not have much control over the classroom acoustics. In newer schools this matter has received attention. However, by keeping doors and windows closed except when ventilation is needed, the teacher can begin to reduce the amount of outside noise that filters into the classroom. Also, noise control can also be maintained by (1) keeping the noise level within the classroom to a minimum, (2) remembering to alert children to keep noise down in the halls by not shouting or conducting other rowdy activities therein, (3) careful planning of the location of the school facility, (4) careful placement of areas that have the potential for a high level of noise (such as shops, playgrounds, and music rooms), and (5) using carpeting and acoustic tile in the construction or remodeling of school facilities.

Water supply. School authorities have a legal and moral responsibility to provide a safe and sanitary water supply for the schools. Availability of a good water supply is a primary consideration when selecting the site for new school construction.

The best way to assure a safe water supply is to receive it from the local municipality, which has a civil responsibility to ensure that the water is safe for consumption for its constituents. In those areas where it is not possible to connect to the municipal water supply, wells can be drilled for water. Wells must be protected from septic tanks and other sources of external contamination.

A deep well is the type that should be used to supply the school. The well shaft itself must be drilled through one or more impervious layers of rock and then tapped into the water table. In general, shallow wells (those that do not pass through an impervious layer) are not acceptable for school water supplies because of their susceptibility to contamination by materials that percolate through the soil and enter the water table.

When the well is in place, it should be closed and encased in a concrete sleeve or other non-invasive type material. It is important that the well be sealed at the top and that the delivery line be large enough to handle peak demands.

The well must be able to provide enough water for all of the daily school activities that require water. Automatic toilet flushing devices used in the school restrooms greatly increase the demand for water. Thus careful planning is needed to ensure an adequate water supply if these devices are to be used in either new or remodeled facilities.

Periodic testing of the water supply should occur to assure that it is free of contamination. This should be done by experienced personnel, usually from the sanitation division of the local health department. Testing should occur at least once a month. If the water supply is found to be questionable, it may be necessary to chlorinate it. The contaminants can usually be rendered harmless, and the water can be used without fear of illness.

FOUNTAINS. Drinking-water fountains should be located in accessible positions and be operable by those who must remain in a wheelchair. Use of "arc stream" fountains is preferable to using the "bubbler" type fountain because the arc stream keeps the person who is drinking away from the direct source of the water. If the individual has a communicable disease, the likelihood of contaminating the bubbler fountain is much greater than that of the arc stream fountain. It is also important that the pressure of the water emitted from the fountain be powerful enough that children will not have to put their mouths too close to the outlet jet to drink.

TOILET ROOMS. The preferred location for the toilet facilities is one with an outside exposure to direct, natural lighting. This is because of the effect of sunlight on select pathogenic organisms. It is important that the toilet facilities be accessible and not located in the basement; there are supervisory reasons for this as well as considerations of distance from the various classrooms in the school. There should be easy access to toilets for the handicapped, which is yet another reason for lavatories to be located on the ground level. Both wash basins and commodes should be accessible to the handicapped. At least one commode that has a closable door for privacy should be provided for the handicapped.

Wash basins in the restrooms (or in classrooms for that matter) should be equipped with hot and cold running water. They should have liquid soap dispensers rather than solid soap. The major problem with bar soap is the possibility of it being involved in an accident when someone steps on it, slips, and is injured.

Sanitation. Students should not be subjected to an unsanitary environment. Provisions must be made for the safe and effective removal of waste from the school. Where daily pick-up of garbage is not possible, refuse should be kept in a secure place where it will not attract animals or vermin that will scatter it around the facility. The use of sturdy disposal cans with tight lids for sanitary storage of waste is advisable.

SEWAGE DISPOSAL. Connection with the municipal sewage system is the best way to dispose of sewage. If this is not possible, septic tanks must be installed. Where running water is not available, chemical holding tanks will have to be used. These tanks are available from many reputable firms and can be used without a great deal of inconvenience. Where chemical tanks are used, they should be kept extremely sanitary and adequately ventilated. Regular disposal of the contents of the holding tanks can be accomplished through a professional sanitary disposal firm.

When installing a septic tank, expert consultation is important. Soil percolation rates (the speed at which liquid seeps through the soil) for the drain field are critical. The septic tank should be located below the source of water in schools that use wells to avoid the possibility of contaminating the water supply. The tank should be accessible for annual cleaning to ensure that there are no pathogenic bacteria contained in the tank.

SCHOOL FOOD SERVICES: ARE THEY ADEQUATE?

The feeding of children in schools is big business. It is also big politics, and it certainly is "no small potatoes" when it comes to the nutrition and health of millions of American children.

Yet for millions of America's students the school breakfast, school lunch, or both is their only chance for a nutritious meal during the day. Repeated surveys show that many school-age children and youth, from *all* socioeconomic levels, are subsisting on diets that are nutritionally marginal if not frankly deficient. There is a pressing need for better school lunches and expansion of the school breakfast program.

School lunch program

Originating in 1935 under Section 32 of Public Law 74-320 (the Agricultural Adjustment Act) under which the federal government bought farm commodities for distribution to schools as a way to absorb farm surpluses and support agricultural incomes, the National School Lunch Act (PL 79-396) was passed in 1946. The purpose of this law was to formalize the process initiated in the mid-1930s, and it authorized financial assistance to public and private schools that had nonprofit lunch programs. Thus the goals of the program were to (1) distribute surplus farm commodities and support farm income, and (2) safeguard the health of school children.

In 1954 the Agricultural Act (PL 83-690), which encouraged fluid milk consumption along with the lunch program, was passed. Since both the National School Lunch Program and the Agricultural Act were basically temporary programs, Congress passed the Child Nutrition Act (PL 89-642) in 1966, giving both prior acts permanent authorization. In 1970 uniform national eligibility guidelines were issued for free and reduced-price meals so more low-income children could participate.

The National School Lunch Program is by far the largest and most comprehensive of any of the six child nutrition programs administered by the Food and Nutrition Service of the United States Department of Agriculture.* Participa-

*Nelson, K., and others: The national evaluation of school nutrition programs: review of research, vol. 1, Santa Monica, Calif., 1981, System Development Corporation.

tion in the program has grown from 6.6 million children in 1946 (approximately 24% of eligible school children) to 27.4 million children (61% of eligible school children) in 1979. At present it is estimated that over 94% of all schools in the United States participate in the National School Lunch Program.

The overall cost of school lunches is almost $4 billion a year. Although the amounts expended in each state differ, about half of the cost is divided between federal and state governments, and the other half comes from "lunch money" from parents. Half of the federal contribution is in the form of food commodities. The federal government contributes to each school meal based on the percentage of students who get free or reduced-price meals. On the average, if less than 60% of the children get reduced-price meals, the school is reimbursed at the rate of 75 cents per meal. If more than 60% of the children get reduced-price meals, the reimbursement is increased to 77 cents per meal. If the school has a high proportion of "especially needy" children, federal assistance may be paid for the full cost of the meals (up to $1.32 per lunch). Overall, the federal government averages about 56% of the total cost of the school lunch program. The state pays 18%, and students pay approximately 26%.

School breakfast program

Because of recognition of the urgent need for many elementary and secondary children to have the opportunity to eat a well-balanced breakfast, pilot breakfast programs have been initiated with the support of the U.S. Department of Agriculture. As in the school lunch program, all public and nonprofit private schools may participate in the breakfast program. In 1980, over 3.6 million children participated.

Study and experience have shown that, as with the lunch program, when students participate in a school breakfast program, they learn better, have fewer complaints of headache and stomach ache, and have fewer behavior problems.

To meet the U.S. Department of Agriculture nutrition standards, breakfasts must serve as often as possible fruit or juice, milk, bread or cereal, and a meat or meat substitute.

The federal government on the average per state contributes to each school breakfast at the following relative rates:

1. All breakfasts—8.75 cents (state-wide average) reimbursement for each breakfast served
2. Free—72 cents additional for all breakfasts served to children who qualify for free breakfasts
3. Reduced price—42 cents in addition to the basic rate paid for all meals served to children who qualify for reduced price breakfasts

The problems

A number of problems have become painfully apparent over the years since the National School Lunch Act was passed during the Truman Administration over 3 decades ago. The program has made substantial contribution to the health of millions of American students, but critics from the field of nutritional science and the congressional arena continue to point up these problems:

1. The *quantity* of food, affected by the changing availability of farm surplus commodities, does not necessarily assure a *quality* diet for growing children and youth.

2. Increasing financial burden has fallen on parents, since, by implicit Congressional sanction, states can count student's lunch payments as part of the matching formula. The result has been a tendency to favor children whose parents can provide lunch money while at the same time limiting the nutritional opportunity of pupils whose parents cannot afford even the modest matching lunch cost.

3. Economic eligibility guidelines—who pays how much for what students—have contributed to administrative, political, social, and—for the student—psychologic problems.

4. Nutritionally superior school lunches are the exception, not the rule. Studies show that many school lunches are deficient in complete proteins and in vitamins A, B_1 (thiamine), B_6 (pyridoxine), C (ascorbic acid), and D, and contain excess fats, salt, and sugar.

5. U.S. Department of Agriculture regulations now permit competitive foods to be sold in vending machines in school lunchrooms to provide students with foods equal in nutrition to meals served in the standard school lunch. Sharp criticism has been leveled at this modification of the national school lunch program, since it opens the door for students to pass up the school lunch for more appealing, but less nutritious, "junk" foods. However, an increasing number of school systems are limiting vending machine sales to milk, fruit juices, and nutritious foods.

6. Food and labor costs are causing a financial crisis for schools and parents in providing nutritious school lunches and breakfasts. A U.S. Department of Agriculture study revealed that a 5-cent increase in meal price resulted in a *10% average decrease* in the number of students able to pay for school lunches.

Too much too soon?

A growing body of evidence indicates that high serum cholesterol levels are a major risk factor in the development of coronary heart disease and premature fatal heart attack. It has also been clearly established that this buildup of blood cholesterol accelerates during adolescence, especially among boys.

In a classic, carefully controlled, study at Saint Paul's School in New Hampshire, researchers were able to substantially lower the serum cholesterol of approximately 500 boys by substituting polyunsaturated foods for those high in saturated fats.* These Harvard School of Public Health investigators modified students' dining hall diets by substituting low-fat milk for whole milk, using polyunsaturated vegetable oil in baked products and for frying doughnuts, re-

---

*Stare, F.J., editor: Atherosclerosis, New York, 1974, Medcom, Inc.

placing butter and regular margarine with a soft margarine, and serving whole eggs just once a week and a low-cholesterol egg mix twice. Other dietary modifications were made with the same purpose in mind—reduction of cholesterol and other hard fats.

Compounding the problem of high cholesterol and coronary heart disease is the hard fact that obesity continues to be a serious threat to health and a high quality of life for millions of American parents and their children. Obesity and malnutrition often go hand in hand—too many calories with too few essential nutrients.

We also have learned that most cases of adult obesity have their beginnings in childhood and adolescence. Yet we continue to serve school lunches and breakfasts dangerously high in fats, salts, sugars, and additives. Surveys of large samples of schools throughout the nation confirm this. Under current standards such hard-fat foods as regular peanut butter, whole-fat milk, processed cheese, fatty meats, frankfurters, and regular margarine or butter qualify for federal reimbursement under the national school lunch program.

Thus boys and girls are fed each day on those high-cholesterol foods as a result of financial expediency and lack of understanding of the role of dietary fats in human health. For the most part, neither school administrators, teachers, food service personnel, nor parents have any idea of the potential danger of these fatty foods.

Too little too late

As previously mentioned, repeated studies show that many school lunches are deficient in complete proteins, iron, and vitamins A and C. More than a few schools also fail to provide adequate amounts of such important nutrients as thiamine, pyridoxine, vitamin D, and magnesium. All of these are needed for optimal growth and development during childhood and adolescence.

Further, the American Heart Association recommends that not over 30% to 35% of the recommended daily allowance of calories be fat.

Too often U.S. Department of Agriculture meals exceed this recommendation. In August 1979 auditors from the Office of the Inspector General reviewed the school lunches served at 62 school districts and found that 70% did not meet minimum meal requirements. Clearly, something must be done to correct this situation.

Streamlining school food services

Perhaps like America's railroad dining car—a nostalgic financial failure—our school lunchrooms need to move into the jet age of airline-type central food service. The day of the haphazardly run kitchen must now give way to a more businesslike organization. Obviously, with over 5 billion lunches served in 1980, school food services have become big business.

Evidence is mounting that the planning and operation of school food services is best done by organizations experienced in large-scale meal delivery systems. Studies show that for the same worker cost centrally located kitchens can provide three times the number of meals that can be served under the existing unit kitchen system where meals are prepared in each individual school.

Recent experience in over 200 school districts has verified the heightened efficiency of the application of new food industry technology to school feeding programs.

The chief drawback to a central kitchen system is the high initial cost. Though such systems usually become economically stable in 1 or 2 years, many school districts cannot afford the initial financial outlay.

Improving school food services

Regardless of the merits or limitations of new school feeding legislation, teachers, school board members, administrators, and others concerned with student health can get information and assistance from the Child Nutrition Division of the U.S. Department of Agriculture (Washington, D.C. 20250), and the American

School Food Services Association (P.O. Box 10095, Denver, Colo. 80210). In addition, teachers and those directly concerned with providing school food services can write or call their state office for specific information.

At local and state levels there is continuing need for studies to determine the most efficient methods—lowest cost and highest nutrient meals—for raising the important contribution of the school feeding program to the health of elementary and secondary school children and youth.

School feeding and nutrition education

Certainly one of the chief advantages of the school lunch or breakfast is the opportunity it provides for relating classroom information on healthful diets to school feeding programs. Teachers can have students keep daily records of what they eat, including school meals, and discussions can be a significant part of a unit on nutrition. Of course, any diary records from students must be anonymous if reliable responses are to be obtained.

A recent news story told about an elementary school principal who was distressed at the food wastage in the lunchroom and had pupils take inventory of what had been thrown in trash cans 1 day. A pupil-prepared report disclosed that students had discarded the following items: forty-one sandwiches, two cartons of milk, two whole pieces of chicken, three bags of potato chips, nineteen apples, thirteen oranges, one piece of cake, an untouched carton of chocolate pudding, four whole carrots, two boxes of raisins, nineteen pieces of candy, and fourteen cookies! Obviously, simply offering food to children does not ensure that they will eat it.

Without sound nutrition education students may discard nutritious foods from the school lunch or breakfast, buy calorie-rich nutritionally poor foods from vending machines, or patronize one of the quick-food commercial establishments in the neighborhood. Again, health education appears as the crucial influence in choices and decisions of students whatever the environmental situation.

WHAT ABOUT SCHOOL BUS SAFETY?

School buses are part of the school environment because once the child steps aboard the bus he or she is under the jurisdiction and responsibility of the schools. The child's health and safety on the bus is just as important as it is when that child is in any other school facility or activity.

Each year about 100 students lose their lives in school bus accidents—35 as passengers and 65 while getting on or off the bus. Every day more than 300,000 school buses carry over 20 million boys and girls to and from school. All in all, the school bus is safer for children than the family or personal car, but there is substantial room for improvement. Unfortunately, parents and the general public usually are apathetic except for brief transient periods of emotional concern following a tragic accident killing large numbers of students.

The National Transportation Safety Board recently reported that 90% of America's school buses are unsafe for one reason or another. The National Highway Traffic Safety Administration has proposed new, tough requirements for all public transport buses, including school buses. Chief among these is the provision for padded, high-backed seats and safety belts for all passengers. The National Conference on school transportation has developed a code that contains minimum standards for school buses. This code is available from the National Education Association.

Congressional legislation, in the face of powerful lobbying and bureaucratic inertia, offers the promise of safer school buses. One of the better recent proposals in the U.S. House of Representatives includes these new national standards:

1. Seating systems including proper padding, firm anchoring to the floor, approved passenger belts, and higher seat backs
2. Improved emergency exits

3. Interior protection for passengers
4. Greater floor strength
5. More crash-resistant bodies and frames
6. Safer vehicle operating systems
7. Improved safety glass for windshields and passenger windows

Safety experts also believe that school bus transportation can be made safer by careful selection and training of drivers, skilled mechanical maintenance, nationwide uniformity of exterior color and bus stopping requirements, and avoidance of overcrowding and unruly pupil behavior.

ARE OUR SCHOOLS FIRETRAPS?*

Not too many years ago some fire safety experts estimated that approximately 30,000 schools in America could be classified as firetraps. Many magazine articles, continued public education by the National Safety Council and local and national fire officials, such popular films as *Towering Inferno*, and the Kentucky nightclub fire in 1977 have tended to increase public concern for fire prevention and protection. In 1980, the cost of fire damage to schools and colleges surpassed $90,000,000.

Still, many schools lack automatic fire alarm systems, and few have automatic sprinkler systems. Such systems should, at least, be installed in shops, chemistry laboratories, boiler rooms, supply rooms, and other fire-hazard areas. Local fire inspectors should be consulted by school administrators for regular inspections and recommendations for eliminating any existing dangerous conditions. The cost of alarm and sprinkler systems is a small price to pay for protecting the lives of children and youth in our schools.

The American Insurance Association urged that the following school fire-hazard conditions be checked and, when necessary, immediately corrected†:

1. Buildings where the walls or ceilings of exit corridors are surfaced with highly combustible finishes
2. Buildings with wood floors and masonry walls, especially if the pupils in the upper floors have no means of exit other than through stairs open to lower stories
3. Buildings of wood construction with pupils housed above the second story
4. Buildings with unventilated space below them where gas may collect and explode
5. Buildings with exit doors to the outside that cannot be readily opened from the inside
6. Buildings in which pupils on upper floors have no means of exit except down stairs that are open to lower stories having combustible walls and finishes or contents in storage that are combustible

With the increasing use of electrical current for audiovisual and other equipment in schools, careful periodic inspection by professionals should be made for faulty or overloaded wiring systems, a major fire hazard.

Monthly fire and disaster drills should be held for students and school personnel, and evacuation plans should be posted in every room. Fire extinguishers should be approved by local fire officials, inspected regularly, and their location and operation understood by teachers and other school personnel. All school personnel and students should be aware of the location of fire extinguishers and manually operated fire alarms in the school and of regular fire alarm boxes near the school.

As with other aspects of a safe and healthful school environment, instruction is essential for optimal fire prevention and protection.

RESPONSIBILITIES FOR HEALTHFUL SCHOOL LIVING

Healthful school living implies a joint responsibility among all persons who come into contact with the school. This would extend to those responsible for developing the physical plant (the board of education and the architect), school administrators, students, parents, custodians, and all ancillary staff.

---

*See the fire safety unit in Chapter 9 for use in educational programs.
†American Insurance Association: Safe schools, New York, 1968, The Association.

Board of education

Probably the most critical role in terms of healthful school living falls on the board of education. This group of individuals decides if, when, and where a school will be built or if existing facilities will be renovated to meet new standards. Their basic authority for these decisions is derived from the voters of the community as their elected representatives. It is these same voters who must ultimately provide the funds for any building or renovation programs suggested by the board.

A responsible board will consider carefully any recommendations for the construction of new or the renovation of existing facilities by holding meetings with school administrators, teachers, architects, and community representatives before they make their decision. The decision to construct a new school is not just a board project but rather a project of the community. The community will ultimately benefit from a well-planned and constructed school building that contributes positively to the students who attend the facility or suffer as the result of a facility that does not meet the needs of the students and the community.

It is the responsibility of the board to retain an architect who is reputable and has experience in school design. It is also their responsibility to approve the basic design presented by the architect. Before accepting a school design, the board should consult with school administrators and teachers to be sure that those persons are satisfied with the basic design, that it meets their needs as professional educators, and that it contributes to the learning of students. By taking this extra step, the board can add a great deal to the overall efficacy of any school planning. By consulting school officials the board develops within those individuals a greater sense of dedication and appreciation of the role they play in maintaining a healthful school environment.

Architect

Once the decision to construct or renovate has been made, the role of the architect be-comes quite formidable. If possible, it is generally advisable to retain an architect who has experience in school building construction. The construction of schools has, in fact, become a specialty within the architectural profession.

Working closely with school personnel and the board of health (which issues the building permits and does construction approval inspections), the architect has the primary responsibility to present a school plant design that embodies the considerations discussed earlier in this chapter. Too often the initial appearance of a school is appealing but on closer examination the school is not as functional as it might be.

To help overcome potential problems, the special needs of not only students but also school personnel should be considered. It is also quite important that the design be compatible with accessibility for handicapped and in compliance with Public Law 94-142, the Education for All Handicapped Children Act of 1975.

Administrators

School administrators have the major responsibility for keeping the board of education informed of needed changes within the educational system. They direct and control the daily operation of the school and must be informed of the needed changes in the physical plant that affect the overall quality of education. School population increases or decreases, deterioration of facilities, and other changes must be reported by school personnel to the superintendent, who then must relay this information with proposals for action to the board of education.

Teachers

The teachers are "on the firing line." They must make administrators aware of any special needs they may have. This far surpasses the mere physical component of the classroom and extends into all facets of school operation.

It is important that the teacher understand the unique features of a particular building so that those features can become an enhancement to the educational experience of the students.

The teacher can also instill a sense of "ownership" of the school into students through the regular instructional program. By keeping the custodial staff informed of needed repairs and the administration aware of any special needs, the teacher can contribute positively to the overall environment of the school.

Students

The pupils stand to benefit most from having a healthful school environment. Teachers must help them learn how to assume responsibility for keeping the school safe, sanitary, and clean. By using trash cans rather than throwing paper on the ground or floor, by refraining from writing graffiti on the restroom walls, by not defacing desks, chairs, and tables, by keeping their feet off the walls, by wiping their shoes on doormats before entering the building, and in other ways students will greatly assist in keeping a healthful school environment.

Custodians

At one time the custodian was the brunt of many jokes and stories about that person's lack of specialized skills. In today's modern school facility, the custodian must possess a broad range of mechanical and carpentry skills, knowledge of safety and sanitation principles, and general concepts of disease control. The custodian must also possess the ability to work with both students and staff.

The custodian must constantly be aware of the advantages and disadvantages of the wide range of cleaning and painting products on today's market and the new equipment available for use in the schools. In many cases the custodian will be called on to repair equipment. This person should periodically attend training workshops designed to update custodial knowledge and skills.

Lunchroom personnel

General sanitation as well as the serving of wholesome and attractive food should be of primary concern to lunchroom personnel. By being aware of and practicing good sanitation and food handling techniques, the lunchroom staff can help control possible food-borne disease outbreaks.

Most states require all persons who deal with feeding the public to undergo a food handler's sanitation course and a medical examination to show that they are free of any type of communicable disease. The food handler's course generally consists of learning about the need for refrigeration and heating, storage of foods, dishwashing, simple equipment maintenance, and various sanitation standards. Personal health habits and their potential for disease causation are also included.

It is important for teachers to keep the lunchroom personnel informed of various nutrition-related projects being conducted in the classroom; thus the lunchroom can become an extension of the classroom. In addition, lunchroom personnel can act in an advisory capacity for the teachers or can assist in the various classroom projects being undertaken. It is also important for parents to keep school officials informed of any possible food allergies of their children. This information must be passed to teachers, school nurses, and the lunchroom staff so that they might be alert for a potential food allergy problem.

SUMMARY

Of course, teachers have no choice in school site or construction unless they are among the few who have the opportunity to serve on a school plant planning committee for a new school. Hence, we must make the very best of what we inherit. Whatever the age or other problems of school site, buildings, and facilities, improvements can be affected by concerned administrators, teachers, school nurses, and others involved with the health and safety of students. School health councils are especially effective as instruments in bringing about favorable change.

Every school building in America should be maintained in accordance with state and local standards of safety, sanitation, and educational utility. Regular inspections of school buildings and facilities should be made by school administrators, local building inspectors, fire inspectors, health department sanitarians and safety experts, and other qualified personnel. Principals, teachers, custodial staff, food service personnel, school nurses, and others in the school should be alert each day for unhealthful or dangerous conditions in the building and on the school grounds.

QUESTIONS FOR DISCUSSION

1. What are the aims of a healthful school environment?
2. What considerations are included in a good program for healthful school living?
3. How can teachers and other school personnel help make improvements in old school buildings and poor school sites?
4. Why are school food service programs important to student health?
5. What are some of the major problems still existing in developing better school lunch and breakfast programs?
6. Why are central food service facilities considered to be better than individual school food preparation facilities?
7. What nutrients are often found lacking in many school lunch programs? What nutrients may be served in excess and too often?
8. What organizations can help start a new school feeding program or improve an existing one?
9. Why are so many school buses considered by safety experts to be dangerous?
10. What changes need to be made in the construction of school buses to make them safer?
11. What changes need to be made in the operation of school buses to make student transportation safer?
12. What are the chief fire dangers in today's schools?
13. How can school administrators and teachers improve programs of fire prevention and protection?
14. Why should the school be obligated to provide a healthful environment for students?
15. What factors have contributed to the school lunch program becoming a national controversy?
16. Discuss how the school physical environment might enhance or detract from the health services program and the health instruction program.

SELECTED REFERENCES

American Academy of Pediatrics: School health: a guide for health professionals, Evanston, Ill., 1978, The Academy.

Boles, H.W.: Step by step to better school facilities, New York, 1965, Holt, Rinehart & Winston.

Callan, L., and Rowe, D.: The role of the school sanitarian, Journal of School Health **43:**360-363, June 1972.

Commission on School Buildings of the American Association of School Administrators: Schools for America, Washington, D.C., 1967, The Association.

Egan, R.: Congress weighs safety standards for school buses, National Observer **48:**May 19, 1973.

Joint Committee of Health Problems in Education: Healthful school environment, Washington, D.C., 1969, National Education Association and the American Medical Association.

Knotts, G., and McGovern, J.: School health problems, Springfield, Ill., 1975, Charles C Thomas.

Means, R.: A history of health education in the United States, Philadelphia, 1962, Lea & Febiger.

Means, R.: Historical perspectives on school health, Thorofare, N.J., 1975, Charles B. Slack, Inc.

Nelson, K., and others, editors: The national evaluation of school nutrition programs: review of research, vol. 1, Santa Monica, Calif., 1981, System Development Corporation.

4
EMOTIONAL CLIMATE AND THE TEACHER

Some teachers are great. . . . They put bandages on my hurts—
on my heart, on my mind, on my spirit. Those teachers cared about
me, and let me know it. They gave me wings.

Thoughts about a drop-out*

When John Locke used the phrase, "mens sana in corpore sano"—a sound mind in a sound body—he expressed the interrelationships that exist between physical and mental health. He envisioned mental health as a condition of the whole personality, not as an entity separate from physical health. He stressed the importance of the total health of children. Current concepts of health also include reference to social and spiritual aspects introduced in Chapter 1.

The mental phase of health today has never had greater meaning. The tremendous anxieties, pressures, and concerns in the world have their effect on children and youth. The young people living in poverty and among bias and prejudice are especially subjected to extensive biological, psychological, sociological, and economic stress. The cultural, ethnic, racial, and economic inequalities, the tensions over world peace, the dichotomy of moral and social values, the stress on materialism, the need for good grades, the conformities to outmoded and antiquated practices and traditions in schools, and the inadequacies of educational opportunities create a social climate conducive to mental illness. The Joint Commission on Mental Health of Children stated*:

The major crisis of our time is a crisis of human relations . . . we have lost our capacity for mutual trust, love and responsibility. . . . Social changes on a major scale are required if all our children and youth are to . . . enjoy optimal mental health.

It is imperative that schools recognize these conditions and that teachers become aware of their roles in the promotion and maintenance of good mental health.

---

*McLeod, A.: Growing up in America: A background to contemporary drug abuse, Rockville, Md., 1973, National Institute of Mental Health.

*Report of Task Force VI and excerpts from the Report of the Committee on Children of Minority Groups by the Joint Commission on Mental Health of Children, New York, 1973, Harper & Row, Publishers, Inc.

In Chapter 3 the physical components of the environment as they relate to healthful school living received consideration. However, healthful school living includes the sum of the internal as well as external factors that act on the individual. Therefore the emotional climate in the school is a critical component affecting the mental health of both students and teachers. The *emotional climate* may be defined as a setting that gives consideration to students—their feelings, their beliefs, their physiological and psychological needs—as well as subject matter. It is a setting that treats pupils with kindness and humaneness. The following anonymous poem illustrates its meaning:

If a child lives with criticism, he learns to condemn.
If a child lives with hostility, he learns to fight.
If a child lives with fear, he learns to be apprehensive.
If a child lives with pity, he learns to feel sorry
for himself.
If a child lives with jealousy, he learns to feel guilty.
If a child lives with encouragement, he learns
to be confident.
If a child lives with tolerance, he learns to be patient.
If a child lives with praise, he learns to be
appreciative.
If a child lives with acceptance, he learns to love.
If a child lives with approval, he learns to like
himself.
If a child lives with recognition, he learns to have a
goal.
If a child lives with fairness, he learns what justice
is.
If a child lives with honesty, he learns what truth is.
If a child lives with security, he learns to have
faith in himself and those about him.
If a child lives with friendliness, he learns the world is
a nice place in which to live.

ANONYMOUS

Observations of pupil behaviors that may indicate mental health difficulties that may be the result of a poor school atmosphere. They may cause teachers to ask:

"Why is Bill always boisterous and rude?"
"Why does Ann cry easily?"
"Why is Susan so hard to reach?"
"Why is Jack so nervous?"

"Why does Sam use drugs?"
"What can I do to help Bob whose parents are alcoholics?"
"Why is Nancy frequently truant?"
"Why is Mary always so quiet and withdrawn?"
"Why does Bill become frightened so easily?"
"Why is Jane always sullen and unhappy?"
"Why is Ed constantly picking on other children?"
"Why is Marion having trouble getting along with her classmates?"
"How can I help, and what should I do to best understand and to help children with behavior problems?"

Architects, builders, and school administrators to a large extent, control the physical aspects of the school whereas teachers exert tremendous influence over the emotional climate in the classroom and in the school. The classroom is the teacher's domain. The atmosphere provided there contributes significantly to student learning. The perceptions pupils have of their physical surroundings, their teachers, and their peers all have impact on learning.

This chapter has been designed to provide (1) understanding about mental health and mental illness and the effect of the school emotional climate on these factors and (2) illustrations of the ways teachers can improve the school atmosphere to reduce student behavior problems, to discover ways to assist children in need of help, and to aid pupils to grow into happy, productive, and useful individuals who will make worthwhile contributions to the society in which they live.

WHAT IS MENTAL HEALTH?

Teachers need to understand the nature of mental health to be able to have an effect on the emotional atmosphere in schools. Although it is very difficult to define mental health to the satisfaction of everyone, for the purpose of this chapter it refers to the adjustment of the individual to self and to society so that the realities of life can be faced and the individual can function most effectively with the greatest satisfaction, cheerfulness, and socially acceptable behavior.

Mentally healthy persons are able to control their emotions and adequately meet situations that occur in their environment; they possess positive self-esteem, insight, and self-acceptance. The observable features of this adjustment may be identified in what is called personality or the individual's personality—the sum of the traits and characteristics that make each person a unique individual. Just as children have numerous combinations of traits and characteristics, many types and varieties of personalities exist.

Mental health is affected by the environment in which a person lives and by that person's experiences. It is an outgrowth of one's total life. Teachers and schools can contribute to the mental health of pupils by helping with the satisfactory fulfillment of their physiological and psychological or emotional needs. The physiological needs include food, air, water, warmth, rest and sleep, clothing, and freedom from disease and other health hazards. The psychological or emotional needs include the following:

1. Affection—love
2. Security—to belong, to have roots, to have protection
3. Acceptance as an individual—free of prejudice or bias, concern for individual differences
4. Achievement—success experiences, recognition
5. Independence—create and develop things, be on one's own, do things under one's own guidance and direction
6. Authority—guidance and direction by adults
7. Self-respect—courteous, fair, and just treatment

Mentally healthy individuals exhibit these characteristics:

1. Pursue reasonable goals using their talents and abilities.
2. Have a sense of self-respect, self-reliance, and achievement; feel worthwhile; have a high level of self-esteem.
3. Know they are liked, loved, and wanted.
4. Have a sense of security and are reasonably

at peace with themselves and their environment; enjoy life.
5. Can think and act rationally and realistically when seeking solutions to problems; are able to withstand frustration and anxiety, to persevere despite difficulty, and to ask for help without loss of self-esteem.
6. Can distinguish between feelings and facts.
7. Can maintain integrity in work and play; exhibit confidence and orderliness.
8. Are able to work in groups; are interested in others.
9. Respect the rights of others.
10. Face the realities of life and are able to accept responsibilities; are self-disciplined.

The mentally healthy individual has a positive self-concept and a realistic view of the culture in which that person lives. The individual can accept bigness or smallness of size, good or poor looks, artistic talent or lack of it, intellectual capacities or limitations. The individual can get along with children and adults in school, at home, in the neighborhood, and elsewhere. Normal individuals can function in the world about them by being able to adjust to its rules and conformities, to express their feelings by behaving in personally gratifying ways that the social order will accept, and to contribute to a changing and challenging society.

Mental health is usually considered a positive aspect of health. If it were placed on a continuum, it would be located at the extreme end and would represent the highest level of health to be achieved. However, it may also be considered to be negative and would be found at the lowest level of health, or mental illness. There are varying degrees of positive mental health just as there are varying degrees and kinds of mental illness. Often these variations are difficult to define or identify.

When basic physical and emotional needs are not met or are threatened, a variety of deviate behaviors may result*:

---

*Adapted from Cornacchia, H., Smith, D., and Bentel, D.: Drugs in the classroom: a conceptual model for school programs, ed. 2, St. Louis, 1978, The C.V. Mosby Co.

1. Overtimidity—withdrawing, crying easily
2. Overaggressiveness—bullying, quarreling, boisterousness
3. Excessive daydreaming—persistent inattentiveness
4. Excessive boasting or showing off
5. Poor sportsmanship
6. Undue restlessness—habit tics, stammering, nail-biting
7. Frequent accidents or near-accidents
8. Abnormal sex behavior
9. Difficulty in reading or reciting
10. Failure to advance in school at normal rate
11. Stuttering or other forms of speech difficulty
12. Lying, stealing, cheating
13. Resistance to authority, constant complaints of unfairness
14. Unhappiness and depression
15. Gradual deterioration and marked sudden drop in educational achievement
16. Lack of interest or motivation
17. Constantly seeking attention or popularity
18. Emotional outbursts such as temper tantrums or antisocial behavior
19. Overuse of various adjustment mechanisms such as rationalization, compensation, or projection

---

WHAT IS MENTAL ILLNESS?

Everyone experiences times of emotional stress. Occasional feelings of anger, loneliness, anxiousness, or depression are normal occurrences. However, when persons are unable to get along with themselves and others, they can become maladjusted and may be considered mentally ill. They cannot or will not adjust to socially acceptable norms for behavior. These pupils are said to be unsocial, emotionally disturbed, and disruptive, with behavior and personality problems. The extent of illness is a matter of degree as well as of kind. Some people have mild emotional disturbances, whereas others have severe mental health problems. Teachers should not interpret every maladjustment or expression of unacceptable behavior as an indication of illness. At times everyone ex-

periences mild disturbances. Students and adults may be unhappy, frustrated, anxious, depressed, angry, rude, boisterous, quiet, withdrawn, worried, unable to resolve problems; they may act irrationally, find it difficult to work with some people, or resort to the use of defense mechanisms without being what is usually thought of as mentally ill or emotionally disturbed. It is the frequent, repeated, and consistent manifestations of such behavior that may lead one to suspect mental or emotional disorder.

The types of mental illness may be categorized as follows:

psychoses Acute or chronic illnesses, the "insanities," that require intensive treatment in hospital settings; affect total personality, can be either organic or functional in origin; characterized by severe mood disturbances with serious changes in thought and feelings, by behavior withdrawal from reality, or by persistent delusions and hallucinations; include such conditions as schizophrenia, paranoia, general paresis, and senile psychosis.

neuroses Less severe disturbances that affect only portions of personality; include anxiety states, fears, phobias, hypochondriases, hysterias, obsessions, and compulsions.

personality disorders Psychosomatic problems of individuals (emotional problems expressed through physical ailments), drug addiction, chronic alcoholism, and delinquencies.

Mental illness is found in children as well as in adults. It is estimated that approximately 10% of pupils (5 million) have emotional problems and maladjustments requiring psychiatric help, with an additional 3% having seriously psychotic or prepsychotic conditions. In the average class of 32 boys and girls, a teacher may expect to recognize emotional difficulties in 3 or 4 pupils and identify 1 child needing psychiatric assistance.

Mental illness is considered to be the leading health problem in the United States. The following estimates have been made:

1. That approximately 20 million people are suffering from some form of mental or emotional illness; approximately 1 in 10 people is afflicted

2. That 1 person in 15 of those mentally ill will need hospitalization

3. That 30% to 60% or more of the patients who consult doctors have complaints caused in part by emotional disturbances

4. That 500,000 children suffer from psychoses and borderline psychotic conditions

5. That 1 million children are afflicted with personality disorders

6. That 1 in 3 of the 15 million youngsters reared in poverty have serious mental and emotional problems

7. That 6 million children and adults are mentally retarded—30 per 1,000; approximately 2 million are under 16 years of age; most are mildly retarded; estimated 40% have personality disorders

8. That approximately 250,000 to 600,000 children and youth are neglected and abused, with an estimated 6,000 deaths yearly. These pupils are subject to physical neglect, emotional neglect and abuse, physical abuse, and the battered child syndrome.

Mental illness is frequently a component of the following:

1. Alcoholism—alcohol is the most abused drug in the United States; there are 9 to 10 million alcohol abusers; approximately 200,000 develop each year; more than 20% of men admitted to mental institutions are alcoholics; problem drinking is a causal factor in almost half of the 54,000 traffic deaths yearly; in some Indian reservations the rate is 25% to 30% as against 6% to 7% in the total United States; almost $30 billion per year is spent on alcohol.

2. Drug addiction—there are approximately 500,000 narcotic addicts; use of amphetamines, barbiturates, hallucinogens (including LSD), and the sedative-hypnotics (marijuana) has greatly increased in recent years; some 55 million Americans have tried marijuana or hashish at least once; there are probably 400,000 to 500,000 daily users, with 22 to 23 million occasional users; in 1975 over $46 billion was spent on legal drugs ($225 for every man, woman, and child); large numbers of young people are using a variety of drugs; over 100,000 people die yearly from the side effects of legal drugs.

3. Juvenile delinquency—over 750,000 young people are in juvenile courts yearly; 30% to 40% have been there before; the rate is rising, particularly among those in the ghetto and the poor.

4. Broken home—one marriage in two ended in divorce in 1981 to 1982; the ratio is higher in teenage marriages.

5. Suicide—34,000 suicides occur yearly; this represents only 10% to 15% of the attempts made; 6.6% of the victims are 15 to 19 years old; boys try three times more than girls; among native Americans the rate is five times the national average, and for black youths it is 50% above the national average; it is one of the 10 leading causes of death in the United States and is the fourth leading cause of death among 15- to 19-year-olds; rates have greatly increased.

6. Emotional maladjustment and personality disorders—these are related to job maladjustments in industry and accidents; mental stress, school failures, criminal behavior, divorce, and absenteeism play an important precipitating role.

WHAT ARE THE CAUSES OF MENTAL ILLNESS?

Mental illness is caused by a multiplicity of complex factors. It may be related to heredity, to environment, and to the reciprocal interaction of these factors. It may develop in a context of interpersonal relations, starting with mother or father and later with other persons. Disturbances are more likely to occur during children's critical growth periods.

Although mental illness is usually not inherited, it is believed that schizophrenia and some types of neuroses, or a predisposition to them, may be inherited. Also, the bodily strengths or weaknesses with which individuals are born may lead to problems that result in illness. The person who is very small or very large in stature, who is unusually obese or thin, who has poor vision or hearing, or who has a deformed limb or body part may not be able to satisfy physiological or psychological needs. Therefore the individual may not be able to make suitable adjustments to these conditions.

Environmentally there are interrelated physical and psychological conditions and situations that may cause illness:

1. Physical or biochemical components
    a. Infections—brain inflammation
    b. Nutritional deficiencies—diabetes, anemia, nervous disorders
    c. Accidents—nervous system damage, loss of limb, physical deformity
    d. Glandular deficiencies or imbalance—abnormal body size and shape, excess nervousness and anxieties
    e. Alcohol—brain softening
    f. Anemia—lack of oxygen to brain, death, or damage to brain
    g. Drugs—death or damage to brain
    h. Physical defects—facial disfigurement, paralysis
    i. Birth problems—premature births, early pregnancy trauma
    j. Excess physical punishment for misbehavior
2. Psychological components
    a. Social relations with group or other persons—cultural and social differences, overly competitive society, peer culture—out-group, prejudice, insecurity, status, lack of self-esteem
    b. Love and marriage—unhappiness, maladjustments, sustained rejection
    c. Family conflicts—constant quarreling, divorce, housing, broken homes
    d. Occupational—work adjustments and pressures, economic status, job, money
    e. Sexual adjustments—inability to satisfy need
    f. Religious conflicts—within family or social group
    g. Parental attitudes—mother domination, rejection, overprotectiveness, discipline, expectations
    h. Parent personalities—chronic alcoholic, neurotic, parental fear and distrust of people, lack of care
    i. School experiences—grade placement, teacher competency and personality, discipline, competition for grades, inappropriate curriculum

After an accident a child may suffer a severe injury such as the loss of a limb. The pupil may not be able to regain a feeling of security or status with peers; the student may not be able to accept or adjust to the physical deformity. Likewise, a student whose parents are chronic alcoholics may not receive adequate nutrition, which may lead to anemia, nervousness, and other conditions.

The heredity and environmental factors in mental illness have a social relationship. The pupils, teachers, and other school personnel; the ministers, priests, rabbis, and others at church; the friends, physicians, and adults in the community; and the parents, grandparents, brothers, and sisters in the home play significant roles in the affection received, the stresses, tensions, and anxieties developed, the security provided—in fact, the total environment of a boy and girl. These people furnish the experiences that help or hinder children in satisfying their physiologic and psychologic needs. The lack of, or the improper, experiences result in the failure of these needs being fulfilled. The signs of maladjustment referred to previously may then begin to appear and be the behavior incipient to more serious mental health problems.

The incidence of mental illness among low-income native Americans, blacks, and other cultural and ethnic groups is greater than in the rest of the population. The poor are those deprived of the basic necessities of food, housing, medical care, education, and employment. They also experience bias, prejudice, and inequality of opportunity. Such omissions and attitudes are related to family conflicts, instability, frustration, failure, lack of personal dignity, and other stresses and problems.

Mental illness is a condition that grows over a period of time; it results from the exposure to many experiences and environments. A teacher viewing the behavior of a student in class must remember that the child has been exposed for 6 to 8 years to parents and others before the child reaches school. Therefore the roots for mental illness may have already been planted and may blossom forth in school when the pupil is faced with an additional unsatisfying or trying atmosphere.

Mental illness is a condition whose start is

difficult, if not impossible, to determine. The body can withstand, within reason, fear, anxiety, worry, and other stressful conditions. However, when stress becomes extreme, the individual can no longer tolerate these conditions and consequently becomes disorganized, disoriented, and maladjusted. This disturbance is often difficult to determine without expert help.

Teachers must realize that stress is experienced by everyone. It is a part of living. How a person responds to stressful conditions is extremely important. Individuals vary widely in their ability to adapt to stress. Also, stress has both positive and negative effects. In the classroom it may stimulate and motivate students positively to increase learning. Repeated negative reactions may result in adverse behaviors previously identified as occurring when needs are unmet. When this occurs, a cycle is initiated wherein the negative behavior evokes negative responses from others, causing more stress, and the cycle repeats itself.

Stress in the classroom setting is part of the process of education. Any teacher requirement or demand will create differing degrees of stress among pupils. It is important that teachers help children learn how to deal with these as well as life's stresses.

WHY SHOULD SCHOOLS BE CONCERNED WITH THE MENTAL HEALTH OF PUPILS?

The school is usually thought to rank second to the family as the most important unit in society affecting the mental health of children and must be concerned for these reasons:

1. The effectiveness of the educative process will be seriously hampered, since approximately 10% of pupils (5 million) are afflicted with emotional disturbances.

2. Educational failure, or the "failure syndrome," is one of the underlying factors that triggers acting-out in schools, depression, drug abuse, truancy, and other maladjustments. Children who exhibit such behavior have a lower self-concept, or self-identity.

3. The experiences to which a child is ex-

posed can help prevent serious difficulties or hasten such problems. Hence, schools play a role in both primary and secondary prevention of mental illness—before conditions occur and in the control of existing conditions. Early identification of children with emotional difficulties is important because remedial help can hopefully be provided at a time when intervention is maximally effective. The increase of problems and the great shortage of community mental health services and facilities add to the need for emphasis on prevention.

4. Behavior is more readily modified at the elementary level than later in life.

5. Children in ghetto and deprived areas must experience success in school with special attention given to their physical and psychological needs. Abrams and associates* reported that 48% of such children were already educationally handicapped in terms of readiness, or probable readiness, to enter school as compared with a black school where 76% of the pupils were affected and a white school of middle income families where 10% were affected. Many will perform poorly in school.

6. The school is the only agency outside the home that reaches practically all children and youths.

The school program in mental health should attempt to achieve the objectives previously referred to by promoting positive mental health in all students, preventing mental illness and emotional disturbances, and assisting children with mental health problems.

WHAT IS THE TEACHER'S ROLE IN IMPROVING THE EMOTIONAL CLIMATE?

There is much being said and written about the effect of schools and school personnel on the emotional health and mental development of children. Most of us have heard the dismal estimate by some psychologists that the average

*Abrams, R.S., Vanecko, M., and Abrams, I.: A suggested school mental health program, Journal of School Health **42:** March 1972.

child is exposed to two emotionally unstable teachers during his school years. Some of us might consider this estimate too conservative.

In any case, the teacher is the person children see day after day during the school year. Next to the parent the teacher probably has more influence on most students than any other persons in their young lives. What a challenge this is; yet what an opportunity!

Practically all certified teachers have had at least some background of study in the field of mental health. Still, teachers find it difficult to deal effectively with the emotional problems presented from time to time in the classroom and in extracurricular settings. The reason for this in most instances is that we know so little about mental health and emotional development. One of the things we do know reasonably well is that people need to be motivated, to have perceivable goals if they are to learn, perform, and develop as individual personalities capable of coping with and contributing to their world.

The single most important contribution to student mental health is the development of a wholesome emotional climate in the classroom. This atmosphere affects students' personal goals, their gaiety and depression; in fact, the moods of the pupils in the room have great influence on all the students. What teachers say, do, and think has great significance on the patterns of behavior that are exhibited by students. Teachers have profound and lasting influences on children. The extent to which teachers can develop good human relationships with their pupils largely determines the extent to which a wholesome classroom atmosphere will exist. The setting in which children work together and are secure in the knowledge and feeling that they are accepted by the group and the teacher is what teachers should strive to achieve. This environment is influenced by teachers' preconceptions of pupils, concern with self, fear of witnessing emotion, values, biases, prejudices, and feelings of social class barriers.

The learning that takes place in school is affected by how people feel and believe, and what they value as well as how people treat each other. Teachers must be concerned with individuals and not just subject matter. There is a need to focus on the learner in the classroom. It is important not only to be concerned with what takes place in school, but also more importantly, to be concerned with what happens to students. An emphasis on humanism or humaneness must take place. Teachers must be concerned with justice, equality, friendship, tolerance, respect for the individual, self-expression, and decision making. These few suggestions should help to provide ways to achieve such a climate:

1. Maximize individual learning through the recognition of individual differences.
2. Encourage and increase student involvement in the education process.
3. Provide a meaningful curriculum that satisfies the needs of students.
4. Provide opportunities for success experiences for all students.
5. Permit freedom of expression in the classroom.
6. Listen to students in a nonjudgmental fashion.
7. Help students to assess their own value systems.
8. Make grades and grading procedures noncompetitive.
9. Aid young people to improve their abilities to cope with the complex world.
10. Aid young people to assume responsibility for their own behavior.

The teacher who is interested in developing the best atmosphere must do the following:

1. Want to help children; establish a classroom environment free from fear and tensions; include an atmosphere of warmth and friendliness; aid in improvement of self-concept.
2. Believe that children are trying to do the best work possible.
3. Get acquainted with children and attempt to develop friendly relations; know their health and guidance records, be cheerful, let children talk, call students by name, talk with pupils, do not be shocked easily, pro-

vide warmth to the room by color and displays, using children to help.

4. Avoid ridicule, sarcasm, and belittling remarks and help pupils to do likewise.

5. Accept the emotional outbursts of children and not condemn or reproach hostility; everyone gets angry sometimes.

6. Understand the many factors that affect the mental health of children, including the family and the home, peer group relations, socioeconomic class, communications media, and the tensions of the times.

7. Be alert for indications of latent skills and interests and encourage pupils in their development.

8. Arouse interest in cultures and religions of all groups and accept pupils regardless of race, creed, or color.

9. Develop trust in students as individuals.

10. Practice tolerance and humanity in dealing with all people in the school—students, teachers, administrators, and staff.

11. Avoid punitive disciplinary action.

12. Provide for individual guidance to help students understand their strengths and weaknesses and how to enhance strengths and overcome weaknesses.

13. Show concern for each student.

14. Make the classroom a friendly place.

15. Make learning fun.

16. Treat all students with kindness and respect.

17. Encourage students to help plan class activities such as field trips or PTA presentations.

Additional factors affecting the emotional climate in the classroom include the following:

1. Clarity and meaning of school activity

2. Excessive competition

3. Curriculum not adjusted to the needs of pupils

4. Uneven and unfair distribution of rewards and punishments (Is the teacher always negative to some students?)

5. Biases regarding students in terms of race, creed, color, or ability

6. Authoritarianism or permissive environment

7. Grades and their uniformity

8. Liberal use of praise and encouragement

9. Attainable goals within pupils' abilities

Anxieties and tensions are acquired and can quickly and easily become evident in class. The teacher can help to ease these conditions by being cognizant of the factors previously mentioned and also by providing relaxation outlets through music, art, drama, play, dance, exercise, or creative reading or writing.

How does teacher health affect the school climate?

Well-adjusted teachers are needed if the most wholesome emotional climate is to be found in the classroom. The teacher who suffers from anxiety and lack of self-confidence will communicate this to children. The teacher's personality is extremely important, since a maladjusted teacher is in a strategic position to do great harm to young people. It is estimated that mentally ill or maladjusted teachers are found in about the same proportion as in the general population—about 10%. One study reveals that 4% of teachers sampled in one school system were severely mentally ill. Teachers, therefore, need to give attention to their personal needs and to make adequate provision for sleep, rest, exercise, appropriate diet, and time for relaxation and need to maintain the highest level of health possible.

It almost goes without saying that the teacher's physical health status, diet, and personal health practices, including the use of alcoholic beverages and mood-altering drugs, may have an impact on the emotional climate within the classroom. It is important for teachers to realize that they become role models for students. As such, the way the teacher reacts to varying stressful situations within the school day will have an impact on the students exposed to that teacher. If the teacher cannot handle the daily stresses of the school day, as well as stresses outside of school, how will that teacher be able to transfer good coping skills to students? The precursors of mental illness include prolonged stress, irritability, loss of sleep, withdrawal from social contacts, and somatic symptoms. Teachers should seek help when these symptoms appear.

The Gallup poll* revealed the following qualities desired in teachers:

1. Ability to communicate, to understand, to relate
2. Ability to discipline, be firm and fair
3. Ability to inspire, to motivate the child
4. High moral character
5. Love of children, concern for them
6. Dedication to teaching profession, enthusiasm
7. Friendliness, good personality
8. Good personal appearance, cleanliness

Health instruction

The need for an educational program as part of the curriculum has been frequently mentioned as a means of promoting positive mental health and of preventing mental illness. Education can help pupils to understand themselves, their drives, their prejudices, their emotions, their ambitions, their growth and personality development, and their values as well as to help them learn how to get along with others, how to live in society, and how to be socially acceptable members of the world in which they live. Satisfaction that comes with self-esteem and self-concept leads to feelings of confidence, worth, strength, capability, and adequacy. Children who attain such attitudes are able to learn with increased interest, enthusiasm, and efficiency. In recent years, *death education* has been introduced into curriculums to help pupils to be able to cope with losses and to better comprehend the meaningfulness of life.

Instruction should include both formal and informal programs (see Chapters 1, 8, and 9). The suggested outline of content for mental health, the concepts that should receive consideration, and the objectives to be achieved through grade level groups in the formal phase

*Gallup, G.H.: Eighth annual Gallup poll of the public's attitudes toward the public schools, Phi Delta Kappan, **58:** Oct. 1976.

may be found in Chapter 9. They can be integrated into all phases of the curriculum, or specific units can be prepared and taught as part of health education using a variety of techniques (see Chapter 12).

Informally, mental health concepts and understandings of self can be learned and modified indirectly through interpersonal relations between teachers and pupils. The wholesome classroom atmosphere provides numerous opportunities for incidental teaching through informal discussion, counseling and guidance, and working with children in many ways. In addition, awareness groups can be convened voluntarily to permit students to express opinions and feelings on a variety of topics through verbal and other forms of communication.

Parent educational programs need consideration for inclusion in schools. Family understandings of children's needs and the need for communication are extremely important for positive mental health.

SUMMARY

In summary, it can be stated that the teacher's role in mental health is to understand and provide for the physical and psychological needs of children, to be alert in their observations for symptoms of emotional disturbance, to refer problem pupils to the appropriate school authorities, to aid in the followup program for deviant students through counseling and guidance and the adjustment of the school program, to provide adequate and appropriate educational experiences for all pupils, to help provide particular educational experiences for special students, to develop a wholesome mental health classroom atmosphere, and to serve on an advisory school mental health committee on request.

The teacher must be aware of the various stresses that face both student and staff each day. The teacher must also understand that the reaction to these stresses varies for each individual. Knowing how children react to stress, however, is not enough. The teacher must also be aware of how he or she reacts to stress, since the teacher becomes a role model for students. If the teacher constantly reacts in a negative way to stress, it is quite likely that the teacher's students will react in the same way.

Personal health practices are important. If the teacher is constantly slovenly in appearance, or lets mood-altering substances provide substitutes for good judgment and professional pride, then that teacher is not doing much to contribute to the total emotional climate of the school. As Plato stated, "Know thyself." By knowing oneself, the teacher is in a better position to positively influence the emotional climate created in the classroom and the total school environment.

QUESTIONS FOR DISCUSSION

1. What is the meaning of the term "mental health"?
2. What are the characteristics of a mentally healthy student?
3. What is the meaning of the term "mental illness"?
4. Why is mental illness a leading health problem in the United States?
5. What are the causes of mental illness?
6. What are the reasons that justify the school's concern for the mental health of pupils?
7. What are some of the procedures teachers may use to help locate children with emotional disturbances?
8. What are the psychologic needs of children? What deviant behaviors are manifested when they go unmet?
9. What can the teacher do to provide an emotional climate in the classroom that promotes good mental health?
10. What might teachers do to be more humane in their dealing with pupils?
11. How can health instruction help the mental health of pupils?
12. What impact does the health of the teacher have on the emotional climate of the classroom?

SELECTED REFERENCES

Abrams, R., Vanceko, M., and Abrams, I.: A suggested school mental health program, The Journal of School Health 42:March 1972.

Allinsmith, W., and Goethals, G.W.: The role of schools in mental health, New York, 1962, Basic Books, Inc. Publishers.

American Medical Association: Mental health and school health services, Chicago, 1965, The Association.

Association of State and Territorial Health Officers, Association of State and Territorial Mental Health Authorities, and Council of Chief State School Officers: Mental health in schools, Washington, D.C., 1966, The Council.

Association for Supervision and Curriculum Development: Learning and mental health in schools, Washington, D.C., 1966, The Association.

Bernard, H.W.: Mental health in the classroom, New York, 1970, McGraw-Hill Book Co.

Burnes, A.J.: Laboratory instruction in the behavioral sciences in the grammar school. In Getz, B., editor: Behavioral sciences in the elementary grades, Second Annual Graduate Symposium, Cambridge, Mass., 1966, Lesley College.

Canfield, J., and Wells. H.C.: One-hundred ways to enhance self-concept in the classroom, Englewood Cliffs, N.J., 1976, Prentice-Hall, Inc.

Caplan, G.: Types of mental health consultation, American Journal of Orthopsychiatry 33: April 1963.

Charles, C.M.: Individualizing instruction, ed. 2, St. Louis, 1980, The C.V. Mosby Co.

Cornacchia, H.J., Smith, D.E., and Bentel, D.J.: Drugs in the classroom; a conceptual model for school programs, ed. 2, St. Louis, 1978, The C.V. Mosby Co.

Cowen, E.L., and others: A preventive mental health program in the school setting; description and evaluation, Journal of Psychology 56: Oct. 1963.

Cowen, E.L., and others: Emergent approaches to mental health problems, New York, 1967, Appleton-Century-Crofts.

Crabs, M.: School mental health services following an environmental disaster, The Journal of School Health 51: 165-168 March 1981.

Crow, L., and Crow, A.: Mental hygiene for teachers, New York, 1963, Macmillan Inc.

Cummings, S.: An appraisal of some recent evidence dealing with the mental health of black children and adolescents and its implications for school psychologists and guidance counselors, Psychology in the Schools 12: April 1975.

Detert, R., and Gatyas, C.: Teacher contact: where students come first, Health Education 11:16-18 May/June 1980.

Deutsch, A., editor: Encyclopedia of mental health. vol. 5, New York, 1961, Franklin Watts, Inc.

Fass, L.: Emotionally disturbed child: a book of readings, Springfield, Ill., 1975, Charles C Thomas, Publisher.

Fishtein, R.: Classroom psychology, Brooklyn, 1974, Book-Lab, Inc.

Gallup, G.H.: Eighth annual Gallup poll of the public's attitudes toward the public schools, Phi Delta Kappan 58: Oct. 1976.

Glasser, W.: Mental health or mental illness? New York, 1960, Harper & Row, Publishers, Inc.

Greenberger, E., and others: The measurement and structure of psychosocial maturity, Journal of Youth and Adolescence 4: June 1975.

Guinn, R.: Promoting mental health in the bicultural classroom, Health Education 8: May/June 1977.

Harris, C.W., editor: Encyclopedia of educational research, ed. 4, New York, 1969, Macmillan, Inc.

Klagsburn, F.: Preventing teenage suicide, Family Health/Today's Health 9: April 1977.

Martin, L.: Mental health/mental illness, New York, 1970, McGraw-Hill Book Co.

McLeod, A.: Growing up in America: a background to contemporary drug abuse, Rockville, Md., 1973, National Institutes of Mental Health.

National Health Education Committee: Facts on major killing and crippling diseases in the United States today, New York, 1971, The Committee.

National Institute of Mental Health: Mental health of children, PHS 1396, Washington, D.C., 1965, Superintendent of Documents.

National Society for the Study of Education: Mental health in modern education, Fifty-fourth yearbook, Part II, Chicago, 1955, University of Chicago Press.

Reinert, H.R.: Children in conflict, ed. 2, St. Louis, 1980, The C.V. Mosby Co.

Report of the Committee on Mental Health in the Classroom, American School Health Association: Mental health in the classroom, revised, Journal of School Health 38: May 1968.

Report of Task Forces IV and V and the Report of the Committee on Clinical Issues by the Joint Commission on Mental Health of Children, The mental health of children; services, research, and manpower, New York, 1973, Harper & Row, Publishers, Inc.

Report of Task Force VI and excerpts from the Report of the Committee on Children of Minority Groups by the Joint Commission on Mental Health of Children: Social change and the mental health of children, New York, 1973, Harper & Row, Publishers, Inc.

Rogers, D.: Mental hygiene in elementary education, Boston, 1957, Houghton Mifflin Co.

Schulman, J.L., and others: Mental health in schools, Elementary School Journal 74: Oct. 1973.

Smith, D.F.: Adolescent suicide; a problem for teachers, Phi Delta Kappan 57: April 1976.

Stickney, S.B.: Schools are our community mental health centers, American Journal of Psychiatry 124: April 1968.

ten Bensel, R.W., and Berkie, J.: The neglect and abuse of children and youth: the scope of the problem and the school's role, Journal of School Health 46: Oct. 1976.

U.S. Department of Health, Education, and Welfare: The protection and promotion of mental health in schools, PHS mental health monograph 5, Washington, D.C., 1964, Superintendent of Documents.

Zolcynski, S.J., and McKee, J.M.: The development of a student mental health record, Journal of School Health 32: June 1962.

PART THREE

Health services

5

HEALTH APPRAISALS OF SCHOOL CHILDREN

Teachers frequently ask such questions as the following:

"Why must I be concerned with the health of boys and girls in my class?"

"How can I find out about the health status of children in my room?"

"Is the failure of children to learn related to their health problems?"

"Can the nurse help me to know more about the health of my pupils?"

"Why must children have periodic vision and hearing tests?"

"What is the teacher's responsibility in preparing children for vision testing, hearing testing, dental inspections, health examinations, and other appraisals?"

"Should I be concerned about a child with a runny nose or a skin infection or one who is always extremely fatigued?"

"What can I do about the overly active, fidgety, aggressive child in class?"

"Why are health records used in schools?"

"What should I do about children in my class who are diabetic or epileptic or who have heart problems?"

Although educators and medical specialists generally believe the home has the primary re-sponsibility for the health of children, schools need to maintain strong supportive programs (1) because of the relationship of good health to effective learning, (2) because there are hazards associated with communicable diseases, and (3) because numerous parents fail to, or do not know how to, accept their responsibilities for maintaining high levels of health in their children. Boys and girls with measles, mumps, tuberculosis, or poliomyelitis may transmit these conditions to others. Children who cannot see or hear well may have difficulty in acquiring an education. Students with emotional problems may have trouble learning to read. Pupils who fail to eat breakfast or who are malnourished may not have sufficient stamina to endure the daily classroom activities. Dental health problems may be of sufficient severity or degree to cause young people constant pain or emotional upsets, which adversely affect their concentration and attention to learning. Children who are diabetic, epileptic, or hyperkinetic need to be identified as such to arrange adjustments of their educational programs.

Unfortunately the home has not always satisfactorily or completely assumed its health role.

In some instances this responsibility has been ignored or has not been recognized. With about 50% of mothers working away from the home, communication with parents has become difficult. Children continue to be sent to school with physical and emotional conditions that are considered to be unimportant or are unknown to parents. The school, therefore, has found it necessary to locate those boys and girls with health problems. The procedures used to identify these children with health problems are called health appraisals.

Health appraisals are part of the comprehensive health services program that should be found in school health programs (see Fig. 1-1). Health services are those actions taken to help children with problems. They also include follow-up and guidance (Chapter 6), emergencies and first aid (Chapter 7), health personnel such as nurses, nurse-practitioners, physicians, and others, and communications with community health agencies and organizations. National, state, and local laws mandate the availability of various service components. However, those services found in schools are uneven in quality and quantity and often barely comply with the letter of the law. Except in large school districts, very little money is appropriated and therefore services are generally inadequate. In most schools, nurses or nurse-practitioners are responsible for segments of the program. The amount of nursing services provided varies widely throughout the United States and is greatly limited in many school districts.

PROBLEMS OF THE POOR

It was pointed out in Chapter 1 that the poor generally have more health problems than those children and youth whose families are at higher socioeconomic levels. The American Academy of Pediatrics* has advocated that where school children do not receive adequate health care,

---

*Committee on School Health: School health; a guide for health professionals, Evanston, Ill., 1981, American Academy of Pediatrics.

school programs may need to provide screening, preventive, and some treatment services. Since 1967, states have been required by Congress to provide early and periodic screening, diagnosis, and treatment (EPSDT) as mandatory services for eligible poor children as part of Medicaid. These procedures have included screening tests (vision, hearing, blood pressure and others), immunizations, dental care, and well-care supervision. Unfortunately, this program has not met the needs of poor children and youth not covered by Medicaid. In California the Child Health and Disabilities Prevention Act of 1975 provided for the early and periodic assessment of the health status of children and youth under 21 years of age. It specifically required that children within 12 months of entering first grade be given a health evaluation (screening) that consisted of a health history; a brief physical examination; developmental assessment; eye and hearing tests; examination of teeth; and laboratory tests, including blood, tuberculosis, anemia, PKU (phenylketonuria), diabetes, urine, and sickle-cell anemia. The evaluation must also include a check of the immunization record to bring up to date the following: DTP (diphtheria-tetanus-pertussis), TOPV (trivalent oral polio virus vaccine), MMR (measles, mumps, rubella), and TD (tetanus and diphtheria toxoids).

WHAT ARE HEALTH APPRAISALS?

Health appraisals refer to a series of procedures to assess or determine the health status of children through the use of teacher observations, screening tests, health histories or inventories, dental inspections, medical examinations, and psychological tests. They are dependent on the cooperation of parents, teachers, physicians, dentists, health educators, nurses, and psychologists in the school program. The nature and frequency of appraisals vary in school districts throughout the United States. The chart on p. 73 illustrates the types, grades, and frequency for the Denver Public Schools in Denver, Colorado.

SCHOOL HEALTH SCREENING PROGRAMS BY GRADE LEVEL AND FREQUENCY, DENVER PUBLIC SCHOOLS, 1980*

Type of service	ECE*	K	1	2	3	4	5	6	7	8	9	10	11	12
Vision screening tests†	X	X	X		X		X		X			X		
Hearing screening tests†	X	X	X		X									
Dental education and/or inspections At selected grades	Spring 1980: 11th grade Fall 1980: 4th grade 5th grade Spring 1981: 6th grade 1981-82 K, 3, 4, 5 (Brush In program included in 3rd grade)													
DMF surveys in high schools (about every 5 years)												X		
Weight and growth measurements on all new and referred pupils (often done cooperatively with P.E. fitness program)	X	X	X	X	X	X	X	X						
Nurse interviews with parents of new children	X	X	X	X	X	X	X	X	X	X	X	X	X	X
Medical and/or school nurse practitioner All pupils with suspected health or learning problems without current or complete reports from family or clinic physicians		X	X	X	X	X	X	X	X	X	X	X	X	X
All pupils being considered for placement in special education without current or complete reports		X	X	X	X	X	X	X	X	X	X	X	X	X
Pupils who participate in swimming classes when private or clinic physician reports are not obtained									X	X	X	X	X	X
Special services Mandatory tuberculin skin tests for those who have not had one within 9 months	No longer mandatory, so not being done at this time. X													
Scoliosis screening							X	X	X					
Inspections for nuisance diseases	(as needed)													
Color vision tests									X		(new pupils)			

Permission to publish granted by the Department of Health and Social Services, Denver Public Schools, Denver, Colorado, 1980.

*Early Childhood Education.

†At certain grades; all new pupils at other grades and referrals.

Appraisals exist for the following reasons:

1. To locate pupils needing medical or dental treatment
2. To locate pupils who are poorly adjusted and in need of special attention at school or treatment by a psychiatrist or child guidance clinic, for example, concerning behavior problems and emotional disturbances
3. To locate pupils who need modified educational programs, for example, those who are hard of hearing, partially sighted, blind, or mentally retarded
4. To locate pupils who need more thorough examinations than provided in school, for example, by means of x-ray examinations, laboratory examinations, or examinations by specialists
5. To inform school personnel and parents about the health status of children and to encourage parents to recognize and accept the responsibility for seeking necessary corrections
6. To help pupils with health problems make adjustments or compensations for their conditions in schools
7. To serve as learning experiences for children, teachers, and parents

The nature of health appraisals and the responsibilities of the teachers are discussed in the pages that follow. The degree to which the teacher participates differs in every school district and is dependent on the extent of the school program as well as on the availability of special school health personnel.

Three important points related to the teacher's role must be recognized:

1. Teachers, nurses, and nonmedically trained people should not attempt to make diagnoses. However, nurses are able to make preliminary diagnoses because of their training and experience. Observations of runny noses, flushed faces, and elevations of temperatures do not permit untrained individuals to identify these conditions as colds, influenza, or other diseases. Signs and symptoms that are noted in young people should result in the referral of these children to the school personnel capable of making diagnoses or of determining necessary action.

2. Ordinarily schools and school personnel should not render medical care, and employees in general should not attempt to provide treatment services; this is the function of physicians, dentists, and other qualified specialists. Some school districts try to make provision for treatment services for poor children.

3. Health information about pupils should remain confidential. Teachers and others in schools who need this knowledge should have access to school health records.

WHAT ARE TEACHER OBSERVATIONS?

Teachers are in a strategic position to observe the appearance and behavior of children because they are with pupils for many hours each day and many weeks each year. They see children perform a variety of activities under different environmental circumstances. They are continually noting pupils with headaches, frequent respiratory infections, and recurrent earaches, or those suffering from overfatigue, skin infections, and emotional disturbances. They are capable of becoming skilled observers of the signs and symptoms of ill health. The constant attention that they give to observing boys and girls throughout the day often results in the identification of pupils who are in the early stages of communicable diseases or who are suffering from physical defects or emotional disturbances needing care. Prompt attention to symptomatic behavior greatly helps in the maintenance and improvement of the children's health.

Teachers must be especially observant of disadvantaged children and those living in poverty. These young people generally have more dental caries and a higher incidence of heart disease, mental illness, tuberculosis, and other health problems than do their classmates of higher socioeconomic standings.

The responsibility of observing children for illness indications does not carry with it the responsibility of diagnosing specific conditions. Diagnosis is a matter that rests with individuals with special professional ability. However, the more detailed and accurate the teacher's noting of pertinent symptoms, the more valuable the information can be for those responsible for diagnosis. A comment such as "George does not seem to feel well today" gives the physician little specific aid; but a brief account of signs and symptoms, such as a runny nose, frequent fatigue, and constant cough, that led the teacher to believe that George was not feeling well is likely to be much more helpful.

Health observations by the teacher (Tables 5-1 to 5-4) are now considered to be a continuous procedure that takes place daily and throughout the entire day. It is no longer the formal type of health inspection that occurred early in the morning and was relegated to a specified few minutes in the schedule. It is much more than the mere checking of the cleanliness of hands, hair, teeth, skin, and other parts of the body. The teacher must realize that pupils' health may change from minute to minute, or from hour to hour, and must constantly be on the alert for these changes. These observations involve the mental and emotional status of pupils as well as their physical status. The foundation of all pupil health appraisal activities is the continual informed observation of students by teachers.

One study* indicated that teacher observations and the use of screening tests are potentially capable of identifying nearly all kinds of health problems that develop after the initial health examination.

Specific learning disabilities or perceptual problems

Teachers will also observe a variety of children's problems that have been characterized as minimal brain dysfunction (MBD), minimal brain damage, or minimal cerebral function. They include such conditions as dyslexia (inability to read more than a few lines with understanding), hyperkinesis, hyperkinetic impulsive disorders or hyperactivity, autism (disturbances

Text continued on p. 82.

*Jenne, F.H.: Variations in nursing service characteristics and teachers' health observation practices, Journal of School Health **40**: May 1970.

TABLE 5-1. Good health characteristics of children

Physical	Social-emotional	Work habits
Endurance: completes a task without undue fatigue	Enthusiastic	Attentive
Enjoys vigorous play	Objective interests: friends, hobbies, games, work, people	Carries a task through to completion
Alert, buoyant, pleasant	Curious: interested in a variety of things	Ability to concentrate
Looks refreshed in morning	Enters into activities	Persistent in work
Assumes good posture	Happy, cheerful, agreeable, friendly	Works independently
Posture expresses buoyancy, alertness, success, happiness	Refrains from quarreling	Orderly in work habits
Prompt, efficient muscular coordination	Confident: expects success, meets failure	Shows originality and initiative
Poise: freedom from unnecessary activity	Shares group responsibility	Creative
Muscles firm	Protects others' property	Takes responsibility
Hair: natural luster	Appreciation and understanding for others	Prompt in meeting appointments
Clear skin, clear bright eyes, clean, neat in appearance, inoffensive breath, wholesome appetite	Does things for the group, not for self alone	Responds quickly and cheerfully to directions
	Shows courage in meeting difficulties	Shares group responsibility
	Cooperative with peers	Cooperative with peers
	Adapts to new situations	
	Exercises emotional control	

TABLE 5-2. Growth and development characteristics

Physical development	Characteristics	Health education implications
	3 to 5 years of age	
Growth continues at moderately rapid rate	Needs vigorous outdoor activity	Rest and sleep: adequate amounts needed; provide rest periods
Permanent body build evident	Becoming more independent; doing things for self; needs freedom	Dental health: emphasis on food selection and care of teeth
Head and upper body reach adult proportions	Needs to learn to get along with others, to share, to take turns	Emotional health: needs attention, freedom, and learning to share and get along; provide restraints with love and care
Legs and arms lengthening	Temper tantrums less likely; may begin to call names, "I don't like you"; much quarreling, hitting, fighting	
Bone growth proceeding and cartilage almost completely replaced by bone	Learns through play; crayons, blocks, large pencils	Nutrition: emphasis on adequate diet and amounts of food; needs protein, minerals, and vitamins
Girls ahead of boys in skeletal development; usually lighter and shorter than boys	Language development increases; understands words; can give simple reasons and explanations; can absorb much information; asks questions	Sex education: answer questions with simple understandings
Height and weight gradually increasing		Safety: provide concern for school and playground accident prevention
Primary teeth usually developed	Can play longer without fatigue	
Heart rate, respiration, and blood pressure usually stable	Begins to identify own sex; asks why mothers and fathers are different	Exercise: allow for vigorous play involving large muscle activities; small muscle coordination not developed
Large muscle weight increasing; boys with more muscle tissue than girls; girls more fatty tissue	Responds when treated as individual	
Brain at 90% of adult weight	More self-reliant; can wash and dress self; attention hard to hold	
	5 to 7 years of age	
Growth is relatively slow: at age 7 may be 2 to 3 inches and 3 to 6 pounds yearly	On entering school may be a resumption of earlier tensional behavior; thumbsucking, nail biting, toilet lapses	Mental health:
Large muscles better developed than small ones; improving by age 7	Eager to learn, exuberant, restless; exaggerates, overactive, and susceptible to fatigue; dawdling may occur	Wants to get along with peers
Some postural defects may have been established by age of 6		Praise, warmth, and patience with independence and encouraging support from adults
Hand-eye coordination is incomplete; 90% are right-handed; small muscle control difficult, especially of fingers and hands	Criticism difficult; thrives on encouragement	Some responsibilities without pressure of being required to make decisions or meet rigid standards
Eyeballs are still increasing in size; tendency toward farsightedness	Attention span short but increasing; interested in activity, not results, learns best through active participation	Help to make adjustments in playground; withdrawn child needs encouragement to find place in group
Heart is in a period of rapid growth	Has difficulty making decisions	
Permanent teeth begin to appear; baby teeth begin to be lost	Self-assertive; aggressive; wants to be first; becoming self-dependent; can take care of own toilet needs and dressing; likes to climb and jump; by 7 is apt to be talkative and prone to exaggeration; competition developing	Provide sense of accomplishment for each child; engage in real tasks; needs freedom
Susceptible to respiratory infections; childhood diseases (measles, mumps, chickenpox, etc.), rheumatic fever		Provide active participation in learning with concrete objects
Lungs relatively small	Interest of boys and girls diverging, less play together; gets along best in small groups	Exercise and safety: active, boisterous games for large muscles; stress safety
Tires easily		Vision care: protect eyes
Teeth: 6-year molars appearing and loss of primary teeth	Able to assume some responsibility concerning right and wrong and simple tasks; acts grown up at times	Sleep and rest: need 11 or more hours of sleep and possibly daytime naps
		Dental health: emphasis on tooth care
		Disease control: development of personal hygiene; cover coughs, sneezes, fingers away from mouth, washing hands, and others

TABLE 5-2. Growth and development characteristics—cont'd

Physical development	Characteristics	Health education implications
	5 to 7 years of age—cont'd	
	Bright eyes, color in face, great vitality	
	Enjoys rhythms, active play, fairy tales, comics, TV, myths, dramatic play and stories	
	Moods fluctuate; quick resistance to bathing	
	8 to 10 years of age	
Growth still slow and steady; some children reach plateau preceding growth of preadolescence; differences in individual bone ossification may vary as much as 5 to 6 years; girls' growth spurts at about 10 years	Wants to do well but loses interest if discouraged or pressured; sensitive to criticism	Mental health:
Small muscles developing; manipulative skill increasing	Gangs strong and of one sex only, of short duration and changing membership; response to structured groups and activities	Self-concept; values
Poor posture may develop; presence may indicate attention; chronic infection, fatigue, orthopedic difficulties, emotional maladjustment, etc.	Allegiance to peers instead of adult in case of conflict; wants a "best friend"	Needs friends and group membership
Hand-eye coordination improved; hands ready for crafts	Capable of prolonged interest; often makes plans and goes ahead on his or her own; increased attention span; realism replacing fantasy	Training in skills without pressure
Eyes ready for both nearsightedness and farsightedness; nearsightedness may develop during eighth year	Enjoys conforming to rules of game, testing his or her skill against perfection; can be fairly responsible and dependable	Wise guidance and channeling of interests rather than domination or overcritical standards
Incisors and lower bicuspids appear; often a period of dental neglect; orthodontia may be necessary	Gaining self-control; conscience becoming strong; awareness of self-energy	Praise, encouragement; warmth from adults
Internal changes in glands and body structure taking place; wide range in beginning of sexual maturity; period of rapid growth comes earlier for girls, it lasts longer in boys:	Fairly good eater; may neglect vegetables	Help gain self-confidence by excelling in one thing
Boys: beginning puberty cycle 10 to 13 years; ends 14 to 18½ years	Decisive, responsible, dependable, reasonable, strong sense of right and wrong; much arguing over fairness of games	Definite responsibility; reasonable explanations; no talking down
Girls: appearance of menstruation 10 to 16 years; average 12 years	Is untidy, deliberately throws over table manners, handwashing, hair combing; protests parents' choice of new clothes; general coolness toward all adults	Exercise:
Lungs and digestive and circulatory systems still developing	Is prone to accidents	Activities involving use of whole body; sports and games
	Health usually good; has much energy	Posture development in need of attention
	Fond of sports and games, collections, comics, adventure stories	Sleep and rest: 10 to 12 hours sleep
		Nutrition: balanced intake of foods
		Dental health: care of teeth reemphasis
		Disease control: handwashing, hair washing, food washing, etc.
		Safety: accident prevention
		Sex education: growth and developmental changes

Continued.

TABLE 5-2. Growth and development characteristics—cont'd

Physical development	Characteristics	Health education implications
	11 to 13 years of age	
A "resting period" followed by a period of rapid growth in height, then weight; usually starts somewhere between 9 and 13 years; girls usually taller and heavier at 11 years than boys	Wide range of individual differences and maturity level	Mental health:
		Self-image; success experiences
	Gangs or groups important; prestige is more important than adult approval; gang interest is changing to interest in one or two best friends (girls more than boys)	Warm affection, approval, no nagging or condemnation
		Increase opportunities for independence
Rapid muscular growth; uneven growth of different parts of body; awkwardness prevalent; posture may be slovenly	Loves parents but does not show it, cool toward adults	Relations with others
		Sense of belonging and peer group relations
	Strong sense of responsibility about matters thought to be important	Values development
Secondary sex charactistics beginning to develop; may cause embarrassment; in girls hip and breast development; in boys voice changes	Girls mature earlier than boys; girls are taller, heavier	Individual health and emotional counseling
		Nutrition: adequate diet importance
	Strong interest in sex, much teasing and antagonism between boy and girl groups; sex consciousness may cause self-consciousness and shyness	Rest and sleep: 9 to 11 hours of sleep
Heart developing; blood pressure may fall; more rest is needed		Exercise: sports and games, both individual and team
		Dental health: care of teeth
Permanent dentition of 28 teeth is completed by 13 to 14 years	Child approaching adolescence often becomes hypercritical, changeable, rebellious, uncooperative; exhibits extremes of conduct from independence to childish dependence; may rebel against rules	Safety: accident prevention and first aid
Resistance to infection may be low		Disease control: acne especially
		Sex education:
	Interest in activities to earn money	Physical and social changes
	Reading differences in ability and tastes apparent	Boy-girl relations
	Ravenous but finicky appetite may develop	Sexually transmitted diseases
	May be overanxious about own health and normalcy	Reproduction
	Competition is keen; development of coordination and skills through games	
	Awkwardness and laziness common because of rapid and uneven growth; may need rest	

TABLE 5-3. Signs and symptoms of health defects and illnesses

Point of observation	Physical signs	Behavior	Complaints
General appearance and behavior	Excessive thinness; excessive overweight; very small or very large in body build for age; pallor; weary expression; poor posture; dark circles under or puffiness of eyes; unusual gait or limp; uncleanliness; lethargic and unresponsive; facial tic	Acts tired or apathetic; is easily irritated; makes frequent trips to toilet; has persistent nervous habits, such as muscular twitching or biting of nails or lips; is subject to spasms (fits), fainting spells, or frequent nosebleeds; gets short of breath after mild exertion and climbing stairs; lacks appetite; vomits frequently; has frequent accidents	Feels tired; does not want to play; has aches or pains; feels sick to stomach; feels dizzy
Hair and scalp	Stringy, lusterless hair; small bald spots; crusty sores on scalp; nits in hair	Scratches head frequently	Head itches
Ears	Discharge from ears; cotton in ear; tired, strained expression long before day is over; watchful, sometimes bewildered expression	Is persistently inattentive; asks to have questions repeated; habitually fails to respond when questioned; mispronounces common words; cocks one ear toward speaker; fails to follow directions	Has earache; has buzzing or ringing in ears; ears feel stuffy; hears noises in head
Eyes	Inflamed or watery eyes; frequent styes; redrimmed, encrusted, swollen lids; crossed eye; recurring styes; sensitivity to light	Holds book too close to, or too far from, eyes; squints at book or blackboard; persistently rubs or blinks eyes; reads poorly; attempts to brush away blur; tilts head to one side; tends to reverse words or syllables; tends to lose place on page; shuts or covers one eye; unable to see distant things clearly	Headaches; dizziness; nausea; eyes ache, itch, smart, or feel scratchy; cannot see well (blurred or double vision); sensitivity to light
Mouth and teeth	Cavities in teeth; excessive stains; tartar at necks of teeth; malocclusion (uneven bite); irregular teeth; bleeding or inflamed gums; swollen jaw; sores in mouth; cracking of lips at corners of mouth	Acts depressed or resentful if many missing teeth or severe malocclusion subjects him or her to teasing or adverse comments from other children; this behavior is especially likely to occur in adolescence	Has toothache; mouth or gums feel sore
Nose and throat (upper respiratory tract)	Frequent or long-continued colds; persistent nasal discharge; persistent mouth breathing; enlarged glands in neck	Is frequently absent from school because of a cold; constantly clears throat or has frequent coughing or sneezing spells; is always sniffling or blowing nose; breathes persistently through mouth	Throat feels sore or scratchy; has difficulty in swallowing; nose feels stuffy or sore
Skin	Rashes or inflamed skin areas; scales and crusts; persistent sores, pimples, and blackheads on face; boils; hives; persistent warts; accidental injuries, such as cuts, scratches, bruises, burns, blisters; dry, red, rough skin	Is always scratching; is subject to skin irritations (hives, eczema, puzzling rashes, etc.), which suggest sensitivity to one or more substances (allergic manifestations); is easily bruised	Skin itches or burns; is concerned about pimples, blackheads, and other skin conditions that affect personal appearance

From Looking for health (previously What teachers see), 1969, New York, Metropolitan Life Insurance Co.

TABLE 5-4. Other signs and symptoms of health defects, illnesses, and problems

Condition	Signs and symptoms	
Allergy	Stuffy and runny nose, sneezing, persistent cough, swollen eyelids, and rash, itching, watery and burning eyes, paleness, mouth breathing	Tired and listless, recurrent headaches, recurrent gastrointestinal cramps, vomiting, diarrhea
Cancer	Leukemia: tires easily, irritable, pale (anemic), recurrent and serious infections, prolonged bleeding from injuries	Brain tumors: irritability, fatigability, decreased appetite and activity, intermittent headache
Child abuse	Bruises, untreated sores, burns, skin injuries; wears long-sleeved shirts or blouses to hide bruises, etc.	Hungry for affection, difficulty relating to others, displays behavioral extremes—timid/fearless, passive/aggressive; undiagnosed learning problems
Child neglect	No one to look after child, inadequate home management; need for health services—dental care, eyeglasses, immunizations	Malnutrition—underweight, fatigue, lack of muscle tone; no breakfast, food, or lunch money
Contagious diseases of childhood	Chill or chilliness; fever (flushed face, lassitude, malaise); sore or scratchy throat; red, watery eyes; watery nasal discharge	Tight, dry cough; sneezing; headache, earache, or aching in back or legs; nausea or vomiting
Diabetes	Constant urination, abnormal thirst, unusual hunger	Rapid loss of weight, irritability, obvious weakness and fatigue, nausea and vomiting
Diabetic insulin reaction*	Excessive hunger, perspiration, pallor, headache, dizziness, nervousness/trembling, confusion, crying	Irritability, drowsiness, fatigue, blurred vision, poor coordination, abdominal pain or nausea
Drug misuse and abuse	Physical: possible odor on breath and clothes; mouth and nose irritations; red, watery eyes; fingers with burns from smoking; poor appetite and/or weight loss; distraction of time and sense of perception; needle marks and scars on body; appearance of intoxication; dryness of mouth and nose	Behavior: changes in attendance, discipline and academic performance; display of unusual degrees of activity and excitement; display of unusual inactivity—moodiness, depression; deterioration of physical appearance and concern for health habits; unpredictable outbreaks of temper and flare-ups
Epilepsy	Dazed look, loss of consciousness	Tremors of any or all groups of muscles, odd gestures or movements (e.g., chewing or lip-smacking), occasional loss of muscle control (involuntary urination)
Heart problems	Pale, blue lips, short of breath on rest of exertion, undersized, deformed chest	Rapid pulse at rest, clubbed fingers, easily fatigued, undernourished, fainting after exertion or excitement
Hyperkinesis	Extreme overactivity, inattentiveness, impulsiveness, emotional explosiveness, short attention span, failure to progress in school at expected rate	Restless, oscillating mood swings, fidgeting, difficulty in sitting still, clumsiness, aggressive behavior, low frustration level
Lead poisoning	Fatigue, lethargy, stomach pains, constipation, vomiting, anemia, irritability	Temper tantrums, severe headaches, unsteady walking, insomnia, convulsions, loss of coordination, poor appetite or paleness; may be no symptoms
Nutrition	General appearance: fatigue slouch or posture; round shoulders or flabby muscles; excessively thin with spindly legs; lack of or finicky appetite; fails to gain weight steadily; excessively fat or poor distribution of fat; strained and worried look; listless and inactive or high-strung and overactive; easily fatigued and possibly irritable and difficult to manage Hair: dry, coarse, brittle, lacking luster, dull	Eyes: tiny red line (engorged capillaries) extending around or across the cornea and inward toward pupil; dark circles under eyes; inflammation and crusting of lids Teeth and gums: decayed teeth; swollen, bleeding, or spongy gums; or abnormal color Tongue: beefy red and magenta Mouth: scarring, fissuring, or sores on angles of lips

*Give sugar immediately in form of sugar, fruit juice, carbonated beverages, or candy.

TABLE 5-4. Other signs and symptoms of health defects, illnesses, and problems—cont'd

Condition	Signs and symptoms
Posture	Skin: small nodules (like gooseflesh) or scaly and rough Chest, knees, legs and feet: pigeon-breasted, knock-kneed, bow-legged, flatfooted—abnormal bone growth Head tilted to side when reading or listening Head tilted forward when sitting, standing, or walking Feet pointed inward or outward; stands with weight on inner ankles (pronated); drags or scuffles feet Shoulders not level: one higher, lower, or forward Round shoulders with protruding shoulder blades One hip higher or more prominent Knees pointed inward (knock-kneed), outward or hyperextended (bowlegs)
Rheumatic fever	Failure to gain weight, or loss in weight; pallor; irritability Poor appetite, repeated colds and sore throats, unexplained nosebleeds, muscle or joint pains
Sexually transmitted diseases	Syphilis: Within 10 to 90 days—small sore (chancre) at sight where germs entered body tissue 6 weeks to 6 months—rash on palms or soles of feet; falling hair; ugly sores on body, in mouth, under arms, between legs or toes Herpes simplex: Blisters on genitalia, sometimes on buttocks and thighs Gonorrhea: Within 3 to 8 days in males—burning sensation on urination, pus from urethra; in females—no pain, male signs may not appear until serious damage to bodily organs occurs Nongonococcal urethritis (NGU): pain on urination
Sickle cell anemia	Pains in arms and legs, swelling in joints, loss of appetite Weakness, pain in abdomen, jaundice
Social-emotional maladjustment	Overtimidity: withdrawing, crying easily Overaggressiveness: bullying, quarreling, boisterousness; cruel behavior Excessive daydreaming: persistent inattentiveness Extreme sensitiveness to criticism: cries easily, temper tantrums Difficulty in reading or reciting Failure to advance in school at normal rate despite good physical health and adequate intellectual capacity Stuttering or other forms of speech difficulty Lying, stealing, cheating, truancy Resistance to authority: constant complaints of unfairness, "picked on," may engage in vandalism Excess boasting or showing off Poor sportsmanship Undue restlessness: hyperactivity, habit tics, stammering, nail biting Frequent accidents or near accidents Poor coordination Abnormal sex behavior Unhappy and depressed Gradual deterioration or marked sudden drop in educational achievement Lack of interest or motivation Withdrawal, shyness, inferiority feelings Intense ambition, especially if inconsistent with potential Inconsistent bladder or bowel control Constantly seeking attention or popularity
"Strep" sore throat	Fever, difficulty in swallowing, swollen neck glands
Suicidal melancholia	Sudden shift in quality of work; excess use of drugs and alcohol; changes in early behavior and learning patterns; extreme fatigue; boredom; decreased appetite; inability to concentrate; truancy; gives away prized possessions Open signs of mental illness—delusions, hallucinations; distress signals—"Notice me; I need help; you'll be sorry when I'm dead"
Tuberculosis	Persistent cough, blood in sputum, nervousness, lack of energy, easy fatigability, fever Loss of weight, chest pain, rapid pulse, night sweats or afternoon fever, pallor, feeling of tiredness

of language, cognition, and human relations—self-centeredness), and developmental aphasia (inability to transmit ideas by language, including reading, writing, and speaking). These central nervous system disabilities are not clearly defined but generally refer to those pupils with near average, average, or above average general intelligence with learning or behavioral abnormalities ranging from mild to severe that are associated with subtle deviant functions of the central nervous system. They are characterized by difficulties in listening, thinking, talking, reading, writing, spelling, and arithmetic. They involve memory and control of attention, impulse, or motor function. There is a significant difference between children's achievement level and their functioning capabilities based on their mental abilities. These conditions are independent of errors of refraction, muscle imbalance, and imperfect binocular vision, including problems caused primarily by hearing or motor handicaps, by mental retardation, to emotional disturbance, or by environmental disadvantage.

Children with specific learning disabilities may exhibit the following behavior:
1. Hyperactivity—constantly moving, poor concentration, short attention span, talkativeness
2. Impulsiveness—easily distracted by stimuli; speaks out of turn
3. Variability and unpredictability—may cry or laugh easily; explosive irritability
4. Emotional instability—overreacts to trips, parties, and such activities; delay and failure may produce tears and temper tantrums; not accepted by peers; gullible and trusting; low tolerance for failure and frustration
5. Perseveration—continuous repetition of an action or response after a successful performance; may write a letter over and over, or talk incessantly about a subject for months
6. Poor sleep habits—easily awakened; hard to fall asleep
7. Muscle coordination—cannot function in sports; exceptionally clumsy; difficulty with buttoning, writing, speech, reading (dyslexia)

Learning disabilities may be found in 10 million children or about 5% of the population. Since the causes for these conditions are not known, the diagnosis of students with perceptual problems is difficult and complex. It is a medical matter. It may involve a team of individuals including school personnel. The procedure involves obtaining a complete medical history, conducting a thorough physical examination, including a neurological survey, as well as a psychiatric and psychological examination and an electroencephalogram. There is question by some authorities regarding the use of the EEG because they claim so-called normal children may exhibit abnormal brain wave patterns.

Treatment for learning disabilities is not easily rendered. It may include helping students to recognize sensory information (perception), to improve memory, to understand oral and written language, or to increase cognitive skills—conceptualizing rational, psychologic, and social factors. It may also include the use of such drugs as stimulants (Ritalin, Dexedrine, Mellaril), tranquilizers, sedatives, antidepressants, antihistamines, and anticonvulsants, which have been beneficial to many children. If drugs are to be administered at school, the role of the teacher should be clearly defined (see Prescribed medications at school, p. 117).

Cardwell* reports there are a number of unproven therapies currently being promoted. The Feingold Diet (removal of additives, especially artificial colors and flavors in foods and beverages) for hyperkinesis has not been substantiated through scientifically controlled studies. Motor patterning therapy for brain-damaged or mentally retarded children (review with child of various motor development stages) is not effective according to the American Academy of Pediatrics. Eye-tracking exercises for reading disability (dyslexia) do not help because the brain learns to read, not the eyes. The hypoglycemic (low blood sugar level) diet for hyper-

---

*Cardwell, M.A., Jr.: The pitfall of unproven therapies, Journal of School Health 49:421, Sept. 1979.

activity or learning disability has not had evidence to support its effectiveness.

Control of communicable diseases

Although local health departments generally have the legal responsibility for the prevention and control of disease, teachers need to be concerned with the control of communicable diseases because of the hazards they present to the pupils attending school. A variety of microorganisms including bacteria, viruses, protozoa, and fungi can enter the body, cause infectious disease, and, if they are transmissible from person to person, are considered to be communicable.

Teachers must be alert for symptoms (Tables 5-3 and 5-4) that will identify suspected disease conditions in pupils. They are expected to isolate those children discovered and send them to the nurse, principal, or appropriate school authority for possible exclusion from school. When such pupils return to school, teachers should be familiar with the readmission procedures to be certain that the pupils have sufficiently recovered to permit their return.

Tables 5-1 to 5-3 provide information that will enable teachers to understand better their role in health observations. Specific details regarding the more common communicable diseases may be found in Appendix A.

It is possible to prevent and control many diseases through immunizations for smallpox, diphtheria, whooping cough, tetanus, poliomyelitis, measles, mumps, and German measles. Some school districts make available these immunizations. (See Appendix B for state regulations.)

Identification of drug users and abusers

The extent of the drug problem in the community and in schools necessitates teacher awareness and assistance in the identification of students with problems. Some children are misusing and abusing drugs at very early ages. The evidence indicates that a large percentage of fourth graders have tasted alcoholic beverages. There is no question that individuals at all ages are using drugs for a variety of reasons and in a variety of ways.

The identification of students who are misusing and abusing drugs may involve any or all of the following:

1. Awareness of observable signs and symptoms; general observations may be found by referring to Table 5-4. Telltale evidence such as syringes, pills, solvents, special cigarette papers, and other items found in student possession and around school are additional clues. Blum* claims that potential users are behavioral problems at school, have mild conduct disorders, and lack self-confidence.

2. Taking prescribed medicines at school; students who have been recognized by nurses, parents, and others may be taking and using drugs while attending school for the control of such conditions as diabetes, epilepsy, and hyperkinesia as well as for other health problems.

3. Peer identification; friends may wish to help friends and thereby be willing to reveal information about drug use.

4. Self-identification; young people who discover their memory is failing, have problems of increased concentration, difficulty in speech, exaggerated feelings of self-confidence, or feelings of futility of life may seek assistance.

Child abuse

Child abuse refers to the physical or mental injury, sexual abuse, negligent treatment, or maltreatment of a child under 18 years of age by the person or persons responsible for the child's health and welfare. Sexual abuse is one of the most underreported and underdiagnosed types of abuse. It may include obscene language, accidental sex stimuli, undesirable touching, exploitation, and rape. It is estimated that 30% to 60% of abusive adults were abused as children.

---

*Blum, H.L., et al.: Drug education: results and recommendations, 1976, Lexington, Mass., D.C. Heath & Co.

The average age of sexually abused children is 11 years. Approximately 20% to 30% of abused children are left with permanent injury. The emotional harm that occurs may lead to crime or violence later in life. Abused children are less likely to become productive members of society and become dependent on welfare, social service, and criminal justice systems.

Some of the signs of child abuse that may be noted in pupils include bone fractures, head injuries, bruises and burns in various stages of healing, discolorations of skin caused by internal bleeding, multiple scratches and parent or guardian identification of the child as a discipline problem. Suspicion of parents as potential abusers may be justified if (1) their attitudes toward school personnel involves irrational hostility, combativeness, abusiveness, and projection of blame on others and (2) there is evidence of alcoholism and drug abuse, assault and battery that has been documented, chronic problems at home with the parent or guardian, sexual promiscuity, unstable job patterns, and a history of psychiatric problems, among others.

Olson* states there are four types of family structures or behavioral patterns that may breed maltreatment of children:

1. Highly structured, authoritarian, inflexibly disciplined family units in which family-school interactions are suppressed or rechanneled into superficial conversation
2. Family units with documented drug addiction or alcoholism of one or both parents
3. Family units with documented psychosis, neurosis, or mental deficiency of one or both parents
4. Family units with loose, ill-defined structure and evidence of emotional immaturity of one or both parents

Teachers and school personnel must become aware of these signs and symptoms to be able to identify and report abused pupils so that preventive action can be taken to protect them from further injury.

---

*Olson, R.J.: Index of suspicion: screening for child abusers, American Journal of Nursing **76:**108-110, Jan. 1976.

WHAT ARE SCREENING TESTS?

Screening tests are those preliminary health evaluations used in schools to assess the health status of pupils. They may include tests for vision and hearing problems, growth and development, tuberculosis, dental problems, posture, nutrition, sickle-cell anemia, and others. They should be low in cost so they can be available to all students. They are likely to be administered by teachers, nurses, technologists, and other school personnel. They serve as rough measuring devices that supplement and complement teacher observations as well as other procedures used to determine the health of pupils. If children are found to be in need, they should be referred to health specialists for diagnostic tests.

State laws widely differ in regard to requirements and frequency for these tests, but many include specific provisions for periodic screening of vision and hearing.

Vision

Vision testing is usually concerned with problems of central visual acuity, direct vision of near and far objects, and ability to perceive the shape and form of objects in the direct line of vision. However, constant alertness for signs of eye diseases and other abnormalities must also be maintained. Children with acuity defects cannot perceive and discriminate the details of objects or printed symbols. Thus they are likely to encounter learning difficulties.

School vision screening usually attempts to reveal the following eye problems:

1. Errors of refraction—eye defects in which images are focused improperly on the retina.
   a. Hyperopia—farsightedness; light rays focus behind the retina, common in those under 10 to 12 years and usually corrects itself as the eye matures
   b. Myopia—nearsightedness; light rays focus in front of the retina
   c. Astigmatism—irregular curvature of the cornea or lens

2. Strabismus—crossed eyes caused by muscle imbalance; the muscles of the two eyes do not work in coordination, resulting in failure of the alignment of the eyes. It is estimated that 1.5% of children are so afflicted. The afflicted eye may not be used and may bring about deterioration of visual acuity, a condition known as amblyopia, which can usually be prevented if treated early; some schools are advising preschool examinations, and others are trying to identify children in Head Start programs.

3. Color blindness—inability to perceive colors; this condition may be congenital or acquired, with the congenital form being more prevalent; congenital defects may be either total or partial; total color blindness is rare, and when it occurs, all colors appear as grays; the partial type is most common and is primarily inherited through the mother who carries the recessive gene and is generally not affected; red and green colors are usually confused in most cases, but blue-yellow defects also occur; acquired defects of color may often develop in the course of ocular, mainly retinal, disease; approximately 3.8%* of children 6 to 11 years of age have color vision deficiencies; by sex, 6.95% of boys and 0.53% of girls are affected; the problem among white boys is about twice as great as among black boys.

The American Academy of Pediatrics states that every child should have a test for visual acuity by the age of 4 years, before entry into school.

Basic minimum recommended procedure. The minimum recommended vision screening program varies in schools throughout the United States. The National Society to Prevent Blindness† claims that where a professional eye examination is not possible a child should have an *annual* test for distance visual acuity. However, realizing that time and personnel may not permit such screenings, the basic minimum using the Snellen charts (Fig. 5-1) should be:

1. Kindergarten or first grade (5 to 6 years)— use symbol "E" chart
2. Second grade (7 years), fifth grade (10 to 11 years), eighth grade (13 years), tenth or eleventh grade (15 to 17 years)
3. All new students and teacher referrals
4. All children who exhibit a change in behavior or learning disability

Continuous observation by the teacher and the tester for symptoms related to eye problems should be correlated with the screening procedure. Several research studies have indicated high correlation of this action with clinical findings by ophthalmologists.

Preschool vision screening is now being recommended. Identification of such defects as cross-eye and amblyopia or so-called lazy eye is important. These conditions can lead to unnecessary loss of vision unless detected and treated before the age of 6 years. Screening with isolated symbols (see Fig. 5-1) is recommended because a "crowding effect" results when more than one letter is used.

Teacher involvement. Who does the screening differs between schools and school districts. Common practice indicates that teachers, nurses, technicians, and volunteers are assigned to perform this service. Some state laws require teachers to administer the tests. Reasons often advanced for teacher involvement in vision testing are the following:

1. They understand better the children with vision problems in their classes.
2. They become more sensitive to and concerned with opportunities for continually observing children with vision problems.
3. They can make the vision screening program a part of the health instruction program.

SNELLEN TEST. The Snellen test is designed to discover those children with myopia, although other difficulties may also be found. It has been widely used in schools because it is simple, economical, and practical. It has been considered by the National Society to Prevent Blindness as well as other authorita-

---

*U.S. Department of Health, Education, and Welfare, Public Health Service, National Center for Health Statistics: Color vision deficiencies in children, United States, Washington, D.C., 1972, U.S. Government Printing Office.
†National Society to Prevent Blindness: Vision screening for children, New York, 1980, The Society.

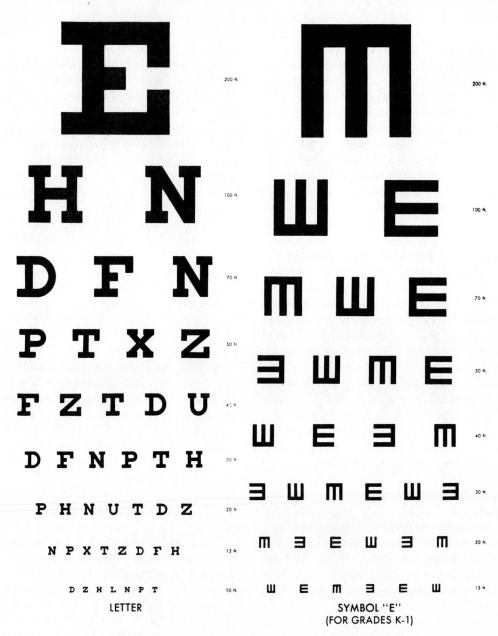

FIG. 5-1. Snellen charts. *(Courtesy National Society to Prevent Blindness, New York, N.Y.)*

tive groups as the best single measurement for vision screening.

The test makes use of a chart that has square-shaped letters or symbols resembling the letter E (Fig. 5-1). These are in specified sizes and in printed rows. The symbol at the top line of the chart is of such a size that a person with normal vision is able to see it from a distance of 200 feet, whereas the person with a vision problem can view it only from 20 feet. In each succeeding row, from the top downward, the size of the symbols is reduced to a point that a person with normal vision can see them at distances of 100, 70, 50, 30, and 20 feet, respectively.

To determine visual acuity, the student stands at a distance of 20 feet from the chart and with one eye covered reads the smallest letter that can be seen. The pupil's acuity is recorded by stating the distance at which the test has been completed and the line the student reads. These numbers are recorded as fractions: 20/20, 20/40, 20/70. They are not actually fractions, but represent a simple method of reporting facts. Thus an acuity of 20/70 means that the student was tested at 20 feet and could read only the letters on line 70. The vision of each eye is tested separately.

Criteria for recommending pupils for a retest may be the following:

1. Four-year-olds through grade 3—20/40 visual acuity or less in one or both eyes; inability to read the 30-foot line
2. Grade 4 and up—20/30 visual acuity or less in one or both eyes; inability to read the 20-foot line

After being retested, children for whom the second findings are the same as those recorded after the first test, provided that the teacher's observations indicate abnormality, should be referred for examination by a professionally qualified person.

Additional tests. The National Society to Prevent Blindness indicates there are several other tests that may be added to the basic minimum procedure. These include the plus sphere lens, muscle imbalance, and color vision tests.

PLUS SPHERE LENS. The plus sphere lens is used to detect pupils with hyperopia. The test is administered by having such children wear a pair of glasses with convex (hyperopic) lenses of specified strength (+2.25 diopters* for the first three grades and +1.75 diopters from fourth grade on) and requiring them to read the 20-foot line of the Snellen chart. Each eye is tested separately. If they read the line, they have failed the test. The convex lens blurs the vision of the children with no refractive error and makes correction for the hyperopic youngsters enabling them to read the chart. Pupils who fail the test should be retested. If the results are the same and there are other signs noted through teacher observations, these children should be referred for professional diagnosis. The plus sphere test should be given only to those pupils who do not wear glasses and who satisfactorily pass the Snellen test.

MUSCLE IMBALANCE. Muscle imbalance refers to the inability of the two eyes to work together. There are a number of instruments to measure this condition such as Maddox's rod but there is no satisfactory screening procedure. A rough, and not very accurate, method still in use is the cover test. It is a simple way to detect latent strabismus (crossed eye not readily noticed). In some children this condition reveals itself only when they are very tired or under emotional stress. Latent strabismus may manifest itself in only one eye, or it may alternate between the eyes.

The cover test determines whether eye alignment is maintained when one eye is covered while the other is fixed on an object. The alignment of each eye should be determined for both distant and near points.

The procedure for testing should be as follows:

1. Have the pupil look at a small light or object 20 feet away.
2. Place a cover card in front of one of the pupil's eyes in a manner so that the light or

---

*Diopter, unit of measurement of strength or refractive power of lenses.

object cannot be seen with that eye. Watch to see if the alignment of the covered eye is maintained; note whether the eye turns in, out, up, or down or holds its fixed position.

3. After a few seconds, move the cover card to the other eye. The previously covered eye is watched for a shift in the direction of its fixation.

4. Repeat the test, having the pupil look at a small light or object 8 to 10 inches in front of the nose. If the muscle balance of the eye is essentially normal, there should be no marked change in its fixation on covering or when the cover is removed.

Pupils who show marked deviation from normal should be retested, and if the same results are discovered, they should be referred for professional diagnosis.

COLOR VISION TEST. The color vision test is a procedure to determine whether a person is color blind, or unable to discriminate between certain colors, usually red and green and sometimes blue and yellow. Two satisfactory tests for school use are the Hardy-Rand-Ritter test and the Ishihara test.

Color blindness is inherited and cannot be corrected. Adjustments to the abnormality are important, and students should be aware of this limitation, especially when making vocational choices, when learning to drive automobiles, or when crossing streets. It is desirable to test young people before they enter junior high school.

Other devices and procedures. Numerous other instruments, devices, and procedures with varied opinions (including that they cause overreferral of pupils) regarding their value are available for vision screening and testing. They include Maddox's rod test (for muscle imbalance), the Telebinocular (a stereoscopic instrument to measure muscle imbalance, visual acuity, and color vision), the Ortho-Rater (similar to the Telebinocular), the Titmus vision tester (for near- and far-sightedness), and the Massachusetts vision kit (visual acuity, plus sphere, and Maddox's rod test). Several modified clinic techniques (MCT) have been used. One involved the cooperative use of optom-

etrists and ophthalmologists; a second used only ophthalmologists. The procedures used to test vision included visual acuity (Snellen "E" Chart), binocular coordination (cover test for muscle imbalance), refractive error (retinoscope for myopia, hyperopia, and astigmatism), and ocular health (use of ophthalmoscope to inspect the internal and external eye structures). It was claimed the MCT procedures reduced the numbers of children in need of eye attention who were missed (underreferrals).

Hearing

The procedure generally used to test the hearing of children is performed with the puretone audiometer. It requires technical training to administer and interpret.

Puretone audiometer. The puretone audiometer (Fig. 5-2) is an individual testing device that measures the ability to hear sounds of varying frequencies* or hertz (Hz) at different intensities of sound called decibels.†

A procedure known as the sweep-check test method has been used in schools to expedite the hearing screening process. Testing each ear separately, the intensity dial is set at 10 decibels; and the tone dial is changed rather quickly through the 1,000, 2,000, 4,000, and 6,000 frequencies and reset at 20 decibels for 4,000 frequencies. The extremely low and high tones may be omitted. Some sweep-check methods involve the 500, 1,000, 2,000, and 4,000 frequencies at 20 decibels. It is estimated that from 5% to 10% of the students will fail this test. Those students who fail to hear one tone or more in either ear in this sweep method should be given a second screening test. Failure to pass the repeated screening should be followed by a threshold test. In this test, pupils listen to all the intensities of sound of each frequency, with the results plotted on audiograms (Fig. 5-3). The findings are then interpreted by tech-

---

*Frequencies, qualities of sound caused by the number of vibrations per second of an object resulting in high and low tones, for example, strings on a piano.
†Decibels, units of sound intensity.

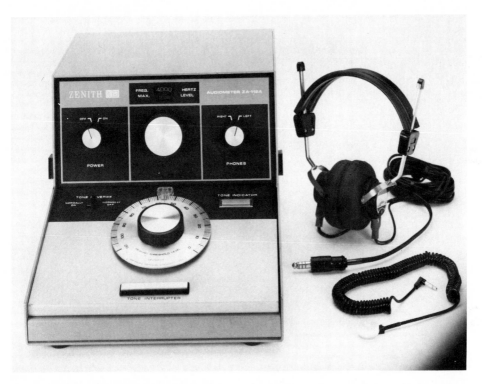

FIG. 5-2. Puretone audiometer. *(Courtesy Zenetron, Inc., Chicago, Ill.)*

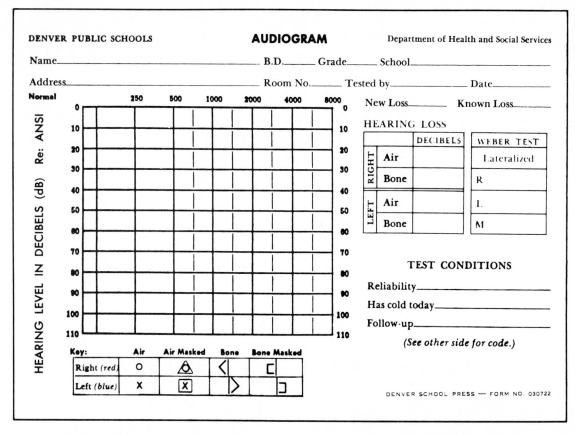

FIG. 5-3. Audiogram. *(Courtesy Department of Health and Social Services, Denver Public Schools, 1981.)*

nologists administering the test, and decisions are made whether to refer these children for specialized examinations. The criteria for referral generally include hearing losses of 20 decibels or more at any two frequencies in either ear, or a loss of 30 decibels or more at any single frequency in either ear. The degrees of hearing disability may be categorized as mild, moderate, moderately severe, and severe.

Audiometers are usually calibrated in round-numbered frequencies such as 125, 250, 500, 1,000, 2,000, on up to 8,000, the range of sounds that are normally heard by human beings. The machines are also calibrated by sound intensities with the step intervals being from 5 or 10 decibels to a maximum of 100 decibels.

The American Academy of Pediatrics* recommends that every child have a hearing test by the age of 4 years. Children with ear disease, language or speech problems, or other indications of possible hearing abnormality should be tested when conditions are first recognized regardless of age. Hearing testing in schools should be done annually in preschool, kindergarten, and grade 1 and then in grades 3, 6, 9, and 12. Children with persistent hearing impairments should be tested annually.

*Committee on School Health: School health: a guide for health professionals, Evanston, Ill., 1981, American Academy of Pediatrics.

CODE: 1. RETEST
2A "HOME REPORT"—*To recommend medical care.*
2B "HOME REPORT"—*With no medical care recommended at present.*
3. REPORT OF HIGH FREQUENCY LOSS
4. EDUCATION AUDIOMETRY

Significant medical history:_____

_____

Significant educational history:_____

_____

Recommendations:_____
Special seating, etc.:_____

_____

_____

General:_____

_____

_____

_____

_____

FIG. 5-3, cont'd. For legend see opposite page.

Growth and development

Periodic measurements of the heights and weights of children will aid in understanding the growth and development of boys and girls in terms of (1) normal progression, (2) extent of overweight, and (3) extent of underweight. However, Eisner and others* state that routine growth measurements have not proved their general usefulness in health service programs and are not of sufficient educational value to justify a large investment of nurse time. Mere observations of weight and height increases, or the failure of children to gain weight, may not in themselves be of much significance in the growth process. Childrens' growth patterns are individual, and unless an instrument is used to show this, school personnel may be led to erroneous conclusions about overweight, underweight, or abnormal growth conditions. Weighing and measuring can be valuable in the appraisal process if the information is recorded and plotted on growth charts for interpretation, as illustrated in the height-weight records shown in Figs. 5-4 and 5-5.

The taking of heights and weights should be done at the beginning, middle, and end of the school year. It is important that measurements be accurately taken and recorded.

*Eisner, V., Oglesby, A., and Peck, E.B.: Health assessment of school children, VI. height and weight, Journal of School Health **42:** March 1972.

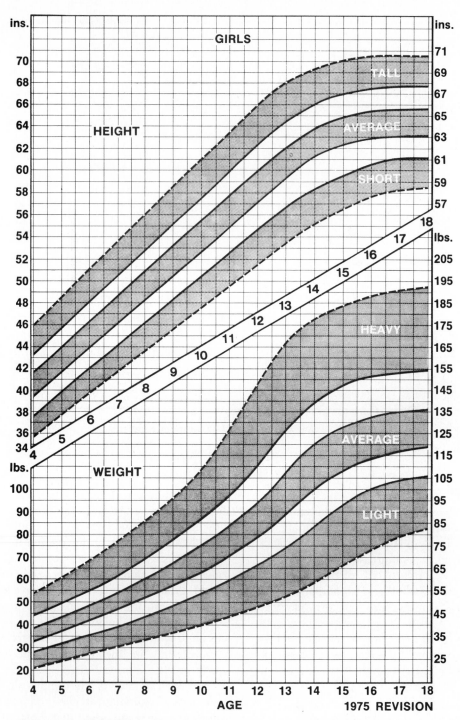

FIG. 5-4. Growth of girls. *(Copyright 1975, 1978, American Medical Association. Publication of A.M.A. Medicine/Education Committee. Material produced by John H. Spurgeon and Howard V. Meredith, University of Southern California.)*

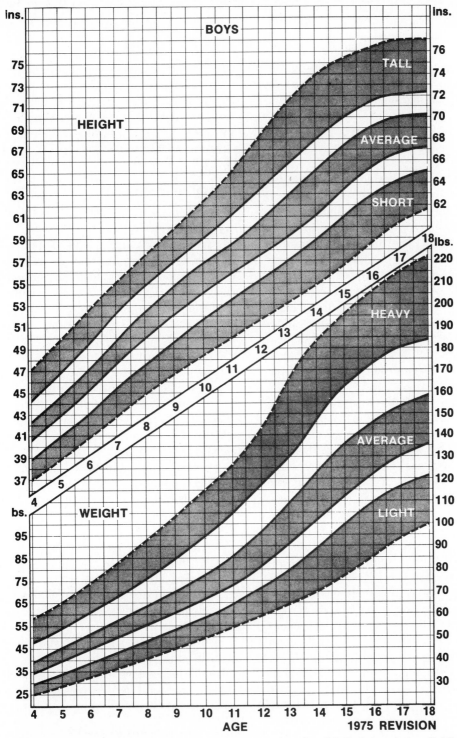

FIG. 5-5. Growth of boys. *(Copyright 1975, 1978, American Medical Association. Publication of A.M.A. Medicine/Education Committee. Material produced by John H. Spurgeon and Howard V. Meredith, University of Southern California.)*

Children in grade 3 and upward can be taught to take these measurements. Teachers, nurses, and/or nurse assistants can aid by recording these data on the growth charts. This activity provides an excellent teachable moment for health instruction about growth and development.

Tuberculosis

The prevalence of tuberculosis in the United States has been on the decline for many years, and its incidence generally is not high except in some communities. A procedure used to detect the disease through the identification of positive reactors is tuberculin testing. In the Mantoux test, a fluid containing proteins extracted from tubercle bacilli called tuberculin is injected intradermally (between the layers of the skin) or into the skin through multiple punctures (tine, Heaf, Mono-Vac, or Sterneedle test). If the test is positive, a reaction, an inflamed or red area, appears in about 48 hours on the skin where the test was made.

A positive reaction to the test (inflammation, redness) does not necessarily mean that a person has active tuberculosis. It is an indication that the person has tubercle bacilli within his or her body and there has been an allergic reaction to these germs. In areas of high socioeconomic conditions less than 2% of positive reactors may be found among elementary children, whereas in low socioeconomic areas this percentage may be as high as 10%. Positive reactors to tuberculin tests should receive thorough medical examinations, including chest x-ray films, to determine whether active tuberculosis exists.

The American Lung Association* recommends that tuberculin testing should be concentrated in areas where the prevalence of infection is constantly high over a period of time. Therefore routine or periodic testing of school children and young adolescents should be stressed in those schools where the reactor rate is 1% or

more and should take place in other schools on a selective basis only. The American Academy of Pediatrics* agrees with this procedure. They also state that schools can determine whether the incidence of tuberculin sensitivity exceeds 1% by testing all those starting school for the first time and children in grades 8 and 9 at intervals of 3 years or by testing randomly selected subsamples annually.

Dental inspections

Dental inspections refer to procedures generally performed by dentists or dental hygienists using mouth mirrors and explorers to locate decayed teeth, as well as to check for diseases of tissues surrounding the teeth and for malocclusion. These inspections are not complete examinations, since they do not include x-ray examinations.

Ideally, children should visit their family dentists twice yearly for appraisal and necessary treatment. There is evidence to indicate only 20% of the population is following this practice.

Opinions differ regarding whether periodic dental inspections should be conducted in schools. Several reasons causing this dilemma include the following:

1. Dental decay is the most common health defect found in school-age children, and there is little need to locate problem cases.
2. Increased pressure on parents by the schools to obtain corrections may make it impossible for dentists to provide the needed services. The schools would be criticized for not being aware of this difficulty.
3. Most school districts do not employ dentists or dental hygienists.
4. There is an inadequate supply of dentists and dental hygienists as well as poor geographic distribution of these specialists.

Dental inspections in schools vary widely as to their inclusion and frequency. In Pennsylvania, dental examinations by a dentist must be

---

*Your patient's risk of tuberculosis, 1975, New York, American Lung Association.

*Committee on School Health, School Health: A guide for health professionals, Evanston, Ill., 1981, American Academy of Pediatrics.

conducted by schools on the original entry of children as well as in the third and seventh grades. In elementary schools, however, substitution is permitted by service from dental hygienists provided it includes a screening process, prophylactic care, and an educational program. In Denver, all pupils are inspected at selected grades by dental hygienists.

Sickle-cell disease

Sickle-cell disease is a disorder of red blood cells caused by abnormal hemoglobin and affects their ability to carry oxygen. The normal red blood cells that usually appear disc shaped are crescent or sickle shaped. The condition is found among the black population and to a lesser degree in individuals with Mediterranean ancestry (Greece, Italy), in Caribbean islanders, and in people in South and Central America. The sickle-cell trait is a genetic factor estimated to be found in 10% of the black population, whereas the disease itself, sickle-cell anemia, is found in approximately 1 in 400 to 500 blacks. The condition results in the swelling of joints, pains in the abdomen, legs, and arms, and fatigue. The anemia cannot be cured, but the "crisis" situation when cells are deprived of oxygen can be treated. The crisis condition can be prevented or ameliorated.

One valid procedure used to identify this condition among junior and senior high school students is to draw venous blood and test it by direct hemoglobin electrophoresis to determine if the blood cells differ from normal ones. Only one test is needed to determine an individual's status. The American Academy of Pediatrics* states that routine screening of well school-aged children is not desirable.

Diabetes

Diabetes is not an infectious disease. It can be detected by urine analysis to determine the level of sugar in the blood. Although schools generally do not conduct such tests, every effort should be made to identify those afflicted children to be able to provide needed help. When students first enter school, parent interviews, completion of health histories, physician contacts, and other means should be used to locate diabetic pupils.

Diabetes results from failure of the pancreas to make a sufficient amount of insulin. Without insulin, food cannot be used properly. Diabetes currently cannot be cured but can be controlled by daily injections of insulin and a prescribed food plan. Afflicted children can participate in all school activities, but should be carefully observed in class. Physical education should not be scheduled just before lunch, nor should a child be assigned a late lunch period. These young people may need midmorning or midafternoon snacks. Teachers should have sugar readily available in the event of insulin shock.

Epilepsy

Epilepsy is a disruption of the electrical impulses to the brain that causes nerves to send out erratic impulses through the body resulting in a seizure, or sudden onset of symptoms, such as convulsions. It occurs in approximately 1 child in 50, with 75% of the cases beginning before the twenty-first birthday. Four out of five seizures, where known, can be controlled with medication; 50% can be totally controlled, and 30% partially. Teachers should be aware that excessive fatigue, overexposure to heat or sunlight, and situations that cause emotional disturbances can affect the seizure threshold in children and increase the incidence of attacks.

Schools must identify students with epilepsy to be able to best provide for their safety and to enable classmates to help these pupils. Screening to locate such children can take place when they first enter school through parent interviews and the completion of health histories, through a review of health records and physician contacts, and by other means.

---

*Committee on School Health: School health: a guide for health professionals, Evanston, Ill., 1981, American Academy of Pediatrics.

Scoliosis

Scoliosis is a condition in which there is a lateral curvature and rotation of the spine. It is found in 0.5% to 2.0% of young people. It occurs in rapidly growing preadolescent and adolescent children aged 9 through 15 years and progresses until skeletal maturity is attained. It is generally the result of poor muscle tone and fatigue and sometimes may reflect depression and lack of self-esteem.

The procedure used in screening for scoliosis should be done with pupils stripped to the waist. Girls may wear brassieres. Pupils should be observed from the back and should stand erect with the shoulders back, head up and looking forward, hands hanging at sides, knees straight, and feet together. Observers should note whether the shoulders, scapulae, arm hang, and hips are in a level plane; one should not be higher or lower than the other. Also, the straightness of the spine should be checked; it should not bend right or left. The pupil should then bend forward at the waist, head hanging relaxed, arms dangling from the shoulders, and knees straight. The screener should observe the surface of the back at eye level to detect prominence of the thoracic ribs and the area around the vertebral column. The chest should be symmetrical, and an imaginary line drawn from scapula to scapula should be parallel to the floor. As the student resumes an upright position, the back movement should be checked to note prominences or spinal curvatures. Abnormalities detected should be referred to a physician for examination and treatment.

The purpose of scoliosis screening is to detect abnormal curvature of the spine at an early stage so that corrective procedures can be instituted. It should take place when skeletal growth is rapid—in girls at 9 to 14 years of age and boys at 11 to 15 years of age. Schools commonly conduct the screening in grades 5 through 9 or 10. The number and frequency of these procedures is dependent on the resources available and local school district policy. The procedure can be completed by nurses and others with special training.

Other screening procedures

A variety of additional types of screening appraisals such as teacher observations of nutritional deficiencies (Table 5-4), speech difficulties, hypertension, and assessment for conditions such as anemia, hemophilia, and muscular dystrophy occur in schools. Their frequency and extent show wide variation throughout the United States.

WHAT ARE HEALTH HISTORIES AND INVENTORIES?

Histories and inventories (Fig. 5-6) are informational accounts of the health practices and behavior of children that take the form of written questionnaires or checklists. They are frequently neglected, yet they are one of the most important parts of periodic health appraisals. The basic content should include information about major past health problems (physical and emotional) and their treatment, an orderly review of body systems, information about current and past special problems of other members of the family, and information about the student's academic achievement and school adjustments. This information provides background data about the health of children not usually revealed by other procedures that are useful in the health appraisals of pupils. The teacher needs to know that a child with diabetes is taking insulin. A periodic health examination may not reveal that a student has asthma or occasional epileptic attacks. These inventories help in understanding the health status of boys and girls and may be particularly useful when school medical examinations are conducted. The forms may be sent to parents of young children for completion or may be finished at school when the child is brought in for enrollment. The data obtained become a part of the child's health record.

WHAT ARE MEDICAL EXAMINATIONS?

Medical, health, or physical examinations refer to those appraisals usually completed by

DENVER PUBLIC SCHOOLS   **SCHOOL NURSE INTERVIEW WITH PARENT**   DEPARTMENT OF HEALTH AND SOCIAL SERVICES

Pupil's name_____ Birth date_____ Date of interview_____

I. BIRTH AND DEVELOPMENT

Pregnancy - Delivery

Gravida_____ Para_____

Birthweight_____

Birthplace_____

Baby's condition at birth_____

Days in hospital_____

Age - sat up_____ crawled_____

    walked_____

    talked_____ words_____ sentences_____

    Any speech problems_____

Weaned at age_____

Toilet training_____ age_____

Constipation_____ Diarrhea_____

Enuresis_____ Encopresis_____

Handedness: Right_____ Left_____ Both_____

Are you satisfied with child's progress and development?_____

Do you have any particular concerns about your child?_____

DENVER SCHOOL PRESS — STOCK NO. 01-030025

II. BEHAVIORAL DEVELOPMENT

How does child get along with

    peers?_____

    siblings?_____

    parents?_____

Assumes responsibility_____

Expresses anger by_____

Expresses insecurity by_____

Method of discipline_____

Habits:

    Eating_____

    Sleeping_____ Nightmares_____

    Thumbsucking_____ Nail biting_____

    Masturbation_____ Other_____

Reading and early listening experiences_____

_____

TV and recreation_____

Attention span_____

School experience_____

III. PAST ILLNESSES (include age of child or date)

Allergies_____

Contagious diseases_____

Serious illnesses or chronic diseases_____

High fever_____

History of convulsions_____

Accidents_____

Head injury or unconsciousness_____

Fractures_____

Surgery_____ Hospitalization_____

Emotional problems_____

Significant family episodes (include dates)

    for example:

    death_____

    severe accident_____

    loss of job_____

    divorce/separation_____

    remarriage_____

    other_____

(OVER)

IV. FAMILY MEDICAL HISTORY

Mother_____

Father_____

Siblings_____

Maternal grandparents_____

Paternal grandparents_____

Others_____

Previous tests or screening of child:

    Sickle cell_____ Speech_____

    DDST_____ Hearing_____ Vision_____

    Dental_____

    Medical care resource_____

V. FAMILY HISTORY

Father's age_____ Occupation_____

_____ Work hours_____

Last grade in school_____

Glasses?_____

Mother's age_____ Occupation_____

_____ Work hours_____

Last grade in school_____

Glasses?_____

Language (s) spoken in home_____

School experience of siblings_____

_____

_____

_____

_____

_____

VI. CONCLUSIONS

How do you think your child will do or does in school?

How would you describe your child?

School nurse and/or family plans, following this interview:

Name of person interviewed and relationship to child

_____, RN

FIG. 5-6. School nurse interview with parent. (*Courtesy Department of Health and Social Services, Denver Public Schools, 1981.*)

physicians who are qualified to make diagnoses and to render treatment. Accurate evaluations of health require medical examinations.

The health examination usually includes the following conditions and parts of the body:

Nutrition
Skin and hair
Head and neck
Lungs
Muscle tone
Nose, throat, and tonsils
Feet
Eyes
Genitalia
Heart
Nervous system
Posture
Thyroid gland
Teeth and gums
Bones and joints
Ears
Pulse resting and after exercise
Blood pressure
Abdomen
Lymph nodes
Inguinal and umbilical region for hernia
Laboratory tests such as urinalysis and blood tests

The American Academy of Pediatrics believes the child's health care provider or family physician is the most desirable source for a health appraisal. Therefore it generally should be performed outside the school setting. However, there may be circumstances such as legal requirements, many deprived children in low socioeconomic areas, and lack of health care resources that necessitate such examinations being conducted in some schools.

The Academy states that routine, periodic, health examinations in schools have proved to have low effectiveness in the identification of serious, uncared for medical problems. They indicate that the continuance of such appraisals is inadvisable.

The frequency of health examinations for children in school is set by law in some states. Where there are no legal directives, local school and medical officials must make these decisions. Appraisals probably should be performed when pupils start school, again in grades 6 or 7, and before leaving school in grades 11 or 12. In addition, they should be conducted for those who have been identified as having particular problems. The Academy states that priority for school examinations should be given to high-risk children, who may be those with low socioeconomic states, poor school performance, existing handicaps, frequent absence, and disciplinary problems.

In recent years nurse-practitioners have appeared who have been trained to perform health examinations. Many are school nurses who have completed a specialized education and training program under the direction of the local medical society or provided by a local medical center at a university. Such preparation may include taking and evaluating medical health history; performing a thorough physical examination including the use of the stethoscope and otoscope; performing a variety of specialized clinical laboratory tests and procedures, such as urinalysis, throat cultures, and hematocrits; and identifying and assessing factors leading to a variety of behavioral, learning, and perceptual disorders. These practitioners work closely with school personnel, school physicians, health personnel, and physicians in private practice.

WHAT ARE PSYCHOLOGICAL EXAMINATIONS AND TESTS?

Psychological examinations and tests include a variety of procedures to test personality, behavior, and social acceptance of pupils as well as intelligence, achievements, and aptitudes. They are usually administered by psychologists and psychometrists who are members of a child guidance or pupil personnel services program. School districts occasionally employ consulting psychiatrists to help with emotionally disturbed students. Mental health specialists and mental health counselors are beginning to be trained and used in some schools. The findings from these appraisals, together with teacher observations, help determine the necessary action. Pupils with suspected emotional difficulties who are located through these evaluations may need to be referred for medical or psychiatric consultation. In California, on a report of the school principal that a pupil shows evidence of impaired mental health and that a mental examination is desirable, the governing body of any school district may, with the written consent of the pupil's parent or guardian, provide for the mental examination of said pupil. The American Academy of Pediatrics states that children with emotional problems are difficult to identify. They claim that the management of children with emotional problems is the most common unmet health need of school children.

Teacher feelings, emotions, and expressions affect pupil emotions. Teacher attitudes are reflected in the attitudes of pupils. The teacher who is kind but firm, sympathetic but exacting, and friendly but reserved exerts a beneficial influence on emotional health. The nagging, scolding, domineering, sarcastic, or emotionally unstable teacher may lead to serious emotional difficulties in pupils.

Locating children with emotional problems

Children who are emotionally disturbed or who exhibit behavior that causes one to suspect mental illness need to be identified and located early if they are to receive the greatest help. The teacher is the main contact person with pupils and is in a strategic position to render valuable service. The importance of teacher observations was stressed earlier; however, the specific signs of maladjustment that the teacher must know and recognize are found on p. 81. It has been estimated that teachers can select 70% of the emotionally disturbed children, and with a clinic team, 90% of their problems can be discovered. The deviant behaviors observed are generally the result of pupil needs (p. 59) not being fulfilled. Teachers must be alert throughout the entire school day and be observant in their informal contacts, conferences,

and interviews with pupils and parents for clues that will help to identify the problems of their pupils. Should the teacher desire to identify more objectively children in need of help, the teacher observation of classroom adaptation (see chart on p. 100) will provide a useful instrument.

Some other procedures teachers may use with discretion to help identify indicators that children may have problems include the following:

1. Sociometric technique—the teacher may ask pupils to list the three classmates they would like to have sit next to them in order of preference. This information can then be plotted on paper, and those pupils with few, if any, friends, can be readily identified. The isolates are easily located through the use of this method.

2. Examination of school records including health records—these contain chronologic reports of children's performances and health status.

3. Written autobiographies—the teacher may have pupils write compositions on such topics as the following:

"What I criticize about myself"
"What others criticize about me"
"What makes me mad"
"The person I would like to be"
"My life 10 years from now"

4. Student survey—the procedure shown in Fig. 5-7 should provide helpful clues when completed by pupils and reviewed by the teacher.

Finding problem children is not easy and is also the responsibility of other school personnel, including nurses and psychologists. Their specific responsibilities vary in schools, but they should be observant of pupil behavior, assess pupil records, use a variety of formal procedures.

School psychologists may use personality adjustment tests, such as the California Test of Personality (elementary series), which covers five levels of personality, including self-relevance, feelings of belonging, and social skills;

Teacher observation of classroom adaptation

Please rate each pupil from 0 to 3 for each of the following kinds of maladaptive behavior observed in the classroom, using the rating scale below. The examples given for each category of maladaptive behavior are merely illustrative suggestions, and should not be thought of as an exhaustive list.

Rating scale (0-3)

0 = Within minimal limits of acceptable behavior
1 = Mildly excessive
2 = Moderately excessive
3 = Severely excessive

_____ 1. Excessively lacking in involvement with classmates: e.g. shy, timid, alone too much, daydreamer, friendless, aloof

_____ 2. Excessively aggressive behavior: e.g. fights too much, steals, lies, resists authority, is destructive to others or property, obstinate, disobedient, uncooperative

_____ 3. Excessively immature behavior: e.g. acts too young physically and/or emotionally, cries too much, has tantrums, sucks thumb, is physically poorly coordinated, masturbates, urinates in class, seeks too much attention

_____ 4. Excessively not working up to his ability; e.g. does not learn as well as your assessment of his ability indicates he is able to

_____ 5. Excessively restless: e.g. fidgets, is unable to sit still in classroom

_____ 6. Global rating of classroom adaptation: This is not a summary of the other behavior ratings but a general overall rating of the child's state of classroom behavior adaptation. However, if a child has been rated as maladapted in one of the classroom behavior categories, he should have a maladapted rating in the global category. If he has received a '0' in each of the boxes above he should have a '0' in this box.

From Kellam, S.G., and others: Mental health and going to school, Chicago, 1975, University of Chicago Press.

	Always 3	Seldom 2	Never 1
1. I can get extra help from the teacher when I need it.			
2. The teacher praises me when I do well.			
3. The teacher smiles when I do something well.			
4. The teacher listens attentively.			
5. The teacher accepts me as an individual.			
6. The teacher encourages me to try something new.			
7. The teacher respects the feelings of others.			
8. My work is usually good enough.			
9. I am called on when I raise my hand.			
10. The same students always get praised by the teacher.			

FIG. 5-7. Student survey. (From Gearheart, B.R., and Weishahn, M.W.: The handicapped child in the regular classroom, ed. 2, St. Louis, 1980, The C.V. Mosby Co.)

the California Test of Mental Maturity; the Goodenough Draw-A-Man test; a semiprojective story completion instrument called "Secret Stories," which is an adaptation of Roger's use of "Wishes"; the Brown Personality Inventory of Children; or Roger's Test of Personality Adjustment, in addition to evaluating the information from school personnel to find emotionally disturbed students.

A variety of other instruments identified by Reinert* as useful devices include the following: (1) Bower-Lambert Scales (grades K to 12), a semiprojective technique; (2) Deveraux Elementary School Behavior Rating Scale (grades K to 6); and (3) Walker Problem Behavior Identification Checklist (grades 4 to 6) for teacher use. Greenberger and associates† developed a Psychosocial Maturity (PSM) Inventory, a self-reporting attitude instrument for use with 8- to 11-year-olds.

Counselors, physicians, nurses, psychiatric social workers, psychologists, and psychiatrists may individually or collectively be involved in case studies of pupils. Teachers and other personnel may also be requested to report their observations. This is a technique whereby the conclusions of a variety of people are brought together to help identify and understand deviant children, to determine needed action to help children, and to suggest school adjustments.

The assessment of the mental health status of pupils is both difficult and complex. Accurate, objective observations of behavior together with the pooling of information obtained from many sources are necessary.

WHAT ARE HEALTH RECORDS?

Health records (Fig. 5-8) refer to those materials that contain all pertinent data about the health status of pupils. Cumulative records should be maintained for all pupils in school and not merely for those with known health problems. They should be accessible to those persons who need to use them and should follow students from grade to grade, from school to school, and from school district to school district.

There is no common type of health record used in schools. However, records information should be kept confidential and should not be available without permission of school health personnel. They should not contain personal observations by the teacher that label children as slow learners, mentally retarded, and the like. Parents or guardians should have access to their contents.

Records usually contain the following information:
1. Teacher observations
2. Screening tests results
3. Findings of medical, dental, and psychologic examinations
4. Notes on health counseling and follow-up procedures

Despite the amount of information found in health records, it is not used with any degree of consistency by teachers and others. This is probably because of any, or all, of the following reasons: (1) there is no central, master file on every student, and retrieval of information is difficult; (2) it takes a great deal of time to transcribe the data by hand; (3) information is frequently lost or misinterpreted, and records may be incomplete; (4) little anecdotal information can be included; (5) if a record is lost, a completely new one must be reconstructed; and (6) an adequate study of the total student population is virtually impossible.

A new approach to records is the Problem Oriented Medical Record (POMR) that was introduced by the Darien Public Schools in Connecticut.* It is organized to acquire such basic data as history, physical examinations, and laboratory results. In addition, it precisely defines student problems and provides monitoring of these problems through the use of progress

---

*Reinert, H.R.: Children in conflict, ed. 2, St. Louis, 1980, The C.V. Mosby Co.
†Greenberger, E., and others: The measurement and structure of psychosocial maturity, Journal of Youth and Adolescence 4: June 1975.

*Boone, S.F.: A new approach to school health records, Journal of School Health 44:156-158, March 1974.

DENVER PUBLIC SCHOOLS • DEPARTMENT OF HEALTH AND SOCIAL SERVICES

DENVER SCHOOL PRESS
STOCK NO. 01-030032

HEALTH RECORD

NAME   BIRTH DATE

ROOM													
YEAR													
GRADE													
HEIGHT													
WEIGHT													
VISION— With Glasses {R. {L.													
VISION— Without Glasses {R. {L.													
VISION REFERRAL													
STEREO TEST													
COLOR VISION													
HEARING, R.													
HEARING, L.													
TEETH													
SCOLIOSIS													
SWIM O.K.													
APPRAISAL													
TUBERCULIN TEST													
CLINIC NAME AND NUMBER													

FATHER'S NAME   MOTHER'S NAME   LIVES WITH (pencil)

NAME AND BIRTH YEAR OF OTHER CHILDREN IN FAMILY:

1.   4.   7.
2.   5.   8.
3.   6.   9.

SCHOOL:
1.   5.   9.
2.   6.   10.
3.   7.   11.
4.   8.   12.

HEALTH CONDITIONS (include year)	IMMUNIZATIONS
	D.P.T.
	Polio
	Rubeola
	Rubella
	Mumps

OTHER PERTINENT DATA (include date)

MEDICAL RECORD (FOR DESCRIPTIVE REMARKS USE A SUPPLEMENTARY SHEET.)

CODE

O = Satisfactory; Otherwise, use code.

MONTH AND YEAR OF APPRAISAL						
I. HISTORY						
II. INITIAL IMPRESSION						
III. NUTRITION						
IV. SKIN						
V. EYES						
VI. EARS						
VII. NOSE						
VIII. MOUTH						
IX. THROAT						
X. THYROID						
XI. HEART BLOOD PRESSURE___/___ RATE						
XII. LUNGS						
XIII. ABDOMEN						
XIV. GENITO-URINARY						
XV. ORTHOPEDIC						
XVI. NERVOUS SYSTEM						
APPRAISED BY:___						

I.   1. Poor eating habits 2. Unsatisfactory sleep 3. Smoking 4. Excessive activities 5. Thumb-sucking or nail biting 6. Enuresis 7. Poor social adjustment 8. Headaches 9. Earaches 10. Stomach aches 11. Excessive absences 13. Drug misuse 14. Battering

II. 1. Anxious 2. Relaxed 3. Well-cared for 4. Responsive 5. Disorganized

III. 1. Underweight 2. Overweight

IV. 1. Acne 2. Eczema 3. Warts 4. Moles 5. Dry 6. Scars 7. Infection

V.   1. Blepharitis 2. Conjunctivitis 3. Strabismus 4. Eye strain

VI. 1. External ear (a. lowset, b. malformed) 2. Canal (a. wax, b. inflamation) 3. Membranes (a. serous otitis, b. discharging, c. perforated, d. scarring)

VII. 1. Nasal obstruction 2. Deflected septum 3. Swollen, red turbinates

VIII. 1. Dental caries (a. deciduous, b. permanent) 2. Malocclusion 3. Gum abnormality 4. Poor oral hygiene 5. Palate defect

IX. 1. Tonsils (a. removed, b. enlarged, c. diseased) 2. Pharyngitis 3. Post nasal discharge

X.   1. Enlargement 2. With symptoms

XI. 1. Murmur (a. systolic, b. diastolic) 1 Apex 2 Pulmonary 3 Aortic 4 Left sternal border 2. Femoral pulse (a. present, b. equal, c. absent)

XII. 1. Dyspnea 2. Wheezing 3. Rales

XIII. 1. Hernia (a. inguinal, b. umbilical) 2. Mass 3. Post-operative scar

XIV. 1. Pubertal changes 2. Dysmenorrhea 3. Menses — date of onset _____

XV. 1. Kyphosis 2. Scoliosis 3. Lordosis 4. Pronated feet 5. Flat feet 6. _____

XVI. 1. Abnormal reflexes 2. Hyperkinetic 3. Poor coordination

FIG. 5-8. Health and medical records. (*Courtesy Department of Health and Social Services, Denver Public Schools, 1981.*)

SCHOOL HEALTH RECORD

Name _____ Smith, Mary _____

Problem list

Entry Date	Problem	Inactive
11-15-75	1. Stomachache	11-18-75
1-8-76	2. Leg injury	2-20-76 normal activity
2-4-76	3. Weight problem	5-28-76 12-pound loss

Date/time	Progress notes*	Signature
11-15-75 9:05 A.M.	1. Stomachache S: "My stomach hurts here." O: Points to lower right abdominal area; T 101° F., diarrhea x3 yesterday, x2 today. A: Gastrointestinal infection? appendicitis? P: Contact parent, send home, advise MD check if symptoms continue.	W. Jones
1-8-76 1:25 P.M.	2. Leg injury S: "I can't walk on it, it hurts to move it. I was running down the stairs and tripped and fell on my right leg." O: Swelling of right ankle, unable to place weight on foot without pain. A: Sprained/fractured ankle? P: Contact parent, advise MD check.	W. Jones
2-4-76 1:30 P.M.	3. Weight problem S: Home Ec. teacher (Mrs. Jones) referred student for weight/diet counseling. Student: "I don't think I'm really fat." O: 5 feet 4 inches 140 pounds = ±15 pounds above recommended height/weight (mod. heavy). A: Student not in agreement with need for weight loss/diet control. P: Personal and diet counseling.	W. Jones

*S = subjective; O = objective; A = assessment; P = plan.

FIG. 5-9. (*Adapted from Oda, D.S., and Quick, M.J.: Journal of School Health* **47**:212-215, *April, 1977.*)

notes. Oda and Quick (Fig. 5-9) illustrate one version that they believe provides simplicity, clarity, and uniformity of data.

Recently in New York an attempt has been made to put the data collected on computer cards so the facts can be more easily stored and more readily accessible. In Ontario, Canada, it was reported by Stennett* and others that a computerized system operative in a large school system (over 10,000 students) and called an Electronic Data-Processing (EDP) oriented record system appears to be successful. The American Academy of Pediatrics stated that computers may be helpful in large school systems to compile statistics, but they may not represent the most cost effective way to maintain and analyze school health records.

Teachers can better understand the health status of students by reviewing these health forms at the beginning of the semester as well as at other times. They may be expected to make notations of observations and other essential information about the health of children in their classes on these cards.

THE NURSE AND APPRAISALS

Nurses have an important role in school health appraisals. Their responsibilities vary depending on the size of the school district, whether physician services are available, and the amount of time they serve in schools. Generally, they are expected to (1) supervise and conduct screening procedures, (2) prepare schedules and logistical arrangements for tests, (3) help teachers with the conduct of certain appraisal procedures, (4) assist with examinations conducted by physicians and other health professionals, (5) aid teachers with pupil observations and referrals, (6) interpret appraisal findings to pupils, teachers, and parents, and (7) maintain health records.

In recent years nurses have assumed expanded duties in the assessment of school-

*Stennett, R.G., and others: Exploring the possibilities of computerized student health records, Journal of School Health **41**: Feb. 1971.

age children. Many have acquired additional special training in schools of medicine and have become *nurse-practitioners*. There are now thousands of nurse-practitioners licensed to practice in most states. They are especially useful in schools with limited or no physician services. In addition, they provide a close relationship with physicians and community health professionals. They are competent to conduct a complete patient assessment including neurologic examinations to screen for learning difficulties. Their functions include completion of health histories, performing developmental and physical examinations, conducting laboratory tests, management of minor illnesses and accidents, and health teaching and counseling.

The number of nurse-practitioners employed by school districts is not known. Most work with physicians in private practice.

TEACHER-NURSE CONFERENCES

A recommended practice in elementary schools is for teachers and nurses to hold periodic meetings during the school year to share their observations and information about the health status of pupils. A general session at the start of the school year followed by individual teacher meetings could be productive. Despite their significance and wide recognition of need, they are infrequently held in many schools because of limited nurse service, time constraints, and other reasons. In general, the following are the reasons for these conferences:

1. To discuss the nature of teacher observations
2. To provide understandings regarding known health problems, such as diabetes, epilepsy, and heart conditions, and to make provisions for individual pupil needs
3. To help teachers know what action to take in emergencies to help pupils with known health problems, such as epilepsy and diabetes
4. To help teachers make adjustments in their classrooms and in school, such as having children sit in the front of the room or having them participate in limited activities

5. To make decisions about referral cases to parents for diagnosis, information, or other action
6. To help teachers with the techniques of discussing health problems with parents
7. To inform teachers about future examinations and screening tests
8. To help teachers identify ways to integrate health instruction into the health services program

Teacher observations serve as supplementary measures to the various screening procedures and examinations that take place in schools. They help to identify pupils with health problems in the interval between medical examinations and to identify children with problems who need special examinations. In schools that do not conduct periodic medical and dental examinations or expect parents to have children examined, teacher observations combined with screening tests and health inventories or histories, together with teacher-nurse conferences, may have to be used in substitution.

THE TEACHER AND APPRAISALS

A review of the various procedures for assessing the health of pupils indicates that the teacher plays an important role in appraisals. The teacher should do the following:

1. Become aware of the characteristics of good health and growth and development of students
2. Observe children for signs and symptoms of health deviations and be familiar with the school's procedures for handling pupils with problems.
3. Understand the meaning and importance of medical and psychologic examinations and observations, dental inspections, and other assessment procedures
4. Be familiar with a variety of screening tests and be prepared to participate in the conduct of several, such as growth and development tests and the Snellen test
5. Know the importance of health records in helping to understand the pupil better and

realize it may be necessary to make periodic notations on these records
6. Be prepared on occasions, when appropriate or where nurse services may be limited or nonexistent, to discuss and/or counsel students and parents in regard to pupil health problems
7. Periodically meet with the school nurse to exchange information about pupils, learn about school adjustments for students, and obtain help with the health instruction program

The teacher should also realize that health appraisals offer numerous opportunities for health education:

1. Teaching about care of the eyes and ears is appropriate when pupils are taking vision and hearing tests.
2. The importance and need for health examinations or dental inspections can have its greatest impact when the instruction period coincides with the examinations or the inspections.
3. The control of communicable diseases should be discussed when tuberculin tests are being administered.
4. Understandings about growth and development can be achieved more easily by relating this process to the periodic taking of heights and weights.

It should be apparent that the more the teacher knows about the health status of pupils the better qualified that teacher will be to understand them, to make necessary classroom and school adjustments, to provide functional health teaching, and to increase the effectiveness of the total educational program.

QUESTIONS FOR DISCUSSION

1. Why must schools be concerned with the health status of students?
2. What is the meaning of the term *health appraisals?*
3. What are the purposes of health appraisals?
4. What is the role of the teacher when observing the health status of children?
5. What are the growth and developmental characteristics of children who are 3 to 5, 5 to 7, 8 to 10, and 11 to 13

years of age, and what are their health education implications?

6. What are some of the signs and symptoms of pupils' health problems that teachers can observe?
7. What are the characteristics of a healthy child?
8. What is the meaning of the term *learning disabilities*, how can a teacher identify such conditions, and what can be done to help children with these problems?
9. What are several of the communicable diseases that children may bring to school, and how may teachers recognize them?
10. Why are teacher-nurse conferences necessary and important?
11. What is the meaning of the term *child abuse*? Identify signs and symptoms that may be observed in children.
12. What are the general categories of health screening tests used in schools, and why are they necessary?
13. What types of vision screening tests may be used in schools?
14. How is hearing tested, and who does it in schools?
15. What are the values, problems, and frequency of periodic height and weight measurements?
16. What is meant by tuberculin testing, and under what conditions should it be completed in schools?
17. What are dental inspections, and why are they valuable?
18. What is sickle-cell disease, what are its signs and symptoms, and how can it be clinically identified?
19. What is diabetes, how can it clinically be identified, and what can schools and teachers do to help such children?
20. Who should administer medical examinations to pupils, and why should they take place?
21. How frequently and why should pupil medical examinations be conducted?
22. What are psychologic examinations and tests, and what can schools and teachers do to help problem children discovered?
23. What is the procedure used in screening for scoliosis and why is it important?
24. What is the meaning of the term *nurse-practitioners*, and how may they help ghetto children with health problems?
25. What behavior may be exhibited by hyperkinetic children, and what understandings are needed by teachers of these students?
26. How can teachers identify drug users and abusers?
27. What is the role of the nurse in health appraisals?
28. What is the role of the teacher in health appraisals?

SELECTED REFERENCES

American School Health Association: The handicapped child in school, the Seventh Annual Schering Symposium, 52nd annual convention of the American School Health Association, Oct. 13, 1978, Journal of School Health 49:137-167, Oct. 1978.

Anderson, C.L., and Creswell, W.H., Jr.: School health practice, ed. 7, St. Louis, 1980, The C.V. Mosby Co.

Baxter, B.P.: School health: the Pennsylvania plan, Journal of School Health 51:129-130, Feb. 1981.

Blum, H.L., Peters, H.B., and Bettman, J.W.: Vision screening for elementary schools; the Orinda study, Berkeley, Calif., 1959, University of California Press.

Buser, B.N.: The evolution of school health services: New York and nationwide, Journal of School Health 50:475-477, Oct. 1980.

Cardwell, M.A., Jr.: The pitfall of unproven therapies, Journal of School Health 49:421, Sept. 1979.

Chang, A., and others: The early periodic screening, diagnosis, and treatment program (EPSDT): status of progress and implementation in 51 states and territories, Journal of School Health 49:454-457, Oct. 1979.

Committee on School Health of the American Academy of Pediatrics: School health: a guide for health professionals, 1981, Evanston, Ill., 1981, The Academy.

Conrad, P.: Identifying hyperactive children, Lexington, Mass., 1976, Lexington Books.

Cornacchia, H.J., Smith, D.E., and Bentel, D.J.: Drugs in the classroom; a conceptual model for school programs, ed. 2, St. Louis, 1978, The C.V. Mosby Co.

Dale, S.: Putting health into school nursing, Health Values 4:15-19, Jan./Feb. 1980.

Dodge, P.R.: Neurological disorders of school-age children, Journal of School Health 46: June 1976.

Gearheart, B.R., and Weishahn, M.W.: The handicapped child in the regular classroom, ed. 2, St. Louis, 1980, The C.V. Mosby Co.

Jenkins, G., Shacter, H.S., and Bauer, W.W.: These are your children, ed. 4, Glenview, Ill., 1975, Scott, Foresman & Co.

Joint Committee on Health Problems: Health appraisals of school children, ed. 4, Washington, D.C., 1969, National Education Association and the American Medical Association.

Knotts, G.R., editor: Guidelines for the school nurse in the school health program, Kent, Ohio, 1974, American School Health Association.

Luther, S.L., and Price, J.H.: Child sexual abuse: a review, Journal of School Health 50:161-165, March 1980.

MacDonough, G.P.: School health, 1977, Journal of School Health 47: Sept. 1977.

National Committee on School Health, Policies: Suggested school health policies, ed. 4, Washington, D.C., 1966, National Education Association and the American Medical Association.

Olson, R.J.: Index of suspicion: screening for child abuses, American Journal of Nursing 76:108-110, Jan. 1976.

Queen, P.S., and Queen, J.A.: Inservice workshop on child abuse, Journal of School Health 50:441-446, Oct. 1980.

Rapaport, H.G., and Flint, S.H.: Allergy in the schools, Journal of School Health 44: May 1974.

Ross, D.M., and Ross, S.A.: Hyperactivity; research theory, and action, New York, 1976, John Wiley & Sons, Inc.

Schneeweis, S.M.: The computer in school health services, Journal of School Health **40:** March 1970.

Schneeweiss, S.M., and Locke, A.: New horizons in school health services; the computer, Journal of School Health **37:** Sept. 1967.

Silver, G.A.: Redefining school health services: comprehensive child health care as the framework, Journal of School Health **51:**157-162, March 1981.

Smith, E.S.: New electronics device zips through mass heart screenings for children with good reliability, California's Health, March 15, 1969.

Starling, K.A., and Shepard, D.A.: Symptoms and signs of cancer in the school-age child, Journal of School Health **47:** March 1977.

Spollen, J.J., and Davidson, D.W.: An analysis of vision defects in high and low income preschool children, Journal of School Health **48:** 177-180, March 1978.

Syre, T.R., and Gold, R.S.: Child abuse and child neglect: two concerns for school health educators, Health Values **5:**265-269, Nov./Dec. 1981.

Vision screening for children: New York, 1980, National Society to Prevent Blindness.

Wallace, A.P.: A scoliosis screening program, Journal of School Health **47:**619-620, Dec. 1977.

Walker, J.E.: What the school health team should know about sickle cell anemia, Journal of School Health **45:** March 1975.

What teachers see, and Looking for health, New York, 1969, Metropolitan Life Insurance Co.

Welner, N.M.: Health care for inner-city school children, Journal of School Health **38:** June 1968.

Wright, G.F.: Hyperactivity and medication, Health Values **4:**26-31, Jan./Feb. 1980.

6

HEALTH GUIDANCE

Identification of children with health problems such as vision and hearing deficiencies, undernourishment, malnutrition, overeating, dental decay, emotional disturbances, skin infections, and heart disease raises the question of whether schools should become involved in providing assistance with these problems. Since health is vital for effective learning and since many parents are not aware of or do not give adequate attention to their children's health problems, the decision by schools whether to aid in the improvement of students' levels of wellness should be obvious. Failure to give attention to discovered pupil conditions will interfere with educational experiences and adversely affect learning. Many schools, therefore, have assumed the responsibility of providing help to students and parents. The methods used are part of the school health services program and are referred to as *follow-up* or *guidance procedures*. They include guidance and counseling, use of community health resources, and adjustment of school programs. The emphasis in this chapter is on the guidance and counseling aspects.

The most important part of the health services program, and the one given least attention, is the follow-up phase. Schools on the whole do not provide enough nurse time and effort to obtain the needed corrective action by students and parents. By way of illustration, Griffith and Whicker* in a study of one school district in North Carolina reemphasized the need for more attention to follow-up activities. They found that over a 6-year period they were able to obtain corrections for their problem children at an average rate of 43%. However, when additional nurse time, nurse aides, and teacher cooperation were tried in an experimental year, they were able to increase this rate to 66%.

WHAT IS HEALTH GUIDANCE?

Health guidance in schools is a broad term that refers to a variety of processes involving the interaction of school and community health personnel, students, and parents that aid in the discovery, understanding, and resolution of health matters through self-effort and self-direction. It includes those activities in which in-

*Griffith, B.B., and Whicker, P.H.: Teacher—observer of student health problems, Journal of School Health **51**:428-432, Aug. 1981.

dividuals participate voluntarily in incidental, individual, or small-group counseling or in "rap" sessions to obtain information regarding health concerns or to seek solutions to health problems. It involves communication with parents to encourage and persuade them to action. The general aim of health guidance is to enable pupils to acquire the highest levels of wellness in accordance with their individual needs. Guidance plays an important role in *primary prevention* (before a condition arises) and in *secondary prevention* (after a condition has been discovered).

Health guidance involves the use of health appraisals and health records; more specifically, it involves counseling to provide information and aid in regard to health problems, immunizations, reports of health examinations, program adjustments, identification of community health resources, relations between pupils and parents with medical, dental, and other health specialists, and numerous other matters. Its objective is not to give advice but to encourage, motivate, and help individuals achieve good health through their own efforts. It is purposeful action and organized effort directed toward intelligent decision making regarding corrections, care, service, treatment, and assistance. It is educational in nature.

Opportunities for health guidance exist in the *formal school health education program.* However, they are not discussed in this chapter. The procedures used in the formal program may be considered to be group guidance methods. Pupils' requests for informal assistance frequently arise from the formal program. Chapters 9 to 13 on organizing, learning, and teaching techniques provide numerous suggestions for helping students in the classroom in a group or formal setting.

The educational procedures used in guidance are frequently referred to as *health counseling.* This is the direct contact between students or parents and counselors (nurses, teachers, physicians and others) on a face-to-face basis, with discussion focusing on information and understanding that will assist in making wise choices

about courses of action. This process may be identified as the *informal phase of the health education program.*

Informal health education

Informal health education must receive greater emphasis in schools if educational programs are to meet adequately the differing health needs of children and youth. It is a phase of the school health education program that has been neglected and has generally been thought the responsibility of the nurse. A great deal of such education has occurred accidentally.

Although the nurse is an important contact person, the nurse's presence in school is frequently limited. Also, there are others who can provide assistance. Any number of students require special, individual attention that cannot be obtained from a formal health education program. These young people need and often desire someone, some group, or some way in schools to be able to discuss concerns and interests about sex, drugs, personality development, stress and pressure, self-care, parent problems, and other health matters. Some young people may wish to talk to their peers about their problems or about where to obtain help in solving problems. The school nurse, a teacher, a counselor, the school psychologist, or someone who will listen in a nonjudgmental fashion and have empathy for student concerns might also help. Informal health education needs to be recognized and established in schools. It would be helpful in secondary prevention of health problems and also could serve a useful purpose in primary prevention.

Informal education is learning that takes place without structure and without much planning. It may occur in the classroom, in the nurse's office, or in other school locations. It may take place in a meeting with a parent or pupil, or by telephone, note, letter sent home, or by other procedures. It may take place outside the school, in the home, watching TV, talking with a parent, friend, or neighbor, while reading a magazine or newspaper, or anywhere else. It usually occurs on a one-to-one basis or in small groups. It is a communication procedure that provides information, counseling, and guidance that is nondirective and nonthreatening to students and voluntary in terms of participation.

Implementation of informal health education may occur in a variety of ways. Several illustrations are provided. A student may ask a teacher a question about health or about the action to be taken because of the sudden appearance of a skin rash. A pupil visits the nurse for information and guidance in terms of excess weight, a severe cold, or fear of one or more aggressive students. The nurse, counselor, or other person encourages children and youth to make visitations to discuss health problems or concerns whenever they are free, at the noon hour, or in after-school rap sessions. The school newspaper prints articles on student health problems written by students. The nurse makes pamphlets and publications available to students. Special voluntary educational programs on drugs, sexually transmitted disease, teenage pregnancies, and emotional problems may be held as needs arise. A parent-teacher-nurse conference is held.

What are the purposes of health guidance?

Health guidance seeks to achieve the following:

1. To provide information about and interpretations of pupils' health status, concerns, or problems
2. To provide understandings to parents of the nature of the health conditions that exist in their children and to encourage needed care
3. To promote pupils' acceptance of the responsibility for the promotion and preservation of their own health
4. To motivate parents and pupils to seek care and treatment when needed for existing health conditions and to accept modifications in the school program where desirable
5. To encourage and promote where necessary the establishment or expansion of school and community health service and facilities especially for needy children and families
6. To encourage pupils and parents to use available medical, dental, and other health resources to the best advantage
7. To contribute to the health education of pupils and parents
8. To assist in the adaptation of school programs to the individual needs and abilities of students with health problems; to keep teachers informed
9. To inform teachers of pupils' health problems and concerns and to identify responsibilities

What are the general problems for which children need health guidance?

Children's health problems requiring guidance may be categorized in the following manner:

In some situations *more detailed examination* of the child is needed to establish a diagnosis. Observations of signs and symptoms might necessitate a chest x-ray examination for tuberculosis or a tuberculin test, special tests for a heart murmur, a blood count for anemia, a urinalysis for diabetes, a medical examination when chronic fatigue, overweight, frequent colds, and blackouts are noted, or a dental examination for decay or periodontal disease.

There are some conditions for which the child needs *treatment services*, such as undernourishment, malnutrition, overfeeding, epilepsy, dental decay, vision and hearing difficulties, skin infections, diseased tonsils, or allergies.

There are conditions that need *home care improvement*. These may include the need for breakfast or help with balanced lunches, cleanliness, dental care, proper clothing, or better sleeping facilities.

Problems of emotional and social adjustment may make *special counseling* mandatory. Opportunities to talk with understanding people may be most helpful to students. Teachers who have success communicating with pupils may be able to assist them with their problems regarding the abuse and use of drugs. It also may be necessary to interpret the emotional problem to parents to encourage their seeking additional help. These problems frequently are difficult and delicate to present to parents.

For some problems, *assistance regarding health practices and behavior* is advisable. This might call for individual discussions with students regarding covering noses and mouths when coughing and sneezing, the importance of washing the hands before eating and after using the lavatory, the misuse and abuse of drugs, using the drinking fountains properly, remaining at home when ill, eating breakfast, and what to do about sexually transmitted disease. Some of these matters may also involve parental communications and should be handled discreetly.

ORGANIZATION FOR SCHOOL HEALTH GUIDANCE

Although practically all schools provide some health guidance, in most cases it is done on an incidental basis. Schools in general do not have well-organized and well-developed health guidance programs, as identified in this chapter. In elementary schools the nurse is usually the key person in the counseling program. Where health guidance does exist on an organized basis, it has been found that best results accrue when the program is carried out cooperatively; all departments and personnel of a school concerned with any phase of mental, emotional, and physical health of children should cooperate and participate in the formulation of health guidance policies. Objectives and responsibilities need clear definition.

Organized health guidance programs may be considered a relatively new development; therefore it may be well to consider some of the fundamental factors that are basic to sound organization. In this respect, it seems essential that recognition be given to such factors as (1) desirable principles of operation, (2) role of the individual who counsels, (3) responsibilities of various school personnel, (4) nurse-teacher/nurse-teacher-parent conferences, (5) tech-

niques for counseling, and (6) use of prescribed medications at school.

Desirable principles of operation

As in other functions of the school, health guidance should be based on certain fundamental principles for effective operation. The following generalized list may serve as a guide for the establishment of such principles in local school situations:

1. The health guidance program should complement and supplement the total educational program within the school.
2. The health program should be such that it serves individual pupil needs.
3. The health guidance program should have the wholehearted support of the school administrators.
4. Policies and procedures that identify purposes and responsibilities of personnel in written form should be provided.
5. School staff members responsible for health guidance programs should be knowledgeable about community agencies and specialists available for referral purposes.
6. The health guidance program should communicate to parents, teachers, and others the objectives of the services.
7. Some means of in-service training in health guidance should be provided for teachers, administrators, and other members of the school personnel whenever necessary or advisable.
8. There should be full cooperation and coordination of all school departments concerned with the health of pupils.
9. The purposes and scope of each school department concerned with child health should be clearly defined to assure the most efficient service to pupils.
10. Responsibility for leadership in the health guidance program should be centered in individuals who possess, insofar as possible, interest, ability, and preparation for such service.
11. The responsibilities of all persons con-

cerned with the program should be clearly defined and designated.

12. The best possible procedures for effective school and community coordination in health guidance should be provided.

13. The health guidance program should be subjected to constant and continuous evaluation so that constructive improvements may be effected.

14. All health guidance personnel should be encouraged to keep abreast of the latest research and changing conditions as they relate to their specific health area.

Role of the individual who counsels

The person who participates as a counselor and is involved in human relations should be competent to interpret findings to pupils and parents and to encourage and motivate them to action. Since parents have the primary responsibility for the health of their children, school personnel should not try to tell them how their children should be raised. School personnel should attempt to acquaint parents with the health conditions of pupils that require attention, to interpret the importance of care especially as it relates to learning, and to inform parents regarding the nature of community health services and the necessary adjustments of the school program.

School personnel must be familiar with blacks, native Americans, Mexican Americans, and those of other ethnic backgrounds. They should understand the cultural heritage and customs, and some should be conversant in the languages for effective communication.

The responsibility for counseling involves a variety of school personnel including teachers, nurses, physicians, psychologists, principals, counselors, and students.

Responsibilities of various school personnel

One of the principles previously mentioned suggested that the responsibilities of all concerned with the health of pupils should be clearly defined and designated. This statement should perhaps be amplified to the extent that *every* person in the school system should accept responsibility for the health guidance of the school population. In other words, every person associated with the school should have the physical, emotional, mental, and social well-being of pupils as a major concern. The fact that pupils' academic and nonacademic interests relate to their physical and mental health cannot be overstressed. For example, the child who is fatigued, hungry, or unable to understand why people do not want him or her around may have difficulty concentrating on learning.

Although all school personnel rightfully should take an interest in health guidance of pupils, the extent of responsibilities naturally must vary. Someone should be available in schools with whom students are able to communicate when necessary about health matters, but especially regarding sexually transmitted disease, drugs, human sexuality, pregnancies, and home and school problems. This might be the nurse or a teacher or some other knowledgeable, capable individual. The following discussion indicates some of the more or less specific responsibilities of various school personnel depending somewhat on the size and existing conditions within the individual school system.

School administrators and officers. The responsibilities of the school board member, superintendent, and principal of the school within the community center on the leadership necessary to carry out a successful health guidance program. These groups actually have the final vote of approval as far as the budgetary needs, the acquisition of new equipment, and the hiring of personnel. It should be strongly emphasized that these kinds of services will entail a cooperative kind of leadership in which the administrator plans with his or her staff on matters pertaining to the broad scope of the program. It is obvious that continued pooling of the competencies of mental health professionals and educators will be needed to achieve the related goals of better mental health and effective learning for more school children.

School administrators need to have adequate

knowledge of the objectives of the program, because they are usually the liaison persons between the school and the community and are expected to interpret the objectives. In addition, administrators should initiate plans for the coordination of school and community relationships and strive to maintain the highest standards for total school health. They may also need to initiate community action to help with the provision of comprehensive health care services, especially for children in ghetto areas.

Health service personnel. One of the main responsibilities of the school physician, school nurse, school dentist, and others in health service is concerned with helping youths who evidence health needs. Frequent follow-up is necessary. For example, certain pertinent information derived from examinations by the school physician can be relayed to teachers and guidance counselors through the proper channels. More and more use is being made of the case study method whereby those people directly working with a child meet and discuss their findings. The various reports add to the separate impressions, and the goal of assisting in the development of the whole child is more fully realized. In other cases either the school nurse or school social worker serves as a direct link between the home and school. The nurse or social worker is in a desirable position to refer to guidance counselors and teachers information that may reveal physical, mental, and emotional health problems that arise out of home situations.

School nurse. The work of the school nurse continues to gain importance in the school health program. The committee on School Health Service of the World Health Organization states that nurses, like physicians, have a different type of task when they work within the framework of the school, for it is not the clinical situation to which they have been accustomed in their hospital experiences. It is a new kind of experience, one with children to whom these nurses must bring warmth, acceptance, and understanding. To the teacher the nurse must be a source of information and guidance. To the parent the nurse must be a friendly counselor,

cognizant of community resources, sympathetic with family problems, and an interpreter par excellence of the child's needs as revealed by medical examination and school behavior.

Although the responsibilities and duties of school nurses are numerous and varied, special emphasis should be placed on their part in health guidance. The following list summarizes some of the ways the school nurse contributes to the health guidance program:

1. Keeping individual health records up to date for general use and for specific use when health counseling is indicated
2. Assisting with examinations and inspections that may reveal a need for guidance and counseling
3. Interpreting the results of health appraisals to pupils, teachers, and parents
4. Providing information and direction concerning community resources available for the care of physical, mental, and emotional problems of children
5. Assisting in motivating pupils to develop and maintain optimum health
6. Helping children to find solutions to their personal problems, particularly those involving or likely to involve physical, mental, and emotional health
7. Assisting in the identification of pupils needing modified education programs
8. Counseling pupils with health problems
9. Counseling parents concerning the health problems of children
10. Serving as a liaison between home, school, and community organizations and agencies
11. Providing care in emergencies and accidents
12. Participating in formal and informal health education

The role of the school nurse is changing, and Oda has identified the expanding duties that include the following*:

1. Greater stress on health education, counseling and consultation
2. Emergence as a school nurse-practitioner in

---

*Oda, D.S.: Increasing role effectiveness of school nurses, American Journal of Public Health **64**: June 1974.

which special training is providing competency to conduct in-depth assessment of physical, psychomedical, and psychoeducational behavior and learning disorders of children

3. Involvement in the development, implementation, and evaluation of health care plans and programs
4. Use of increased technological health assessment skills

The number of nurses found in schools varies because standards are not uniform or consistent throughout the United States. It is generally believed there should be one nurse for every 800 to 1,200 pupils. However, common practices differ widely. Many schools have no nurse services, while in others nurses are limited to one-half day weekly. In recent years nurse services have been eliminated in some districts because of budget limitations.

Some school districts are using nonprofessional *health aides* to assist school nurses. These individuals may perform a variety of clerical responsibilities such as answering the telephone, entering data in health records, and arranging schedules. These individuals may be volunteers and occasionally are paid employees. Health aides free nurses from certain routine procedures, allowing them to devote more time to professional duties.

Health coordinator. The person assuming the responsibilities of school health coordinator should be professionally trained and should direct, supervise, and coordinate all activities concerning the health of students. The success or failure of health guidance programs may depend on the extent to which proper use of information is made. For example, many schools have an excellent program of health appraisal, yet they do not have adequate organization, ways, or means of following up the findings of the appraisals. The school health coordinator should fill any gaps that may exist by coordinating all information that might be used to guide the pupil in health matters.

Another important function of the school health coordinator is that of conducting needed research. All too often records are kept and up-to-date entries made so that the pupils' growth and development are charted, with little if any attempt made to use these data for study purposes. The analysis of records could certainly aid in pointing out trends, changes in physical, social, and emotional patterns of both boys and girls, and the limitations of the school's health program, to name a few.

Unfortunately, health coordinators per se are not commonly employed in school districts. Where they are found, these individuals may be nurses, physicians, health educators, or others.

Guidance personnel. Guidance directors, psychometrists, and other guidance personnel have the responsibility of helping pupils in their efforts to handle their health problems. If counselors and others expect to have pupils referred to them for individual help, then a knowledge of the objectives of the health guidance program is essential. They should have not only sufficient background in the psychodynamics of behavior, but also an understanding of health education, since most of the problems found among children involve, either directly or indirectly, physical, mental, social, and emotional health. They may also contribute to the health guidance program by offering in-service education to teachers and other school personnel with respect to the counseling methods that would be most effective with those pupils needing counseling and guidance.

Because guidance personnel are generally involved in a helping relationship, children, parents, teachers, and others often share with them various types of personal concerns, some of which may relate to the school environment. It is possible, without breaking confidence, for the guidance personnel to assist in calling attention to health problems that are not receiving care.

School psychologist. In school systems in which the services of a psychologist are available, many contributions can be made to the health guidance program by the person serving in this capacity. At the present time one of the major functions of the school psychologist is more like that of a psychometrist who administers group and individual psychological tests. In addition to this primary function, many school psychologists confer with parents and teachers about individual pupils with problems that particularly concern emotional health. The school psychologist should be in close contact with the school administrators, school physician, school nurse, school social worker, teachers, and family physicians and psychiatrists who may be in a position to act on his or her recommendations regarding children who are in need of adjustment to problems that concern their health. Although most school personnel have taken course work in the area of the behavioral sciences, the school psychologist can be most helpful in aiding in the understanding of unusual behavioral patterns. Often the school psychologist will administer various types of tests and submit a report of these findings for the school to keep on record. Since these reports are more often than not psychologically descriptive, care must be taken in their use and circulation.

Elementary school teachers. Classroom teachers are actually the hub in a successful health guidance program at the elementary school level. As mentioned previously, in the majority of cases elementary school teachers are in a position to observe pupils day by day. It becomes their responsibility to detect physical, social, and emotional behavior patterns that are unusual and refer them to the nurses, physicians, and administrators. Elementary teachers probably are the most important people, outside of the family, in providing for the cultivation of health attitudes and values through the health instruction program. The student will seek out the teacher for information if communication has been established in incidental and informal settings.

Special teachers. Teachers dealing with special groups, as in rehabilitation, special education, and the various special subjects, such as physical education, home economics, and health education, very definitely have considerable re-

sponsibility in all matters of pupil health, including health guidance, since they ordinarily come in closer contact with situations that deal with health status. For instance, the physical education teacher has an opportunity to observe the growth and development of pupils as well as peer acceptance of the group members. Whether physical educators are aware of their responsibility for health guidance has been questioned, but it is the feeling that physical development should not be their only concern.

Drug counselor. A person known as a drug counselor has been available to students in some upper elementary and junior and senior high schools in recent years. This person may be considered to be a counselor with responsibilities related to drugs and drug use. The duties of the drug counselor may include communication with drug users, misusers, and abusers; student and parent guidance; liaison with community resources, including the police and the courts; and the preparation of policies and procedures for the school or school district. This individual should be one who is approachable by students, is readily available and accessible, is willing to talk and not preach, is honest and trustful in approach, is willing to discuss any topic of interest to pupils, and is knowledgeable about the drug scene.

Students. There have been a variety of attempts by schools to use student peers in an attempt to help pupils with drug problems. Upper elementary school youths have made formal presentations to sixth graders and other students in their own schools. They have also been available for indirect, informal individual and group meetings. Students who are familiar with drugs have been able on occasions to establish rapport with drug misusers and abusers. The value of such activities has not been clearly defined, but indications reveal they create interest and enthusiasm on the part of both the participants and the performers. The use of students in a variety of health counseling situations should receive greater consideration and experimentation in schools.

Nurse-teacher/nurse-teacher-parent conferences

Casefinding and follow-up in the interest of the child requires a three-cornered arrangement—nurse or medical professional, teacher and parent. The absence of participation of any one of these members makes effective action on behalf of the child much less likely.

George A. Silver, M.D.*
Professor of Public Health,
Yale University School
of Medicine

The need for communication within as well as between the school and the home is clearly identified in Dr. Silver's remark. He adds that nurse-teacher conferences are the exception rather than the general practice. He states that nurse-parent-teacher conferences rarely, if ever, occur. Unquestionably, limitations of nurse services in many schools, extensive teacher responsibilities, and the fact that 50% of mothers are working are factors that make the problem more complicated. In any event, it should be evident that effective guidance of pupils is not going to take place without improved communication procedures. Perhaps teachers will need to take more initiative in attempting to overcome the problems that interfere with this communication by assuming greater responsibility if the health needs of their pupils are to receive adequate attention.

Techniques for counseling

The specific procedures for communicating with students and parents include informal and formal talks, notes home, home and school visits with parents, and telephone calls.

When counseling parents or students, or both, the following suggestions should receive consideration:

1. Try to develop rapport and thereby improve the effectiveness of the communication.

---

*Silver, G.A.: Redefining school work health services: comprehensive child health care as the framework, Journal of School Health 51:157-162, March 1981.

Attempt to be friendly and nonofficious in approach. Demonstrate sincerity in wanting to be helpful. Create the feeling that information and aid, if desired, is the intent of the meeting. Refrain from telling the parent or student what action to take; hopefully a request for help will be forthcoming. Be tuned in on expressions and language indigenous to inner-city children. Be familiar with differences in values and cultural conflicts without becoming judgmental. Permit cultural identification to emerge in the development of a source of pride.

2. Help parents and pupils analyze or recognize the problem. A child's heart murmur may be very threatening to the parents and frightening to the child. Although this condition is abnormal and may be serious, it may not be serious for that particular child. Only medical help can determine the extent of the problem.

3. Help parents and pupils understand the nature and significance of the problem by encouraging questions and by supplying information as requested. Be certain understanding and clarity occur.

4. Help parents and pupils determine the various courses of action to be taken and discuss the consequences. The solution may be relatively simple if parents have a family physician. However, if parents do not know where to go or do not have a physician or funds, the problem may be more complex in resolving.

5. Encourage parents and students to choose a particular course of action, but indicate that the decision will rest with them.

When contacting parents about student health problems that are not unusual, such as vision or hearing difficulties, the school nurse may send home a form notice because it is the quickest and easiest way to communicate with a large number of parents. The use of this reporting method has these limitations: the note may not reach home; parents may not read it; parents may not be able to understand or interpret it; and it may be cold, formal, and impersonal. Therefore the procedures used to get in touch with parents must receive careful consideration.

From recent studies on effective ways of communicating with parents to get action, it has been found that children of parents at high socioeconomic levels are more likely to receive attention than those at low socioeconomic levels; children whose parents give defects a high urgency rating are more likely to receive attention; notification about a child's defect by more than one contact technique (written notice, telephone call, home or school visit, and others) are more likely to secure attention than if parents are notified by one contact only. Those contacts involving personal interaction by telephone or visitation are significantly more productive than those using a written medium. Also, parents who receive two notifications of children's defects are more likely to pay attention than parents who receive only one notification. Three notifications do not appear to be worth the effort.

Research findings conclude the most effective techniques of communication for parent action are notices written by a physician and telephone calls by school nurses. However, a study in San Diego* of sixth grade pupils revealed that the face-to-face contact by a home call or a nurse-parent conference at school or at the parent's place of work resulted in over 70% of defects identified through health appraisals receiving attention.

Prescribed medications at school

Increasing numbers of severely handicapped and emotionally disturbed children are attending school who must take physician-prescribed medications during regular school hours. It is therefore necessary for schools to establish written policies and procedures in regard to this matter. A study completed by Kinnison and Nimmer† revealed that less than 32% of the school districts reporting (48 of 159) had carried

out this responsibility. Jones* has suggested these procedures should be included in the policies:

1. The school nurse should supervise the administration.
2. A record should be maintained of the medication given, the time, and by whom.
3. Teachers should be alerted to the children receiving the drugs, the side effects of the drugs, possible adverse reactions, and what to do in an emergency.

Jones further recommends that the regulations established should include those prepared by the Committee on School Health of the American Academy of Pediatrics, as follows:

1. Written orders from a physician should detail the name of the drug, dosage, time interval that the medication is to be taken, and the diagnosis or reason for the medication to be given.
2. Written permission should be provided by the parent or guardian requesting the school district comply with the physician's order.
3. Medication should be brought to school in a container appropriately labeled by the pharmacy or physician.
4. One member of the staff should be designated to handle this task, ideally the health personnel if available.
5. A locked cabinet should be provided for the storage of medication.
6. Opportunities should be provided for communication between the parent, school personnel, and physician regarding the efficacy of the medication administered during school hours.
7. A designated member of the school staff should notify the parent or guardian as quickly as possible after an emergency occurs. The parent's telephone number should be available in the student's record specifically for this purpose.

---

*Brophy, H.E.: Project pursuit: a health defect follow-up activity, Journal of School Health 40: April 1970.
†Kinnison, L.R., and Nimmer, D.N.: An analysis of policies regulating medication in the schools, Journal of School Health 49:280-283, May 1979.

*Jones, E.H.: PL 94-142 and the role of school nurses in caring for handicapped children, Journal of School Health 49:153-155, March 1979.

WHICH COMMUNITY HEALTH RESOURCES ARE ESSENTIAL?

School personnel should be familiar with and use all local community health resources that can help meet the health guidance needs of pupils. Schools must take the initiative to learn about the services available and establish communications with the various physicians, dentists, psychiatrists, and other health specialists in private practice, health clinics and hospitals, voluntary health agencies, health departments, child guidance clinics, social service agencies, family service agencies, civic and service organizations, welfare agencies, and religious services located in the community.

By way of illustration, resources in the community for emotionally disturbed children may include privately practicing psychologists and psychiatrists, child guidance clinics, general and mental hospitals with inpatient and outpatient care, youth agencies, associations for the physically handicapped, special schools, family service agencies, welfare agencies, and a variety of professional and voluntary organizations.* They offer services including diagnosis, treatment, transition, rehabilitation, education, information, and consultation. In several states, public health departments make available some or many of these services. The extent of community mental health services differs in school districts, with many of them being in short supply. Services for the poor are frequently inadequate. The cost for help may be part or full pay, depending on the need of the patient. Some organizations provide free services.

Health problems that schools experience when dealing with poor people are of greater

*Professional organizations include American Academy of Child Psychiatry, American Association for Mental Deficiency, American Association of Psychiatry Services for Children, American Orthopsychiatric Association, American Psychiatric Association, American Psychological Association. Voluntary organizations include National Association for Mental Health, Child Study Association of America, Council for Exceptional Children, National Society for Autistic Children, Inc., Al-Anon Family Group Headquarters and Alateen.

magnitude and more complex in solution than for other students. Many children in ghetto areas do not receive the basic health services needed to attain high levels of wellness. It will be necessary for schools to take the initiative to stimulate community action to provide such assistance or to enter into a cooperative arrangement for such services. In California the state Department of Education* developed a plan to provide health services for 29,000 children in 176 school districts in 27 counties. Medical services were provided by private physicians and part-time school physicians, and clinics were established for school children in migrant camps. Dental treatment was also made available through the use of a mobile unit. Nurses and nurses' aides were based in the camps. Through the assistance of the Office of Economic Opportunity numerous neighborhood health centers have been established in deprived areas in an attempt to provide better systems for delivery of health care. These centers have worked closely with school personnel. The drug and sexually transmitted disease problems demand additional community resources.

It will be necessary for at least one person in the school to be familiar with the kinds and variety of resources available so the best guidance can be provided to students and parents. Frequently the school nurse assumes this responsibility and is the best-informed person. Where nurses are not available, teachers may have to (1) try to locate someone in the school or school district who knows the resources or (2) contact the local health department for assistance.

HOW DO SCHOOLS ADJUST PROGRAMS?

Teachers who recognize symptoms of mental or emotional disturbances in children should initially examine their own activities in class or their relations with the pupil to determine

*Eisner, V.: Health services under the Elementary and Secondary Education Act, Journal of School Health **40:** Nov. 1970.

whether they may be the cause of, or a factor contributing to, the behavior exhibited. It is conceivable that student maladjustments may be prevented by teachers modifying their activities or pupil relationships. The teacher may find it advisable to provide additional help to a child who is having difficulty in reading or to motivate the gifted student with additional responsibility. They may have to help pupils who have trouble controlling their emotions. Teachers may have to provide success experiences for a boy or girl. They may need to be friendlier with a pupil. They may have to try to gain acceptance of a child rejected by his or her peers. These are some of the considerations that teachers must make before determining that the problem is one needing referral to others.

After appropriate care or treatment has been received by a student, it may not always mean that the child has been cured or that the child's health problem has been corrected. A child with a severe vision problem may have to wear corrective lenses but still may not be able to read the type in a textbook. A pupil with a heart problem may be under treatment and need controlled activities or to have all classes on one floor. A student with epilepsy may be receiving medication to control seizures but may have to take the drug while at school. It therefore becomes necessary for schools to adjust programs to fit the needs of students with health problems.

Among the numerous ways schools have modified and adjusted educational programs are the following:

1. Special consideration for students in the regular classroom. The visually handicapped or hard-of-hearing child may need to be placed near the front of the room. Special rest periods during the day may have to be provided for some pupils. For others, midmorning snacks may be necessary.

2. Special teachers for certain handicapped children provided in the regular classroom. The partially sighted child may need to have special large-print textbooks and other materials prepared. The pupil with speech difficulties may need special attention. Children with learning disabilities may need special guidance.

3. Special classes in the regular school. Those who are mentally handicapped, blind, or deaf may be grouped into special classes with specially prepared teachers. Greater attention to a curriculum to satisfy the needs of these children may therefore take place.

4. Special day schools. Cerebral palsied children, those who are emotionally disturbed, and those who are severely mentally retarded may be housed in a facility entirely separate from the regular school.

5. Special residential schools. Blind and deaf students may need to remain overnight for extended periods of time in these schools to receive the best education.

6. Home teachers. Those children who are ill or injured and who must remain at home for long periods of time may need to have teachers go directly to their homes.

7. Hospital teachers. Those students who must remain in hospitals for extensive periods of time may need service of teachers while confined.

Schools differ in the nature and extent of the educational services provided for handicapped pupils. The larger school districts and those with more funds are usually able to provide greater services. Federal and state funds are frequently available to subsidize local programs.

Gary, Indiana, schools have several classes for children with severe emotional problems, with the local child guidance clinic supplying psychiatric supervision. In Chicago, classes are held for boys less than 12 years of age with normal intelligence and severe problems of truancy. New York City has the "600" schools, also referred to as social adjustment schools, with the curriculum devised to fit the needs of the pupils. Classes are also being formed for brain-injured or brain-damaged pupils, hyperactive children, and those with perceptual difficulties who need medical supervision and who are educable. Many schools have special classes for mentally retarded and severely mentally retarded children. Some residential institutions for mentally ill children, especially those with severe emotional problems, are sending their pupils to the local public schools. Other educational approaches include having a school in a psychiatric hospital, an entire school for those with narcotics problems, and programs of play therapy for younger children. In addition, there are now appearing so-called opportunity classes and schools for unsuccessful and emotionally disturbed pupils.

It is essential to understand that health guidance is an important and essential part of the school health services program. It should receive adequate consideration in schools. Without follow-up procedures to obtain corrections, treatment, and care including the adjustment of school programs, health appraisals by themselves are not important to the educational process. Assistance in guidance should be forthcoming from a variety of school personnel. School nurses spend a considerable portion of their time in health guidance and are important resources not only for teachers, but also for parents, students, and others. Teachers should clearly understand their responsibilities in health guidance.

QUESTIONS FOR DISCUSSION

1. What procedures are necessary when children with health problems have been discovered in schools?
2. What is meant by the term *health guidance*, and what is its relationship to informal health education?
3. What is informal health education, why is it necessary, and how can it occur in schools?
4. How would you differentiate between health guidance and health counseling?
5. What are some of the pupil health problems needing health guidance?
6. What are the major purposes of health guidance in schools?
7. How can the health problems of children needing health guidance be generally categorized?
8. What organizational factors must receive consideration when a school health guidance program is being introduced?
9. What are the guiding principles necessary for an effective school health guidance program?
10. What should be the role of the individual who counsels in the health guidance program?
11. What are the responsibilities of a school drug counselor, and how can such a position be justified?
12. What are some of the duties of the school nurse as the nurse's responsibilities expand?
13. What are the responsibilities of the various school personnel in health guidance?
14. What are some effective techniques for health counseling?
15. What guidelines should be used when students or parents are being counseled?
16. What health resources may be available in the community to help with student health problems?
17. What ways have schools tried to adjust programs to help pupils with health problems?
18. What policy regulations should be established in schools in regard to the use of physician-prescribed medications?

SELECTED REFERENCES

Anderson, C.L., and Creswell, W.H., Jr.: School health practice, ed. 7, St. Louis, 1980, The C.V. Mosby Co.

Ayers, G.E.: Communicating with inner-city children, School Health Review 3: Jan./Feb. 1972.

Bryan, D.S.: School nursing in transition, St. Louis, 1973, The C.V. Mosby Co.

Brophy, H.E.: Project pursuit; a health defect follow-up activity, Journal of School Health 40: April 1970.

Burney, L.E.: New missions in health service; to act or react, Journal of School Health 40: Jan. 1970.

Caufman, J.: Factors affecting outcome of school health referrals, Journal of School Health 38: June 1968.

Cornacchia, H.J., Smith, D.E., and Bentel, H.J.: Drugs in the classroom; a conceptual model for school programs, ed. 2, St. Louis, 1978, The C.V. Mosby Co.

Cowen, D.L.: Denver's preventive health program for school-age children, American Journal of Public Health 60: March 1970.

Dinkmeyer, D.C.: Guidance and counseling in the elementary school, New York, 1968, Holt, Rinehart & Winston.

Eiseman, S.: The need for effective health counselors in schools, Health Education 6: Sept./Oct. 1975.

Eisner, V.: Health services under the Elementary and Secondary Education Act, Journal of School Health 40: Nov. 1970.

Griffith, B.B., and Whicker, P.H.: Teacher: observer of student health problems, Journal of School Health 51:428-432, Aug. 1981.

Griffin, J.: Follow through; parents, school, and community work together to provide health care for good classroom performance, School Health Review 5: July/Aug. 1974.

Hummel, D.L., and Bonham, S.J.: Pupil personnel services in schools—organization and coordination, Chicago, 1968, Rand McNally & Co.

Hutson, P.W.: The guidance function in education, ed. 2, New York, 1968, Appleton-Century-Crofts.

Jones, E.H.: PL 94-142 and the role of school nurses in caring for handicapped children, Journal of School Health 49:153-155, March 1979.

Kinnison, L.R., and Nimmer, D.N.: An analysis of policies regulating medication in schools, Journal of School Health 49:280-283, May 1979.

Knotts, G.R., editor: Guidelines for the school nurse in the school health program, Kent, Ohio, 1974, American School Health Association.

Meyer, H.: Guiding children to better health through health counseling, Journal of School Health **37:** May 1967.

Oda, D.S.: Increasing role effectiveness of school nurses, American Journal of Public Health **64:** June 1974.

Paige, J.C.: Health programs for the disadvantaged; implications for school health, Journal of School Health **40:** March 1970.

Robey, D.L., and Dickey, B.A.: Health counseling, Journal of School Health **36:** April 1966.

Silver, G.A.: Redefining school health services: comprehensive child health care as the framework, Journal of School Health **51:**157-162, March 1981.

Stafford, R.L., and Meyer, R.J.: Diagnosis and counseling of the mentally retarded; implications for school health, Journal of School Health **38:** March 1968.

Wilson, C.C., editor: School health services, revised, Washington, D.C., 1964, National Education Association and the American Medical Association.

Woody, R.H.: Counseling in Health Education, Journal of School Health **41:** Jan. 1971.

7

EMERGENCY CARE PROCEDURES

Since children are required to attend school, all school personnel have an ethical and legal responsibility to assure that pupils have a safe and hazard-free environment and be provided care in emergencies when accidents or illnesses occur.

Accidents and illnesses may be considered unplanned occurrences at school that all employees should be prepared to handle with promptness and efficiency when they happen in the course of the elementary school day. Regardless of the care with which a school facility is constructed, and regardless of the diligent care rendered to prevent accidents, it is not possible to provide a completely safe environment. Illnesses and accidents frequently cannot be anticipated.

This chapter will contain basic elements of emergency care including first aid procedures that will enable both the teacher and the staff of schools to assist children. It is preferable that one person trained in emergency care procedures be present at all times when children are in the school facility. We believe that all school personnel should be adequately trained in current emergency care procedures whether provided by the American National Red Cross or through a certificate awarded by a college or university that certifies the individual is qualified to render first aid to the ill or injured.

For all ages accidents have consistently ranked among the top five leading causes of death. Accidents are the leading cause of death and disability for all persons age 1 to 44. In 1978, accidents cost $68.7 billion in lost wages, medical expenses, insurance costs, fire losses, property damage, and indirect work loss.*

By and large elementary teachers have apparently been doing a good job in safety education. Over the past half century the accident death rate for children in the 5- to 14-year age range has dropped more than 65%. Yet there is still room for improvement when we lose some 6,000 elementary school children each year through accidents. More tragic is the fact that approximately half of these accidents could have been prevented.

While it is true that major advances have been made in medical, surgical, and hospital care and rehabilitation of injured children, it would be better if these accidents had never occurred.

---

*Data from National Safety Council.: Accident facts, Chicago, 1981, The Council.

WHAT CAN TEACHERS DO?

Because health and safety are so closely related from the viewpoint of the optimum welfare of the school child, it is very important that teachers have a clear understanding of the relationship of health and safety in the school program.

Teachers, parents, and others interested in and responsible for the optimum growth and development of children should be cognizant not only of the problems in health education, but of those in safety education as well. For many years the schools have accepted responsibility in health education in attempting to help each child develop to his or her greatest possible capacity not only academically, but also emotionally and physically. Naturally, teachers and others have attempted to do everything possible to educate children concerning health as well as to try to help them maintain good health and to protect them from ill health and disabling diseases and disorders. It is recognized that safety ranks in the same category in the attempt to assure optimum growth and development of children. If teachers think in terms of protecting and providing for the optimum health and growth of children, then they must assume responsibility for safety at school.

WHAT PROVISIONS SHOULD BE MADE FOR EMERGENCY CARE OF INJURED AND ILL PUPILS?

When illnesses or injuries occur, school personnel frequently are not prepared to handle them properly. Every school regardless of size should have carefully organized written plans and procedures for the proper care of injured and ill pupils. These plans should be made for emergency care of both mass and individual injuries and illnesses.

Organization and administration of the school emergency care program are the responsibility of the board of education. This responsibility, however, is usually delegated to the superintendent, principal, and other school administrators.

A school district should establish a uniform policy for the emergency care of the injured and ill. The policy established by a particular school will depend on a number of factors, including the size of the community and school; availability of nurses, physicians, hospitals, and ambulances; effective communications; and trained first-aid personnel. In formulating the emergency care policy, school administrators should seek the aid, advice, and cooperation of school and community safety councils, parents, local medical and public health groups, and any of the community organizations or agencies, such as the police department, fire department, and ambulance and auxiliary services that may be able to lend aid and assistance when necessary.

The main responsibilities of the school in emergency care are to give *immediate and proper first aid, to notify the parents, and to be certain that the injured or ill are placed under the care of parents or a physician designated by the parents.* The school policy including plans, procedures, and responsibility assignments should be made available *in writing* to all teachers and other school personnel who may be involved in any way in emergency care. Also, it is advisable to make the *parents* acquainted with the policy for emergency care.

Since new teachers usually join the school faculty beginning with the fall term, it is advisable for school administrators to make them familiar with the emergency care program at the beginning of the term or before the school term begins. Also, the beginning of the fall semester is a good time to review the emergency care program for all teachers and to acquaint them with any changes in policy, plans, or procedures. It is the duty of school administrators to make teachers who join the faculty at times other than at the beginning of the fall season familiar with the policy concerning school emergency care.

In the final analysis, a community's emergency care program depends on (1) availability of *trained first-aid personnel* at the scene; (2) quick and effective *communication;* (3) prompt, safe, well-equipped, and well-attended *transportation;* and (4) access to *hospitals with specialized emergency care equipment and medical and nursing personnel.*

Plans for emergency care

Detailed written plans and procedures should be developed that cover all emergency situations. It is practically impossible to list the detailed plans that may be necessary for every community, but there are a number of common procedures to which all schools should be prepared to adhere.

Emergency transportation. Every school should have plans for transporting injured or ill children to their homes, to a hospital, or to physicians' or dentists' offices. Previous arrangements should be made to have available school buses, ambulances, or other suitable transportation such as private cars. Frequently it may be advisable for the school nurse or other school personnel to transport children in private vehicles. When children are transported in private vehicles, proper insurance coverage should be carried on those vehicles. Regardless of the means, some acceptable type of transportation should be available to the school at all times when children are in attendance.

Facilities and equipment. Proper first aid and emergency care imply that there will be sufficient facilities and equipment in every school. There should be emergency lounges for both boys and girls, containing cots, blankets, lavatories, towels, chairs, and a table. The emergency room should be equipped with adequate first-aid supplies for any type of injury or sudden illness. The first-aid supplies should be maintained in accordance with the best standards for first-aid care. The kinds and amounts of first-aid material will depend on the size of the school and the availability of community resources for assisting with emergency care. In addition to the first-aid supplies found in the emergency room, classroom teachers should have on hand such things as soap and small dressings for minor wounds. A suggested list of first-aid supplies is found on p. 143.

Reports and records. An adequate report of each and every emergency injury or illness arising in the school should be made. The National Safety Council standard accident report form is shown in Fig. 7-1. Ordinarily, the principal delegates this responsibility to the school nurse, the teacher, or some other member of the school personnel. In any case, teachers are likely to have a part in making reports, particularly when children under their supervision are injured or become ill. The report should contain such information as the name of the pupil; time, location, and nature of the accident or illness; witnesses, teachers, or other persons present; possible causes of the illness or injury; description of the illness or injury including the part of the body seemingly injured; first aid given; notification of parents; and disposition of the case.

School policy on emergency care. Minor injuries and illnesses happen frequently among school children. At such times, the classroom teacher should follow the policy of the school in caring for the pupil. If an illness is mild, the child should be kept warm and on a cot and be under constant or regular supervision. If the illness seems to be progressive, the parent should be called, and the usual procedure invoked for caring for more serious illness. The teacher should remember that no medication of any kind should be given. In minor injuries the policy of the school often is that the classroom teacher cares for them. First aid for such injuries as minor cuts and scratches usually can be safely cared for by the teacher. The teacher should permit limited bleeding and stress the importance of cleanliness by washing the wound with soap and water and applying a sterile dressing.

For certain seemingly major illnesses, the school policy concerning the notifying of parents and taking whatever steps necessary should be put into operation immediately. The child should rest on a cot, and body temperature should be maintained. Someone should be in constant attendance with the child until the school has fulfilled its responsibility of carrying out the parents' instructions or, in case the parents cannot be contacted, in getting the services

STANDARD STUDENT ACCIDENT REPORT FORM
Part A. Information on ALL Accidents

1. Name: _____ Home Address: _____
2. School: _____ Sex: M ☐; F ☐. Age: _____ Grade or classification: _____
3. Time accident occurred: Hour _____ A.M.; _____ P.M. Date: _____
4. Place of Accident: School Building ☐   School Grounds ☐   To or from School ☐   Home ☐   Elsewhere ☐

5. NATURE OF INJURY		DESCRIPTION OF THE ACCIDENT

5. **NATURE OF INJURY**

Abrasion /_____   Fracture _____
Amputation _____   Laceration _____
Asphyxiation _____   Poisoning _____
Bite _____   Puncture _____
Bruise _____   Scalds. _____
Burn _____   Scratches _____
Concussion _____   Shock (el.) _____
Cut _____   Sprain _____
Dislocation _____
Other (specify) _____

DESCRIPTION OF THE ACCIDENT

How did accident happen? What was student doing? Where was student? List specifically unsafe acts and unsafe conditions existing. Specify any tool, machine or equipment involved. _____
_____
_____
_____
_____

PART OF BODY INJURED

Abdomen _____   Foot _____
Ankle _____   Hand _____
Arm _____   Head _____
Back _____   Knee _____
Chest _____   Leg _____
Ear _____   Mouth _____
Elbow _____   Nose _____
Eye _____   Scalp _____
Face _____   Tooth _____
Finger _____   Wrist _____
Other (specify) _____

6. Degree of Injury: Death ☐ Permanent Impairment ☐ Temporary Disability ☐ Nondisabling ☐
7. Total number of days lost from school: _____ (To be filled in when student returns to school)

Part B. Additional Information on School Jurisdiction Accidents

8. Teacher in charge when accident occurred (Enter name): _____
    Present at scene of accident: No: _____ Yes: _____

9. **IMMEDIATE ACTION TAKEN**

First-aid treatment _____ By (Name): _____
Sent to school nurse _____ By (Name): _____
Sent home _____ By (Name): _____
Sent to physician _____ By (Name): _____
Physician's Name: _____
Sent to hospital _____ By (Name): _____
Name of hospital: _____

10. Was a parent or other individual notified? No:___ Yes:___ When:_____ How: _____
     Name of individual notified: _____
     By whom? (Enter name): _____
11. Witnesses: 1. Name: _____ Address: _____
     2. Name: _____ Address: _____

12. **LOCATION**

Specify Activity	Specify Activity	Remarks
Athletic field _____	Locker _____	What recommendations do you have for preventing other accidents of this type? _____
Auditorium _____	Pool _____	
Cafeteria _____	Sch. grounds _____	
Classroom _____	_____ shop _____	
Corridor _____	Showers _____	
Dressing room _____	Stairs _____	
Gymnasium _____	Toilets and	
Home Econ. _____	washrooms _____	
Laboratories _____	Other (specify) _____	

Signed: Principal: _____ Teacher: _____

(National Safety Council—Form School 1)   Printed in U.S.A.   Stock No. 429.21
Rep. 100M106002

FIG. 7-1. National Safety Council accident report form. (*Courtesy National Safety Council, Inc., Chicago, Ill.*)

of the family physician or taking the child to a hospital. In cases of major injuries the school policy for rendering first aid under such circumstances should be put into effect.

Information for emergencies

It is imperative that certain kinds of information be readily available to facilitate the rapid and proper handling of emergency cases. The following kinds of information should be carefully listed, organized, and placed near a telephone in the principal's office where it is accessible to all teachers or other school personnel who may be expected to assist in any way with emergency care of injured and ill children:

1. A list of all pupils with full and correct names
2. The names of both parents
3. Home address
4. Home telephone number
5. Business address of both parents
6. Business telephone numbers of both parents
7. Name of family physician
8. Business telephone number of family physician
9. Home telephone number of family physician
10. Physician of choice, in case family physician cannot be reached
11. Telephone number of physician of choice if family physician cannot be reached
12. Relatives to be called in case the parents cannot be reached
13. Telephone number of relatives to be called in case parents cannot be reached
14. Hospital of choice
15. Hospital telephone number
16. Any special directions from parents concerning the handling of emergency injury or illness
17. List of homeroom teachers
18. List of pupil's daily class schedule
19. Telephone number of local ambulance services
20. Telephone number of fire department
21. Telephone number of police department

Recently an increasing number of communities have centralized their emergency communication systems. Through the efforts and cooperation of the telephone companies a growing number of towns and cities have begun an emergency communication plan, with 911 as the all-purpose number to dial. School administrators and teachers as well as other school personnel should be aware of the local emergency communication system.

Notification of parents

Schools frequently request parents to sign a permit authorizing the proper emergency care of their children in case of injury and certain illnesses. This is particularly helpful in situations in which parents or guardians cannot be immediately contacted. The school is then free to call the designated family physician or hospital or take any other action it thinks necessary for the best welfare of the child.

Parents or guardians should be notified immediately in case of serious injury or illness. When notifying parents by telephone, the person making the call should speak in a calm, reassuring voice to allay any fear or anxiety the parent may suddenly develop. A full description of the child's injury or illness should be given so far as it is evident and possible. Parents should be told whether immediate medical attention seems needed. Sometimes emergency room hospital care may be advised and stressed to the parent. The person making the call should learn from the parents whether they will come to school for the child or whether they wish the pupil to be brought home. Parents should be encouraged to call for children whenever possible. Occasionally, it may be the desire of the parents that the family physician call at school if it seems necessary. If an ambulance is needed, parents should give permission to summon one before the school takes this action.

Sometimes it may be necessary for the child to go directly to the hospital emergency room or the family physician's office. In some cases the parent may wish someone from the school to accompany the child. Usually the nurse or principal will provide transportation and provide any other assistance necessary.

Since most physicians are not well prepared to provide emergency care in their office in critical life-death situations, it is usually most advisable to call 911 or another emergency phone number and have the child quickly transported to the emergency unit of the nearest hospital. It is important to call the hospital and to inform them of the nature of the injury or illness while the child is en route to the emergency room. This gives hospital personnel time to set up whatever equipment and medicines may be required for a specific case. It also alerts them to possible need for a surgeon or other specialists whom they may need to call to the emergency room.

Sick or injured children should never be sent home unless accompanied by a responsible adult and unless the parents or some responsible person designated by the parents is there to care for them. In cases in which parents or guardians cannot be immediately contacted, school authorities must proceed according to their best judgment. It may seem necessary to call a physician or dentist directly, or in some cases it may be necessary to call an ambulance and take the child to a hospital. In every case school personnel should give the parents every possible aid in caring for a sick or injured child. Often if specialized medical attention is indicated, the parents may be at a loss concerning the selection of a physician. In this case the school authorities should be prepared with a roster of names of various medical specialists available such as pediatricians, otorhinolaryngologists, orthopedists, ophthalmologists, surgeons, and dentists so that they can consult with the parent in making a selection.

It is advisable that the school follow up emergency cases. Parents or guardian should be called within 24 to 36 hours to learn the condition of the injured or ill child. If the condition is serious, periodic telephone calls from the school might be made until the child is well on the way to full recovery. The follow-up of emergency cases costs little and usually brings a great deal of goodwill to the school. It is also important that school officials know the recovery period needed for any injury or illness so that the child's schedule can be altered appropriately.

TEACHER'S ROLE IN EMERGENCY CARE

Every teacher should be prepared to assume some responsibility for the school emergency and first-aid care program. Even though physicians, nurses, and others highly skilled in emergency and first-aid care may be available at practically all times, the teacher must be prepared to accept certain responsibilities, such as the following:

1. Assist with any emergency in which large numbers of pupils are injured or become suddenly ill
2. Render first aid or contact those who are officially designated to give first aid when a pupil under the teacher's direction is injured or becomes ill
3. Assist those who are officially designated to give first aid when necessary by doing such things as calling parents or physician
4. Give first aid for minor injuries such as small and insignificant wounds that do not require the attention of a physician, nurse, or others officially designated to give first aid

The legal duty of school personnel falls into four categories:

1. To foresee possible hazards and take reasonable steps to correct the hazard
2. To provide warnings about hazards that are not immediately remediable
3. To render proper first aid to the injured
4. Not to increase the severity of the injury

Although the situations are likely to be relatively few in which the teacher does not have assistance with first aid, nevertheless, the teacher should be prepared to assume full responsibility for those few times when there is no immediate help. The teacher should keep in mind that providing first aid does not involve medication of any kind. The teacher should never use antiseptics on a wound unless it is an established policy of the school to use them. Then *only* those that are indicated in the written policy of the school should be used. The teacher should not give the child any type of medication, even including such seemingly harmless things as aspirin tablets, unless directed to do so by a physician. All first-aid supplies in the schools should have the approval of those responsible for formulating the policy for emergency and first-aid care.

WHO IS LIABLE AND RESPONSIBLE FOR SCHOOL ACCIDENTS?

Although teachers have always been concerned about accidents involving school children, a study of the accident situation in the schools shows that in the past there has been a lack of proper understanding on the part of some teachers as to their full responsibility in accidents involving school children.

The changing attitude of the public regarding the accident situation in the United States has resulted in greater emphasis being placed on the responsibility of the schools for the safety of the school-age child. Also, the accident problem in schools is greater than in earlier years because of the extended school program and wider variety of activities offered. Programs of physical education, athletics and recreation, science laboratories, and bus transportation of pupils are some of the additions within the modern school program that increase hazards for school children.

Legal responsibility

The question is frequently asked, "Why is there a greater tendency today to attempt to hold the teacher financially liable for injuries to pupils?" The answer to this question in part is that today most people have come to expect accidents to be paid for. When an accident occurs that results in injury to an individual, usually the first question asked is, "Who is to pay for the accident?"

Since the teacher is supposed to be acting in loco parentis (in the place of a parent), any time a student is injured at school, the teacher runs

the risk of being sued for negligence. Negligence is generally based on failure to act as a reasonably prudent and careful individual would act given the same or similar circumstances. In general, negligence may take three forms: (1) failure to perform an expected duty (nonfeasance or an act of omission), (2) performing a duty incorrectly (misfeasance or an act of commission), or (3) performing an illegal procedure or performing a procedure without consent (malfeasance or an act of commission).

Until a few years ago, the common law in the United States, in the absence of specific state legislation, held that boards of education or school committees could not be held financially liable for accidents to school children. In other words, the school funds, raised by taxation in most cases, could not be used for any purpose other than education. This left the teacher practically the only source through which remuneration could be gained. However, at least five states (Washington, California, New York, New Jersey, and Connecticut) have either passed legislation that permits school boards to be sued or have repealed their school board immunity statutes.* Even so, the wise teacher will purchase liability insurance.

It is now commonly understood that a teacher or a school board, or both, in case of *negligence*, can be held responsible and financially liable for accidental injury to a pupil. Increasing numbers of court procedures and damage suits for injuries through accidents to school children are being recorded. Each year there are some 8,000 schools involved in lawsuits resulting in payments of over $15 million.

Teachers should familiarize themselves with the school law in their own state regarding negligence and liability to civil suit.

The law of negligence is partly based on the theory that everyone has the right to live safely and must be protected from the negligence of others in this right. In the school situation the teacher owes a duty to the school child. In many

---

*Anderson, C. and Creswell, W.: School health practice, ed. 7, St. Louis, 1980, The C.V. Mosby Co.

cases the failure to act to prevent an accident to a school child would be considered negligence on the part of the teacher.

The law of negligence implies, so far as the duty of the teacher to the pupil is concerned, that there must be *foreseeability*. The teacher acting as a reasonably careful and prudent person should anticipate danger or an accident.

For negligence to be established, the court must determine that*:

1. The student was injured as a result of a school-related incident.
2. The action or inaction of the school official resulted in additional injury or caused the severity of the injury to increase.
3. The school official acted in a manner different from the way a reasonable and prudent person would have acted under the same or similar circumstances.
4. The school official did, in fact, have a duty to act.

Some conditions that may make teachers liable to legal action include:

1. Permitting pupils to play unsafe, unorganized games
2. Maintaining attractive nuisances (conditions of school environment, apparatus, equipment, machinery, and the like)
3. Permitting pupils to use dangerous devices
4. Inadequate planning and organizing for field trips
5. Permitting use of defective equipment
6. Failing to provide adequate supervision or instruction for pupil activities

Although these six points may seem rather obvious, the basic laws associated with liability were developed to protect and compensate innocent victims of accidents that might have been prevented through prudent action on the part of school officials. The laws were also enacted to protect the school official from frivolous lawsuits, which are often leveled at teachers.

In addition to the possibility of the teacher's being held financially liable for the injury of a child, especially in a case of negligence, there is another factor that should be taken into consideration. In many cases the teacher may not be vulnerable from the viewpoint of financial liability. However, the teacher may be quite vulnerable from the viewpoint of failing to take proper responsibility in case of an accident to a child. That is, although the teacher could not be held financially liable for the accident, nevertheless, the superintendent of schools or the board of education could hold the teacher negligent, perhaps resulting in discipline or even discharge for failing to use reasonable care in providing safe conditions for the child.

Legal defense

Fortunately, teachers generally exercise a great deal of caution in their dealings with students. Further, the courts have realized the difficulty of controlling or keeping under close supervision as many as 35 to 40 students who are all full of energy. Also, there has not been a successful prosecution for negligence against any person who has followed established first-aid procedures when providing aid to an injured individual. The low cost of personal liability insurance is also mute testimony to this low incidence of successful prosecutions.

Several defenses are generally used in lawsuits against teachers. These are as follows:

assumption of risk The person injured failed to heed warnings or voluntarily and with full knowledge of the possible consequences entered a hazardous situation (e.g., climbed over a fence surrounding a hazard)

contributory negligence The failure of the injured person to use due care for his or her own personal safety

vis major An irresistible natural cause that could not be guarded against or anticipated by a person acting in a reasonable and prudent fashion (e.g., an earthquake or other act of God)

Obviously the best defense is not to become involved in litigation initially. This means that a well-planned safety program should be func-

---

*Adapted from Hafen, B.: First aid for health emergencies, ed. 2, St. Paul, 1981, West Publishing Co.

tioning within the school and that the teacher and other school staff should be prepared to handle emergency situations as they arise.

WHAT FIRST-AID PROCEDURES SHOULD TEACHERS USE?*

The emergency care given at the time a person is injured or becomes suddenly ill is known as first aid. It is the care given before medical aid is available. Under most circumstances, medical aid is readily available. The duties of the person giving first aid end immediately when medical assistance is obtained.

It should be kept in mind by teachers that *first aid is the emergency care given at the time an injury or sudden illness first occurs.* It does not mean attempting to care for injuries or illnesses after medical aid has been obtained. Therefore such actions as repeated bandaging of wounds or attempting to care for extended illnesses is not a responsibility of the teacher and should not, under any circumstances, be attempted. Every elementary school classroom teacher should have a knowledge of first aid. Some states now require that elementary teachers have completed a university credit course in first aid or have had comparable Red Cross instruction. Every person employed by the school district, every parent, and every boy and girl should have some understanding of first aid.

The following basic points should be kept in mind when giving first aid:

1. First aid is given to an injured person for the purpose of preventing further harm.
2. First aid is given for the purpose of reducing suffering and discomfort.

3. Many children injured in accidents receive further injury through improper emergency care.
4. Sometimes the failure to receive proper first aid may result in permanent injury or even death.
5. The first-aider should know what *not* to do, as well as what to do.
6. Hurry is seldom necessary, especially if it is likely to cause further damage to the injured person, except in cases of severe bleeding, stoppage of breathing, and poisoning.
7. If the injury is serious, a check should be made for suspended breathing, hemorrhage, shock, obstructions to breathing caused by a foreign body in the mouth or throat, back and neck injuries, and broken bones.
8. If the child is vomiting, the head should be turned to one side to facilitate breathing.
9. Clothing should be loosened about the neck and chest, particularly if breathing is difficult.
10. The child's body temperature should be maintained by covering with blankets or coats to reduce or prevent shock.
11. An injured person should not be moved, unless it is absolutely necessary, until the exact nature of this injury is known and provisions have been made to prevent further damage.
12. An unconscious person must not be given liquid, food, or medication of any type because of the danger of strangling.

The teacher or person responsible for giving first aid should remember that there are three emergency situations that require immediate and instant action to save life (hurry cases): serious bleeding, suspended breathing, and poisoning. Although shock may be extremely serious, the first-aider usually has more time to act.

Serious bleeding

Severe bleeding must be stopped immediately. In addition to danger due to loss of blood it is likely to bring about serious shock. Further-

*Adapted in part from American National Red Cross: Advanced first aid and emergency care, Garden City, N.Y., 1973, Doubleday & Co., Inc.; Standard first aid and personal safety, Washington, D.C., 1973, American National Red Cross; Fishbein, M., and Irwin, L.W.: First-aid training, Chicago, 1961, Lyons & Carnahan; Kennedy, R.H., editor: Emergency care, Philadelphia, 1966, W.B. Saunders Co.; U.S. Department of Health, Education, and Welfare; the U.S. Department of Defense: Family guide emergency health care, Washington, D.C., 1966, U.S. Government Printing Office; and Hafen, B.: First aid for health emergencies, ed. 2, St. Paul, 1981, West Publishing Co.

more, children are usually frightened by the sight of their own blood if it is serious. Fright may add to the seriousness of shock. If a large blood vessel is severed, a quart of blood can be lost from the body within 1 minute. Consequently, in an emergency of this kind the teacher must act instantly. Direct pressure with elevation is the method recommended to stop bleeding. In most cases hand pressure with a sterile dressing or clean napkin, towel, or cloth is the accepted procedure. A compress directly on the wound with a tight bandage will control the blood flow in a majority of cases. Blood flow from the head and face can usually be controlled in this way.

If a large artery of the arm or leg is cut, it may be necessary under some circumstances to apply a tourniquet. A tourniquet is used only on an arm or leg when a large artery is cut. Because a tourniquet is an extremely dangerous piece of equipment in the hands of the average first-aider, its use is highly restricted and may indicate the limb should be sacrificed to save the life of the individual. Some results of improper use of a tourniquet are the following:

1. The artery may be permanently damaged through crushing by too much pressure.
2. Keeping the supply of blood from a part of the body too long may cause gangrene.
3. Additional bleeding resulting from removing the tourniquet too soon may prove serious.
4. Removing the tourniquet after an extended period of application may increase shock.

A tourniquet can be applied to the arm about midway or slightly above the midpoint between the elbow and the shoulder. For the leg, it can be applied about 3 inches below the groin. It should not be too close to the edge of the wound. Any material fairly thick and soft that can be tied around the arm or leg and twisted tight enough to stop the bleeding can be used as a tourniquet. *It must not cut or bruise the flesh.* Such materials as wire or rope should never be used as a tourniquet.

It is important to remember that a tourniquet should be used *only in case of very serious bleeding that threatens life* and cannot be stopped by other recommended means. A tourniquet is seldom necessary and if a tourniquet is applied, it should not be released other than by a physician. When a tourniquet is applied, the time of application should be attached to or, if possible, written on the forehead of the victim.

Artificial respiration

A person cannot live more than a few minutes without breathing. Most people would die within 5 or 6 minutes if breathing completely ceased. It is extremely important to begin artificial respiration immediately after the cessation of breathing because the heart continues to beat only a short time after breathing has stopped.

Some of the causes of complete or partial cessation of breathing or serious interference with the oxygen supply of the body are electric shock, drowning, certain gases, choking, strangling, certain chemical fumes, and some drugs such as morphine, barbiturates, and alcohol. From the viewpoint of the school situation, however, mechanical obstruction is likely to be the most common cause of suspended breathing or serious interference with breathing. The mechanical causes include foreign bodies in the throat and windpipe, submersion in water involving drowning, and strangulation.

There are many ways of administering artificial respiration. However, the mouth-to-mouth or mouth-to-nose method is recommended as the most efficient and usually the most practical. The following directions briefly explain how to give mouth-to-mouth and mouth-to-nose artificial respiration.

First, shake the person gently and ask if he or she is all right. If you get no response, place your ear near the mouth to see if you detect breathing. Simultaneously, check to see if you can feel a carotid pulse (in the neck, near the Adam's apple). If you feel a pulse but detect no breathing, place the person on the back with arms at sides. Check the mouth to be sure that it is free from any kind of foreign matter. Remove anything from the mouth that may obstruct breathing by wiping it out with your finger or with a cloth. Place one hand under the person's

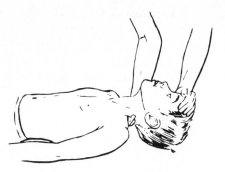

A, Move the head so that the chin is pointing upward.

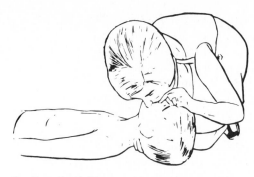

B, Close the child's nostrils and place your mouth tightly over the child's mouth.

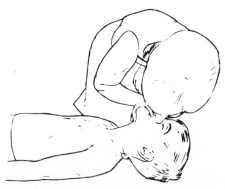

C, If the mouth-to-nose method is used, close the mouth and place your mouth over the nose.

D, In the case of a young child hold the child's jaw in place with one hand and place your other hand on the stomach. Place your mouth over both the nose and mouth of the child.

FIG. 7-2. Administering artificial respiration.

head and your other hand on the forehead. Move the head so that the chin is pointed upward with the lower jaw in a jutting position as shown in Fig. 7-2, A. In this position the base of the tongue tends to move away from the back of the throat to give clear passage to the air.

In the mouth-to-mouth technique close the person's nostrils with your fingers or cheek. Place your mouth tightly over the person's mouth as shown in Fig. 7-2, B. If you do not wish to come in contact with the person, place a handkerchief over his nose and mouth. If you use the mouth-to-nose technique, close the person's mouth and place your mouth over his nose

as shown in Fig. 7-2, C. Exhale into the person's mouth or nose. Remove your mouth and turn your head to one side while you inhale. Repeat the exhaling of air into the person's nose or mouth and remove your mouth to inhale. The rate of breathing in this way should be about *12 to 16 times per minute.* Exhale vigorously in giving artificial respiration to an adult or older child.

If at any time obstruction to breathing develops that makes it difficult to get air into and out of the person's lungs, quickly turn the victim on the side and slap the back several times between the shoulders with the palm of your hand. Then quickly resume artificial respiration.

There are a few differences in using the mouth-to-mouth method of artificial respiration on small children and on grown people.

Place a small child on his/her back with chin pointed upward and lower jaw in a jutting position. Place your mouth over *both* the child's nose and mouth tightly enough so that air cannot escape as shown in Fig. 7-2, *D*. Hold the child's lower jaw in position with one hand and then place your other hand on the child's stomach just below the ribs. Exhale gently and smoothly into the child's nose and mouth until the chest rises. While breathing into the nose and mouth, with your hand apply a little pressure to the child's stomach to keep it from filling with air. When you have breathed enough air into the child's lungs, as indicated by the rising of the chest, raise your head and allow the air to pass from the child's lungs. Keep one hand under the jaw and the other on the stomach and *repeat this cycle about 20 times a minute.*

If there is any obstruction to getting air into the child's lungs, quickly bend the child over with the head down and administer three or four quick pats between the shoulders. Then continue artificial respiration immediately.

If no pulse can be felt in the carotid artery on the neck under the angle of the lower jaw, the *CPR technique* should be used as described next.

ABC of life support*

This emergency first-aid procedure consists of recognizing stoppage of breathing and heartbeat —then applying cardiopulmonary resuscitation (CPR), which involve (A) opening and maintaining victim's *Airway;* (B) giving rescue *Breathing;* and (C) providing artificial *Circulation* by external cardiac compression (heart massage). CPR should be performed by people with special training. For information, get in touch with

your local Heart Association or Red Cross. To refresh your memory, these are essential ABCs:

A *Airway open.* Turn victim on back and quickly remove any foreign matter from the mouth. Place your hand under person's neck and lift, tilting head back as far as possible with other hand. This provides an airway.

B *Breathing restored.* If person is not breathing, place your mouth tightly over his mouth, pinch nostrils, and blow into airway until you see chest rise. Remove your mouth. Give four breaths and check for neck pulse (Fig. 7-3). If pulse is present, continue rescue breathing at 12 times a minute. For small child or infant, cover nose and mouth tightly with your mouth. Blow gently 20 times a minute.

C *Circulation maintained.* Quickly feel for neck pulse; keeping victim's head tilted with one hand, use middle and index fingers of other hand to feel for carotid pulse, in neck artery, under side angle of lower jaw. If no pulse, start rescue breathing and external cardiac compression.

Victim's back should be on firm surface. Place heel of your hand on center of lower breastbone with fingers off chest and other hand on top. Gently rock forward, exerting pressure down, to force blood out of the heart. Release pressure. Alternate (B) Breathing with (C) Circulation.

Two rescuers: Give 60 chest compressions a minute—one breath after each five compressions. *One rescuer:* Perform both artificial circulation and rescue breathing giving 80 chest compressions a minute—two full breaths after each 15 compressions.

FOR SMALL CHILDREN AND INFANTS: Use only the heel of one hand and, for infants, only the tips of index and middle fingers. Give 80 to 100 compressions per minute with two breaths after each five compressions.

REMEMBER: These basic ABCs only briefly outline what to do for a person unconscious from drowning, electrocution, suffocation, accident, heart disease, or stroke. Time is crucial. Rescue efforts must begin at once and continue until

---

*From the Metropolitan Life Insurance Co., New York, 1974.

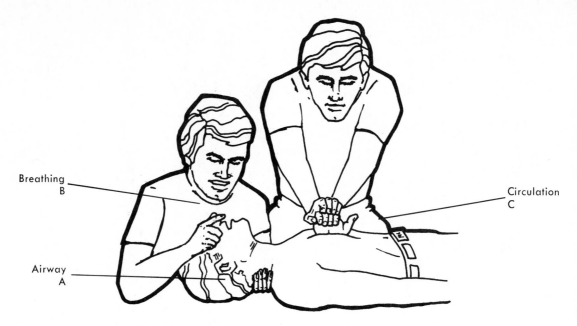

FIG. 7-3. The ABC life support (Cardio-Pulmonary Resuscitation, CPR). *(From the Metropolitan Life Insurance Co., New York, 1974).*

professional help arrives. To be fully effective, special training and periodic refreshers are vital.

There are a few other measures that should be followed in suspended breathing:

1. The body temperature of the person should be maintained.

2. Artificial respiration should be continued without interruption.

3. The person should not be moved until normal voluntary breathing returns.

4. If it is necessary to move the person, resuscitation should be carried on during the time the child is being moved.

5. When the person is revived, body temperature should be maintained. The victim should remain quiet for a while and should be treated for shock by a physician.

6. Since in some cases of suspended breathing recovery is unusually slow and discouraging to those giving first aid, artificial respiration should be continued for at least 3 hours, or longer, or until rescue squad or hospital emergency personnel and equipment are available.

Choking

The following article, authored by Henry J. Heimlich, is adapted from *Emergency* and is reprinted with their written authorization.

Heimlich maneuver: the thrust of life.* The effectiveness of the Heimlich maneuver in saving the lives of those choking on food and other objects is based on its simplicity. The technique was not easily discovered but resulted from extensive scientific investigation.

The principle of the Heimlich maneuver is easily understood from the following definition:

Heimlich maneuver Technique for saving the life of a person choking on food or another object; consists of external compression of the air in the lungs in order to provide a flow of air from the larynx sufficient to expel the obstructing object.

DIAGNOSING A CHOKING VICTIM. There should be no difficulty in differentiating a choking victim from one having a heart attack because there are clearly distinguishing factors. In

---

*Adapted from Heimlich, H.J.: Heimlich maneuver; the thrust of life, Emergency, Carlsbad, Calif., 1977, pp. 64-67.

FIG. 7-4. Heimlich maneuver.

more than 90% of instances the victim is seen to choke on food or another object. The choking victim cannot breathe or speak, becomes cyanotic, and collapses. The heart attack victim, on the other hand, is able to breathe and usually can talk. Furthermore, it has been shown that over 98% of persons dying suddenly in an eating establishment have choked on food and only slightly more than 1% have had a heart attack. There is obviously a life-threatening danger to the choking victim if the Heimlich maneuver is not applied because an observer thinks only of heart attack. There should be little possibility that the Heimlich maneuver will be performed unnecessarily in a heart attack victim.

In an article in the *Journal of the American Medical Association*, Dr. Heimlich introduced a

FIG. 7-5. Heimlich sign.

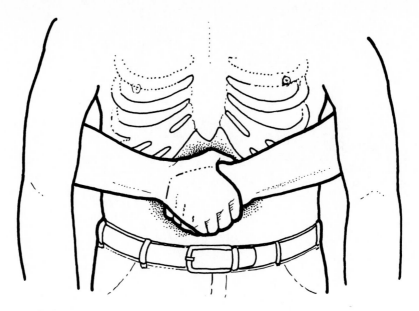

FIG. 7-6. Rescuer standing when using the Heimlich maneuver.

signal that has come to be known as the "Heimlich sign," which indicates, "I am choking on food." Victims grasp their neck between their thumb and index finger to indicate the choking situation (Fig. 7-5). Should this sign become universal, the diagnosis of food choking will be 100% accurate.

HEIMLICH MANEUVER. To be safe and effective, the Heimlich maneuver should be performed in one of the following prescribed ways:

1. When the rescuer is standing and the victim is standing or sitting (Fig. 7-4), the rescuer takes these steps.
    a. Stand behind the victim and wrap your arms around the victim's waist.
    b. Place your fist, thumb side, against the victim's abdomen slightly above the navel and below the rib cage (Fig. 7-6).
    c. Grasp your fist with your other hand and press into the victim's abdomen with a quick upward thrust.
    d. Repeat several times if necessary.
2. When the victim is sitting, the rescuer stands behind the victim's chair and performs the maneuver in the same manner as for a standing victim.

3. When the rescuer is kneeling and the victim is lying face up (Fig. 7-7), the rescuer takes the following steps:
    a. With the victim lying on his back, face the victim, and kneel astride his hips.
    b. With one of your hands on the top of the other, place them on the victim's abdomen slightly above the navel and below the rib cage (Fig. 7-7).
    c. Press into the victim's abdomen with a quick upward thrust.
    d. Repeat several times if necessary.

The standing and sitting positions are used most often; however, it is extremely important that rescuers learn the supine position (victim lying down, face upward). Only in that position, with the rescuer astride the victim's thighs, can a small person—slight woman or child who cannot reach around the victim's waist or who is not strong enough to press a fist upward around the diaphragm with sufficient force—save a heavy victim. In the supine position, the rescuer uses his weight, not strength, to press upward on the diaphragm.

The choking victim has 4 minutes to live from the onset of choking; however, when a victim is

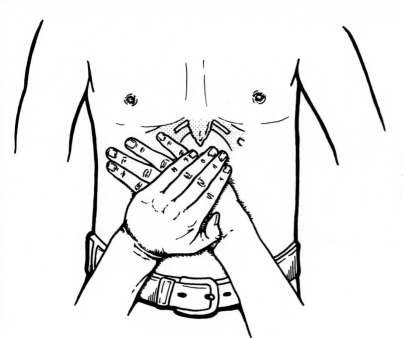

FIG. 7-7. Rescuer kneeling when using the Heimlich maneuver.

on the floor unconscious, he does not have the full 4 minutes but only a matter of seconds. It is necessary to straddle the victim's thighs immediately and apply the Heimlich maneuver without delay. Backslaps, fingers in the mouth, or mouth-to-mouth resuscitation will cause delay and diminish the possibility of rescue.

COMMUNITY INVOLVEMENT. The Heimlich maneuver is similar to a vaccine—unless the entire population receives it in adequate repeated doses, some people will die. Communitywide Heimlich maneuver teaching programs have led to the saving of many lives. Individuals and organizations have started such ongoing programs by involving an entire city through advance TV and newspaper publicity and participation of officials, devoting a full day to the programs. Dr. Heimlich has had the privilege of speaking at many such "opening day" meetings. Since 25% of choking victims are children, and children have saved lives (an 8-year-old saved his 6-year-old brother, a 13-year-old saved his mother's life), schools should be involved.

Shock

In a state of shock the body processes are usually greatly reduced. Broken bones, poisoning, severe burns, hemorrhage, perforation or inflammation of internal organs, reactions to drugs or proteins, or strong emotions may cause shock. Intense pain, loss of blood, tissue destruction, and sometimes strong emotions may interfere with the nervous system's control of the circulatory system. There may be a fall in blood pressure to a level so low that circulation is inadequate. The brain fails to get enough blood to supply sufficient oxygen and nutrition, and, as a result, consciousness may be lost.

Shock may not be clearly noticeable following most minor injuries. However, some degree of shock may follow any injury, particularly if it is accompanied by strong emotional reactions.

Some people are much more subject to shock than others. An injury that causes only slight or moderate shock in one person may cause serious shock in another. Severe shock usually follows serious injury. Consequently, the teacher should always be alert and expect shock in giving first aid to pupils who are accident victims. Shock may appear soon after an injury, or it may appear many hours later.

The question is often asked as to how it is possible to prevent shock. The answer is that it may not be possible to prevent shock, but the proper first-aid care may greatly reduce its seriousness. There are a number of ways by which shock can be detected. Some of the signs are the following:

1. The lips and fingernails are blue or grayish.
2. The skin is cool to the touch, yet it is covered with moisture, making it feel clammy.
3. The injured child may be nauseated.
4. The injured child may vomit.
5. The victim may be partially conscious and complain of feeling cold.
6. The face becomes pale, almost a gray color.

First aid for shock consists of keeping the person lying in a supine position with the head lower than the feet. Precaution should be taken, however, in placing the head lower than the feet. *In head or chest injuries, or if breathing becomes more difficult* with the head low, the *child's head and shoulders should be raised a few inches* higher than his feet. This can be done by placing a pillow or coat under the victim's head and shoulders. If the child develops difficulty in breathing with the head and shoulders elevated, lower them. The pupil should be kept comfortably warm with blankets or coats *but not overheated.* Pain contributes to shock. Unnecessary movement of an injured person makes unnecessary pain. Fear may increase shock. The child should be reassured and should not be bothered with unnecessary questions. The first-aider should never give a person in shock any kind of liquids or stimulants.

Poisoning

Once poison is swallowed and reaches the stomach, it is only a matter of time until it is absorbed. In most cases of poisoning it is important that the poison be diluted and as much of it as possible emptied from the stomach by vomit-

ing. Poisoning from foods occurs frequently. Food poisoning may be caused by spoiled or partially spoiled foods. Certain types of mushrooms, wild berries, roots, and some types of leaves are poisonous. The poisonous type of mushrooms are frequently called toadstools. Small children are often poisoned by aspirin and petroleum products, such as kerosene and gasoline.

The symptoms of poisoning may vary greatly, depending on the substance swallowed and the time elapsed after ingestion. Some of the general symptoms are nausea, stomach cramps, pain, and sometimes vomiting. Sometimes poisons are absorbed before symptoms become evident. The corrosive poisons, such as acids and alkalis, may burn the lips and mouth and cause very marked shock. Poisoning caused by foods may cause vomiting, diarrhea, and collapse. There is usually some degree of prostration present.

When first aid for poisoning is given, the first step is to call the hospital emergency room or the nearest poison control center. When first aid for poisoning other than strong acids, petroleum products, and alkalis is administered, an attempt should be made to dilute the poison and to induce vomiting. Fluids suitable for use in diluting the poison and filling the stomach are plain water and milk. If baking soda is available, a few teaspoons should be added to each glass of water, because it tends to induce vomiting. Although water is always the most readily available fluid, milk is good to use, because it gives some protection to the lining of the digestive tract. Four or five glasses of fluid should be given. Vomiting should not be induced if acids or alkalis were swallowed, because the poison coming up may do further damage to the lining of the food passages.

With the rapid increase in the number of over-the-counter and prescription drugs available to children in the home, opportunities for poisoning or dangerous overdose are much greater today than in past years. Sometimes children will ingest medicines or drugs in the home, yet effects may not be noticed until later in the day at school.

Diabetic reactions

Diabetic reactions occur as the result of too much (insulin reaction) or too little (diabetic coma) insulin. In an insulin reaction the first sign noted in the child is general irritability in which the pupil may be despondent, cry readily, or be exuberant or belligerent. In addition, the student may be hungry, perspire excessively, tremble or be unable to concentrate, and complain of dizziness. The symptoms vary in duration and will often disappear in 10 to 15 minutes by providing the child with any of the following: sugar cube, pop, candy, raisins, fruit juice with sugar, or any other carbohydrate. If the symptoms do not subside after this action, then the pupil's parents should be notified. A diabetic coma, a rather rare condition, is caused by the failure to take insulin, an illness, or neglect of a proper diet. It is slow in onset and may be observed by these symptoms: thirst, frequent urination, flushed face, labored breathing, nausea, and vomiting. The teacher should keep the child in a resting state and maintain body temperature. In addition, the school nurse, the principal, or the parents should be immediately notified.

Epileptic convulsions

Most elementary school classroom teachers at one time or another are confronted with the problem of dealing with epileptic convulsions in children. The minor form of epilepsy is not a particular problem for the teacher. The seizures in major or grand mal epilepsy require emergency care on the part of the teacher. The seizures are usually marked by loss of consciousness, convulsions, and thrashing about. The convulsive state is then followed by prolonged stupor.

In giving a child first aid for a seizure, the teacher should not resist his/her thrashing about. Keep calm and let the convulsion run its course, which it will do in 2 to 5 minutes. The child should be kept in the open where he/she will not be injured by striking any hard or sharp objects. *Do not force anything between the patient's teeth.* The child's collar should be loosened to prevent breathing from being obstructed. Turn the victim's face to one side so that liquid emitted does not fall back into the throat. Place something soft, such as a rolled-up coat, beneath the person's head. After the convulsion the child should be taken to the emergency room to lie down and sleep. However, the parents should be notified because they may wish to call for the student at once. Ordinarily, if it is known that the child is epileptic, arrangements should have been made with the parents and physician concerning the routine to follow.

Fainting

Just before fainting, a child is likely to feel weak and dizzy. Vision becomes blurred, the face becomes pale, and the victim may be covered with a cold sweat. When a child faints, he or she should be placed on the back with head lowered. The color of the face indicates to some extent the amount of blood being supplied to the brain. If the face is very pale, the head should be kept lowered until the color of the face improves. If, on the other hand, the face is extremely red, it may be desirable to keep the head level or slightly raised. After the fainting victim has recovered consciousness, the victim should lie quietly for a few minutes. The child should then sit up for a few minutes before taking a standing position. The fainted person should have plenty of fresh, cool air. After regaining consciousness, a cool, wet cloth may be applied to the face or chest as a stimulant to recuperative action.

Nosebleed

Nosebleed is frequent following a blow on the nose, although there may be other causes. Some of the small blood vessels in the mucous lining of the nose can be ruptured very easily. It is often unnecessary to give first aid for nosebleed as many, if not most of them in children, will stop without emergency care. For minor cases pressure can be applied by closing the nostrils by pinching them with the fingers and tilting the head back. In giving first aid for more persistent nosebleed, it is preferable to place the child flat in a prone position. It keeps the blood from flowing back into the throat. Cold packs may be applied to the nose, or it may be temporarily packed with sterile gauze. If a nosebleed cannot be readily stopped, a physician is required.

Wounds

Any injury to the skin or tissue is classed as a wound. The person giving first aid is primarily concerned with wounds in which the skin or mucous membrane is broken. Any tiny break in the skin is considered a wound if germs are allowed to enter.

Wounds may be classified according to the way the injury occurs, the type of wound made, and the kind of first aid required. The general types of wounds with which the first-aider is likely to be concerned are incisions or clean-cut wounds, torn or lacerated wounds, abrasions or scraping, or rubbing types of wounds made by the body sliding on the floor or on a rough surface. Puncture or stab wounds are made by such objects as pins, needles, and nails.

Clean-cut wounds usually bleed freely, and they are not so likely to become infected. Wounds made by machines or other rough objects, however, are more likely to become infected. They may not bleed freely, and frequently there are dirt and grease in the wound. Puncture wounds are ordinarily more serious than other types of minor wounds. They usually do not bleed freely, and they are hard to cleanse properly. Furthermore, there is danger of tetanus, or lockjaw, from puncture wounds.

Infection is a chief danger from a majority of wounds. Although thousands of germs may enter even a tiny wound, not all wounds in which germs enter become infected. The body may resist and overcome the germs, depending on a number of factors, or the germs may not have the strength to grow and multiply.

In giving first aid for wounds in which serious bleeding is not a factor, a main purpose is to prevent infection if possible and to keep germs from entering a wound once it is made. If a physician will be available soon, all the first-aider will need to do as far as the wound itself is concerned is to cover it with a sterile dressing. The first-aider should never try to clean a wound or to apply an antiseptic if the services of a physician are needed and readily available. If it is necessary to cleanse a wound, use plain soap and running tap water adjusted to room temperature. The first-aid care of ordinary small wounds requires only that the first-aider apply a sterile compress and bandage to keep dirt from entering the wound.

Punctures and stabs are particularly dangerous types of wounds for the following reasons:

1. Tetanus, or lockjaw germs, may grow readily when there is a lack of air, such as in a puncture wound.
2. Punctures do not bleed freely; consequently, dirt and germs are not washed out as in an open wound.
3. It is extremely difficult to clean the wound, and germs may have been deposited in the bottom of it by the instrument making the wound.

A physician is needed to treat a puncture wound as protective measures may be needed against tetanus. If a physician cannot be secured for some time, the first-aider should encourage bleeding without bruising the tissue.

Eye injuries

Since the eyes are very delicate organs, they should be treated with the greatest of care. Children should not be allowed to use most sharp-pointed instruments because of the danger of injuring the eye or falling on the instrument. The following points should be remembered in caring for eye injuries:

1. If any type of chemical gets into the eyes, it should be washed out immediately with plenty of water.
2. The use of any kind of sharp object should be avoided in removing foreign particles from the eye.
3. The first-aider should *never* attempt to remove an embedded object from the eye.
4. If a foreign object gets into the eye, the eye should not be rubbed. Rubbing the eye with a foreign object in it, especially if it is a sharp particle, such as a cinder, may drive it into the eyeball tissue.
5. If a child gets an object in the eye, the teacher should attempt to remove it with a sterile cloth. If the object cannot be removed readily, a physician is needed.

Burns

There are three general types of burns—*chemical*, *thermal*, and *solar*. Burns and scalds are from heat of such a degree as to cause injury to the skin and tissue of the body. Burns from hot liquids or steam are classified as scalds. Burns are sometimes classified as follows: first-degree burns are those in which the skin is reddened; second-degree burns are those in which the skin is blistered; third-degree burns are those in which there is a destruction of deeper tissue and are very serious, since growth cells that form new skin are destroyed.

Giving first aid for a burn depends somewhat on the extent of the burn. If it is extensive or if tissue has been destroyed, a physician is needed as soon as possible. The main duty of the first-aider in this case is to try to prevent and care for shock until a physician is in charge of the individual. Nothing should be put on the burned area. However, relief of pain and control of tissue damage can often be achieved in first- and second-degree burns by application of ice, "instant-cold" chemical bags, or immersion in ice water. Chemical cold sprays should not be used because of the danger of frostbite and possible tissue damage.

Fractures

Although there are many classifications of fractures, for the purpose of first aid they can be classed as (1) simple or closed fractures, in which a bone is broken but the skin is not broken and (2) compound or open fractures, in which a bone is broken and a wound extends from the break through the tissue and skin.

Physicians have classified fractures into many different categories, depending on the extent of the injury in most cases. For example, in a simple fracture the bone is broken, and there has been some injury to tissue around the bone, but the skin is not broken. In a compound fracture the bone is broken, and the skin is also wounded so that the wound communicates directly with the area of the broken bone. Sometimes a portion of the bone itself will penetrate the skin. A complicated fracture is one in which the bone is broken, the skin is broken, and there may be serious damage to blood vessels or organs around the broken bone.

Fractures are also described in relation to the nature of the injury to the bone. In a greenstick fracture the bone is split. In a comminuted fracture the bone may be broken into several pieces; for example, there may be a combination of several kinds of fractures, so that one may have a compound comminuted fracture.

The symptoms of fracture include swelling, pain, and bruising. If a portion of a limb swings in any direction that it could not do unless the bone were broken, that is sure proof that there has been a fracture. If a bone that ordinarily appears straight suddenly assumes an angular position, the irregularity of the line indicates a fracture. Not all symptoms will necessarily be present in every fracture.

If fracture is suspected, a physician is needed. The usual policy of the school should be followed in this case. Shock may follow a broken bone. The first-aider should give first aid for shock. If medical aid is readily available, the child should not be moved. If it is necessary to move the patient, a splint should be applied if the arms (Figs. 7-8 and 7-9) or legs are involved;

FIG. 7-8. Board splint for fractured arm.

FIG. 7-9. Splint and sling for fracture of upper arm.

if the neck or back is involved, extreme care should be used in handling the person. If it is necessary to move the injured person with a neck or back injury before medical aid is available, it should be remembered that the body should never be allowed to sag, especially the head or neck. The child should be prevented from moving in any way if at all possible. Some rigid material should be used on which to move the person. A wide flat board or door will keep the body straight and prevent it from sagging. Plenty of help should be available for carrying the injured person.

Skull fracture may result from any type of hard blow on the head or by the head striking a hard surface. Some of the symptoms of skull fracture are bleeding from the nose, mouth, or ears, unconsciousness, pupils of the eyes unequal in size, and face flushed or pale, depending on the seriousness of the injury, and there may be evidence of a blow on the head, such as a cut or a bump. All of the symptoms may not be present in every case.

First aid for skull fractures involves keeping the person in a lying position with the head and shoulders *slightly elevated if the face is flushed.* If the face is pale or ashen, the head and shoulders should not be elevated. The child's body temperature should be maintained, but no heated object should be applied. A physician should be secured as soon as possible. If a person

must be moved before medical aid is available, the victim should be kept in a lying position.

Dislocations

A dislocation is a bone out of place at a joint. The ligaments may be injured by being torn, the blood vessels and nerves may be injured, and the ends of the bones may be chipped. A physician is needed to reduce a dislocation safely. The parts of the body that may be dislocated are the fingers, shoulders, jaw, elbows, knees, and hips. The first-aid care for a dislocation consists of placing an ice bag or cold compresses over the joint and securing a physician. There should be no movement of the joint, since there is danger of chipping the bone.

Frostbite

In some areas of the country, school children may occasionally suffer from frostbite. It results from loss of circulation because of constriction of arteries at low temperatures. Consequently, the tissues are deprived of oxygen. Injury from frostbite varies with circumstances, and the kind of emergency care given.

The fingers, toes, nose, ears, and cheeks are the parts of the body most likely to be frostbitten. The signs of frostbite are a sensation of intense coldness, then numbness, then finally almost complete loss of sensation in the frozen part. The frostbitten part may be flushed at first and then become very white or grayish white. Because of numbness and loss of sensation, people may not realize that their nose, cheeks, or ears are frostbitten until someone calls attention to it.

In giving first aid for frostbite, the teacher should be careful not to damage the tissue. Rubbing or careless handling of a frozen part may bruise the tissue and cause further damage. If a person is outdoors, the frozen part should be covered with the hand or with cloth, preferably woolen. The child should be brought indoors and placed in a warm room, and the frostbitten part should be covered with a warm cloth such as a blanket. However, hot objects of any kind should be kept away from the frostbitten part.

Sprains

In sprains, ligaments and other tissues may be damaged. Wrists and ankles are most frequently sprained. In giving first aid for a sprain, the teacher should apply cold compresses or an ice bag for 20 or 30 minutes after the injury. The injured part should be kept elevated and the child not allowed to put any weight on the sprained part. A sprained ankle may be helped by a crisscrossing bandage, elastic bandage, or adhesive around it to keep it immovable. The usual school procedure in contacting the parents concerning a physician should be followed.

First-aid supplies

Every elementary school should have adequate first-aid supplies, depending on the enrollment as well as the location of the school and the availability of medical assistance. In most elementary schools the first-aid supplies are likely to be under the care of the principal. They should be kept in a central place, such as the health service room, the emergency room, or the principal's office. Periodic stock taking should be done to assure that first-aid kits are complete and up to date. The following list

shows the usual first-aid supplies needed by the school:

Absorbent cotton
Adhesive tape
Compresses of various sizes
Sterile gauze of various sizes
Roller bandages of various sizes
Triangular bandages
Cotton swabs sterilized in packages
Scissors
Eye dropper
Aromatic spirits of ammonia
Tourniquet
Tincture of green soap
Meat tenderizer (for bee stings)
Wooden applicators
Hand brushes
Elastic bandages, 2 and 3 inches wide
Blankets
Splints
Pillows
Paper cups
Safety pins
Tweezers
Hot-water bottle
Ice bag
"Instant cold" chemical bags

It is important to remember that *no medicines of any kind* are part of a first-aid supply cabinet!

SUMMARY

The concept of school safety has received a great deal of attention over the past few years. Whenever a child is injured at school, the question, "Who is going to pay for this injury?" arises. There is an increasing trend for people to recover costs from accidents, and the attitude that has begun to emerge is that parents expect teachers to pay for accidents that result in injuries to students.

The teacher has a duty to care for those who are injured and ill but must realize that the possibility of litigation exists. In general, teachers should carry personal liability insurance even though school boards may increasingly be sued for damages in injury cases.

Although it is best if trained and certified

first-aid personnel are on duty whenever children are present at school, techniques for handling select emergency situations have been presented in this chapter. It is hoped that these suggestions will motivate the individual to seek additional first-aid training and that any certification acquired will be kept up to date.

QUESTIONS FOR DISCUSSION

1. Whose responsibility is the promotion of safety in the elementary school?
2. What are the basic components of a school's emergency care procedures?
3. Why should the school emergency plan be a written document?
4. How would you characterize the role of the teacher in emergency care?
5. What is meant by the phrase, "a reasonable and prudent individual?"
6. What is probably the best way to avoid becoming involved in liability litigation?
7. Under what circumstances is the teacher liable in the event of pupil injury?
8. Briefly discuss the basic principles that should be followed in administering first aid to the injured.
9. What legal duties would a teacher be expected to perform in terms of a school safety program?
10. Do you feel that the school board should be exempt from legal liability in cases of pupil injury? Why or why not?
11. Some individuals maintain that school boards should be required to purchase personal liability insurance for all employees. What is your viewpoint on this issue?
12. Why is it desirable that a person certified in first aid be present at all times that students are in the school facility?
13. Why should all pupil accidents be reported on accident report forms?
14. What is meant by "The ABC of Life Support?"
15. Why are school personnel admonished not to give a pupil any type of medication unless that medication has been specifically prescribed by a physician?

SELECTED REFERENCES

Aaron, J., Bridges, F., and Ritzel, D.: First aid and emergency care, New York, 1977, MacMillan, Inc.

American Alliance for Health, Physical Education, Recreation, and Dance: Safety education review, Washington, D.C., published annually, The Alliance.

American Alliance for Health, Physical Education, and Recreation: School safety policies (report of the Joint Committee on Health Problems in Education of the National Education Association and the American Medical Association), Washington, D.C., 1968, The Alliance.

American National Red Cross: Standard first aid and personal safety, Washington, D.C., 1973, American National Red Cross.

Anderson, C., and Creswell, W.: School health practice, ed. 7, St. Louis, 1980, The C.V. Mosby Co.

Baker, S.: Injury control; accident prevention and other approaches to reduction of injury. In Sartwell, P., editor: Preventive medicine and public health, New York, 1973, Appleton-Century-Crofts.

Consumer Product Safety Commission: Banned products, vol. II, Part 1, Washington, D.C., Oct. 1, 1973, The Commission.

Craig, A.B.: Some hazards of aquatics, American Journal of Diseases of Childhood, June, 1973.

Green, M.I.: A sigh of relief; the first-aid handbook for childhood emergencies, New York, 1977, Bantam Books, Inc.

Hafen, B.: First aid for health emergencies, ed. 2, St. Paul, 1981. West Publishing Co.

Hartley, J.: First aid without panic, New York, 1977, Popular Library.

King, B.G.: Man and the control of accidental injuries, Public Health Review, Dec. 1973.

Kuntz, R.: How to help your attorney win your case when your school district is sued, The American School Board Journal 160:35-37, Jan. 1973.

Market Facts, Inc.: Household safety study, Chicago, 1971, Market Facts, Inc.

McFarland, R.A., and Moore, R.C.: Childhood accidents and injuries, Boston, 1970, Harvard School of Public Health.

Meyer, R.: Childhood injury and pediatric education; a critique, Pediatrics (Suppl.), 1969.

National Safety Council: Accident facts, Chicago, published annually, The Council.

National Safety Council: School safety magazine, Chicago, published quarterly, The Council.

School Health education Study: Health education: a conceptual approach to curriculum design, Washington, D.C., 1967, The School Health Education Study.

Smith, V.: A study of injuries, Journal of School Health, Feb. 1971.

Stack, H.J., and Elkow, J.D.: Education for safe living, Englewood Cliffs, N.J., 1972, Prentice-Hall, Inc.

Trubitt, H.: Legal responsibilities of school teachers in emergency situations, The Journal of School Health **36:** Jan. 1966.

Westaby, J.R.: A bookshelf on injury control and emergency health services, American Journal of Public Health, April 1974.

PART FOUR

Health education

8

HEALTH EDUCATION TODAY

Effective health education early in life can help to prevent the major diseases of adulthood . . . as children grow older, we must teach them how to become responsible informed consumers of health care . . .

Joseph A. Califano, Jr.
Former Secretary of the U.S. Dept. of Health, Education, and Welfare*

Health education in America's schools has been slowly approaching a threshold of awareness, growth, and emphasis that should have a profound future influence on the children and youth of the United States. Acceptance of the need for preventive health care with a focus on adopting life-style behaviors that promote good health is now widely advocated by all leaders in the health and medical community. The concept has received general approval by parents and the public at large.

Elementary school health education is not without support from governmental, professional, and health and education organizations, voluntary health agencies, commercial companies, and parents. In 1975 the Comprehensive School Health Education Act was under consideration by the U.S. Congress to provide financial support for the development of pro-

grams in elementary and secondary schools. Although the act was never passed, recognition of need and public awareness were greatly increased.

Approximately 25% of the 50 states have mandated comprehensive school health education, but its definition varies widely. Other states have required specific curriculum areas such as alcohol, tobacco and other drugs, safety, and sexually transmitted disease. Still others have additional permissive legislative provisions. The introduction of health education into schools has been advocated by the American Academy of Pediatrics, the American Association of School Administrators, the American Dental Association, the American Medical Association, the American Public Health Association, the American School Health Association, the Association for the Advancement of Health Education, the Council of Chief State School Officers, the National Association of State Boards of Education, the American Cancer

*Speech delivered at the National School Health Conference, Minneapolis, May 12-13, 1977.

147

Society, the American Heart Association, and the American Lung Association. The National Dairy Council, the United Way, the Kellogg and Robert Wood Johnson Foundations, and Blue Cross and Blue Shield, among others, have supported financially the development of programs in various U.S. communities.

A significant position paper adopted by the Governing Council of the American Public Health Association in 1974 stated that:

The school is a community in which most individuals spend at least twelve years of their lives . . . the health of our school-age youth will determine to a great extent the quality of life each will have during the growing and developing years and on throughout the life cycle.*

In 1981 the Education Commission of the States† proposed that state education agencies should do the following:
1. Encourage local school boards and administrators to include health education in the curriculum in elementary and secondary schools
2. Promote health education as a responsibility shared by the family, school, and community
3. Promote the development of comprehensive school health education programs

Despite the legislative provisions and the efforts of the various organizations and agencies previously identified, health education programs are not common nor universally found in schools in the United States. The paucity of curricula is caused primarily by the lack of understanding of the need for and the significance of such programs of learning. It is estimated that only several hundred formal health instruction programs may be in operation in the 1,500 school districts and 65,000 schools in the United

States. However, the number of programs has been on the increase in recent years. Most health education programs were probably introduced within the past 20 years. Where programs have started, many are fragmented or piecemeal in scope. Some may be broad based (include a variety of topics) but few are what might be considered comprehensive. Some lose their priority status and become obsolete a few years after their initiation. Little has been done to assess the effectiveness of such programs on children's behavior. The situation is best described by the U.S. Department of Health and Human Services in its publication *Better Health for Our Children:*

Many school health education programs at present are neither sufficiently comprehensive nor sufficiently attuned to the influence of peer culture and other important determinants of youthful behavior to be truly effective in promoting good health habits.*

Teachers, nurses, administrators, and others who may desire to or have a duty to develop curricula for their classrooms and schools or those who wish to assume leadership to promote the introduction of health education programs in their districts will find practical material in this text. Programs may be prepared from the information found in the chapters that follow or from the illustrations and sources identified in this chapter.

WHY IS HEALTH EDUCATION NEEDED?

Education regarding health should be an essential component of the school curriculum at all grade levels.*

Julius B. Richmond, M.D., former Surgeon General of the United States, advocated that efforts of the Public Health Service (PHS), of

---

*Governing Council of the American Public Health Association: Education for health in the school community setting: a position paper, New Orleans, Oct. 23, 1974. (see Appendix C.)
†Education Commission of the States: Recommendations for school health education: a handbook for state policymakers, Denver, 1981, The Commission.

---

*U.S. Department of Health and Human Services, Public Health Service: Better health for our children: a national strategy, vol. 1, major findings and recommendations, Washington, D.C., Superintendent of Documents, 1981.

the U.S. Department of Health and Human Services, can best serve Americans through a preventive approach to health. As a result, the PHS has supported health programs in schools for a number of years by providing funds for curriculum development and demonstration projects and through evaluative studies.

The need for education about health and health care has been growing in recent years and has reached a high level of acceptance. There is increasing awareness among the public in general of the need for increased information and actions that will help persons, families, and communities. Federal and state laws have been passed mandating instruction in various aspects of health in curriculums. Parents and many community organizations have supported and actively campaigned for the inclusion of health education in school programs. The numerous student health problems and conditions identified in Chapter 1, many of which can be reduced by preventive action, clearly demonstrate the need for health education. There are a variety of specific reasons that justify the inclusion of school health instruction.

High cost of illness and medical care

In 1980 the expenditure for health care in the United States was approximately $246 billion,* and it has been rising each year at a rate of more than 10%. This sum represented 9.5% of the gross national product. The per capita outlay of funds for health care was in excess of $1,067. Physician fees for office visits ranged in cost from $20 to $35 depending on geographic location. The cost of room and board for a day in a hospital can exceed $200 and when other costs are added, the total may amount to $2,000. The so-called working poor and the elderly are the people chiefly affected when a continuing or

catastrophic illness causes a severe financial burden. However, middle-income families also pay a heavy price for health services because long and expensive illnesses may reduce them to poverty. It should be obvious that information provided at an early age that aids in preventive action could help reduce the costs of illness and medical care.

Gullible public

It is estimated that $10 billion annually is spent on worthless health products and services, many of which may even be harmful. Millions of dollars each year are wasted on valueless cancer and arthritis remedies. Approximately $150 million is spent on useless and fake remedies ordered through the mails. Over $1 billion is spent on questionable foods, fraudulent weight-reduction schemes, and fad diets, and another $1 billion goes for vitamins and minerals. In 1980 over $13 billion went for over-the-counter drugs and drug products, many of which were unnecessary. Quacks and quackery are rampant throughout the United States. Children and young people need to learn to make intelligent decisions regarding the purchase and use of health products and health services and know how to identify charlatans.

Health misconceptions

Children as well as adults lack accurate scientific health information. A study conducted by the U.S. Food and Drug Administration* identified many commonly held misconceptions, among which were the following:
1. Extra vitamins give more pep and energy.
2. The major reason for bad health is that people do not eat the right foods.

---

*Cornacchia, H.J., and Barrett, S.: Shopping for health care: a guide to products and services, St. Louis, 1982, The C.V. Mosby Co.

*Food and Drug Administration: A study of practices and opinions, Springfield, Va., 1972, National Technical Information Services, U.S. Department of Commerce.

3. Substantial weight loss can occur through perspiring.
4. A daily bowel movement is necessary for good health.
5. Most things that advertisements say about health and medicines are true.
6. Most things people buy in drugstores to treat themselves are practically worthless.

These inaccuracies expressed by adults are unquestionably related to the lack of information they received as children.

Health information confusing

Health information that people read or receive from friends, neighbors, and family members may be inaccurate or never clearly defined for a variety of reasons. Testimony from individuals may be based on opinions rather than scientific data. Often, factual information becomes distorted in transmission. The causes, prevention, and treatment of many illnesses including arthritis, cancer, and heart disease have not been completely identified. The media often dramatize the significance of preliminary data from limited scientific studies and mislead the public to believe the information is conclusive. The tremendous expansion of newspapers, magazines, books, and radio and television stations has produced an overwhelming amount of health information that is difficult for people to understand and interpret. The dissemination of false and inaccurate information by authors and writers is protected by the constitutional provision of "freedom of speech." One study conducted by the American Council on Science and Health* rated 19 popular magazines on the accuracy of nutrition information provided and revealed that four were reliable, eight were inconsistent in reliability, and six were unreliable. These factors make it virtually impossible for consumers to determine the reliability and validity of what they read and hear. The question

may be asked, "How does one determine fact from fiction?" Young people must learn to locate and use reliable sources of information to be able to identify truths from falsehoods.

Media influence on behavior

What people read or hear through the media influences their decisions to purchase and use health products and services. Advertising, however, is frequently unclear, misleading, and deceptive, often deliberately so. The intent is to capitalize on the ignorance of the consumer by describing a product in terms of a mystical ingredient physicians are said to recommend rather than in terms of specific contents and value. J. Thomas Rosch, former Director of the Bureau of Consumer Products of the Federal Trade Commission, stated that advertising claims have multiple meanings, one or more of which may be false or unsubstantiated from a technical standpoint.*

Children need help in learning how to analyze advertising to be able to determine the accuracy of information provided by the media.

Life-style and disease

American life-styles contribute to the high incidence of certain diseases such as cancer, heart disease, diabetes, and dental decay. Data reveal that people who exercise regularly, eat nutritious foods, obtain proper sleep and rest, control their weight and the use of alcoholic beverages and drugs, eliminate cigarette smoking, and reduce stress increase their potential to live longer. People who expose themselves to the identified risk factors increase their chances for ill health. One study that assessed the relative contributions of a variety of factors to the 10 leading causes of death suggested that about one half of the mortalities were caused by unhealthy

---

*Hudnall, M.: ACSH survey: how popular magazines rate on nutrition, American Council on Science and Health News and Views 2:1-2, Jan./Feb. 1982.

*Federal Trade Commission News, Feb. 26, 1974.

behavior and life-styles.* Schools can help children to eliminate or reduce the risk factors involved through a health education program.

Peer and adult pressures

Young people are under pressures by their peers to conform to group behavior patterns in such activities as smoking, alcohol and drug use, and sexual activity. In addition, young people wish to become adults and emulate adult behaviors. Students need to be prepared to know how to deal properly with these pressures as well as those they will encounter as adults. A comprehensive school health instruction program will help pupils acquire the skills needed to cope with the health problems and pressures confronted by both teenagers and adults.

Self-care

The focus on preventive aspects of health places emphasis on wellness rather than illness. Since good health has a high correlation with life-styles and behaviors, the concept of self-care needs development and implementation in the health instruction program. Children must learn to assume responsibility for their own bodies. They must be taught at an early age to make intelligent decisions on ways to reduce or eliminate risk factors that lead to ill health.

WHAT IS THE CURRENT STATUS OF HEALTH EDUCATION?

Despite the greatly increased awareness of the need for health education, the implementation of programs into local schools and school districts continues to leave much to be desired. Comprehensive curricula are being advocated but their numbers are not rapidly increasing. Most programs continue to be piecemeal and fragmentary. They consist of one or several

---

*Healthy people: the surgeon general's report on health and disease prevention, Washington, D.C., 1979, U.S. Department of Health and Human Services.

health subject areas at selected grades. However, the outlook for improvement in the future is optimistic. Events at national, state, and local levels support the positive outlook for school health education.

National

A chronology of recent significant legislation, activities, and offices established in support of health education includes:

1973: President Richard Nixon's Committee on Health Education reported that school health education in elementary schools was not, or was poorly, provided.

1974: The Bureau of Health Education (now the Center for Health Promotion and Education) was established in the Center for Disease Control, U.S. Public Health Service.

1975: The National Center for Health Education, a nongovernmental agency, was established in San Francisco to promote health education.

1975: A variety of federal agencies including the Public Health Service of the U.S. Department of Health, Education, and Welfare established as priorities for national health planning and resources development the prevention of disease and the development of effective methods for health education of the public.

1975-1976: The U.S. Congress gave consideration to the passage of the Comprehensive School Health Education Act. The bill never passed but it gave health education greater visibility, which was reflected in the amendments to the Elementary and Secondary Education Act in 1978.

1976: The Office of Health Information and Health Promotion was created in the U.S. Department of Health, Education, and Welfare (now the Department of Health and Human Services).

1978: Amendments to the Elementary and Secondary Education Act of 1965, Title III, authorized funds for states and local districts to develop and implement comprehensive school health education programs. Although no funds have been appropriated to date, local school districts now have legal sanction to expend funds awarded to states by the federal government under the so-called block grants provision for health education programs.

1979: The Office of Comprehensive School Health in the United States was established in the Department of Education to coordinate the variety of efforts in school health services, instruction, and environmental programs. Funds for the office staff were not continued under the new administration, and the office is not operative at this time.

1975-1980: The National Parent-Teacher Association Comprehensive School/Community Health Education Project was contracted for by the Bureau of Health Education (now the Center for Health Promotion and Education) to increase community awareness and understanding of health education needs and to develop support for more effective health education.

1980-1981: The U.S. Surgeon General's Office* expressed support for school health education programs.

State

In most states, laws require health instruction as part of the curriculum. This requirement is usually general in nature and not adequately

*U.S. Department of Health and Human Services, Public Health Service: Better health for our children: a national strategy, vol. 1, major findings and recommendations, Washington, D.C., 1981, Superintendent of Documents.

defined in terms of scope, sequence of topic, and time allotment. However, most state departments of education have prepared recommendations, guidelines, and frameworks for health instruction.

A summary of state requirements is found in Table 8-1. It reveals that 13 states require comprehensive health education, 4 mandate health education, 17 make health education optional for the local district to introduce, and 16 have no requirement. Every state requires certain health topics. This has led to fragmented rather than comprehensive programs. Alcohol, tobacco, and drug education is required in 38 states but the quality of instruction is not known.

Local

It is estimated that 300 to 400 health instructional programs may be found in the 1,500 elementary school districts in the United States. These vary in nature from individual topical programs to broad-based, comprehensive ones. Their impact on children has not been adequately evaluated. They have been financed by federal, state, and local district funds as well as by voluntary health agencies, private foundations, and a few industrial corporations.

The National Center for Health Education* prepared a report that contained limited infor-

*National Center for Health Education: A compendium of health education programs available for use in schools, San Bruno, Calif., 1982, The Center.

TABLE 8-1. State requirements for health education in general and by specific selected areas of health

Program	Health education	Alcohol, tobacco, drugs	Venereal disease	Family life/ sex education	Nutrition	Safety	Dental health	Consumer health
Mandated	4	38	13	8	13	16	10	9
Optional	17	4	12	16	16	13	13	14
No requirement	16	8	25	26	21	21	27	27
Comprehensive	13	—	—	—	—	—	—	—

Casile, A.S., Allensworth, D., and Noak, M.: School health in America: a survey of state school health programs, ed. 3, Kent, Ohio, 1982, American School Health Association.

mation about 102 instructional programs of which 78 were for elementary schools. Eleven of the 78 were developed by voluntary and government agencies and organizations and were not identified with specific school districts. A review of elementary programs, in which 30 states and the District of Columbia were represented, revealed the following types of programs:

39 broad-based (several topics covered)

9 comprehensive

1 School Health Curriculum Project (SHCP)*

1 Primary Grades Health Curriculum Project (PGHCP)*

28 individual topics: nutrition, 5; drugs, 5; vision, 4; heart, 3; human sexuality, 3; emotional health, 2; alcohol, 2; epilepsy, 1; fire safety, 1; parenting education, 1; dental, 1

Preschool children

The introduction of early education and day-care programs for children 3 to 5 years of age has resulted in new opportunities for health-related education for 3 million pupils. The federal government has advocated instruction and has developed health instruction materials for use in such programs as Head Start. Stress has been on the development of habit patterns relating to such areas as nutrition, safety, disease control, and dental health. In this text, the content material for teachers in Chapter 9 and the teaching/learning activities in Chapter 12 are useful in the development of health instruction programs for preschool children.

Special services for handicapped children

The passage of Public Law 94-142, the Education for All Handicapped Children Act of 1975, has resulted in greater emphasis on providing equal educational opportunities for handicapped young people. The act enables handicapped children to be integrated (main-

streamed) into regular academic classes. A number of school districts are now giving consideration to providing health instruction for these students. Suggestion for content may be found in Chapter 9. Many of the activities in Chapter 12, with modification, are useful.

WHAT ARE THE ADMINISTRATIVE PROBLEMS?

The major administrative problem is the low priority given to health education as a subject field by superintendents and school boards despite the increased recognition of need and the progress made in program development. The problem is compounded by these concerns now facing all U.S. public schools: (1) the questioning by the community of the quality of education, (2) the desire of parents for a return to an emphasis on basic subjects (reading, writing, arithmetic) in the curriculum, and (3) the curtailment of federal and state financial support.

These difficulties are formidable but are not insurmountable. Health instruction can be introduced into school curricula despite existing problems. School boards make the decisions regarding the adoption of health instruction as well as any other curriculum. As community representatives school board members are expected to serve the people they represent. Coordinated pressures by parents and health professionals can affect such decisions.

The presence of a health instruction program in a school is no assurance that it will have a positive effect on children. A quality program is dependent on the thorough consideration of a variety of administrative problems.

How should health instruction be included in the curriculum?

The question of whether to have a pattern of instruction that includes *direct* teaching or *integrative* teaching or both must be answered.

Direct teaching. The direct teaching approach is one in which health is identified as a separate subject in the curriculum with a specified amount of teaching time allocated in the

*See Chapter 10.

school day similar to that given to other subjects. Direct teaching provides status to health instruction as a necessary curriculum area. Its inclusion more likely provides the opportunity for a sequential program of learning throughout the grades. Direct teaching in health education allows for the attainment of attitudes and practices of healthful living by students that will enable them to develop life-styles conducive to good health.

The direct method of teaching must receive priority as the best approach to use in health instruction.

Integrative teaching. The integrative teaching approach is one in which health is taught throughout the many subject fields in the curriculum. For example, social studies may include information about health organizations and personnel—health departments, physicians, and nurses. When covering addition, subtraction, and multiplication in arithmetic, the teacher can relate these procedures to the numbers of oranges and apples in boxes or to determining the cost of 1 day's food supply; the structure and function of muscles and body organs may be included in science; language arts may include reading and writing about "Who Am I?" or a show-and-tell visit to the dentist; and the physical education program may cover safety on apparatus or on the playground. Actually, health-related matters can be integrated with any school subject.

The integrative approach presents two important problems for health instruction: (1) the major emphasis in the learning may be on a special subject area rather than health and (2) the learning objectives stressed may be on the acquisition of information, on factual data, or on the skills of writing, reading, or computation rather than on healthful living. By way of illustration, a lesson in reading from a nutrition text may focus on teaching students how to read rather than on eating the proper foods. If the health program's objective is to get pupils to eat nutritious foods, reading may be used to help students analyze the nutritional content of breakfasts, lunches, and dinners.

The integrative method can provide positive health learnings especially when used for reinforcement and repetition. It should not be the basic, nor the only, approach to the teaching of health. Health can serve as the core of the curriculum with all other subjects correlated.

Integrative health teaching is the only health program found in many schools that claim to have a health education program. The quality of such programs in terms of their impact on student health life-styles can frequently be questioned.

What about grade placement?

The determination of grade placement for any or all of the health instruction areas in the curriculum is a complex task. It has not been clearly defined by professional health educators nor by curriculum specialists. The reason is probably the variety of pupil and community health problems that must be locally identified and introduced. There is no single grade arrangement that will function best for all school districts. The pattern to be used must be selected on an individual basis. The suggestions that follow are based on our many years of curriculum experience.

Grade placement in health education is determined through the use of several curriculum principles and a number of additional factors. Three principles in need of attention are (1) that student needs and interests are fundamental, (2) that instructional areas should be sequentially organized through the grades, and (3) that repetition of subject areas is necessary for the reinforcement of learning.

Student needs and interests used in curriculum development may or may not be felt. Therefore in addition to pupil involvement through surveys and other means further information must be derived from state laws (some mandate specific content areas by grades or grade level groups), review of the growth and developmental characteristics of children, examination of local community health problems, identification of ethnic, religious, and racial factors, observations of pupils by parents, and data from physicians, dentists, and other health professionals, including those in health departments.

The sequence of subject areas in health instruction through the grades must follow a pattern that is related to children's growth and development (for example, dental health at the first grade level because of the appearance of the 6-year molar; menstruation for girls at the fifth or sixth grade level), and to their felt and unfelt needs and interests. The curriculum information presented to pupils must flow from simple facts to more complex concepts as students move upward in grade level.

The content and objectives provided in the sequence of learning must give consideration to reinforcement of learning without repetition throughout the grades. It may be advisable to space or cycle some health areas. For example, nutrition can be introduced in kindergarten or earlier and repeated in grades 1, 3, 5, and 7. Not every health area needs to be taught at every grade. There may not be enough time in the total school curriculum for such consideration.

The several additional factors that affect grade placement include the amount of time to be devoted to health instruction at each grade, whether the instruction is to be through direct or integrated teaching, and whether the educational program will be both formal and informal.

Adequate amounts of time are needed in the formal instruction program for direct teaching to have a positive effect on student life-styles. Such provision will enable the spacing procedure to be introduced into the health curriculum and help reduce the problem of excessive repetition of information, yet allow for the necessary reinforcement of learning to take place.

Informal health instruction has always existed in schools when, for example, students went to visit the nurse or asked a teacher about a specific health problem. This generally occurred incidentally, on an unplanned basis. Although the word *informal* connotes actions that take place spontaneously, there is need for a limited amount of planning. In recent years, except perhaps in drug education, little informal health instruction has occurred. Drug counselors or people knowledgable about drugs have been available to meet with students individually or in small groups on a voluntary basis for information or guidance. In a few schools, voluntary student group meetings, in which opportunities were provided for pupils to ask questions or merely listen to discussions on specific health problems, have been held after hours. Informal gatherings of this nature need to be included into health instruction programs, although planning will need to be limited in an informal learning setting. They should be correlated with the direct teaching program. Presently there are no guidelines for the conduct of this kind of instruction.

The sample school health Scope and Sequence chart found in Table 9-1 provides an illustration of grade placement for health instruction. The content areas were determined through a survey of pupil needs and interests, with consideration given to growth and development characteristics, and through the use of a variety of other information and procedures. The areas have been cycled and are not taught at every grade; however, the individual teacher in any given grade can use judgment to repeat health areas in immediate higher grades depending on student needs. This curriculum provides for direct teaching in the formal instructional program.

How much time should be allotted?

The amount of time needed to teach health instruction adequately at any given grade level or throughout the grades has not been adequately researched. Therefore the best information available today is based on expert professional opinions.

By way of illustration, a curriculum project for fire prevention for elementary schools sponsored by the National Fire Protection Association,* in which 200 teachers from seven cities participated, attempted to determine the

---

*National Fire Protection Association: Learn not to burn curriculum, Boston, 1979, The Association.

amount of time needed to teach this content area adequately. The results showed that, on the average, 5 hours (about 20 minutes weekly for one semester) was needed to adequately cover the material.

Some health education experts have advocated that the time provided for health teaching at any grade level should be roughly equal to that given to any other basic subject or area of learning in the elementary school curriculum. This perhaps is the ideal arrangement, but it is unrealistic today because of the many school problems and the low priority for health education. The following suggested minimum amounts of time are reasonable expectations that more easily can be adapted to fit present crowded school curricula:

Primary grades: 15 minutes daily for at least one semester per grade per year

Intermediate grades: 20 minutes daily for at least one semester per grade per year

Upper grades: 45 to 50 minutes weekly for at least one semester per grade per year

The organization and use of this time in classrooms should be discretionary with teachers. They may wish to have extended learning periods on given days and use the allotted weekly time in 1 or 2 days.

The question of the amount of time to be provided at specific grades must be based on pupils' needs and interests, the patterns of instruction, and the total elementary school curriculum. Local schools and school districts must individually determine the amount of time to allot for health instruction.

Who is responsible for the program?

The development, maintenance, and continuance of a health instruction program will not take place without one person in the school or school district who has supervisory or administrative responsibility. This individual should be professionally qualified in the field of health education. A person designated as the health coordinator, supervisor, or consultant could be a health educator, a physician, a nurse, or a teacher. Someone is needed who has access to the school superintendent and the school board. This person must be given the responsibility (1) to develop the curriculum, (2) to seek funds for support of the program, (3) to conduct in-service teacher preparation programs, (4) to communicate with parents and community organizations and agencies, (5) to order and help select teaching aids and equipment, and (6) to supervise and administer the program. Unfortunately, except perhaps in some large districts, there are not many such people employed in local school districts.

Many school nurses have become qualified in the field of health education and have assumed or been assigned health education responsibilities in schools. These are some of the ways nurses may provide assistance:

1. Help with the selection and location of teaching aids
2. Locate resources for community materials and speakers
3. Assist in curriculum and lesson planning
4. Teach classes on occasions
5. Serve as school health committee members
6. Consult with teachers regarding instructional possibilities of health services programs
7. Aid in evaluation of the programs
8. Assist in curriculum development

Despite the lack of administrative or nurse assistance in schools that have no program, individual teachers who feel competent and wish to introduce health instruction into their classrooms will find sufficient information in this text to develop a program. These teachers should also understand that the variety of state and local government offices, health departments, and voluntary and professional health agencies and organizations in the local community have many services to provide on request.

Who should teach health education?

At the elementary level the primary responsibility for the teaching of health should rest with the classroom teacher. This person is familiar with teaching methods and is in the best position to maintain, coordinate, and integrate the program into the curriculum. Where nurse services are readily available, teachers should not hesitate to use them as a resource and bring them into the classroom to discuss specific health topics and to use them in other ways.

Although some nurses are qualified to teach health education, for them to serve on a full-time basis and in all classes would be logistically impossible. Many districts may provide only limited nurse services. Besides, if nurses are expected to be involved in the health services program and possibly the environmental health aspect of the program, their multiplicity of responsibilities would not permit them to participate extensively in health education.

In-service training programs should be provided for teachers who are expected to teach health and do not feel qualified. Those teachers who wish to become prepared in health education or desire to upgrade their competencies can do so by taking college and university courses and workshops, reading current health literature, and seeking help from the many available community health resources.

What about financing?

School districts must provide funds in their budgets for the development, supervision, personnel, and teaching aids needed for health instruction programs. No program can start or continue to exist without adequate financial support by school boards.

The present economic situation may necessitate that schools seek community help for the development and maintenance of health instruction programs. Two sources of funds that have been used with varying degrees of success by some districts are (1) voluntary health agencies, local health departments, and other governmental offices, and (2) solicitations from industrial corporations. In recent years more businesses including banks and insurance companies have been providing funds for school health instruction programs.

Should parent education be included?

The need for both formal and informal education of parents is justified on the basis that many health behaviors occur outside the classroom, in the home and the community. Without parental support and cooperation, the effectiveness of school health instruction will be greatly reduced. Parents need to approve the objectives of the program, especially if it includes sex education and drug education. They need to understand the nature of the school program.

Parent education, although difficult to make operational, can be achieved through planning and concerted effort. Formal education can take place through lectures, films, group discussions, and other procedures. Information regarding the inclusion of controversial areas must be communicated to parents.

Informal education may occur through parent-teacher, nurse-parent, or nurse-parent-teacher conferences, special bulletins, telephone calls, notes home, newspaper articles, radio and television presentations, and in many other ways. Counseling and guidance can be effective in handling individual student problems.

The extent of parent health education is believed to be sporadic in U.S. schools, and its effectiveness is not known.

What controversial areas should be included in the curriculum?

Sex education and education about sexually transmitted diseases, drug education (including alcohol and tobacco), and values education are curriculum areas parents generally have the greatest concern about including in the health instruction program. The primary arguments raised in the controversy are as follows:

1. Students will be encouraged to experiment with sex and drugs.
2. The home and/or church should be responsible for this education.
3. Schools are not capable of dealing with moral and ethical issues, that is, with values education.

4. Schools may teach values that are in conflict with the home or church.

5. Parents generally prefer teaching abstinence in the use of drugs and sexual involvement rather than moderation or intelligent decision making.

6. Teachers are not competent to teach these subjects.

Many student problems are connected with these controversial areas. Unfortunately numerous parents are unable, unwilling, or lack the information to provide the counseling and guidance their children need. Schools have a responsibility to attempt to help students and parents cope with these problems through programs of instruction and in other ways. Should schools decide to introduce any or all of the controversial areas into the curriculum, these factors must receive consideration:

1. Parents, with community support from health departments, physicians, voluntary health agencies, churches, and others, should give approval to the inclusion of those curriculum areas identified. Involvement of these individuals and organizations in the preparation of the curriculum will provide understanding and enhance the chances of approval.

2. Curricula must be approved by the school board. School board members are representatives of the people and will supply the funds to implement and support the program.

3. Teachers must be qualified to teach the subject areas. In-service programs may be necessary to develop curricula and teacher competencies. Teachers must be interested in, feel comfortable with and capable of teaching the subject to which they are assigned.

4. Teachers should be well-adjusted, emotionally stable, mature persons with a wholesome and positive outlook on life. They must be individuals who are acceptable to parents and the community. Parents should be provided the opportunity to meet the teachers who will conduct the instructional programs. Parents need to feel comfortable and assured that these teachers will give proper consideration to their educational wishes.

5. Parents should be provided the opportu-

nity to view teaching materials. This is mandatory for sex education in some states.

6. The curriculum areas in terms of objectives, content, and materials should be periodically reviewed and approved by parents and appropriate community groups. School districts cannot expect that a program approved in any given year will have support in later years. The needs and problems of students and the nature of families and community representatives are constantly changing.

Controversial areas have been approved for inclusion in the curriculum and have generally been successful in school districts where these factors have received adequate consideration.

What should be the role of the community?

The school as a part of the community must involve parents and health and safety organization representatives in the development, maintenance, implementation, and assessment of health instruction programs. The extent and nature of their specific participation must be determined by each school or school district.

Parents can provide valuable assistance in a variety of ways that include (1) identification of student health problems, (2) help in the conduct of pupil need and interest surveys, (3) service on health instruction committees, (4) organization of community support for instructional programs, (5) persuasion of school boards to develop and conduct health education, and (6) assistance with evaluation procedures. Health departments, voluntary health agencies, medical and dental organizations, and individual physicians and dentists can participate in parent activities and in addition can help to (1) determine the nature and accuracy of the curriculum content, (2) determine the feasibility of the program objectives, and (3) provide, select, and assess teaching aids.

Is evaluation necessary?

The health instruction program periodically should be quantitatively and qualitatively assessed to determine the extent to which school objectives have been achieved. Quantitatively it is important to know whether the curriculum is adequate. Some of the questions that should be answered include: Are the subject areas provided sufficient to meet student needs? Is the curriculum guide useful? Are the teaching aids effective? It is more important, however, to discover the quality of the program in terms of its impact on student behavior. It is necessary to learn life-style changes in terms of student practices, attitudes, and knowledge.

The evaluation process in health education has not been greatly used nor adequately developed. Qualitative assessment of the health program has rarely occurred except to determine the extent of knowledge students have acquired. Chapter 14 provides information that will help with the evaluation process.

SUMMARY

The awareness of the need for health instruction programs, although fairly well-established, continues to require development. Many parent and community health organizations and agencies support the inclusion of health education in school curricula. Despite the establishment of several national and governmental health education agencies and organizations, as well as the existence of numerous state requirements, few comprehensive health instruction programs may be found in schools. Fragmented curricula consisting of one or more content areas are evident in many school districts. Health instruction programs may be justified because of the spiraling costs of medical care, health misconceptions, a gullible public, confusion about health information, the media influence on behavior, the relation of life-style to disease, and the need for self-care. The implementation of effective programs in schools can be achieved through the resolution of a variety of administrative problems.

QUESTIONS FOR DISCUSSION

1. What evidence exists that indicates there is increased support for health instruction programs in U.S. schools?

2. What factors identify the need for the health education of elementary school children?
3. What is the current status of health education in the United States today at the national, state, and local levels?
4. What are the administrative problems in need of school attention to ensure effective health instruction programs?
5. Identify and describe the patterns of health instruction that may be used in schools. What are the advantages and disadvantages of their use? Illustrate their application to health instruction.
6. What principles are used in the determination of the grade placement of health education in schools? Illustrate their application to the health instruction program.
7. How much time should be provided in the elementary school curriculum for health education? What factors are used in determining the amount of time for health education?
8. Who should teach in the elementary school health instruction program? Why?
9. Why should parents be included in the elementary school health education program? How can this be achieved?
10. Why are some topics considered to be controversial in health education? What factors need school consideration for decisions to include these topics in the instruction program?

SELECTED REFERENCES

American Academy of Pediatrics: School health; a guide for health professionals, Evanston, Ill., 1981, The Academy.

American Public Health Association, School Health Section: Education for health in the school community setting, Washington, D.C., 1975, The Association.

Anderson, C.L., and Creswell, W.H.: School health practice, ed. 2, St. Louis, 1980, The C.V. Mosby Co.

Castile, A.S., Allensworth, D., and Noak, M.: School health in America, ed. 3, Kent, Ohio, 1982, American School Health Association.

Cornacchia, H.J.: Elementary health education curriculum, Journal of Health, Physical Education, and Recreation, April 1958.

Cornacchia, H.J., and Barrett, S.: Consumer health, a guide to intelligent decisions, ed. 2, St. Louis, 1980, The C.V. Mosby Co.

Cornacchia, H.J., and Barrett, S.: Shopping for health care: the essential guide to products and services, New York, 1982, Mosby Medical Library.

Culliton, B.J.: Preventive medicine, legislation calls for health education, Science, Sept. 26, 1975.

Don't teach us what you want to teach, teach us what we want to know, Journal of School Health, May 1969.

Education Commission of the States: Recommendations for school health education: a handbook for state policymakers, Denver, 1981, The Commission.

Federal Trade Commission News, Feb. 26, 1974.

Food and Drug Administration: A study of practices and opinions, Springfield, Va., 1972, National Technical Information Service, U.S. Department of Commerce.

Hill, P.: Health education needs of preschool and school age children, School Health Review, Sept./Oct. 1972.

Hudnall, M.: ACSH survey: how popular magazines rate on nutrition, American Council on Science and Health News and Views 3:1-2, Jan./Feb. 1982.

Joint Committee on Health Problems in Education: Why health education in your school? Washington, D.C. and Chicago, 1974, National Education Association and the American Medical Association.

Levin, H.M., editor: Community control of schools, New York, 1976, Simon and Schuster.

McGavran, E.G.: The role of primary prevention in public health, Health Education, July/Aug. 1977.

Metropolitan Life Insurance Company: Longevity in the United States at a new high, Statistical Bulletin, May, 1977.

Miller, A.C.: Health care of children and youth in America, American Journal of Public Health, April 1975.

National Commission on Community Health Services: Health is a community affair, Cambridge, Mass., 1966, Harvard University Press.

Russell, R.D.: Health education, Washington, D.C., 1975, Joint Committee on Health Problems in Education of the National Education Association and the American Medical Association (available from the American Alliance for Health, Physical Education, and Recreation and Dance, Washington, D.C.).

Sliepcevich, E.M.: School health education study: a summary report, Washington, D.C., 1964, School Health Education Study.

Sliepcevich, E.M.: Curriculum development: a macroscopic or microscopic view? The National Elementary Principal, Nov. 1968.

U.S. Department of Health, Education and Welfare: Health services and mental health administration: the report of the President's Committee on Health Education, Washington, D.C., 1973, Superintendent of Documents.

U.S. Department of Health and Human Services: Healthy people: the Surgeon General's report on health and disease prevention, Washington, D.C., 1979, Superintendent of Documents.

U.S. Department of Health and Human Services, Public Health Service: Better health for our children: a national strategy, vol. 1 major findings and recommendations, Washington, D.C., 1981, Superintendent of Documents.

Why teachers are under fire, U.S. News & World Report, Dec. 12, 1977.

Willgoose, C.E.: Health education in the elementary school, Philadelphia, 1974, W.B. Saunders Co.

9

ORGANIZING FOR HEALTH TEACHING

There is general agreement among authorities on the importance of planning and organizing for health education. This is critical if objectives are to be attained in the cognitive (knowledge), affective (attitudes), and action (behavior) areas of child development in schools. Clear definitions should be provided in curricula in terms of what pupil goals teachers should be seeking, what content should be included, what methods and materials are to be used, and whether the purposes established have been achieved. Ideally, experiences for pupils should be provided in a humanistic setting that are both scientifically fact oriented and pupil inquiry oriented. The purpose of this chapter is to provide information and direction to this end.

Health education must be organized in both formal and informal ways if the differing needs and interests of students are to receive proper consideration. Pupils with drug problems, including alcohol and tobacco, with sex concerns, and with emotional and psychologic difficulties frequently cannot be helped except on one-to-one or small group arrangements. To date, insufficient attention has been given to the informal approach in schools. Chapter 6 provided a variety of ways to guide and counsel young

people. This chapter and succeeding chapters focus on organizing for formal health teaching.

Curriculum development and implementation is basic to organizing for formal health and safety teaching. A variety of tasks need attention, including determination of what shall be taught and the preparation of units for teacher reference and use. In addition, teachers need help in developing their own plans for teaching and guidance through illustrative units.

Before presenting material in regard to curriculum development and teacher planning, it is important to understand some basic principles involved, to be familiar with the conceptual approach, to be aware of the usefulness of values clarification as a strategy in health education, and to have knowledge about personnel responsibility for the preparation of the curriculum.

WHAT ARE THE BASIC PRINCIPLES FOR CURRICULUM DEVELOPMENT IN HEALTH EDUCATION?

For any educational function to proceed on a sound basis, it must be predicated on certain valid principles or assumptions. If we begin with a firm foundation of fact and philosophy, we cannot stray far from the path of excellence. To choose learning experiences on the basis of established principles is to assure worthwhile education for pupils; to select on the basis of popularity, newspaper headlines, tradition, personal bias, and yesterday's problems is to run the risk of failure in preparing children to live most and serve best in a complex, changing society.

Fundamentally, a sound curriculum must be based on the needs, problems, and opportunities of society and the individual. Beyond this broad approach are certain principles and assumptions that may be used as guidelines for curriculum planning and development in health education:

1. Provision for a sequential, comprehensive program of instruction that includes the ascending spiral effect allowing for an increasing depth of information from kindergarten through grade 12

2. Provision for repetition of content areas without excessive duplication through the cycling of such areas, or in other appropriate ways

3. Adaptability and flexibility to allow for changes and modifications, introducing new content, new information, and new materials as they develop and emerge in society

4. Use of the concept approach in curriculum development with particular emphasis on health, concepts, and objectives

5. Emphasis on the preventive aspects of health in the instructional program with a focus on self-care responsibilities

6. Health emphasis that includes physical or physiological, sociological, psychological, and spiritual aspects

7. Emphasis on the needs and interests of students in forming the basis for the curriculum so it will be appropriate to the local community or communities and the social climates in which pupils reside; special consideration must be given to the children and youth problems of minorities and those with ethnic and cultural differences

8. Provision for writing goals in behavioral terms, including cognitive, affective, and action domains*

9. Provision for goals observable in the classroom, nonobservable, and delayed in their attainment in the action domain where it is appropriate and possible.

10. Provision for goals, with the following differential emphasis at the grade level groups indicated whenever possible:

   a. Primary grades—focus on physiological aspects of health with limited psychological and social aspects

   b. Intermediate grades—focus on physiological aspects of health with greater inclusion of psychological and social aspects and limited spiritual emphasis

   c. Upper grades—focus primarily on psychological and social aspects with decreasing emphasis on the physiological aspects but with concern for the spiritual phases

11. Provision for inclusion of all the alternatives to action so that students can make intelligent decisions regarding behavior

12. Allowance for students to make their own decisions regarding behavior

13. Current content, accurate and nonbiased, derived from scientific sources; both positive and negative aspects to be included whenever possible

14. Use of the principles of learning (see Chapter 11) in the selection of the methods or techniques of teaching for behavioral changes that stress student involve-

---

*The drug problem resulted in new educational terminology, such as humanistic, affective, and confluent education, and emphasis being introduced in schools. The need for students to develop positive self-concepts, to express feelings and aspirations, to reach social maturity, and to participate in values clarification has led authorities to support affective-humanistic education. It is believed such emphasis will enable persons to more effectively cope with life's problems. Confluent education refers to the integration of affective and cognitive elements in learning. These are worthwhile directions for inclusion in health education. The clearly written objectives found in the units in this chapter include these new ideas.

ment, decision making, critical thinking, discussions, problem solving, self-direction, development of values, and responsibility

15. Use of a variety of resource materials that are interesting, current, accurate, carefully screened, and appropriate for the grade level intended

16. Involvement of students, parents, and community representatives in the development and evaluation of the curriculum

17. Provision for periodic assessment of various aspects of the curriculum

These principles and assumptions may seem to be self-evident, yet so often elementary school programs of health education blatantly ignore one or more of these guidelines. The material that follows is based on these principles and their application.

THE CONCEPTUAL APPROACH

For many years researchers in psychology and education have attempted to better understand how children learn so they can help pupils learn more effectively. The concept approach is one of the more promising methods to evolve from their efforts.

Concept formation

Learning involves thinking. The thinking process may include one or more of these six types of thinking: *perceptive, associative, inductive-deductive, creative, critical,* and *problem-solving.* The formation of concepts involves the use of the perceptive process.

Percepts are simplified conclusions that students obtain from seeing, hearing, touching, tasting, and smelling. They are the raw materials of thinking that result from environmental stimuli. In the classroom these stimuli are generally provided and controlled by the teacher and may include the teacher's oral presentation, other pupils' comments, content of health textbooks, films, bulletin board information,

and a host of others. Perception is essential to concept formation.

Inhelder and Piaget* indicate that children's ability to understand broad concepts, or generalizations, and abstractions depends on their ability to have direct sensory experiences. These experiences help them to construct and reconstruct percepts. Modern research show that sensory-motor experiences (for example, manipulation and construction) are most effective in developing percepts. Then, through use and application of these raw materials of health instruction, children can understand and deal with more abstract concepts. For example, "use of substances that modify mood and behavior arises from a variety of motivations," is a concept. It is a rather obtuse statement that necessitates specific sensory experiences for understanding and comprehension. Pupils may need to discuss, hear comments by drug abusers, and review literature about why people use drugs to grasp the meaning of the concepts.

Thus children are exposed to, screen, and select stimuli. The stimuli produce percepts that lead to the formation of concepts, which are conclusions or generalizations.

Concepts applied to health education

The concept approach to health education emerged from the School Health Education Study conducted under the leadership of Dr. Elena Sliepcevich† that was introduced in the mid-1960s. It continues to be a valid and useful procedure for use in curriculum development. It was prepared using current educational philosophy, was innovative, and was the first and only attempt to scientifically develop a health education curriculum that followed the basic principles used for all other educational

---

*Inhelder, B., and Piaget, J.: The growth of logical thinking from childhood to adolescence, New York, 1958, Basic Books, Inc., Publishers.

†Lieberman, E.J., editor: Mental health: the public health challenge, Washington, D.C., 1975, American Public Health Association.

curricula. It is fundamental to the eclectic plan identified in this text, which gives consideration to a variety of other significant prevalent ideas, including holistic health (physiological, psychological, social, and spiritual), student needs and interests, prevention, and ecology.

Health concepts are conclusions or generalizations that result from learning experiences to which students have been exposed. They cannot be taught directly. They emerge from exposure to the variety of activities introduced by teachers from which students derive perceptions. They serve as the organizing framework to use in determining the content and in preparation of the objectives of the curriculum. Thus after students have completed their learnings, they should be able to conclude that, "Most dental diseases and disorders are preventable and treatable," "Proper use of drugs may be beneficial," or, "The selection of nutritious foods in a balanced diet is necessary for growth and health."

Examples of realistic and effective applications of the conceptual approach are the health education curriculum illustrative partial units, which are represented on pp. 175-230.

VALUES IN THE CURRICULUM

Family life-style changes, the influence of the mass communications media, technologic innovations, world events, materialism, conflict of conformity and self-reliance, ethics, and affluence among others are creating difficulties in the establishment of values by young people. As a result, youth are searching for meaning in life. They are asking, "Who am I? Why am I here? What really matters?" They desire to cope with daily problems, to develop life coping skills, to understand themselves, and to be able to make wise decisions. Because of the failure to answer these questions a variety of patterns of behavioral problems have been appearing in schools. Such problems include apathy, inconsistent behaviors, drifting, dropping out, overconforming, and overdissenting. Schools have a major role in helping children

and youths at early ages to begin to clarify their values.

Raths and others,* among other leaders in the field of psychology, have indicated the need for individuals to have a sense of purpose in their lives. People actively search for meaningfulness and identity in life, although some may never be able to clearly define or to achieve such a goal. The achievement or failure of achievement of a sense of purpose may affect an individual's mental health either positively or negatively.

There is no single, clear definition of values. They have been said to be deep, long-lasting commitments to a concept or doctrine that is highly prized and about which action will be taken in satisfying ways. They are characteristics or attitudes about human experiences that are strongly desirable to an individual or group of individuals. Values give direction to life and may be considered to be determinants of behavior. They aid in the making of decisions and judgments. They have been identified in the concept of health described in Chapter 1 as part of the *spiritual* aspect of health in the isosceles triangle illustration (see Fig. 1-2). They have been included in the units in this chapter in the affective domain objectives.

Values may be learned through a variety of meaningful experiences and through interaction with the environment. Thus the sources of values are adults, peer cultures, the family, the church, the communications media, friends, social groups, and the school.

Raths and others believe the focus—probably starting in the intermediate grades—should be on value clarification and not on the teaching of values per se. They believe values will emerge through this process. Didactic value clarification involves a series of strategies or methods for helping students learn values. They state that a *value* must meet these seven criteria:

---

*Raths, L.E., Harmin, M., and Simon, S.: Values and teaching; working with values in the classroom, Columbus, Ohio, 1966, Charles E. Merrill Books, Inc.

Choosing

1. Choosing freely—individual should not be coerced and should have freedom of selection.
2. Choosing from alternatives—a variety of alternatives must be provided.
3. Choosing thoughtfully—consideration should be given to the consequences of each alternative
4. Affirming—when something is cherished, it is publicly and verbally supported: doing something

Prizing

5. Prizing and cherishing—choice has a positive tone and is held in high esteem.

Action

6. Acting on choices—life is affected through reading, spending money, and budgeting time.
7. Repeating—persistency and endurance become a pattern of life.

Ten value-rich areas identified by Raths and others are useful in the clarification process: money, friendship, love and sex, religion and morals, leisure, politics and social organization, work, family, maturity, and character traits.

Value clarification has a place in health education as part of both content and methodology. It has particular application to the areas of mental health, drugs, human sexuality, alcohol, smoking, health care, and environment, but it is also useful in other health areas. The outlines of content found in the illustrative units in this chapter contain suggestions. Some of the strategies that are useful are found in Chapter 12.

The inclusion of values clarification in health teaching may be considered controversial by parents in some communities. The suggestions for arriving at a decision on whether to include them in the curriculum are found in Chapter 8, p. 157.

Loggins* claims that the value clarification process may only superficially treat values. It cannot be assumed that students will evaluate or decide on their own values. The conceptualization and organization of values may require cognitive elements for analysis, synthesis, and evaluation. The method does generate interest and stimulate student discussion, but Loggins is not sure about the contribution of the method of values education.

---

*Loggins, D.: Values clarification revisited; clarifying what and how well, Health Education 7:March/April 1976.

WHO IS RESPONSIBLE FOR DEVELOPING THE CURRICULUM IN HEALTH AND SAFETY?

Curriculum development and improvement have become a major function of modern education. Not too long ago the curriculum was shaped largely by experts in the various disciplines. However, in recent years the subject-matter authority has been joined by teachers, pupils, and lay citizens in planning curricula. This does not mean that the opinions of experts are minimized or disregarded. It means simply that a curriculum can be developed to fit a certain school and community best if opportunity is provided for teachers, pupils, and lay groups to adapt the curriculum to local interests and needs.

For example, an elementary school in Florida might want to give time in the curriculum to hookworm infestation and "creeping eruption" (a skin infestation caused by dog and cat hookworms), instead of spending time on frostbite and winter sport safety. An impoverished area school in the inner city might decide to stress the problems of unwanted pregnancy and sexually transmitted disease at an earlier grade level than a school in suburbia. A rural school might emphasize the importance of water purity and sanitation, whereas an urban school might take more time for air pollution. A school whose pupils come from families where ethnic and racial backgrounds shape their daily meals would surely want to stress the place of Italian, Mexican, Oriental, Indian, and "soul" foods as they apply in choosing a balanced diet.

Thus we find real need for adapting the curriculum to best meet local problems in many areas of health and safety. Yet fundamentally the subject matter is the same for all schools and all children. It is the fringe areas and the manner of illustrating basic concepts that offer the best opportunity for adaptation.

Curriculum development is a shared responsibility. Even though the approach may differ from one community to another, the curriculum in health and safety should reflect the interests, concerns, and efforts of teachers, pupils, parents, physicians, dentists, public health specialists, law enforcement officials, civil defense authorities, school board members, fire department officials, representatives of voluntary health agencies, school nurses, principals, curriculum specialists, and school health coordinators. These people, working together at the local level, can fashion the most fundamental and functional curriculum for their local school situation while retaining the common learnings in health and safety. Often the local group will need to make only a few minor changes in a course of study that has been prepared by the state department of education, by a county school office, or perhaps by some other school district.

Again, the matter of cooperative planning and action can be very helpful. The school health council at the district level, under the direction and guidance of the health coordinator or consultant, can give considerable support to the curriculum development program. The health council usually represents the thinking of most, if not all, concerned persons and organizations. Moreover, it provides a ready-made mechanism for resolving many variances in philosophy and for implementing group decisions.

Experience in the national School Health Education Study showed that very few school districts throughout the country have the personnel resources to develop a sound, up-to-date health education curriculum on their own. If a health coordinator is not available, schools should seek guidance from state or local colleges and universities.

Most important of all is the fact that critical analysis of the curriculum in health education must be a continual process if the instructional program is to be truly functional in the lives of children. The rapid advances in the health sci-ences no longer permit the schools to "stand pat" for very long on content. Sequence too is affected by the increasingly frequent medical and health science developments and problems. These are in the main accurately and promptly reported in newspapers, magazines, telecasts, and other media. Often such health science reporting provides the teacher with a "teachable moment"—a time when pupils are more likely to be motivated—for a topic that had not been planned. Examples are many: new vaccines for measles and German measles, the sexually transmitted diseases, zero population growth statistics, elimination of smallpox vaccination from the standard schedule, toxic shock syndrome and tampon use, the energy crisis, radiation hazards, new drugs being used and abused, quackery and fraud in the health marketplace, and a host of others.

The wise teacher will be flexible enough to depart from the lesson plan and take full advantage of the heightened interest of pupils when these stories "break." The unimaginative teacher will cling steadfastly to the planned sequence and, ignoring publicized fresh facts of importance, plow ahead with the predetermined unit on a less relevant topic. The choice separates the truly innovative teacher from the inferior journeyman.

HOW IS THE CURRICULUM DETERMINED?

To determine what should be taught in health education, it is necessary to identify the health interests and needs of pupils from which a scope (content) and sequence (grade levels) chart (see Table 9-1) is prepared for use in determining what units need to be constructed. Consideration must be given to the special problems of minorities.

Interests and needs

The following is a variety of information sources useful in determining the scope and sequence of the curriculum.

Pupil interests. Pupils learn better when they have interest in the subject matter. In essence, interest is an attitude favorable to learning. Beyond this, interest hinges on the values, desires, wants, and purposes of the pupil. As children perceive the relationship of a topic to their personal advantage and well-being, they become interested. The *active interests* are those that relate here and now to the child's daily life and world. *Latent interests* are those that the child may have had at an earlier age, but that were stifled because parents and other adults would not or could not encourage and develop them. Finally, since interests depend heavily on past experiences, there are many areas in which pupils have practically no interest. It is one of the central purposes of education to amplify and diversify the interests of children. Thus pupil interests, although vital to motivation, cannot be considered in themselves as complete indicators of the relative importance of topics in health and safety.

Yet teachers should identify pupil interests and emphasize those already developed. This is simply good motivation. Latent health interests (for example, "What makes me grow?" "Where do I go when I sleep?" "Where do babies come from?") will have to be further developed and new interests will need to be created if health teaching is to be effective.

A 1969 report* by the Connecticut State Department of Education provides remarkable insight into the health interests, concerns, and problems of elementary school pupils. To date there has not been a more complete research project. This study involved more than 5,000 students from kindergarten through the twelfth grade. It showed, among other things, that basic health interests were common to all pupils whether they lived in a city, rural, suburban, or high socioeconomic environment. The questions and comments of elementary-age children were grouped according to three levels: kindergarten through grade 2, grades 3 and 4, and grades 5 and 6.

Boys and girls in kindergarten and first and second grades showed interest in a broad variety of health problems but were unsure of what health is and had only a vague concept of it. They were more interested in not being sick than in being healthy; when not sick, they can run, play, and have fun. Most of the questions they asked were related to their health, growth, and development. Sample key interests and concerns in the various areas of health and safety are cited.

KINDERGARTEN THROUGH GRADE 2
What is good health?

"You don't have measles or mumps."
"You eat lots of vegetables and fruits and no coffee."
"You brush the dirt off of your teeth."
"You take vitamin pills."

About the body

"How does my body get made?"
"What makes you stop growing?"
"Why do men have big muscles and ladies don't?"

About aches, pains, and diseases

"How can I tell if I have a fever?"
"Does a vaccination keep you healthy?"

About family health

"My mom gets us new babies; she feeds us, picks me up when I fall, cleans me off."
"I help my mom and dad."
"I don't think I have enough love for two fathers."

About relations with peers

"You don't do anything right, you don't do it the way we do."
"He doesn't take a bath, his ears are dirty."

GRADES 3 AND 4
What is a healthy person?

"Isn't too fat or too skinny."
"Doesn't play with matches."
"Doesn't go to the hospital."
"Eats everything he should, the right vegetables, not too much fattening food or candy, has a well-balanced diet."

---

*Byler, R.V., Lewis, G.M., and Totman, R.J.: Teach us what we want to know, New York, 1969, Mental Health Materials Center, Inc. for the Connecticut State Department of Education.

About accidents

"The doctor is nice."
"I like the hospital."
"I was glad to come home."

About personal health and safety

"I don't want your germs."
"I didn't mean to do it. Frank was chasing me, and I ran into the street."
"A car might come along and hit him, and he'll end up in the hospital."
"How many hours should you sleep to keep healthy?"
"How does toothpaste help to keep your teeth clean?"
"Should you bite your fingernails?"

About family health

"How can you tell which is a cow or a bull?"
"They use the bull so the cows can have babies who will grow up to be milk cows."
"You can't have babies, if you're too young."
"Where does a baby come from?"
"How does it get out of the mother's stomach?"
"Do you know what abortion means?"

What would you like to study in health?

"The eyes—why do they become bloodshot?"
"Why do some people become mentally ill?"
"Why do some people go blind?"
"Why should we destroy LSD?"

About the body

"What is healthy blood?"
"How do lungs grow when we grow?"
"Why do we lose baby teeth?"

About food and nutrition

"What kinds of liquids should you drink to keep healthy?"
"How do people get fat?"
"How do vitamins help keep us strong?"

About exercise and physical education

"Does exercise help you?"
"How does exercising really take off fat?"
"What are the best exercises to do?"

About first aid and safety

"If you fall and think you are hurt, what should you do?"
"If you are way out in the woods a long way from a doctor, and someone got killed, what would you do?"

About mental health

"If you worry too much, will you get sick?"
"Why do I get so lonely?"
"How do you get mental illness?"

About problems of the entire society

"How many people in the world are healthy and how many aren't?"
"What illness do you get from smoking?"
"What is the difference between a doctor and a surgeon?"
"What do nurses do?"

About drugs, smoking, and alcohol

"Why do so many people take shots of marijuana, STP, LSD, 'snow,' and 'speed'?"
"Is marijuana a dangerous drug? How does it affect you?"
"Why do so many people smoke?"
"Why do people drink so much?"

GRADES 5 AND 6
What is a healthy person?

"He eats right and drinks milk."
"Doesn't smoke and drink."
"Goes for a checkup."

What is health?

"Health is exercising; keeping yourself fit; maintaining a strong body and preventing defects."
"Health is physical and mental."

About the body

"How does a body grow? I'd like to know *all* about the body."
"Why do we have hair?"
"Why do girls grow up faster than boys?"
"Why do girls have periods and boys don't?"

About food and nutrition

"What are the best foods for a person to eat?"
"What foods are bad for you?"
"What should we eat for a good diet?"
"What vitamins should you have and what are the effects of a lack of vitamins? This is fun to learn about."
"What makes you fat?"

About personal health

"We should know about care of the teeth and about cavities, about bathing, keeping clean, and having good breath."

About exercise and physical education

"The health plan in Connecticut should consist of a very good gym system. Have good, well-trained teachers. Have large playgrounds. Have more track meets and different sports."

About babies

"How is a baby formed?"

"How can birth control pills stop birth?"

"Why can't you have a baby when you are not married?"

About mental health

"It's the way kids get along together."

"I would like to understand my personality."

"Why do I act happy, sad, angry?"

"Why can't I control my temper?"

"I would like to help others and to understand them."

About social-emotional development

"Why do I sometimes hate my friends? What is a real friend, what can I do to make friends?"

"I am well-liked at school, but in trouble at home."

"Why can't I get along with my brother or sister?"

About drugs, alcohol, and smoking

"Why do people take drugs?"

"What do they do to you?"

"Can anyone ever break the drug habit?"

"How does it feel to go high on LSD?"

"When do people want to smoke?"

"Smoking is our greatest health problem."

"Why do they sell cigarettes?"

About environmental health

"When will air pollution, alcohol, smoking, and other things like these be cured or stopped?"

"Factories pollute the air and water."

"Why don't people stop killing and start loving?"

Surely these provocative questions and stimulating statements confirm the adage that "out of the mouths of babes" come some of the most perceptive comments. While these are randomly selected responses of elementary school children included in the Connecticut study, they reflect some of the more important interests and concerns of children across the nation.

Pupil needs. Student needs may be considered as falling into two groups: those that are *felt* by children and those that are prevalent

health and safety problems but are *unfelt* by children. *Felt needs* are the wants and desires of students that can be expressed in *interest surveys* such as the one completed by the Connecticut State Department of Education. *Unfelt needs* are health problems and concerns from other sources and those expressed by people other than pupils. Such information comes from mortality and morbidity statistics, accident statistics, growth and development characteristics of children, state laws regarding health instruction areas, local, state, and national health departments, voluntary, commercial, and professional health agencies and organizations, pupils' health records and absenteeism records, and other sources. Some of the people who can provide information about health problems of children include parents, teachers, nurses, physicians, dentists, and health officials in health departments and health agencies.

Using the wide variety of sources and people identified may be logistically difficult if not impossible to handle in determining the nature of the health instruction curriculum, even with computers. Local schools and school districts may find it more convenient to select a sampling of procedures to provide the best representative information on the needs of their pupils. However, large districts and statewide curriculum projects may find it advantageous to conduct extensive surveys of student interests and needs.

The illustrative units found in this chapter include a broad approach to pupils' interests and needs.

SCOPE AND SEQUENCE

To determine the scope and sequence of health teaching in the elementary school program, it is necessary to consider the needs and interests of children at all age levels from kindergarten throughout the elementary school. The material developed by the Ellensburg public schools in the state of Washington is a good illustration of how one school system provided for these needs in their scope and sequence (Table 9-1). It should be noted that recent evidence indicates learning about alcohol, tobacco,

TABLE 9-1. A sample public school health scope and sequence

Areas	K	1	2	3	4	5	6	7	8
Alcohol							X	√	X
Anatomy and physiology	X	√	√	X	X	X	X		
Community	√	√	√		X		X		
Consumer	√	√	√		√	√	√		X
Dental health	√	X	X	X	X		√		√
Disease	√	√	√	√	X		√	X	X
Drugs							X	√	X
Family	X	X	√	√	X	X	X	X	X
Health careers									√
Mental health	√	X	√	√	√	√	√	√	√
Nutrition	X	X	X	X		X			√ First aid
Safety	X	X		X	*√	*X	*X		X
Smoking					X	X		X	√
Exercise, rest, and sleep	√	√	√	√	√	√	√	√	

X = Study in depth with relationship to the level of the learners.

√ = Unit developed and will be taught; however, depth will be left to the judgment of individual teacher.

* = Special emphasis on recreational safety to coincide with camping program

and other drugs may take place at earlier grades than shown; perhaps at the fourth grade.

Organized health instruction should be provided at all grade levels throughout the elementary school. There are a number of important reasons why it should be offered at all levels. First, the body of knowledge concerning health and healthful living in the modern world is so extensive that it is necessary to offer it over a period of years to adequately impart the knowledge needed. Second, there is a need for a certain amount of health knowledge at all ages, even including kindergarten children. The degree of maturity of children in the elementary grades is such that they cannot be given the extensive knowledge needed for adult life. Yet it is highly important that instruction be given and that the various phases of health and healthful living be introduced to the children as rapidly as their maturity and level of intelligence will permit.

From the viewpoint of psychology it is much easier to establish proper habits of health and healthful living early in the child's life. Also, the child needs to practice good health and safety habits just as much at an early age as later. Therefore it seems psychologically sound to teach as much as possible about health as early

as possible, considering the stages of maturity of the children. An example of this is in the area of nutrition, which is a phase of the health education program at practically all grade levels. The subject of nutrition should be introduced and developed as far as the ability of the children at any particular age level permits, for nutrition is a functional part of the life of the primary-age child just as it is of an older child. If by educating children in nutrition to their capacity at the primary level we can better assure their optimum nutrition, then it is obvious that the subject should be introduced in school just as early as possible. Even though primary-age children are not mature enough to be given all the safety information they need for life, it is highly important that they know as much about safety as possible to safeguard their lives while growing up. As an example, the failure to teach elementary school children certain facts about traffic safety could result in a child's death or permanent disability.

What then can we consider to be properly included in the course of study for health and safety in our elementary schools? As we know, the needs of communities, states, and regions may differ somewhat in that some problems are specific for certain localities but not for others.

Yet, in the main, the fundamental concepts are essentially the same. Content of safe and healthful living, which research and experience have shown to be necessary to a sound, productive program of health education in elementary schools, is outlined here.

Health content for the child in primary grades

What it means to be healthy
Why we need good health
How our bodies are made and how they work
How we grow
Good food for growth and health
Taking care of our feet
Rest and play for good health and growth
Seeing and hearing well
Caring for our teeth
Drugs, alcohol, and smoking
Fighting diseases that are catching
Working and playing with others
People in our town who help keep us healthy

Safety content for the child in primary grades

What it means to live safely
Why we need to act safely each day
Safety in our homes
Safety in our neighborhood
Playing safely
Safety in walking or riding to school
Preventing fires
Safety in the water
Safety on the school grounds
Safety in our school buildings
People in our town who help us keep safe

Health content for the child in intermediate and upper grades

The meaning of physical, mental, and emotional health
The importance of health in living happily and usefully
The machinery of our bodies
Growing up physically (including growth problems that begin at about the fifth- or sixth-grade level)
Choosing the best foods for energy, growth, and health
Proper food and drink to protect our health
Fresh air and sunshine for everyone
Exercise, relaxation, and sleep for better health
The eyes and ears of our world

Good teeth for better health and appearance
Helping our feet support us
Caring for our skin, hair, and nails
Immunization and fighting infection
Looking and feeling best in proper clothing
Growing up socially and emotionally
Drugs, alcohol, and smoking
Wise choice of health products and services
Living healthfully in the family
Emergencies and accidents action
Working for the health of our town

Safety content for the child in intermediate and upper grades

Adventure and safety
What the accident problem means to us
Safety on our streets and highways
Safety at the beach and in the pool
Sports safety
Safety at home (including farm safety where appropriate)
Safety at school
Using firearms with care
The danger of fire
Bicycle safety
Safety as a passenger in motor vehicles
Safety in hiking and camping
Checking safety hazards in our neighborhood
People in our town who work for our safety

In general, surveys have shown that the elementary health curriculum should include units on nutrition; consumer health; growth; exercise; sleep; rest and relaxation; dental health; eyes and ears; family life and health; mental health; safety; first aid; alcohol, tobacco, and other drugs; body mechanics; structure, function, and care of the body; control of diseases; medical and dental care; community health problems; and chronic diseases. Many of these areas are covered in the illustrative units found on pp. 174-230.

Special education

Pupils in special education classrooms need to be provided learnings in health education. They have problems and interests similar to those of the so-called normal students. For those who

TABLE 9-2. Health education for special children

	Levels*				
Areas	**I**	**II**	**III**	**IV**	**V**
Safety	*Emergencies* Awareness and simple first aid Communication Report	*Traveling* Pedestrian Passenger Bicycle	*School* Classroom Building Playground	*Home* General Fire and electricity Appliances and equipment	*Recreation* Environment Use of equipment and games Bicycle and camping
Mental health	*Self-acceptance* Physical abilities and limitations Mental abilities and limitations Cultural and social differences	*Acceptance of others* Physical abilities Mental abilities and limitations Cultural and social differences	*Values* Personnel Home and school Community and national	*Adjustment to stress* School Home Community	
Family living	*Roles in family* Recognizing roles Learning roles Accepting changing roles	*Home management and maintenance* Supervised responsibilities Simple independent responsibilities Self-directed responsibilities	*Family and child care* Supervised responsibility Simple independent responsibilities Self-directed responsibilities	*Sex education* Sex organs Reproduction	
Nutrition	*Foods* Sources Types Components	*Diet* Selection of basic food Planning of daily menus Effects of components	*Preparation and preservation of foods* Cleaning and storing Preparation of food for meals Preservation of foods	*Health problems* Weight Vitality Allergies	
Body care and personal hygiene	*Cleanliness* Routine Grooming Body changes	*Respect and protection of body parts* Dental care	*Rest and exercise* Awareness of need Understanding of need Ways and means	*Proper clothing and shelter* Awareness of need Understanding Ways	
Disease and illness	*Communicable disease* Symptoms Causes Treatment	*Sanitation* Personal Home and school Community	*Personal care* Awareness Communication Treatment	*Health services* Knowledge of community Knowledge and location of services When and how to use	

Prepared by a group of special education teachers in Ellensburg, Washington.
*Refers to stages of learning progression. Children move from level to level upward when ready regardless of grade.

are mentally retarded, much of what is used in the regular program in sex education can be adapted to simpler presentation. Also the use of more visual aids and repetition is necessary. For those who have cerebral palsy, special tooth-brushes and prophylactic implements can be prepared for oral health. For blind students, braille materials should be created. Teachers will need to develop their own items, make adaptations, or explore community resources for assistance.

A suggested health education program usable in a classroom where there are different types of handicapped children is found in Table 9-2.

Health education curriculum for preschool programs

Children regardless of their ages should be exposed to educational programs about health. Many habit patterns are established early in life, and numerous health problems are preventable in the formative years. The school setting offers opportunities to influence the development of behaviors and to reduce problems. Preschool programs should include curricula in health education. The information in this chapter including the unit materials that are categorically listed as well as the activities in Chapter 12 at the primary grade levels are useful. Teachers will need to extrapolate the applicable sections and to adapt and organize them into suitable units and lessons. However, the U.S. Office of Child Development Project Head Start prepared a curriculum guide useful to teachers. The following represents a suggested content outline adapted from that reference.*

All about me
My body (inside, outside, functions of body systems)
Who am I? (sex, race, ethnic group)
Real me (How do I feel inside? happy, sad, angry, afraid, lonely, and so forth)

---

*Adapted from the Office of Child Development Project Head Start: Healthy that's me; a health education curriculum guide for Head Start, Washington, D.C., 1971, U.S. Department of Health, Education, and Welfare.

Accident prevention and first aid
Home
Fire
Playground
To and from school
Dangerous strangers

Disease control
Germs
Infections
Colds
Coughs
Immunizations and other control

Dental health
Decay
Brushing and flossing
Sugar foods

Nutrition
Selection of nutritious items

Rest, sleep and exercise
Need for and adequate amounts

Who helps to take care of health
Family (parents, physician, teacher, school nurse; vision and hearing testing, and others)

THE UNIT IN HEALTH TEACHING

Few concepts in education are less understood than is the unit or the unit method. Unit teaching is basically a good way of organizing for teaching.

It is common for both prospective and certified teachers to become confused about the definition, concept, nature, and purpose of the unit approach. This is entirely understandable when one reviews the educational literature. It seems that each writer places his or her own interpretation on the unit and its use in improving instruction in the classroom. But through the fabric of a multitude of definitions is woven the common thread of organization. Both topics and learning experiences are organized in such a manner that they are related to a central theme or problem. Thus units in health are built around fundamental concepts in health and the major problems of children and society in safe and healthful living.

Most statements of unit organization and content include certain essential elements: objectives, content, teaching aids, activities, and evaluation procedures.

Certainly the unit is far superior to teaching in a hit-or-miss fashion. Yet the most carefully planned and thoroughly detailed health unit falls short of its purpose and potential if it deals with trivia. Occasionally teachers may be led to believe that the process is more important than the learning products. When this happens, teachers may become so infatuated with the procedures and techniques of the unit approach that they fail to pay enough attention to the significance of the knowledges, attitudes, and practices they seek to develop among pupils.

The unit approach is one of the best means available for organizing more meaningful learning experiences. Beyond this, the unit helps assure a sound, logical presentation of subject matter. It represents an effective blending of psychological and logical organization of topics and concepts.

In the preparation of the objectives for the units found in this chapter, the taxonomy (classification) of educational goals that was developed by Bloom and associates* and has been widely used in curriculum development in the United States was used.

---

*Adapted from Bloom, B., editor: Taxonomy of educational objectives. Handbook I: Cognitive domain, New York, 1956, David McKay Co., Inc. and Krathwohl, D.R., Bloom, B.S., and Masia, B.B.: Taxonomy of educational objectives. Handbook II: Affective domain, New York, 1964, David McKay Co., Inc.

TAXONOMY OF OBJECTIVES

Cognitive domain (knowledges/understandings)

Know—define, name, relate, list, recall, explain, state, recite, tell

Comprehend—predict, draw conclusions, diagram, illustrate, discuss, classify, recognize, identify, report, review, describe

Apply—solve, translate, demonstrate, dramatize, illustrate

Analyze—identify, distinguish, establish criteria, conclude, interpret, translate, classify, criticize, debate, question, examine

Synthesize—plan, integrate, summarize, develop, compare, design, create, prepare, construct, formulate, compose

Evaluate—compare, contrast, differentiate, judge, rate, appraise, select, assess, measure, estimate

Affective domain (attitudes: feelings, appreciations, values)

Attend (be receptive)—talk about, be supportive, listen, display interests, be attentive

Respond (be impressed)—ask questions, react, give opinions, bring things to class

Value (rate highly)—accept, support

Action domain (practices)

Act, eat, wash, brush, buy, avoid, refrain from, demonstrate, choose, place, obey

Illustrative partial units for primary, intermediate, and upper grades

The illustrative partial units that follow, covering many of the important health content areas teachers may use in planning for health instruction, include such areas as consumer health; dental health; disease control; exercise, rest, and body control; drugs; family health; mental health; nutrition; safety and first aid; and vision and hearing. Note that they follow the basic principles previously identified and give consideration to the new definition of health, the concept approach, and values.

COMMUNITY HEALTH UNIT
Outline of content

Physiological

Definitions: public health (community health), preventive medicine, preventive health care, immunity, screening tests

Community health problems: communicable diseases (sexually transmitted disease, tuberculosis, upper respiratory infections, hepatitis, measles, German measles, polio, rabies, tetanus, typhoid, mononucleosis, food infections); noncommunicable diseases (heart and circulatory disorders, cancers and leukemias, emphysema and chronic bronchitis, diabetes, arthritis, allergies, ulcers, skin conditions); blindness and other eye defects; dental problems; maternal and child health; mental health; suicide; drug abuse, including alcohol and tobacco; accidents; malnutrition; pollution, accidental pollution

Psychological

Why public health? lack of public understanding of purposes and activities of community health personnel and organizations; improvement of individual, family, and group health; preventive approach; need for group efforts to prevent or correct certain health and accident problems

Social

Public health organizations: U.S. Public Health Service; state health department; local health department; World Health Organization; The American Heart Association; The American Cancer Society, Inc.; The American Lung Association; The National Society to Prevent Blindness; The National Association for Mental Health, Inc.; The National Foundation; The National Association of Hearing and Speech Agencies; National Clearinghouse for Drug Abuse Information; The Planned Parenthood Federation of America, Inc.; The American Social Health Association; The American National Red Cross; The American Diabetes Association, Inc.; National Sickle Cell Anemia Research Foundation; Muscular Dystrophy Association of America, Inc.; The National Safety Council

Community health programs and activities: prevention and control of diseases (communicable and chronic); infant and maternal deaths; malnutrition; mental illness; drug abuse; accidents; dental and oral defects; hearing problems; blindness and vision disorders; suicide; accidental poisoning; environmental pollution

Public health personnel: increasing need for community health personnel; career opportunities in public health (health educator, public health physician, public health dentist, public health nurse, sanitarian, environmental specialist, safety consultant, mental health counselor, hospital administrator, school nurse, and dental hygienist)

Professional societies: medical society; dental society; osteopathic association; optometric association

Spiritual

Values: value of public health in protecting, maintaining, and improving human health

Moral issues: Should citizens contribute money voluntarily to private agencies and through taxes to official organizations for the support of community health programs? Is each individual responsible for the health and safety of others?

Humanism: concern of community leaders for the health and safety of all citizens

Concepts

Concept	Application of health definition
1 Public health programs protect, maintain, and improve the health of people in a community through group effort.	Social-spiritual
2 As members of the community, children and youths are entitled to public health services and resources.	Social-spiritual
3 Public health agencies and organizations function at the local, state, national, and international level.	Social
4 Community health programs are carried out by official and voluntary organizations.	Social-spiritual
5 All citizens can help improve individual, family, and community health by supporting the work of health departments and health agencies.	Social-spiritual-psychological
6 Community health organizations conduct preventive and control programs for diseases, infant and maternal deaths, malnutrition, mental illness, drug abuse, accidents, blindness and other visual defects, hearing problems, dental neglect, poisoning, and environmental problems.	Physical-social
7 Public health departments generally are not adequately supported by tax funds.	Social
8 Through careers in the health sciences, many individuals contribute to the health of the community.	Social-spiritual-psychological
9 The school health program is part of the overall community health program.	Social

Objectives for grades K-3

Domain	Objectives for students	Basic concepts
Cognitive	1. Explains the general purpose of public health.	1
	2. Identifies several local health agencies.	3, 4
	3. Explains why public health services should be available to everyone.	1, 2, 6
	4. Lists reasons why people should support community health programs.	5, 7
Affective	1. Displays interest in learning more about health departments and agencies.	3, 4, 6
	2. Asks questions about who pays for community health programs.	5, 7
	3. Asks questions about the work of physicians, school nurses, dentists, public health workers, and other people concerned with community health.	2, 5, 8
	4. Shows interest in the value of group effort in preventing and solving certain health problems.	1, 5, 6
Action	1. Cooperates with teachers, school nurses, and others involved in the school health program.	2, 5
	2. Assists wherever possible with school or community health efforts.	2, 5

Objectives for grades 4-6

Domain	Objectives for students	Basic concepts
Cognitive	1. Lists the major purposes of health departments.	1
	2. Cites examples of public health organizations and agencies.	3, 4
	3. Explains the chief differences between official and voluntary health agencies.	4
	4. Understands the importance of school health and other community programs concerned with child health.	2
	5. Explains the need for community support of public health programs.	5, 7
	6. Cites examples of health careers.	8
	7. Lists health problems that may be prevented or solved by community health programs.	6
Affective	1. Displays interest in the basic philosophy of public health.	1
	2. Asks questions about the different programs and aims of official and voluntary health agencies.	3, 4
	3. Accepts the need for community health programs and personnel.	1, 2, 5
	4. Appreciates the need for financial and other public support of community health programs.	1, 5, 7
	5. Shows interest in and concern for major community health problems.	5, 6
	6. Displays interest in career possibilities in public health work.	8
Action	1. Seeks reliable sources of information regarding community health programs.	2, 5, 6
	2. Visits the health department and other local agencies when recommended as part of a community health project.	2, 5, 6
	3. Cooperates with school health projects.	2, 9

Objectives for grades 7-8

Domain	Objectives for students	Basic concepts
Cognitive	1. Discusses the importance of public health for all communities.	1
	2. Lists reasons why community health programs are especially important for children and youth.	2
	3. Explains the nature and functions of health departments at the local, state, national, and international levels.	3
	4. Explains differences between official and voluntary agencies with regard to personnel, financing, relative emphasis on services, research, and education.	4, 5, 7
	5. Compares the need for the group approach with that of private medical and dental care.	1, 6, 8
	6. Cites the reasons for public support of community health programs.	5, 7
	7. Identifies by purpose, activities, and location major health agencies in the community.	3, 4
	8. Explains the three basic phases of the school health program.	9

Domain	Objectives for students	Basic concepts
Affective	1. Appreciates the social values of community health programs.	1, 5
	2. Shows interest in the quality of local community health services.	2, 5, 7
	3. Asks questions about the most pressing needs in public health at the local, state, national, and world levels.	3, 6, 7
	4. Appreciates the purposes of the school health program.	9
	5. Offers opinions on the responsibility of government to provide effective public health programs for all citizens.	1, 3, 7
	6. Displays interest in differences between official and voluntary health agencies.	4, 5
	7. Inquires about public health career opportunities.	8
	8. Shows concern for the quality of the school health program.	9
Action	1. Cooperates whenever possible with special projects of the health department or voluntary agencies.	2, 4-6
	2. Talks with parents about the values of a good community health program.	1, 3, 5-7
	3. Takes part in school health projects.	2, 9
	4. Seeks information on needed legislation for the improvement of local, state, and federal public health programs.	1, 4, 5, 7
	5. Seeks information on educational requirements and opportunities in one or more public health careers.	8

CONSUMER HEALTH UNIT*
Outline of content

Physiological

Definitions: consumer health (economics of health), health products, health services, self-diagnosis, self-medication, prevention, effects of health products, nature of various health examinations, medical care, health insurance

Psychological

Why consumer health? self-diagnosis and self-medication; advertising inducement; spiraling costs; misinformation and lack of information; vast amount of scientific information; preventive medicine concept

Why do people purchase health products and services? self-diagnosis and self-medication; less expensive treatment; improvement of health status; advertising; the need for help; condition minor in nature; ignorance of hazards; lack of information; religious beliefs; friend or peer recommendations

Why do people go to quacks? lonely; refusal of physician to listen to problem; hopeless case for treatment or cure; mysticism; the desire for pleasant, easy cure; physician's limitation in dealing with problem; psychological problems

Budgeting for health care: estimate of yearly costs of products and services; insurance; emergencies

---

*See also Cornacchia, H.J., and Barrett, S.: Consumer health: a guide to intelligent decisions, ed. 2, St. Louis, 1980, The C.V. Mosby Co.

How to act as an intelligent health consumer: a skeptic; critical and analytical of what is read, seen, or heard regardless of source; initiator of investigation; identification of quacks and quackery, fads and frauds, or suspicious of same; knowledge about when to call or visit doctor, dentist, or other health professionals; knowledge about how to select a doctor, dentist, and other health professionals; knowledge of what to expect from a physician, dentist, and other health professionals, and also what is expected by these individuals of patient; application of sound criteria in purchase of health products or services; reading of labels; knowledge of where to seek, how to obtain, and how to seek reliable health information; initiative taken to go to protection agencies and organizations for help

Social

Health products
Arthritis—cures, devices
Athletics and fitness—drugs, vitamins, weight reduction, mechanical aids, spot reducers, vibrator machines, isometric versus isotonic exercises
Cancer—Krebiozen, Laetrile, Hoxsey treatments and cures
Cosmetics—deodorants, hormone creams, and wrinkle removers
Dental—toothpaste, toothbrushes, Water Pik, and others
Drugs—use and misuse, aspirin, over-the-counter, and others
Hearing—hearing aids, mail order of aids
Mechanical—bust developers, rupture devices, silicones, vibrators, seawater
Nutrition—vitamins, food additives, weight control diets, organic and natural foods
Tobacco—smoking cures and filters
Vision—glasses by mail, sunglasses, and contact lenses
Others—cough and cold remedies, laxatives, preparations for hemorrhoids, skin blemish removers, allergic conditions, bad breath, hair restorers, and impotency cures

Health services
Health examinations—what, when, who does, frequency, and cost
Types of health specialists
    Physicians—general practitioners, internal medicine, pediatrics, or surgery
    Dentists—general practice, orthodontics, oral surgery, and others
    Psychologists—general, clinical, and family counselor
    Also podiatrists, pharmacists, optometrists, osteopaths, and nurses
Hospitals and clinics—types, licensing, standards
Health insurance—types, services, costs
Criteria for selection of health specialists—license to practice, preparation and training, member of local health profession society in good standing, night calls, discussion of fees in advance, opinion of others, hospital affiliation
When to call health specialist—complaint or symptoms too severe to be endured; persistence for more than few days; symptoms' repeated return; accident

Role of business in health products: self-control versus governmental control; psychology of selling; mass communication media; analysis of advertising

Protection of the consumer
Agencies and organizations
    Government—FDA, FTC, Post Office, health departments
    Professional—AMA, ADA, American Pharmaceutical Association
    Voluntary—cancer, arthritis, heart, lung, Better Business Bureau
Laws—federal Food, Drug and Cosmetic Act; advertising limitations; labeling of products
Education—formal and informal, sources of information from family, friends, and school

Sources of reliable health information: reputable individuals, such as physicians or dentists; also from scientific books, magazines, and publications; questions such as, What is reputation, training, and experience of authors and sources? Is there a profit motive involved in the writing? Are the data accurate and up to date? What do other sources say about the topic or material?

Quacks and quackery

Definition—boastful pretender to medical skills; a charlatan; ignorant or dishonest practitioner

Motivational factors—money, power, prestige

Identifying factors—disregard or misinterpretation of scientific evidence; acceptance of money for worthless or questionable treatments, products, or services

Why some quack cures work? spontaneous remission of some diseases, placebo effect, psychosomatic effect of encouragement of patient

Spiritual

Values: differing healing philosophies or cult values—medicine, osteopathy, acupuncture, herbalists, faith healers, Christian Science, Jehovah's Witnesses, and chiropractic

What is the effect of differing values on the selection, purchase and use of health products and services?

Moral issues: Is an ethical code needed in advertising, in the business world? Is an ethical code needed in medicine, dentistry, and the health professions?

Humanism: What should be the relationship between medical practitioners and patients?

Concepts

Concept	Application of health definition
1 Health products and health services may have beneficial and harmful effects on individuals.	Physiological
2 Self-diagnosis and self-medication and the use of quacks and quackery may be hazardous and costly to individuals.	
3 Individuals purchase and use health products and services for a variety of reasons.	Psychological
4 Wise decisions regarding the selection, purchase, and use of health products and services necessitate individuals acting as "intelligent health consumers."	
5 The use of scientific information is necessary for the effective evaluation, selection, purchase, and use of health products and services.	
6 Appraisal, selection, purchase, and use of health products and services are influenced by past experiences and the environment.	Social
7 There are reliable and unreliable sources of health information.	
8 The community provides a variety of organizations, agencies, and laws to protect the health consumer.	
9 Individuals differing in values and philosophies regarding the healing and health treatment of individuals influence the selection, purchase, and use of health products and services.	Spiritual
10 Ethical considerations involved in the selling of health products and the rendering of health services.	

Objectives for grades K-3

Domain	Objectives for students	Basic concepts
Cognitive	1. Identifies people who can help promote and protect one's health.	8
	2. Identifies people who can help when injured or ill or who prescribe medicines.	8
	3. Explains the reason for caution when taking medicines.	1, 2, 4
	4. Lists the reasons adults should help to supervise the taking of medicines.	1, 4, 8
	5. Concludes that medicines may be necessary at times for health.	1, 4, 7
	6. Explains the effect of mass media on the purchase and use of health products.	3-6, 8
	7. Identifies a variety of sources of health information.	4, 5, 7
Affective	1. Asks questions about the hazards involved in taking medicines without adult supervision.	1, 4, 8
	2. Is attentive to the discussion regarding the dangers involved in the consumption of unfamiliar food and liquids.	1, 3
	3. Supports the need for medicines when prescribed by physicians.	1, 2, 4, 8
	4. Is attentive to discussion about the various people who can help when a person is ill or injured.	8
	5. Displays interest in the effect of the mass media on the purchase and use of health products.	3-6, 8
Action (observable)	1. Informs parents, teachers, and others when injured or not well.	8
	2. Demonstrates limited skill in analyzing mass media advertising.	3, 4, 7, 8
	3. Seeks health information from a variety of sources.	4, 5, 7
(nonobservable or delayed)	4. Refrains from taking medicine without adult supervision.	1, 4, 8
	5. Refrains from consuming unknown foods and liquids.	1, 2, 4

Objectives for grades 4-6

Domain	Objectives for students	Basic concepts
Cognitive	1. Lists the hazards of self-diagnosis and self-medication.	2
	2. Identifies reliable sources of health information.	7
	3. Explains factors that affect the reliability of health information.	4, 5, 7
	4. Lists the types of mass media that may have an influence on the purchase and use of health products and health services.	6
	5. Is able to apply criteria in analyzing labels and advertisements of various kinds.	1, 3, 6, 8
	6. Explains the influences of friends and family on the plans to purchase and use health products and health services.	6, 8
	7. Identifies a variety of health products that are used in self-treatment and explains problems related to their use.	1, 2, 8
	8. Discriminates between reliable and unreliable health information and advertising.	7
	9. Cites examples of agencies and organizations that protect the consumer.	8

Domain	Objectives for students	Basic concepts
Affective	1. Displays interest in the need for reliable sources of health information.	5, 7
	2. Asks questions in regard to the hazards of self-diagnosis and self-medication.	1, 2
	3. Accepts the need for establishing criteria for use in the selection of health products and health services.	4, 5, 7
	4. Is aware of the significance of the influence of religious beliefs, customs, superstitions, fads, and family on consumer health purchasing.	3, 6, 9
Action (observable)	1. Seeks reliable sources of health information when necessary.	5, 7
	2. Seeks appropriate health services personnel when injured or ill.	8
	3. Can analyze labels and advertisements using established criteria.	3, 4, 8
(unobservable or delayed)	4. Avoids self-diagnosis and self-treatment.	2
	5. Uses established criteria when making decisions to purchase and use health products.	4, 5, 7

Objectives for grades 7-8

Domain	Objectives for students	Basic concepts
Cognitive	1. Identifies a variety of health products available and explains their effects on individuals.	1
	2. Recalls the laws that attempt to protect the health consumer.	8
	3. Explains quacks and quackery and their effects on people.	1-4
	4. Describes the nature, frequency, cost, and significance of health examinations.	2, 4, 8
	5. Identifies the various types of health specialists and services available to help individuals.	2, 4, 8
	6. Compares the healing or health treatment philosophies or cults found in society.	6, 8, 9
	7. Identifies the criteria to follow to become an "intelligent health consumer."	4
	8. Compares the role of a variety of community organizations and agencies in protecting the health consumer.	8
	9. Identifies the reasons why individuals purchase and use a variety of health products and services.	3
	10. Explains the reasons supporting a code of ethics for business establishments making health products available and for those rendering health services.	10

Domain	Objectives for students	Basic concepts
Affective	1. Accepts the need for reliable sources of health information.	4, 5, 7
	2. Displays interest in the need for skepticism in consumer health.	4
	3. Supports the need for laws and community organization and agencies to protect the people in consumer health.	8
	4. Is supportive of the need to understand quacks and quackery.	1, 2, 4, 5, 7
	5. Is attentive to the need for health examinations.	1, 8
	6. Listens to the discussion regarding the types of health specialists available.	2, 8
	7. Asks questions about the different healing and health treatment philosophies.	6, 9
	8. Displays interest in the need for the application of a code of ethics in the business world for manufacturers, advertisers of health products, and those rendering health services.	10
Action (observable)	1. Seeks reliable sources of health information.	4, 5, 7
	2. Is skeptical regarding health information from advertising and other sources until it can be verified.	4, 5, 7
(nonobservable or delayed)	3. Uses the criteria for an "intelligent health consumer" when considering the purchase or use of health products and health services.	4
	4. Seeks the help of community agencies and organizations when information or assistance is needed in regard to health products and health services.	8
	5. Refrains from the purchase and use of health products that are detrimental to one's health.	1, 2

DENTAL HEALTH UNIT
Outline of content

Physiological

Structure and functions of teeth

Structure—divisions—crown (top), neck, root (base); layers—enamel, dentin, cementum, pulp

Types and numbers of teeth—primary (deciduous), twenty (incisors, cuspids, molars); permanent, thirty-two (eight incisors, four cuspids, eight bicuspids, twelve molars)

Functions—chewing; speech; appearance; primary hold spaces for permanent teeth

Diseases and disorders

Dental caries—tooth decay

Causes—bacteria plus sugars = acid = decay; pathway—enamel, dentin, pulp; plaque—gluey, gelatinlike substance adhering to teeth where bacteria collect and act on food

Contributing factors—heredity, tooth structure, saliva, bacteria, sugar

Periodontal diseases

Gingivitis—inflammation of gums; pyorrhea—advanced gingivitis involving gums and bone

Symptoms—"pink" toothbrush from bleeding gums; red, swollen, tender, gums

Causes—irritation from dental calculus that results from substances secreted by bacteria in plaque; sharp edges of badly decayed teeth, worn-out fillings rubbing on gums; malocclusion, poor nutrition, systemic diseases

Prevalence—major cause for tooth loss over 35 years

Malocclusion—improper bite; effects—interferes with chewing, speech, and appearance; harder to clean

Causes—heredity, acquired factors—pressures on teeth including thumb sucking, mouth breathing, tongue twisting, lip sucking, sleep and sitting habits

Stains—(1) extrinsic—food pigments, tobacco and caffeine, metallic dusts; green stain in children—bacteria, fungi plus inorganic elements (calcium); (2) intrinsic—within tooth structure; caused by pigments in blood; imperfect tooth development

Abscess—infection affecting blood, lymph vessels, and nerves in pulp; due to neglect of decay

Halitosis—bad breath; caused by poor dental hygiene, carious teeth, unclean mouth, periodontal disease, pyorrhea, infection, and others

Plaque—sticky, almost colorless layer of organized microcolonies of bacteria in a gelatinous substance; clings to teeth, especially near gum line

Calculus—calcified (hardened) plaque, also known as tartar; mineral deposits around gum lines that harden and are removed only by scaling

Nutrition

Need for balanced diet from basic four food groups; excess vitamins and minerals (calcium and phosphorous) not generally needed

Good "snack" food—no or minimal sugar and refined sugars: (1) potato chips, corn chips, popcorn, nuts, cheese, hard boiled eggs, raw fruits and vegetables, unsweetened fruit juices, milk; (2) detergent foods (cleanse teeth and provide exercise), raw vegetables—carrots, celery, green peppers, cauliflower, radishes; raw fruits—apples, oranges

Poor "snack" foods—candy, pastry, cookies, chocolate milk, sweetened beverages, syrups, jellies, and carbohydrate foods that are sticky and cling to teeth

Psychological

Why oral health? proper tooth functioning necessary for chewing; speech; affects appearance, acceptance and rejection by peers; prevents diseases and disorders

Care of teeth and proper oral hygiene by individual

Toothbrushing—clean teeth and mouth; eliminate food particles; remove plaque; massage; prevent stains and calculus, when to brush, after eating; if not, "swish and swallow"

Toothbrush—rinse and let dry in sunlight; selection—three to four rows of bristles in straight line

Mouthwash—removes excess particles; can do with water; commercial products not effective in removing film, neutralizing acids, curing halitosis, or preventing decay; temporarily freshens and sweetens mouth; may mask disease

Flossing for plaque control with waxed or unwaxed floss between the teeth

Dentifrice—no best kind; possibly one with fluoride

Fluorides—possible use in toothpastes or powders, in tablet form, in bottle water

Periodic dental visits

Proper nutrition

Avoidance of injuries and accidents—follow safe practices; avoid detrimental habits—thumb-sucking, tongue-thrusting, chewing hard objects

Social

Problem: 90% or more of all children and youths need better oral health

Care of teeth

By dentists who examines mouth for diseases and disorders, fills cavities, provides bridges and crowns, applies topical application of fluoride, cleans and polishes teeth, replaces missing teeth, teaches dental hygiene, helps with orthodontia, and uses x-ray films, different types of fillings—silver amalgam, gold, porcelain—mouth mirror and explorer, scaler, drill, and other equipment; when to visit dentist—preferably twice yearly

By community through fluoridation of water supply (1 ppm); sodium fluoride is a chemical that becomes part of the tooth and strengthens it against decay; applied by topical application, in water, and by taking pills; favorable claims—inexpensive; reduces tooth decay significantly; reaches all people; reduces costs of repairs; unfavorable claims—forces people to drink fluoridated water against their will; dangerous to health; type of socialized medicine

Types of dentists—general practice, orthodontia; prosthetics, periodontia; pedodontia, oral surgery, and endodontia

How to select dentist—call local dental society for three names; call reputable hospital and ask chief of dental services for suggestions; see if dentist is member of local dental society; does postgraduate work; attends clinics and does not advertise; ask family dentist in previous community; call nearby dental school; check neighbors who are satisfied with dentist

Effects of mass media including advertising on dental health products and services

Dental health insurance

Costs of products and services for dental care

Spiritual

Values: importance of dental health to self-identity; self-esteem

Moral issue: fluoridation of water supply

Humanism: responsibility of individual and community (including schools) to help needy students without funds to obtain dental health products and services

Concepts

Concept	Application of health definition
1 Positive oral health and oral health neglect have differing effects on individuals.	Physiological
2 Most dental diseases and disorders are preventable and treatable.	
3 Differing motivations influence decisions regarding dental health.	Psychological
4 A variety of environmental factors are important contributing causes of dental diseases and disorders and influence the purchase and use of dental health products and services.	Social
5 The community has a responsibility in the control and prevention of oral health diseases and disorders.	
6 All individuals are affected by dental health neglect.	
7 Community resources are available to assist individuals with oral health problems in varying kinds and amounts	
8 Dental health is affected by an individual's values.	Spiritual
9 Fluoridation of the water supply is a moral issue.	
10 Equality and justice demand that dental health services and products be available to, or provided for, all individuals.	

Objectives for grades K-3

Domain	Objectives for students	Basic concepts
Cognitive	1. Explains ways to clean teeth as well as when this action should take place.	1,2
	2. Recalls foods that help in promoting dental health.	1, 2
	3. Identifies the different teeth and their functions.	2
	4. Lists ways to prevent tooth decay or other disorders.	1, 2, 4, 7
	5. Explains the proper way to brush teeth.	1, 2
	6. States the practices that may be harmful to oral health.	4
	7. Identifies the reasons why the dentist or dental hygienist can help individuals.	2, 7
	8. Explains the procedures to follow in preparing an inexpensive dentifrice.	2
	9. Explains the proper way to floss the teeth.	1, 2
Affective	1. Displays interest in brushing teeth properly.	1, 2
	2. Listens carefully to the ways to prevent tooth decay and other disorders.	
	3. Asks questions about teeth and their functions.	2
	4. Brings pictures to class, or is attentive to discussion of foods that may be helpful and detrimental to dental health.	1, 2, 4
	5. Talks about the need for daily health care.	1, 2, 6
	6. Accepts the dentist or dental hygienist as a friend.	2, 7
Action (observable) (nonobservable) (nonobservable, or delayed)	1. "Swishes and swallows" when brushing the teeth is not possible.	1, 2
	2. Prepares an inexpensive dentifirice in the classroom.	2
	3. Eats nutritious foods, including "snack" foods.	1, 2
	4. Attempts to refrain from harmful dental health practices.	
	5. Brushes teeth properly after eating when possible.	1, 2, 4
	6. Attempts to floss teeth once daily.	1, 2, 4
	7. Uses own toothbrush and gives it proper care.	1, 2, 4
	8. Visits the dentist periodically.	2, 7

Objectives for grades 4-6

Domain	Objectives for students	Basic concepts
Cognitive	1. Explains the type, structure, functions, growth, and development of teeth.	1, 2
	2. Identifies ways in which oral health influences appearance and social relationships.	3, 4
	3. Summarizes the procedures to follow for dental health.	2, 5, 7
	4. Lists the factors that control and prevent tooth decay.	2, 5, 7
	5. Recalls the diseases and disorders that occur from oral health neglect.	1, 4, 6
	6. Explains the causes of tooth decay.	1, 2, 4
	7. Identifies the reasons for topical application of fluorides to the teeth.	1, 2, 6
	8. Recites the services that a dentist can render to an individual.	5, 7
	9. Demonstrates the proper way to floss the teeth.	1, 2

Domain	Objectives for students	Basic concepts
Affective	1. Accepts the responsibility for personal dental health care.	1, 3, 6-8
	2. Talks about the need for dental care including periodic dental visits.	1, 2, 7, 8
	3. Displays interest in wanting to learn more about the role of nutrition in dental health.	1, 2, 4
	4. Listens to discussion about the importance of the individual's oral health.	2, 6, 8
	5. Reaches the conclusion that dental health plays a role in the social acceptance and self-esteem of individuals.	2, 4, 8
	6. Supports the need for flossing teeth as an important preventive dental health procedure.	1, 2, 6
Action (observable and non-observable) (nonobservable, or delayed)	1. "Swishes and swallows" when brushing is not possible.	2
	2. Refrains from using teeth in hazardous ways.	1, 2
	3. Eats nutritious foods and especially detergent foods.	1, 2, 4
	4. Limits the consumption of sweets.	1, 2, 4
	5. Attempts to floss teeth daily.	1, 2
	6. Brushes teeth properly after eating when possible.	1, 2
	7. Visits the dentist periodically.	1, 2, 7
	8. Uses care in the treatment and storage of the toothbrush.	2

Objectives for grades 7-8

Domain	Objectives for students	Basic concepts
Cognitive	1. Compares the claims made for and against fluoridation.	5, 9
	2. Compares advertising claims of the product effectiveness on dental health.	4
	3. Identifies the community resources available to assist in dental health care.	7
	4. Explains the use of x-ray films in the dental care process.	1, 2, 7
	5. Lists the importance of teeth to appearance, speech, and digestion.	1, 3
	6. Lists the variety of dental specialists and the kinds of services they render.	7
	7. Compares the costs of dental services with and without proper dental care.	4, 7
	8. Identifies sources of reliable and current scientific dental health information.	4, 5, 7
Affective	1. Talks about fluoridation of the water supply as a moral issue.	9, 10
	2. Displays interest in learning about dental health and its relations to social acceptance and appearance.	3
	3. Asks questions regarding the costs of dental services with and without proper dental care.	4, 7
	4. Discusses the place of dental health in an individual's values.	8
	5. Is attentive to information presented about the variety of dental specialists and auxiliary dental personnel available in the community.	4, 7
	6. Asks questions about the benefits and hazards in the use of x-ray films by dentists.	1, 2, 7

Action (observable and non-observable) (nonobservable, or delayed)	1. Is able to differentiate between reliable and unreliable dental health information.	4, 7
	2. Supports community efforts to fluoridate the water supply.	5, 6, 9, 10
	3. Supports community efforts to make dental health services and products available to needy students.	6, 10
	4. Is able to make wise decisions regarding personal dental health care.	3, 4, 8

DISEASE CONTROL UNIT
Outline of content

Physiological

Definitions: disease, communicable disease, noncommunicable or chronic disease, host (focus), avenue, susceptible, acute, chronic, antigen, antibody, immunity, pathogen, vaccine, serum, antibiotic, resistance, epidemic

Types

Communicable—respiratory—colds, bronchitis, pneumonia, influenza; tuberculosis, "strep" throat; infectious hepatitis; mononucleosis; skin diseases; sexually transmitted diseases; gastrointestinal—food poisoning; childhood—measles, mumps, smallpox, chickenpox, and poliomyelitis

Causes—microorganisms-bacteria (sexually transmitted diseases, tetanus, tuberculosis, "strep" throat); viruses (colds, infectious hepatitis); fungi (ringworm); protozoa (dysentery; malaria); parasites (worms)

Contributing causes—heredity; lack of sanitary procedures; individual susceptibility; lack of nutritious food; and exposure

Modes of transmission: air, food, water, direct contact, insects, and animals

Portals of entry—mouth, nose, breaks in skin, and other body openings

Disease process—fever, pain, infection, redness, loss of weight, bleeding, shortness of breath, and other signs and symptoms

Body defenses—skin and mucous membranes; fever; white blood cells; antibodies

Noncommunicable—heart, cancer, allergy, arthritis, diabetes, mental illness, and acne

Contributing causes—heredity; food; dysfunctioning of body organs; irritations; pressures, and a variety of other environmental factors

Effects—damage, destruction, and altered function of cells, tissues, organs, and systems; illness, disability, death

Prevention and treatment—individual—isolation, health habits; community—control of environment through laws and regulations; immunization; sanitation; water and food controls; drugs and medicines; surgery; radiation; and medical help

Psychological

Effect of diseases and disorders on mental and emotional health: adjustment of self and others; success in social world

Importance of early diagnosis and treatment

Individual responsibility in disease control

Fear of disease, disability, and death

Disease and death in the family

Social

School and community responsibilities for prevention and control

Control procedures: laws and regulations; sanitary procedures; immunizations; availability of health department services; adequate supply of physicians and hospital and clinic facilities

Sources of help: physicians; health departments; voluntary health agencies

Spiritual

Values: appreciation of healthy body; differing religious and healing philosophies toward disease

Moral issues: ethics of disease prevention and treatment on the part of individuals and the community

Humanism: attitudes toward people with disease; appreciation of healing arts; concern for others

Concepts

Concept	Application of health definition
1 Diseases can cause disability, temporary or permanent, and sometimes death.	Physical-social-spiritual
2 Communicable diseases are caused by germs and may be transmitted directly or indirectly from an infected person, or host, to someone who is not immune.	Physical-social
3 For a communicable disease to spread, there must be a host (focus of infection), an avenue or means of transmission, and a susceptible person.	Physical-social
4 Noncommunicable—sometimes called chronic—diseases are caused by hereditary factors, metabolic disorders, aging, diet, stresses, and unknown influences.	Physical
5 Acute diseases are of short duration; chronic diseases are long-lasting.	Physical
6 Elementary-school pupils should be routinely immunized against measles, polio, German measles, diphtheria, whooping cough, and tetanus.	Physical-social
7 Parents are responsible for having their children properly immunized.	Social-spiritual
8 Communicable diseases are often spread in elementary schools because of inadequate control measures at home and in school.	Physical-social-spiritual
9 Diseases occur more often among poor children and contribute to lower learning achievement for all elementary pupils.	Social-spiritual
10 Adequate medical care and public health services are necessary for control of disease in a community.	Social-spiritual

Objectives for grades K-3

Domain	Objectives for students	Basic concepts
Cognitive	1. Tells why it is important to avoid disease.	1, 9
	2. Explains the reasons for covering coughs and sneezes in the classroom.	2, 3, 8
	3. Lists the ways a communicable disease may be spread.	2, 3, 8
	4. Identifies some communicable diseases fairly common among children.	2, 3, 8
	5. Tells why it is necessary to be immunized against certain diseases.	2, 3, 6
Affective	1. Displays interest in preventing and controlling disease.	1, 8
	2. Asks questions about different kinds of diseases.	2, 4
	3. Is aware of spread of "catching diseases" among children.	2, 3, 6, 8
	4. Accepts the value of immunizations.	3, 6
	5. Appreciates the effect of illness on learning.	9
Action	1. Covers coughs and sneezes, and follows other sanitary practices in school.	2, 8
	2. Cooperates in school or community immunization program.	6, 7
	3. Remains at home when ill with a communicable disease.	8
	4. Talks about reasons why poor people are sick more often than others.	9

Objectives for grades 4-6

Domain	Objectives for students	Basic concepts
Cognitive	1. Lists the major disease causes of death for all Americans and for children of elementary school age.	1
	2. Explains the differences between communicable and chronic diseases.	1-5
	3. Cites the differences between a vaccine and a serum.	2, 6
	4. Compares acute diseases with chronic diseases.	5
	5. Gives reasons for higher rates of disease among poverty groups.	4, 7, 9, 10
	6. Lists the communicable diseases against which elementary pupils should be immunized.	6
	7. Explains causes, prevention, and medical care for major chronic diseases.	1, 4, 10
Affective	1. Is attentive to information presented on methods for individuals, families, and communities to control diseases.	1, 3, 4, 9, 10
	2. Accepts the responsibility for taking steps to avoid spreading disease to others.	3, 6, 8
	3. Appreciates the responsibility of parents to have children immunized against certain diseases.	6, 7
	4. Supports local, state, and federal efforts to control communicable and chronic diseases.	1, 10
	5. Displays interest in government plans for health care of older people and other Americans.	1, 9, 10

Domain	Objectives for students	Basic concepts
Action	1. Follows personal and family practices to prevent disease.	1, 8
	2. Seeks medical care when symptoms of illness are present.	1, 10
	3. Cooperates with school policy by keeping immunizations up to date and staying home when ill.	3, 6, 8, 10
	4. Reports symptoms of illness to parents, teacher, or school nurse when feeling ill.	3, 8, 10

Objectives for grades 7-8*

Domain	Objectives for students	Basic concepts
Cognitive	1. Explains specific causes, preventive measures, and community control of heart diseases, cancers, stroke, and other major diseases.	1, 4, 9, 10
	2. Cites differences between communicable and noncommunicable and acute and chronic diseases.	1, 2, 4, 5
	3. Lists recent medical and health science advances that have helped control disease.	1, 10
	4. Illustrates ways that individuals, families, and communities can help control disease.	1, 8, 10
Affective	1. Appreciates the fact that some diseases can be controlled more easily than others.	1, 4, 5, 10
	2. Displays interest in plans to provide better medical and hospital care for all Americans.	1, 9, 10
	3. Realizes the importance of immunizations for self-protection and the protection of others.	3, 6, 7
	4. Supports government and other research efforts to improve preventive and control measures for disease.	1, 10
	5. Accepts responsibility for having periodic medical checkups.	1, 10
Action	1. Has regular medical checkups.	1, 10
	2. Has all routinely recommended immunizations.	3, 6, 8
	3. Follows personal and family practices to prevent disease.	1, 8
	4. Avoids smoking, drinking, drug use, and other practices that may cause illness.	1, 9
	5. Avoids or minimizes physical, chemical, or emotional stresses that may cause disease.	1, 4

*Special attention may be given to heart disease and risk-taking factors and cancer.

DRUG UNIT
(INCLUDING ALCOHOL AND TOBACCO)
Outline of content

Pharmacological

Definitions: drug, drug use, misuse, and abuse, addiction, dependency, habituation, tolerance, toxicity, slang terms, tobacco, alcohol, alcoholic beverages, alcoholism

Alcohol synonyms: ethyl alcohol, ethanol, alcohol

Identification of abused drugs: technical help needed

Classification of drugs:

Legal and illegal
   Legal—over the counter and prescription
   Illegal—marijuana, heroin, LSD, and others
Pharmacological
   Stimulants—amphetamines, tobacco, coffee, cocaine
   Depressants (sedatives-hypnotics)—alcohol, barbiturates, inhalants, marijuana
   Psychedelics—LSD, psilocybin, peyote, STP
   Narcotics—heroin, morphine, opium, codeine, methadone
   Tranquilizers—Thorazine, Compazine, Serpasil
   Over-the-counter—aspirin, antihistamines, cough medicines, diet pills, sleeping pills
Common or trade name (brand) and generic (chemical) identity

Alcoholic beverages: distilled spirits (40% to 50%)—whiskey, brandy, scotch, gin, vodka; wine (12% to 20%); beer (4%)

Tobacco: cigars, cigarettes, pipes, chewing tobacco.

Physiological

The nervous system

Drug effects: dependent on dose response, biologic variability, potency, tolerance, body size

Medical uses: dependent on drug used

Abuse potential: physical and psychological dependence, tolerance

Alcohol:

Short-term effects: intoxication, reaction time slowed, released inhibitions and relaxation at low dosages, dulling effects at high dosages; also, absorption, metabolism, excretion, brain effects
Long-term effects: alcoholism, liver malfunction, brain damage

Tobacco:

Short term effects: stimulation, irritation of mucous membrane, improvement in short-term performance, chronic use affects interchange of O_2, CO, CO_2
Long-term effects: lung cancer, emphysema, heart disease, and other circulatory disorders

Duration of action: dependent on drug used

Method of administration: pills, capsules, injections, sniffing, liquid, smoking, chewing

Benefits:

Alcohol: antiseptic, diet stimulation (small amounts), tonic when prescribed by physicians
Tobacco: stimulation

Psychological

Why people use, misuse, and abuse drugs: curiosity, personal conflicts—insecurity, escape, boredom, rebelliousness; kicks; peer pressures; search for identity-adulthood; rejection of culture including schools; television; commercial exploitation

Why people don't use: alcohol: religion, no wish to impair physical/mental health, do not like taste, personal convictions against use; tobacco: odor, taste, cost

Characteristics of potential drug abusers: high-risk youths are those with behavioral problems at school with mild conduct disorders; lack of self-confidence; maybe self-centered and self-indulgent

Alternatives to drugs: athletics and recreational activities; counseling and group therapy in personal development; improved communications; social service participation; political service activities; intellectual motivation—reading discussion, creative games; participation in creative art activities; philosophic discussions on ethics, morality, values; spiritual involvement; survival training

Social

Patterns of drug use and abuse: classification of users and abusers

Nature and extent of drug use and abuse: legal and illegal; youth (alcohol—60% to 90%; tobacco—40% to 60%), adults

Factors affecting drug use and abuse

    Conflicts in reality—escape, values

    Economics—business and communication media

    Social and political climate

    Youth life-styles—counter-culture, youth identity, adolescent revolt

Role of home, school, community: prevention, control, treatment, and rehabilitation

Rehabilitation and treatment: multimodality concept

    Crisis intervention

    Detoxification

    Aftercare

        Pharmaceutical—Cyclazocine, methadone

        Psychiatric—individual counseling in psychiatric hospital

        Psychosocial—Syanon, Daytop Village, and others

        Religious—Teen Challenge, AA

Courts and the law: laws; enforcement procedures and problems; criminal justice process

Community resources: federal, state, and local governmental agencies—FTC, FDA, OE, NIMH; private sources; mass media and the business world; education; laws and enforcement; facilities—crisis centers, clinics, hotlines, ongoing groups, self-help groups; drug abuse council or committee

Identification of drug abusers

    Observations of signs and symptoms

        General and specific—change in attendance, discipline, and performance; unusual activity or inactivity; deterioration of personal appearance and health habits; unpredictable outbreaks of temper

        Characteristics of potential users

        Tell-tale evidence

    Peer identification, self-identification, clinical test

Spiritual

Values: developing a value system; self-identity and self-concept

Moral issues: implications of use and abuse of drugs on self, home, and community; drug use by students and adults; commercial interests; the mass media; the sale of drugs; the justice of laws controlling drugs

Humanism: individual and community responsibilities for drug abusers; the job market for rehabilitated drug abusers or drug abusers in industry

Concepts

Concept	Application of health definition
1 Drugs differ in kind and degree; they have multiple uses with a variety of effects on individuals.	Pharmacological
2 Proper use of drugs may be beneficial to individuals, the family, and the community.	
3 Improper use of drugs may result in health and safety problems to individuals, the family, and the community.	
4 Numerous factors and forces influence the availability as well as the use and misuse of legal and illegal drugs by individuals and the community.	Psychological-social
5 The individual, the family, and the community have interrelated and reciprocal responsibilities to help control the availability, to prevent the misuse and abuse, and to assist individuals who become misusers and abusers of drugs in society.	Social
6 The use and misuse of drugs by individuals involve moral principles and issues and are related to one's sense of values as well as to the humane and just treatment of all people in society.	Spiritual

Objectives for grades K-3

Domain	Objectives for students	Basic concepts
Cognitive	1. Identifies drugs commonly used.	1
	2. Illustrates ways common drugs are used by individuals.	1
	3. Lists beneficial effects of drugs.	2
	4. Identifies substances that can be harmful or misused.	3
	5. Lists responsible people who can help when medicines are needed.	2, 3
	6. Explains why medicines should be taken under supervision of parent as prescribed or recommended by a physician or dentist.	4
	7. States conditions under which individuals show lack of responsibility when using medicine.	5
	8. Cites ways in which individual shows respect for drugs.	5
Affective	1. Is aware of differences between alcohol and other drugs and of their usage by individuals.	1, 4
	2. Displays interest in learning about the beneficial as well as harmful effects of drugs.	2, 3
	3. Desires to use drugs in useful and responsible ways.	4, 5
	4. Shows interest in discovering people who can help when medicines are needed.	5
Action (nonobservable, or delayed)	1. Uses only substances that aid in proper responsible supervision.	3
	2. Takes medicines and drugs only under responsible supervision.	3
	3. Refuses to accept substances from strangers.	3-5
	4. Limits or refrains from use of drugs, except medicines prescribed and recommended, until adulthood.	

Objectives for grades 4-6
(introduce alcohol/tobacco at this level)

Domain	Objectives for students	Basic concepts
Cognitive	1. Identifies varieties of drugs used by individuals.	1
	2. Lists reasons for drugs in society.	3
	3. Explains medical uses of commonly used drugs.	2
	4. Explains physiological effects of some of the commonly used drugs.	1
	5. Lists reasons persons react differently to chemicals contained in drugs.	1
	6. Cites examples of misuse and abuse of drugs.	3, 4
	7. Identifies difficulties or possible problems from misuse and abuse of drugs.	3
	8. Explains why misuse and abuse of drugs may start early in life.	4
	9. Lists ways society tries to protect individuals from abuse of drugs.	4
	10. Identifies ways to protect self against misuse and abuse of drugs.	3, 4
	11. Starts to analyze information about drugs on television, in newspapers and magazines.	4, 5
Affective	1. Displays interest in learning about varieties of drugs and their effects on the body.	1-3
	2. Asks questions about problems involved with misuse or abuse of drugs.	3, 5
	3. Seeks further information about community efforts to help people who misuse and abuse drugs.	5
	4. Discusses ways to protect self against misuse and abuse of drugs.	5, 6
	5. Expresses desire to use drugs responsibly and usefully.	2, 6
Action (nonobservable, or delayed)	1. Uses only substances that aid in proper growth and development.	2
	2. Takes medicine and drugs only under responsible supervision.	3
	3. Limits or refrains from use of drugs, except medicines prescribed or recommended, until grown up.	3
	4. Refuses to use illegal drugs.	3, 6
	5. Starts to develop own practices and habit patterns to protect self against abuse of drugs.	3, 4

Objectives for grades 7-8
(including alcohol and tobacco)

Domain	Objectives for students	Basic concepts
Cognitive	1. Recalls varieties of drugs used by people.	1
	2. Describes how medicines can be used to benefit individual.	2
	3. Lists variety of individual and social factors that influence misuse and abuse of drugs.	4
	4. Interprets role of business and advertising in sale of drugs.	4, 5
	5. Identifies differing effects of variety of drugs on the body.	1, 4
	6. Compares benefits of smoking, drinking, and using drugs with possible detrimental effects.	2, 3
	7. Identifies reasons why people do and do not use, misuse, and abuse drugs.	4
	8. Illustrates ways to cope with social and emotional pressures of life other than through use of drugs.	4, 5

Domain	Objectives for students	Basic concepts
	9. States procedures used by community to control availability, sale, and use of drugs.	5
	10. Discusses need for development of a value system.	6
	11. Recalls signs and symptoms of drug misusers and abusers.	1
Affective	1. Is attentive to information presented on varieties of drugs used by people, their benefits, their hazards, and their differing physiological effects.	1-3
	2. Shows interest in comparisons of benefits and detrimental effects of alcohol, tobacco, and drugs on individuals and society.	2, 3
	3. Gives opinions regarding role of business and advertising in sale and availability of drugs.	2, 3, 5
	4. Asks questions about alternatives to drug use.	4, 5
	5. Displays interest in developing a value system.	6
	6. Is aware and discusses long-term results from frequent and regular misuse and abuse of drugs.	4, 5
Action (nonobservable, or delayed)	1. Make judgments about drugs and drug users after reviewing all aspects of problem.	4-6
	2. Seeks to discover one's own identity and purposes in life.	6
	3. Participates in a school-education-information program.	5
	4. Seeks help from school personnel if having a drug problem.	4, 5
	5. Refrains from regular use of drugs that may lead to dependency, disease, or disability.	3-6
	6. Avoids use of drugs that may affect ability to think clearly and react normally.	3-6
	7. Refuses to use illegal drugs.	3-6

EXERCISE, REST, RELAXATION, AND BODY CONTROL UNIT
Outline of content

Physiological

Definitions: physical fitness, physiology, physiology of exercise, body mechanics, muscular system, cardiovascular system, strength, speed, endurance, posture, rest, sleep.

Exercise

Muscles—types—skeletal (external body control), heart, and smooth (internal organs—blood vessels, glands, others)

Characteristic—contractility when stimulated by nerves

Skeletal muscles:

Structure—attached to bones of body

Locations—back, chest, abdominal wall, arms and legs

Functions—movement of body (exercise), maintenance of posture, production of body heat

Kinds of exercise—many forms; light or heavy, including walking, running, bicycling, hiking, sports, recreational activities

Effects—muscle tone, strength, size and control of skeletal muscles; aid in individual's meeting demands of daily activity; help in creation of reserves for emergencies and safety; aid in cardiovascular, respiratory, and nervous system functioning; improvement of posture; stamina, endurance; relief from tension; fun and pleasure; aid in mental health; control of body weight; one factor involved in heart disease

Rest, relaxation, and sleep

Requirements—need for a balance of work, play, rest, relaxation, and sleep daily; sleep requirements—8 to 10 hours daily for children and adolescents

Fatigue—types—physical, mental or emotional

Causes—intense or prolonged physical activity; psychologic factors—nervousness, boredom, worry, tensions and stress, emotions, noise; infections and disease conditions

Effects—less attention, drowsy, irritability, lowered resistance to fatigue, less alert to possible hazards—more accident prone, less ability to perform effectively

Procedures for relaxation—sleep, rest, exercise, change of activity, music, art, and other pleasurable activities

Body control

Dependent on proper exercise, practice of bodily movements, adequate rest, relaxation and sleep, nutrition, and other environmental factors

Poor posture because of lack of, or improper, exercise, rest, and sleep; poor habits of sitting, standing, reclining, or walking; improper nutrition; ill-fitting clothes and shoes

Psychological

Importance of relaxation in helping endure stress

Importance of exercise, rest, and sleep to the individual

Selection of activities to fulfill individual needs

Competition and its psychological effects on children and youths

Games and sports and their provision for success experiences and self-reliance opportunities

Social

Role of school, home, and community: providing facilities and opportunities for exercise, rest, and relaxation

School curriculum: its inclusion of an education program to help students with postural or exercise problems or to fulfill pupil needs

Social interaction: through games, sport, dance, or other forms of exercise and activity

Improvement of teacher-pupil relationships

Spiritual

Values: appreciation of physical fitness, rest, sleep, relaxation, and posture to health and effective living; appreciation of differing attitudes of individuals toward exercise and physical activity

Moral issues: fair play and good sportsmanship in games and sports

Humanism: teacher-pupil relations in an informal atmosphere through play experiences; guidance by providing for the differing physical abilities of pupils

Concepts

Concept	Application of health definition
1 Physical fitness is one aspect of total health and requires regular vigorous exercise.	Physical
2 Regular exercise produces good muscle tone and efficient circulation and helps maintain desirable body weight.	Physical-social
3 Everyone needs a balance of exercise and rest for optimal health.	Physical-psychological
4 Sports and dance provide opportunity for healthful exercise and pleasant social interaction.	Physical-social-psychological
5 Sound body dynamics improves efficiency and appearance.	Physical-social-psychological

Objectives for grades K-3

Domain	Objectives for students	Basic concepts
Cognitive	1. Tells why exercise, rest, and relaxation are important for good health.	1-4
	2. Identifies ways to relax.	3
	3. Recalls pleasant experiences in games or dance activities.	4
	4. Identifies the values of good posture and sound body mechanics.	5
	5. Explains the importance of rest, relaxation, and sleep to optimal health.	3
Affective	1. Appreciates value of exercise, rest, and relaxation in maintaining good health and growth.	1, 2
	2. Desires to learn and play games regularly.	1, 2, 4
	3. Shows interest in individual and group games and dances.	1, 2, 4
	4. Shows interest in using own body most efficiently.	5
	5. Is aware of the daily need for rest, relaxation, and sleep.	3
Action	1. Takes an active part in games and dances at school and after school.	1, 2, 4
	2. Practices good body dynamics in daily activities.	5
	3. Sleeps 8 to 10 hours each night and rests occasionally during the day.	3
	4. Demonstrates good sportsmanship and a spirit of cooperation in games and dances.	4

Objectives for grades 4-6

Domain	Objectives for students	Basic concepts
Cognitive	1. Explains physiological reasons for regular, vigorous exercise.	1, 2
	2. Understands emotional health values of sports and dance.	4
	3. Can demonstrate the basics of functional body movement.	5
	4. Lists reasons for adequate rest, relaxation, and sleep.	3
	5. Identifies ways to relax at home and school.	3

Domain	Objectives for students	Basic concepts
Affective	1. Appreciates the values of physical fitness as a part of total good health.	1, 2, 4
	2. Asks questions about the physiological and mental benefits of exercise.	1, 2, 4
	3. Desires to learn more about basic skills, strategy, and rules of sports.	4
	4. Is attentive to information on the importance of rest, relaxation, and sleep.	3
	5. Appreciates the esthetic and physiological values of efficient body movement.	5
Action	1. Takes an active part in games and dance activities at school.	1, 2, 4
	2. Participates in sports after school and on weekends.	1, 2, 4
	3. Sleeps 8 to 10 hours each night and rests when fatigued during the day.	3
	4. Demonstrates good sportsmanship in sports and dance activities.	4
	5. Practices good body dynamics in daily activities.	5
	6. Takes time daily to participate in some type of relaxation activity.	3

Objectives for grades 7-8

Domain	Objectives for students	Basic concepts
Cognitive	1. Explains specific changes in muscular and circulatory systems during exercise.	1, 2
	2. Describes mental health values of sports and dance.	4
	3. Understands the kinesiology of fundamental body movements as in standing, sitting, walking, lifting, pushing, and pulling.	5
	4. Cites the physical and mental values of proper sleep, relaxation, and rest.	3
	5. Lists health values of regular exercise.	1, 2, 4
Affective	1. Believes that physical fitness is one of the values in the good life.	1-5
	2. Appreciates the physiologic and emotional values of regular exercise.	1, 2, 4
	3. Desires to learn more about basic skills, strategy, and rules of sports.	4
	4. Appreciates the physical and mental values of adequate rest, relaxation, and sleep.	3
	5. Believes that one's appearance and efficiency are enhanced by sound body dynamics.	5
Action	1. Participates regularly in sports, dance, or other forms of physical exercise.	1, 2, 4
	2. Sleeps 8 to 10 hours each night and rests when fatigued during the day.	3
	3. Demonstrates cooperation, leadership, and good sportsmanship in sports or dance activities.	4
	4. Maintains desirable muscle development and figure control through exercise.	1, 2
	5. Follows principles of sound body dynamics in daily activities.	5
	6. Relaxes daily using a satisfactory method.	

FAMILY HEALTH UNIT
Outline of content

Physiological

Life: purpose and order, a life cycle or pattern of growth, all living things from living things

Characteristics—a beginning, changes, and death; reproduction; need for food, water, air, protection; movement; response to light, sound, cold, pain, danger

Differences—form, structure, functions, life cycle, pattern of growth, dependency and needs, methods of reproduction

Types—plant, animal, and human; plant reproduction—budding, runners, seeds, pollination; animal reproduction—asexually—cell division or fission; sexually—internally with males and females, and externally as in some fish that lay eggs

Human life: human being—unique; rational; decision maker; possessor of freedom, self-awareness, consciousness, and dignity; controller of actions; similarities and differences—heredity, race, size, intellect, ethnic background

Human growth and development

Definitions—"growing up," puberty, maturity

Puberty—special growth stage reaching physical adulthood; girls reach this stage 1½ years earlier than boys

Maturity—growth stage in which the person is more cooperative; has positive sex attitudes; is not easily hurt, is not dominated by moods, is able to meet problems constructively, is able to meet responsibilities, is able to make wise decisions

Cause—action of endocrine glands and their hormones

Results—a variety of physical, emotional, and social changes

Physical—size and shape changes; appearance of secondary sex characteristics; boys—muscle development; hair on face, chest, and pubic areas; seminal emissions; appearance of sex drive; girls—hair under arms and pubic areas; breasts, widening of hips; menstrual cycle; appearance of sex drive

Emotional—physical attraction; fears and emotions with possible moodiness

Social—increase in boy-girl relations; need for friends

Role of heredity—physical characteristics; chromosomes and genes

Human reproduction

Start of life—union of male (sperm) and female (ovum) cells; need for father and mother

Reproductive organs

Male—external—penis, scrotum, testicles, pubic hair; internal—urethra, bladder, prostate, seminal vesicles, vas deferens, epididymis

Female—external—pubic hair, labia majora and minora, urethral opening, clitoris, vaginal opening, hymen; internal—vagina, cervix, uterus, oviduct, ovaries, urethra, bladder

Other concepts—fertilization, conception, implantation, fetus growth, birth, menstruation, birth control

Psychological

Understanding self: strengths and weaknesses; personality; worth; ability to succeed, but ability to accept failure; understanding and control of emotions; experience of joy through self-fulfillment; wholesome relations with others; decision making by problem solving process; good use of abilities

Sex drive—normal reaction; perpetuation of mankind; provides pleasure

Sex behavior in adolescence—interest in one's body and sex normal; questions of sex before marriage; sex deviation—homosexuality, exhibitionism, rape

Factors influencing sex drive—biologic makeup; early childhood experiences; parental attitudes; environmental influences

Purpose of family—satisfaction of physical and psychological needs; stability and security important for good mental health; guidance of individuals to adulthood

Social
The family

Nature—size; structure, or composition; culture or ethnic; religion; changes

Types—two parents; one parent; no parents, guardian; step-parents; mixed ethnic

Needs—physical, psychological, and emotional

Functions—different roles because of different types of families and geographic location, but inclusion of sharing and transmission of feelings, ideas, heritage, and income; security by fulfilling needs; aid in education; growth and development; affection, worthy use of leisure time

Role of individual family members—assumption of responsibilities; cooperation in functioning of home; respect of others' rights; consideration; acceptance of differences; trying to understand members; not making unreasonable demands; working together; helping in different ways including financial support; use of constructive ways to solve differences

Status in family of oldest child—only child; only boy in group of girls; only girl in group of boys

Family influence on ability of members to make adjustments in society dependent on—cultural background of parents; family dwelling and location; health practices of members; economic status; type of structure; values

Problems and conflicts—parents; siblings; grandparents; money; use of car; discourtesy; failure to assume responsibilities at home, school, or elsewhere; use of drugs; choice and selection of friends; use of time

Boy-girl relations

Development—building of friendships; popularity; qualities boys and girls are seeking

Purpose—sense of belonging; affection; getting along with opposite sex; enjoyment; learning of social behavior

Dating—types: purposes; responsibilities; choosing a date; dating behavior and society's moral code; drinking and drugs

Steady dating—why; advantages and disadvantages; parents' attitudes and reactions

Values of sex in marriage—legal; emotional; social; medical; spiritual

Family planning

Love

Spiritual

Values: finding a purpose and meaningfulness in life; a philosophy of life; importance of friendships; interpersonal relationships with adults and peers; influence on personality development; relation to acquisition and use of money

Moral issues: premarital sex; failure to assume home responsibilities; relations with others, including parents

Concepts

Concept	Application of health definition
1 All living things come from living things.	Physiological
2 Individuals in some ways are like all individuals, in some ways like some individuals, and in some ways like no other individual.	
3 The sex drive and reproduction are normal functions of humans.	Psychological
4 Maturity is dependent on a variety of physical, social, and emotional factors.	
5 The family, with its unique features that are subject to change, is the basic unit in American society.	Social
6 Individuals influence and are influenced by the family and its members.	
7 Boy-girl relationships are important preludes to family life and family relations.	
8 Values and moral issues affect attitudes and behaviors regarding the family and sex.	Spiritual

Objectives for grades K-3

Domain	Objectives for students	Basic concepts
Cognitive	1. Identifies the differences that exist between boys and girls.	2
	2. Concludes the human baby grows and develops inside the mother.	1, 2
	3. Recites the correct vocabulary for body parts and body functions.	1, 2
	4. Lists the responsibilities to be completed at home and at school.	5, 6
	5. Explains how humans reproduce.	1
	6. Compares how families differ in their composition and functions.	5
	7. Recalls that living things come from living things.	1
	8. Explains the way parents and family members help individuals.	4-6, 8
	9. Identifies the rights of others in need of respect.	2, 4-8
	10. Describes the role and responsibilities of family members.	5
Affective	1. Displays interest in learning about the differences between boys and girls.	2
	2. Asks questions about the growth of the baby inside the mother.	1, 2
	3. Is interested in wanting to learn the correct vocabulary for body parts and body functions.	1, 2
	4. Believes there are responsibilities individuals must give their attention to at school and at home.	5, 6
	5. Is attentive to the discussion regarding human reproduction.	1, 2
	6. Talks about the differing compositions and functions of families.	5, 6
	7. Accepts the conclusion that living things come from living things.	1
	8. Believes that parents and family members may be helpful to individuals.	4-6, 8
	9. Is supportive of the need to respect the rights of others.	2, 5-8
	10. Is attentive to the discussion about the role and responsibilities of family members.	5
Action (observable) (observable and non-observable)	1. Uses the correct vocabulary for body parts and body functions.	1, 2
	2. Assumes responsibilities at school and at home.	5, 6
	3. Tries to respect the rights of others, including their right to privacy.	5, 6

Objectives for grades 4-6

Domain	Objectives for students	Basic concepts
Cognitive	1. Identifies the responsibilities that need attention as a family member.	5, 6
	2. Lists the rights of others in need of respect.	2, 4-8
	3. Is familiar with the terminology used in describing the human reproductive process.	1
	4. Summarizes the meaning of puberty and its effect upon growth and development.	1-4
	5. Explains the responsibilities of all members of a family.	5, 6
	6. Recalls that sex is a basic life function.	1-4
	7. Identifies the role of heredity in the growth and development of individuals.	2-4, 7
	8. Lists the variety of characteristics displayed by the family.	5, 6
Affective	1. Believes that it is necessary as a family member to assume home responsibilities.	5, 6
	2. Supports the concept that the rights of others must be respected.	2, 4-8
	3. Is interested in learning the terminology necessary to describe the human reproductive process.	1
	4. Listens to the discussion about puberty and its effect on growth and development.	1-4
	5. Displays interest in the responsibilities of all family members.	5, 6
	6. Accepts sex as a basic life function.	1-3
	7. Asks questions regarding the role of heredity on the growth and development of individuals.	1, 2, 4
	8. Accepts the basic life function of menstruation as an important phenomenon.	2, 3
	9. Believes it is necessary to cooperate with other family members to achieve a happy family unit.	5, 6
	10. Is aware that families display a variety of characteristics.	5
Action (observable, nonobservable, or delayed)	1. Assumes responsibilities at home as a family member.	5, 6
	2. Tries to cooperate with family members to achieve a happy family unit.	5, 6
	3. Makes efforts to consistently respect the rights of others.	2, 4-8
(observable)	4. Is able to discuss human reproduction using appropriate terminology without embarrassment.	1

Objectives for grades 7-8

Domain	Objectives for students	Basic concepts
Cognitive	1. Explains the sex drive and its effect on individuals.	1-4, 7
	2. Identifies factors that may influence one's sex drive.	3, 4, 6-8
	3. Differentiates between physical, emotional, and social maturity.	4
	4. Summarizes the human reproductive process from conception through birth.	1-3
	5. Concludes that the family is the basic unit of American society and is familiar with its changing roles.	5
	6. Identifies the importance of boy-girl relationships and the qualities boys and girls seek in one another.	7
	7. Prepares criteria for behavior on dates.	3, 4, 7, 8
	8. Compares the advantages and disadvantages of steady dating.	7, 8
	9. Discusses sexual behavior in adolescence and before marriage.	3-5, 8
	10. Explains the meaning of love.	7
	11. Identifies the social, economic, and cultural influences on family life.	5, 6, 8
	12. Selects values or a value system having meaning in life.	8
	13. Is familiar with the problem solving process to help make decisions about the family and sex behavior.	4, 5, 8
	14. Concludes there are moral issues involved in premarital sex, acceptance of responsibilities in the home, and others.	3-5, 8
	15. Describes the concept and purpose of family planning.	3-5, 7, 8
Affective	1. Accepts sex as a natural drive and function of individuals that is accompanied by related responsibilities.	1-4, 7
	2. Believes that maturity in life is essential for successful living.	4
	3. Displays interest in the human reproductive process from conception through birth.	1-3
	4. Is sensitive to the acceptance of the family as the basic unit of American society and its changing roles.	5
	5. Is aware of the need to develop boy-girl relationships and procedures for building friendships.	7
	6. Asks questions regarding the advantages and disadvantages of steady dating.	7, 8
	7. Is interested in discussing and preparing criteria for behavior on dates.	3, 4, 7, 8
	8. Displays a readiness to want to discuss sexual behavior in adolescence and before marriage.	3, 4, 7, 8
	9. Accepts the meaning of love to be more inclusive than physical attraction.	7
	10. Is aware of the variety of social, economic, and cultural influences on family life.	5, 6
	11. Believes that individuals need to determine the values that help them develop a philosophy of life.	8
	12. Supports the problem solving process as a useful method in making decisions about sex and family behavior.	4, 6
	13. Is sensitive to the moral issues involved in premarital sex relations, acceptance of responsibilities in the home, and others.	3-5, 8
	14. Is aware of the importance of family planning.	3-5, 7, 8

Domain	Objectives for students	Basic concepts
Action (observable and non-observable or delayed) (nonobservable or delayed)	1. Attempts to act as a physically, emotionally, and socially mature individual.	4
	2. Tries to become a contributing and effective member of the family.	5, 6
	3. Demonstrates the ability to achieve a balance between expression, behavior, and the sex drive.	1-4, 7, 8
	4. Develops wholesome relationships with members of the opposite sex.	7
	5. Behaves in socially accepted ways with members of the opposite sex.	7
	6. Attempts to develop values or a value system that will give life meaningfulness.	8
	7. Uses the problem solving process to help make decisions about the family and sex behavior.	3, 4, 6

MENTAL HEALTH UNIT*
Outline of content

Physiological

Definitions: mental health—adjustment to self and society; faces realities of life; functions effectively

Mental illness—varying degrees of emotional disturbance; in severe forms—psychoses, neuroses, personality disorders

Death †—physiological, social, and psychological aspects and concepts, causes, and effects

Growth and development of individual: factors influencing

Heredity—nervous system and endocrine glands; effect on thinking, feeling, acting

Environment—economically rich or deprived; stresses and pressure of parents, peers, of teacher; physical atmosphere—housing, climate

Interrelationship of biologic and environmental influences—heredity sets limits; environment determines level of attainment; stress situations may cause biologic reactions and anxiety; pleasant environment brings feelings of calmness and tranquility

Psychological

Mentally healthy individual: pursuer of reasonable goals; self-respect; knowledge of being liked and loved; sense of security; ability to think and act rationally; distinguishes between facts and feelings; maintenance of integrity in work and play; ability to work in group; respect for rights of others; faces realities of life; acceptance of responsibilities

Needs of individuals: physical—food, air, water, rest and sleep, housing, clothing, freedom from disease

Psychological—affection, security, acceptance as an individual, achievement, independence, authority, self-respect, success

---

*See Chapter 4.

†Death education has been introduced into school curriculums. It is believed to be a part of mental health. References at the end of the chapter provide selected readings. Chapter 12 contains suggested activities.

Mature personality: a clear self-concept*

Definition of personality—involving total physical, social, mental, and emotional aspects of individual including interests, size, shape, dress; the way the individual walks, talks, thinks, feels; ability to get along with people

Understanding of own strengths, weaknesses, and academic, intellectual, and physical potentials

Understanding of emotions' role in development

Types—anger, fear, love, hate, jealousy, happiness, prejudice, sorrow, joy

Effects—helpful or harmful

Relief from effects by talk with someone, play, work, hobbies

Influence on personal health—sleep and rest; eating; posture; physical activity

Control—sense of humor; ability to accept criticism, disappointment, failure, and unhappiness in normal fashion.

Understanding of the physical growth changes taking place

Ability to make adjustments, develop coping skills

Solving of problems and making decisions after weighing alternatives and consequences about study, work, sex, parent relations, peer relations

Establishment of realistic goals within potentials; achievable to reduce stress

Assumption and carrying out of responsibilities at home, school, and community

Ability to handle stress

Nature—tensions or pressures build attempting to carry out responsibilities, to achieve goals, or to solve problems resulting in anxieties, fears, worries and other emotional responses; degree dependent on factors involved

Causes—competition, desire to succeed, failure, sibling rivalry, parent expectations, school demands

Values and limits—some individuals work better under slight stress; may be motivational; may interfere with normal response

Relief from—modification of goals; activity change; balance of work and play; assumption of responsibilities; talking it out; taking one thing at a time; working off

Risk taking—positive and negative; includes financial gambles, risks of bodily harm and physical injury, ethical, self-esteem, and social risks

Coping with death and dying; bereavement and grief

Adjustment mechanisms: result from inability to adequately solve problems; individual resorts to other procedures to gain satisfaction, such as rationalization, projection, identification; misuse results in maladjusted behavior

---

*Stenner and Katzenmeyer claim that children during the early school years who have positive self-concepts are confident of their ability to meet everyday problems and demands and are at ease in their relationships with other people. These children tend to be independent and reliable and are relatively free from anxiety, nervousness, excessive worry, tiredness, and loneliness. They are seldom considered behavior problems. They tend to be above average in reading and mathematics. They view school as a happy, worthwhile place.

Causes of mental illness: multiplicity of complex environmental factors

Physical and chemical—infections, nutritional deficiencies, accidents, gland deficiencies, alcohol, anemia, physical defects

Psychological—social relations, love and marriage, family conflicts, sibling conflicts; sex adjustments, religious conflicts, parental attitudes and personality, school and peer experiences

Emotional maladjustment or mental illness: mental illness is a matter of degree and kind; for some individuals, mild emotional disturbances; for others, severe mental health problems manifested in a variety of symptomatic behaviors

Death: meaningfulness and relation to birth and life, to individuals, animals, and pets; bereavement and grief—stages of grief, need for others, need to be alone, helping others grieve; coping mechanisms—denial, anger, bargaining, depression, acceptance; feelings—perception of death; suicide—causes, signs, and symptoms

Social

Building of satisfying human relations: effective interaction with adults, peers, and opposite sex

Acquisition and retention of friends: sharing possessions and time; development of trust and fair play; respect of people as individuals; willingness to work with people; courteous and considerate; ability to give as well as to take

Choice of friends: need to establish criteria

Influence of people: rewards; threats; authority; expertness

Warm, safe, and secure home and school climate

Alternative life-styles

Successful group functioning involving respect and acceptance of all members; participation of all members; acceptance of responsibilities by each member; need for authority; a must to have constructive ways to resolve differences

Recognition of worth: realization that all individuals have differing human worths; ability to give consideration to rights of others; value of individual differences including race, religion or ethnic origin

Community resource available to help with problems: school—nurse, teacher, counselor; home—parents; church—clergymen; community—physicians, psychiatrists, organizations and agencies, public health departments

Death: death rituals and funerals—cultural and ethnic differences; communication with terminally ill; costs; suicide—sources of help

Spiritual

Values: the individual needs to attempt to define own values or value system; the individual's acceptance of differing values and value system of others

Moral issue: basic principles to use in the development and retention of relationships with others

Humanism: recognition that all individuals should receive equal and just treatment regardless of socioeconomic status, religious, cultural, or ethnic backgrounds

Death: right to life; euthanasia

Concepts

Concept	Application of health definitions
1 Mental health is influenced by biological and environmental factors.	Physiological
2 Each individual is like all others, like some others, and like no others.	
3 Understanding and acceptance of the concept of one's self is important in mental health.	Psychological
4 All individuals have dignity and worth.	
5 Individuals should be able to face the realities of life with emotional maturity.	
6 Stress can be beneficial and detrimental to individuals.	
7 The ability to get along with others is important in mental health.	Social
8 The community has a variety of sources available to help individuals with mental and emotional problems and difficulties.	
9 Values help to provide meaningfulness to life.	Spiritual

Objectives for grades K-3

Domain	Objectives for students	Basic concepts
Cognitive	1. Explains the reasons why sharing and taking turns are necessary.	7
	2. Lists ways to respect the feelings, rights, and property of individuals.	4, 7
	3. Lists ways of making and keeping friends.	7
	4. Identifies basic emotions.	5-7
	5. Discusses ways emotions may be helpful and harmful and their effects on personal worth.	5-7
	6. Recalls possible ways to sublimate or control emotional reactions.	1, 3, 5-7
	7. Recites ways to assume responsibilities in school and at home.	7
	8. Identifies ways to have success and to be independent at school.	3, 5
	9. Explains ways to prevent hurting someone or causing hard feelings.	1, 4, 5, 7
	10. Explains life and death in terms of loss of pets and animals.	5
Affective	1. Is interested in sharing and taking turns.	7
	2. Talks about the feelings, rights, and property of individuals.	4, 7
	3. Is attentive to discussion regarding emotions and their effects on individuals.	1, 5-7
	4. Asks questions regarding ways to prevent hurting people or causing hard feelings.	1, 4, 5, 7
	5. Accepts the need for successful and independent school experiences.	3, 4
	6. Displays interest in wanting and learning how to make and retain friends.	7
	7. Supports the need to assume responsibilities in school and at home.	7
	8. Realizes that living things must die.	5
Action (observable, nonobservable, and delayed)	1. Participates in sharing and taking turns.	7
	2. Experiences success and independence in a variety of ways in school.	3, 4
	3. Is able to acquire friends and to maintain them.	4, 7
	4. Respects the feelings, rights, and property of others.	4, 7
	5. Attempts to control emotions.	1, 5-7
	6. Is able to express feelings in a mature fashion.	1, 5-7
	7. Refrains from behavior that will hurt someone or cause hard feelings.	1, 4, 5
	8. Assumes responsibilities expected in school and at home.	7

Objectives for grades 4-6

Domain	Objectives for students	Basic concepts
Cognitive	1. Identifies adults who are receptive to talking over problems.	8
	2. Identifies adults who are available to help with problems.	8
	3. Lists the rules necessary for classroom behavior.	1, 7
	4. Identifies the characteristics in which individuals are alike, different, or unique.	1, 2
	5. Identifies goals that are within the possibility of achievement by the individual.	3, 5
	6. Describes ways emotions can be controlled.	1, 3, 5-7
	7. Explains the reasons for treating all individuals with dignity and respect.	4
	8. Discusses the biological and environmental factors affecting mental health.	1
	9. Lists situations when stress may occur and discusses helpfulness or harmfulness.	1, 6
	10. Recalls the scientific principles need to solve problems.	5
	11. Illustrates ways to be able to work productively as an individual in small groups.	3, 4, 7
	12. Recalls a variety of interesting leisure time activities.	1, 3, 8
	13. Identifies ways individuals try to adjust to demands of daily living.	5
	14. Explains the role of the brain, nervous system, and endocrine glands in mental health.	7
	15. Explains risk-taking behavior.	6
	16. Discusses life and death, meaning and causes.	5
Affective	1. Believes a variety of individuals are willing and available to help solve problems.	8
	2. Accepts the realization that there are adults willing to help students with problems.	8
	3. Is attentive to the preparation of rules for classroom behavior.	1, 7
	4. Talks about the significance of establishing realistic goals.	3, 5
	5. Displays interest in characteristics that identify individuals as alike, different, or unique persons.	1, 2
	6. Believes emotions need to be controlled.	1, 3, 5-7
	7. Is attentive to the importance of treating all individuals with dignity and respect.	4
	8. Asks questions regarding the biological and environmental factors affecting mental health.	1
	9. Believes stress situations may be helpful and harmful.	1, 6
	10. Supports the need to try to solve problems using scientific principles.	5
	11. Displays interest in being able to work productively as an individual and in small groups.	3, 4, 7
	12. Enjoys and is interested in participating in a variety of leisure time activities.	1, 3, 8
	13. Believes that risk-taking behavior may be hazardous.	6
	14. Realizes that grief is part of death and must cope with loss of loved ones.	5

Domain	Objectives for students	Basic concepts
Action (observable, nonob- servable, and de- layed)	1. Participates in the formulation of rules for classroom behavior	1, 7
	2. Seeks help when facing unsolvable problems.	8
	3. Talks over problems with trusted adults.	8
	4. Attempts to establish realistic goals.	3, 5
	5. Treats all individuals with dignity and respect.	4
	6. Attempts to control emotions.	1, 3, 5-7
	7. Attempts to avoid or reduce stressful situations.	1, 6
	8. Tries to solve problems using scientific principles.	5
	9. Is able to work productively as an individual and in groups.	3, 4, 7
	10. Participates in a variety of interesting leisure time activities.	1, 3, 8

Objectives for grades 7-8

Domain	Objectives for students	Basic concepts
Cognitive	1. Describes the values believed to be important to self.	9
	2. Explains the interrelationships between biologic and environmental influences on mental health.	1
	3. Identifies the characteristics of the mentally healthy individual.	3, 5
	4. States the strengths, weaknesses, and potential abilities of the self.	1, 2, 3
	5. Describes the growth and developmental changes taking place in the individual.	1, 2
	6. Concludes an individual's personality is comprised of a variety of components and is unique.	2
	7. Discusses the procedures necessary and problems faced in attempting to improve relationships with parents and teachers.	7
	8. Compares the helpful and harmful aspects of friends and friendships.	7
	9. Explains the scientific principles usable in solving problems.	5
	10. Translates all the evidence needed to make decisions.	5
	11. Interprets the effect of peer pressures on individual behavior.	6
	12. Indicates ways stress produced by peer pressures can be handled.	6
	13. Identifies the types and symptoms of maladjustive behavior and the community sources and services available.	1, 8
	14. Discusses positive and negative aspects of risk-taking behavior.	6
	15. Identifies awareness of death and life.	5
	16. Lists ways to cope with death.	5
	17. Analyzes suicide in terms of causes, signs and symptoms, and sources of help.	5

Domain	Objectives for students	Basic concepts
Affective	1. Believes that establishing values or a value system is necessary to find meaningfulness in life.	9
	2. Is attentive to discussion about the interrelationships between biological and environmental influences on mental health.	1
	3. Displays interest in the characteristics of the mentally healthy individual.	3, 5
	4. Is supportive of the need to constantly improve individual abilities.	2, 3, 5
	5. Asks questions regarding the growth and developmental changes that take place in the individual.	1, 2
	6. Is interested in identifying own personality; characteristics and uniqueness.	2, 3
	7. Believes that parent and teacher relationships are important.	7
	8. Accepts the fact that friends can be helpful as well as harmful to individuals.	5, 7
	9. Supports the need to solve problems using scientific principles.	5
	10. Listens to the idea that decisions cannot be made without careful consideration.	5
	11. Displays interest in learning the effect of peer pressures on behavior.	2, 3, 5, 6
	12. Believes that stress created by peers may not always be beneficial.	6
	13. Asks questions regarding the types and symptoms of maladjustive behavior and the treatment sources and services available in the community.	1, 8
	14. Realizes the positive and negative aspects of risk-taking behavior.	6
	15. Asks questions regarding funerals, rituals, and bereavement.	5
	16. Is attentive to discussion about euthanasia.	5
Action (observable, nonobservable, and delayed)	1. Tries to develop a set of values or a value system.	9
	2. Attempts to improve the strengths, weaknesses, and potential abilities of the self.	3-5
	3. Endeavors to improve parent and teacher relationships.	7
	4. Chooses friends after careful consideration of a variety of factors.	2, 5, 7
	5. Solves problems using scientific principles.	5
	6. Tries to make decisions after viewing all the alternatives and consequences.	5
	7. Attempts not to be unduly influenced by stress created by peers.	2, 3, 5, 6
	8. Seeks help when maladjustive symptoms of a persistent nature appear.	8
	9. Attempts to help others in times of death of loved ones.	5

NUTRITION UNIT
Outline of content

Physiological

Definitions: food, nutrition, calorie

Purposes of food: energy, tissue building, protection and maintenance of bodily functions

Nutrients needed: reasons; good sources of proteins and fats; daily recommended allowances by age, sex, size, activity

Food needed: basic 4 food groups; daily recommended allowances by age, sex, activity

Planning for meals or sample meals: breakfast, lunch, dinner, snacks, camping, picnics, sports, children, aged, pregnancy, parties

Diet and weight control: desirable weights—age, sex, size; identification of overweight and obesity; food intake; role of exercise; reducing fads and fallacies; sources of help; reliable and unreliable sources of information

Body processing of foods: digestion; absorption; use

Effects on the body: performance—mental, nervous stability, motor, disease; body structure and size—teeth, bones, soft tissues; length of life; energy needs—internal and external body activities

Disorders and diseases: appendicitis, constipation, allergies, diabetes, cancer, food poisoning, heart disease (genetic and environmental risk factors)

Psychological

Food = Power: security; prestige and status; symbol of hospitality and friendship

Effect and outlet for emotions: joy, sorrow, conflict, comfort, fear, worry, anxiety

Motivations for modifying food habits

Specific—weight reduction; weight control; lower blood pressure; pregnancy; sports; looks and personality; old age

General—good health; longer life

Social

Eating patterns and preferences: influencing factors including cultural, ethnic, religious, racial and social customs and traditions—Italian, Mexican, Chinese, native American, black; economic factors; age, sex, size; sensory reactions to food—texture, color, odor, taste, looks; social climate and atmosphere including companionship; education influences—TV, radio, newspapers, magazines, school, family, community, friends, neighbors

Sanitation and safety: home, school, community (restaurants); laws; protective agencies

Preparation, processing, preservation, and storage: procedures—canning, frozen, dehydrated, powdered, refrigerated, pasteurized, irradiated, adulterated

Consumer protection: laws—additives, advertising, safety, adulteration, pasteurization, sanitation, food production, processing; agencies—FDA, FTC, health departments

Fads and fallacies: misconceptions, weight control, "soul," natural and organic foods

Selection and purchase of foods: wise economic expenditures

Problems of hunger in society: role of individual and community

Spiritual

Values: value of food in human life; importance of food for health of individuals

Moral issues: Does society have the obligation to feed the hungry and the poor? Should the hungry and the poor receive food?

Humanism: How should people treat individuals who are hungry and in need of food?

Concepts

Concept	Application of health definition
1 Foods differ in kind, sources, and nutritive value and serve a variety of purposes for individuals.	Physiological
2 Individuals require the same nutrients but in varying amounts throughout life.	
3 The selection of nutritious foods contained in a balanced diet are necessary for the proper growth, good health, and everyday functioning of the individual.	
4 Lack of nutritious food resulting from a variety of factors may be detrimental to the health of individuals.	
5 Differing motivations influence the types and amounts of food consumed by individuals.	Psychological
6 Foods help to satisfy the emotional needs of individuals.	
7 Cultural, social, economic, and educational factors affect an individual's food selections.	Social
8 Production, processing, storage, preparation, and dispensing of foods influence their nutritional value, safety, and consumption.	
9 The social atmosphere present at meals, or when food is consumed, may have positive and negative effects on individuals.	
10 Food should be made available to all individuals regardless of their cultural, social, economic, or educational status.	Spiritual

Objectives for grades K-3

Domain	Objectives for students	Basic concepts
Cognitive	1. Identifies the basic 4 food groups.	1-3
	2. Recalls the importance of milk in the daily diet.	1-3
	3. Explains the purposes of food and relates to the basic 4 food groups.	1, 3
	4. Lists nutritious snack foods.	3
	5. Is able to limitedly plan nutritious breakfasts, lunches, and dinners from the basic 4 food groups.	1, 3
	6. Recalls the sources of foods from plants and animals.	1
	7. Explains the reasons for sanitary practices in the preparing, serving, and eating of foods.	9
	8. Identifies the cultural and social differences in foods consumed by people.	8
Affective	1. Is attentive to discussions about the basic 4 food groups.	1, 3
	2. Displays interest in eating a variety of foods.	1, 3
	3. Raises questions regarding the sources of food from plants and animals.	1
	4. Accepts the importance of tasting new and different foods.	1, 3
	5. Listens to the discussion for socially acceptable behavior at mealtime.	10
	6. Talks about cultural and social differences in foods consumed by people.	8

Domain	Objectives for students	Basic concepts
Action (observable)	1. Eats breakfast before attending school or while at school.	3
	2. Eats nutritious snack foods.	1, 3
	3. Acts in a socially acceptable manner at mealtime.	10
	4. Follows sanitary practices in the preparing, handling, and eating of foods.	9
(nonobservable and delayed)	5. Eats well-balanced meals selected from the basic 4 food groups.	1, 3
	6. Demonstrates willingness to try and eat a variety of foods, including new ones.	1, 3
	7. Takes only the amount of food that can be eaten.	8

Objectives for grades 4-6

Domain	Objectives for students	Basic concepts
Cognitive	1. Recalls the basic 4 food groups.	1-3
	2. Identifies the nutrients found in foods as well as the foods in which they are found.	1
	3. Is able to plan nutritious meals with some degree of efficiency.	1, 3
	4. Identifies the reasons why individuals need the same nutrients but in varying amounts throughout life.	2
	5. Recalls how the body processes foods in terms of digestion, absorption, and use.	2, 3
	6. Compares the foods and eating practices of various community, ethnic, religious, racial and cultural groups of people to the basic 4 food groups.	7
	7. Explains the relationships of poorly balanced diets and lack of food to diseases and disorders.	4
	8. Lists factors that affect choices of foods by individuals.	5
	9. Compares the nutritive values of highly advertised foods to the basic 4 food groups and to the nutrients needed by individuals.	1, 2, 7
	10. Identifies reliable sources of nutrition information.	7
Affective	1. Listens to discussions about the importance of nutritious foods for growth and health.	1-3
	2. Displays interest in the selection of nutritious foods.	1, 3
	3. Accepts the fact that new and different foods can add interest to eating.	1-3
	4. Questions the value of highly advertised foods.	1, 3
	5. Reacts to class discussions by raising questions regarding how foods satisfy differing emotional needs of individuals.	6
	6. Raises questions regarding reasons individuals require different types and amounts of food.	2
	7. Displays interest in learning more about the relationships of food to disease and disorders.	4
	8. Is attentive to discussions regarding the cultural and ethnic patterns and eating practices of individuals.	7
	9. Supports the need to locate and use reliable sources of nutrition information.	7

Domain	Objectives for students	Basic concepts
Action (observable)	1. Eats nutritious foods at mealtime and at snacktime.	1, 3
	2. Eats breakfast before attending school or while at school.	3
	3. Follows sanitary practices in the preparation, serving, storing, and eating of food.	8
(nonobservable, or delayed)	4. Eats a variety of foods and is willing to try new ones.	1, 3
	5. Uses reliable sources for nutrition information.	7

Objectives for grades 7-8

Domain	Objectives for students	Basic concepts
Cognitive	1. Explains how it is possible to obtain all the essential nutrients by eating a balanced diet selected from a variety of foods.	1, 3
	2. Describes diseases and disorders that may be associated with nutritional practices.	4
	3. Lists the dangers to growth, health, and body functioning through the consumption of improper foods or poor eating habits.	4
	4. Identifies the differing motivations that bring about changes in food consumption habits, such as sports, weight control, length of life.	5
	5. Analyzes TV and other commercials about food and their nutritive value.	1, 3, 5, 7
	6. Identifies federal, state, and local agencies and their functions in the control of the purity and quality of foods.	8
	7. Explains how weight can be controlled in many individuals through proper diet and exercise.	2
	8. Summarizes the current food fads and misconceptions.	5, 7
	9. Illustrates the differing effects of food and lack of food on the body.	4
	10. Compares the cultural or ethnic food patterns of community groups to the basic 4 food groups.	1, 7
	11. Concludes that all people need food and that efforts should be made to assure that it is available when needed.	10
	12. Examines food consumption at breakfast, lunch, dinner, and snacktime and compares with basic 4 food groups.	1, 3
	13. Identifies the genetic and environmental risk factors related to heart disease.	4
	14. Lists reliable sources of nutrition information.	7
Affective	1. Displays interest in attempting to help individuals in need of food.	10
	2. Accepts the importance of weight control through proper diet and exercise.	2
	3. Accepts and understands the cultural and ethnic differences in foods consumed by individuals.	7
	4. Asks questions in regard to agencies and their functions that have responsibility for the control of the purity and quality of foods.	8
	5. Is attentive to discussions regarding current food fads and misconceptions.	5, 7

Domain	Objectives for students	Basic concepts
	6. Displays interest in the differing motivations for food habits.	5
	7. Talks about food as a socializing agent by participating in discussions.	7, 9
	8. Is supportive of the concept that a balanced diet selected from a variety of foods is necessary for proper growth and health.	1, 3
	9. Believes that advertising about foods and food products must be carefully analyzed in terms of nutritional value.	1, 3, 5, 7
	10. Realizes the role of nutrition as a risk factor in heart disease.	4
	11. Accepts the importance of the use of reliable sources of nutrition information.	7
Action (observable) (nonobservable, or delayed)	1. Eats breakfast before attending school or while at school.	3
	2. Eats nutritious foods at mealtime and snacktime.	1, 3
	3. Periodically provides assistance by helping needy individuals obtain food.	10
	4. Attempts to keep weight and intake of foods under control through the wise selection and consumption of nutritious items.	2, 3
	5. Refrains, or attempts to encourage parents to refrain, from purchasing highly advertised foods unless they have been analyzed for nutritional value.	1, 3, 5, 7
	6. Reduces intake of foods related to heart disease.	4
	7. Uses reliable sources of nutrition information.	7

SAFETY AND FIRST AID UNIT*
Outline of content

Physiological

Definitions: injury, sudden illness, hemorrhage, respiration, concussion, fracture, shock, abrasion, laceration, resuscitation, burn classifications, poisons, sprains, strain, contusion, heat stroke and heat exhaustion, "g" levels, defensive driving

Effects of accidents: disability and death

Areas: home; school; community; fire and electric; bicycle; farm; sports and recreation; firearms; winter and summer

Psychological

Individual responsibility for safety
Accident proneness
Emotional factors in accidents and emergencies
Alcohol and other drugs in accidents
Emotional effects of accidents and emergencies on first aiders
Emotional influence in shock
Attitude toward mouth-to-mouth resuscitation
Importance of safe practices

---

*Also see Chapter 7.

Social

Accident costs in money, diability, and death responsibility: safe construction of motor vehicles, highways and information signs, toys, household appliances, farm and ranch equipment, houses and hotels, schools, business and industrial plants, children's clothing, and industrial equipment

Accident insurance and legal liability
Dangerous strangers
Responsibility for community emergency care programs
Sources of aid in accidents and emergencies

Spiritual

Values: importance of safety and health for all
Moral issues: protection of life and health of others in school, home, and other places
Humanism: responsibility of individual and community to prevent accidents and provide emergency care

Concepts

Concept	Application of health definition
1 Accident hazards and unsafe conditions exist in all environments.	Physical
2 An individual's safety depends on own ability to adjust to own environment.	Physical
3 Accidents are the leading cause of death and injury among elementary-school pupils.	Physical
4 Combinations of factors and forces contribute to the occurrence of accidents.	Psychological-social
5 Individuals, families, and community groups should be prepared to act effectively in the event of injury or sudden illness.	Social
6 Everyone has an obligation to reduce accident hazards in the environment.	Social
7 Safety and emergency care procedures are based on appreciation of the value and quality of life.	Spiritual

Objectives for grades K-3

Domain	Objectives for students	Basic concepts
Cognitive	1. Identifies accident hazards in own immediate environment.	1, 2, 6
	2. Explains the reasons for protecting people from accidents.	1-3
	3. Lists ways of avoiding accidents.	2, 4
	4. Cites examples of disrespect for safety procedures in motor vehicle, home, school, and public activities.	4, 6, 7
	5. Explains why first aid is important.	5, 7
	6. Identifies ways to care for minor injuries.	5, 7
	7. Cites best methods for getting help in emergencies.	5, 7
	8. Lists most common kinds of accidents among kindergarten to third grade pupils.	3, 4

Domain	Objectives for students	Basic concepts
Affective	1. Asks questions about hazards in the environment.	1, 2, 6
	2. Shows interest in the causes of accidents.	2, 4, 6
	3. Reacts to class discussions on loss of life and health by accidents.	2, 3, 6
	4. Expresses a desire to do something about the accident problem.	1, 3, 6
	5. Is attentive to information presented on simple first-aid measures and procedures for obtaining expert assistance.	5, 7
	6. Displays interest in helping others who may be sick or hurt.	5, 7
Action	1. Follows safe practices in classroom, lunchroom, hallways, and playground.	1-6
	2. Acts in a safe manner enroute to and from school—in bus or car, as pedestrian, or cycling.	1-4, 6
	3. Seeks aid from school personnel for injury or sudden illness.	5
	4. Helps other pupils when they are hurt or sick.	5, 7
	5. Improves safe practices at home and in the immediate environment.	1-4, 6
	6. Provides care for minor injuries.	5

Objectives for grades 4-6

Domain	Objectives for students	Basic concepts
Cognitive	1. Identifies the four classes of accidents: motor vehicle, home, public, and occupational.	1, 2
	2. Lists new environmental accident hazards resulting from technologic advances.	1, 2, 4
	3. Explains ways to reduce potential for accidents.	1, 2, 4, 6
	4. Tells how mental upsets may help cause accidents.	1, 4
	5. Lists the steps in first aid to help someone who has been injured or becomes ill.	5, 7
	6. Explains the most common emergency care procedures.	5
Affective	1. Asks questions about specific potential causes for various types of accidents.	1-4, 6
	2. Shows interest in environmental improvement to remove hazards.	1-4, 6
	3. Displays an appreciation of the accident toll on children, youths, and adults.	3, 7
	4. Is aware of the indifference and ignorance of the public with regard to safety.	2, 4, 7
	5. Inquires about ways to improve safety conditions in and around the school.	1, 3, 6, 7
	6. Expresses desire to become competent in first aid methods.	5, 7
	7. Shows concern for need to improve emergency care programs.	5, 7
Action	1. Acts in a safe manner in school and in the community.	1-4, 6
	2. Starts to develop habits of helping others in preventing accidents.	3, 6, 7
	3. Assists safety patrol or other school personnel when occasion arises.	3, 6, 7
	4. Seeks information on underlying causes of accidents.	4, 6
	5. Administers first aid for minor injuries.	5, 7
	6. Secures information on the community's emergency aid program.	5, 7

Objectives for grades 7-8

Domain	Objectives for students	Basic concepts
Cognitive	1. Lists deaths and injuries by age groups for the four major classes of accidents.	1, 2
	2. Explains the ways in which modern environment can threaten own safety.	1, 2, 4, 7
	3. Contrasts of pleasures and dangers of motorcycling, aquatic sports (scuba and skin diving, surfing, and water skiing), snow skiing, and other locally popular sport activities.	1, 4, 6
	4. Identifies reliable sources of safety information.	1, 3, 6
	5. Identifies safety organizations at the national, state, and local level.	1, 6
	6. Explains and illustrates specific major first-aid procedures.	5
	7. Lists reasons for needed improvements in community emergency care programs.	5, 7
	8. Lists school and community resources that can render assistance in emergencies.	5
Affective	1. Displays interest in doing own part to reduce hazards.	2, 6
	2. Accepts the need for improving environmental conditions and human behavior.	1, 2, 4, 6, 7
	3. Supports the concept that safety is everyone's responsibility.	6, 7
	4. Believes that improved safety measures could reduce deaths and injuries among elementary-age children and youths.	2, 3, 7
	5. Supports the work of the National Safety Council and other organizations in accident prevention.	6, 7
	6. Is aware of the need for better first-aid training for youth and adults.	5, 7
	7. Believes that there is an urgent need to improve community programs for emergency care.	5, 7
	8. Realizes there are school and community resources that provide assistance in emergencies.	5
Action	1. Attempts to act in a consistently safe manner under all conditions.	1, 2, 6
	2. Shows leadership in helping others avoid accidents.	2, 3, 6
	3. Demonstrates acceptance of the values of safe behavior.	2, 7
	4. Seeks solutions to accident problems in a scientific manner.	2, 4, 6
	5. Demonstrates leadership in school, home, or community emergency care program.	1, 5, 7
	6. Uses school and community resources in emergencies.	5-7
	7. Effectively carries out sound first-aid measures if and when an emergency occurs.	5, 7

SAFETY-FIRE UNIT*
Outline of content

Physiological

Effects

Harmful—3 million fires, 300,000 injuries (50,000 hospitalized), 8,800 deaths, $4 billion property damage yearly

Beneficial—warmth, cook food, manufacture products, scientific research, others

Leading causes of fire: electrical, smoking and matches, heating and cooking equipment, incendiary, children and matches, open flames, flammable liquids, lightning, chimneys and flues, and spontaneous ignition

Types of fires: slow-burning, flash, explosion

Classes of fires: combustibles (A); flammable liquids, grease, and oil (B); electrical (C); and metals (D)

Fire essentials: heat, fuel, oxygen

Where fires start in homes in rank order: living room, den or family room, basement, kitchen, bedroom, bathroom

Fabric flammability: cotton, linen, and silk burn more easily; tight-weave materials and those treated with flame-resistant substance and also nylon, acrylic, or polyester materials are more difficult to ignite; nylon, and so on, when ignited melts and causes severe burns

Control of fires: remove fuel (turn off electricity, dispose of wood, trash, and so forth), remove heat (cool), remove oxygen (smother)

Psychological

Risk-taking behavior hazards: injuries, deaths, property damage

Prevention behaviors

Before fires occur

Public places—hotels, theaters, restaurants, and others—identify escape exits and plan for escape; schools—participate in fire drills

Homes

Escape plans, periodic inspection of hazards, installation of smoke and flame detectors

Safety procedures

General—good housekeeping—trash removal, as well as clutter in basements, attics and other places, safe storage of flammable materials, remove damaged wires

Specific

Matches—close matchbook before striking, extinguish completely, do not play with

Outside fires—burn trash only when permitted, do not burn unless with adult, do not use flammable liquid to start and rekindle, among others

Lightning—stay indoors; be away from metal objects, such as wire fences; if outside avoid trees and small sheds, get away from water

Flammable liquids—do not use for home dry cleaning

Electrical appliances—turn off when not in use, do not use if fuse blown, keep away from objects that can burn, inspect regularly

Electricity—do not overload circuits, remove broken or bare wires, replace blown fuses

Clothing—wear sturdy jeans, tight-fitting jerseys, blouses without frills, jersey pajamas, tight-fitting or short-sleeve clothes

Baby-sitter—know all exits, escape plan, emergency telephone number; do not leave children alone

Holidays—do not use fireworks, use flashlight rather than candles on Halloween, do not use paper decorations, keep Christmas trees moist and in water and turn off lights when not at home or nearby

---

*National Fire Protection Association developed and launched a fire prevention and safety program in American schools in 1979.

After fires occur

    General—survival, escape, alarm, rescue, first aid

    Specific

        Home or building—follow escape plan

        Report of fire—telephone, alarm box

        When trapped—*crawl low* and get out of room, check door before opening and if hot fill cracks, signal for help in window with light-colored cloth or use telephone

        First aid—burns, asphyxiation, summon medical aid

        Clothing—drop to ground and roll

Social

Fire department: sole responsibility to fight fires, services usually available 24 hours daily, telephones readily available

Fire alarm boxes: purpose to summon fire fighters quickly, false alarms delay saving of lives and property

Fire codes, regulations, and laws

Spiritual

Values: importance of fire prevention and safety to prevent injuries and death and protect property

Moral issue: protection of people and property is a responsibility of all individuals

Concepts

Concept	Application of health definition
1 Fire has both beneficial and harmful effects.	Physical
2 Risk-taking behavior is the result of a variety of motivations.	Psychological
3 Individuals, families, and communities can prevent fires, save lives, and prevent injury and loss of property.	Psychological-social
4 Fire fighters are friends and necessary community helpers who render necessary services.	Social
5 Fire codes, regulations, and laws are necessary for the protection of individuals and property	Social
6 Individuals have responsibility to protect their own lives and property as well as their neighbors'.	Spiritual

Objectives for grades K-3

Domain	Objectives for students	Basic concepts
Cognitive	1. Identifies the benefits and harmful effects of fire.	1-3, 6
	2. Describes the actions to take in a fire drill.	3-6
	3. Demonstrates the proper stop, drop, and roll technique when clothes are on fire.	3, 6
	4. Describes the crawling low method to exit from a smoke-filled room.	3, 6
	5. Lists the procedures to follow when smoke or fire is discovered in a building.	3, 6
	6. Explains the reasons for reporting fire and smoke conditions immediately.	1, 3, 4, 6
	7. States reason to look for two exits from every building.	1, 3, 5, 6
	8. Lists the dangers of playing with or using matches improperly.	1-3, 6
	9. Recalls the dangers and safety procedures around heat-producing appliances.	1-3, 6
	10. Lists the types of electrical hazards in homes.	1, 3, 5, 6
	11. Recites the need for fire-safe holidays.	1-3, 6
	12. Recalls the way combustibles can be ignited.	1-3, 6
Affective	1. Values fire and smoke drills as necessary for fire safety.	3, 5, 6
	2. Supports the need to use the stop, drop, and roll technique when clothes are on fire.	3, 6
	3. Is interested in learning the crawling low procedure to exit from a smoke-filled room.	3, 6
	4. Values the need for prompt action when smoke or fire is discovered.	1, 3, 4, 6
	5. Realizes why fire and smoke conditions should be reported immediately.	1, 3, 6
	6. Realizes the importance of identifying and being able to locate two exits at all times.	3, 6
	7. Wishes to protect self and others from the hazards of improper use of matches.	1-3, 6
	8. Is interested in learning about fire safety around lighted stoves, heaters, and small appliances.	1-3, 6
	9. Wishes to keep family members fire safe when camping, picnicking, or cooking outdoors.	1-3, 5, 6
	10. Recognizes that electrical hazards may result in fire, injury, death and loss of property.	1-3, 6
	11. Believes in identifying and removing fire hazards.	1, 3, 4, 6
	12. Supports the need for fire-safe holidays.	1-3, 6
	13. Realizes the hazard of inserting objects into electrical outlets.	3, 6

Domain	Objectives for students	Basic concepts
Action (observable and non-observable)	1. Participates in fire and smoke drills at schools.	3, 5, 6
	2. Participates in the planning of a home evacuation plan.	3, 4, 6
	3. Immediately reports fire, heat, or smoke conditions to a responsible adult.	3, 4, 6
	4. Refrains from playing with or improperly using matches in home, school, or outdoors.	1-3, 6
	5. Refrains from playing near stoves, heaters, or fireplaces.	1-3, 6
	6. Reports electrical hazards to responsible adults.	1, 3, 4, 6
	7. Is able to crawl low to exit from a smoke-filled room.	3, 6
	8. Prepares evacuation plan for multistoried building when necessary.	3, 6
	9. Applies cold water on minor burns if no adult is present.	3, 6
	10. Seeks help for severe burns.	3, 6
	11. Practices and encourages family members to practice fire safety when camping, picnicking, or cooking outdoors.	1-3, 5, 6
	12. Practices and encourages fire safety on holidays and special occasions.	1, 3, 6

Objectives for grades 4-6

Domain	Objectives for students	Basic concepts
Cognitive	1. Describes the actions to take in fire drills.	3-6
	2. Demonstrates the proper way to stop, drop, and roll when clothes are on fire.	3, 6
	3. Identifies hazardous types of clothing.	3, 6
	4. States reason for crawling low in a smoke-filled room.	1, 3
	5. Lists procedures to follow when smoke or fire is discovered.	1, 3, 4, 6
	6. Explains reasons for reporting fire and smoke conditions immediately.	1, 3, 4, 6
	7. Describes the purpose of two exits from buildings.	3, 4, 6
	8. Identifies the first-aid procedures for burns.	3, 6
	9. Explains the procedures for fire safety when serving as a baby-sitter.	1, 3, 6
	10. States the reason for remaining clear of fire fighters while fires are in progress.	4
	11. Recites the reasons for refusing to turn in false fire alarms.	2, 4
	12. Lists the dangers of playing with or using matches improperly.	1-3, 6
	13. Identifies fire safety behavior around lighted stoves, heaters, and small appliances.	1-3, 6
	14. Recalls how to store flammable liquids safely.	1-3, 5, 6
	15. Explains the ways to extinguish outdoor fires.	1, 3, 6
	16. Identifies the types of electrical hazards in homes.	3, 6
	17. States the reasons for conducting periodic home hazard inspections.	2, 3, 6
	18. Recalls the need to use gasoline in well-ventilated places outside of buildings.	2, 3, 6

Domain	Objectives for students	Basic concepts
Affective	1. Values fire and smoke drills for fire safety.	3-6
	2. Values the need to use the stop, drop, and roll technique when clothes are on fire.	3, 6
	3. Is interested in learning the crawling low technique to exit a smoke-filled room.	3, 6
	4. Realizes the importance for prompt action when smoke or fire is discovered.	1-4, 6
	5. Appreciates the importance of locating two exits from buildings.	3, 4, 6
	6. Realizes the need for immediate attention to burns.	3, 6
	7. Supports the need to refrain from interfering with fire fighters while fires are in progress.	4
	8. Believes that false fire alarms are dangerous.	4
	9. Wishes to protect self and others from the misuse of matches and lighted objects.	1-3, 6
	10. Realizes the hazards when around lighted stoves, heaters, and small appliances.	1-3, 6
	11. Recognizes the hazards of improperly stored flammable liquids.	1-3, 5, 6
	12. Supports the need to extinguish outdoor fires properly.	1, 3, 5, 6
	13. Believes in the importance of the use of nonflammable substances inside homes and buildings.	1-3, 6
Action (observable) (observable and non-observable)	1. Helps teachers in the conduct of fire drills.	3, 6
	2. Helps family in the preparation and the following of a home evacuation plan.	3, 6
	3. Immediately reports fire, heat, or smoke observed to a responsible adult after leaving a building.	1, 3, 4, 6
	4. Refrains from improperly using matches and helps to store them properly.	1-3, 6
	5. Practices and encourages others to practice fire safety when outdoors.	1-3, 5, 6
	6. Assists in regular inspection of buildings and grounds.	3, 6
(nonobservable)	7. Performs accurately the stop, drop, and roll technique when clothes are on fire.	3, 6
	8. Properly performs the crawling procedure to exit a smoke-filled room.	1, 3, 6
	9. Establishes an evacuation plan in case of fire in a multistoried building.	3, 5, 6
	10. Applies cold water to a minor burn if no adult is present or seeks help with a severe burn.	3, 6
	11. Aids fire fighters on arrival regarding location of fire and whether persons are in building.	4, 5
	12. Refrains from turning in false fire alarms.	4, 5
	13. Helps to maintain storage of flammable liquids in proper containers.	1-3, 5, 6
	14. Encourages safe smoking habits in buildings, outdoors, and other places.	2, 3, 6
	15. Persuades others to use gasoline and other volatile substances in well-ventilated places.	1-3, 6

Objectives for grades 7-8

Domain	Objectives for students	Basic concepts
Cognitive	1. Identifies reasons for fire drills.	3-6
	2. Demonstrates proper technique for stop, drop, and roll technique to use when clothes are on fire.	3, 6
	3. Identifies reason to crawl low to exit from smoke-filled room.	1, 3, 6
	4. Lists procedures to follow when smoke or fire is discovered.	1, 3, 4, 6
	5. Explains reasons for reporting fire and smoke conditions immediately when discovered.	1, 3, 4, 6
	6. Demonstrates first aid for use with burn victims.	3, 6
	7. Describes procedure to plan a baby-sitter safety plan.	3, 6
	8. States the importance of remaining clear of fire fighters while fires are in progress.	4
	9. Lists the hazards of false fire alarms.	4
	10. Lists the hazards of the improper use of matches.	1-3, 6
	11. Recalls the dangers and safety procedures when around cooking, heating, and other heat-producing appliances.	1-3, 6
	12. Describes the flammability dangers from volatile substances.	1-3, 6
	13. Identifies the safety procedures for use in outdoor fires.	1-3, 5, 6
	14. Explains the purposes of fuses and the safe way to replace them.	1, 3, 6
	15. Lists procedures used in the conduct of regular inspection of buildings for fire hazards.	3, 6
	16. Lists the procedures to follow for fire-safe holidays.	3, 6
	17. Recalls the need for safe smoking habits in buildings, outdoors, and in automobiles.	1, 3, 5, 6
	18. Explains the types, costs and operation of fire and smoke detectors.	3, 5, 6
	19. Describes the significance of the use of the UL label on electrical appliances and equipment.	3, 5, 6
	20. States the reason for licensed or certified personnel performing electrical repairs and maintenance.	3, 5, 6
Affective	1. Supports the need for fire drills and accepts responsibility for sharing in their conduct.	3-6
	2. Values the need to use the stop, drop, and roll technique when clothing is on fire.	3, 6
	3. Is interested in learning the crawling low method to exit from a smoke-filled building.	3, 6
	4. Values the need for prompt action when smoke or fire is discovered.	1, 3, 4, 6
	5. Is interested in learning the first aid for burn victims.	3, 6
	6. Believes it is necessary to help children to escape from fire when serving as a baby-sitter.	3, 6
	7. Supports the need to refrain from interfering with fire fighters while fires are in progress.	4
	8. Believes that false fire alarms should not be turned in.	4
	9. Realizes the importance of using matches safely.	1-3, 6
	10. Willingly accepts the responsibility to protect children when around heat-producing equipment.	1-3, 6
	11. Recognizes the hazards of improperly used and stored flammable liquids.	1-3, 6

Domain	Objectives for students	Basic concepts
	12. Desires to practice fire safety outdoors.	2, 3, 5, 6
	13. Realizes the need for fuses and circuit breakers to protect from electrical overloads.	3, 5, 6
	14. Values the importance of periodic building inspections for fire hazards.	3, 6
	15. Supports the need for fire-safe holidays and special occasions.	3, 5, 6
	16. Recognizes the high risk of smoking in bed and the improper disposal of smoking materials.	2, 3, 6
	17. Supports the need for fire and smoke detectors.	3, 5, 6
	18. Is interested in learning the importance of the UL label.	3, 5, 6
	19. Recognizes the need for the repair and maintenance of electrical equipment by licensed or certified personnel.	3, 5, 6
	20. Is aware that lightning may cause fires and personal injury.	1, 3, 5, 6
Action (observable) (observable and non-observable) (nonobservable)	1. Willingly participates in fire and smoke drills at school and assumes responsibility to help conduct same.	3-6
	2. Participates in helping family and others develop and follow a home escape plan.	3, 6
	3. Prepares evacuation plan in case of fire for use in multistoried building.	3, 5, 6
	4. Conducts or assists in periodic building fire safety inspections.	3, 6
	5. Performs stop, drop, and roll technique to use when clothes are on fire.	3, 6
	6. Performs crawling low procedure to exit from smoke-filled room.	3, 6
	7. Immediately reports observed fire, heat, or smoke after leaving a building to responsible adult or fire department.	1, 3, **4**, 6
	8. Administers first aid for minor burns and shock and seeks medical help for major burns.	3, 6
	9. Plans safety procedures with parents when babysitting.	3, 6
	10. Assists fire fighters regarding location of fires and persons in burning buildings.	3, 4, 6
	11. Refrains from turning in false fire alarms.	3, 4, 6
	12. Refrains and discourages others from the improper use of matches.	1-3, 6
	13. Helps keep children away from heat-producing equipment and appliances.	3, 6
	14. Aids in the proper use and storage of flammable liquids.	1, 3, 6
	15. Assists with the removal of electrical hazards in the home.	3, 6
	16. Encourages safe smoking habits in buildings, outdoors, and automobiles.	1, 3, 6
	17. Persuades others to install fire and smoke detectors and to purchase electrical equipment with the UL label.	1, 3, 5, 6
	18. Encourages adults to install lightning protection on buildings where appropriate.	1, 3, 6

VISION AND HEARING UNIT*
Outline of content

Physiological

Definitions: hyperopia, myopia, astigmatism, amblyopia, glaucoma, color blindness, night blindness, strabismus, conjunctivitis, ophthalmologist, optometrist, optician, otitis media, otitis externa, conduction deafness, nerve deafness

Structure and function of eyes and ears

Eye structure—cornea, iris, lens, retina, optic nerve

Eye function—vision, appearance

Ear structure—outer ear, middle ear, inner ear, auditory nerve

Ear function—hearing

Refractive errors; eye diseases and ear disorders

Signs and symptoms of problems (see Chapter 5)

Psychological

Emotional problems: caused by strabismus, nearsightedness and farsightedness, partial or complete blindness, partial or complete deafness, learning difficulties

Purposes of testing and care of vision and hearing

Social

Selection of eye specialist

Selection of physician for earache or hearing problem

Choice of glasses, contact lenses, or hearing aid if needed

Periodic eye and ear examinations or screening tests—types, frequency

Spiritual

Values: importance of eye and ear health to self-image

Moral issues: provision of eye and ear care by government funding or private sources; protection of workers' vision and hearing in certain industries

Humanism: attitudes toward blind and deaf people; responsibility to help blind and deaf persons

---

*Also see Chapter 5.

Concepts

Concept	Application of health definition
1 Vision and hearing are the two most important senses for life and health.	Physical
2 Vision should be clear, sharp, and bright, with good distinction of color.	Physical
3 Common eye disorders include nearsightedness, farsightedness, and astigmatism.	Physical
4 One in five elementary pupils has a visual problem requiring professional care.	Physical-social
5 Visual disorders may cause learning difficulties or psychological problems.	Psychological-social
6 Good hearing depends on efficient function of the outer, middle, and inner ear as well as the auditory nerve.	Physical
7 Most hearing loss in childhood is a result of middle ear infection.	Physical
8 Nerve deafness may be caused by long-term exposure to loud noise, birth defects, certain diseases or medicines, head injury, or heredity.	Physical-social
9 One in twenty elementary school pupils has a hearing problem requiring professional care.	Physical-social
10 Hearing disorders may cause learning difficulties or psychological problems.	Psychological-social
11 During the elementary schools years, parents have the primary responsibility for correction of hearing or vision problems in pupils.	Spiritual
12 Prompt professional care can correct or improve most disorders of vision and hearing.	Physical-spiritual

Objectives for grades K-3

Domain	Objectives for students	Basic concepts
Cognitive	1. Tells why good eyesight and hearing are important.	1
	2. Explains the reasons for having vision and hearing tests.	2-4, 7, 9, 12
	3. Identifies the main parts of the eye and ear.	1, 2, 6
	4. Lists ways that good sight and hearing can help learning.	5, 10
	5. Discusses factors that may impair vision or hearing.	3, 7, 8
	6. Recalls any experiences of visual difficulty or earache.	3, 7
Affective	1. Is aware of the importance of good vision and hearing.	1
	2. Accepts the need for vision and hearing tests.	4, 9, 12
	3. Displays interests in how the eyes and ears function.	2, 6
	4. Listens carefully to the ways to protect vision and hearing.	1, 5, 10
	5. Shows interest in finding professional specialists in eye and ear health.	11, 12
Action	1. Participates cooperatively when vision or hearing tests are given at school.	4, 5, 9, 10
	2. Tells about any personal seeing or hearing difficulty.	4, 9, 12
	3. Uses textbooks and other printed materials in a proper, efficient manner.	2, 5
	4. Does not habitually ask the teacher or others to repeat what they have said.	6, 10

Objectives for grades 4-6

Domain	Objectives for students	Basic concepts
Cognitive	1. Explains the basic structure and function of eyes and ears.	1, 2, 6
	2. Identifies ways to protect vision and hearing.	1, 3, 7, 8
	3. Cites major causes of visual and hearing disorders.	3, 4, 7-9
	4. Illustrates how middle ear infection can cause hearing loss.	6, 7
	5. Describes effect of glare on visual acuity and eye fatigue.	2
	6. Explains important effects of color blindness and night blindness.	1, 2
	7. Explains the importance of regular eye and ear checkups and follow-up for corrections.	4, 9, 11, 12
Affective	1. Understands and appreciates the critical value of good vision and hearing.	1, 5, 6
	2. Accepts responsibility along with parents for care of eyes and ears.	1, 4, 9, 11, 12
	3. Displays interest in the effects of heredity on eye and ear disorders.	3, 8
	4. Appreciates the role of teachers, school nurses, and health specialists in the prevention and correction of eye and ear defects.	4, 5, 9-12
	5. Believes that healthy vision and hearing are necessary for a good education.	5, 10
Action	1. Takes an active, cooperative part when vision or hearing tests are given at school.	4, 5, 9, 10
	2. Protects own eyes and avoids endangering the eyes of others in sports and other physical activities.	1
	3. Reports any personal problem of seeing or hearing to the teacher, school nurse, or other professional person.	4, 9, 12
	4. Avoids probing ears with sharp objects, looking directly at sun, or other practices that can be harmful.	1
	5. Does not habitually ask the teacher or others to repeat what they have said.	6, 10
	6. Avoids exposure to excessively loud rock music or other high-decibel noise.	1, 8

Objectives for grades 7-8

Domain	Objectives for students	Basic concepts
Cognitive	1. Explains major errors of refraction in terms of altered structure and function and professional care.	3, 12
	2. Cites causes, prevention, and reasons for professional care of middle ear infection.	7, 12
	3. Lists types of environmental noise that can damage hearing.	8
	4. Analyzes differences between and among ophthalmologists, optometrists, and opticians.	12
	5. Describes possible effects on studying and learning of eye and ear disorders.	5, 10
	6. Describes possible emotional effects of eye and ear disorders.	5, 10
	7. Compares advantages and disadvantages of glasses and contact lenses.	12
	8. Cites dangers of delayed treatment for amblyopia (lazy eye) and glaucoma.	12

Domain	Objectives for students	Basic concepts
Affective	1. Understands and appreciates the critical value of good vision and hearing.	1, 5, 6
	2. Accepts responsibility for protecting and caring for own eyes and ears.	1, 4, 9
	3. Recognizes the responsibility of parents to seek professional care for children with eye or ear problems.	1, 4, 9, 11
	4. Inquires about the relative merits of various types of eye and ear specialists.	4, 9, 12
	5. Discusses the problem of providing medical care for the poor who have eye or ear problems.	1, 12
	6. Recognizes and appreciates the growing problem of noise pollution in the environment.	1, 8
Action	1. Takes an active, cooperative part when vision or hearing tests are given at school.	4, 5, 9, 10
	2. Protects own eyes and avoids endangering the eyes of others in sports, laboratory work, and other physical activities.	1
	3. Is able to make wise decisions regarding personal eye and ear care.	1
	4. Supports school and community efforts to protect and improve eye and ear health.	1, 4, 9, 11, 12
	5. Seeks reliable information on eye and ear health.	1, 3, 7, 8
	6. Consistently wears glasses or hearing aid if prescribed.	1, 5, 10
	7. Avoids exposure to excessively loud rock music or other high decibel noise.	1, 8

HOW DOES THE TEACHER PLAN?

There are a variety of ways teachers can plan for health instruction programs in schools. They involve procedures that organize learning experiences into a number of useful patterns. The materials presented in this chapter together with those provided in Chapters 11 through 14 will be helpful. These guidelines should be followed in the sequence listed for the *direct* teaching of health in classrooms where there are no health curricula:

1. Identify the needs and interests of students and use this information to establish a scope and sequence of content.
2. Identify student learning objectives.
3. Identify school and community resources for health instruction curriculum guides, teaching aids, and health education specialists.
4. Prepare a series of units from the scope and content previously identified.
5. Prepare lesson plans or modules from the units.

In those school districts where curriculum guides are available, teachers may wish to start with procedure 2 or 3 in this list.

Scope and sequence

A health instruction program should be related to the specific, local needs and interests of children in a particular school or school district. Using the material or one of the procedures described in this chapter will enable a teacher to identify these needs and interests. A meeting with the school nurse may help to obtain this information quickly. These data can then be grouped into topical areas as illustrated in Table 9-1 and Table 9-3 (under *Area*). The sequence in terms of a monthly schedule as seen in Table 9-3 is merely illustrative and may need modification during the school year. The mental

TABLE 9-3. Second grade teacher plans for health education, Ellensburg, Washington, public schools

Month	Area	Concepts	Learning activities	Teaching aids	Integration
September	Mental health	New experiences may give satisfaction. Home, school, church, and community can be warm, safe places.	Have children act as "big brother" or "big sister" to new students. Encourage drawings about things they love, how it feels when hurt or scared, how to be helpful. Encourage art work to relieve tensions. Discuss leaders and followers, forgiveness, and other topics. Dramatize putting self in others' shoes. Films	Films: We play and share together Courtesy at school Health text: Second and third grade	Language arts: Write short experiences. Music: Listen to quiet music if tense. Physical education: Suggest activities to relax. Social studies: Discover community helpers.
October	Dental health	Daily care promotes dental health. Dentists help maintain healthy teeth. Community resources provide for dental care.	Demonstrate, using model, brushing teeth. Make toothpowder in class. Show films and filmstrips and discuss them. Survey for number of dental visits. Have vocabulary bingo game. Write creative story about detergent foods.	Films: The beaver tale Learning to brush Salt and baking soda Toothbrush dental kit Pictures: Detergent foods and other foods	Mathematics: Count teeth; subtract missing teeth. Social studies: Characterize dentist as community helper. Art: Make detergent-food mobile.
November	Family health	Families help each other in the community.	Make pictures of the family. Tell experiences. List ways neighbors can be helpful. Arrange bulletin board about good neighborhood. Keep home duty chart.	Health text Record: Community helpers, Bowman Family fun with familiar music	Language arts: Employ creative dramatics. Music: Play records and songs. Art: Draw pictures.
January	Consumer and community health	Doctors and dentists who help us are our friends. Hazards of the environment can cause discomfort and problems. Many people keep water and air safe. Individuals can improve their surroundings.	Use atomizers to show how odors disperse. Show films and filmstrips. Make notebook on community helpers' relation to environment. Dramatize how children help at home. Locate on map local family and health agencies. Decorate flannelboard with creative story with characters. Leave food out, covered and uncovered, to relate to improper storage.	Film: Magic touch Filmstrip: Dentist School nurse Record: Community helpers Personal pictures Map of community	Social studies: Relate to community helpers unit. Language arts: Encourage reports or notebooks. Art: Make mural of community helpers.

Continued.

TABLE 9-3. Second grade teacher plans for health education, Ellensburg, Washington, public schools—cont'd

Month	Area	Concepts	Learning activities	Teaching aids	Integration
February	Nutrition	There are many kinds of foods. Some foods may be better than others for you.	Try new foods at tasting party. Experiment with white rat. Make vegetable soup. Make grocery store; use food models and shop for nutritious foods. Make clay or paper maché fruit. Select basic 4 foods, using magazine pictures.	Film: Eat for health Filmstrip: The food we eat Transparencies: See unit Food models of cardboard cutouts Health text	Art: Draw basic 4 food groups; prepare mural. Mathematics: Sell items in grocery store and add costs. Science: Experiment with white rat. Social studies: Take trip to store.
March	Anatomy-physiology	Good posture helps prevent fatigue, enables the body to work better, and makes use more attractive.	Use horizontal ladder for proper alignment. Use plumbline to check posture. Decorate bulletin board with stick figures or pipe cleaners. Show film and discuss.	Film: Beginning good posture Filmstrip: Let's stand tall	Physical education: Relate to apparatus activities. Art: Make silhouettes and individual pictures. Language arts: Show and tell.
April	Disease control	Good health habits help to keep us well. When ill, certain practices help us get well. We depend on others for good health.	Use poster to illustrate ways to protect others. Stage choral reading and speaking. Use chart to show ways germs are transmitted. Write reports. Grow germs on cloth in warm and cool places. Dramatize going to doctor for help. Experiment with potato and agar in petri dish.	Films: Common cold; Soapy the germ fighter Milne: We are six (Wheezie and Sneezie)	Language arts: Relate to experiences when sick, effects of care, creative stories. Science: Experiment with potatoes and agar.
May	Family health	An egg grows into a baby.	Discuss charts of mammal reproduction. Prepare chart on life cycle of animal reproduction. Hatch egg in incubator. Chart and discuss fish egg development. Make mural of animals caring for own babies. Show films and filmstrips.	Eye Gate charts of mammal reproduction series and fish egg development Films: Baby animals; animals growing up Filmstrip: The zoo trip	Science: Hatch egg; relate to insect unit. Art: Prepare mural.

health unit permeates the entire school curriculum, and portions may be covered whenever it is deemed appropriate. Teachers should feel free to modify this arrangement if a teachable moment arises that will permit introduction of an area when it will have greater student interest and motivation.

Unit construction

By definition, a unit in the curriculum refers to a procedure that organizes the learning experiences that are related to a particular topic or unifying purpose, for example, nutrition or dental health. The content of a unit generally includes these elements: topic, grade level, number of lessons or time, concepts, goals or objectives, content, teaching/learning activities, teaching aids, evaluation, and integration relationships. The partial illustrative units in this chapter contain the content, concepts, and objectives. The teaching techniques, the teaching aids, and the evaluation suggestions can be selected by the individual teacher from the material found in Chapters 11 through 14.

Table 9-3 is a partial illustrative unit or a series of units that is also a yearly scope-and-sequence arrangement prepared by an individual teacher. This unit outline can serve to help teachers plan a health instruction program for a semester or for an entire year. It will be necessary to develop lesson plans or modules from this material that will also include the objectives to be achieved and other relevant information.

It is important that consideration be given to the amount of time to be devoted to the unit. Assuming that 20 minutes per day is allotted for health instruction, approximately 100 minutes weekly or 1,800 minutes (30 hours) per semester would be provided for the instruction. Thus a teacher in a given semester might distribute this time as follows:

Nutrition—15 hours
Safety—10 hours
Dental health—5 hours

It might be advisable to provide information about ways to integrate this unit into language arts, social studies, science, and other curriculum areas. Table 9-3 provides an illustration of how this material might be included.

In planning the development of the unit, the teacher should check local school and community resources for material that will help in unit construction or lesson planning. These are some of the items that need to be identified: resource personnel, curriculum guides, films, filmstrips, models, charts, books, pamphlets, and other teaching aids. School nurses can often be of considerable help in this regard.

Lesson plans/modules

Lesson plans or modules are step-by-step procedures to be followed by the teacher in one session or for a given period of time. A lesson or module therefore may not be completed in one day. Lesson plans/modules are segments of instruction that are related to a particular subject matter area. They are prepared from the units previously discussed in this chapter, and their content may include concepts, objectives, content, and other information. They should also provide for a presentation or learning sequence that enables teachers to know exactly what to do at any time, how to introduce content, how to use the teaching aids, and how to involve students. A module may differ somewhat from a lesson plan in that it contains all of the teaching aids such as charts, illustrations, tests, and such materials ready for use by any teacher. A teacher may have to prepare a lesson plan without all of the items found in a module and therefore have to develop them before using the lesson plan. In some instances a unit around an instructional area may not be prepared but rather several modules centering on a given subject area are developed. This arrangement could be considered to be equivalent to a unit in organization.

The box on p. 234 provides an illustration of a lesson plan.

ILLUSTRATION OF A LESSON PLAN

Unit: To smoke or not to smoke
Level: Grade 7 or 8
Time needed: About 45 minutes
Previous lesson: Strategies used in advertising
Concept: Advertising may influence the use of tobacco
Objectives: The student:
  1. Identifies the appeals and slogans used to influence the use of cigarettes
  2. Realizes the importance of slogans and advertisements in influencing the use of cigarettes
Content: Advertising appeals: attractive people; glamour and elegance; sex or love; macho image; better taste; beautiful scenery; better filter; low tar and nicotine; sign of adulthood
Slogans: "You've come a long way, baby"
            "The coolest taste around"
            "Where a man belongs"
Some reasons for use: sell more cigarettes by trying to appeal to people's psychological needs through social influences—adulthood, peer acceptance, love, beauty, less hazardous to health, strong/powerful/controlled person
What are advertisers trying to sell? Hope; to be like others

Learning activities/procedures:
  1. On chalkboard teacher introduces some slogans and appeals obtained from cigarette advertisements brought to class by students.
  2. Organize class into small discussion groups with one student as chairperson in charge of each and provide each group with three advertisements. Ask each group to take 20 minutes to analyze the advertisements in terms of: (1) identification of the advertising appeals and slogans and (2) the reasons why these slogans and appeals are used.
  3. Reassemble the class, have chairpersons report their information, and tally the findings on the backboard.
  4. Teacher summarizes the essential points and students put information in notebooks.
Evaluation: Teacher observations of student interest in lesson together with the extent of pupil participation
Materials and resources needed: Numerous magazine and newspaper cigarette advertisements; chalkboard
Assignment: Students bring empty cigarette containers to class and be prepared to orally comment on the meaning of the "warning against smoking" found on the package. Also identify the amount of tar and nicotine in the brand of cigarettes. Read appropriate chapter in the assigned text.
Next lesson: Alternatives to use of cigarettes: develop own personality; better self-care; self-image; success in school, job, and recreational skills.
Vocabulary: glamour, elegance, beautiful, nicotine, advertisements, adulthood, attractive

Adapted from Middleton, K.: Back to some basics in health lesson planning, Health Education **12**:4-8, Jan./Feb. 1981.

QUESTIONS FOR DISCUSSION

1. Who should be responsible for curriculum development in the school?
2. What are the basic principles on which the health curriculum should be based?
3. Why is both formal and informal health education necessary in schools?
4. What is the meaning and significance of the inclusion of values in the curriculum?
5. What is the meaning of the concept approach, and how can it be applied to health education?
6. Who should be responsible for the development of the health and safety education curriculum?
7. How is the curriculum in health education determined?
8. To what extent would you use the health interests of children as shown by the Connecticut study?
9. What are some of the sources of helpful information in determining health content for elementary pupils?
10. What are the procedures to be followed in determining the health education curriculum for elementary schools?
11. What is the fundamental purpose of the unit in health teaching?
12. What is the meaning of the phrase *scope and sequence*?
13. What are the common, essential elements of a good *teaching* unit?
14. What should be the nature of the health education curriculum for students in special education and preschool programs?
15. What must the teacher do to plan for health instruction?
16. How can the broad concept of health (holistic) identified in Chapter 1 be utilized in the development of the health education curriculum?
17. What does the phrase *taxonomy of objectives* mean as identified by Bloom and others, and how can it be used in health education?

SELECTED REFERENCES

Allen, R.E., and Holyoak, O.J.: Evaluation of the conceptual approach to teaching health education: a second look, Journal of School Health **43**: May 1973.

Anderson, C.L., and Creswell, W.H.: School health practice, ed. 7, St. Louis, 1980, The C.V. Mosby Co.

Bloom, B., editor: Taxonomy of educational objectives. Handbook I: Cognitive domain, New York, 1956, David McKay Co., Inc.

Bouchard, R.P.: Behavioral objectives; a change agent for improved instruction. Paper presented at the annual meeting of the Association for Supervision and Curriculum Development, Atlantic City, N.J., March 1968.

Byler, R.V., Lewis, G.M., and Tottman, R.J.: Teach us what we want to know, New York, 1969, Mental Health Materials Center, Inc.

Corliss, L.M.: A report of the Denver research project on health interests of children, Journal of School Health **32**: Nov. 1962.

Cornacchia, H.J.: How we developed our elementary health education curriculum, Journal of Health, Physical Education, and Recreation **29**: April 1958.

Cornacchia, H.J., and Barrett, S.: Consumer health: a guide to intelligent decisions, ed. 2, St. Louis, 1980, The C.V. Mosby Co.

Cornacchia, H.J., and Barrett, S.: Shopping for health: an essential guide for products and services, St. Louis, 1982, Mosby Medical Library.

Dearth, F.: Construction and utilization of visual aids in dental health education, Thorofare, N.J., 1974, Charles B. Slack, Inc.

Fodor, J.T.: A conceptual approach to curriculum development in venereal disease education, Journal of School Health **43**: May 1973.

Fodor, J.T., Gmur, B.C., and Sutton, W.C.: Framework for health instruction in California public schools (adapted by California State Board of Education), Sacramento, Calif., 1970, California State Department of Education.

Goodlad, J.I., Stoephasius, R., and Klein, M.F.: The changing school curriculum, New York, 1966, Fund for the Advancement of Education.

Havighurst, R.J.: The values of youth. In Issues in American education, New York, 1970, Oxford University Press.

Hoyman, H.S.: Health ethics and relevant issues, Journal of School Health **42**: Nov. 1972.

Hoyman, H.: A synthetic health curriculum design in ecologic perspective, Journal of School Health **47**: Jan. 1977.

Krathwohl, D.R., Bloom, B.S., and Masia, B.B.: Taxonomy of educational objectives. Handbook II: Affective domain, New York, 1964, David McKay Co., Inc.

Lieberman, E.J., editor: Mental health; the public health challenge, Washington, D.C., 1975, American Public Health Association.

Loggins, D.: Values clarification revisited; clarifying what and how well, Health Education **7**: March/April 1976.

Mayshark, C.: Health education. In Encyclopedia of educational research, New York, 1968, Macmillan, Inc.

Middleton, K.: Back to some basics in health lesson planning, Health Education **12**:4-8, Jan./Feb. 1981.

Murphy, M.L.: Values and health problems, Journal of School Health **43**: Jan. 1973.

Pollock, M.B.: Curriculum planning; a gamesmanship approach, Journal of School Health **39**: Oct. 1969.

Raths, L.E., Harmin, M., and Simon, S.: Values and teaching: working with values in the classroom, Columbus, Ohio, 1966, Charles E. Merrill Publishing Co.

School Health Education Study, Inc.: Health education; a conceptual approach, St. Paul, Minn., 1967, 3M Education Press.

Sliepcevich, E.M.: Curriculum development; a macroscopic or microscopic view? The National Elementary Principal **48**: Nov. 1968.

Stenner, A.J., and Katzenmeyer, W.G.: Self-concept development in young people, Phi Delta Kappan **58**: Dec. 1976.

Tyler, R.: Basic principles of curriculum and instruction, Chicago, 1969, University of Chicago Press.

Valett, R.E.: Humanistic education; developing the total person, St. Louis, 1977, The C.V. Mosby Co.

Werden, P.K.: Health education for Indian students, Journal of School Health 44: June 1974.

SELECTED DEATH REFERENCES

Farberow, N.E., and others: Research in suicide. In Resnik, H.L.P., and Hawthorne, B.C., editors: Suicide prevention in the 70's, Washington, D.C., 1973, U.S. Department of Health, Education, and Welfare Publication HSM 72-9054, U.S. Government Printing Office.

Feifel, D., editor: New meanings of death, New York, 1977, McGraw-Hill Book Co.

Frederick, C.J.: Crisis intervention and emergency mental health. In Johnson, W.R., editor: Health in action, New York, 1977, Holt, Rinehart & Winston.

Frederick, C.J.: Suicide in the United States, Health Education 8: Nov./Dec. 1977.

Gray, V.R.: Dealing with dying, Nursing, June 1973.

Hafen, B.Q.: Death and dying, Health Education 8: Nov./Dec. 1977.

Hart, E.J.: Philosophical views of death, Health Education 8: Nov./Dec. 1977.

Hendin, D.: Death as a fact of life, New York, 1973, Warner Paperback Library.

Kastenbaum, R.: Death, society, and human experience, ed. 2, St. Louis, 1981, The C.V. Mosby Co.

Kübler-Ross, E.: On death and dying, New York, 1969, Macmillan, Inc.

Kübler-Ross, E.: Death; the final stages of growth, Englewood Cliffs, N.J., 1975, Prentice-Hall, Inc.

Switzer, D.K.: The dynamics of grief, Nashville, Tenn., 1970, Abingdon Press.

10
HEALTH EDUCATION APPROACHES

SELECTED CURRICULA IN ELEMENTARY SCHOOL HEALTH EDUCATION

Elementary school health education programs in the United States have been developed over the years by many health education and curriculum specialists and others without the use of a consistent and educationally sound philosophy and through a variety of haphazard procedures. Few individuals, including health educators, understand completely the process of curriculum development, know how to prepare functional programs using pupils, teachers, and community resources, have been engaged in successful experiences in terms of completion and implementation, or have been able to assess the effectiveness of their programs. Often programs and curricula have been prepared based on what others have done without adequate consideration of their quality or the nature of their impact on children. A basic set of principles and procedures that are universally acceptable or that can be generally implemented by professionals has not emerged. The development of health education curricula

cannot take place without such guidelines. The first major organized effort in this regard that used talented health education experts occurred in the School Health Education Study project in the 1960s under the direction of Dr. Elena Sliepcevich. Despite these problems, a number of curricula have been prepared at national, state, and local levels that have been found useful, gained popularity, and show promise of fulfilling the basic principles for development found in Chapter 9.

It is the purpose of this chapter to provide illustrations of selected programs that should receive study by schools. It is hoped the resources provided will encourage the examination of additional curricula before the adoption of one.

At this time there are no clear-cut procedures for developing and implementing health education curricula in U.S. schools. Numerous approaches have been used, and many programs are available. However, each program must be reviewed in terms of its particular strengths and weaknesses. Therefore schools wishing to introduce a health education curriculum should peruse other successful programs to be certain they are sufficiently flexible to meet local student and community needs and interests as well as meet the legal mandates of the state.

Before presenting the selected health education curricula, it is important to become familiar with the National Diffusion Network, a federal dissemination system designed to assist schools in locating exemplary programs in all areas of the curriculum, including health instruction programs.

NATIONAL DIFFUSION NETWORK

The National Diffusion Network (NDN) is a federally funded system that makes exemplary and proven educational programs available for adoption by schools, colleges, and other institutions. It was formed in 1973 under the Elementary and Secondary Education Act (ESEA) of 1965.

Many locally developed programs have proved to be extremely successful in helping children learn. However, few of these projects have been used away from the sites where they were first developed. Because of this, there was a need for a nationwide means of disseminating information about the programs. The NDN was formed in response to the wishes of Congress to formulate such a dissemination system.

The goals of the NDN are as follows:
1. To stimulate positive educational change in local schools
2. To help parents, teachers, and administrators find programs for children that match local needs
3. To move programs quickly and cost-effectively to classrooms nationwide
4. To help public and private schools secure information about new programs and support for their implementation in the district
5. To ensure that nationwide communication about these programs continues among local school districts, intermediate service agencies, and state departments of education

By reaching these goals, the NDN supports the flow of new ideas and increases the impact of educational investments that have already been made.*

The NDN can provide limited funds to help create an awareness of exemplary school programs, to aid schools with adoption decisions, to provide in-service training and follow-up assistance, and in selected instances, to purchase teaching aids for classroom use.

What is an exemplary program?

To be considered "exemplary" by the NDN, a program must have proved itself educationally effective for children and be cost-effective with reasonable per pupil cost. If a program developer feels that the program meets these criteria, the developer can submit the program to the NDN for consideration.

The Joint Dissemination Review Panel

Before being accepted for inclusion in the more than 300 previously NDN-approved programs, the program is reviewed by the Joint Dissemination Review Panel (JDRP). The JDRP was first appointed in 1972 and was created specifically to review evidence (generally research) presented by any program developers who stated that what they had developed was effective in attaining the goals set forth for that particular program.

Consisting of approximately 25 education and evaluation experts from the U.S. Department of Education, the JDRP convenes periodically to review programs that have been nominated as exemplary. Nomination for review is dependent on the source of funding for initially developing the project. If federal funding was used for project development, the state officer responsible for administering the federal funds can nominate it. A second means is for those who develop a program using state funds to contact the state

---

*The information contained in this section comes from a filmstrip and cassette on the National Diffusion Network prepared in 1979 by the U.S. Office of Education. It is available from the U.S. Department of Education.

program officer and request nomination. If other than federal or state funding sources were used for project development (such as foundational or other agency support), the person responsible for developing the program can contact the Director of the Division of Replication in the U.S. Department of Education directly and request nomination consideration.

Once a program has been nominated, it undergoes a preliminary review by the Director of the Division of Replication to determine its social fairness and the accuracy of the supporting evidence presented for the claims of program effectiveness. If this preliminary review is positive, a brief summary of the project is prepared by the persons requesting nomination. This summary is reviewed by the federal program office to determine if the program should be reviewed by the JDRP. If the program is approved for review, a public meeting, including a person or persons knowledgeable in the techniques used to evaluate the program's effectiveness, is convened. A minimum of seven experts, appointed by the Secretary of Education, review the evidence submitted and vote to determine if the nominated project does, in fact, do what it purports to do. This decision is made immediately following the review discussion.

If a project is approved, it becomes eligible for diffusion funds either from the NDN or through other federal funding programs. If the program is not approved, the reasons for rejection are explained. In the case of rejection, the project can be revised or new evidence of effectiveness can be prepared and the project resubmitted for consideration at a later date.

An approved program receives several direct benefits:
1. Recognition of the program by both professionals and the public through awareness workshops
2. Increased chances for obtaining competitive federal funds
3. Entry into a federal diffusion system

NDN state facilitators

Each state has one or more individuals specifically designated as State Facilitators for the NDN. These persons are in key positions to aid local school district planners who want to examine a variety of approaches to a given curricular area before the development of a local curriculum. The state facilitator is often in close communication with the Elementary and Secondary Education Act (ESEA) Title IV director for the state and will be able to convene an awareness workshop of proven programs for districts that ask to see exemplary projects available through the NDN. These "showcases" are conducted several times each year in each state at no cost to the local district and generally prove quite useful, since they provide information about a wide range of programs in any given curricular area.

The state facilitator may also assist a local school district match their needs with appropriate NDN projects, help develop and plan local workshops, help search for alternate sources of funding, and help local program developers prepare the information needed to nominate a program for JDRP review. Further, the state facilitator has limited funds to support school personnel who wish to visit sites of demonstration projects.

SELECTED ELEMENTARY SCHOOL HEALTH INSTRUCTION PROGRAMS

Presented here are some examples of the more widely known elementary health education programs available in the United States. This listing is in no way meant to be exhaustive, since many districts have developed some type of health instruction program. It should also be pointed out that inclusion of a given program does not suggest our endorsement of the program nor does omission of a program suggest our rejection. These programs are presented as examples of nationally validated programs (included on the NDN), state-based programs, locally based programs, programs available through various health-related agencies, and commercially prepared programs. A listing of sources of selected programs may be found in Appendix D.

Programs included in the NDN

In May 1979 the JDRP approved the first health instruction program to ever be nationally validated for inclusion on the NDN. One year later a second program underwent review and was approved. These two programs are the only health instruction programs currently approved for inclusion in the NDN.

School Health Curriculum Project. The School Health Curriculum Project (SHCP) is claimed to be a comprehensive program of health instruction specifically designed for children in grades 5, 6, and 7. There is also a grade 4 program currently under review by the JDRP.

The goals of the SHCP are as follows:

1. To increase students' knowledge and decision-making abilities about a wide range of behaviors and in a number of health education areas
2. To help students learn how their bodies function and how their personal choices affect their health
3. To integrate classroom learning with other life situations
4. To offer students and teachers an experienced-based understanding of the physical, social, mental, and emotional dimensions of their own health

Designed as a direct method of teaching health, the units of instruction also lend themselves to integration with other elementary school curricular topics. The SHCP is a broad-based program that includes an intensive, 60-hour teacher-training component; a wide variety of teaching methods; and strategies for involving both parents and community resources. It incorporates a variety of useful teaching aids. It has been called a student-centered, hands-on, multimedia approach to health instruction. The program provides many opportunities for each student to engage in self-expression and individual exploration. The class-

room organization incorporates large and small group activities as well as individual activities that allow the concept of individualization of instruction to become a reality.

Although the specific content varies by grade level, the overall organization of each grade level unit remains rather constant. The basic grade level organization of the SHCP is as follows:

Introduction: Activities to motivate children to study health.

Awareness: The interaction between body systems.

Appreciation: The unique contribution of a given body system to the optimal functioning of the human organism.

Structure and function: How a specific body system is organized and how it functions when it is in a healthy state.

Diseases and disorders: What are some major health problems that have initial impact on a specific body system and can cause dysfunction within the entire organism? What factors may be precursors to development of a particular health problem?

Prevention: What can the individual do to avoid the precursors of a particular disease, thus reducing the chance of incurring a health problem?

Culmination: An overview of the major concepts learned throughout the unit, which are then presented by the students to their parents in a special parents' night.

The various units of instruction are designed to be taught approximately one class period per day (40 to 50 minutes in a class period), 5 days per week for an 8- to 10-week period of time. Although the scope of the content within each unit of study is broad, each unit was developed around a central theme. The titles of the four grade level units of instruction are as follows:

Grade 4: About Our Digestion and Our Nutrition

Grade 5: About Our Lungs and Respiration

Grade 6: About Our Hearts and Circulation

Grade 7: Living Well with Our Nervous System

Initially funded for dissemination through a contract with the National Clearinghouse for

Smoking and Health in 1965, the SHCP has attracted funds from a wide range of local and state agencies as well as private foundations and businesses. Each school district wishing to adopt the program has the responsibility for obtaining funds for teacher training and materials.

At present the SHCP has been adopted by over 300 school districts in 37 states. It is also being used in a modified form in Sheffield, England, and in the Arabian-American Oil Company schools in Saudi Arabia.

Primary Grades Health Curriculum Project. A companion to the School Health Curriculum Project, the Primary Grades Health Curriculum Project (PGHCP) was developed in the Seattle, Washington, Public Schools through a combined contract between them, the Bureau of Health Education (now the Center for Health Promotion and Education of the U.S. Department of Health and Human Services), and the American Lung Association. The PGHCP was validated by the JDRP in 1980 for inclusion in the NDN.

The PGHCP follows the same basic organizational format as the SHCP in terms of the internal structure of each unit. The various unit titles for the PGHCP include the following:

Kingergarten: Happiness is Being Healthy
Grade 1: Super Me
Grade 2: Sights and Sounds
Grade 3: The Body: Its Framework and Movement

As with the SHCP, the PGHCP also has a teacher-training component. However, the actual training workshop for the PGHCP is only 30 hours. Further, the classroom implementation is somewhat shorter because the class periods in the lower elementary grades are generally shorter than one finds in the upper elementary grades.

To implement the program in the classroom, approximately one class period per day (20 to 30 minutes), 5 days per week for 8 to 10 weeks is required. This means that approximately 100 to 150 minutes per week is spent in direct health instruction. In addition, numerous activities included in the program can be integrated with other topics in the curriculum. Thus the pupils are exposed to more than direct health instruction.

The learning and teaching methods included in the PGHCP include small- and large-group activities and experiments, the use of different media, field trips, and the involvement of other teachers in the school (for example, music, physical education, and art teachers), parents, and health professionals from the community. The materials used for the program include books, films, supporting filmstrips, games, records, audiotapes, and overhead transparencies. All of these materials are included in the program to assure that a broad-based use of the senses as well as the reading levels and learning opportunities are integrated into the curriculum.

Since the inception of the PGHCP, there has been an ongoing program of research to determine the effectiveness of the PGHCP in selected demonstration centers from four school districts across the United States. The evaluation reports are available from the American Lung Association.

At present the PGHCP is being used in approximately 200 school districts in nearly 30 states and in Saudi Arabia.

State-based progams

A number of states require some sort of health instruction to be included in the curriculum of the school. Most of these states require the teaching of drug, alcohol, and tobacco use and misuse. Seven states (California, Colorado, Florida, New York, Illinois, North Carolina, and Vermont) have gone beyond this, however, and have provided specific guidelines for the development of health instruction curricula. Both New York and Illinois have passed legislation allowing the Superintendent of Public Instruction to set minimum guidelines for the development of health instruction programs. California and North Carolina have developed rather detailed frameworks for health instruction. Others recognize exemplary programs operating within the state and have initiated validation procedures for these programs.

According to a report recently published by the U.S. Department of Health and Human Services entitled *School Health in America,* education codes in 42 states require instruction about health as a part of the school curriculum. A total of 33 states have published curriculum or planning guides for health education and 49 state education agencies employ an individual who has responsibility for health education. Within the past 5 years, 18 states have completed some sort of evaluation of health education.*

California framework. The Framework for Health Instruction in California Public Schools† was originally published in 1970 by the California State Department of Education. The Framework incorporates a conceptual approach with an emphasis on the achievement of selected behavioral objectives and the development of health knowledge and attitudes. The document is an attempt to provide a comprehensive set of guidelines for school districts so that with minimal effort, through the addition of teaching/learning activities, teaching aids, and evaluation procedures, a health instruction curriculum can be developed.

The Framework evolved from an assessment of the health needs of school-age children in California and was developed by a team of health instruction experts. The needs assessment included literature reviews and numerous discussions with various health authorities from around the state. Ten content areas emerged: consumer health; mental-emotional health; drug use and misuse; family health; oral health, vision, and hearing; nutrition; exercise, rest, and posture; disease and disorders; environmental health hazards; and community health resources. The Framework is organized to include an overview, major concepts, specific

grade level concepts, and suggested behavioral objectives and content for each content area.

The publication is updated periodically to include new developments in the health field as they arise. The document has been distributed widely in California as well as elsewhere across the United States. It forms the basis for many of the health instruction programs that have been developed by local school districts in California as well as in other states.

New York strands. In 1969 the New York State Education Department organized health knowledges, attitudes, and practices into five major conceptual areas or "strands": (1) Physical Health; (2) Sociological Health Problems; (3) Mental Health; (4) Environmental and Community Health; and (5) Education for Survival. Teacher guides were prepared for each of the strands at four grade levels (grades K to 3, 4 to 6, 7 to 9, and 10 to 12). The guides contain specific pupil objectives and provide the teacher with an outline of the content needed to reach those objectives. Major understandings and fundamental concepts, suggested teaching aids, suggested learning activities, and supplementary information for the teacher such as additional sources of free or inexpensive health instruction aids are included. Provision is made for modification of the content or sequence to satisfy local needs and interests in the health instruction program.

Locally based programs

A number of local school districts have developed programs that are said to be comprehensive in scope. For example, Project Prevention in The Dalles, Oregon; the Cleveland County School Health Education Program in Shelby, North Carolina; and the North Clackamas, Oregon School District Health Education Program. Still others have focused on fewer content areas of health instruction such as a program called "Here's Looking at You Two," in Seattle, Washington.

Project Prevention. Primary prevention of health problems through a comprehensive

---

*Castile, A.S., Allensworth, D., and Noak, M.: School health in America: a survey of state school health programs, ed. 3, Kent, Ohio, 1982, American School Health Association.
†California State Department of Education: Framework for health instruction in California, Sacramento, 1972, The Department.

framework of health instruction is emphasized in Project Prevention. This health instruction program was initially developed in The Dalles, Oregon, using funds from ESEA Title IV C. This was one of the development and demonstration grants provided through the NDN process.

The program was designed for students in grades K through 12. An advisory committee consisting of parents, grade level teachers, medical specialists, school administrators, social workers, counselors, clergy, and students from grades 6 through 12 developed the guiding philosophy for the program. Program goals, scope and sequence, and lesson plans were then developed. The program can be entirely or partially adopted and integrated into the existing instructional program. It is designed primarily as a program of direct instruction, although many of the activities integrate well with other topics in the curriculum.

Emphasis is placed on each student developing a positive self-concept, applying decision-making skills in a variety of situations, developing effective communication skills for effective, healthful living, and evaluating various health resources and services available in the community. Teachers who use the program must participate in an intensive 2-day training program designed to acquaint them with the various methods and materials to be used. The teacher's guide includes lesson plans, a guide to free or inexpensive health materials, a guide for adopting the program, individual test booklets designed for each lesson plan, 35-mm slides, audiotapes, and overhead transparencies. Approximately 150 teachers in approximately 30 schools in eastern Oregon and southeastern Washington are currently using the program.

Cleveland County School Health Education Program. The Cleveland County School Health Education Program is an adaptation of the state framework for health developed in North Carolina and is funded by the North Carolina State Board of Education. Central to achievement of the overall program goal is the development of community support for the program. This is accomplished through the use of a broad community-representative local school health council with the assistance of the school PTA, the local college, and numerous community agencies.

The basic goals of the program are to:
1. Help students accept responsibility for their own health
2. Improve student decision-making skills especially as these decisions affect their health needs
3. Provide students with a basis for developing healthy life-styles and the ability to meet life's challenges without taking undue risks
4. Help students evaluate the various factors that affect individual health status
5. Improve students' comprehension of the interaction between health status, personal needs, stress, and developmental characteristics as manifested throughout the human life cycle

Audiovisual aids, including posters, audiotapes, and films, are used, and various community agencies, including the Agency for Instructional Television, provide materials for classrooms. In-service workshops for teachers are conducted and supported by health education specialists, university personnel, and school administrators.

North Clackamas, Oregon School District Health Education Program. As evidenced by these goals, the prevailing theme in the North Clackamas health instruction program is the prevention of health problems:
1. Promoting good health through prevention
2. Assisting parents to help their children develop skills for effective functioning in varied roles and life-styles
3. Encouraging self-responsibility for personal health
4. Providing opportunities for students to develop adapting and coping skills that can be applied in a variety of situations

There are four major areas of concentration (physical health, mental health, community health, and safety) in the program. These four areas encompass 23 different content areas that articulate with the goals, competencies, activities, and teaching resources.

The teacher's guide includes grade level competencies and activity cards that specify the philosophy, suggested activities, and resources that can be incorporated into the lesson for a student to reach a given competency. Teachers are free to select activities best suited to their students' needs and abilities, as well as to the teacher's personal teaching style. Numerous techniques gleaned from existing U.S. programs, commercially prepared materials, and teacher suggestions are provided. The teaching aids include a wide variety of classroom supplements and duplicated materials; the program does not rely on a specific textbook. Teachers can use currently available school resources as well as free or inexpensive materials from many community agencies.

Here's Looking at You Two. "Here's Looking at You Two" is a school-based alcohol and drug education program originally developed by personnel from Educational Service District 121 in Seattle, Washington, in 1975 through a grant from the National Institute on Alcohol Abuse and Alcoholism.

The overall goals of the program are to:
1. Assist students make responsible decisions about alcohol and other drugs
2. Foster coping skills and a positive self-concept
3. Provide information about alcohol and drugs and their effects
4. Improve student attitudes about the use and nonuse of alcohol and drugs

The program consists of 15 detailed plans at each grade level, which can each be integrated with other subject matter normally included in the elementary school curriculum. Thus the program can be taught as a 3-week unit in a regular health instruction program or can be integrated throughout the school year. A 3-day teacher-training workshop for classroom teachers, school counselors, nurses, and school administrators is designed to acquaint these persons with the methods, materials, activities, and content of the program.

Schools in 45 states and 5 foreign countries are currently using the program.

Programs available through various health-related agencies and associations

The American Heart Association, the American Cancer Society, the National Dairy Council, and the National Fire Protection Association are some of the many voluntary health agencies that have developed programs that can be integrated into an existing health instruction program.

Putting Your Heart into the Curriculum. "Putting Your Heart into the Curriculum," developed by the American Heart Association, is specifically designed as a series of teaching modules and strategies to be used in grades K through 12 by teachers as an addition to their regular health instruction program. It is designed to affect those attitudes and value judgments of young people that may have an effect on their behaviors.

The following areas are included:
1. Choosing not to smoke
2. Making informed and healthy food choices
3. The importance of having a blood pressure within normal limits
4. Recognizing the various risk factors of cardiovascular disease and how to lessen their impact on the individual
5. Developing and keeping a regular program of weight control and physical exercise

In-service training for teachers is available from the Association or through selected universities that participate in the program. Teaching aids and materials are available free of charge from local chapters of the American Heart Association.

An Early Start to Good Health. "An Early Start to Good Health" instruction program for grades K through 3 developed by the American Cancer Society consists of four separate units and includes teacher guides, filmstrips, posters, phonograph records, and activity sheets. It is designed to develop health awareness and to supplement existing programs.

The four units of instruction include the following:

Unit 1: My Body—introduction to basic body organs

Unit 2: My Self—the difference between the inner and outer self

Unit 3: My health—activities needed to maintain health

Unit 4: My choice—personal choices and the effects of those choices

Health Network. Health Network was also developed by the American Cancer Society and is designed as a companion to the Early Start to Good Health program. Health Network consists of three units of instruction designed specifically for use in grades 4, 5, and 6. Each unit contains a filmstrip and either a phonograph record or tape cassette that provides the story for the unit. Also included are a teacher's guide with an introductory lesson and several group activities, reproduction masters to make handouts for the students, and either a game or poster that exemplifies the basic content of the unit.

The three units of instruction each have objectives for students that aid the teacher in planning to use the program. The three units of instruction are as follows:

Unit 4: Special People—cigarettes don't improve one's self-image and one need not be a "star" to be a valuable person.

Unit 5: Health News—a simulated television news broadcast that reports on how the respiratory system uses oxygen in the process of breathing

Unit 6: Starga's World—a girl from outer space visits Earth and learns how to make decisions about herself and her health.

Food: Your Choice. The National Dairy Council designed "Food: Your Choice" a nutrition education program, for students in grades K through 6. The program is sequential and activity oriented. Its purposes are to: (1) foster an understanding of key concepts of nutrition, (2) convey the importance of nutrition in preventing health problems, and (3) encourage maintaining a healthy body.

The program consists of three levels:

Level 1: Specifically designed for use in grades K through 2, nutrition concepts are learned through hands-on experiments and meal preparation.

Level 2: Designed for use in grades 3 and 4, this level is designed to further expand the concepts learned in Level 1. Students have the opportunity to examine more closely the role of food in society. They classify foods and learn the consequences of poor food selection and eating habits.

Level 3: Designed for grades 5 and 6, this level focuses on a study of nutrients in food as well as analysis of those factors that influence eating patterns, food selection, and food advertising. Special materials have been developed to integrate nutrition teaching into social studies, science, and home economics.

Most state dairy council office staff members will conduct teacher-training workshops designed to acquaint school personnel with the program.

Learn Not to Burn. The "Learn Not to Burn" program was developed between 1975 and 1978 by the National Fire Protection Association to provide a comprehensive fire prevention program for grades K through 8. A survey revealed that little coordination between fire departments and school districts in terms of fire prevention curricula existed in the United States. The program is unique in that it involves parents as well as fire department personnel.

The basic goals of the program are as follows:

1. Protection of the individual and others from fires

2. Prevention of fires

3. Motivation of persons to practice fire prevention and safety

The program consists of three major segments that are reflected in the program goals. It includes 25 key fire prevention and protection behaviors in the three major segments of protection, prevention, and persuasion. Each of the 25 behaviors has at its core an action domain determined to be the most direct means of saving life and property together with knowledges and attitudes necessary to achieve the action.

Commercially prepared programs

Many school health instruction programs rely on commercial companies for the teaching aids and other materials they use in their programs. Therefore some of these business firms have prepared curricula that incorporate the variety of teaching aids they manufacture for sale. Two such programs are "Being Healthy," developed by the A.J. Nystrom Company, and the "Health Activities Project," distributed by the Hubbard Scientific Company.

Being Healthy. The three units of instruction of the "Being Healthy" program, digestion, respiration, and circulation, correspond to the equivalent grade level units of the SHCP. Each unit of the program comes individually packaged and is complete with a set of activity cards, reproduction for duplicating student worksheets, and a teacher's guide that outlines the program philosophy. Specific behavioral objectives for each activity are stated, and performance indicators are included. Student logs and progress reports for the students are contained in each unit, and the student can learn in a self-paced manner.

The company offers a brief teacher orientation to be sure that the teacher understands the basic activities and philosophy of the program before implementing it.

Health Activities Project. The "Health Activities Project" gets students involved with personal health and safety using hands-on, discovery-type activities. It is assumed that students can realize how to improve their health and safety by learning how their bodies function.

The program uses a variety of teaching aids for the 58 different activities. The teacher's guide contains a description of each activity, the health background for it, the space requirements necessary to conduct the activity, and the materials that are needed. The activities are specifically designed to supplement and enrich existing school health, physical education, and science curricula.

SUMMARY

The programs described in this chapter represent but a few of the different types of health instruction programs available in the United States. The critical elements in each program that must be identified are its flexibility in terms of meeting student and community needs and how local teachers can use the program in terms of direct and integrated health instruction. For those persons faced with having to develop a health instruction program, these illustrations provide suggestions for use in newly developed curricula.

We recognize that anyone who is not familiar with health education curriculum development and desires to develop a program should obtain expert assistance before undertaking such a project. This aid might be obtained from the state department of education, from professional health educators in colleges or universities, or from neighboring school districts. Programs should be developed that are responsive to student and community needs and that are based on sound principles of curriculum development such as those presented in Chapter 9.

QUESTIONS FOR DISCUSSION

1. Why do you think that no clear-cut procedures for developing and implementing health instruction curricula in U.S. schools have been developed?
2. What do you perceive is the value of the National Diffusion Network?
3. Why might state National Diffusion Network facilitators be considered the most important links in the network?
4. What are three ways a program might be considered for inclusion in the National Diffusion Network, and what is the basic process for including a program in the network?
5. Briefly critique the process and procedures used by the Joint Dissemination Review Panel in reviewing "exemplary" programs.
6. How would *you* define an "exemplary" health instruction program? How does your definition differ from that used by the Joint Dissemination Review Panel?
7. What benefits might accrue to a program that is included in the National Diffusion Network?

8. You have been asked to make a recommendation to a school district about how to initiate a comprehensive school health instruction program. How would you go about formulating your recommendation and what basic advice would you give to the school district about curriculum development?

9. What factors appear to have been key elements in the success of the specific programs illustrated in this chapter?

10. What factors do you feel have kept many state legislatures from enacting comprehensive school health instruction legislation?

11. What factors exist in common between the four locally based health instruction programs presented in the text?

12. What factors exist in common between the five programs available through health-related agencies that are discussed in the text?

SELECTED REFERENCES

American Heart Association Subcommittee on Health Education of the Young: We've put our heart into the curriculum, Health Education 13:20-23, Jan./Feb. 1982.

Byler, R., Lewis, G., and Totman, R.: Teach us what we want to know, New York, 1969, The Mental Health Materials Center Inc., for the Connecticut State Board of Education.

California State Department of Education: Framework for health instruction in California, Sacramento, 1972, The Department.

Castile, A., Allensworth, D., and Noak, M.: School health in America: a survey of state school health programs, ed. 3, Kent, Ohio, 1982, American School Health Association.

Evans, N.: Advancing school health education via the National Diffusion Network, Health Education 12:10-13, Sept./Oct. 1981.

Gilbert, G.: Organizing for health education, Health Education 10:22-23 May/June 1979.

Health education curriculums in action, Health Education 10: Nov./Dec. 1979.

Health instruction: suggestions for teachers, Journal of School Health Special Edition, May 1969.

Kupsinel, N.: A look at state health curriculum guides, Health Education 11:25-27, May/June 1980.

National Parent-Teacher Association: Comprehensive School/Community Health Education Project, Chicago, 1981, The Association.

Olsen, L., Redican, K., and Krus, P.: The school health curriculum project: a review of research studies, Health Education 11:16-21, Jan./Feb. 1981.

Parcel, G.: Skills approach to health education: a framework for integrating cognitive and affective learning, Journal of School Health 46:403-406, Sept. 1976.

Pennsylvania Department of Education: Conceptual guidelines for school health programs in Pennsylvania, Harrisburg, 1970, The Department.

Price, J.: Learn not to burn: a K-8 curriculum, Journal of School Health 51:543-547, 1981.

Talmage, H.: Evaluating nutrition education curricula, Health Education 11:14-19, Sept./Oct. 1980.

The School Health Curriculum Project: Focal Points, Feb. 1976.

The School Health Education Study: Health education: a conceptual approach to curriculum design, Washington, D.C., 1967, The Study.

Willgoose, C.: Saving the curriculum in health education, Journal of School Health 43:19-23, March 1973.

PART FIVE

Methods and materials in health education

11

BEHAVIOR MODIFICATION IN HEALTH EDUCATION

Health education frequently has been attacked for its failure to help individuals develop practices and habits that prevent illness and maintain and promote good health. It often has been guilty of solely providing information of a physiological nature. However, the problem of how to modify or whether to try to modify the health behavior of people has not been adequately resolved. Human health behavior is a complex process that may be resistant to change but is influenced by a variety of factors previously identified in the concept of health (see Chapter 1) that include physiological, psychological, social/cultural, and spiritual components (holistic health*). Home atmosphere, racial, ethnic, or cultural background, peer influences, adequacy of housing and food intake, affection received, achievements, self-respect, and bias and prejudice have specific impact on children and youth. The needs, motivations, beliefs, values, experiences, and environment of people affect the health habit patterns they develop. They enable people to make responsible

health decisions and to cope with or adjust to problems they face in the society in which they live. These factors are in need of recognition and use if educational programs are to aid individuals to achieve high levels of wellness.

It is the purpose of this chapter to provide understanding in regard to behavior modification that will (1) help teachers to become better informed in regard to the learning process necessary for successful teaching in health education and (2) demonstrate the application of essential principles of learning to be used in the selection of methods and techniques (see Chapter 12) for effective instructional programs.

WHAT IS BEHAVIOR MODIFICATION?

Health behavior modification refers to the changing of health knowledges, attitudes, and practices acquired by individuals. It is an internal process that is influenced by personal needs and environmental exposures. It is not something done to pupils but rather involves educational procedures or methods used to help individuals adapt, adjust, solve problems, or

---

*Holistic health is a term in vogue that refers to the health of the total person and not merely the physiological aspects.

cope with situations in regard to their health. Health education should attempt to aid students to make intelligent and responsible decisions.

The question of the extent to which educators should try to modify health behavior is a moot one. Should the use of alcohol or tobacco be condemned or condoned? Should all individuals exercise at regular intervals and in the same manner? Should the use of contraceptives be promoted? Should pupils reduce their consumption of foods containing high levels of sugar and cholesterol? Should the flossing and brushing of teeth be universally advocated? Hochbaum* states that in controversial aspects of health behavior, no attempt should be made to make modifications in line with rigid criteria (not to drink, not to smoke). He believes that students should be helped to develop skills and motivation that will enable them to arrive at rational and intelligent decisions. Smith and Ojemann have identified a four-step model for decision making that is worthy of consideration.†

1. Examine the motivating forces operating in a given situation; identify the needs individuals are trying to satisfy through their behavior.
2. Devise and examine the probable intermediate and remote effects of possible alternative ways of satisfying these motivations.
3. Apply your personal standard to the proposed course of action to determine if the effects of the action are compatible.
4. Decide either for or against the selected behavior at this point in time.

WHAT IS LEARNING?

Learning is a complex process that is dependent on factors taking place both inside and outside the individual. It refers to the physical, in-

---

*Hochbaum, G.M.: Behavior modification, School Health Review **2**: Sept. 1971.

†Smith, L.V., and Ojemann, R.H.: A decision making model, School Health Review **5**: Jan./Feb. 1974.

---

tellectual, and emotional changes that occur in human organisms as a result of their interaction with the environment. It is the growth and development process that goes on within individuals as a result of their participation in a variety of experiences, feelings, attitudes, and interests. The health-educated pupil, having been exposed to a variety of health opportunities and activities, is better able to promote and maintain good health.

There is evidence that the brain consists of two hemispheres, a left brain and a right brain, and that each has different yet coordinated functions. This should be considered in health education. It is believed that memory, reading, writing, language, and analytical thinking are responsibilities of the left brain, while the formation of new ideas involving the intuitive process, the understanding of complex relationships that cannot be defined, and the comprehension of patterns that might not be logical but involve qualities essential to creative insight are responsibilities of the right brain. Despite these differences in function and organization, both brains, as a result of complex creative interaction, contribute to visual perception, voluntary movement, speech production, and other intellectual and physical procedures. The literature in educational journals indicates that the development of the right brain often has been neglected in traditional education. Health education therefore will need to consider the inclusion of appropriate learning experiences.

It should be made clear that the process of learning happens within the individual but is influenced by the experiences to which pupils are exposed through the teaching methods and techniques (see Chapter 12) selected by the teacher. Knowledge of the nature and conditions of learning is basic to an understanding of the teaching process in the health instruction program.

HOW DO CHILDREN LEARN?

The exact nature of learning is not known. However, the process does involve a series of

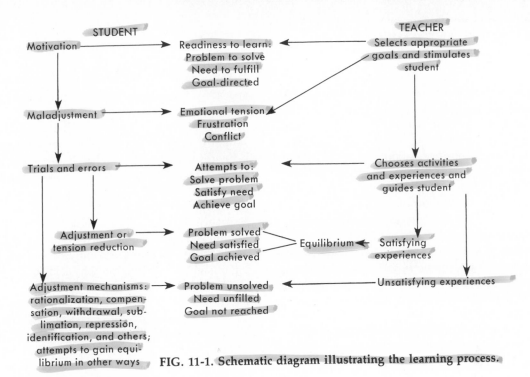

FIG. 11-1. Schematic diagram illustrating the learning process.

rewards and punishments of both a desirable and undesirable nature. Positive reinforcers may include money, candy, privileges, grades, peer approval, praise, attention, and self-interest. Negative reinforcers that result in the elimination of behavior may include loud sounds, disapproval, punishment, poor grades, and use of unpleasant substances. It is believed that learning takes place most efficiently and effectively when someone wants to learn something (positive learning). This person is then said to be motivated to action—to be goal directed. A diagram best illustrates the learning process as it probably occurs (Fig. 11-1).

The process of learning may be illustrated by the example of the teacher who desires to have a student learn procedures that will help to prevent and control communicable disease. The goal having been set and the student ready to learn, the teacher provides a variety of activities that will aid in achieving the goal. These experiences may include reading about germs, discussing the hazards of respiratory infections, the importance of washing hands before lunch, and looking at bacteria under a microscope. The extent to which emotional tension, or conflict, is created in the pupil will depend on a number of factors, such as the intensity of the motivation, the difficulty encountered in reaching a solution, the amount of work required to be completed, and the desire for a good grade. If the activities provide satisfying experiences in learning for the child, the goal will be reached and the pupil will return to a state of equilibrium. Should the goal not be reached, the pupil may react by making such excuses as, "There was too much work to do," "The teacher didn't help me enough," or "I didn't understand what to do."

Learning occurs when a learner encounters new experiences in the environment. However, teacher guidance can help to motivate this learning and reduce the errors a pupil may make in the learning process by controlling, manipulating, and selecting the appropriate kinds of activities.

LEARNING AND THE CONCEPT APPROACH TO HEALTH EDUCATION

One effective approach to teaching health is through the emphasis on concepts. Today, it is important to help students develop big ideas or reach conclusions about health that will enable them to take positive action and to make wise decisions regarding their own, their families', and their community's health. Teachers must be aware of these generalizations and help students to achieve them. Such concepts as smoking may be harmful to the human body, drugs are mood modifiers, certain foods are needed for proper growth and development, and there are ways to protect ourselves from disease help teachers to determine more relevant and effective health education goals (see illustrative units in Chapter 9). These "big ideas" are more likely to be remembered and hopefully will provide greater potential for pupil action.

LEARNING AND THE GOALS OF HEALTH EDUCATION

Knowledge of the objectives of health education is important to the learning and teaching processes. Goals give direction to the learning that enables pupils to acquire the concepts needed for healthful living. It is necessary therefore that teachers clearly understand the purposes of health education for the most effective teaching. Precisely defined health objectives have particular meaning, since learning should be centered on behavior outcomes as well as on factual achievements. Learning should lead students to the acquisition of health education concepts.

The present aim of health education is to develop practices and attitudes of safe and healthful living through the understanding of scientific health information. Individuals should be able to make intelligent decisions about the physical, mental, and social aspects of health. Health behaviors are therefore related to and dependent on the cognitive learning acquired

by pupils. It is important that children obtain correct understanding about health. Attitudes also affect health habits.

The precise interrelationships of knowledge and attitudes to practices are not known today except that they are interdependent. Present evidence, however, indicates that the possession of understanding by itself does not necessarily result in good health habits. Knowing how to brush the teeth does not mean that this practice will be followed. Knowing that some snack-time foods are more nutritious than others is no assurance that they will be eaten. Knowing that immunizations protect against diseases does not always result in these preventive measures being obtained. Knowing the physiological effects of drugs does not necessarily reduce their usage. There are also data that support appreciation and feelings as the means of bridging the gap between the "knowing" and the "doing" in health. Some authorities therefore believe that stress must be placed on the attitudinal effects of knowledge in health teaching. In any event, attitudes are significant in health education; and although knowing may not always lead to doing, there will be no doing without knowing.

Consideration must be given to the fact that behavioral and attitudinal changes in health do not necessarily take place immediately after teaching. Cultural, social, and other values and beliefs that pupils bring from home and community relating to health habits are extremely difficult to change within short periods of time. However, some behavior changes may be observable in the classroom and are subject to measurement; those occurring in the home and elsewhere outside of school may not be seen and may be extremely difficult to assess. It should be recognized that the impact of health learning frequently takes time to have its effect on children. Despite these difficulties, health education must provide correct understanding if appropriate health behaviors are to be acquired by pupils.

Good health behavior is significant only in terms of its effect on the lives of pupils. Good health therefore should be a means to an end and not an end in itself. Being healthy should enable children to obtain a better education, to be happier, to have fun, to be able to play for longer periods of time without undue fatigue, to be more productive in the world, and to be better citizens in the community. When good health is an end in itself, pupils are likely to become overly concerned about their health and become health neurotics.

Teachers should be aware of the fact that all students may not be able to acquire the same health levels because of hereditary and environmental factors. Children who are blind or deaf may never have these senses restored. Pupils who are paralyzed from poliomyelitis may never be able to walk as others do. Boys and girls with uncorrectable heart defects may never have the stamina to play in strenuous games. Students without food may be hungry and malnourished. Despite these handicaps, students need to maintain the best health status possible for themselves within their own limitations. Numerous illustrations of handicapped people leading well-adjusted, happy, and productive lives are found in society. The goals in health education therefore may need to be modified to fit the individual differences of children.

Inspection of the specific outcomes of health education that teachers seek to achieve reveals them to be categorized into the following:

1. Practices, habits, skills—action domain
2. Attitudes, feelings, ideals, interests, appreciations—affective domain
3. Knowledge, understanding, information—cognitive domain

Illustrations of these goals in health education that reflect the psychological, social, and spiritual as well as the physiological aspects of health (see Chapter 9) include the following:

Practices—action domain

The pupil:

1. Eats the proper foods for growth.
2. Obtains adequate sleep, rest, and exercise.
3. Acts safely.
4. Critically analyzes and evaluates health advertising and publicity.
5. Uses community health resources effectively.

6. Takes proper care of teeth.
7. Faces the realities of life.
8. Obtains proper immunizations.
9. Refrains from the use and abuse of drugs.
10. Refrains from the use of tobacco.
11. Attempts to develop a value system.

Attitudes—affective domain

The pupil:

1. Appreciates the dangers to self and others of communicable diseases.
2. Supports the need to have a concept of self.
3. Realizes that health departments and other community health organizations are needed in society.
4. Appreciates the need for periodic health examinations.
5. Is aware of the health hazards of the use of tobacco.
6. Is interested in providing for the rights of others.

Knowledge—cognitive domain

The pupil:

1. Explains how to protect self against disease.
2. Identifies the procedures to follow when ill.
3. Recalls how to care for the skin, feet, ears, and eyes.
4. Summarizes how growth and development occurs.
5. Demonstrates how to administer first aid.
6. Identifies the physiological, sociological, and psychological effects of drugs on individuals.
7. Discusses ways emotions may be helpful and harmful.

The health objectives listed are not all inclusive, nor are they appropriate for all grades (see Chapter 9). It is necessary to study the needs and interests of children in individual schools and school districts to determine the total program and the grade placement.

The *decision-making process* must receive attention by teachers. Pupils are growing and developing organisms that are exposed constantly to environmental influences affecting health and about which decisions must be made. Young people must have the opportunity to make their own decisions and not be expected to follow the dictates of the teacher. However, such decisions must be based on complete awareness of the consequences. To make wise decisions, it is important that students be exposed to the possible alternatives for action. Such teacher consideration is vital to health teaching because it aids in the establishment of credibility, it allows for the free choice of action, and it prepares students to think and act for themselves. It is teaching for the future. By way of illustration, young people find cigarettes available in their communities and are constantly being persuaded to use them. If these individuals are to be able to determine intelligently whether to smoke or not to smoke, they must learn the positive as well as the negative effects of smoking on the human organism. Merely condemning cigarettes may create distrust among students who talk to peers and adults and obtain conflicting evidence regarding the beneficial or detrimental aspects. This is not to imply the use of tobacco is not hazardous but rather to emphasize that wise decisions will come about when the total spectrum of tobacco's effects is provided.

HOW CAN TEACHERS RELATE KNOWLEDGE TO BEHAVIOR IN THE INSTRUCTION PROGRAM?

The importance of health practices and habits points out the need for the use of teaching procedures that will help bridge the gap between the knowledge and behaviors to preserve and maintain health. Unfortunately the precise methods are not known today. However, there is significant evidence that indicates that attitudes play an important role in student health behaviors. It is believed that the acquisition of feelings, interests, and appreciation will lessen the time needed to convert the basic understanding that pupils receive into desirable practices.

An attitude refers to a mind set to action; it is an internal readiness to perform or behave. Therefore what pupils believe, feel, or value affects what they do. Children who feel they are not susceptible to diseases may not think it

necessary to be immunized against these diseases. Pupils who do not believe that excessive sugar consumption might lead to dental decay may not attempt to eat nutritious snack-time foods. Boys and girls who do not realize the dangers of jaywalking may not cross streets at the proper places. Young people may need to be helped to develop an interest in the concept of self. Effective learning in health education therefore must give consideration to including teaching methods that will attempt to develop appropriate student health attitudes as well as proper understanding.

A health education program that tries to stress the development of health attitudes is difficult to achieve, particularly since children are coming to school with ideas, interests, values, and feelings developed and influenced by their home and community experiences. For example, in arithmetic or spelling the child may come to school lacking any information. Yet in matters relating to health and safety the child may not only lack scientifically sound information but also, and more important, may have strong beliefs affirmed by family and community that are false and perhaps even dangerous. Getting pupils to take responsibility for their own lives, whereby they seek to protect and maintain good health, takes much teaching skill and thoughtful planning. It involves initiative, ingenuity, creativity, and fortitude on the part of teachers who aspire to reach this goal.

Learning about health and safety does not always necessarily start with the provision of information or knowledge. There will be occasions when students will be expected to behave in certain ways and develop habit patterns of conformity that precede understandings from which positive or negative attitudes will emerge. These will be situations in which adults take authoritative or arbitrary action that is considered to be in the best interests of students, for example, when a fire breaks out in the school, the candy and soft drink machines are removed from the halls, a school lunch program is provided for all children, or an accident occurs to the school bus that is taking pupils home.

The applied principles of learning that follow, as well as the specific methods and materials found in succeeding chapters, should provide guidelines and specific teaching aids that will help teachers to enable pupils to acquire the behaviors necessary for healthful living.

WHY ARE PRINCIPLES OF LEARNING IMPORTANT IN HEALTH?

Knowledge of the principles of learning is important to teachers in health instruction programs because:
1. Learning is a complex process.
2. Behavior-centered emphasis in learning compounds the complexity of the learning process; attitudes are difficult to assess, and many practices are nonobservable in the classroom.
3. Understanding about motivation and behavior is necessary for effective teaching.
4. Teaching methods and learning are interrelated.

WHAT ARE THE PRINCIPLES OF LEARNING?
Motivation is essential to learning

Health behavior is determined by individuals' motives and beliefs or values about various courses of action open to them. Since all behavior is motivated, the extent to which health behavior of individuals can be understood, predicted, or controlled depends on the ability of teachers to identify these motives and beliefs and to use them in their health teaching.

Positively, motives refer to those drives, needs, urges, or inner compulsions that stimulate individuals to want certain things. They are classified as the following:
1. Physiological needs, such as food, water, sleep, rest, air, sunshine, and exercise
2. Psychological needs, such as security, love, achievement, independence, responsibility, and authority

Motives may also be considered in a negative sense, as barriers that individuals must overcome.

Values are the strong beliefs or attitudinal concerns that have influence on positive or negative motives. The use of alcohol and tobacco, the significance of immunization, periodic visits to physicians, daily exercise, playing safely, and support for health departments depend on individual beliefs of the importance of these actions on their lives. People have to feel that their practices will enable them to play longer, have more fun, and be more productive citizens.

Values are acquired from a variety of sources including the family, social groups, television and other mass media, adults admired by children, and peer cultures in school. When they are consistent with the goals of health education, they will reinforce learning, but when they are in conflict, learning may be limited or restricted. They are not completely resistant to change despite the cultural and social factors that may have influenced their formation. The earlier in the lives of children that attempts are made to acquire proper health behaviors, the greater are the possibilities that these practices will be highly valued by pupils. The school therefore has both a responsibility and an opportunity to modify beliefs and attitudes as well as to develop new ones that will promote and maintain good health.

Principles of motivation. Several principles of motivation based on current research provide some important information about health behavior:

Preventive health action is determined by the degree to which a person sees a health problem as threatening in terms of the following:
1. Its probability of susceptibility or occurrence. Will smoking cause lung cancer?
2. Its seriousness, severity, or urgency of the consequences. Is dental caries sufficiently important to warrant attention? Will an infection be painful?
3. Its benefits or courses of action open that will reduce or remove the threat to the individual's health. What health practices should individuals follow, and will these practices be

beneficial? Are vision screening and hearing tests important, and will they reveal important findings? How much will it cost?

Individual motives and beliefs about various courses of action are often in conflict with each other, and behavior emerges as the conflicts are resolved. The kinds of conflicts referred to include the following:

1. When two motives compete with each other for dominance, the one of greater importance or the more highly valued one will become dominant. A family may spend what little money it has for food, shelter, and necessities rather than on medical or dental visitations. A child who must wear glasses because of poor eyesight may not wear them because the peer group at school disapproves of this practice. A pupil will smoke cigarettes to gain social acceptance.

2. If a pupil is motivated to act in a healthful manner (sees a course of action open), but the action is unpleasant, painful, time-consuming, or inconvenient, the pupil may not complete the action.

3. A pupil may not accept a teacher's beliefs or opinions that there are ways to prevent or help a specific health condition and therefore does not see an effective way (course of action) to resolve the problem. A girl with a boil on her leg may have been advised to visit a doctor but fails to do so because she may not believe the condition is serious or because she does not see how this action can help her. She may try self-medication, but as the infection grows worse she may find that her concerns and fears increase because she is not sure what action she should take. A man who is told he might have incurable cancer may not wish to believe the authority who gave him the diagnosis and may resort to magic and mysticism to find a solution. Later, his fears may become so great that he is no longer able to think rationally because his own attempts to find a solution were not effective.

Health-related motives may sometimes lead to behavior unrelated to health, and conversely some behavior that has the appearance of being health related may in fact be determined by motives unrelated to health. A hungry child may not reveal hunger to a teacher and may be untruthful when asked whether he or she has eaten any food. An illustration of the converse part of this principle is one in which a child may drink milk in class because other students are drinking it.

It should be evident that teachers play an important role in health instruction programs by motivating children to seek appropriate health goals as well as by helping boys and girls to acquire beliefs and values related to these motives. Teachers must provide pupils with experiences and activities that will improve their values of good health so that they will be better prepared to resolve conflicts in motives when they occur.

Fear can lead to rational as well as irrational behavior. It serves to protect, and it can be destructive to individuals. The fear of cancer may help students to refrain from smoking. The fear of becoming overweight may lead pupils to reduce food intake. However, a teenager with a genital sore or infection may be afraid to learn that a sexually transmitted disease has been contracted and may not have the condition checked by a physician.

Risk-taking is normal and necessary and demands selectivity on the part of individuals after determination of benefit and harm. Everything people do involves risks of varying degrees. The decision to take them is dependent on whether the rewards outweigh the penalties. Crossing the street or eating food in a restaurant or lunchroom involves risk. However, they are minimal in comparison to the advantages. Surgery is hazardous, but if the chances of survival are increased, the benefits predominate in the decision. The dangers of using heroin or driving an automobile when under the influence of alcohol may be greater than the pleasures derived. Young people need to be taught to compare the advantages and disadvantages of risk-taking behavior in order to make responsible decisions.

Subprinciples of motivation. The subprinciples of motivation that follow will point out additional aspects valuable in both the learning and teaching processes.

Cultural and social factors may be barriers to learning. The traditions and practices in the home, at play, in social groups, with adults, in the peer culture at school, and in the total environment in which children live affect and influence the values, prejudices, and perceptions that pupils bring to class. There is a relationship between the socioeconomic status of families and the amount of money spent for health services and products. Families that rank highest generally spend more of their income on health services. Some families may not have funds to purchase glasses, toothbrushes, or food or to provide health examinations for children. Some parents may be concerned with immunizations or dental care. The nutritional and dress habits of certain ethnic and racial groups may differ somewhat from those advocated in school. Working parents may not be able to adequately supervise the eating habits and behaviors of their children. Certain religious groups may not believe in health examinations and appraisals, treatment, services, fluoridation of the water supply.

Teachers should be cognizant of these cultural and social factors and realize that they may have an effect on the health education program. They may support the health instruction program, or they may adversely affect it.

Size of objects, use of color, and movement in instructional materials may aid in attracting attention and developing interest in learning. The principle concerning size, color, and movement emphasizes the importance of using a variety of teaching aids in the health instruction program. These materials aid in gaining attention, increasing interest, and helping to make teaching more effective, therefore making learning more concrete and specific.

The use of a variety of films, filmstrips, tape recorders, television and radio programs, phonograph records, exhibits, flannelboards, magnetic boards, objects, specimens, graphs, and charts will stimulate interest in the learning experiences provided by the teacher.

The use of such models as the human torso, heart, eyes, ears, and teeth serve as valuable teaching tools. Exhibits of the contents of first-aid kits or the hazardous objects found in the home help to create interest in the area of safety. Use of food models and flannelboards will increase attention when nutrition is being taught.

Chapter 13 provides detailed information about teaching aids usable in the health instruction program.

Extrinsic motivation is less effective than intrinsic motivation. Should children perform good health habits because of some material reward they will receive or because of the inherent values of the practices performed? Should teachers award gold stars to children who come to school with clean handkerchiefs, when they have brushed their teeth, and for other such reasons? Is it advisable to present a special scroll to classrooms that report 100% attendance of their pupils? Should pupils receive candy or toys as rewards for visits to dentists or doctors? The external stimuli described may obtain the health action desired, but the results are usually of temporary duration. The procedures described are questionable practices because:

1. Some parents do not give their children clean handkerchiefs to bring to school.

2. Some parents do not buy toothbrushes for their children, nor do they take them to physicians.

3. Pupils not able to have clean handkerchiefs or not having brushed their teeth may be embarrassed when special note of these practices occurs in class. The mental health implications may be of greater importance than the rewards themselves.

4. Children who are ill may infect others in school.

Teachers should motivate children to good health practices through the use of meaningful experiences and other approaches that develop intrinsic values for good health rather than through the use of artificial stimuli. This kind of health teaching will more likely provide the lasting behaviors desired. Further illustrations of this point will be found in other principles of learning.

Moderate tension facilitates learning, but severe tension may inhibit learning. Teachers often question the degree to which they should pressure children into desirable health behaviors and practices. The illustrations that follow provide examples that give some guidance.

The cause of a child's dislike for or never having tried celery and carrot sticks may be related to some unpleasant home experience involving pressure or punishment. This same pupil, however, is more likely to try these foods in the classroom during a tasting party where the pressures of group approval are not quite as severe and there is an accompanying pleasant experience.

The teacher who is consistently sarcastic, rude, and unfair, who expects absolute quiet at all times, or who seldom has a sense of humor or permits pupil planning or decisions in the classroom undoubtedly provides a mental health environment that is less conducive to learning, whereas the teacher who is generally courteous and fair and who frequently uses democratic procedures in class presents a more permissive atmosphere that probably provides a better balance of tension that will facilitate learning.

The fear approach in health education, in which the teacher exhorts and admonishes children by saying, "If you don't do this, here's what will happen," may create tensions that will inhibit the acquisition of the desired health behaviors. The teacher who strongly urges poliomyelitis shots because failure to do so will bring on the dreaded disease and paralysis may create such great tensions that fewer pupils participate in the program. Although children may be afraid of having a needle injected into the skin, they are more likely to obtain these immunizations if some understanding of their nature and values is provided in a positive manner and if their classmates are obtaining them.

Learning is generally greater when praise is used more often than blame or reproof, when success occurs more often than failure. Success and praise reinforce learning, but constant frustration and failure adversely affect learning. The importance of the application of this statement to the mental health of children is extremely significant to classroom teachers. It emphasizes the need for teachers to recognize improvement based on individual standards rather than on general levels of achievement. Pupils with poor vision, defective hearing, or other physical ailments may need special praise or opportunities for success experiences in the classroom or on the playground.

Achievement standards should be individual. From a mental health viewpoint, the expectation level of children toward the health goals established should be constant with their powers of accomplishment. A few specific illustrations of the application of this principle to a behavior-centered health education program are the following:

1. Children's needs for sleep may vary in amount.
2. The brushing of teeth after meals may not be possible in those homes that do not provide toothbrushes or dentifrices.
3. Some children may be allergic or diabetic and should not be expected to drink milk or to eat all the foods prepared by the cafeteria at lunch.

Knowledge of results is a strong incentive to learning. The principle of knowledge as a strong incentive to learning refers to evaluation of the instructional program in terms of the achievement of the health education goals discussed earlier. Teachers as well as pupils want to know whether they are progressing toward the attainment of these purposes. They will want to know whether the practices, attitudes, and knowledge of healthful living have been acquired. This assessment of learning serves as a stimulus as well as an aid in redirecting the learning when necessary. Through the use of paper and pencil tests, demonstrations, observations, surveys, and other such techniques, some of the following questions may be answered:

1. Are children receiving the appropriate immunizations?
2. Do children know what to do when injured or ill at school?
3. Can children identify hazardous play areas?

4. Do children know how to administer simple first aid?
5. Are children getting adequate sleep, rest, and exercise?

A more complete discussion of evaluation can be found in Chapter 14.

Maturation and readiness of the child affect learning

Heredity, or the constitution of the pupil, sets the limits of learning of that individual by determining the individual's native intelligence and other capacities as well as physical and mental disabilities. However, maturation, or the physiological growth and development of the pupil, is a determining factor whether the pupil is mentally, physically, socially, or emotionally ready to learn. It provides a state of readiness important in health education as well as in all learning.

In dental health 6- and 7-year-old children may have difficulty accurately learning the proper toothbrushing technique. This coordination involves use of the small muscles of the fingers and hands, and pupils may not be ready to learn this difficult procedure as completely or as accurately as desired. Although the brush is a fairly large implement, expertness of performance will take time and may be delayed until the child physically matures. Nevertheless, the brushing habit needs to be started early, and teachers should introduce this motor skill in school.

In the area of safety, children may not be ready to learn to manipulate sharp-pointed implements, to use apparatus safely, to operate bicycles safely, or to perform other motor skills. Teachers need to be aware of these pupil limitations in their education programs.

The taking of heights and weights in school is a time when pupils are ready to learn about their individual physical and emotional growth patterns. Pupils will be able to better understand their constitutional limitations in weight, height, size, and shape at this time.

The menstrual process generally begins in girls in the fifth and sixth grades, and an educational program is appropriate when this growth change appears.

Adolescence is a time when students are interested in the growth changes taking place in their bodies.

In the early grades especially, pupils are not completely ready to learn to be social individuals. However, it becomes necessary for children to learn to get along with others, to respect authority, and to cooperate in school if they are to grow into emotionally healthy individuals.

Experiences and the environment affect learning

Despite the variety of health behaviors that children bring to school, provisions must be made for learning experiences and environmental conditions that are conducive to good health. Teachers and other personnel have responsibilities to control the daily activities and conditions under which pupils learn. Some of the health experiences and conditions that should be included are the following:

1. The curriculum should include opportunities for children to learn how to live healthfully and safely.
2. Nutritious snack-time foods should be sold at lunchtime or used at parties and social gatherings, rather than candy, cakes, and soft drinks that may not be conducive to good dental health.
3. Provision of a hot lunch at noon may help to develop good nutrition habits.
4. Playgrounds, classrooms, halls, and other places should be free of hazardous conditions and should be safe areas for learning.
5. Classrooms, halls, and playgrounds should be maintained in a neat, clean, and sanitary fashion.
6. Lavatories should provide soap and water for use when necessary.
7. Teachers should be free of communicable diseases and in good physical and mental health.
8. Adequate lighting, heating, and ventilation should be provided.

9. A democratic atmosphere in the classroom and the school will result in greater learning than an autocratic atmosphere where discipline is severe or nonexistent.

Guidance is necessary for the most effective learning

Health instruction must be a part of the school curriculum if the greatest health learning is to occur. An organized education program is necessary if children are to learn to play fairly and to get along with others, to understand fears, to know how to prevent and control diseases, to know what to do when injured, to realize the importance of adequate sleep and rest, and to follow numerous other health practices and attitudes. Inclusion of this program means that schools must make teachers available to teach the subject area and must also provide materials that will enable them to carry out this teaching responsibility. These items should include teachers' guides or units that have been developed around pupils' health problems as well as a variety of teaching aids and materials.

The teacher aids children in the health instruction program by motivating them to learn, by selecting the goals to be achieved, by determining the content to teach, and by choosing and arranging the experience or activities to be used. Teachers help children learn to wash their hands properly, to brush their teeth properly, to assume responsibilities, to have success experiences, and to ride bicycles safely by using a variety of experiences and techniques including dramatizations, demonstrations, experiments, and discussions.

The teacher serves to facilitate learning by controlling motivation, distributing the learning at appropriate intervals, and organizing the learning process. Use of the learning principles found in this chapter will aid in this organization process.

Learning is a self-active process

The behavior-centered emphasis of health education makes the active participation of the learner particularly important and appropriate. Merely telling pupils "you should eat the proper foods," "you should take the safest route home," or "you should play fairly" will not achieve the desired health behaviors. Bridging the gap between knowledge and practices is more likely to come through pupil participation. Children must feel, see, discuss, act out, manipulate, and even taste things if the attitudes that affect good health practices are to be developed. The teacher has the important role of determining the nature of the experiences to be used in the learning process. Whenever possible, children should have two, three, or more of their senses involved in learning. It is believed that the greater the pupil participation, the greater will be the possibility of developing the appropriate behaviors.

To illustrate the application of this principle, the following specific activities are listed:

1. Have children learn about good snack-time foods by conducting a tasting party in which they eat appropriate nutritious foods.
2. Have children learn the proper way to brush their teeth by actually performing the exact procedure in class. Merely demonstrating this technique will not be satisfactory.
3. Have children make a survey of the unsafe conditions in the school and help to develop solutions for their elimination.
4. Take the class on a field trip and actually follow the safest way to the home of one class member.
5. Teach fair play, honesty, getting along with others, or waiting turns by including them in a softball game, a tag game, or as part of apparatus play.
6. Have pupils collect and analyze a variety of advertisements relating to health products.

Most effective learning occurs when there are good personal relationships between the pupil and the teacher

The dominant factor in any learning situation is the combination of personal and social relationships that exist between the pupils and the teacher in the classroom. Learning should take place in a democratic setting with the opportunity for free expression and participation by all children. Consideration must be given to the fair, just, and humane treatment of all pupils, regardless of race or ethnic background. The school and classroom should provide a warm, comfortable, and friendly environment. The teacher should be understanding and permissive but must also provide guidance and security. The emotional climate that pervades a school is extremely important to the effectiveness of the learning process.

Teachers should realize that their personal values, beliefs, prejudices, enthusiasms, and perceptions of health are brought to the classroom. They may affect the human relationship's atmosphere if they conflict with those of their pupils, peer groups, or families. They may influence the health behavior of children in a way that is contrary to best practice. Illustrations of these differences include the following:

1. Cleanliness and appropriate clothing
2. Amount of sugar consumed and significance to dental health
3. Appropriate foods for parties and snack times
4. Food faddism—use of vitamins and other food supplements
5. Food aversions—spinach, milk, liver
6. Fluoridation of the water supply
7. Use of alcohol and tobacco
8. Exercise and play
9. Choice of medical practitioner or health adviser

Teachers who make conscious efforts to avoid permitting their prejudices to influence pupils' health and who are willing to objectively permit children to look at scientific evidence do not necessarily have to compromise their own beliefs and values. This approach should enable teachers to maintain the good relations previously established.

Much learning is soon forgotten, and only a fraction of what was once learned is ultimately remembered

Studies reveal the greatest forgetting by pupils occurs when emphasis in learning is placed on the recall of factual material; evidence shows that meaningful information related to attitudes and practices is more easily learned and is remembered more completely and for longer periods of time. Understanding and knowledge should be provided in a context other than that of unrelated, isolated, factual information. Mere memorization or regurgitation of the names of the teeth, the digestion of foods, or the body systems will not be remembered unless the facts are more closely associated with the attitudes and habits of healthful living. They should lead to the acquisition of big ideas or generalizations, to concepts of health.

This principle emphasizes the need to stress the psychological approach over the logical or structure-and-function approach to teaching. It indicates the importance of the greater use of problem solving in the health instruction program. It demonstrates the importance of learning centered around health needs and problems of pupils. Here are several illustrations to demonstrate this principle:

1. Pupils' appreciations of the possible hazards of using tobacco and narcotics must be more meaningfully related to the ingredients of tobacco and various drugs. Pupils must feel that these substances may affect their performances in athletics, in recreation, and in school as well as their growth and health.

2. Pupils' interests in immunizations against diseases and the prevention of infections' spread will be greater if the diseases considered are those they or their parents may acquire or have acquired.

3. Pupils' appreciation for eating the proper foods will be increased if the lack of vitamins, minerals, and other substances is related to their own or their families' food needs or deficiency diseases.

Well-organized, meaningful material is more easily learned and is remembered longer than meaningless or nonsense material

The content of the health education program should be based on the needs and interests of pupils if it is to be meaningful. Various studies indicate the following areas to be representative of these needs and interests: cleanliness and grooming; community health; consumer health; dental health; control and prevention of disease; care of the eyes, ears, and feet; exercise and fitness; family health; growth and development; mental health; nutrition; rest, sleep, and fatigue; safety; and alcohol, tobacco, and drugs. Learning organized around these areas will result in the most effective health behaviors.

Schools should have teacher guides to health education containing units of instruction focused around the health areas identified in the previous paragraph. These manuals should define the learning that should take place at the various grade levels. They should provide a sequence of learning that avoids excessive overlapping and duplication of content.

Teachers should capitalize on incidents that occur at school or in the home and use these "teachable moments" (see Chapter 12) in their instruction programs, thus making health education practical as well as functional. Such incidents as the following are usable:

1. The class is going to use the playground apparatus.
2. The nurse is coming to do the vision screening.
3. Fire Prevention Week is emphasized in the community.
4. A child reports a visit to the dentist.
5. Children wash their hands before lunch and after going to the lavatory.

The ability to solve problems, to reason, and to do reflective thinking involves training and must be learned

Reasoning ability does not appear suddenly, but rather it develops gradually with age and experience. Differences in the reasoning ability of children and adults are differences in degree and not in kind. Children should be taught how to think rather than what to think. In the primary grades this process can be done more simply using questions that challenge pupils' thoughts.

The many quacks, charlatans, and pseudo-medical people who live in our communities together with the millions of dollars spent yearly on unnecessary drugs, vitamins, and patent medicines make it necessary that children begin to be able to do reflective thinking in health as they do in other phases of learning. Children and adults need to know whether health information they are hearing is valid and to know reliable sources of health facts.

Illustrations of problems that teachers may use for children to solve may include the following:

1. What should you do when you are injured?
2. What should you do when you are ill?
3. Who can help you when you are ill or injured?
4. How can you make friends?
5. What kinds of clothing should you wear to protect your body?
6. How does the health department protect the health of the people?
7. Should we believe what we read and hear about health products?
8. What hazards in the home may cause accidents?
9. Where can you get help if you have a sexually transmitted disease?

The learning process must specifically include teaching for transfer of training or learning if this transfer is to occur

Health knowledge that carries over into or transfers to pupil activities outside of school is the most significant kind of learning. Transfer does not happen by chance but rather by design. Teachers must include teaching for carryover in their planning if school health activities are to occur in the home and community.

The most effective transfer of learning happens when the learning in school is as near real-life situations as possible. Learning, therefore, must be lifelike to obtain the greatest transfer.

When teaching pupils about safety at street corners, it may be necessary either to go to the corner itself and perform the safe behavior or to simulate a street corner on the school grounds using traffic lights, small cars, and other props with the children participating in a role-playing activity.

To obtain the greatest safety in the home, it may be necessary for children to survey the hazards therein and to suggest ways to reduce or remove these hazards.

To expect children to eat balanced meals at home, it may be advisable to provide such meals in schools at noontime.

To expect children to reduce their consumption of sugars and sweets, it will be necessary to curtail, or remove, their availability in schools, at lunchtime, at snacktime, during parties, and during other social occasions in school. However, some health educators believe that foods containing sugars should be available but controlled as an educational means of teaching children their proper use.

The use of repetition and reinforcement is necessary in learning

Health learnings must be repeated and reinforced if they are to have the greatest effect on the health behavior of individuals and if they are to be useful in the children's daily lives. A brief exposure in a classroom, or elsewhere, to a discussion, demonstration, or report of the safest way home from school, the safe way to act on the bus, the use of hand signals when riding a bicycle, the importance of eating the proper foods, the hazards of smoking, what to do when someone is injured, or the proper way to brush teeth does not assure that these actions will be followed consistently for any length of time. Activities used to achieve health and safety objectives must be used on several occasions either during the unit, during the semester, or during the entire school year.

In psychological terms, this type of learning is frequently referred to as spaced learning—a repetition of what has been taught after intervals of time have elapsed. These time intervals may occur during or at the end of a lesson, in the middle or end of a unit, or during the semester, or there might be longer spacing. To illustrate, when teaching the proper technique

for brushing the teeth during a unit on dental health, a demonstration of the correct procedure might have to be made again during the lesson and followed by the pupils actually performing the correct technique. The entire sequence, or some modification, may have to be repeated óne time or more during the unit and possibly reviewed during the semester. Had this learning occurred in the first or second grade, it may be advisable and necessary to repeat or reinforce it in the third or fourth grades and possibly again in the fifth, sixth, or seventh grades.

The extent and degree of repetition will vary and will be dependent on any or all of the following:
1. The individual differences in pupil abilities
2. The health values pupils bring to the classroom
3. The nature of the health environment in the home and in the community
4. Parental cooperation and assistance

SUMMARY

The chapters that follow will be of specific help to teachers in the planning and teaching of health education in their schools. However, when selecting and using methods and materials for the instruction program, teachers should be concerned with the behavior-centered emphasis and the principles .of learning. A summary of these principles for quick reference follows:

1. Motivation
   a. Principles
   b. Subprinciples
      (1) Cultural and social factors
      (2) Size of objects, color, and movement
      (3) Extrinsic versus intrinsic
      (4) Moderate versus severe tension
      (5) Praise versus blame
      (6) Individual achievement standards
      (7) Knowledge of results
2. Maturation and readiness
3. Experiences and environment
4. Guidance
5. Self-active process
6. Good personal relationships

7. Much learning forgotten
8. Meaningful material
9. Problem solving
10. Transfer of training or learning
11. Repetition and reinforcement

QUESTIONS FOR DISCUSSION

1. What is the meaning of the term *behavior modification?*
2. What is believed to be the process of how children learn? Apply this to health education.
3. What is the role of the teacher in the learning process in health education?
4. Why must the teacher be familiar with the goals of health education?
5. What are the goals of health education?
6. What is the aim of health education? Discuss its relationship to pupils and their individual differences.
7. What are the general as well as specific objectives that the teacher should achieve in health education?
8. What is meant by "bridging the gap" between health knowledge and health behavior?
9. Why are the principles of learning important in health teaching?
10. What are the principles of learning that will help the teacher in the health instruction program? Provide specific illustrations of their application to health education.
11. What are the principles of motivation that have an effect on learning in health education?
12. What is the significance of pupil values and beliefs in health education?
13. Why are good personal relationships important and necessary for effective health teaching?
14. What are several illustrations of ways the teacher can make health learning a self-active process?
15. What is the meaning of the term *decision-making process* when applied to health education?
16. What is the significance of fear and risk taking in behavior modification in health education?

SELECTED REFERENCES

Bernard, H.W.: Psychology of learning and teaching, ed. 3, 1972, Oregon State System of Higher Education.

Carroll, H.A.: Motivation and learning; their significance in a mental-health program for education. In National Society for the Study of Education: Mental health in modern medicine, forty-fourth yearbook, Part II, Chicago, 1955, University of Chicago Press.

Cassell, R.N.: The psychology of instruction, Boston, 1957, Christopher Publishing House.

Clarke, K.S.: Values and risk-taking behavior; the concept of calculated risk, Health Education 6: Nov./Dec. 1975.

Derryberry, M.: Health education in transition, American Journal of Public Health 47: Nov. 1957.

Eastern States Health Education Council: Psychological dynamics of health education, New York, 1951, Columbia University Press.

Fodor, J.T., and Dalis, G.T.: Health instruction; theory and application, ed. 3, Philadelphia, 1981, Lea & Febiger.

Fransen, F.J., and Landholm, J.: Changing behavior by personalized learning, Journal of School Health 41: Feb. 1971.

Gagne, R.M.: Some new views on learning and instruction, Phi Delta Kappan 7: May 1970.

Galdston, I., editor: The epidemiology of health, New York, 1953, Health Education Council, New York Academy of Medicine.

Grandsen, A.N.: How children learn, New York, 1957, McGraw-Hill Book Co.

Hanna, L.A., Potter, G.L., and Hagaman, N.: Unit teaching in the elementary school, New York, 1955, Holt, Rinehart & Winston.

Harris, C.W., editor: Encyclopedia of education research, ed. 3, New York, 1960, Macmillan, Inc.

Hochbaum, G.: Research in behavioral sciences, presented at the Regional Institute on the Science of Health Education at the University of California at Los Angeles, June 12-14, 1961.

Hochbaum, G.: Learning and behavior; alcohol education for what? Alcohol Education Conference Proceedings, March 1966, U.S. Department of Health, Education, and Welfare.

Hochbaum, G.: Effecting health behavior, presented at the annual meeting of the New York State Public Health Association, Buffalo, May 23, 1967.

Hochbaum, G.: How we can teach adolescents about smoking, drinking, and drug abuse? Journal of Health, Physical Education, and Recreation 39: Oct. 1968.

Hochbaum, G.: Changing health behavior in youth, School Health Review, Sept. 1969.

Hochbaum, G.: Health behavior, Belmont, Calif., 1970, Wadsworth Publishing Co., Inc.

Hochbaum, G.: Human behavior and nutrition education, Nutrition News 40: Feb. 1977.

Jordan, A.M.: Educational psychology, ed. 4, New York, 1956, Holt, Rinehart & Winston.

Katz, J.: Responsible decision making, Health Education 6: March/April 1975.

Kegeles, S.S.: Why people seek dental care; a review of present knowledge, Journal of School Health 51: Sept. 1961.

McKennell, A.: Implication for health education of social influences on smoking. American Journal of Public Health 59: Nov. 1969.

Mossman, M.: How we can motivate in health education, Journal of Health, Physical Education, and Recreation 24: Sept. 1953.

Ripple, R.E., editor: Learning and human abilities; education psychology, New York, 1964, Harper & Row, Publishers, Inc.

Rosenstock, I.M.: Motivation bases for health education practices, presented at the fifty-first annual meeting of the Wisconsin Anti-Tuberculosis Association in Milwaukee, Wis., April 24, 1959.

Rosenstock, I.M.: Psychological forces, motivation, and nutrition education, American Journal of Public Health **59:** Nov. 1969.

School Health Education Study: Health education; a conceptual approach to curriculum design, 1967, St. Paul, Minn., 3M Education Press.

Springer, S.P., and Deutsch, G.: Left brain, right brain, San Francisco, 1981, W.H. Freeman and Co., Publishers.

Tyler, R.W.: Health education implications from behavioral sciences, Journal of Health, Physical Education, and Recreation **31:** May/June 1960.

12
METHODS AND TECHNIQUES IN HEALTH TEACHING

Health cannot be given to people, it demands their participation.

Rene Saud

Now that the role of the learner in health education has been considered, let us look at the role of the teacher in the behavior modification process with specific reference to the learning process.

The teacher is the most important single factor in the health education program. The responsibility for organizing, guiding, and directing the learning toward health objectives rests with the teacher. This is accomplished through a familiarity with a wide assortment of teaching activities and experiences. The selection of those methods and techniques that will most efficiently and effectively aid learning and lead to health-educated pupils is necessary. The variety of procedures used by teachers to achieve the practices, attitudes, and knowledge goals of healthful living are called methods or methods of teaching.

WHAT IS METHOD?

Method is a broad term in teaching referring to the organized and systematized ways used by teachers to achieve purposes or objectives. They are often said to be the "how to" of teaching.

Techniques is a concrete word describing more specific ways to attain goals. They may be called activities, experiences, or teaching/learning activities. In health education, these procedures help to interpret and translate scientific information to pupils.

The mere selection of appropriate activities or experiences by the teacher does not ensure effective learning. These related factors must also receive consideration:

1. The maintenance of good pupil relationships provides an atmosphere conducive to learning. Understanding children's physical, emotional, social, and intellectual characteristics, treating pupils fairly and firmly, and using democratic procedures contribute to an appropriate social climate in the classroom.

2. Teachers must recognize and provide for differences in abilities, aptitudes, and achievements in pupils. Some students may need more help in learning how to floss and brush teeth. Others may require special guidance to complete survey and research projects.

3. Methods may be teacher or pupil centered. Teacher-centered methods are those dominated by the teacher and are usually more

formal in approach. They may include recitations, question-and-answer sessions, and lectures. Pupil-centered methods refer to the nondirective processes that allow for greater student participation. They may include demonstrations, excursions, constructive activities, and peer group involvement. Greater emphasis must be given to those activities involving pupils if health attitudes and behavior changes are to occur.

WHAT ARE THE TYPES OF METHODS?

Methods are difficult to categorize because the variations and combinations used by teachers are so numerous. In addition, their close relationships to instructional materials add to the complexity of grouping. Nevertheless, the types listed here are classifications that have been found effective and useful in health instruction programs in elementary schools.

1. Problem solving
   a. Brainstorming
   b. Values clarification
2. Construction activities
3. Creative activities
4. Demonstrations
5. Discussions
   a. Questions and answers
      (1) Question box
      (2) Quizzes
      (3) Self-tests
   b. Experience charts and records
   c. Buzz groups
   d. Problem solving—answers to questions
6. Dramatizations
   a. Dramatic play
   b. Role playing or sociodrama
   c. Plays
   d. Puppet shows
   e. Stories and storytelling
7. Educational games and simulations
8. Excursions and field trips
9. Experiments
10. Individual and group reports
11. Illustrated presentations
12. Resource people—guest speakers
13. Show and tell time
14. Surveys
15. Others—films, filmstrips, tape recordings, videotapes, slides, and additional instructional aids

Problem solving

Problem solving is perhaps the most important and practical method available for teacher use in the development of pupil health behaviors—in helping students make decisions. It is a general process whereby children learn to solve personal and community health problems through the use of the scientific approach. Pupils learn how to investigate, to reason, and to think reflectively so that they can differentiate facts from fiction and truth from superstition. It includes the use of a variety of activities, such as discussion, sociodrama, experimentation, dramatic play, and storytelling.

Several illustrations of health problems that may be solved are: How can we protect ourselves from disease? Who are some of the people who help us to stay healthy? What foods do we need for growth? Should we drink alcoholic beverages? Should we smoke? How can we prevent accidents?

The sequential steps that teachers can use to guide pupils in solving health problems are as follows:

1. Recognition of the problem
2. Definition of the problem
3. Selection of methods of procedure
4. Collection of pertinent data
5. Selection, interpretation, and organization of data
6. Preparation of conclusions or alternatives
7. Application of conclusions or alternatives to the solution, problem, or plan of action
8. Possible evaluation of solution or solutions

Brainstorming, a type of problem solving. Brainstorming is a group attempt to solve a well-defined problem by offering any solution that comes to mind, no matter how extreme. It attempts to generate ideas quickly and in large quantity by the free association of ideas.

These procedures should be followed:

1. Encourage a free flow of ideas no matter how far out. Permit freewheeling.
2. Do not permit critical judgments, negative comments, or evaluations.
3. Restate the problem and start sorting out and refining ideas.
4. Evaluate the ideas objectively and narrow them to one or more solutions.
5. Summarize, and assign responsibilities.

These problems are illustrations of ones suitable for brainstorming. How can we encourage pupils to refrain from smoking cigarettes? How can we improve safety at school? How can we convince pupils to refrain from the misuse of drugs?

This procedure has value because it allows for freedom of expression, an exchange of ideas, and creative thinking. It has limitations in that the teacher may find it difficult to maintain class control, and it may not be productive if the class is too large. It also demands clarification of ideas, well-planned organization, and follow-up for effective results.

Values clarification, a type of problem solving. Values clarification involves a series of strategies or methods for helping students learn about values. It does not attempt to teach values per se. Illustrations of strategies can be found in Chapter 12. The seven criteria* used in the process are found in Chapter 9.

Values clarification will help students to critically review their own as well as society's values. It will aid pupils in identifying the concept of self and in searching for meaning in life.

Construction activities

Construction activities involve pupil and teacher planning as well as pupil participation in the preparation of a variety of items (using paper, wood, cardboard, glue, crayons, and other materials). Illustrations of specific items that may be made include a fire alarm box, a traffic light standard with stop and go signals,

papier-mâché models of fruits and vegetables, plaster-of-paris models of teeth, the heart, and other organs of the body, and construction of paper models. These items have use in dramatic play, sociodramas, exhibits, bulletin board displays, and other techniques of teaching.

Creative activities

The free expression of children's thoughts, ideas, and feelings through such media as stories, poems and verses, dramatic plays, murals, and other creative activities may be useful and productive in the health instruction program. (See Chapter 12 for illustrations.)

Demonstrations

Demonstrations are procedures that help to make abstract verbal descriptions and symbols more concrete and meaningful in health education. They may include involvement of the sense of sight and touch as well as the auditory sense. They are helpful ways to improve the teaching process and may be performed by teachers or pupils.

Five important reasons for the use of demonstrations in teaching are the following:
1. They stimulate interest and thereby motivate learning.
2. They help to clarify learnings.
3. They help improve and speed up the learning process.
4. They may be used to initiate a unit.
5. They provide a visual image helpful in the retention of things learned.

Some demonstrations usable in health education are (1) the importance of oxygen in fires; (2) the proper way to brush teeth; (3) the safest way to ride a bicycle on sidewalks, streets, and highways; and (4) the proper use of fire extinguishers.

Discussions

The discussion as a method of teaching is probably the most familiar and commonly used procedure in health instruction. All activities

---

*Raths, L.E., Harmin, M., and Simon, S.B.: Values and teaching; working with values in the classroom, Columbus, Ohio, 1966, Charles E. Merrill Books, Inc.

and methods include or should include some type of discussion. These methods generally permit children to ask questions, make recitations, perform surveys, and participate in numerous other ways in the teaching process. They provide opportunities for the exchange of information between pupils and teachers. Group discussion is especially valuable, since it is conducive to helping children to gain understanding and respect for each other's feelings and viewpoints.

Discussions need teacher guidance, and several of the following helpful points should aid in directing the conversation along constructive channels:

1. Encourage and stimulate pupil questions, since they provide information about needs, interests, and concerns. Pupils should be helped to think through their own experiences and relate them to the discussion.

2. Try to get all children in the class to participate or be involved.

3. Do not hurry discussion.

4. Listen carefully to all contributions and relate them to the topic. Compliment and encourage children who make significant remarks. It may be necessary to have students amplify their statements.

5. When groups are reluctant to engage in discussions, mention of a personal experience or anecdote may help to get children to participate.

Discussions may take place in a variety of ways, and the suggestions that follow merely serve to illustrate the numerous variations that may be used in the health instruction program.

Questions and answers. Questions may serve to introduce a health area, they may be part of the teaching process used during the presentation of a unit or lesson, and they may serve as a review or summary of a class discussion.

The best results are obtained when careful thought, planning, and organization are given to building sets of questions. As a general rule, question-and-answer periods and sessions should be planned in detail and in advance as carefully as other teaching procedures.

QUESTION BOX. Occasionally, children are reluctant to ask questions in class because they fear embarrassment or for other reasons. This situation can be solved by having a receptacle of some kind available where pupils may anonymously place questions of interest or concern. This procedure may be especially appropriate when the topic of sex education or social hygiene is being considered in class.

QUIZZES. Quizzes can be oral, written, or performance based in nature. They have value when used for drill, review, or grading purposes. They serve to motivate learning and are important in the instruction program. They have evaluation limitations, since they tend to measure only the cognitive learning (understandings) acquired by pupils.

SELF-TESTS. Self-tests are a series of teacher-prepared, easily answered questions that help to stimulate discussion about a particular health topic. The number and difficulty of questions can vary, depending on the purpose of the test and the grade level in which it is used.

These tests are not given for grading purposes. They have value because they can be duplicated and distributed at the start of the class and immediately get all pupils participating and thinking about the lesson. They may also be used to initiate a unit as well as to help determine additional class activities.

The following is an illustration of a partial self-test:

What do you know about tuberculosis?

Please circle the correct answer to the statements that are listed below. If you do not know the answer, circle the letter "D."

1. Tuberculosis is caused by a germ.   T   F   D
2. Tuberculosis is a contagious, or communic-   T   F   D
   able, disease.
3. A person with a persistent cough may have   T   F   D
   tuberculosis.
4. Tuberculosis can be cured.   T   F   D
5. You can have tuberculosis without feeling   T   F   D
   sick.
6. The tuberculin test is used to find people   T   F   D
   with tuberculosis.

Experience charts and records. Experience charts and records are lists of phrases or brief stories that are dictated by children to the teacher who records their suggestions, or ideas, or thoughts, on the blackboard or on large sheets of paper. This procedure has been used in the primary grades to introduce reading, but it also serves as a good technique when teaching health education. It is usable at other grade levels as a way to list or record questions that need to be answered about a particular health topic. It may be considered part of the problem-solving technique in teaching.

An illustration of a partial experience chart used in the first grade shows the following:

Milk

Milk is good for us.
Milk helps us grow.
Milk helps us play.
Milk makes us strong.
Drink milk each day.

Buzz groups. The buzz group method is one in which the class is divided into small groups of from five to eight pupils to discuss a specific problem or series of problems for a limited time, usually of 3 to 5 minutes' duration. Each subgroup selects a chairperson to keep the discussion on the topic and to give everyone an opportunity to speak. A recorder is chosen who not only will jot down key points but will also be prepared to present these verbally to the entire class on request. The teacher's role during the buzzing is to move from group to group to be certain that the topic is being discussed, to see that students know what is expected of them, and to clarify questions relating to the problem under discussion. At the conclusion of the buzz groups, the teacher permits the spokespersons to report their answers, and a pupil summarizes the main points on the blackboard. Further discussion is encouraged by the class members during the summary period.

This technique has a number of important advantages for use in the health instruction program:

1. It provides a way to have several committees in class study different aspects of a given topic.

2. It allows greater pupil participation in the discussion.
3. It provides an atmosphere conducive to discussion.
4. It may serve as a diagnostic procedure to find out what pupils know about a particular topic.
5. It may lead to further pupil activities or experiences.

Buzz groups may be used (1) to discuss a particular problem or question, (2) to determine what action to take regarding a particular problem or question, and (3) to determine questions to ask a resource person who may be coming to class the following day.

Illustrations of several problems suitable for this method are the following: Should we drink alcoholic beverages? Is exercise good for us? Should we smoke cigarettes?

This procedure has limitations especially if pupils have no background information about the discussion topic; it may result in a rehash of ignorance. Also, a buzz group takes careful planning for the optimal results, for the prevention of a few students dominating the conversation, and for the confining of the comments to the topic being discussed. Selection of a subject about which students have controversial and varying opinions increases the chances of success for this method.

Problem solving—answers to questions. Problem solving is a teaching technique whereby children are presented with specific health questions or situations and they attempt to provide solutions through class discussions. An illustration of this activity can best describe it. A teacher may present the following situations for pupil reactions:

1. What would you do if you were injured at school?
2. What would you do if you were injured a long way from home?
3. What would you do if a friend tried to persuade you to smoke a cigarette?

A modification of this procedure would be to present a problem in written form, such as the following:

You were playing in the school yard at lunchtime and cut your leg on a sharp object. The wound was bleeding quite a bit, and you were in pain. Place a check in the box beside the statement below that would best describe what you would do. Be prepared to tell why you would take this action.

1. Take out my handkerchief and wrap it around the □
   cut.
2. Wash the cut with water. □
3. Press my hand on the cut to try to stop the □
   bleeding.
4. Report to the nurse or to my teacher. □
5. Wait until I arrived at home before doing anything. □
6. Not do anything. □
7. Go home. □

Critical review of quotations found in the literature and analysis of newspaper articles, lyrics from popular songs, scenes from movies, and value strategies are additional problem-solving possibilities.

Dramatizations

Dramatizations are ways for children to express their feelings and urges through make-believe, imitation, and imagination. It is believed that children are more likely to remember facts when they are portraying them. These procedures are interesting to children and apparently contribute to the development of health attitudes and values, since pupils tend to identify themselves with characters in the situations.

Dramatic play. Dramatic play is an informal, spontaneous, natural way for children to act out what they have been reading, discussing, or seeing in health.

Children who have visited a fire station or read about one may construct an imaginary station in the classroom and play fire fighter. A visit to a grocery store may result in such a store being established in school. The presence of the school doctor may encourage children to establish a corner in the room as a physician's office.

Role playing or sociodrama. Role playing or sociodrama is a more formalized procedure than dramatic play. It is spontaneous and unre-

hearsed and focuses on a health problem of interest or concern. It provides a considerable amount of emotionalism and realism that apparently communicates to individuals.

The steps to follow in conducting a sociodrama generally include the following:

1. Selection of a problem of interest and importance to children
2. Explanation of the technique in simple terms
3. Provision of enough of the story to set the scene
4. Selection of children to participate
5. Definition of the problem and role of each pupil
6. Definition of the audience role
7. Cues to begin or opening remarks needed by first actors to get started
8. Stopping sociodrama at the point where action drops or when discussion should be started; may be after a 2- or 3-minute presentation
9. Conducting discussion afterward, asking such questions as: "What was being presented?" "What was good about the way the situation was handled?" "What might have been changed in the situation?"

Illustrations or dramatizations suitable in health education include (1) walking across the street, (2) riding a bicycle on the street, (3) helping a person who is lost, (4) how a person behaves when teased by someone, and (5) how to say "no."

Plays. Plays are more formal in nature because they have a prepared script and involve memorization of dialogue. They may or may not be pupil written. They can serve as culminating activities with presentations made to parent groups or to school assemblies.

Puppet shows. When children are involved in making the puppets and planning the stories, the result on health behaviors can be very beneficial. These experiences are enjoyed by young children both as spectators and as participants. They have great attitudinal effects on pupils. Puppets may also be used in dramatic play or with spontaneous dialogue.

Many areas including dental health, nutrition, and safety provide suitable materials for these shows.

Stories and storytelling.* Children enjoy stories and storytelling to the extent that various health topics can serve as themes. They can be used to initiate a unit in health, or they may be part of the on-going activities. They help stimulate questions and answers.

Some illustrations of how this procedure may be used are (1) read stories about fear, courage, honesty, truthfulness, and other phases of mental health; (2) read stories about fire and traffic safety; (3) prepare a puppet or a construction paper character having some such name as Bozo the dog, Chippy chipmunk, or Ronny raccoon and create a story in which this animal discusses mental health or nutrition; (4) prepare a flip chart with a series of humorous or otherwise interesting drawings that relate to how to take care of the eyes, ears, or feet; and (5) show pictures of toothbrushes, wash cloths, combs, and other such items and encourage pupil discussions relative to the importance of these items to health.

Educational games and simulations†

These activities are ways to stimulate interest in health education by increasing student attention and making learning an active process. The techniques may be used by individuals or groups of individuals. They are found in many forms and include crossword puzzles, anagrams, quiz shows, bingo, nonverbal and verbal communication, tic-tac-toe, and baseball. They have received increased attention in recent years, and numerous commercial materials are available. Teachers must learn to be selective in those games to be used in the classroom. They should contribute to the achievement of the established health education goals.

---

*See Appendix E for specific story references.
†Specific activities are found in Chapter 12. These references provide teacher information. Packer, K.L.: Peer training through game utilization, Journal of School Health **45:** Feb. 1975. Sleet, D.A.: The use of games and simulations in health instruction, California School Health **13:** Jan. 1975.

Excursions and field trips

Excursions are designed to enrich classroom teaching procedures by making health more meaningful. Field trips may be limited to the school plant and the school neighborhood, or they may be distant journeys requiring bus transportation.

Some places to visit that may be part of the health instruction program are the school lunchroom, the school grounds, a grocery store, the corner crosswalk, the first-aid station, a dairy, a hospital, a dentist's office, and the health department.

Experiments

Experiments are procedures that use the scientific method to test suggested truths or to illustrate known truths. They are ways to solve problems and may also be classified as demonstrations. They differ from demonstrations because the techniques employed are more exacting and precise and controls are used to ensure valid results. The specific sequential steps may include the following:
1. Define the problem to be solved or the hypothesis to be tested.
2. Select the methods of procedure to be used.
3. Identify and assemble the necessary materials.
4. Conduct the experiment.
5. Collect and record data.
6. Select, organize, and interpret the data.
7. Prepare conclusions.

Experiments stimulate interest and attention in learning. They provide realism to abstract concepts and make learning more meaningful.

Following are illustrations of experiments that have been helpful in the health instruction program:
1. The effect of good and poor diets on growth and development may be shown by the white rat feeding experiment. This demonstration may be done with kindergarten or first-grade children to encourage the drinking of milk and to discourage the consumption of excess sweets.

Details of the exact procedure are available from the National Dairy Council.*

2. The importance of washing hands with soap may be demonstrated through the use of a series of sterile agar plates (petri dishes from science department). Children place fingers in one dish before washing with soap and water and in a second dish after washing. The dishes are then incubated or kept in a warm place for 24 hours or longer, and the extent of germ growth can be compared in the two dishes.

Individual and group reports

Individual and group reports are methods whereby oral or written reports, or both, are made about assigned or special interest health topics by individual pupils or groups of pupils. They involve critical reading and analyses, research, independent study, interviews, investigations as well as excursions or field trips. Questions and answers become necessary, since they may precede, be part of, or follow the reports. They may include panel and forum presentations and independent study.

Illustrated presentations

Illustrated presentations are activities whereby teachers present phases of health using audiovisual materials such as charts, models, pictures, and specimens. Children should be encouraged to participate in discussions and provided opportunities to ask questions.

An example of this procedure would be the use of food models on a flannelboard to illustrate the basic 4 food groups or appropriate breakfasts, lunches, and dinners.

Chalk, both colored and white, could be used effectively to make cartoons, sketches, and schematic drawings of germs, body parts, foods, maps, illustrated slogans (such as "Germs hate soap"), charts, and a variety of other valuable and useful visual presentations.

*National Dairy Council, 111 N. Canal St., Chicago, Ill. 60606.

Resource people—guest speakers

The use of community resource people who are experts in their chosen fields often enriches the health instruction program. Such individuals may include physicians, dentists, health officers, police officers, fire fighters, and nurses.

The following points should be discussed with resource people or guest speakers who are invited to schools:

1. The choice of a topic appropriate to that being covered in class
2. The grade level of the class
3. The material covered in class before and what will happen after the speaker departs
4. The nature of the vocabulary to use
5. The use of audiovisual aids whenever possible
6. The use of demonstrations, experiments, and illustrations whenever possible
7. Permission for children to ask questions; pupils should prepare their questions in advance

Peer group action. This is a method whereby students prepare materials for use or are able to discuss one or more health topics with their peers in formal and informal educational settings. By way of illustration, these procedures may include the preparation of audiovisual materials for presentation, the conduct of rap sessions, participation and leadership in a variety of discussions, and writing and producing newspaper articles and special bulletin materials for distribution.

This approach has had measurable success with students having drug problems. Former drug users have been able to reach drug users more effectively in selected situations. Junior high pupils have been able to improve communications with their peers or young people in sixth grade. Also, the concept is conceivably useful in the areas of sexually transmitted disease, family health, and mental health if knowledgeable and interested students are involved. This idea is worthy of consideration in the upper grades and possibly also in the intermediate grades.

Show and tell time

Show and tell time is an appropriate time to discuss health matters as well as other topics. This activity is especially useful in the primary grades for children to tell about visits to dentists or physicians, accidents at home, or fires that happened in the community. Some children with parents who are physicians, dentists, fire fighters, police officers, or health officers may have special health items that they will bring to school and share with their classmates, such as stethoscopes, teeth, models, charts, books, and pamphlets.

Surveys

Surveys are procedures in which students use checklists, interviews, questionnaires, and opinionnaires to collect information about the nature and extent of pupil or community health problems or practices. They may be considered part of the problem-solving process.

The survey provides excellent opportunities to integrate health with language, art, and arithmetic. The survey forms will need to be prepared by pupils, and oral and written reports and research may also be necessary. In addition, arithmetic tabulations and computations must be completed.

Some areas in health that lend themselves to surveys are (1) the types and amounts of snack-time foods consumed by pupils; (2) the amount of candy and soda consumed daily, or weekly, by children; (3) the kinds of foods eaten for breakfast, lunch, and dinner by children; (4) the extent to which students smoke cigarettes or use drugs; and (5) the safety hazards in the school or home.

Others

There are many variations of the methods of teaching described in this chapter that can be used in health education. Teacher ingenuity and creativity are necessary to develop the variety of other possible techniques. Communication media including television, radio, tape record-ings, films, filmstrips, videotapes, and slides as well as models, charts, exhibits, displays, bulletin boards, posters, flannelboards, and other audiovisual aids may be combined with the procedures just presented to provide numerous additional activities and experiences.

WHAT METHODS SHOULD TEACHERS USE?

There is no one best method or combination of methods to use in the health instruction program. If any procedure is to be singled out as a basis from which to start selecting, perhaps the problem-solving approach must be given first consideration. This is a meaningful and scientific way to teach health education, it involves other activities, and it is behavior centered as well as pupil centered.

The process of developing health-educated individuals is complex and difficult. The techniques teachers employ should be those, however, that help pupils to understand the concepts needed to acquire the practices, attitudes, and knowledge for healthful living. It is important therefore that teachers be familiar with the nature, values, and limitations of many methods so that they may choose the ones that will aid pupils to achieve these objectives.

Teachers should review the following questions and use them as criteria when selecting procedures for the health instruction program:
1. Will the objectives be achieved?
2. Will they have educational value?
3. Will pupils participate actively?
4. Will interest be attracted and maintained?
5. Will information be communicated to pupils?
6. Will the teacher feel comfortable using the procedures?
7. Will the methods be appropriate for the abilities and aptitudes of pupils?
8. Will the methods be suitable for the grade level?
9. Will they be adaptable to the supplies, equipment, and facilities that are readily available?

Kindergarten and primary grades

The health education program in kindergarten and the primary grades should be centered around daily activities in school, the home, and the community, such as safety, disease control, nutrition, rest and sleep, the doctor, the police officer, the fire fighter, and the nurse.

Health can be integrated very easily into other areas of the curriculum, such as language arts (Fig. 12-1), social studies, and science; however, there will always be need for direct teaching.

The methods selected for these grades should be those that include doing, experiencing, and observing. The techniques that will achieve the best results will probably include reading, stories, games, problem solving, excursions, discus-

FIG. 12-1. Integration of mental health into language arts. *(Courtesy Mary Wilbert Smith, Educational Service District #121, Seattle, Wash.)*

sions, show and tell periods, creative activities, construction activities, questions and answers, experience charts and records, and dramatizations.

Intermediate grades

Children in intermediate grades have acquired a new level of curiosity and enthusiasm. They begin asking more questions and want to know the "whys" of health. They are seeking more exact answers to their questions.

The growth changes occurring in pupils provide the need for learning about the structure and functions of the human organism. Girls particularly need information about menstrual hygiene.

The beginning of group activities and the wider use of community resources and problem-solving procedures become possible and should be considered for use by teachers in their health instruction programs.

Health continues to be integrated to some extent with other subjects, but more direct teaching begins to be necessary.

The methods that teachers may use in their programs include discussions, problem solving, educational games, surveys, excursions, illustrated lectures, role playing, experiments, demonstrations, resource people, and individual and group reports.

Upper grades

Children in the upper grades are adventuresome, want to experiment, and desire more activity than ever before in their lives. Therefore the health experiences must go far beyond the confines of the textbook. Pupils can be involved in cooperative planning and sharing of experiences.

The early adolescent period indicates the need for additional content areas to be included in the health instruction program. Tobacco, alcohol, and the use of drugs begin to have added meaning for these children, although these areas should receive consideration in the lower grades. In addition, exercise takes on impor-

tance, with dental and nutritional problems and sexually transmitted disease having special significance.

Some of the methods that may be included in the health instruction program are surveys, panels, debates, excursions, peer group action, exhibits, tape recordings, independent and group work, demonstrations, experiments, buzz groups, and problem solving.

ARE INCIDENTS METHODS?

Incidents by themselves are not methods. However, they are teachable moments that stimulate learning by setting the stage for meaningful health education. They can serve to initiate units or lessons. They may be considered as health problems that lend themselves to solutions through the use of the problem-solving process as well as other procedures. They lend themselves to both formal and informal educational approaches. Therefore they may be considered a part of method.

Teachers must be constantly alert for the numerous occasions that happen in schools, homes, and communities that are usable in health instruction programs. The newspapers, magazines, and television are sources of these incidents as are student and adult reports. Teachers who consistently capitalize on these motivating events will undoubtedly be more successful in getting children to acquire the appropriate health behaviors.

The teacher must recognize that there are values as well as limitations in the use of incidents in health teaching. When they are improperly used, they may result in serious emotional disturbances among children. A teacher who discusses the cleanliness habits or the decayed teeth of a particular pupil in class not only may embarrass the child but also may make the child unnecessarily conspicuous before the other students. From a psychological viewpoint, therefore, this action may be very harmful to the child. The teacher must use discretion in choosing incidents as well as the appropriate occasion for capitalizing on such situations. Incidents in health teaching may be used in several ways:

1. To discuss individual health problems with pupils in private or with parents.

2. To discuss health and safety problems that have been observed in school or elsewhere without reference to any special pupil or groups of pupils.

3. To discuss special events or occasions involving health and safety that will take place in the school or in the community.

4. To discuss a particular pupil health problem when the child is not in the room. This is probably the rare occasion but may be necessary for the protection of the child. For example, if a child has had an epileptic seizure in class, it will be necessary for the teacher to seek the support of the child's classmates to help the pupil when necessary. This attack could occur on the playground or on the way home when the teacher or other adult was not nearby. Therefore a brief explanation of the nature of seizures and first-aid procedures is important. This action may help to prevent the pupil from being injured and being rejected by the other classmates.

The following incidents that occur in the school setting illustrate opportunities available for health instruction:

1. Students smoking in school.
2. Many children absent because of the flu.
3. Pupils come to school with colds.
4. Children prepare refreshments for a party at school.
5. A student tells how a friend's hand was burned while playing with matches.
6. The school conducts a fire drill.
7. A child reports a visit to the dentist.
8. Pupils make fun of children wearing eyeglasses or hearing aids.
9. The food served for lunch at school.
10. Children have their vision and/or hearing screened at school.
11. A student asks about dental health or nutrition claims in TV commercials.
12. A child is bitten by a dog on the playground.
13. A student has an epileptic seizure in class.
14. An accident occurs to a student on the way to or at school.
15. Students eating candy and sweets in excess.

A third-grade teacher who took advantage of a report in the newspaper of a bicycle accident that occurred to a school child and resulted in a broken arm will serve to illustrate how to use an incident in the instruction program. The morning after the accident the teacher asked the class how it happened. Discussion brought out such matters as careless riders, unsafe conditions, and unsafe equipment. The conversation led the pupils to list the actions that often lead to accidents: bicycle riding, car driving, walking, living in school, and living at home. The teacher then asked the question: "If these may lead to accidents, how can we act safely?" The pupils began to mention safety rules but finally decided they needed more information to be able to answer this question satisfactorily. At this point the teacher suggested that continued planning go on the next day.

When the discussion resumed the following day, the children decided to participate in a variety of experiences to learn more about safety. These are some of the activities they selected:
1. Read stories in safety books and pamphlets.
2. Create bulletin board displays of safety posters.
3. Create a checklist of "Ways to make my home safe."
4. Invite a police officer to visit the class to discuss safety.
5. Conduct a culminating activity that dramatizes a typical day of children who do not practice safety and a typical day of children who do.

Special community and school events are also important occasions to motivate for health education in schools. The "Monthly Health Specials Calendar" approach that follows offers useful suggestions.

MONTHLY HEALTH SPECIALS*

September
Find safest way to school
Walk *left* on rural highways

---

*Adapted from Schneeweis, S.M., and Jones, R.: Time linked health problems; the monthly health specials calendar approach for use in grades K-6, Journal of School Health 38: Oct. 1968. (Reprinted by permission of editor, Journal of School Health, with minor revisions.)

Bus safety
Bike safety
Classroom safety
Doctor, nurse, and dental hygienist are your friends
Emphasize good nutrition
Wash hands before eating
Know phone numbers: home, police, and fire department
National Child Safety Week

October
Fire Prevention Week—discuss fire drills. Emphasize home clean-up for fire safety
Halloween safety

November
Winter hazards

December
Christmas tree: use safe lights, turn off if no one in the room; inspect lights carefully
Vacation safety
Smoking and alcohol education

January
Snow and ice are still with us
Stress good sportsmanship and courtesy and their relationship between popularity and good mental health

February
Dental Health Week
First aid

March
High water and dangerous slippery banks: *stay away*
Vacation safety again
Bike safety
Save Your Vision Week

April
Cancer drive: relate this to dangers of smoking, polluted air, and emphasize early examinations of adults
Good-Vision Week
Bike Safety Campaign
Beware of strangers; never get in a car with an unknown person

May
Child Health Week
Mental Health Week
Stress swimming and other water safety
Mention farm animals and their danger
First aid

June
Sunburn is a real burn! Poison ivy is a danger
Water safety
Camping safety

Other seasonal events offer opportunities for health education: (1) the appropriate time to discuss safety to and from school, bicycle safety, and playground safety may be when children return to school in September; (2) fall and winter may be significant times to discuss respiratory diseases and other communicable diseases; and (3) spring may be the time when camping, picnic, and water safety become especially important.

IS THE USE OF THE HEALTH TEXTBOOK A METHOD?

The health textbook is a very important teaching aid that should serve as a reference or resource to provide information necessary to solve health problems. It should be used in conjunction with pupil activities and experiences and therefore may be considered to be a part of or related to method. It may be used in the preparation for discussions, panels, individual and group work, and so on. It can help to provide continuity and direction to learning experiences.

A textbook, however, should not be used as a passive reading lesson. Children will not acquire the necessary health behaviors if their experiences are limited to a 10- or 15-minute daily reading assignment in a health text. This procedure is contrary to the principles of learning discussed in Chapter 11. Teachers must be more imaginative and creative and use a variety of the methods and activities described in this chapter if the goals of health education are to be achieved.

WHAT ARE THE RELATIONSHIPS BETWEEN METHOD AND MATERIAL AIDS?

Material or teaching aids such as models of the teeth, health films and filmstrips, flannelboards, exhibits, or displays of the contents of first-aid kits are valuable supplementary items that enrich learning experiences. They are aids to learning that make abstract health concepts specific, concrete, and meaningful in the lives of students; they serve to attract and maintain attention; they help to stimulate interest in the teaching process; they assist in encouraging greater student participation in the learning process. Teachers should be familiar with the variety of such items that are available and use many of them in their teaching. Chapter 13 provides comprehensive coverage of the nature of these aids.

Instructional aids should not be considered teaching methods in themselves. However, they are important and necessary supplementary and complementary aspects of the procedures used in learning. They are part of the "how to" methods of teaching.

At times it is difficult to distinguish between methods and teaching aids. An example or two serves best to illustrate this point. A film by itself is a teaching aid. When children are expected to look for specific information as they view the film and, after its showing, discuss what they saw, then it becomes part of the teaching process. Therefore discussion may be the method used in the learning, with the film being a part of this procedure. A flannelboard and food models are teaching aids. When these items are used in a discussion to demonstrate the food items needed for an adequate breakfast, they become a method.

Using a variety of teaching aids can greatly contribute to the emphasis on pupil-centered teaching. They will assist in providing more pupil participation in the learning process.

WHAT TEACHING TECHNIQUES ARE USABLE IN HEALTH INSTRUCTION?*

The wide variety of specific teaching techniques that are presented next will aid the teacher in the achievement of the objectives in health education. They include more than 1,200 ideas for use in the instructional program. They are organized alphabetically into 15 subject areas, and the appropriate grade level group for each activity is identified.

When the procedures for health teaching are selected, it will be helpful to keep in mind these essentials:

1. The purposes of health education go beyond an emphasis on information alone; they also consider the development of health attitudes and practices.
2. The principles of learning described in Chapter 11 are important.
3. The specific technique or combination of techniques to be used should help to achieve a desired goal or goals.
4. Activities should be continually evaluated to determine the extent of learning taking place.

Despite the many and varied types of activities presented, the procedures that follow do not provide a comprehensive coverage of all health teaching experiences, nor do they include the use of films and filmstrips. Rather they serve a fourfold purpose:

1. To provide specific, tested techniques that will give spark and vitality to the health instruction program. The numerous experiences listed have been used by many teachers in their classrooms.
2. To provide a broad selection of activities.
3. To provide suggestions of teaching techniques that will stimulate the creative and imaginative teacher to modify, change, or devise completely new procedures.
4. To provide methods that may be used to initiate new units or may be used as culminating activities.

It should be noted that the following teaching procedures have been organized in a functional and practical manner for easy reference by the teacher. The letters or numbers found on the right of the page in the activities or experiences that follow refer to the *suggested* grades or grade level in which they may be used: P, primary; I, intermediate; U, upper.

---

*An excellent culminating activity that involves much student, parent, and community participation is the conduct of a *health fair*. The reference at the end of this chapter prepared by the American School Health Association is one worthy of review.

ALCOHOL

		Grades
Bulletin board	1 Illustrated display of accidents and other losses attributed to alcohol.	U
	2 Illustrated display of the alcohol content of the various kinds of beverages.	U
Buzz group	3 Conduct a buzz session on the questions "Should I drink alcoholic beverages?" "Why do people drink alcoholic beverages?"	6, 7, 8
Chart	4 Prepare a chart or poster that shows the effect of alcohol on the body and the level of alcohol in the blood after beverages are consumed.	6, 7, 8
Demonstration	5 Place a small (3-inch) goldfish in a solution of ½ ounce of alcohol in ¾ pint of water (the amount in a 12-ounce bottle of beer). In almost 20 minutes the fish will be "under the influence" (floating to the surface). When the effect of the alcohol can be seen, remove the fish and place in fresh water to be revived.	I, U
Discussion	6 The physiological, psychological, and sociological effects of alcohol on the human body.	6, 7, 8
	7 The nutritional elements of a glass of milk, an ounce of whiskey, and a bottle of beer.	6, 7, 8
	8 The nature of the alcohol content in beer, wine, and whiskey.	6, 7, 8
	9 Collect ads from newspapers and magazines on alcoholic beverages and analyze them in class.	U
	10 Safe and unsafe use of alcohol.	U
	11 Predisposing factors to alcoholism.	U
	12 Effects on families of individuals with alcohol problems.	U
Dramatization	13 High school drama class depicts scenes of pressures put on sixth-, seventh-, and eighth-grade students to drink alcoholic beverages. Follow with discussion of junior high school pupils' suggestions for handling such situations.	6, 7, 8
Exhibit	14 Display whiskey, wine, and beer glasses and discuss the amount of alcohol contained in each beverage and in each glass.	6, 7, 8
	15 Display a variety of magazines, pamphlets, and other materials for students to read, do research, and prepare oral and written reports on alcohol.	U
	16 Pupils display lables taken from medicine bottles and other containers and prepare a list of the amount of alcohol found in these substances.	U
Graph	17 Compare the amount of money spent nationally on alcohol and the amount spent on education, cancer, tuberculosis, and other health projects.	U
Guest speaker	18 Invite a member of Alcoholics Anonymous to discuss the services rendered by this organization to help alcoholics.	U

Grades

19 Invite a physician to discuss the physiological effects of alcohol on the human body.   U

Individual and group reports

20 Pupil committees write letters to organizations having materials on alcohol and request copies for use in class.   6, 7, 8

21 Pupils prepare oral and written reports on recent magazine articles about alcohol.   6, 7, 8

22 Pupils prepare oral and written reports on the effect of alcohol on a person in sports, driving an automobile, flying, typing, and using industrial skills.   U

23 Pupils prepare individual and group reports on such topics as the preserving quality of alcohol, alcohol as a fuel, alcohol in medicine, and alcohol as a disinfectant.   U

Interview

24 Interview a member of the sheriff's office or police department to find out the effect of alcohol on the crime rate and the accident rate in the community.   U

25 A pupil committee interviews a physician and the health officer on the benefits and adverse features of the use of alcohol.   U

Panel

26 Have a panel discussion on the topic "Why people drink alcoholic beverages."   U

Problem solving

27 Pupils do research and prepare oral and written reports about a series of problems such as: "Why do people drink?" "Should teenagers drink alcoholic beverages?" "What effect does alcohol have on the body?" "What effect does alcohol have on the mind?" "Is alcohol a food?" "What are the uses of alcohol?" These may also serve as introductory questions to stimulate student discussion to determine ways to find solutions.   U

Reports

28 Pupils prepare reports on Alateen and Alanon programs; relationships of alcoholism and nutritional problems; state laws; community resources to treat alcoholism; alcohol and use in religious ceremonies.   U

Resource persons

29 Invite member of Alcoholics Anonymous to class.   U

30 Have police officer talk about alcohol intoxication tests.   U

Role playing

31 Saying no when offered an alcoholic beverage.   U

32 Pressures of peer groups to consume alcoholic beverages.   U

Scrapbook

33 Pupils make scrapbooks to include pictures, magazine and newspaper articles, stories, and other items about the use and effect of alcohol.   U

Self-test

34 Pupils complete a self-test and conduct a discussion afterward.   U

What do you know about alcohol?

Circle the correct answer to the right. If you do not know the answer, circle the letter "D."

1. Alcohol is a narcotic drug.	T	F	D
2. Scientists consider alcohol to be a good food.	T	F	D
3. Alcohol has good uses outside the body.	T	F	D
4. A person can get drunk on beer.	T	F	D
5. A person can do things better after a few drinks.	T	F	D
6. A drink of whiskey helps to overcome a cold.	T	F	D
7. Alcohol slows down digestion.	T	F	D
8. Football coaches permit their players to drink small amounts of alcohol.	T	F	D
9. More accidents are caused by drivers with "just a few" drinks than by drunk drivers.	T	F	D
10. The use of alcohol is related to the crime rate.	T	F	D
11. Drinking is related to the causes of divorce.	T	F	D
12. If people want to drink, it is their own business.	T	F	D
13. Drinking is a good way to solve a difficult problem.	T	F	D
14. Most people begin to drink because they like the taste.	T	F	D
15. It is easy to tell who may become an alcoholic.	T	F	D
16. Alcohol is a stimulant.	T	F	D
17. Alcohol is a disinfectant.	T	F	D

			Grades
Survey	35	Conduct a survey among pupils to find out the kinds and amounts of alcoholic beverages they have tasted or now drink.	U
Tape recording	36	Have students interview a former alcoholic about attitudes toward use of alcoholic beverages.	U

COMMUNITY HEALTH

			Grades
Bulletin board	1	Display illustrated drawing or pictures of the functions of various community health agencies.	I, U
	2	Show the life cycle of the mosquito or the fly.	I, U
Chart	3	Make illustrated charts and posters about community health helpers.	P
	4	List ways the children can help to promote good health in the community.	P, I
	5	Make a chart listing the professional, official, and voluntary health agencies in the community.	I, U
Checklist	6	Prepare a checklist for use in rating the school health environment and the community health environment.	U
Construction	7	Make a bear's head out of papier-mâché and a large ice cream carton; have the mouth open for paper deposits—"Litter Bear."	P, I

FIG. 12-2

			Grades
Demonstration	8	The correct use of the drinking fountain.	P, I
	9	How water may be purified by filtration as illustrated in Fig. 12-2.	I, U
	10	Have pupils examine some swamp water under a microscope and a second sample of this same water after it has been treated with chlorine.	U
	11	Show how a small amount of oil on water forms a thin layer that causes mosquito larvae to die because they cannot penetrate the film to breathe. Obtain swamp or other stagnant water containing mosquito larvae for this demonstration.	U
Diorama	12	Prepare a diorama showing the locations of the agencies and the helpers involved in community health.	P
Discussion	13	Discuss and illustrate with pictures and stick-figure drawings the various kinds of community helpers who take care of our health, such as the fire fighter, the police officer, the doctor, the nurse, and the dentist.	P
	14	Collect pictures of ponds, lakes, rivers, and reservoirs and ask the class whether they think it is safe to drink water out of or to swim in these places.	P, I
	15	The proper use and maintenance of drinking fountains and lavatories.	P, I
	16	The maintenance of a healthful school environment including cleanliness, lighting, heating, and ventilation.	P, I
	17	The danger of petting strange animals and the procedures to follow if bitten by one.	P, I
	18	The importance of sanitation including the disposal of lunch papers and refuse in the school and classroom.	P, I, U
	19	The community rules and regulations concerning garbage and rubbish disposal.	I, U
	20	The relationship of water supply to the sewage disposal systems in schools, homes, and rural areas.	I, U
	21	The importance of restaurant sanitation.	I, U

Grades

22 The responsibilities of individuals to keep public places clean, such as picnic grounds, parks, campgrounds, and public rest rooms.   I, U

23 The effects of water pollution and how local health laws protect against pollution.   I, U

24 The need for periodic health examinations.   I, U

25 The use of chemical sprays and dusts in agriculture and the possible dangers involved.   I, U

26 Ways used by the city to remove and dispose of garbage and trash.   I, U

27 The sanitary procedures necessary for swimming pools.   I, U

Dramatization
28 Prepare and present a play to the Parent-Teacher Association on the work of the health department.   I, U

29 Prepare and present a play to a school assembly that will dramatize community health problems with possible solutions.   I, U

Drawing
30 Make drawings showing the sanitary procedures used in the school cafeteria.   I

Excursion
31 Take an excursion to the lavatories in the school and discuss use and maintenance.   P

32 Visit a grocery store or food market to observe how perishable foods are stored and how cleanliness is practiced.   P

33 Take a trip to a dairy to observe the sanitary procedures used in the handling of milk.   I, U

34 Visit a water purification plant, a sewage disposal plant, or a health department.   I, U

35 Visit food markets, restaurants, and other establishments to observe sanitary ways of handling and dispensing food.   I, U

36 Visit a local hospital.   I, U

Exhibit
37 Display larvae, eggs, pupae, and adult mosquitoes and flies to observe development.   I, U

38 Display pamphlets, books, and other reading material relating to community health.   I, U

Experiment
39 To demonstrate the need for refrigeration in preserving foods, obtain two glasses of milk and cover them. Put one in the refrigerator and leave the other outside at room temperature. Compare the milk in each glass for several days, noting the differences in appearance, texture, and taste.   I, U

Guest speaker
40 Invite the custodian to discuss ways used to protect the health of pupils in school.   I, U

41 Invite a member of the mosquito abatement office to discuss the control of mosquitoes and flies in the community.   I, U

42 Invite members of the health department staff such as sanitarians, laboratory technologists, statisticians, and health officers to discuss community health.   I, U

43 Invite a sanitarian from the local health department to discuss health laws regarding public eating places, public rest rooms, and the sale of food in the community.   I, U

Grades

44 Have a guest speaker from the community health council or committee describe the organization and its functions.   U

45 Have a panel of speakers discuss possible health careers, such as nurses, doctors, dentists, and dietitians.   U

Individual and group reports

46 Write an individual or group letter to the city water department requesting literature on how water is filtered and purified.   I, U

47 Write a group letter to the health department asking about its role in the health of the community.   I, U

48 Write a group letter to the local health officer requesting materials that tell how he or she helps to protect the health of the community.   I, U

49 Pupils prepare a list and conduct a study of the common insects and animals that carry disease and create sanitation problems.   I, U

50 A pupil committee writes to the mosquito abatement office for information concerning the control of mosquitoes and flies.   I, U

51 Report on the procedures used to make water safe for drinking in the community.   I, U

52 Investigate the nature of air pollution and the role of the health department in this problem.   I, U

53 Pupils write to the World Health Organization, the U.S. Public Health Service, and the state department of public health for information about their services and activities.   U

54 Consult the local health officer and report on the morbidity and mortality statistics of the community.   U

55 Pupils report on the health heroes in history and their contributions to community health.   U

56 Investigate ways that the community is protected against disease from people who come from foreign countries by ship and plane.   U

57 Report on the services rendered to the community by such agencies as the heart and tuberculosis organizations.   U

58 Pupils write reports on the methods of sewage disposal in the community and the problems related to these procedures.   U

59 Write reports on ways to purify water and compare them with the procedures used in the community.   U

Interview

60 Pupils interview parents on the major community health problems.   I, U

61 Interview health officials and obtain information about food poisoning   I, U

62 A committee of pupils visits the cafeteria manager to discuss ways used to sanitize dishes, dispose of garbage, and store food.   I, U

63 A committee of pupils interviews someone from the county or city health department for information about housing laws.   U

Mural

64 Draw a mural showing the location and functions of the various community health helpers.   P, I

Panel

65 Have a panel discussion of the major community health problems and present viewpoints of the nurse, physician, health officer, and others.   U

		Grades
Posters	66 Make illustrated posters and charts about keeping clean public places, such as parks, public rest rooms, and campgrounds. Include slogans: "Did you use the garbage can?" "Did you leave the campground clean?"	I, U
	67 Pupils prepare drawings and posters after a trip to the dairy to observe the procedures used in the sanitary handling of milk.	I, U
Scrapbooks	68 Prepare scrapbooks containing pictures of and newspaper and magazine articles on community health helpers.	I, U
	69 Make illustrated booklets of the work of the health department or a local hospital or both.	I
Show and tell	70 Have a child tell of a recent visit to a hospital.	P
Sociodrama	71 Children dramatize an unclean classroom or improper sanitation in the cafeteria or a restaurant.	I
Story	72 Write a cooperative story about "Jeremiah Germ" who delights in bad health habits that help him get around the community.	P
Survey	73 A pupil committee surveys the school environmental conditions, such as light, heat, and flies, that influence health.	I, U
	74 Have a committee survey the community to determine its "clean-up" needs and plan a campaign.	U

CONSUMER HEALTH*

		Grades
Attitude opinionnaire	1 Prepare a series of statements as illustrated below:	U

Check the appropriate box for each statement below (SA = strongly agree; A = agree; N = neutral; D = disagree; SD = strongly disagree).

	SA	A	N	D	SD
1. A physician is the best person to see when ill.	☐	☐	☐	☐	☐
2. Nurses provide reliable health information.	☐	☐	☐	☐	☐
3. People should treat themselves when ill.	☐	☐	☐	☐	☐
4. Acupuncture helps people with certain illnesses.	☐	☐	☐	☐	☐
5. Special foods and diets help people with arthritis.	☐	☐	☐	☐	☐
6. Books and pamphlets are good places to find out about health.	☐	☐	☐	☐	☐

		Grades
Bulletin board	2 Display health products advertised in newspapers and magazines for student review and analysis.	I, U
	3 Display magazine and newspaper articles related to consumer health students bring to class.	I, U
	4 List local consumer health agencies and organizations and the services they render. Include addresses and telephone numbers.	I, U

*Teacher information is available in Cornacchia, H.J., and Barrett, S.: Consumer health: a guide to intelligent decisions, ed. 2, St. Louis, 1980, The C.V. Mosby Co.

			Grades
Discussion	5	Pupils bring a variety of labels from health products to class for discussion.	I, U
	6	Pupils bring advertisements of health products to class for critical analysis.	6, 7, 8
	7	Television and radio advertisements of health products.	6, 7, 8
	8	The Pure Food, Drug, and Cosmetic Act.	U
	9	Health food fads and fallacies.	U
	10	Superstitions and quacks in health.	U
	11	Role of the physician, nurse, dentist, and other health practitioners.	P, I, U
	12	Use of products in the medicine cabinet at home.	P, I
	13	Alternative healing philosophies—acupuncture, faith healing, chiropractic, and others.	U
	14	Self-diagnosis and self-medication.	I, U
	15	The intelligent health consumer.	P, I, U
	16	Reliable sources of health information.	P, I, U
	17	Community agencies and organizations to protect the health consumer.	U
	18	Food fads—vitamins, wheat germ, yogurt, and others.	I, U
	19	Use of aspirin and aspirinlike compounds.	P, I, U
Excursion	20	Visit a Food and Drug Administration laboratory.	6, 7, 8
Exhibit	21	Display a variety of items that are available in the various health food stores and discuss.	6, 7, 8
	22	Display labels of a variety of over-the-counter drugs available in drugstores.	6, 7, 8
	23	Have a place in the classroom where pamphlets and publications relating to consumer health are available for pupil use.	6, 7, 8
	24	Have the Food and Drug Administration, the Arthritis Foundation, or other organizations display gadgets and items sold by quacks in the community.	U
Guest speaker	25	Invite the school nurse or a physician to discuss answers to such questions as "How can I choose a competent physician?" "Should I choose my own medication at the drugstore?" "What are the various kinds of specialists who can help me when I am sick and what do they do?"	I, U
	26	Invite a speaker from the Food and Drug Administration to relate how that organization protects the health of the consumer.	6, 7, 8
	27	Invite speakers from such organizations as the Federal Food and Drug Administration, the Better Business Bureau, the state Food and Drug Administration, the Post Office Department, the Federal Trades Commission, or the American Medical Association to discuss how they protect the health of the consumer.	6, 7, 8
Individual and group reports	28	Children prepare lists of the health products, or the products that affect health, advertised on radio and television as well as in newspapers and magazines.	I, U
	29	Pupils collect lists of superstitions, sayings, or customs related to health and health practices.	6, 7, 8
	30	Pupils prepare reports on the meaning of the terms *quack* and *nostrum*.	I, U

Grades

31 Write to the Food and Drug Administration, the Better Business Bureau, the American Medical Association, and other organizations for information and materials about consumer health. U

32 Pupils write reports on the different kinds of health specialists found in the community. U

33 Pupils prepare individual and group reports on consumer health found in current magazine articles. U

34 Compile a list of community sources from which reliable and accurate health information can be obtained. U

35 Students prepare a list of services rendered by community health agencies and organizations protecting the consumer. I, U

36 Students prepare reports analyzing health publications available for sale. U

Interview

37 A committee of pupils interview a member of the Food and Drug Administration, the Better Business Bureau, the Post Office, and other agencies that play a role in consumer health. U

38 A pupil committee interviews a representative from the advertising department of a local newspaper to learn whether newspapers have criteria for accepting advertising for health products and services. U

Panel

39 Have a panel discussion of the question "What are the dangers of self-medication?" Present viewpoints of parent, nurse, and physician. 6, 7, 8

40 Have a panel discussion on the question "How should I choose a physician?" Present viewpoints of parent, nurse, and physician. 6, 7, 8

Self-test

41 Prepare a self-test on superstitions, quackery, or health fads. U

Nutrition facts or fiction?

Place a check mark in the box under the appropriate answer.

	FACT	FICTION	DON'T KNOW
1. Dry cereals are necessary for body energy.	☐	☐	☐
2. Raw eggs are more nutritious than cooked.	☐	☐	☐
3. Eating an egg a day is harmful.	☐	☐	☐
4. Fish and celery are brain foods.	☐	☐	☐
5. Frozen orange juice has less nutritive value than fresh.	☐	☐	☐
6. Vegetable juices have magic health-giving qualities.	☐	☐	☐
7. All fruits and vegetables should be eaten raw.	☐	☐	☐
8. It is dangerous to leave food in a can that has been opened.	☐	☐	☐
9. Water is fattening.	☐	☐	☐
10. Drinking ice water causes heart trouble.	☐	☐	☐
11. Wine makes blood.	☐	☐	☐
12. If one vitamin pill a day is good, two or three are better.	☐	☐	☐
13. Meat is fattening.	☐	☐	☐
14. Toast has fewer calories than bread.	☐	☐	☐

Survey

42 Students ask parents and friends about the kinds and extent of use of over-the-counter drug products purchased in drugstores. U

43 Students ask parents and friends about the kinds and extent of use of foods purchased in health food stores. U

DENTAL HEALTH

			Grades

Bulletin board   1 Display a collection of magazine pictures about dental health.   P, I

2 Display illustrated captions on dental health such as the following: P, I

> Here is little Billy
> Doesn't he look silly?
> He was pulled out by Carol
> When he fell in a barrel.
> I would have been just fine
> If I had kept my place in line
> To the faucet I did run
> Broke this tooth and that's no fun.
> Here's a tooth so very loose
> As you can see it's not much use.
> 'Cause Tommy refused to look ahead
> And ran into someone else's head.

3 Prepare posters or displays on dental health as illustrated in Figs.   P, I, U
12-3 to 12-6.

4 Students help the teacher in the preparation of a health chart of   P, I
practices that contribute to dental health as follows:

PRACTICES	PRODUCTS NEEDED	SERVICES NEEDED
Brush teeth	Brush	See dentist twice
Floss teeth	Toothpaste	yearly or when
	Dental floss	problem develops

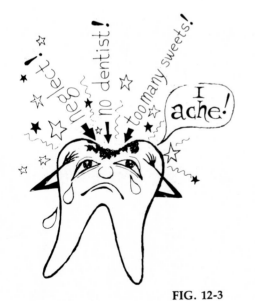

FIG. 12-3

FIG. 12-4

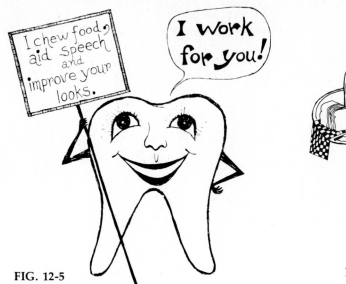

FIG. 12-5

FIG. 12-6

			Grades
Brush-in	**5**	Provide toothbrushes and toothpaste to be used in practicing tooth-brushing procedures. Use disclosing tablets to determine effectiveness.	P, I
Checklist	**6**	Children prepare a daily brushing chart to be taken home and hung in the bathroom to record when their teeth have been brushed.	P, I
	7	Have students complete and discuss "How do I rate?"	I, U

How do I rate?	YES	NO
1. I have had a thorough examination of my teeth in the last 6 months.	☐	☐
2. All dental treatment recommended by my dentist has been completed.	☐	☐
3. I brush my teeth or rinse my mouth with water immediately after eating.	☐	☐
4. I understand the importance of having missing teeth replaced.	☐	☐
5. I do not eat sweets between meals.	☐	☐
6. I have my teeth cleaned by a dentist or dental hygienist regularly.	☐	☐
7. I know that sugar in candy and soft drinks can lead to tooth decay.	☐	☐
8. My teeth have been treated with a fluoride solution at the recommended ages.	☐	☐

Construction	**8**	Children make large construction paper toothbrushes. Each day the child reports the removal of plaque from brushing, the child may hang the brush on the wall-long toothbrush holder.	P
Debate	**9**	Have a debate or panel discussion on fluoridation of the water supply.	U

Grades

Demonstration

10 Teacher demonstrates the proper way to brush teeth, and students practice the technique using the flexed fingers of one hand on the cheeks and lips. Distribute toothbrushes and small tubes of toothpaste for all children to take home and use. P, I

11 Make tooth powder in class. Students mix the following ingredients in the proportions indicated: 1 teaspoon salt, 2 to 3 teaspoons baking soda, and a drop or two of oil of peppermint, wintergreen, or cinnamon. Pupils take home some of the mixture to use when brushing teeth. P, I

12 Have pupils show the acidity or alkalinity of the mouth using nitrazine paper. Give pupils strips of paper, instructing them to soak sterile cotton swabs with saliva and apply to the paper. The degree of acidity or alkalinity can be determined by comparing the resulting color of the paper strips with the color chart provided by the manufacturer. A pH of 7 indicates a neutral mouth, less than 7 indicates an acid mouth, and greater than 7 shows an alkaline mouth.* P, I, U

13 Demonstrate the proper way to brush the teeth using a large toothbrush and a large set of teeth. Children participate in a toothbrush drill using tongue blades instead of toothbrushes. Pupils also practice rinsing their mouths and swallowing—"swishing and swallowing." Pupils may also be given disclosing tablets to take home and use.†

14 Show spoonful amounts of sugar found in candy, soft drinks, and other foods by placing equivalent quantities in test tubes or other containers. Each container should be labeled and placed on exhibit. I, U

Discussion

15 The value of certain foods, such as apples, celery, carrots, and oranges, as tooth cleaners. P

16 Display and discuss magazine pictures brought by children showing good and bad foods for teeth using "the happy and sad tooth" chart. P

17 The loss of primary teeth (deciduous) as a normal process unless there is tooth decay or an accident. P

18 The importance of teeth in speaking after having children pronounce such words as thirsty, thank you, thistle, and sister Susie sitting on a thistle. P

19 Show and discuss pictures of people smiling. Illustrate how some of these people would look with missing teeth by blackening a few teeth. P

20 The reasons why the dentist is a friend. P

21 Have the class discuss how teeth grow by examining a model of the teeth and jaw. I, U

22 The types and functions of teeth, using models: incisor—cuts, cuspid—tears, bicuspid—crushes, molar—grinds. P, I

23 The qualities and care of a good toothbrush. Draw on blackboard or bring models of toothbrushes to school. P, I, U

---

*Rich, R.: Tests for acidity of the mouth in relation to susceptibility to dental caries, Journal of School Health 33: Feb. 1963.
†Your dentist or local dental society can provide information about securing a supply of these tablets.

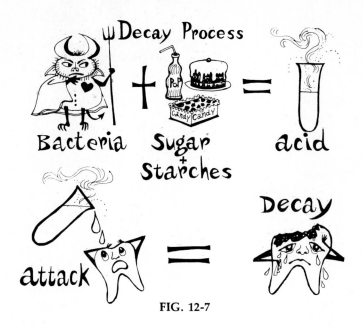

FIG. 12-7

		Grades
	24 During discussion of teeth have pupils label mimeographed diagrams.	I, U
	25 The value of the use of tooth pastes or tooth powders.	I, U
	26 Fluoridation.	U
	27 Discuss the decay process, using the illustration in Fig. 12-7.	P, I, U
Dramatization	28 Children set up a dentist's chair and dramatize cleaning teeth and visiting a dentist. A discussion should precede this activity on how to clean teeth and why visits to the dentist are necessary.	P
	29 To show that acid will weaken substances containing calcium (such as tooth enamel), place a whole egg in a bowl of vinegar (acetic acid) for about 24 hours. The eggshell should become soft as the vinegar decalcifies the shell.	P, I, U
	30 Dramatize a visit to the dentist's office.	P
	31 Have class write a play on dental health and present it to the Parent-Teacher Association or at a school assembly.	P, I, U
Drawing	32 Children draw, color, and possibly animate different teeth as well as different parts of teeth.	P, I
Excursion	33 Visit the community water plant and observe how water is fluoridated.	U
Exhibit	34 Display pencils, unshelled nuts, buttons, and other hard objects and discuss the dangers to teeth when these items are bitten or chewed.	P, I
	35 Display an explorer and mouth mirror and other implements used by the dentist to examine the teeth and discuss them.	P, I
	36 Build a toothbrush holder and supply each child with a new toothbrush (possibly obtain from the Parent-Teacher Association) for noon brushing. Be certain that each brush is properly labeled with each child's name on it.	P, I

Grades

37 Display several types of toothbrushes.	I, U
38 Display booklets, pamphlets, teeth, models, and other items relating to dental health.	I
39 Display x-ray films and discuss their use in dental care.	I, U
40 Obtain extracted teeth from a dentist and display to illustrate decayed teeth.	I, U
41 Display models of orthodontia showing before and after results.	U
42 Exhibit mouth protectors used in sports such as football and boxing.	U
43 Show the relative amounts of sugar in different foods, such as candy bars and soft drinks.	U

Experience chart

44 Prepare an experience chart or record listing significant points about dental health, such as: **P**

> Teeth are our helpers.
> Teeth must be cleaned.
> Teeth help us to chew.

45 Prepare a chart listing the foods that are good for teeth.   **P**

Experiment

46 Observe the progress of decay in two apples by breaking the skin of one and leaving the other intact. Place both apples in a place where they can be seen for a few days and relate what happens in the dental decay process.   **P, I**

47 Have each child eat a cracker and with the tongue feel the coating of food on the teeth. Then have each student eat a piece of carrot, celery, or apple and note how much cleaner the teeth feel.   **P, I**

48 Demonstrate the relative value of brushing the teeth, swishing with water and swallowing, and chewing such raw fruits and vegetables as apples, carrots, and celery right after eating a snack. Have six children each eat a chocolate cookie. One should then brush using water and no dentifrice, a second should swish with water and swallow, a third should eat an apple, a fourth should eat a piece of raw celery, a fifth should eat a carrot, and a sixth should do nothing. All pupils should receive a paper cup that is ¾ full of water and be instructed to rinse their mouths (using water in small amounts) and empty into a second cup. The amount of chocolate food debris in each cup will serve as a measure of the cleansing effectiveness of the different methods used.   **I, U**

Flannelboard

49 To show the presence of bacteria in the mouth, sterilize some gelatin (sweetened with sugar) in a pressure cooker for 15 minutes (or heat in oven at 100° to 120° F. for 1 hour). Prepare two shallow dishes of the gelatin. Carefully scrape between the teeth and near the gum line to remove food debris (may use a toothpick). Place these scrapings in one dish. Cover both dishes, label, and place in a warm place. After several days fungus growth should appear in the dish exposed to the mouth bacteria, but little or none will be seen in the uncontaminated dish.   **I, U**

50 Compose a story of how a rabbit or other animal took care of its teeth and illustrate the procedures using a flannelboard.   **P**

Grades

51 Prepare models to compare the parts of a tooth with a hard-cooked egg or an apple. — P, I
Enamel—skin of apple or egg shell
Dentin—white of apple or egg white
Pulp—core of apple or egg yolk

52 Discuss appropriate foods for dental health by preparing models for use on the flannelboard and include poor food (candy and soft drinks) models, but do not put sandpaper on the backs of these items. When an attempt is made to place them on the board, they will fall off, indicating their poor quality. — P, I, U

53 Show the parts of the tooth and how decay proceeds by using colored flannel cutouts with black for decay, gray for a filling, pink for the pulp, yellow for the dentin, white for enamel, and red for infection and abscess. Use name tags (enamel, dentin, crown, and others) made of paper with sandpaper backing to identify the flannel parts. — P, I, U

54 Illustrate the decay process (Fig. 12-7). — P, I, U

55 Illustrate the progressive stages of dental caries. — P, I, U

Field trip — **56** Students visit a dentist's office. — P, I

Flip chart — **57** Make a flip chart that shows the importance of retaining all of one's teeth. Show pictures of appetizing foods, such as steak, apples, oranges, and celery. Also illustrate types of baby food that would have to be eaten if children did not have teeth. — I, U

Floss-in — **58** Demonstrate proper way to use dental floss and have students practice this skill in class. Relate to brush-in and use of disclosing tablets to determine effectiveness. — P, I, U

Guest speaker — **59** Invite a dentist or dental hygienist to class to discuss dental care. — P, I, U

Individual and group reports — **60** Children write brief summary paragraph in answer to the question "What must we do to take care of our teeth?" — P, I, U

61 Children prepare lists of good dental snack-time foods. — P, I, U

62 A pupil committee sends a composite letter to the American Dental Association requesting materials on dental health. — I, U

63 Pupils write reports on the values of x-ray films in dental health. — I, U

64 Pupils investigate the use of fluoride in preventing tooth decay. — U

65 Pupils write a group letter to the water commission requesting information about the natural supply of fluoride in the water supply. — U

66 Students identify foods consumed in 1 day and determine the amount of sugar in each item and total the daily intake. Provide plans for reduction of amount eaten. — I, U

Kit — **67** Prepare a plaque control kit containing a toothbrush, flossing material, and disclosing tablets for use at school or at home. — P, I, U

Models — **68** Children construct plaster-of-paris models of their own teeth. — P, I

Grades

Mural | 69 Make a mural in which each child draws a self-portrait and writes a slogan under the picture describing good dental health practices. | I

Poems | 70 Create original poems. | P

> We brush the teeth as they grow
> Down from the top and
> Up from below.
> Your teeth look swell
> When you brush them well.
> But your teeth decay
> When you keep the brush away.

Puppets | 71 Children participate in puppet shows emphasizing a visit to the dentist, brushing the teeth properly, or eating the proper foods for dental health. | P

Scrapbooks | 72 Children prepare scrapbooks of picture cutouts showing good and bad teeth as well as proper and improper foods for dental health; also drawings of toothbrushes, dental floss, and toothpaste. | P, I

Show and tell | 73 Children share a visit to the dentist or the experience of losing a tooth. | P

Songs | 74 Create simple toothbrushing or dental health songs. | P

> TUNE: *A Hunting We Will Go*
> A brushing we will go,
> A brushing we will go,
> We'll brush our teeth so white and clean,
> A brushing we will go.

> TUNE: *Mulberry Bush*
> This is the way we brush our teeth,
> Brush our teeth, brush our teeth,
> This is the way we brush our teeth
> Right after eating food.

Stories | 75 Have children make up a short story about the care of the teeth. | P

Survey | 76 Survey the class to determine how many pupils have visited the dentist within the past year. | I, U

77 Have children keep records of the amount of candy, soft drinks, and other such items consumed and estimate the total amounts of sugar being eaten. | I, U

Tasting party | 78 Have a bunny rabbit party in which celery, green peppers, and carrot sticks are served and discuss their importance in helping to clean the teeth. | P, I, U

79 Plan a dental health program for parents and serve nutritious snacktime foods. | P, I, U

DISEASE CONTROL AND PREVENTION

		Grades

Bulletin board

1 Display a list of good health rules and practices that will protect children from disease.   P

2 Display illustrations of animals and insects that carry disease.   P, I

3 Display pictures or drawings showing how to cover the face when coughing or sneezing.   P, I

4 Prepare posters to illustrate ways to protect others from communicable diseases, such as: P, I

> Catch that sneeze (use of handkerchief or tissue)
> Cut the apple to share it (rather than taking a bite)
> Use your own comb or towel or washcloth

5 Display the signs, symptoms, control, and treatment of a particular disease. Different diseases can be featured. Community health organizations often have materials to help with the bulletin board.   U

6 Prepare pictures of such items as soap, washcloth, toothbrush, comb, and towel. Place caption below reading "We need these to keep clean."   P

7 Display the hands of all the children in class by tracing them on paper and making cutouts. Place the caption below to read "We wash our hands."   P

Chart

8 Prepare a chart that lists the ways germs are transmitted from one person to another: talking, sneezing, coughing, dirty hands and objects, carelessness in handling foods, utensils, and dishes.   P, I

9 Make a "Good health habits" chart to include statements with illustrations of the following: P

> My hair is combed.
> My face is clean.
> I wash my hands and nails frequently.
> My clothes are neat and clean.
> My shoes are clean.

FIG. 12-8   FIG. 12-9

Grades

Choral
speaking

10 Children participate in choral speaking.   P

My hanky

See my hanky white as snow,
I use it when my nose I blow,
It's not to play with,
Oh, my, no!!

Construction

11 Prepare a disease prevention railroad train for bulletin board dis-   P, I
play using construction paper. The various freight cars should be
hauling a comb, toothbrush, handkerchief, washcloth, soap, and
other items needed. Each car can be labeled "Comb car", "Toothbrush car," and other appropriate names. The total train might be
called "The disease prevention train" or the "Getting ready for
school train."

Demonstration

12 The proper way to blow the nose.   P, I
13 The way to cover coughs and sneezes.   P, I
14 The proper way to wash hands.   P, I
15 The proper use of handkerchief or tissue.   P, I
16 How to use a paper bag as a sanitary way to discard disposable   P, I, U
tissues and other contaminated objects.
17 Darken the classroom and flash the light from a movie projector on   I, U
the wall so that the dust particles in the air may be seen. This will
show how germs may be spread by the dust to which they attach.
18 Have a member of the health department demonstrate tuberculin   I, U
testing.
19 The use of the clinical thermometer in class and its importance in   I, U
illness.
20 Demonstrate how germs may be transformed by putting fluorescent   I, U
dye on some coins or other appropriate objects with several pupils
handling the items. Have one or two of these pupils wash their
hands with soap and water. Using "black light" (ultraviolet) in a
darkened room, observe the hands of the children who handled the
objects as well as those who washed their hands. If the dye remains
on the hands, it will be clearly visible by glowing in the "black light"
and thus showing how germs may be spread. The washed hands
may or may not fluoresce, depending on the thoroughness of the
washing. Ultraviolet light may be damaging if shone directly into
the eyes. The nurse may have a Wood's light for use in this demonstration.
21 Show pictures of a boy washing hands, a girl washing hands, and   P
hands being washed with soap. Discuss how and when to wash
hands. Demonstrate the proper way and follow by having all children practice the proper way to wash hands.
22 Demonstrate the proper way to wash the hands and face.   P
23 Make soap in the classroom.   P, I
24 Show the proper way to clean and file fingernails.   P, I
25 Have children use a magnifying glass to examine the creases and   I
folds of the skin and the dirt on one hand. After washing the hand
have pupils again examine the skin.

		Grades
	26 Examine samples of different kinds of clothing material with magnifying glass. Discuss seasonal appropriateness of each.	I
	27 Demonstrate "hidden dirt" on the skin of a child who appears to be clean but has perspired by washing an area of the skin with rubbing alcohol using a piece of cotton. Show the cotton to the class after the demonstration.	I, U
	28 Display two beakers containing warm water in one and cold water in the other with each having a tablespoon of oil and a tablespoon of liquid soap. Stir both beakers and compare the results. Warm water disperses the oil globules more effectively and hence is better for washing.	I, U
	29 Using charts and models, study the structure of the skin and relate this to cleanliness and disease control.	I, U
Discussion	30 Disease control in terms of sleep and rest requirements.	P
	31 Briefly discuss some of the common childhood diseases, their symptoms, prevention, and control.	P
	32 The need for immunizations.	P
	33 Why children should stay at home when not feeling well.	P, I
	34 How to protect ourselves and others from contracting contagious diseases.	P, I
	35 The importance of washing hands before lunch and after the toilet. Have children practice these habits at the appropriate times.	P, I
	36 Cleanliness in handling and consuming food; washing of fruits and vegetables before eating and refusing to share bites of food or to eat food that has been dropped on the floor.	P, I
	37 The causes of disease.	P, I
	38 Colds and other contagious diseases in terms of prevention.	P, I
	39 Beneficial and harmful germs. Beneficial germs give cheese its flavor, make bread rise, and turn apple juice to cider. Harmful germs cause disease and illness.	P, I
	40 The importance and significance of poliomyelitis immunization.	P, I, U
	41 The use of disinfectant in the control of disease.	I, U
	42 The methods that help to destroy bacteria; soap and water, pasteurization, sterilization, light and air.	I, U
	43 Tuberculin test and its meaning.	I, U
	44 Food poisoning and how it may be prevented.	I, U
	45 The heart and heart disease using a model of the heart and a chart of the circulatory system.	U
	46 Weather and seasonal changes that require different kinds of clothing.	P, I
	47 Pictures of appropriate shoes and clothing for work and play as well as for different kinds of weather.	P, I
	48 The correct disposal of tissues.	P, I
	49 Such questions as "Why should I keep clean?" What should I do before I eat?"	P, I
	50 Need, frequency, and methods of bathing.	P, I
Dramatization	51 Dramatize a visit to the doctor to be immunized or to obtain treatment for a contagious disease.	P

Grades

52 Getting ready for school using towels, soap, nail file, mirror, nail brush, comb and brush, cloth to wipe shoes, toothbrush, and clean handkerchief. — P

Excursion 53 Visit the school health office and meet the school nurse. — P

Exhibit 54 Display pamphlets and materials on communicable diseases for student use. — I, U

55 Display samples of clothing for use in different kinds of weather. Have children discuss and select appropriate apparel for the weather indicated by the teacher or by pupils. — P

Experience chart 56 Prepare an experience chart about good health rules and practices in preventing and controlling communicable diseases. — P

Experiments 57 To show the existence of germs on the hands, wash with soap and water and place salt on them. Try to rub off the salt until none is visible. By touching the tongue to the hands it can be shown that salt still remains. Wash hands again with soap and water and touch tongue to hands to show that the salt has been removed. — P, I

58 To discover the conditions that may affect the growth of germs, have pupils wet two pieces of cloth and place one in a dark, warm place and the other in sunlight and air for 1 week. The results will show that warmth, moisture, and darkness help molds and bacteria to grow whereas sunshine prevents this process. — P, I

59 To discover that hands are germ carriers, have pupils with dirty hands touch a piece of bread and place it in a labeled jar. Have children with freshly scrubbed and dried hands touch another piece of bread and place it in a second labeled jar. After a week or more, the piece of bread that was touched with the dirty hands will have much more mold than that touched with clean hands. — P, I

60 To discover how germs are spread, push a needle into the moldy part of an orange. Pierce a second orange with the contaminated needle. Clean and sterilize the needle by boiling and pierce a third orange. Label all oranges and observe the changes that occur daily for a week or more. Mold will grow on the contaminated orange. — I, U

61 To discover the presence of germs, wash, dry, and sterilize (heat directly on an electric plate at medium temperatures for 1 hour on each side) two petri dishes (may use metal lids and glass squares). Prepare a sterile solution by dissolving ½ ounce of plain gelatin in 1¾ cups of water and boil for 1 hour. Pour this substance into the petri dishes. Cough into one petri dish and cover. Merely cover the second dish. Place these dishes in a warm dark place and observe them daily for 1 week. Colonies of bacteria will develop in the contaminated dish. — I, U

62 To discover that sunlight kills bacteria, inoculate two petri dishes (prepared as previously described) from a dish where bacteria are growing. Place one dish in the open sunlight and the other in a warm dark place. After one dish has been in the sunlight for several hours, place it in the dark, warm, place with the other dish. Examine the two dishes each day for several days. — I, U

Grades

63 Using a magnifying glass, study the molds that have grown on stale bread, fruit, or other material. Bring a microscope to class for each child to view this mold.   I, U

64 To show the growth of germs, boil some small, peeled potatoes until still firm and place one in each of four sterile pint jars with lids. Maintain one jar as a control, but contaminate the potatoes in the other three jars by (a) rubbing with dirty hands, (b) rubbing with hands after washing with soap and water, and (c) rubbing with tissue after blowing nose. Put lids on all jars, label, and place in a warm but visible location. Observe daily the growth of bacteria and compare with the control potato.   I, U

65 Touch different articles in the classroom with swabs and touch these to petri dishes containing agar. Incubate the dishes so that the germs will grow. Ask a laboratory technologist from the health department to identify some of the germs.   I, U

66 To teach the importance of cleanliness, put some dust on a sterile agar petri dish (may use gelatin if agar not available), cover, and place in a warm, dark place. use a sterile petri dish as a control, cover, and place with the first dish. Observe results daily for about 1 week and compare the growth of germs.   I, U

67 To show how flies spread disease, have one crawl across a sterile agar petri dish (may use thin layer of gelatin if agar not available), cover, and place in a warm, dark place. Use a sterile petri dish as a control; cover, and place with the first dish. Observe results daily for about 1 week and compare the growth of germs.   I, U

Finger plays

68 Children participate in finger plays.   P

Here is my little washcloth,	Here is Johnny, ready for bed,
Here is my bar of soap.	Down on the pillow he lays his head.
This is the way I wash my face,	He pulls up the covers over him tight,
Until it's clean, I hope.	This is the way he sleeps all night.
This is the way I brush my teeth,	Morning comes, the sun is bright,
Until they are so white.	Back with a kick the covers fly.
I drink my milk and eat my cereal	He jumps up and gets dressed
So when at school I feel just right.	And goes to school to play with the rest.

Flannelboard

69 Use paper dolls on a flannelboard to illustrate the appropriate clothing for school and different kinds of weather.   P, I

Guest speakers

70 Invite the health officer or nurse to discuss communicable diseases.   P, I, U

71 Invite guest speakers from the heart, cancer, and tuberculosis associations to discuss the nature of chronic diseases.   U

72 Invite a nurse, dermatologist, or other physician to discuss skin problems or care of the skin.   U

Individual and group reports

73 Children write a brief summary paragraph or two in answer to the question "Why is it necessary to wash our hands and when should this be done?"   P, I

74 Children write a brief report on "Why I should stay home when I am ill."   I, U

Grades

75 Pupils read about such health heroes as Leeuwenhoek, Koch, and   I, U
Pasteur and write about their contributions to the control of disease.

76 Pupils read and write reports about communicable diseases trans-   I, U
mitted by insects or animals to man including methods of control.

77 Pupils write to the health department, requesting materials about   I, U
the control of diseases.

78 Pupils prepare written reports for publication in the school news-   I, U
paper on tuberculosis, poliomyelitis, colds, and other communicable diseases.

79 Form pupil committees to report on diseases such as tetanus and   I, U
smallpox.

80 Pupils read and write about harmful bacteria in drinking water,   I, U
milk, or food.

81 Pupils write reports on television or radio programs they have seen   I, U
or heard on the control of disease.

Interview   82 A pupil committe interviews health department officials about the   I, U
prevention and control of disease in the community.

Mobile   83 Make a mobile showing a toothbrush, comb, washcloth, nail file,   P
and other items needed for cleanliness and disease control.

Pantomime   84 Discuss the various procedures a child should follow when getting   P
ready for school. Have children pantomime these procedures and
let the class guess the activities being dramatized.

Poem   85 Children or teacher or all create poems.   P, I, U

If you cough,
or if you sneeze,
Cover your mouth
With a tissue, please.

Cover your mouth when you sneeze,
'Cause if you don't
Someone might get the disease.

The man with the flying sneeze

Germs fly through the air with the greatest of ease,
Whenever you cough or whenever you sneeze.
So don't be a goose,
A clean handkerchief use,
Anytime with a flying sneeze.
   Ah - - Choooooooo - - - - - -

Good food we should eat,
And get plenty of sleep.
When water is deep,
Away from it keep.
Be on the alert
And don't be a jerk
Anytime with a flying sneeze.

Dirt

Dirt is fine:
    For gardens and roads,
    For worms and toads,
    For puppy to dig—
    And maybe for pig—
    For cats
    For rats
    For night-flying bats,
    For lambs
    and clams
    and even for dams,
    For slugs and snails,
    but
      Under my nails,
    Not mine!

DORIS HAMMER

			Grades
Posters	86	Children make posters about the control and prevention of communicable diseases.	P, I, U
Problem solving	87	Jimmy and his parents are going on a camping trip for a week where there are no modern facilities such as tap water, electricity, or other conveniences. Help Jimmy answer the following questions: How can we keep clean? How can we obtain safe drinking water? What should we do if we get a cut knee? What other things must be done to protect ourselves from disease?	I, U
Puppets	88	Make two puppets and call them "Healthy Harry" and "Sick Sam." Dramatize children coming to school who feel sick.	P
Quiz	89	Show students a series of pictures and have them orally tell or write the answers to these questions:	P, I

PICTURES	QUESTIONS
Washing hands	1. When do we do this?
Brushing teeth	2. When do we do this?
Going to bed	3. How much sleep do we need?
Coughing or sneezing	4. What must we do?
Wearing raincoat	5. Why do we need this?

			Grades
Research	90	Children read and write reports on how disease germs are spread and controlled.	I
	91	Committees prepare oral and written reports on the following diseases: heart, cancer, diabetes, asthma, allergies, and arthritis.	U
Riddle	92	Make up riddles such as "I'm thinking of something we should do after we play and before we eat. What is it?"	P, I
Scrapbooks	93	Prepare scrapbooks of magazine and newspaper articles and pictures relating to communicable diseases.	I
	94	Pupils collect magazine articles, pictures, and other information on chronic diseases and prepare scrapbooks.	U

			Grades
Self-test	95	Prepare a self-test on the prevention and control of disease.	I, U
Show and tell	96	Children report experiences about illnesses at home.	P
Sociodrama	97	The school health examination.	P, I
	98	Conduct a sociodrama on the immunization procedure.	P, I
	99	The procedures for the proper handling of foods.	P, I
	100	The role of the nurse and the doctor in the prevention of disease.	P, I
Stories and songs	101	Prepare creative stories and songs about the doctor, nurse, and health habits.	P
Survey	102	Survey the nature of illness and the extent of immunizations of the children in class.	I, U
Television box	103	Construct a television box and prepare a series of panels on various aspects of cleanliness. Children or teacher could make the panels, which might include soap, comb, washcloth, children washing, and others. Have a television show when everything is ready.	P

DRUGS*

			Grades
Advertisements	1	Students bring drug advertisements to class for analysis.	U
Brainstorming	2	Have students identify ways they can contribute to the control of drugs in the school and the community.	U
Bulletin board	3	Display magazine and newspaper articles brought to class by pupils.	U
	4	Display illustrations of popular drugs used and abused.	I, U
	5	Display pamphlets and other reading materials and permit students to select items they wish to read or report on.	U
	6	Display of ways to say no.	I, U
Buzz groups	7	Discussion questions: Should students use drugs? Should marijuana be legalized? Why do students use drugs? Does "everybody's using drugs" mean everyone should do so?	U
Comparative analysis	8	Have students seriously think about something they like to do above all else—art, music, reading, football—and ask them to jot down in several brief, concise phrases their feelings of what this activity does to and for themselves. Teachers list all the phrases on the chalkboard without reference to the activity. Give students a copy of a list of phrases extracted from drug abusers about their feelings of what drugs do for them. Compare this list with the chalkboard list, which might include:	U

> It makes you aware.
> My mind is broadened.
> It does something to my perception.
> I notice differences more.

*For additional techniques, see Cornacchia, H.J., Smith, D.E., and Bentel, D.J.: Drugs in the classroom: a conceptual model for school programs, ed. 2, St. Louis, 1978, The C.V. Mosby Co.

Grades

It increases my potential.
The world is more interesting.
It gives you a sense of awe of nature.
It's an intense total experience.
You appreciate your senses better.
It puts me in a world by myself.
I don't understand why people find boredom in living.
I am totally involved in the environment.

Ask students to identify the similarities and differences in the two lists and give the reasons why. This procedure should encourage a discussion of alternatives to drugs rather easily and profitably.

Discussion   9 The kinds of medicines that are used by members of the family such   I, U
as cough medicine (codeine), sleeping pills, aspirin, and others. Also
talk about the effects of these drugs on the body: sleep induction,
sedation, relief of pain.

10 Read current newspaper articles about drugs and have pupils pre-   U
pare questions that they wish to have answered. List these questions
on the blackboard and have pupils determine how to find answers.

11 The importance of taking drugs under parents' and doctors' supervi-   P, I
sion.

12 The effect of coffee, tea, and cocoa on the body.   P, I

13 Why people use drugs.   U

14 The physiological effects of drugs such as marijuana, heroin, mor-   I, U
phine, barbiturates, amphetamines, volatile chemicals, hallucinogens and others on the body.

15 Sociological factors, including laws of drug use and abuse.   U

16 Drug usage by students in schools.   U

17 Poisonous substances in the home.   P, I

18 Emergency procedures when poisonous substances are ingested.   P, I, U

19 How young people are introduced to drugs.   I, U

20 The federal and state regulations concerning the sale and use of   U
drugs.

Dramatization   21 A student is urged by friends to ingest an unknown substance.   I, U

Exhibit   22 Display a variety of containers that contain drugs obtainable at drug   U
stores.

23 Display a variety of pamphlets, magazine articles, and other materi-   U
als for pupil use in writing and preparing reports.

Field trip   24 Students attend a court session involving illegal drugs.   U
25 Students visit and talk with drug abusers.   U
26 Entire class visits a teenage rehabilitative resource center.   U

Guest speaker   27 Invite a member of the sheriff's office, the local police department,   U
or the state narcotics office to discuss narcotic drugs.

28 Invite a physician or pharmacist to come to class to discuss the effects   U
of drugs on the human body.

29 Invite a drug abuser to class.   U

Grades

Individual and group reports	30 Vocabulary lists and definitions of such drugs as narcotics, heroin, morphine, marijuana, barbiturates, amphetamines, hallucinogens, volatile substances.	U
	31 Use of drugs by individuals and their effects on the body.	I, U
	32 Oral and written reports on the uses of drugs in medicine.	U
	33 Origins of drugs.	U
	34 Federal, state, and local laws about the sale and use of drugs.	U
Music	35 Have students relate rock music, or music in general, to the drug scene.	U
Newspaper articles	36 Students collect articles about drugs for discussion in class.	I, U
Interview	37 A committee of pupils interviews a physician to obtain information about the values, dangers, and abuses of the use of drugs.	U
Panel	38 Have a panel discussion describing the effects of such drugs as aspirin, sleeping pills, and tranquilizers on the human organism.	U
Peer group	39 Upper-grade students prepare presentation for sixth-grade pupils or seventh and eighth graders.	U
Posters	40 Students plan a drug education program for schools, using a variety of posters.	U
Pretest	41 Give a pretest to determine the extent of pupils' knowledge about drugs.	U
Problem solving	42 Place the following terms on the blackboard (or assign pupils to locate their meaning): bennies (benzedrine pills), coke (cocaine), cook a pill (heat opium for smoking), fix (injection), get high (smoke marijuana), hemp (marijuana), horse (heroin), junk (narcotics), mainliner (addict), pusher (peddler), and weed (marijuana cigarette). Ask pupils to identify these words. Continue the discussion by defining the terms and providing additional information about drugs. Pupils may raise further questions that need exploration.	U
	43 Procedures to be followed to ensure the proper use of medicines.	P, I
	44 If you discovered your brother, sister, or friend using drugs, what would you do? What should you do?	U
	45 What might be the consequences if you are attending a party or are in a car where drugs are being used?	U
Puppets	46 Prepare stick or other types of puppets and dramatize use of medicine in the home.	P
Questions and answers	47 Pupils prepare anonymous questions that they would like answered about drugs.	U
Rap session	48 Provide opportunities for students to meet voluntarily in small groups or on a one-to-one basis with a school person who communicates easily with students and is knowledgeable about the drug scene.	U

Grades

| Reports | 49 Have students prepare reports on: my philosophy of life; what I value; peer pressure and drug use; drug laws and minors. | U |

| Records | 50 Play records of rock bands related to drugs. Prepare verses to songs and discuss contents. | U |

Role playing	51 Students dramatize trying to influence others to use illicit drugs, and class analyzes the situation presented.	U
	52 Students dramatize a parent giving medicine to a sick child.	P
	53 Students dramatize someone refusing an offer to smoke a marijuana cigarette.	I, U

| Scrapbook | 54 Pupils make scrapbooks containing drawings, newspaper and magazine articles, and written reports on drugs. | U |

| Sociodrama | 55 Conduct a sociodrama of a peddler who approaches a group of pupils and tries to sell them marijuana cigarettes. | U |

| Student information center | 56 Establish a location in school manned by students where pupils seeking information may go for help. | U |

| Survey | 57 Students attempt to discover the extent of the use of drugs in school. | U |

| Tape recording | 58 Interview drug users and abusers, physicians, and others. | U |

| Television | 59 Students view a current program about drugs and prepare a report for class. | U |

CARE OF THE EARS

Grades

| Bulletin board | 1 Display drawings or pictures that show how the ears help us to hear. | P, I |
| | 2 Prepare a bulletin board showing the head of a clown and place a large pupil-drawn ear on the clown. Put a caption at the top of the display "We use our ears to:" and then put various other statements around the clown, such as "use the telephone," "hear bells," "hear danger signals," and "enjoy music." | P, I, U |

| Cartoons | 3 Draw cartoons illustrating rules about the care of and hazards to the ears. | P, I |

Demonstration	4 The proper way to wash the ears.	P
	5 The proper way to blow the nose. Have children practice the procedure following the demonstration.	P
	6 Show a drum and relate it to the functions of the eardrum and sound vibrations.	P, I
	7 Demonstrate lip reading to show how handicapped a deaf person might be. Discuss the importance of protecting one's hearing.	P, I
	8 How a drum head may be punctured from a severe blow and relate the possibility of this occurring to the eardrum from a loud noise or blow.	P, I, U

Grades

	9 Sound vibrations using a tuning fork. Drop a rock in water to show how vibrations travel in all directions.	I, U
	10 Test hearing using the whisper and watch test.	I, U
Discussion	11 How infections, accidents, and foreign objects may affect hearing.	P, I
	12 How the ear helps us to hear.	P, I
	13 The need for reporting pains or other symptoms of ear problems.	P, I
	14 The dangers of putting objects in the ear.	P, I
	15 How we hear. Use rhythm instruments to produce sounds and relate these to hearing.	P, I
	16 How to protect ears from loud noises such as yelling in someone's ear, and the television or radio turned on too loud.	I, U
	17 The structure and function of the ear, using charts and models to illustrate.	I, U
	18 The prevention of ear injuries when swimming, blowing the nose, cleaning the ears, playing, and receiving blows to the ears.	I, U
	19 How colds and other diseases may result in deafness.	I, U
	20 How to help the person with poor hearing: hearing aids, talking into the good ear, making distinct words for the lip reader, and removing wax from the ears.	I, U
	21 Motion sickness.	I, U
Dramatization	22 Dramatize hearing testing or a doctor's examination of the ears.	P
	23 Have children dramatize the following procedures: proper way to blow nose, wash ears, whispered conversation, loud voice, and normal conversation.	P, I
	24 Dramatize a situation in which a person is wearing a hearing aid and is overly conscious of it. Bring out the relationships of hearing problems to emotional stability and the importance of understanding on the part of friends.	U
Exhibit	25 Display an otoscope (instrument to look into ears) and discuss how the doctor uses this instrument.	P, I
	26 Permit children to examine an ear model.	P, I
	27 Display several types of hearing aids.	I, U
Experience chart	28 Prepare an experience chart on the care of the ears.	P
Game	29 Play "listening" game. Have each child blindfolded or with closed eyes and ask individual players to identify different sounds: bell, bottle half full of water being shaken, horn, clock, crumpling of paper, and others.	P
	30 Play the game "ask-it basket." Divide the class into two teams and place in a basket questions prepared on the care of the ear. Team captains draw one question at a time and ask the opposing team for answers.	I, U
	31 Have pupils prepare a list of common terms relating to the ear and use these words to construct a crossword puzzle.	I, U

			Grades
Guest speaker	32	Invite the audiometrist to demonstrate hearing testing and discuss care of the ears.	P, I, U
	33	Invite the teacher for the hard-of-hearing to discuss hearing.	I, U
Individual and group reports	34	Pupils prepare written reports on care of the ears.	I, U
	35	Pupils prepare oral and written reports about people who have succeeded in life despite hearing difficulties.	U
Posters	36	Prepare a series of posters showing how the ear may be injured.	I, U
	37	Prepare drawing of the ear and label the major parts.	I, U
Pretest	38	Give a pretest to determine the extent of pupil understanding of the structure, function, and care of the ears.	I, U
Story	39	Children and teacher cooperatively write stories about the care of the ears.	P
Tape recording	40	Record voices on the tape recorder and permit children to hear their own voices.	P, I, U

EXERCISE AND BODY MECHANICS

			Grades
Bulletin board	1	Display drawings or pictures of proper sitting, standing, and walking posture.	P, I, U
	2	Display charts of the muscles and bones (skeleton) with captions or illustrations showing their relation to exercise, movement, and body mechanics.	P, I, U
	3	Display a series of pictures or drawings of beneficial activities and exercises.	I, U
Debate or panel	4	Have a debate or panel discussion on the "Soft American." Bring in viewpoints of physicians, parents, and others.	U
Demonstration	5	Children observe own posture in a full-length mirror.	P, I, U
	6	The correct way to pick up objects.	P, I, U
	7	Correct sitting, standing, and walking posture. Conduct drills in which pupils practice these procedures.	P, I, U
	8	Correct body alignment using a plumb line.	I, U
	9	Have pupils walk attempting to carry a book on their heads after they have assumed the correct posture.	I, U
	10	To show the effect of exercise on pulse rate, have pupils take own pulses while sitting or at rest. Permit them to stand in the aisles and jump up and down about 10 times and again take own pulse rates. Ranges of pulse rates before and after exercise can be noted on board with individual differences and relationships to exercise discussed.	I, U
	11	Conduct posture parade monthly in which the class votes on the boy or girl demonstrating the best walking posture. Children should determine in advance how they plan to make their selection.	I, U

		Grades
	12 To show the effect of exercise on breathing and oxygen intake, have children count the number of breaths they normally take per minute using a watch with a sweep second hand. Have pupils stand in the aisles, jump up and down about 10 times, and again count the number of breaths needed after exercise.	I, U
Diorama	13 Prepare a diorama of suitable physical education activities and exercises using pipe cleaners for figures.	I, U
Discussion	14 The importance and need for exercise in the maintenance and development of physical fitness.	P, I, U
	15 The relationship of muscles and bones to good body mechanics.	P, I, U
	16 The factors that influence posture such as food, sleep, exercise, and mental attitudes.	I, U
	17 The relationships of exercise and eating to good posture.	I, U
	18 The types of exercise and sports activities that are beneficial.	I, U
	19 The importance of muscular strength in preventing fatigue and in performing daily activities.	I, U
Game	20 Have pupils play "Indians" by walking on a straight line with heads held high. The leader (the "chief") has children vary their arm positions while walking; out to side, overhead, or bent at elbow in front of chest.	P, I
	21 Play "puppet" and "pull" self straight up as though using an imaginary string at the top of the head.	P, I
	22 Children stand against a wall and try to make their heads, shoulders, hips, and heels touch the wall. Follow this action by having pupils walk away from the wall retaining this position.	P, I, U
Guest speaker	23 Invite the physical education teacher or supervisor to discuss and demonstrate good body mechanics.	P, I, U
	24 Invite the physical education teacher or supervisor to visit the classroom to discuss "keeping in condition" and its importance in daily living.	I, U
Individual and group reports	25 Pupils write or give oral reports on such topics as "How I exercise each day," and "The sport I like best."	I, U
	26 Pupils prepare written or oral reports on the values of exercise.	I, U
	27 Children prepare written reports about their favorite sports and list the parts of the body that are exercised most in these activities.	I, U
Model	28 Pupils make a posture model (use heavy cardboard) for use in the discussion of body mechanics.	I, U
Mural	29 Make a mural of the variety of kinds of beneficial pupil activities and exercises.	I, U
Music	30 Walk to music, exhibiting good posture.	P, I
Poems, songs, and plays	31 Children create poems, songs, and plays about exercise and its values.	P

Posters   32 Make posters showing the importance of exercise in daily living.   P, I

Scrapbook   33 Make a series of drawings and collect magazine pictures and stories   P, I
                   demonstrating proper body mechanics.

Shadowgram   34 Children make shadowgrams of each other. Using a piece of craft   I, U
                   paper as large as a child, with two students holding the paper, have a
                   third pupil stand between the paper and a source of light. A fourth
                   boy or girl outlines the shadow of the third child using a piece of
                   charcoal or crayon. Discuss these drawings individually in terms of
                   good body mechanics.

Stories   35 Children write illustrated stories of how exercise helps us.   P, I

Survey   36 Survey the amount of exercise pupils receive by completing the   I, U
                   following:

How much exercise do I get?

Fill in the amount of time in hours or in fractions of hours.

	S	M	T	W	Th	F	S
Riding bicycle or walking to and from school							
Playing at recesses							
Playing before school, in the morning, and at noon							
Exercising during the physical education class							
Active playing after school and before bed-time							
TOTALS							

                37 Survey the kinds of activities in which pupils participate.   U

Television box 38 Make a television or motion picture box and have children prepare a   P
                   series of pictures showing the importance of exercise and body
                   mechanics.

CARE OF THE EYES

		Grades
Bulletin board	1 Display pictures and drawings about care of the eyes.	P, I
Chart	2 Prepare a chart containing important terms to know about the eye.	I, U
	3 Have pupils complete the names of the parts of the eye on a mimeographed diagram.	I, U
Demonstration	4 The correct way to carry objects such as sticks, knives, and tools.	P, I
	5 The procedure for removing foreign objects from the eye.	P, I, U
	6 The proper lighting for reading and working.	P, I, U
	7 Have a child read or look at a book or picture in direct sunlight or under a bright light. Discuss such questions as "Why is it difficult to read?" "Do your eyes hurt?" "Must you squint or frown to see?"	P, I, U
	8 Blindfold a child, turn him around several times, and have him try to walk to different places in the room. Discuss blindness.	P, I, U
	9 The importance of sight by having children cover their eyes and explain their reactions to a variety of situations.	P, I, U
	10 Teacher or nurse demonstrates the vision screening procedure.	P, I, U
	11 Demonstrate the blinking response using one pupil in class. With the corner of a soft paper, touch the lashes near the inner corner of one eye. Have children note the blinking reaction. Discuss the closure of the eyelid when sand lands on the eyeball, which is accompanied by a flow of tears to try to flush away the particle.	P, I, U
	12 Completely darken the room for a few minutes and then lighten it. Discuss what happens to sight when you first enter a darkened movie theater and also when later you first come into the bright sunlight.	P, I, U
	13 Demonstrate or draw a comparison between the function of the eye and a camera.	I, U
	14 Display various types of paper showing those with low and high gloss and discuss their importance in vision.	I, U
	15 Use a light meter to show the amount of light in the classroom.	I, U
	16 Have pupils hold their thumb at arm's length and look at it. Have pupil close their right eye and line up their thumb with the corner of the room. Without moving the arm, have them close their left eye and look with the right eye. Pupils should see a different view with each eye, demonstrating that binocular vision helps to adjust to space relationships.	I, U
	17 Have pupils close one eye and hold a pencil from 12 to 14 inches from the other eye. Have pupils look at the pencil and then at a distant object and report how the pencil appeared in each instance. Pencil looks blurred when the eye is focused a distant object or the reverse is true. This indicates the need for occasional resting of the eyes because muscles are involved in eye focusing changes.	I, U
	18 Have pupils look at a neighbor's eye in a darkened room. Lighten the room quickly and have pupils note contractions of the pupils of the eye. The eye must adjust to various amounts of light; therefore, a well-lighted room involves fewer eye adjustments and is less fatiguing.	I, U

Grades

19 Where the optic nerve enters the eyeball, there is a blind spot that   I, U
can very easily be demonstrated. Have pupils draw a black dot (¼
inch in diameter) on a white sheet of paper, and about 1½ inches to
the right draw a black cross (¼ inch). Have the pupils close their left
eye and stare steadily at the black dot with their right eye while the
paper rests on the table. Have pupils pick up the sheet of paper and
move it slowly toward the eye while staring at the dot. They will find
a point where the image of the cross to the right will disappear. The
blind spot for the left eye can be found by closing the right one and
staring at the cross. When the sheet is brought close to the eye, the
black spot will disappear.

20 With curtains or blinds drawn, hold a lighted 40-watt electric lamp   P, I, U
exactly 2 feet above an open book. This is approximately the amount
of illumination needed for comfortable reading. Show that light
rapidly diminishes as the lamp is moved further away. At a distance
of about 3 feet a 100-watt bulb is needed to provide the same illumination that a 40-watt bulb gives at 2 feet.

Discussion

21 The possible danger to the eyes of throwing things including sand,   P, I
rocks, and dirt.

22 The importance of vision to animals, showing pictures to illustrate.   P, I

23 An accident on the playground that resulted in an injury to a child's   P, I
eye.

24 The importance of wearing glasses when necessary.   P, I, U

25 Show pictures of artists, surgeons, pilots, and others and discuss   P, I, U
the importance of vision in their work.

26 Care of the eyes and television.   P, I, U

27 Have children roll a sheet of paper to make a cylinder and look   P, I, U
through it with one eye. Discuss tunnel vision.

28 The importance of symptoms of vision difficulties such as inability   P, I, U
to see the blackboard, words look fuzzy, or vision is blurred. Emphasize importance of notifying parent or teacher when these signs appear.

29 The hazards to vision of looking directly at the sun.   P, I, U

30 The ways eyes are protected in various sports.   P, I, U

31 The structure and function of the eye, using charts and models.   I, U

32 The importance of periodic eye examinations.   I, U

Dramatization

33 Dramatize the school nurse doing the vision screening test on a   P, I
child.

34 Dramatize the correct sitting distance and lighting for various tele-   P, I
vision.

35 Dramatize good reading habits and a visit to an eye doctor.   P, I

Exhibit

36 Display a model of the eye and permit children to take it apart and   P, I
put it together.

37 Display samples of Braille material and discuss how a blind person   P, I, U
uses it to learn to read.

38 Display various materials used in the vision screening program and   P, I, U
discuss.

39 Display pamphlets, magazines, and other reading materials on vision   I, U
and make available for reading and research.

Grades

40 Display different styles of glasses including sunglasses and goggles used to protect the eye in various activities. — I, U

Experience chart or record

41 Make an experience chart or record about the care of the eyes. — P

Game

42 Play the game "Pin the tail on the donkey" and discuss the importance of vision. — P, I

Guest speaker

43 Invite the school nurse to discuss vision screening. — P, I, U

44 Invite an eye doctor to discuss care of the eyes. — I, U

Individual and group reports

45 Pupils prepare oral or written reports about signs and symptoms of vision problems as well as common eye difficulties. — I, U

46 Pupils prepare oral or written reports on eye infections: conjunctivitis, styes, and others. — I, U

47 Pupils prepare oral or written reports on the various kinds of eye specialists in the community. — I, U

48 Pupils write reports on the various ways eyes are protected in sports. — U

Mural

49 Make a mural on care of the eyes or hazards to the eye. — P, I

Panel

50 Have a panel discussion of the various ways eyes are protected in sports. Get opinions on football, basketball, baseball, and others from appropriate sources. — U

Poems, stories, and plays

51 Create poems, stories, and plays about care of the eyes. — P

Posters

52 Make a series of pictures or drawings about proper lighting for reading as well as care of the eyes. — P, I

Self-test

53 Give self-test on the structure and function of the eye. — I, U

Self-test illustration

eyeball	pupil	retina
iris	lens	optic nerve

Fill in the blanks using the words above.

_____ Small, dark, round hole in center of eye.

_____ Carries pictures from retina to brain.

_____ Moves up, down and sideways.

_____ Light passes through lens, falls on lining at back of eyeball.

_____ Front part of eyeball, blue, brown or gray (in color) in circle.

_____ Behind the pupil and inside the eye.

Show and tell

54 Children relate a visit to an eye doctor or tell how wearing glasses helps those who need them. — P

Sociodrama

55 Role-play parents and children watching a television program, a visit to an eye doctor, having to wear glasses, and others. Discuss the significance to vision. — P, I

Survey

56 A pupil committee determines the amount of light in the classroom, halls, and other areas of the school using a light meter. — I, U

FAMILY HEALTH

		Grades
Bulletin board	1 Collect pictures of boys and girls of approximately the ages of students in class for a display illustrating differences in size and body build among children of the same age.	I
	2 Show pictures of ways families spend their time in recreation and during holidays.	I
	3 Collect pictures on family life and magazine and newspaper articles about birth and display them.	I, U
	4 Show pictures of happy families and have students describe what makes the families happy.	P
Charts	5 Construct a chart showing varying ages when boys and girls mature.	I
Discussion	6 What can I do to help my family be happy?	P
	7 Ways in which the community helps the family.	P
	8 Differences in growth rates between boys and girls.	I
	9 Inherited characteristics, such as eye and hair color, and curly or straight hair.	I, U
	10 Meaning of "growing up."	I
	11 Anonymous questions prepared by students.	I, U
	12 Living things come from living things.	P
	13 Family rules and family problems.	I, U
	14 Home responsibilities.	I, U
	15 What family members can do to show love, especially at certain times.	P,I
	16 Family customs, traditions, race, religions, and patterns.	I, U
	17 Care of pets.	P
	18 Nature and functions of the endocrine glands.	I, U
	19 Secondary sex characteristics of boys and girls as they relate to body shape, size, and growth.	I, U
	20 Moral and ethical values and their relation to sexual activities.	U
	21 Different ways of reproduction, asexual and sexual.	I, U
	22 Human reproduction.	I, U
	23 Good sources of information on sex, reproduction, and family living.	I, U
	24 Attraction between sexes and sexually transmitted disease.	U
	25 Ways to resolve family conflicts.	P, I
	26 Animal and plant reproduction.	P
	27 Compare the development of human babies before birth with animal babies.	P
	28 Family changes due to death, divorce, or separation.	P, I
	29 Responsibilities at home, at school, and elsewhere.	P
	30 Freedom and responsibility.	I
	31 Terms, such as mating, stud, heat, foal.	I, U
	32 Puberty and maturity.	I, U
	33 Love—marriage, children, family.	U
	34 Sex drive, birth process, masturbation, wet dreams, behavior on dates, marriage.	U
	35 People, organizations, and agencies that help people with family problems.	U
	36 Behavior on dates.	U

Grades

		Grades
	37 Steady dating.	U
	38 Determination of personal values.	I, U
Demonstrations	39 Have male and female guinea pigs or hamsters in the classroom. Pregnancy of the female will offer an opportunity to discuss the creation of new life.	P
	40 Hatch chicks from eggs.	P
	41 Observe the growth of seeds in relation to new life.	P
	42 Observe the growth of frog eggs.	P
Display	43 Make available pamphlets and magazine and newspaper articles about sex, reproduction, and values, for student optional reading.	I, U
Drawings	44 Illustrate ways in which families have good times together.	P
	45 Children draw their own family groups and list various family patterns.	P
	46 Illustrate pupil's own family or animal families.	P
	47 Depict mother's, father's, or own work.	P
Exhibit and health fair	48 Students prepare bulletin board displays, posters, charts, and other visual materials for display and exhibit these materials at school. Pupils should be available to discuss their projects, to provide information requested, and to distribute pamphlets.	I, U
Field trip	49 Tour the school building and include a visit to boys' and girls' bathrooms. This should lead to a discussion of anatomic differences of boys and girls and correct names of body parts.	P
	50 Visit a farm and observe the animals.	P
	51 Visit a local museum, hospital, or clinic to view exhibits of before birth and birth of a baby.	P, I, U
Films	52 Observe films on birth and growth of animals.	P
	53 See and discuss films on human growth, menstruation, and reproduction.	I, U
Guest speakers	54 Invite a physician or nurse to discuss reproduction, childbirth, and other matters.	I, U
	55 Invite ministers, priests, and other religious representatives to discuss moral and ethical values.	I, U
Graph	56 Prepare a graph that shows the heights and weights of class members; compare with national norms.	I
Mural	57 Develop a mural showing animals and human beings caring for babies.	P
Pretest	58 Develop a test relating to puberty, mate selection, reproduction, sex drive, and other matters.	U
Problem solving	59 Develop relevant situations with alternative solutions concerning dating, behavior on dates, selection of marriage partners, sexual relations. Use these as a basis for class discussion.	U
	60 Have children try to provide answers to these questions: How do you grow? What helps you grow? Why do you grow?	I

		Grades
Individual and group reports	**61** Rh factor, sex drive, marriage, dating, and others.	U
	62 Different ethnic, religious, and cultural backgrounds of people.	I, U
	63 What things do I do that make my family happy or unhappy?	P, I
Puppets	**64** Prepare a skit to show how parents help us.	P
Question box	**65** Provide a box in an appropriate location for students' anonymous questions.	I, U
Role playing	**66** Provide skits relating to family roles of mothers and fathers, getting along with brothers and sisters, helping to care for a new baby.	P
	67 Develop skits depicting manners and etiquette.	P
Scrapbook	**68** Include illustrated materials "All about me," all the items in terms of family, friends, and things that cause different emotional responses.	I
Story	**69** Prepare an open-ended story about the family, its activities, responsibilities of children. Allow pupils to fill in some of the words.	P
	70 Teacher starts with "I love my father and mother because . . ."	P
	71 Read appropriate stories about families and family relations.	P, I

CARE OF THE FEET

		Grades
Bulletin board	**1** Prepare a bulletin board display using magazine pictures and drawings of appropriate types of shoes for play, school, parties, and other occasions.	P, I, U
Chart	**2** Prepare a chart listing the important rules to consider when purchasing shoes.	P, I, U
	3 Prepare a chart listing the important rules to consider in caring for the feet.	P, I, U
Demonstration	**4** The proper way to walk with the feet parallel and have children practice this method.	P, I, U
	5 The proper way to wash and dry the feet.	P, I, U
	6 To demonstrate the proper way to walk, have a pupil make footprints on paper and make cutouts of these prints. Draw a straight line on the floor with chalk and have the pupil tape the footprints to the floor so that the inside of each print is parallel to the line and the toes point straight ahead. Now permit the child to walk the chalk line stepping in the footprints.	I, U
	7 Have pupils trace the outline of their shoes on a piece of paper. Have them remove the shoes and trace the outline of the foot on top of the shoe outline. Compare the two drawings and determine whether the shoe is the proper size.	I, U
	8 The importance of the feet to posture. Illustrate how walking with pronated or inverted feet may cause undue back and leg pressures with possible result that posture will be affected.	I, U

		Grades
	9 High and low foot arches by having pupils walk on pieces of paper with wet feet.	I, U
Discussion	10 The importance of changing shoes and socks when wet.	P, I, U
	11 The proper way to cut toenails.	P, I, U
	12 The importance of drying the feet properly.	P, I, U
	13 The proper care of the feet.	P, I, U
	14 The importance of shoes and socks or stockings that fit well and provide the best protection for the feet.	P, I, U
	15 The signs and symptoms of foot problems and who to see when they appear.	P, I, U
	16 How posture is affected by shoes that do not fit properly or are in poor condition.	P, I, U
	17 How to prevent athlete's foot and what to do about it when you have the condition.	I, U
	18 The importance of the bones and arches of the feet to posture and walking using a chart, drawing, or model.	I, U
Dramatization	19 Dramatize buying a new pair of shoes.	P, I, U
Exhibit	20 Display a variety of shoes for different kinds of activities.	P, I
	21 Display an instrument used in a shoe store to measure feet for new shoes. Have pupils determine their correct sizes and compare these with the shoes they are wearing.	I, U
	22 Display various types of materials found in socks, such as wool, nylon, and cotton, and discuss their significance in foot care.	I, U
Experience chart or record	23 Prepare an experience chart or record to show the proper ways to care for the feet.	P
Guest speaker	24 Invite a shoe salesman to discuss the way to select a properly fitting shoe.	I, U
	25 Invite a chiropodist to discuss the care of the feet.	U
Poems and plays	26 Children write poems, jingles, and plays about the proper care of the feet.	P
Posters	27 Make drawings or posters illustrating the importance of properly fitting shoes and socks.	P, I
Scrapbook	28 Prepare a scrapbook of magazine pictures and drawings of different styles of shoes for various activities and also stories about the care of the feet.	P, I
Story	29 Have children create a story about the kinds of shoes to wear for various types of weather.	P

GROWTH AND DEVELOPMENT

		Grades
Bulletin board	1 Teacher prepares a series of large drawings that show the progressive stages of the development of a chick embryo into a full-grown chick. Appropriate colors may be necessary to make these illustrations more attractive.	P, I
	2 Children collect pictures showing differences in growth patterns of adults for a bulletin board display: midgets and giants as well as tall and short persons. Discuss these differences as they relate to the pupils themselves.	P, I, U
	3 Pupils bring to class pictures of well-known, important people and prepare a bulletin board display of these individuals. Discuss the differences in body build.	I, U
	4 Teacher prepares a display showing the relationship of cells, tissues, organs, and systems to the organism as shown in Fig. 12-10.	I, U
Buzz group	5 Have a buzz group discussion about the meaning of the term *growing up*.	I, U
Demonstra-tion	6 Put several articles in a bag and observe whether children can identify the articles by merely touching them and not seeing them. This introduces the fact that the nerves send messages to the brain.	I
	7 Bring an earthworm to class and point out that it has no bones and its only means of locomotion is muscular movement. Mention that without a skeletal system human beings would probably move around like an earthworm. This leads to the concept that each part of the skeleton is shaped for its particular function and that muscles are necessary for locomotion.	I, U
	8 Demonstrate what happens when a person breathes by measuring the size of the chest before and after taking in a deep breath.	I, U

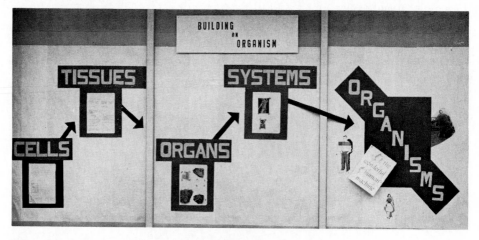

FIG. 12-10. Growth and development bulletin board. (*Courtesy Jefferson Union Elementary School District, Daly City, Calif.*)

Grades

9 Bring a stethoscope to class to demonstrate how a physician uses this instrument. — I, U

10 Line up pupils in class and have them note the differences in height. Discuss the fact that children do not have the same growth rate due to many factors: heredity, nutrition, illness. — IU

11 Dissect a hog's or cow's heart and identify its parts. — I, U

Discussion

12 Provide an illustrated discussion of the nervous and digestive systems using suitable charts and models. — I, U

13 Provide an illustrated discussion of the respiratory system using suitable charts and models. — I, U

14 Provide an illustrated discussion of the heart and the circulatory system using suitable charts and models. — I, U

15 Provide an illustrated discussion of the muscles of the body, using suitable charts and models. Demonstrate how muscles fasten to bones. — I, U

16 Discuss the nature and function of the skeletal system using suitable charts and models. — I, U

17 Discuss the endocrine glands and their role in growth and development. — I, U

18 Discuss and compare the human body with a machine (automobile). Mention the intake of fuel and the conversion to energy. — I, U

19 Disassemble a model of the human torso and ask pupils to identify the separated parts. Pupils might also try to reassemble the torso at the conclusion of this discussion. — I, U

20 Provide pupils with diagrams of the nervous, digestive, respiratory, skeletal, and circulatory systems and have them label the parts. — I, U

21 Discuss growth as an individual matter and show the differential patterns. — I, U

22 The story of heredity. — I, U

23 Ask such questions as: How do you know you have a heart? How big is your heart? What is pulse? Can you feel it? How many times does your heart beat, and how many times do you breathe in 1 minute? — I

Display

24 Bones from a variety of animals including human beings; have students try to identify them. — I, U

Dramatization

25 Dramatize a small boy trying to pick a fight with a large boy. Discuss the implications in terms of growth and development. — I, U

Drawings

26 Children draw, color, and label various systems and organs of the human body. — I, U

Exhibit

27 Display pamphlets and other publications on growth and development in the classroom for review by interested children. — P, I, U

28 Display animal bones obtained from a meat market. Show some cross sections and longitudinal sections of bones. — I, U

Experiment

29 Demonstrate how baby chicks, ducks, or other animals grow when given the proper food. The white rat experiment may also be used to illustrate the growth process. — P, I

Grades

		Grades

30 Provide a flannelboard and a box containing cutouts of the bones of the human body. Permit children to try to build the human skeleton on the flannelboard. — I, U

Films 31 Show and discuss films on human growth and menstruation. — I, U

Game 32 Play the game "Who am I?" A child describes the function of a particular organ of the body and pupils try to identify the organ. Another version of this game is to have children mention bones of the body and then have other pupils name bones to which they attach. — I, U

Graph 33 Construct a giraffe out of plywood and place measurements on its neck. Have children periodically measure themselves and record these findings on a graph that they have prepared. — P

34 Have each child prepare a height and weight graph. Children take their measurements once a month and plot their findings. Separate graphs using height and age or weight and age may also be advisable to make and use. — I, U

Guest speaker 35 Invite the school nurse to meet with the girls to discuss menstruation. — I, U

36 Invite the school nurse to come to class to discuss the process of human reproduction. — I, U

37 Invite a physician or other qualified person to class to discuss sexual growth with the boys. — U

Individual and group reports 38 Pupils compile a list of causes for individual differences in growth. — I, U

39 Pupils find the meaning of the words *heredity* and *environment*. — I, U

40 Pupils prepare lists of the characteristics they have inherited and acquired. — I, U

Model 41 Children make clay models of different organs of the body after they have seen pictures or drawings of these parts. — I, U

42 Children make a stethoscope using the material shown in Fig. 12-11. Have pupils hold funnel firmly over the heart and listen to heart sounds. Discussion of structure, function, and related diseases could follow. — I

43 Display real organs or plastic models of the heart and other body organs. — I, U

Problem solving 44 Encourage pupils to raise questions about growth and development and list these on the blackboard. Have pupils determine ways to find answers to the listed problems. — I, U

45 Present these or similar questions to pupils for discussion: What does *growing up* mean? How do individuals grow? Do boys and girls grow at the same rate? Why doesn't everyone grow at the same rate? How does one know when growth is taking place? What factors are involved in growth? — I, U

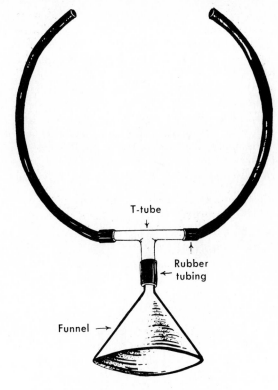

T-tube

Rubber
tubing

Funnel →

FIG. 12-11. Stethoscope model.

			Grades
Question box	46	Provide a question box for pupils' anonymous questions about menstruation, reproduction, and other aspects of growth and development.	I, U
Self-test	47	Prepare a self-test on the various aspects of growth and development, systems of the body, endocrine glands, heredity.	I, U

MENTAL HEALTH

			Grades
Bulletin board	1	Collect and display pictures and drawings of happy children and families as well as of people showing kindness.	P, I
	2	Display work by each child as often as possible to encourage responsibility in doing his or her best work.	P, I
	3	Display a list of class helpers for a week, eventually giving everyone in class a chance to be a leader.	P, I
	4	Prepare a bulletin board of examples found in newspapers and magazines that show good deeds, good sportsmanship, and other qualities.	P, I, U

Grades

5 Display an illustrated list of the hobbies of the children in class.   P, I, U

6 Prepare a bulletin board with a variety of illustrated mental health phrases such as "Meet friends halfway," "Be cheerful," and "Control your anger."   I, U

7 Display pictures of a variety of emotions with the caption: "Emotions we live with."   P, I

8 Pupils collect for display magazine and newspaper articles that describe mental health problems of concern to pupils.   U

9 Prepare the display illustrated in Fig. 12-12. The teacher can prepare questions in first panel and pupils can bring pictures for second panel and also help to obtain definition and lists for third panel.   I, U

Brainstorming   10 Students prepare lists of problems they consider important and develop plans to resolve them.   I, U

Buzz group   11 Conduct a buzz group discussion on the character traits a pupil likes or dislikes in a person.   U

12 Have a buzz group discussion of how boys and girls may become better acquainted.   U

13 Discuss such questions as: What is reality? Does "everybody's doing it" mean everyone should do it?   U

Checklist   14 Pupils complete checklists and teacher either holds individual conferences with pupils or anonymously discusses some of the problems in class. Some sample statements on this list might include: I, U

> I do not get along well with my parents.
> I am frequently embarrassed when with others.
> I usually do not know how to act in company.
> I usually feel inferior to my classmates.
> I lack self-confidence.

Consequences   15 Students periodically prepare written statements for discussion of the questions that follow regarding any or all of the actions identified or others deemed appropriate: I, U

Questions—Do you consider the consequences before taking action? Should you? How frequently? Why? What are the possible consequences of your actions?

Actions—smoking; using marijuana; using heroin; selecting dates; getting angry or emotional with friends or others; refusing the help of parents, teachers, and others when problems arise; sex activities; eating foods that may be harmful to health; racial and ethnic prejudice

Demonstration   16 Choose a child to be "big brother" or "big sister" to a new pupil during the first week in school.   P

17 Demonstrate ways for children to "let off steam" through such activities as play, music, hobbies, creative work, dramatization, and talking about things.   P, I, U

18 Teacher provides opportunities for all children to have chances in leadership roles.   P, I, U

19 Teachers provide a warm, friendly atmosphere in the classroom with many centers of interest.   P, I, U

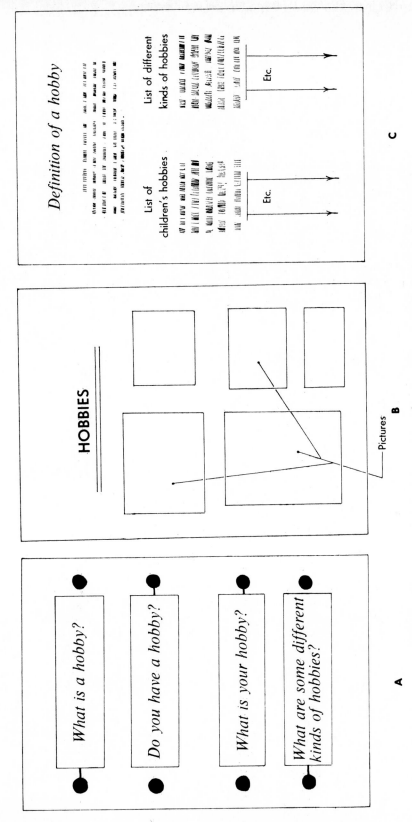

FIG. 12-12. Mental health bulletin board. **A**, Left panel. **B**, Middle panel. **C**, Right panel.

			Grades
Discussion	20	Children have opportunities to experiment with planning, to carry out plans, and to evaluate results of a variety of experiences.	P
	21	Talk about how to make friends.	P
	22	Ways to be helpful at home, happy times with the family, and ways to be unselfish about listening to the radio and television.	P
	23	The use of the words *please* and *thank you*.	P
	24	The necessity for proper rules and manners in the cafeteria.	P, I
	25	Children's feelings and the need for control over such actions as crying easily, temper tantrums, and fighting.	P, I
	26	Behaviors in class and in school in terms of getting along with one another and related problems.	P, I
	27	What it means to be a leader and a follower.	P, I
	28	When playing games in physical education, discuss the need to rotate positions to give opportunities for all.	P, I
	29	Discuss what to do when one feels sad, what to do to help others who are unhappy, and ways to behave when something unfortunate happens.	P, I
	30	The need to forgive children who have made mistakes.	P, I
	31	The need for the development of self-responsibility by keeping desk clean, hanging clothes in closet, taking care of pets.	P, I
	32	The quality of friendship.	P, I
	33	How people differ in their abilities to do things.	P, I, U
	34	Have class elect officers, with children establishing rules on voting and rules of behavior.	I
	35	Ways to cope with and solve problems* when they arise. What specific procedures should a pupil follow when faced with a situation for which he can find no answer?	I, U
	36	What it means to put oneself in another person's shoes.	I, U
	37	How people can be considerate of the feelings of others and how to handle hurt feelings.	I, U
	38	Honesty and truthfulness.	I, U
	39	Develop standards for acceptable behavior in the classroom, on the playground, to and from school, on the bus, in the library, on study trips, and at home.	I, U
	40	Children who are embarrassed by physical defects and what others can do to help these individuals.	I, U
	41	Inadvisability of keeping emotional tensions, worry, and fear bottled up inside. Discuss the need for friends to talk to, hobbies as outlets, being able to face up to problems, and other solutions.	I, U
	42	Have pupils prepare a list of qualities they like in a person as well as those qualities they do not like and post these on the bulletin board or put them in the school newspaper.	I, U
	43	The following personality traits: kindness, helpfulness, reliability, tactfulness, cheerfulness, good sportsmanship, good manners, intelligence, sense of humor, loyalty, and honesty.	I, U

Inside/Out is a series of 30 films that are 15 minutes each in length and are designed for 8- to 10-year old children. *Self-Incorporated* is a series of 15 films that are 15 minutes each in length and are prepared for 11- to 13-year-old children. These series are available from National Instructional Television Center, Box A, Bloomington, Ind. 47401.

		Grades
	44 Evaluate ways boys and girls have of gaining acceptance through such means as conforming to clothing fads, using current slang, forming clubs, and participating in school-sponsored social activities, plays, and other projects.	U
	45 Discuss the question "At what age should one start dating?"	U
	46 Habits and ways of behaving that will give parents confidence in allowing boys and girls increasing freedom to make decisions and to participate in activities outside the home.	U
	47 Reactions to other individuals who do not act, look, or believe as you do.	U
	48 The values of people.	U
Dramatization	49 Dramatize the following: thoughtfulness, courtesy, self-reliance, sharing, playing and working together, helping at school, following directions, respecting each other's property, lost and found, self-control, rudeness, good manners, and criticism.	P, I
	50 Dramatize emotional behavior exhibited such as anger, fear, jealousy, sorrow, hate, love, and temper.	P, I
	51 Dramatize such incidents as the following:	P, I, U

Things that make me happy.
Things that make others happy.
Things that make me sad.
Problems on playground or in classrooms.
Things I like to do.
How to make new friends.
Other kids can always do things I can't do.
It's not my fault others won't play with me.

		Grades
	52 Dramatize introductions to and conversations with other people in public places, bus, school, dance, party, theater, and street.	U
	53 Dramatize how it feels to be different from others in terms of race, nationality, beliefs, and customs.	U
Drawings	54 Have children make drawings illustrating: things I love; how I feel when hurt, scared, and angry; when I've wanted something I couldn't get.	P, I
	55 Draw a picture illustrating a way to be helpful to someone.	P, I
	56 Draw pictures of objects or animals that make us afraid.	P
Emotion box	57 Prepare an emotion box and have students periodically complete form in which their names, dates, types of emotion experienced, and the reason for same is identified. Teacher occasionally reviews and uses the material as a basis for class discussion and problem solving without indicating students by name.	I
Exhibit	58 Display pictures brought to class by children of places they would like to visit or where they would like to live. Discuss the reasons these places have been selected.	I, U
Finger paint	59 Provide children opportunities to finger paint to help release tensions and to explore creative abilities.	P

Grades

Flannelboard | **60** Use the flannelboard to illustrate situations of fair play and good sportsmanship and to create stories about fear, anger, hate, friendship, and others. | P, I

Good-deed box | **61** Prepare a good-deed box and have children deposit in writing good things that they have seen classmates do during the day. At the end of the day the teacher reads these to the class without mentioning names. | P, I

Guest speaker | **62** Invite a psychologist or psychiatrist to discuss the meaning of the term *personality*. | U

Individual and group reports | **63** Children write brief stories or reports on "How to be a better leader or follower." | P, I

64 Children write a brief summary paragraph or two in answer to the question "Why should we learn to get along with others?" | P, I

65 Pupils complete an individual written assignment on the topic "When my feelings were hurt." | I, U

66 Prepare oral or written pupil reports on good manners and courtesy. | I, U

67 Write a brief paragraph about good citizenship and draw pictures to illustrate. | I, U

68 Prepare reports on jealousy, prejudice, anger, and others for the school newspaper. | I, U

69 Boys make up lists of the qualities they like and dislike in other boys and have the girls do the same. Discuss the common characteristics found in both lists and their meanings to the pupils. | I, U

70 Pupils prepare written reports about what they do well and what they would like to improve in themselves. | I, U

71 Pupils write about and discuss the following: what makes me angry, happy, sad, or afraid; what I wonder about; three persons I love; three wishes; what I would like to change at home or at school; what I like about people; what I like about my friends. | I, U

72 Pupils write reports about the racial, religious, and other prejudices they have noticed that people have against individuals. | I, U

Mobile | **73** Using colored construction paper, children trace and cut out their hands and feet as well as other parts of the body they consider important. Various lengths of string are attached to each cutout and attached to a coat hanger or short pieces of dowling and hung around the classroom. | P, I

Murals | **74** Make murals, charts, and booklets that emphasize sharing in terms of carrying dishes to the table, going to the store, taking care of pets, making the bed, hanging up clothes, putting away food, running errands, and putting things away. | P, I

Music | **75** Use of various types of music to help calm and relax children to help create a beneficial classroom atmosphere. | P, I

Grades

Poems

76 Discuss the meaning of lyrics found in a variety of popular songs.   U

77 Prepare original poems.   P

> So little hands, be careful please
> Of everything you do
> For if you are sent to bed
> I'll have to go there too.

78 Read poems   P, I, U

Joy*

Joy is like a magic cup,
I lift it to the sky,
And all the more I offer up,
The fuller joy have I.

A smile*

A smile is like a little wedge
That often keeps us from the edge
Of getting sad, or feeling blue—
I love to see a smile, don't you?

Words*

I love the sound of kindly words—
I try to make them sing,
And I hope I never send one out
To be a hurtful thing.

Politeness*

Hearts, like doors, will open with ease
To very, very little keys,
And don't forget that two of these
Are "Thank you, Sir," and "If you please."

A level head*

It takes a level head to win,
A level hand, a level eye,
But sometimes, even when you try
Your level best, things go awry.
You drop the ball, you miss your aim,
You slip a cog and queer the game.
Then comes the test. Don't make excuse;
Don't crumple; stand up in your shoes.
Remember, in a certain sense,
It takes a level head to lose.

---

*Los Angeles City School Districts, California: Speech in the elementary school, pub. No. 479, 1949, Office of the Superintendent of Schools, pp. 190, 262, 263.

Grades

Problem solving	79 Describe a human relations episode to the class, such as lying, stealing, rudeness, or poor sportsmanship, and have children write or orally discuss how they would solve the problem.	I, U
Puppets	80 Make stick, paper bag, or hand puppets and prepare stories or plays around such themes as fear, anger, and jealousy.	P, I
	81 Construct a shadow box or puppet stage with children working together.	P, I
Questionnaire	82 Students complete short answers to the following:	I, U

Happiness is _____.
Sadness is _____.
I am fearful of _____.
I am angry when _____.

Question box	83 Have a question box in class and encourage children to put in questions concerning worries, fears, and other areas of trouble that they would like discussed.	I, U
Reports	84 Students write about: "Me as I see myself"; "Me as I would like to be"; "When I wanted something I could not have, what did I do?" "What should I have done?"	I, U
Role playing*	85 Teacher acts out such emotions as anger, fear, and hate. Students are requested to close their eyes before the teacher performs and on signal to open them as the demonstration occurs. Pupils try to identify the emotion and discuss beneficial and hazardous uses.	P
	86 Students act out such situations as how to make friends; getting along with others; facing dangers; solving problems.	I, U
Scrapbook	87 Children prepare a scrapbook or notebook with illustrated writings on "What to do when I get angry," "How to play fairly."	P, I
	88 Prepare a scrapbook of pictures and magazine and newspaper articles that illustrate good sportsmanship.	I
Self-test	89 Have pupils complete the following:	I, U

Friendliness test	YES	NO
Do you smile easily?	☐	☐
Are you a good listener?	☐	☐
Are you courteous?	☐	☐
Are you a good sport?	☐	☐
Do you refuse to tell tales?	☐	☐
Do you have a hobby?	☐	☐
Can you laugh at a joke on yourself?	☐	☐
Are you usually in a good humor?	☐	☐
Can your friends depend on you?	☐	☐
Do you try to talk about what interests other people?	☐	☐

Show and tell	90 Provide time for jokes, funny stories, and riddles.	P
	91 Provide opportunities for all children to show and tell something as frequently as possible.	P

*Also refer to Hawley, R.: Value exploration through role playing, Amherst, Mass., 1974, Educational Research Press.

Grades

Sociogram	92 Prepare a sociogram to find out if children in the classroom have friends. Have each child list the three children he or she would like to sit near.	P, I
Stories*	93 Read, make up, and discuss stories showing thoughtfulness of individuals to other individuals, about fears, cooperation, sharing, fair play, courtesy, sportsmanship, honesty, truthfulness, courage, friendliness, and other personality traits.	P
	94 Tell and read stories about helping at home, sharing of toys, caring for baby, and family living.	P
	95 Read and discuss stories of famous people who have overcome handicaps and failures such as Edison, Helen Keller, Pasteur.	I, U
	96 Have students write an ending to an unfinished story. Have several read aloud and follow with discussion.	P, I
	97 Read and discuss such stories as:	P

"Boo, Who Used to Be Afraid of the Dark," Leaf Munro
"Noise in the Night," Anne Alexander
"A Friend Is Someone You Like," J.W. Anglund
"Having a Friend," Betty Miles
"Behave Yourself," B.A.M. Briggs

	98 Read stories* about death and dying.	P, I, U
Survey	99 Conduct a survey regarding the qualities or traits that the pupils like in their friends. Have a committee tabulate the results and prepare a chart for display titled "Our best friends."	I, U
	100 Conduct a survey of interests, tabulate, and prepare a series of discussion questions on the findings. Some sample questions that could be included are the following:	I, U

I wish I had better grades.
I wish I didn't get headaches when I read.
I wish I didn't get into trouble at school.
I wish I could change some of my teachers.
I wish my folks didn't quarrel at mealtime.
I wish my parents got along better.
I wish my parents really loved me.
I wish I could take my friends home.
I wish my father could spend more time with me.
I wish I weren't afraid of things.

Tape recordings	101 Record conversations of a group of children and then have pupils listen to the tone of voices. Point out the emotions expressed and consider ways to modify them.	P, I

*See Appendix E for sample fiction and nonfiction books.

FIG. 12-13. Self-concept identification. *(Courtesy Miss Betty Jane Mobley, teacher, Tacoma Public Schools, Tacoma, Wash.)*

        Grades

Television box   **102** Make a television box with a series of drawings illustrating captions   P
such as the following:

> This little girl is too lazy to make her bed.
> Are you a good sport?
> Are you helpful at home, at school?
> Do you lose your temper and fight?
> Do you cry easily?
> Are you kind to others?

VALUE CLARIFICATION PROCEDURES*

Clarifying of   **103** Have students write their opinions regarding such questions as: U
values   Are people treated fairly in this school or community? Is money
the most important thing in life? What do you really believe in? Do
you want war or peace, violence or rational action? Do people treat
others justly, honestly, and equally? What do you want to be? Discuss these questions and raise others in an attempt to help in the
clarification of values.

---

*Adapted from Simon, S.B.: Promoting the search for values, School Health Review **2**:Feb. 1971; also, Raths, E.L., Harmin, M., and Simon, S.B.: Values and teaching; working with values in the classroom, Columbus, Ohio, 1966, Charles E. Merrill Books, Inc.

Grades

Consequences   **104** Have students prepare reports or discuss these behaviors: self-medication and self-diagnosis; smoking; use of marijuana or heroin; sexual intercourse; destroying or damaging someone else's property; stealing a book or money; having no friends; being a failure; telling people untruths; conflicts with parents; being rude to friends and others; sexually transmitted disease; exceeding the speed limit while driving an automobile. They should respond to these questions: Do you consider the consequences before you act? Should you? Why?   I, U

DUSO*   **105** Developing Understanding of Self and Others involves a variety of activities, including a story, role playing or puppets, posters, and discussion picture. It focuses on such developmental tasks as self-identify, self-acceptance, feelings of adequacy, responsibility, and value judgments.   P

Incomplete questions   **106** Have students complete such questions as those that follow and discuss answers using the value clarification technique:

I believe the three most important things in life are _____ .
If I could change the school program, I would _____ .
If I could be any person in the world, I would be _____ .
If I had three wishes, they would be _____ .
If I could change myself, I would _____ .   I, U

Me   **107** Students select words, pictures, symbols, and the like from magazines and newspapers that represent who they are and prepare a collage of these items on large pieces of construction paper.   P, I

Language of self   **108** Pupils write five words that describe themselves on a sheet of paper. They turn over this paper and write five words they wish would describe themselves. Discussion may take place in class.   I, U

Self-confidence chart   **109** Students check rating to the right of the following for discussion: I, U

	NO				YES
	1	2	3	4	5
Am easily upset emotionally.	☐	☐	☐	☐	☐
Dislike meeting people.	☐	☐	☐	☐	☐
Find criticism hard to take.	☐	☐	☐	☐	☐
Have trouble solving problems.	☐	☐	☐	☐	☐
Feel inferior most of the time.	☐	☐	☐	☐	☐
Will not try anything if it means failure.	☐	☐	☐	☐	☐

Self-rating personality scale   **110** Students cooperatively prepare a self-rating scale that contains such criteria as: makes friends easily; talkative; moody or happy-go-lucky; accepts responsibilities; good sport; is considerate. An individual self-analysis is followed by class discussion.   I, U

---

*Dinkmeyer, D.: Developing understanding of self and others, Circle Pines, Minn., 1970, American Guidance Service, Inc.

Grades

Things I like to do	111 Students identify the five things they like to do in order of importance on a sheet of paper. They indicate using a dollar ($) sign if they cost money to do, indicate the date last performed, and place an X beside those they enjoy doing with others. These may be discussed in class.	I, U
Unfinished sentences	112 Provide students with a variety of unfinished sentences to be completed such as: "If I were older . . ." "I wish . . ." "I would like to be . . ." "My favorite fun is . . ." "I make mistakes when . . ." Children can be encouraged to respond to answers by choice in class.	I, U
Value analysis	113 Ask students a series of questions and following responses ask why to: What aspect of health do you value most? If you had to give up one of your senses, which one would it be? If you had 6 months to live, what would you do? What do you like or dislike about yourself?	U
Value challenges	114 The teacher periodically raises value issues with students by introducing provocative, controversial statements found in newspapers, magazines, books, and elsewhere about values. Quotations, pictures with or without captions, scenes from plays or movies, lyrics from songs, and advertising slogans may also be used. These should be duplicated or shown to students for reading and viewing and followed by a series of questions such as: what is your reaction to the statement, item, photo, or scene? Would you be proud of this action? Was it right or wrong? Why? Does it make you want to change your life? How would you have helped? How would you have handled it?	I, U
Value questionnaire	115 Prepare a series of questions for student responses and discussion such as: What do you most like to do with your free time? What adult qualities do you admire? Where will you be and what will you be doing in 10 years? What injustices exist in the community? How do you feel about money and material possessions? Would you marry outside your race or religion?	U
Value report card	116 Students turn in weekly anonymous 4 by 6 inch value cards on which they describe things they care about deeply, or value highly. One card is turned in each time containing one value. Some cards are read and discussed in class periodically.	U
Value time diary	117 Students maintain a time diary for 1 week; a daily chart divided into 30-minute time blocks. Actual uses of time are identified. This information should be considered personal and not for viewing by anyone. An attempt should be made to help student locate those things they most like to do, to discover wasted time, to identify inconsistencies, and to focus on the difference between what one says and what one does. After students tabulate and clarify activities, students make individual efforts to determine what they really value.	I, U

Grades

Who am I?   **118** Students write about themselves and discuss those questions they   I, U
wish, such as: What are my emotions like? How can they be controlled? What do I look like? How can I tell? Can I change what I look like? Which is the most important: money, security, education? Why? What do I want to be? How can I get there? What makes me sad, glad, angry, hateful, worry?

NUTRITION

Grades

Bulletin board   **1** Prepare a display of new foods tried by children. Include the food   P
item, a picture or drawing of the food, and the name of the student who had eaten the food.

    2 From cereal boxes and milk and other cartons construct a food train   P
with an engine and four cars containing the basic 4 foods. Place food models made from construction paper, clay, papier-mâché, or cutouts from magazines in the cars.

    3 Prepare a bulletin board display depicting a rocket ship and in the   P, I
pilot's seat insert animated fruits or vegetables. Illustrated caption might read:

Mr. Carrot: "Fly high with me and grow big and strong."
Mr. Milk: "I fly high and fast because I give lots of pep and energy."

The captions and food items can be changed periodically.

    4 Prepare bulletin board displays, showcase exhibits, dioramas, and   P, I, U
others using real foods, food models, attractive pictures, children-made cutouts, and papier-mâché models showing:

A well-balanced breakfast, lunch, or dinner
Wholesome "snack" foods
Milk products, such as whole milk, skim milk, dried milk, cottage cheese, cream, butter, and indicate their importance
Foods containing vitamins, minerals, proteins, carbohydrates, and fats
Food sanitation including the preparation, serving, cleanup, washing of utensils, and storage of food
Meals or foods to be served in the school lunchroom
Recent newspaper and magazine articles
The amount of sugar contained in various kinds of candy and soft drinks
A model of the basic 4 boy and girl with the foods they need pinned to them
World food problems

    5 Construct a "Mr. Breakfast" (Fig. 12-14) out of construction or draw-   P, I, U
ing paper as follows:
Hat—bowl of cereal   *Hands*—fruits, eggs, bacon, and bread
Head—an orange   *Arms*—may substitute bananas
Body—bottle of milk   *Legs*—may substitute bacon strips

    6 Assign a group of students the responsibility of locating pictures and   I, U
newspaper and magazine articles related to nutrition. Students should provide statements or comments below each item.

FIG. 12-14

Mr. Breakfast

Grades

Chart

7 Prepare a cooperative chart, or charts, on the kinds of foods (carbohydrates, fats, proteins, minerals, and vitamins) with food pictures to
illustrate.

P, I

8 Cut pictures of foods from magazines and make a basic 4 classification
chart for the classroom.

P, I

9 Prepare a chart of the food nutrients as follows:

U

NUTRIENT	WHAT IT DOES	FOODS IN WHICH FOUND
Proteins		
Vitamins		
Carbohydrates		
Fats		
Minerals		

Grades

Demonstration

10 Make butter from cream and serve on bread to children in class. P
Permit each child a chance to shake the jar containing the cream.

11 Make giant paintings of favorite fruits or vegetables on paper bags. P
Cut holes for the head and arms and have children wear these bags
while they tell pupils in other classes what they like about these
fruits and vegetables.

12 With the help of parents or teachers, prepare and serve a nutritious P, I
breakfast.

13 With Parent-Teacher Association members, plan, prepare, and serve I, U
a meal that contains foods from a foreign country.

14 Children participate in the planning and preparation of nutritious I, U
foods for class or school parties. Avoid the usual cakes, candies, and
soft drinks, substituting such items as fruit, fruit juices, popcorn, and
nuts.

15 Pupil committee tries to improve the attractiveness of the cafeteria I, U
through the use of posters, table settings, and flowers.

16 Demonstrate ways to test foods for content. I, U

Starch—Soften, crush, and dissolve foods in water. Place in a test
tube with some water and add a drop of iodine (1% solution). If
solution turns blue, starch is present.

Fat—Place foods on pieces of paper. Remove foods and place papers
on radiator to heat. Fatty foods will leave grease spots.

Protein—Burn foods in direct flame of Bunsen burner. Protein foods
(raw, lean meat; cheese; dried beans) will emit odor of burning
feathers. May need to burn a feather first so that pupils recognize
odor.

Minerals—Burn various foods on a small asbestos or metal plate.
High mineral content foods (dried milk, beans, peas, and egg yolk)
will leave a gray ash containing one or more minerals such as
calcium. Nonmineral foods such as sugar will leave only a small
residue of black carbon.

Water—Expose fruits, leafy vegetables, and other foods containing
high water content to air and they become shriveled after a while.
They may be weighed before and after dehydration to determine
the amount of water lost.

Discussion

17 Establish the EE (eat everything) and FF (fussy feeder) clubs. Have I
children read the cafeteria lunch menu each day and compare this
with the balanced food chart found on the bulletin board. On their
return from lunch, pupils report themselves as EE or FF members.
Discuss why they acted as they did.

18 Discuss and help plan a school lunch menu. I, U

19 Discuss a well-balanced lunch in class and select menus to show I, U
foods containing the necessary vitamins and minerals needed for
growth. Pupils discuss items purchased in cafeteria and best ways to
spend money to obtain proper foods.

20 Obesity, weight reducing, and vitamin pills. U

21 The kinds and purposes of foods necessary for growth as well as the U
deficiency diseases.

	22 Participate as a member of a school health advisory committee to help solve school nutrition problems.	U
Dramatization	23 Dramatize visits to the dairy, grocery store, and food markets by constructing a store having shelves filled with empty food cans, boxes, and other such items. Also play house and dramatize foods eaten for breakfast, lunch, and dinner.	P
	24 Children prepare and participate in plays, radio, and television broadcasts presenting various aspects of nutrition.	P, I, U
Drawings	25 Have children draw pictures of foods, using a worksheet like the one below.	P

MILK	ORANGE JUICE	BUTTER
BREAD	CELERY	MEAT
EGGS	APPLE	CARROTS

Excursions	26 Visit the dairy, grocery store, and local food markets to observe the availability and storage of different foods.	P
	27 Visit the school lunch room to observe foods being prepared for the noon meal.	P, I
	28 Observe the sanitary methods used in the preparation, serving, and storage of foods in a restaurant or in the school cafeteria.	I, U
	29 Visit milk or food processing plants.	I, U
Exhibit	30 Prepare a display or exhibit of well-balanced breakfasts, lunches, and dinners using real foods or food models.	P, I, U
	31 Construct a man or woman from a variety of dairy product cartons.	I, U

Head—cottage cheese carton
Buttons—other cheese cartons
Body—ice cream carton
Legs—milk cartons
Arms—cubed butter wrappers or cartons

Grades

32 Have a "Food Fair" during which children display various kinds of foods, adequate lunches, dinners, and breakfasts, and appropriate snack-time foods. Pupils may construct murals, bulletin board displays, write-ups for the newspaper, and invitations to parents.   I, U

33 Set up a nutrition corner displaying pamphlets, books, magazines, and other materials for pupil reference and use during the nutrition unit.   I, U

Experiment

34 Place grass seed in a sponge, add some water, and watch the sprouts grow. This activity shows the need of food for growth.   P, I

35 Participate in the white rat experiment to learn the importance of food for life and growth.   P, I

36 Soak a corn seed in water overnight, remove the bran coat, and then discuss the significance of this outer coat to the white part underneath.   I, U

37 Use two sibling rats, conduct a feeding experiment in which one of the rats receives milk to drink and the other receives coffee in addition to food. The rat drinking the milk will grow and look much better than the coffee-fed rat.   I, U

38 Soak a small uncooked bone in vinegar for 3 days. The mineral matter will dissolve and the bone will lose its strength and firmness so that it can be easily bent. This experiment demonstrates the presence of minerals (especially calcium and phosphorus) in bones. It points out the importance of minerals in the diet.   I, U

Finger play

39 Prepare finger play, such as: P

TUNE: *Mulberry Bush*
This is the way we drink our milk,
Drink our milk, drink our milk,
This is the way we drink our milk,
Every night and morning.

This is the way it makes us grow,
Makes us grow, makes us grow.
This is the way it makes us grow,
Every single day.

Flannelboard

40 Read the following poem and have children (as many as possible) place the appropriate foods mentioned on the board.   P

Three little pigs and their dinners

There were three little pigs so happy and gay,
As each started to go his way one day.
Said the first little pig, in his house of straw.
"Now I can eat all the candy I want, hurrah."
So he filled his tummy with candy and cake,
'Till it began to ache and ache.
"Oh I wish I had listened to Mommy," he said,
As he rolled over and over in his bed.

The second little pig in his house of twigs,
Said, "Now I have no Mommy to make me eat figs."
So he had doughnuts, popsicles, and root beer.
Soon he yelled loud, "Oh dear! Oh dear!
My tooth is aching, my tummy's in pain.
I'll never do that, no never again."

The third little pig, remembering what his Mommy said.
Had meat, fresh vegetables, milk, and bread.
He ate oranges and apples, singing their praise,
As he felt peppy and strong all of his days.
"I'm always healthy, happy, and strong
I get my sleep and nothing goes wrong."

MARY STULTZ

		Grades
	41 Place the following food pictures on a flannelboard and have children prepare three different breakfasts: oranges, whole wheat bread, butter, cocoa, eggs, bacon, milk, and cereal.	P, I
	42 Have food models available and permit children to show the foods they ate for breakfast, lunch, dinner, and snack-time, and also the foods they should eat for breakfast, lunch, dinner, and snack-time.	P, I
	43 Use food models to illustrate the basic 4 foods as well as a balanced breakfast, lunch, and dinner.	I, U
	44 Pictures from magazines are brought to class and children cut out good food items. Pupils paste these foods on cardboard plates, shellac them, and use them to play "Going to the cafeteria" and "What to eat."	P
Individual and group reports	45 Pupils prepare lists of foods they like and dislike and make comparisons with the basic 4 food groups.	I, U
	46 Read and write words and sentences about nutrition.	P
	47 Children write a brief summary paragraph or two in answer to the question "What are the proper kinds of foods to eat, and why must we eat them?"	P, I

Grades

48 Serve as a class committee member to meet with the school lunch   I, U
manager to learn how nutritious lunches are prepared and report
findings in oral or written reports to the entire class.

49 Pupils write letters of request to various companies for available   I, U
nutrition materials for use in class.

50 Prepare magazine articles regarding school lunch menus, weight re-   U
duction, and other important phases of nutrition for publication in
the school newspaper.

51 Analyze weight-reducing procedures advertised in newspapers and   U
magazines.

52 Analyze several newspaper or magazine advertisements about foods   U
and food products.

53 Pupils prepare lists of food fallacies and do research to discover why   U
these are considered to be such.

54 Students prepare notebooks of food pictures cut out of newspapers   P
and magazines and grouped according to the basic 4 food groups.

55 Students identify one favorite food and determine the nutrients,   I, U
caloric value, and contributions to health.

Mobile   56 Make a food mobile illustrating individual foods found in the basic 4.   P, I

57 Teacher prepares a large block (at least 12 inches square) and places   P, I
pictures of the basic 4 food groups on each side. The block is hung as
a mobile during the time that nutrition is being discussed. Manila
cardboard can also be used to construct the block because it can be
folded and stored more easily.

Model   58 With colored construction paper, teacher and children make a 5-foot   P
"Mr. Breakfast." The following day the teacher mimeographs the
model on a smaller scale, the children color it, put their names at the
bottom, and take it home to their parents.

59 Prepare food models from clay, sawdust mixtures, cardboard, news-   P, I
paper clippings, and other materials to be used for exhibit purposes
or in the discussion on nutrition.

60 Prepare papier-mâché fruits and vegetables using real foods as forms.   P, I
These items can be used in dramatic play and in the discussion of
nutrition.

Panel   61 Participate in a panel discussion of the problem "Diet and its re-   U
lationship to weight control."

Poem　　　　　　　**62** Create original poems about nutrition, such as the following:　　　　P

> There was an old woman
> Who lived in a shoe.
> She had so many children
> But she knew what to do.
> She fed them milk, fruit,
> And vegetable greens.
> So they were the best children
> You have ever seen.

> Iggildy, piggildy, wiggildy, doo!
> I'm Ms. Carrot, How do you do!
> I'm lean and crisp,
> I come in a bunch.
> Eat me and see that I'm so good to munch.
> I'm good for teeth.
> I make them chew.
> I make them exercise.
> That's what I do.
> I'm good for eyes to see things, too!

> Oodle, doodle, humpty dumpty!
> I'm white and smooth and never lumpy.
> Drinking me keeps you in trim.
> Drink me well 'cause I'm filled to the brim.
> Strong bones and teeth is what I give.
> Drinking me makes you really live!
> My vitamins make skin smooth as silk.
> You should know me,
> I'm Mr. Milk.

Puppets　　　　　**63** Make puppets from construction paper and tongue blades (Figs.　　　P
12-15 to 12-17). The puppet heads should be about 12 inches high
with the following rhymes written on their backs:

> *Celery:*　　"I'm Madam Celery
> 　　　　　So much fun to eat
> 　　　　　Serve me at your snacktime
> 　　　　　Then you'll want no sweet."

> *Apple:*　　"I'm Mr. Apple.
> 　　　　　A juicy, swooshy bite
> 　　　　　Eat me every day
> 　　　　　To keep your teeth just right."

> *Orange:*　"I'm Madam Orange
> 　　　　　The sunshine color you see
> 　　　　　I protect you from illness
> 　　　　　Because I give you vitamin C."

> *Milk:*　　"I'm your nice, sweet milk
> 　　　　　I'll make your bones and teeth grow strong.
> 　　　　　Drink and drink and drink some more
> 　　　　　Then you'll be healthy your whole life long."

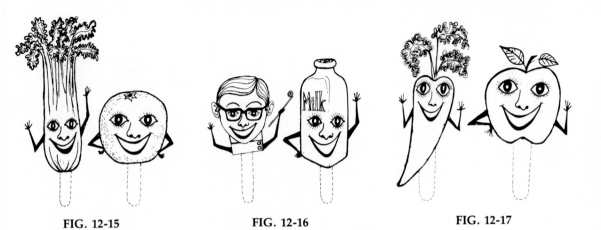

FIG. 12-15   FIG. 12-16   FIG. 12-17

Carrot: "I'm Ms. Carrot
So much fun to eat.
I go crunch, crunch, crunch, crunch
Between your strong, white teeth."

Dentist: "I am your friend the dentist
Come see me any day
I'll hunt out all cavities,
And fill them right away."

Grades

64 Have a puppet show centered around a boy visited by Mr. Candy and Ms. Pop, who persuaded him to eat these items as snacks instead of oranges and other fruits. Later the fruit (Mr. Orange) and vegetables (Ms. Carrot and Mr. Celery) come along and persuade the boy to try them as snack foods.   P, I

65 Use puppets or marionettes made in class to dramatize nutrition concepts, such as drinking milk daily, eating fruits and vegetables, importance of a good breakfast.   P, I

Riddle   **66** Have children write such riddles as the following: P, I

> You find me in the garden,
> I'm orange with long green hair,
> You might find me on your table
> So look for me there.
> Who am I?

Scrapbook   **67** Locate pictures and information in magazines, newspapers, and pamphlets for making different kinds of sandwiches and preparing lunch boxes more attractively and put them into a booklet to be taken home.   P, I, U

68 Prepare scrapbooks using pictures from magazines and other sources of such foods as fruits, vegetables, cheese, milk, butter, eggs, meat, fish, and poultry. Also organize these items into nutritious breakfasts, lunches, dinners, and snack foods.   P, I, U

		Grades
Shadow box	69 Make shadow boxes depicting the basic 4 foods as well as nutritious breakfasts, lunches, and dinners.	P
Speakers	70 Invite such resource people to class as nutritionists, school lunch managers, and others to discuss various aspects of nutrition.	U
Stories, songs, and rhymes	71 Write stories, songs, and rhymes as well as plays about nutrition.	P, I
Survey	72 Survey the number of children in class who eat breakfast, as well as the nature of the food consumed.	I, U
	73 Survey the number of children purchasing plate lunches at school and compare this figure with the number who bring their lunch to school.	I, U
	74 Conduct a 1- to 3-day survey of snack foods eaten by pupils.	I, U
	75 Participate in a 3-day diet survey.	I, U
	76 Survey the number of children who eat candy or soft drinks at lunch time, as well as the amounts consumed.	I, U
Tasting party	77 Have a bunny party in which children make head bands with paper ears and all eat raw green vegetables and carrots.	P
	78 Participate in the eating of nutritious snack foods by having milk, fruit, fruit juices, nuts, celery, and carrot sticks instead of cake, candy, and soft drinks.	P, I, U
	79 Plan, prepare, and serve nutritious food items for parties and social gatherings at school.	U
Vegetable garden	80 Grow such vegetables as lettuce, tomatoes, and carrots to provide understandings of some of the foods needed for growth and development.	P, I

REST AND SLEEP

		Grades
Bulletin board	1 Display pictures that children bring to class or draw showing sleep, work, play, and relaxation.	P, I
	2 Display humorous illustrations of the basic rules of sleep and rest.	P, I
Chart	3 Make a construction paper clock chart and put two sets of hands on it. Use red hands to indicate the time to go to bed and green hands to tell the time to get up.	P, I, U
	4 Construct a clock chart that shows children how to budget their time to get adequate amounts of rest, sleep, and exercise.	P, I, U
Demonstration	5 Demonstrate a variety of exercises that can help one to relax.	P, I, U
Discussion	6 Collect, show, and discuss pictures of animals at sleep and rest.	P
	7 Have children suggest ways to rest and relax and list these on the blackboard: warm bath, lying down, sit with head on desk, listening to music.	P
	8 Importance of sleep and rest and the amount needed.	P, I
	9 Rest, relaxation, and music.	P, I
	10 Children plan the work, play, and rest periods for the day.	P, I

Grades

11 Discuss the following questions in class: What happens when we sleep? When did you get up this morning? Did you sleep well? Did you feel rested? What time did you go to bed last night? — P, I

12 Discuss the best conditions for sleeping and include comments about air, bed, and the room itself. — P, I, U

13 Discuss the meaning of the terms *relaxation* and *tension.* Demonstrate by having the pupils flex muscles in their bodies and then relax them. — I, U

14 The causes of fatigue, the signs of fatigue, what to do when fatigued, and the effects of overfatigue. — I, U

15 Sleep and rest in terms of their value, how one feels and acts when sufficiently rested, and the need for balance between sleep, rest, and exercise. — I, U

16 Why we tire; how rest affects posture, work, and play; and how anxiety, fear, anger, and eating before bedtime may affect sleep. — I, U

Dramatization

17 Children play house and devote part of their play to stressing sleep and rest. — P

18 Children dramatize going to bed at night. One child stands in front of the class and makes suggestions while others pantomime the action during the singing of the tune "Mulberry Bush." — P

19 Prepare a play emphasizing desirable habits of sleep and rest to be presented in class, to a school assembly, or to the Parent-Teacher Association. — I

Drawings

20 Draw pictures about sleep, rest, and relaxation. — P, I

Experience chart

21 Prepare an experience chart or record of important points about sleep and rest. — P

Experiment

22 Tie a weighted string near the tip of the left third finger of a pupil volunteer. Have the pupil raise and lower his finger as long as possible. Allow the child to rest for a minute and then repeat the procedure. Try this experiment using different fingers on both hands. The results show that exercise is fatiguing and there is need for rest and relaxation. — P, I, U

Finger plays

23 Have children participate in finger plays. — P, I

> This little boy is going to bed,
> As down on his pillow he lays his head.
> Tuck him in with the covers tight
> And this is the way he sleeps all night.

> **Rest and listen**
> I like to rest and listen.
> Let me listen while I rest.
> My eyes are closed so I can't see.
> I'll listen while you count for me.
> Sh—whisper, count to ten . . .
> Now listen while I rest again.

> Time for us to take a rest.
> Lock the door up tight (lock lips).
> Pull the little window shades (close eyes)
> We'll play that it is night.

Let's play rag doll

Let's play rag doll.
Don't make a sound.
Fling your arms and bodies
Loosely around.
Fling your hands!
Fling your feet!
Let your head go free!
Be the raggediest rag doll
You ever did see.

		Grades
Individual and group reports	**24** Pupils prepare oral and written reports on rest, sleep, fatigue, and relaxation.	I, U
	25 Write a story on the three R's: rest, relaxation, and recreation.	I, U
Music	**26** Play restful and relaxing music in class.	P, I, U

Brahms' Lullaby
Clair de Lune, Debussy
Air from Suite No. 3 in D major, Bach
The Swan from Carnival of the Animals, Saint-Saens
The Lake from Adventures in a Perambulator, Carpenter
White Peacock, Griffes

Poems	**27** Children listen to, participate in the reading of, and act out poems on sleep, rest, and relaxation.	P, I, U

I am a limp rag doll,
I have no bones,
My feet are flat and still,
My hands are in my lap,
My head is limp,
Now my head rests on my knees
And my hands hang at my sides.

SARAH T. BARROWS

Close your eyes, head drops down
Face is smooth, not a frown
Roll to left, head is a ball
Roll to right, now sit tall
Lift your chin, look at me
Deep, deep breath, one, two, three
Big, big smile, hands in lap
Make believe you just had a nap
Now you're rested from your play
Time to work again today.

I went into a circus town
And met a funny Bunny Clown,
He winked his eye, he shook his head,
"This is splendid exercise," he said.
He shook his head, he shook his feet,
He wobbled, bobbled, down the street,
He moved his jaw both up and down
This funny little Bunny Clown.

He played that he was a lazy man
And then sat down like a Raggedy Ann.
His head fell down and his arms fell, too,
And he went to sleep for an hour or two.

The stretching game*

Link your thumbs;
Raise your arms
Straight up and past your ears,
Stretch and pull;
Pull and stretch;
Try to touch the sky.
Pull and stretch;
Stretch and pull;
Pull—pull—pull!
Drop your arms, now sigh.

FRANCES C. HUNTER

			Grades
Posters	28	Make posters or pictures illustrating activities conducive to play, sleep, and relaxation.	P
Puppets	29	Make two puppets and call them "Sleepy Head" and "Wide Awake." Have children dramatize aspects of rest and sleep.	P, I
	30	Make paper-bag puppets and dramatize a problem, such as a boy who wants to stay up past his bedtime to watch television.	P, I
Scrapbook	31	Prepare scrapbooks of pictures showing restful and relaxing activities.	P, I
Stories	32	Read and create stories about rest, sleep, and relaxation.	P, I

---

*Los Angeles City School Districts, Calif.: Speech in the elementary school, pub. No. 479, 1949, Office of the Superintendent of Schools, p. 90.

SAFETY

BICYCLE SAFETY

		Grades
Bulletin board	1 Display children's drawings on bicycle safety.	P, I, U
	2 Display bicycle safety posters and other printed materials available from the American Bicycle Institute and such organizations.	P, I, U
	3 A committee of pupils prepares a bulletin board display showing an outline of a bicycle labeled with its main parts and the safety rules. See Fig. 12-18.	I, U
Chart	4 Children prepare a chart listing the bicycles safety rules.	P, I, U
Checklist	5 Pupils prepare a checklist for use in the inspection of the mechanical safety of bicycles. The assistance of a bicycle repairperson may be necessary.	I, U
	6 Organize a bicycle club in school.	I, U
Demonstration	7 Children demonstrate the following procedures correctly: getting on a bicycle, getting off a bicycle, guiding a bicycle, applying the brake, and stopping and parking the bicycle.	P, I, U
	8 Pupils demonstrate and practice the proper hand signals when riding bicycles.	P, I, U
	9 Demonstrate the mechanical inspection of a safe bicycle in class. It is advisable to bring a bicycle into the room.	P, I, U
	10 Have a demonstration of minor bicycle repairs. It may be necessary to invite a bicycle repairperson to class.	I, U
	11 Conduct a bicycle field day in which pupils participate in a variety of activities that show their ability and skill to ride bicycles safely. Automobile clubs and other organizations in the community often will provide assistance with this program.	I, U
	12 Pupils prepare a demonstration of bicycle safety to be presented to a school assembly.	I, U

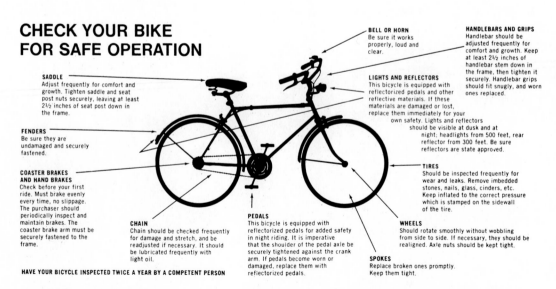

FIG. 12-18. Bicycle safety check. (*Courtesy the Bicycle Institute of America, Inc., New York.*)

Grades

Discussion	13 The motor vehicle laws and regulations in terms of licensing of bicycles, need to comply with rules, proper hand signals, parking, motor vehicle rules, and others.	P, I, U
	14 Safety factors involved in riding a bicycle to school.	P, I, U
	15 Pupils bring newspaper and magazine articles about bicycle safety or accidents to class.	I, U
	16 Pupils discuss the causes of bicycle accidents and how to prevent them. This could lead to a series of unanswered questions and start the problem-solving approach to bicycle safety.	I, U
Dramatization	17 Children dramatize riding a bicycle and demonstrate the necessary safe practices.	P, I, U
Excursion	18 Visit a bicycle repair shop to observe how bicycles are repaired.	I, U
Experience chart	19 Prepare an experience chart or record of bicycle safety rules.	P
Guest speaker	20 Invite a police officer to class to discuss bicycle safety traffic rules.	P, I, U
Individual and group reports	21 Prepare oral and written reports on the safest way to ride bicycles to and from school.	I, U
	22 Prepare oral and written reports on bicycle safety.	I, U
	23 Prepare school newspaper articles titled "Bicycle safety tips."	I, U
	24 Write a group letter to the police department or some other organization requesting a speaker to discuss bicycle safety.	I, U
	25 Children prepare a code of safety for bicycle riders. This can be posted on the bulletin board or may be printed in the school newspaper.	I, U
	26 Children write to the Bicycle Institute of America or other organizations for bicycle safety materials.	I, U
	27 Pupils prepare reports on the yearly accidents occurring on bicycles in the nation, state, county, and city.	U
Interview	28 Interview a police officer or some other authority on bicycle safety.	I, U
Scrapbook	29 Prepare a scrapbook containing newspaper and magazine articles, pictures, stories, and other obtainable materials on bicycle safety.	P, I, U
Self-test	30 Prepare a self-test or pretest on bicycle traffic safety.	I, U

Sample questions	YES	NO
1. A bicycle can be ridden on the sidewalk in a business area.	☐	☐
2. A bicycle rider should obey all traffic signs, lights, and devices.	☐	☐
3. Pedestrians do not have the right-of-way in crosswalks.	☐	☐
4. You should walk your bicycle across heavily traveled streets.	☐	☐
5. Night riding without a light and reflector is unsafe.	☐	☐
6. It is safe and proper to carry a passenger on a bicycle.	☐	☐
7. Hitching to a moving truck is safe if you are careful.	☐	☐
8. It is best to ride three abreast when riding in a group.	☐	☐
9. You should give hand signals when turning at all times.	☐	☐
10. On a country road you should ride on the left of the highway.	☐	☐

Survey	31 Pupils conduct a survey of bicycle traffic violations noted on the way to and from school.	I, U

Grades

BUS SAFETY

Bulletin board	1 Display pictures, drawings, slogans, cartoons, and posters about bus safety.	P, I, U
	2 Make a bus out of construction paper and display this along with appropriate captions about bus safety.	P, I, U
Demonstration	3 With a small toy truck and blocks demonstrate why it is necessary to be seated at all times in the school bus. Show how blocks will fall when a sudden stop is necessary.	P, I
	4 Have children practice bus loading and unloading and discuss safe behavior while riding.	P, I, U
Discussion	5 The need to cooperate with the bus driver when riding the school bus.	P, I, U
	6 Discuss bus safety with children preparing a list of safe behavior rules.	P, I, U
Dramatic play	7 Make a bus out of large cardboard boxes and use dramatic play to practice safe bus rules.	P
Dramatization	8 Arrange chairs in classroom to represent a school bus and have children act out the right way and the wrong way to get on and off the bus.	P, I
	9 Dramatize getting on and off a bus safely and also safety on the bus.	P, I
Excursion	10 Visit a bus and have the driver discuss safe behavior while boarding and riding.	P, I
Experience chart	11 Prepare an experience chart or record of safe procedures on the bus.	P
Guest speaker	12 Invite the bus driver to discuss bus safety.	P, I
Mural	13 Prepare a mural depicting safety on the bus.	P, I
Scrapbook	14 Construct a scrapbook of pupil drawings about bus safety.	P, I
Songs and poems	15 Compose songs and poems about bus safety.	P, I

DISASTER SAFETY

Bulletin board	1 Display pictures, drawings, or diagrams of procedures to follow in the event of an atomic attack.	P, I, U
	2 Prepare an illustrated display of foods suitable for storing for emergency use.	P, I, U
Chart	3 Prepare a wall chart for each classroom, showing the floor plans, exits and entrances to the building, and the shortest route to the nearest shelter.	P, I, U
Demonstration	4 The signals in schools that signify alerts or attack and practice identification.	P, I, U
	5 Demonstrate and practice ways to protect the eyes, ears, nose, and mouth when under simulated attack.	P, I, U

Grades

	6 Demonstrate and practice thorough washing of hands, nails, face, and hair to decontaminate these areas.	P, I, U
	7 Demonstrate and practice emergency drills for evacuation or under-cover.	P, I, U
	8 Have pupil committees prepare to demonstrate decontamination and other emergency procedures to children in school or to the community.	I, U
	9 Food pollution through the use of simple fungi and bacteriologic experiments.	I, U
	10 How and where to store foods safely at home during an attack.	I, U
	11 How to preserve perishable foods without refrigeration.	I, U
	12 How to properly dispose of polluted food.	I, U
	13 Demonstrate and display an appropriate first-aid kit for civil disasters.	I, U
	14 How to preserve and package foods for emergencies.	I, U
	15 First-aid procedures after civil disasters.	I, U
Discussion	16 What children may do (activities) while waiting in a shelter at school until the all-clear signal is sounded.	P, I, U
	17 The procedures to follow if caught outdoors during an attack or if an alert is on.	P, I, U
	18 The location of emergency shelters in the school and community.	P, I, U
	19 The meaning of civil defense and why it is necessary.	P, I, U
	20 The nature of radiation and its effect on human beings.	I, U
	21 The hazards from atomic, biologic, and chemical warfares.	I, U
	22 The procedures to follow if one has survived an atomic attack.	I, U
	23 The problems of emotions, panics, and other behaviors that will occur during an atomic catastrophe.	I, U
	24 First-aid procedures necessary in civil disasters.	I, U
	25 The contamination of food and water and ways to protect these items.	I, U
Dramatization	26 Dramatize proper conduct during disasters.	P, I, U
Exhibit	27 Display pamphlets and other printed materials for pupil reference and use.	I, U
Guest speakers	28 Invite civil defense and Red Cross speakers to discuss aspects of atomic, biologic, chemical, or other civil disasters.	I, U
Individual and group reports	29 Have individual or group oral or written reports on the civil defense recommendations for the protection of people in the event of atomic, biologic, or chemical warfare.	I, U
	30 Pupils write articles for the local newspaper or school paper on how individuals can protect themselves at home, at school, or when outdoors during an atomic attack.	U
Interview	31 Interview civil defense authorities and others about the feasibility of building home shelters or community shelters.	I, U
	32 Pupils interview local health officers and medical personnel about the availability of services and hospital facilities in the event of civil disasters.	U

Grades

	33 Pupils interview the health officer or a representative from the civil defense office on that person's role in civil defense.	U
Survey	34 Survey the school and community to locate the designated shelter areas.	I, U

FARM SAFETY

Bulletin board	1 Children obtain pictures or make drawings of tools and machinery found on the farm such as tractors, cotton pickers, cotton trailers, harvesters, plows, and discs and place caption "Dangerous equipment" below. Pictures may be obtained from pamphlets available from farm machinery companies or from farm organizations.	P, I, U
Discussion	2 Safe practices when riding on trucks and other farm machinery.	P, I, U
	3 The hazards of insect stings, poisonous sprays, canals, irrigation ditches, tools, and other unsafe places and equipment on the farm.	P, I, U
	4 The hazards of sharp implements such as pitchforks, hoes, saws, and axes used on the farm.	P, I, U
	5 Safety around horses, bulls, and other farm animals.	P, I, U
Experience chart or record	6 Children help to prepare an experience chart or record on farm safety rules.	P
Exhibit	7 Display a variety of sharp implements used in farm work and discuss the dangers of their improper use.	P, I, U
Individual and group reports	8 Children prepare oral and written reports on farm safety.	I, U

FIRE SAFETY

Bulletin board	1 Prepare an illustrated bulletin board display about fire prevention using construction paper, real clothing materials, or crayons.	P, I, U
	2 Display pictures or news items about fires in the community.	P, I, U
	3 Use pictures and drawings to display the varieties of types of fire extinguishers.	I, U
	4 Display pictures of drop and roll and crawling in smoke-filled room procedures.	P, I, U
	5 Pictorially illustrate the action to be taken when fires occur or smoke appears at home and include escape plan and other procedures.	P, I
Chart	6 Prepare a list of illustrated fire safety rules.	P, I
	7 Make an illustrated chart listing the common causes of fires in the home.	P, I, U
	8 Make an illustrated chart of the fire exits in school.	P, I, U
Demonstration	9 Light two candles and fan one of them to show how moving air causes a flame to burn more vigorously.	P, I
	10 Sound the fire alarm bell and have children practice responding to it for fire drill.	P, I, U
	11 The way to report a fire using an alarm box and the telephone.	P, I, U
	12 Ways of putting out fires using a variety of fire extinguishers.	P, I, U

Grades

13 How to put out a fire when someone's clothing is ablaze. — P, I, U

14 How to use matches safely—use only safety matches and strike match with the cover closed; dispose of burned matches by breaking them and placing in a glass or tin container. — P, I, U

15 Drop and roll and crawling low in smoke-filled room procedures. — P, I, U

16 Demonstrate the making of a fire extinguisher by putting some vinegar in a bottle and adding some baking soda. (Wrap the soda in a tissue before adding it to the vinegar. This will delay the formation of the carbon dioxide gas.) Put a rubber stopper and a pipet in the bottle, turn it upside down and pour the fluid into a pail or sink. — P, I, U

17 The combustibility of a variety of materials such as asbestos, glass, paper, water, cotton, cloth, wood, kerosene, and various types of clothing. Also discuss spontaneous combustion. — P, I, U

18 Place a piece of cardboard against a small light bulb and show the brown spot that occurs. Explain in terms of the fire triangle. — P, I

19 Teacher lights a candle in class, and pupils watch it burn. A glass is placed over the candle, and children attempt to explain action in terms of the triangle of fire why the flame was extinguished. — P, I, U

Discussion

20 Fire safety rules and reasons for fire drills. — P, I

21 Beneficial and hazardous effects of fire. — P, I

22 Fire hazards on special occasions, such as Christmas and the Fourth of July. — P, I, U

23 Discuss and practice fire drills in school. — P, I, U

24 Discuss these questions: What causes fires? How do fires start? What materials burn? Where should matches be kept? What should you do in case of fire? How should you put out a picnic fire? How can fires be prevented? — P, I, U

25 The value of the home inspections conducted by firemen. Introduce common electrical terms, such as wire, plug, socket, bulb, fuse,and and fuse box. — I, U

26 Ways to prevent fires by good housekeeping procedures, proper disposal of rubbish and ashes, safe storage of fuel, correct installation and care of stoves, electric equipment, and furnaces. — I, U

27 The types of fires and how they may be extinguished. — I, U

28 Pupils participate as members of the fire-safety patrol to inform other pupils about fire prevention. — I, U

29 Baby-sitting. — I, U

30 Smoke detectors. — P, I, U

31 Fire escape plans from homes and other buildings. — P, I, U

32 First-aid procedures for burns. — P, I, U

33 Hazards and use of electricity and flammable materials. — I, U

34 Identity and proper storage of flammable liquids. — P, I, U

35 Fires reported in newspapers and magazines in terms of causes and prevention. — I, U

36 To whom and how to report fires and smoke discovered. — P, I

37 Combustibility and flammability of various types of clothing and other substances. — I, U

38 Importance of drop and roll and crawling low procedures. — P, I, U

39 False alarms. — I, U

40 Ways to call fire department. — P, I, U

		Grades
Dramatization	41 Build a fire engine using large blocks, cardboard boxes, and other items. Children participate in dramatic play by having a corner in the classroom as a firehouse. Pupils bring their toy telephones to practice reporting fires.	P
	42 Dramatize the procedures to follow when reporting a fire by telephone.	P, I, U
	43 Dramatize fire safety through sociodramas, puppet shows, and plays.	P, I, U
Drawings	44 Children make drawings of ways to prevent fires, escape from fires, and signal when fire is discovered.	P, I
	45 Draw pictures of wires, plugs, sockets, electric appliances, and other items with descriptions placed below telling of the safe ways to use these items.	I, U
Excursion	46 Visit the firehouse.	P, I, U
	47 Children walk around the school to locate fire hazards or become familiar with the locations of extinguishers, exits, and alarm boxes.	P, I, U
	48 Visit a fireboat.	
Exhibit	49 Invite the fire department to display fire-fighting equipment and its uses.	P, I, U
	50 Display a variety of combustible materials, such as paper, wood, cloth, gasoline, and kerosene.	P, I, U
	51 Display books, magazines, pamphlets, and stories about fire safety for pupil use.	P, I, U
	52 Show pictures and materials of fire hazards, such as overload of electrical circuits, trash accumulation, frayed electric wires, and gasoline storage containers.	P, I, U
Experience chart or record	53 Prepare an experience chart or record about fire safety.	P
Experiment	54 Place a lighted candle on a table and let the class watch it burn. Cover the candle with a clear glass so that no air can enter. Have pupils note what happens to the candle—it goes out when the oxygen supply has been used. Relate this to extinguishing fires.	P, I, U
Flip chart	55 Prepare a series of illustrated flip charts for a discussion about fire safety. Include answers to these questions: how is fire helpful? What are the causes of fire? How many fires occur in our community? How can we prevent fires?	P, I
Games	56 Make crossword puzzles, riddles, and other games about fire prevention and fire safety.	P, I, U
Guest speaker	57 Invite a fire fighter to discuss fire safety.	P, I, U
	58 Invite the fire chief from your local fire department to discuss the junior fire marshall program and to encourage children to participate.	I
	59 Request the local fire department to conduct a demonstration of the types of fire extinguishers and smoke detectors.	U
	60 Invite a member of the National Board of Fire Underwriters Laboratory to discuss the work of this organization in fire safety.	U

Grades

Individual and group reports	61 Write stories about their experiences in fire safety.	P, I
	62 Write to insurance companies and others concerned with fire safety and request materials for display and class reading.	I, U
	63 Prepare oral or written reports on the causes, effects, and prevention of fires.	I, U
	64 Write articles for the school newspaper about fire safety.	I, U
	65 Students prepare reports on baby-sitting and fire safety.	I, U
Inspection	66 Prepare checklist to search for fire hazards in home or school.	I, U
Map	67 Prepare a map of your community identifying the locations of fire-houses, hydrants, alarm boxes, and other fire safety features.	I, U
	68 Students prepare home escape-from-fire plans in consultation with parents.	P, I
Models	69 Construct a fire alarm box, a firehouse, and fire prevention equipment for use in dramatic play.	P
	70 Make fire fighter hats out of construction paper.	P, I
	71 Draw or build a home that is free of fire hazards.	I, U
Mural	72 Prepare a mural of ways to prevent fires.	P, I
Poems and songs	73 Create and learn poems, songs, jingles, and stories about fire safety.	P, I
Posters	74 Conduct a contest for the best school poster on fire safety.	I, U
Scrapbook	75 Pupils prepare scrapbooks containing pictures, photos, stories, poems, newspaper articles, and written reports about fires and fire prevention.	P, I, U
Self-test	76 Give the following self-test:	I, U

Fire safety

Circle the correct answers to the right. If you do not know the answer, circle the letter "D."

1. A grease fire may be put out by pouring water on it.	T F D	
2. One should run to extinguish flames when clothes are on fire.	T F D	
3. A frayed wire on an electric appliance is a dangerous fire hazard.	T F D	
4. Fire drills are not necessary at schools.	T F D	
5. It is safe to run a lamp cord under a rug.	T F D	
6. The leading causes of fire are matches and smoking.	T F D	
7. A penny is good substitute for a blown-out fuse.	T F D	
8. "EXIT" on a door means the door leads to the outside.	T F D	
9. A wood fire may be put out by pouring water on it.	T F D	
10. Gasoline can be stored safely in glass bottles.	T F D	
11. Oily rags can catch fire without a match.	T F D	
12. One should always close the cover of a safety match book before striking a match.	T F D	

Show and tell	77 Children tell of their experiences with fire, fire engines, and fire fighters.	P
	78 Children identify names, addresses, and home telephone numbers.	P

		Grades
Survey	79 Pupils make survey forms to check their homes for fire hazards.	P, I, U
Television box	80 Students make a movie with a title such as "The day Mary's house burned." Pupils draw pictures of the discovery of the fire and what they did.	P
Word lists	81 Prepare a list of new words learned about fire prevention.	P, I, U

FIRST AID

Bulletin board	1 Show pictures and drawings that display first-aid procedures to be followed at school.	P, I, U
	2 Display pictures or drawings of poisonous snakes, insects, and plants.	P, I, U
Demonstration	3 Have nurse or other person demonstrate how to cleanse a wound with soap and water, apply a sterile dressing and bandage, and stop a nosebleed and other bleeding.	P, I, U
	4 Demonstrate the correct procedure for removing foreign objects from the eye.	I, U
	5 Provide for a demonstration of the mouth-to-mouth procedure of artificial respiration.	I, U
Discussion	6 What to do when injured at school, home, or when away from home.	P, I, U
	7 First-aid procedures for sunburn, chapped skin, poison oak or ivy, insect bites and stings.	P, I, U
	8 Discuss reasons for cleansing wounds and applying sterile dressings and bandages.	P, I, U
	9 First-aid procedures for minor cuts, burns, and bruises.	P, I, U
	10 Dog bites and the necessary first-aid procedures as well as other action that must be taken.	P, I, U
	11 First-aid procedures for bone fractures.	I, U
	12 The general first-aid procedures when accidents occur.	I, U
Dramatization	13 Children play doctor or nurse attending a child who has been injured.	P
	14 Dramatize the reporting of an accident at school, at home, and elsewhere.	P, I
	15 The procedure to follow in an emergency or when someone is injured.	P, I, U
	16 Dramatize a series of injuries and then permit the class to try to determine the first-aid procedures to be followed: A boy is using a penknife at school and whittling on some wood; a girl is running her hand along a wooden bench that is full of splinters; a boy is tackled playing touch football and falls, striking his wrist on the ground.	I, U
Drawings	17 Pupils prepare drawings of first aid being administered to injured children.	P, I
Exhibit	18 Display a variety of poisonous substances or containers that hold such materials.	P, I
	19 Display the contents of a simple first-aid kit. Nurse may be helpful in determining items to be included.	I, U

Grades

		Grades
	20 Display an assortment of materials such as dressings, bandages, triangular bandages, and splints used in first aid.	I, U
Experience chart or record	21 Construct an experience chart or record that describes what to do when injured at school.	P
Guest speaker	22 Invite the school nurse to come to class to discuss first-aid procedures.	P, I, U
Individual and group reports	23 Children prepare reports on first-aid procedures for snake bites, epileptic seizures, frostbite, fractures.	I, U
	24 Children prepare a letter inviting a member of the Red Cross to come to class to discuss first aid.	I, U
Problem solving	25 Present a series of first-aid problems to individuals or committees and let them try to solve them. Such problems might include:	U

What would you do if your mother cut her finger while preparing dinner?
What would you do if your sister swallowed a poison, such as ammonia?
What would you do if a pupil at school fell from the horizontal bar that is 7 feet high?

		Grades
Scrapbook	26 Make scrapbooks containing stories, pictures, magazine articles, and drawings about first aid.	I, U
Self-test	27 Prepare a self-test for use in the discussion on first aid.	I, U
Show and tell	28 Children tell of what they experienced when they were injured.	P

HOME SAFETY

		Grades
Bulletin board	1 Display pictures and magazine and newspaper articles on home accidents and safety.	P, I, U
	2 Pupils construct for display a graph or pie-shaped chart showing the numbers and types of home accidents.	U
Discussion	3 Children's prepared lists of hazardous conditions in and around the home.	P, I
	4 Student-planned "pick-up" day at home to remove hazards.	P, I
	5 Children's observations of safe and unsafe practices in the home and elsewhere.	P, I
	6 The causes and possible ways to prevent the accidents reported in newspaper articles brought to class by students.	I, U
	7 The safe handling of blasting caps and the procedures to follow when they are found.	I, U
	8 How to turn off the electricity and the gas at home.	U
	9 Prepare a list of responsibilities of baby-sitters and discuss the safety problems that sitters may have to handle.	U
Dramatization	10 Children play house the safe way by storing knives and matches properly, by using scissors carefully, by keeping stairs and closets clear of objects, and by putting away pins, needles, and other sharp objects when not in use.	P

Grades

11 Children act out such situations as a stranger offering a ride, a cross dog barring the sidewalk, and one child double-daring another to do something reckless. Ask pupils to consider these questions: "What would you do?" and "Would you be acting safely?" — P, I

12 Dramatize an accident in the home, such as slipping on a scatter rug that has no rubber backing, and discuss how this could have been prevented. — I, U

13 Prepare a play on home safety for presentation to the Parent-Teacher Association or to a school assembly. — I, U

Drawings

14 Following a discussion on safe play areas at home, children draw pictures of where they play at home. — P

15 Following a unit on home safety, each child draws pictures of what he or she does at home to make it a safer place. — P

Exhibit

16 Children bring some of the dangerous objects found in their back yards for display. — P, I

17 Children construct a medicine cabinet using cardboard boxes and construction paper and have all items properly labeled. — P, I

18 Prepare an exhibit of hazardous objects or materials found in the home such as metal toys with sharp edges, sharp knives improperly stored, rugs without rubber backing, and oily rags improperly stored. — P, I, U

19 Display pamphlets, booklets, and other resource materials on home safety for pupils' use. — I, U

20 Display poisonous substances found in the home, such as ammonia, disinfectants, drugs, chocolate laxatives, moth balls, and crayons. — I, U

Experience chart or record

21 Prepare an experience chart on home safety containing such activities as walking carefully on polished floors, picking up toys when finished with them, and not playing with matches. — P

Flannelboard

22 Prepare home safety stories and use a flannelboard to illustrate them. — P

Game

23 Make a human train that must stop at railroad crossings before picking up full speed again. Signals to start and stop are given by the teacher. — P

Guest speaker

24 Invite a representative from the National Safety Council or the local safety council to come to class to discuss home safety. — I, U

Individual and group reports

25 Pupils use drawings or pictures to illustrate daily activities that will keep themselves safe. — I, U

26 Collect newspaper articles about accidents in the home and categorize them by types. Committees then do research and write reports about how they could have been prevented. — I, U

Model

27 Make a container for father's used razor blades. — P

28 Pupils construct a cross section of a house out of cardboard or wood and illustrate the possible hazardous places within. — I, U

Mural

29 Make a large cooperative mural of safe play areas in the neighborhood. — P, I

Grades

Newspaper	30 Pupils prepare a home safety newspaper to be published periodically containing stories about safety in the home.	I, U
Panel	31 Have a panel discussion on the topic, "Making a safe home."	I, U
Posters	32 Make posters showing how to correct hazardous conditions found in the home, such as not touching radio or electric light cords when bathing, proper position of cooking utensils on stove with handles turned in, and using a step-ladder rather than a chair to stand on.	I, U
Scrapbook	33 Children prepare a scrapbook with pictures, stories, and newspaper articles on "Safety at home."	P, I, U
Show and tell	34 Children tell about home accidents.	P
Songs and poems	35 Create home safety songs and poems.	P
Survey	36 Survey the neighborhood and prepare a report on the safe and unsafe places to play.	I, U
	37 Conduct a survey of home hazards using a checklist prepared by children. Discuss how these problems can be changed. Emphasize specific areas such as unlighted, cluttered stairs; unscreened fireplaces; electric outlets and wiring; proper place to store garden tools, matches, nails, pins, sewing needles.	I, U
	38 Prepare a home safety checklist for inspection of home workshops.	U
Telephone card	39 Make a card to be hung by the telephone with the number of the fire and police departments, an ambulance, the family doctor, the nearest relative, and also the home address.	P, I
Telephone number	40 Children dial home telephone number and give the last name of parent, address, identity of road and street landmarks.	P, I

PEDESTRIAN SAFETY

Bulletin board	1 Prepare a display of student drawings about pedestrian safety.	P, I, U
	2 Develop pedestrian safety slogans for use on the bulletin board such as "Courtesy is safety," "Cross at the crosswalks," and "Wait for the traffic signal before crossing streets."	P, I
	3 Make a series of charts or graphs for display showing the number and kinds of pedestrian accidents.	U
Chart	4 Prepare a chart that lists the pedestrian safety rules.	P, I
Demonstration	5 Demonstrate and practice the proper way to cross streets.	P, I
	6 Prepare a table simulating a street corner using small cars, bicycles, policeman, and traffic lights and demonstrate safe pedestrian practices.	P, I
	7 Darken room and have students dressed in various colored clothes walk in front of the room. Be sure to have someone wearing white among these students. Children discuss which colors were more easily seen.	P, I, U

Grades

8 In a darkened room have two lighted flashlights representing auto headlights. Have a student with dark clothes and one with white clothes walk in front of the lights to show the difference in the reflection of light. — P, I, U

Discussion

9 The importance of knowing names, addresses, and telephone numbers. — P

10 What action to take if a stranger invites you to take a ride in an automobile. — P, I

11 The school safety patrol and its role in helping children to cross streets safely. — P, I

Dramatization

12 Children bring small toy cars, trucks, and buses for use in dramatic play about pedestrian safety. — P

13 Using a large space in the classroom or on the playground, lay out an intersection with strips of tape or chalk, including crosswalks, and have children cross the street properly. Prepare a number of crossing signal models, such as a traffic light with appropriate color, a walk-wait signal, and a stop sign. — P

Drawings

14 Children make drawings about pedestrian safety. — P, I

15 Children draw pictures of how they come to school, pointing out safe practices. — P

Excursion

16 Visit the street corner nearest the school to see the traffic signals, the police officer, the yellow crossing lines, and other safety features. — P

Exhibit

17 Display variety of traffic signs and discuss their meanings for traffic and pedestrian safety. — I, U

Experience chart and record

18 Prepare an experience chart or record of safety pedestrian rules that may include: — P

> Red means stop.
> Yellow means wait.
> Green means go.
> Cross at the crosswalks.

Flannelboard

19 Prepare illustrations to tell a story of pedestrian safety with emphasis on the danger of playing between parked cars. — P, I

Game

20 Write safety rules on strips of tagboard and cut them in half to form a simple puzzle. Children try to match the cut pieces and locate the correct safety rules. — P, I

Guest speaker

21 Invite a police officer to discuss pedestrian and traffic safety. — P, I, U

22 Invite a member of the school safety patrol to discuss correct ways to cross streets. — P, I

Individual and group report

23 Record the number and type of pedestrian accidents listed in local newspapers for a designated period. — I, U

24 Write letters to the National Safety Council, automobile clubs, and other community organizations requesting material on pedestrian safety for use in class. — I, U

Grades

Interview

25 Pupils prepare oral or written reports on the number, kinds, and cause of pedestrian accidents. U

26 Pupils interview a traffic police officer and a representative of the automobile club about pedestrian accidents and how to prevent them. I, U

Map

27 Prepare a large map showing the route each child takes to school and discuss the safest ways to come to school. P, I

Model

28 Make a traffic signal box with red, green, and yellow lights or signals for use in dramatic play. P

Poems

29 Children create and learn poems about pedestrian safety such as the following: P

> Red says stop,
> Green says go.
> Yellow says wait,
> You'd better go slow.
> When I reach a crossing place,
> To left and right I turn my face.
> I walk, not run, across the street
> And use my head to guide my feet.

> Stop, look, and listen
> Before you cross the street.
> Use your eyes, use your ears
> Before you use your feet.

Posters

30 Prepare posters and enter them in the school contest on pedestrian safety. I, U

Problem solving

31 Have children discuss this problem: "You come to a street corner that you must cross, but there is no signal. How will you get across?" P, I

Puppets

32 Make puppets and dramatize ways to be a safe pedestrian. P

Quiz

33 Have children write the five numbers listed below on a piece of paper and place yes or no answers beside the appropriate number. P

1. We should cross streets at crosswalks.
2. We should cross streets when the traffic light is green.
3. We should look one way when crossing streets.
4. We should always go with the traffic when walking on highways.
5. We know the yellow light at a crosswalk means wait.

Riddle

34 Children make up riddles, such as the following: P

> It stands near the corner.
> It turns red and green.
> It helps keep us safe.
> What is it?

Scrapbook

35 Make illustrated scrapbooks with pedestrian safety rules, slogans, rhymes, and limericks. P, I, U

36 Prepare a scrapbook of pictures and drawings showing safety as a pedestrian. P, I

Self-test   37 Pupils take following self-test.   I, U

		Do you	YES	NO
	1.	Cross streets only at intersections or marked crosswalks?	☐	☐
	2.	Look left and right before crossing, making sure that the entire crossing can be made safely?	☐	☐
	3.	Cross only on green light or "go" signals?	☐	☐
	4.	Obey directions of safety patrols or officers?	☐	☐
	5.	Walk on the left side facing traffic if walking on roadway and give way to approaching vehicles?	☐	☐
	6.	Wear white at night or carry a light?	☐	☐
	7.	Always get into and out of a vehicle on the side nearest the curb?	☐	☐
	8.	Give the motorist the right of way where there are no signals?	☐	☐
	9.	Stay out of streets when playing?	☐	☐
	10.	Watch for oncoming traffic when catching or leaving a bus?	☐	☐

Score ("yes" answers)

9-10—You may live to a ripe old age.

6-8—You may expect to get hurt before long.

5 or less—Stay in your own yard; you're living on borrowed time.

Show and tell   38 Children tell about pedestrian hazards they have seen.   P

Television box   39 Make a shadow box or television box and have students prepare a   P
series of drawings about pedestrian safety. Include such illustrations
as wearing white at night, crossing at street corners, and waiting for
the green light.

RECREATION SAFETY

Bulletin board   1 Prepare displays of pictures and drawings of water skiing, hunting,   P, I, U
camping, picnicking, fishing, skating, hiking, and vacation safety.

2 Display posters or drawings showing the correct and incorrect ways   P, I, U
to get in and out of rowboats, canoes, and motorboats.

Chart   3 Pupils prepare and complete charts of summertime safety for refer-   I, U
ence and use at home during vacation.

Summertime safety

My summer activities

1. _____

   _____

2. _____

   _____

3. _____

   _____

4. _____

   _____

Grades

What could hurt me

1. _____
   _____

2. _____
   _____

3. _____
   _____

4. _____
   _____

How to keep safe

1. _____
   _____

2. _____
   _____

3. _____
   _____

4. _____
   _____

Demonstration	4 Have the Red Cross conduct a demonstration of swimming, boating, and beach safety at one of the local swimming pools, lakes, or rivers.	P, I, U
Discussion	5 Safety on special occasions, such as Halloween and the Fourth of July.	P, I, U
	6 The people who can help when you are injured or lost.	P, I, U
	7 Safety on picnics and outings.	P, I, U
	8 Show pupils pictures of recreational equipment, such as a canoe, gun, skate, sled, ski, baseball bat, and fishhook, and have them tell of a good safety practice when using these items.	P, I, U
	9 Safe and unsafe features of swimming in lakes, rivers, oceans, canals, and other places. Learn how to choose a safe swimming area.	I, U
	10 The laws with which pupils should be familiar when hunting, fishing, and camping.	I, U
	11 Methods of protection while participating in various sports, such as football, baseball, basketball, and skiing.	I, U
	12 Safety in skin and scuba diving.	I, U
	13 Safe hunting procedures.	U
Dramatization	14 Children participate in dramatic play of safe practices while camping or picnicking.	P
	15 Prepare and present a skit on snow safety to an assembly, the Parent-Teacher Association, or broadcast it over the local radio station.	I, U
	16 Pupils write a play ("Comedy of Errors") on how not to go on a camping trip.	I, U

Grades

Drawings	17 Make drawings of safe practices while boating, swimming, skiing, playing in the snow or at the beach.	P, I, U
Exhibit	18 Display the items of a "Lost" kit that may be usable when camping or out in the woods that contains such things as a single-edge razor blade, fishhooks, fish line and wet flies, pencil and notebook, Band-aids, soap and disinfectant, nail magnet and thread (for compass), sugar lumps, strong string (shoe laces), and matches water-proofed with paraffin. Seal the contents in a pipe tobacco can and attach with a belt strap.	P, I, U
	19 Display such hazardous objects as fishhooks, darts, sharp-pointed sticks, and blasting caps.	P, I, U
	20 Display the appropriate clothing to wear in various outdoor activities, such as hiking, camping, hunting, skiing, and boating.	P, I, U
	21 Display the equipment needed for skin and scuba diving and discuss safety features.	I, U
	22 Display safety items that give protection in various sports: football—mouth protectors; baseball—mask; skiing—safety binders.	I, U
Experience chart or record	23 Make an experience chart or record about safe procedures on vacations, when swimming, and at other times.	P
Game	24 Play the game "Little child lost." The teacher is a police officer and a student is lost. Have children determine what they would do, or should do, if this happens to them.	P
	25 Children collect pictures from magazines and newspapers of safe and unsafe ways of playing. Place all of these in a box and permit each child to select one item and tell whether it is a safe or unsafe procedure.	P, I, U
Guest speaker	26 Invite a member of the Red Cross or the school nurse to discuss first-aid procedures for possible recreation emergencies, such as sunburn, poisonous plants and insects, and blisters.	P, I, U
	27 Have a forest ranger discuss safe procedures in parks and playgrounds.	P, I, U
	28 Have a representative from the Red Cross or a skin and scuba diving club discuss the safety aspects of this sport.	I, U
	29 Invite guest speakers to discuss safety in such activities as football, basketball, skiing, tennis, and swimming.	I, U
	30 Have a member of the local rifle club demonstrate and discuss safety while hunting or the safe handling of guns.	U
Individual and group reports	31 Pupils prepare oral and written reports on the safety rules when camping, boating, hiking, fishing, swimming, hunting, skiing, and roller or ice skating.	I, U
	32 Pupils write report of their favorite recreational activities and include the safety rules that should be observed when participating.	I, U
Map	33 Prepare a map showing the safe swimming area in the immediate vicinity and within a comfortable driving distance from the local community.	I, U

Grades

Mural	34	Make a mural of safe places and safe ways to play while skiing, boating, swimming, hiking, skating, and others.	P, I, U
Puppet	35	Prepare a puppet show or dramatization of a safe camping or hiking trip.	P, I
Scrapbooks	36	Pupils prepare scrapbooks containing pictures, newspaper and magazine articles, stories, and other items on safety categorized into such areas as fishing, camping, swimming, boating, hunting, skiing, and skating.	I, U

SCHOOL SAFETY

Bulletin board	1	Prepare a display of pictures and drawings showing safety at school.	P, I, U
Cartoon	2	Conduct a school safety cartoon or slogan contest.	I, U
Chart	3	Pupils prepare a chart or graph of the nature, number, and location of accidents that occur in school.	I, U
Demonstration	4	The safe use of tools, blocks, and other equipment.	P, I
	5	The safe way to use stairways, drinking fountains, and school equipment.	P, I
	6	The safe way to use playground apparatus and equipment, such as slides, swings, bats, and tetherballs.	P, I
Discussion	7	School safety helpers, such as the teacher, nurse, custodian, and bus driver.	P
	8	The dangers of throwing sticks, climbing fences, throwing balls improperly, and running in the halls or crowded areas.	P, I
	9	The proper use of fountain pens, scissors, and other implements in class as well as the proper way to open doors and walk in the corridors.	P, I
	10	Prepare a list of safety rules for the classroom and the playground that may include:	P, I

> I walk in the halls.
> I use the slides properly.
> I use scissors and pencils carefully.
> I do not push when in line.
> I do not throw rocks and other objects.

	11	What to do when injured at school.	P, I, U
	12	School and playground hazards and accidents.	P, I, U
Dramatization	13	Make puppets and dramatize safety practices at school.	P
	14	Dramatize safety precautions when playing softball, lining up in the cafeteria, waiting for the bus, and other situations.	P, I, U
Drawings	15	Make drawings of play areas and equipment and write captions about school safety below.	P, I
Excursion	16	Walk around the school and locate hazards to safety.	P, I
Exhibit	17	Children prepare drawings on safety in school, such as keeping feet under tables and desks, not pulling chairs away from others, and the incorrect way to use the drinking fountain.	P, I

		Grades
Experience chart or record	18 Prepare an experience chart or record of safe practices in school.	P
Flannelboard	19 Make two children out of construction paper (or make drawings) and call them "Safety Sam" and "Silly Billy." Tell a story about school safety including these two characters and use drawings to illustrate their activities.	P, I

Safety Sam
    waits in line.
    stops the swing and gets off.
    uses pencils properly.

Silly Billy
    pushes in line.
    jumps off the swing.
    jabs pencils in his hand.

		Grades
Guest speaker	20 Invite a physical education teacher or the supervisor of physical education to discuss and demonstrate safety on the playground.	P, I, U
Handbook	21 A committee of pupils prepares an illustrated handbook of safe practices at school for distribution to all students.	I, U
Individual and group reports	22 Pupils or pupil committees prepare articles for the school newspaper on school safety.	I, U
	23 Pupils prepare written reports on the causes of school accidents and ways to prevent them.	I, U
Interview	24 A committee of pupils interviews the school nurse to find out how accidents occur in the school. After reporting their findings in class, they formulate a plan of prevention.	I, U
Map	25 Prepare a composite map of the neighborhood indicating the location of the traffic lights, stop signs, police officers, and sidewalks. Have students draw the safest way home using colored crayons or yarn. Children may also prepare individual maps to be taken home to parents.	P, I
	26 Draw map of the school grounds and illustrate safe and unsafe places to play.	I, U
	27 Plot locations of accidents on map of school and school grounds.	I, U
	28 Teacher prepares map of school showing drinking fountains, bicycle racks, incinerators, and other places. Place on bulletin board and children mark the hazardous places in school and locate accidents that occur.	P, I
Panel	29 Have panel discussion on "Safety at school."	I, U
Problem solving	30 Discuss solutions to these safety problems:	P, I

A boy runs from the cafeteria with an ice cream stick in his mouth.
Two groups walking in the corridor meet at a corner.
One student opens a door and bumps two boys standing in the corridor.
A boy throws his bat while playing in a softball game.
A girl steps in front of another girl who is using the swing.

Grades

		Grades
	31 Form a school safety committee to locate hazardous school areas and to plan ways to prevent accidents.	I, U
Questionnaire	32 Prepare a "Do you remember?" questionnaire as a concluding activity to the unit on school safety. Include 15 to 20 questions to be answered verbally by yes or no, such as, "Do I always walk down the halls and stairways properly?"	P, I
Songs and poems	33 Create songs, poems, stories, and drawings about school safety.	P
Survey	34 Children conduct a hazard hunt on school property and safely remove such objects as glass, rocks, wire, tacks, and nails.	P, I
	35 Children are "safety detectives" and locate examples of safety at school.	P, I
	36 Pupils prepare a safety checklist and then survey the school for hazards.	I, U

TOBACCO*

		Grades
Buzz group	1 Conduct a buzz group discussion on the question, "Should teenagers smoke tobacco?"	U
Chart	2 Pupils prepare charts for bulletin board displays regarding the rise in death rates of major diseases associated with smoking; comparison of overall death rates of smokers and nonsmokers; location of disorders associated with smoking on an outline figure of the human body; computation of the cost of smoking one to two packages of cigarettes a day or a week for 1 year and listing of other uses of the same amount of money.	I, U
Debate	3 Have a debate on the use of tobacco by teenagers. Try to answer the questions: "Should teenagers smoke?" "Should tobacco advertising in newspapers and magazines be controlled?	U
Demonstration	4 Prepare materials as shown in Fig. 12-19. Open and close pinch clamp (acts as siphon—water may need to be replaced several times) to stimulate puffing on cigarette and observe (a) smoke collecting, (b) color of water after shaking flask, and (c) residue on walls of flask. Later discuss relationships to lung tissue in persons who smoke. Place pieces of cotton in glass tube between cigarette and flask without stopping up tube. After smoking several cigarettes (use siphon action previously mentioned), remove cotton and examine. Wipe tar-stained cotton on growing plants and observe results (abnormal growths will appear).	I, U

*Check the local lung association or the American Cancer Society for resources and material aids.

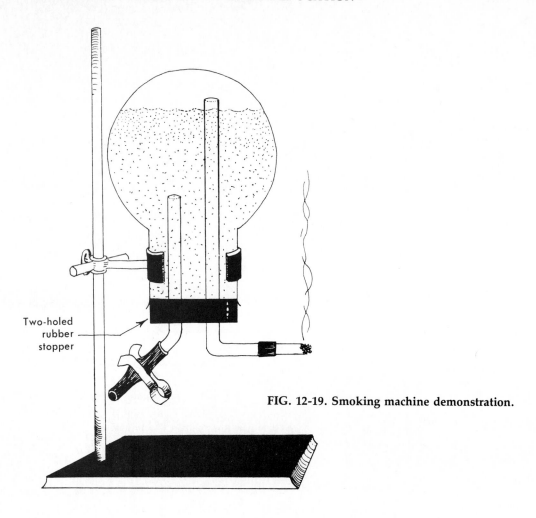

Two-holed
rubber
stopper

FIG. 12-19. Smoking machine demonstration.

	Grades
5 Blow cigarette smoke through a clean handkerchief or paper tissue with and without inhaling. Observe difference in amount of residue and relate to lung tissue.	I, U
6 Place a drop of solution containing paramecia on a microscopic slide and observe movement under the low-power lens of a microscope. Blow smoke on the slide and observe the effect on the paramecia.	I, U
7 Wipe a cotton pellet that has been saturated with tobacco tars on the tongue of a live frog and note the frog's temporary collapse.	I, U
8 Make a nicotine insecticide by soaking cotton pellets from a smoking machine or cigarette tobacco in water. Test and use as a spray on insects.	I, U

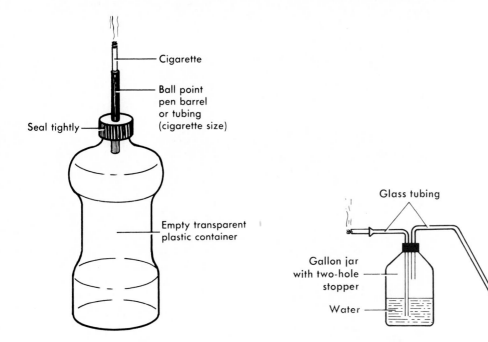

FIG. 12-20. Smoking machine demonstration.   FIG. 12-21. Smoking machine demonstration.

Grades

9   Prepare a smoking machine, using materials shown in Fig. 12-20.   I, U
    Insert loosely packed cotton into the tubing and put a cigarette into
    the open end of tubing. Press firmly on the plastic container to force
    air out before lighting the cigarette, and then proceed with slow
    and regular pumping action. Later, cotton can be withdrawn from
    tubing to show the accumulation of tar.

10 Prepare a smoking machine using materials shown in Fig. 12-21.   I, U
    Light the cigarette and pump the vacuum so as to draw smoke from
    cigarette into gallon jar and water until the cigarette is burned com-
    pletely. Use additional cigarettes until tars can be seen in the water
    and around the jar. Cotton can be inserted in tubing behind the
    cigarette and examined later for tars.

Discussion   11 The nature of tobacco smoke.   I, U
               12 The physiological effects of tobacco on the human body.   I, U
               13 The relationship of the use of tobacco to lung cancer.   I, U
               14 Analyze the claims of several tobacco advertisements.   6, 7, 8
               15 Why people smoke.   6, 7, 8
               16 Laws related to smoking.   6, 7, 8

Dramatization 17 Prepare a skit illustrating social pressures used by students to get   U
                   others to smoke. Follow with a discussion regarding actions pupils
                   should take to handle such situations.

Grades

Exhibit
18 Display a variety of brands and kinds of cigarettes. Break open several and show the types of filter tips.   6, 7, 8
19 Display magazines, pamphlets, and other materials for student reference and use.   6, 7, 8
20 Display newspaper and magazine articles on the use of tobacco.   6, 7, 8
21 Display a variety of advertisements found in newspapers and magazines.   6, 7, 8
22 Display a variety of charts and graphs available from the American Cancer Society on the extent and effect of smoking.   U
23 Obtain samples of lungs of smoker and nonsmoker from the American Cancer Society.   I, U

Experiment
24 Obtain some nicotine and dissolve it in water in a fish bowl. Place a tadpole in the bowl and observe the results.   6, 7, 8
25 Prepare two bowls or jars. One should contain plain water and a tadpole or small fish and the other should contain nicotine or tobacco smoke (Fig. 12-19) dissolved in water. After pupils observe the activity of the fish in the plain water, remove the fish and place it in the bowl with the nicotine and smoke. Have pupils observe results and draw conclusions. Promptly remove fish to plain water to revive soon after observations.   I, U

Graph
26 Pupils prepare graphs showing the incidence of heart disease, lung cancer, and emphysema among smokers and nonsmokers as well as the costs of smoking cigarettes yearly.   U

Guest speaker
27 Invite a physician to discuss and answer questions about the effect of tobacco on health.   6, 7, 8

Individual and group reports
28 Pupils investigate the laws regarding the sale of tobacco to minors.   U
29 Pupils prepare oral and written reports on recent magazine articles about tobacco.   6, 7, 8
30 Pupils prepare oral and written reports on emphysema, chronic bronchitis, lung cancer, effectiveness of filter-tipped cigarettes, and number of cigarettes sold.   6, 7, 8
31 Students prepare individual notebooks on tobacco and health, including analysis of advertising, magazine article summaries, research data, and pictures.   I, U

Interview
32 Interview the local health officer for information about the incidence of lung cancer in the community.   U
33 A committee of children interviews one or more physicians about the effect of tobacco on health.   U
34 Ask people who smoke and do not smoke for their advice on making decision to smoke or not to smoke.   U

Grades

Newspaper
35 Prepare articles for the school newspaper as part of an antismoking campaign.
U

Parents
36 Involve parents in an antismoking campaign program with students writing letters against smoking, distributing pamphlets, or inviting them to see a film at school.
6, 7, 8

Self-test
37 Conduct a self-test on tobacco.
6, 7, 8

What do you know about smoking?

Circle the correct answers to the right. If you do not know the answer, circle the letter "D."

1. Smoking reduces the appetite.   T F D
2. Smoking irritates the throat.   T F D
3. Inhaling causes a smoker to absorb more nicotine.   T F D
4. Smoking may become a habit.   T F D
5. Teenagers frequently start smoking because they want to act like adults.   T F D
6. Some people smoke to relieve tension.   T F D
7. Smoke from tobacco may be annoying and unpleasant to other persons.   T F D
8. Smoking causes lung cancer.   T F D
9. Filter-tipped cigarettes prevent the absorption of nicotine into the body.   T F D
10. The use of tobacco causes a shortness of breath.   T F D

Survey
38 A committee of pupils conducts a survey of opinions of parents, friends, doctors, coaches, and teachers on the use of tobacco by teenagers.
U

39 Conduct a survey of the smoking habits of pupils in the class. Have pupils post results on the bulletin board in the form of a bar graph.
U

Smoking questionnaire

Check only one statement that best describes your smoking habits at present.

☐ 1. I smoke half a pack of cigarettes or more just about every day.
☐ 2. I smoke cigarettes just about every day, but less than half a pack a day.
☐ 3. I do not smoke cigarettes every day, but I do smoke them at least 1 day a week.
☐ 4. I have smoked cigarettes (including trying them to see what they were like) but do not now smoke them regularly, at least 1 day a week.
☐ 5. I have never smoked cigarettes at all.

Check one: ☐ Boy   ☐ Girl
Present school grade: ☐ 7   ☐ 8
Age: ☐ 11   ☐ 12   ☐ 13   ☐ 14   ☐ 15

SUMMARY

Methods and techniques of teaching health are extremely important in the instruction program that seeks the development of health practices and attitudes based on scientific information. Teachers who are familiar with the variety of activities described in this chapter and are competent in the selection of appropriate ones will have effective health education programs.

QUESTIONS FOR DISCUSSION

1. What is the role of the teacher in the learning process in health education?
2. What are the meanings of the terms *method* and *technique?*
3. What factors related to learning must receive teacher consideration?
4. What are the types of methods that contribute to effective health teaching and what are illustrations of each to health education?
5. What are the advantages and disadvantages of the various types of teaching methods that may be used in the health instruction program?
6. What guidelines help the teacher determine the methods of health teaching to be used in the primary, intermediate, and upper grades?
7. What is meant by the term *incidents* or *incidental teaching* in health education? Provide illustrations.
8. What are the limitations and possible problems in the use of incidents in health teaching?
9. How should the textbook be used when teaching health?
10. How can instructional materials be used effectively with methods in health teaching?
11. What are several ways students may be used in peer education programs?
12. What are the relationships between the objectives of health education and the techniques in teaching?
13. What factors should receive consideration when selecting activities and experiences for health teaching?
14. What are several activities or experiences suitable for health teaching in the primary, intermediate, and upper grades?
15. What are several health areas in which bulletin boards may be used in health teaching?
16. What are several demonstrations suitable for the primary, intermediate, and upper grades when teaching health?
17. In what grades is the use of buzz groups and self-tests probably most appropriate?
18. What are several experiments suitable for teaching fire safety, dental health, nutrition, and communicable disease control?
19. What are several illustrations of dramatic play that are usable in health teaching?
20. What are some examples of the use of the flannelboard in the health instruction program?
21. How can models, charts, and graphs be specifically used in the teaching of health?
22. What are several teaching techniques that may be used in the value clarification process?

SELECTED REFERENCES

Alameda County, California: Dependency-producing substances; a teaching unit grades one through twelve, 1968, Office of the Superintendent.

American School Health Association: Health instruction; suggestions for teachers, Journal of School Health, revised, May 1969.

American School Health Association: How to plan and present a school-community health fair, Journal of School Health 45: Dec. 1975.

Arrigoni, E.A.: Teenage antismoking campaign in elementary schools, School Health Review 3: March/April 1972.

California Interagency on Cigarette Smoking and Health: Teachers resource kit on smoking and health, Sacramento, Calif., 1964, State of California.

Calsbeek, F.: Brainstorming health problems; a creative approach, Journal of School Health 38: Oct. 1968.

Canfield, J., and Wells, H.C.: One-hundred ways to enhance self-concept in the classroom, Englewood Cliffs, N.J., 1976, Prentice-Hall, Inc.

Clark, K.M.: A multimedia approach to mental health, School Health Review 3: March/April 1972.

Cornacchia, H.J., Smith, D.E., and Bentel, D,.J.: Drugs in the classroom; a conceptual model for school programs, ed. 2, St. Louis, 1978, The C.V. Mosby Co.

Dearth, F.: Construction and utilization of visual aids in dental health education, Thorofare, N.J., 1974, Charles B. Slack, Inc.

Dinkmeyer, D., and Ogburn, K.D.: Psychologists' priorities; premium on developing understanding of self and others, Psychology in the Schools 11: Jan. 1974.

Ellensburg School District, Washington: Health instruction guides, grades kindergarten-6, 1968-69, Office of the Superintendent.

Fodor, J.T., and Dalis, G.T.: Health instruction; theory and application, ed. 3, Philadelphia, 1981, Lea & Febiger.

Griffith, M.: Techniques for relating health instruction to the real world, School Health Review 3: March/April 1972.

Gross, R.E., and McDonald, F.J.: Classroom methods; the problem-solving approach, Phi Delta Kappan 39: March 1959.

Henry, C.D.: Ideas that worked with black teenagers, School Health Review 4: Jan./Feb. 1973.

Kellam, S.G., and others: Mental health and going to school, Chicago, 1975, University of Chicago Press.

McGuire, R.: Flintstones and Snoopy join the antismoking campaign, School Health Review 3: March/April 1972.

National Clearing House for Smoking and Health: Smoking and health experiments, demonstrations and exhibits, 1968, U.S. Department of Health, Education, and Welfare, Public Health Service.

Osman, J.D.: Value growth through drug education, School Health Review 5: Jan./Feb. 1974.

Raths, L.E., Harmin, M., and Simon, S.B.: Values and teaching; working with values in the classroom, Columbus, Ohio, 1966, Charles E. Merrill Publishing Co.

Rich, R.: Tests for acidity of the mouth in relation to susceptibility to dental caries, Journal of School Health 33: Feb. 1963.

Scheer, J.K., and Williams, C.: Using children's stories to teach something we don't talk about (death education), Health Values 1: May/June 1977.

Schneeweis, S.M., and Jones, R.: Time-linked health problems; the monthly health specials calendar approach for use in grades K-6, Journal of School Health 38: Oct. 1968.

Simon, S.B.: Promoting the search for values, School Health Review 2: Feb. 1971.

Simon, S.B., Howe, L.W., and Kirschenbaum, H.: Value clarification; a handbook of practical strategies for teachers and students, New York, 1972, Hart Publishing Co., Inc.

Sleet, D.A.: The use of games and simulation in health instruction, California School Health 13: Jan. 1975.

Toohy, J.V.: Beatle lyrics can help adolescents identify and understand their emotional health problems, Journal of School Health 40: June 1970.

Valett, R.E.: Humanistic education; developing the total person, St. Louis, 1977, The C.V. Mosby Co.

Vincent, E.P.: Early safety education, Health Education 7: July/Aug. 1976.

13
INSTRUCTIONAL AIDS FOR HEALTH TEACHING

The quality and value of health instruction depends largely on the classroom teacher's effective use of appropriate methods, techniques, and strategies and the careful selection of the best available teaching aids. The teacher faces a challenging task in the selection and use of instructional aids for health education.

Health instruction must be sensitive to the latest and most reliable research and information from the broad spectrum of the biological, social, and physical sciences. Unlike some other areas of the elementary school curriculum, content and concepts in health and safety often change markedly and abruptly with new developments in medicine, public health, dentistry, nutrition, pharmacology, physiology, psychology, physical fitness, first aid and emergency care, and many other areas.

Therefore the classroom teacher—involved in a diverse range of subject matter areas—must keep abreast of the significant and applicable contributions of all those fields that bear on personal, family, and community health. To do this, the teacher needs to know where to locate scientifically accurate information and appealing teaching aids.

Resources and instructional aids are what the teacher makes of them. The best materials may be of little value when used improperly or ineffectively.

WHAT ARE INSTRUCTIONAL AIDS IN HEALTH EDUCATION?

Instructional aids are those materials used to enhance pupil learning. They are meant to complement effective teaching. Everything in the pupils' environment that contributes in any degree to learning may be considered an aid. Defined in these broad terms, instructional aids include all items that teachers and pupils use such as bulletin boards, cartoons, charts, pictures and photographs, maps, objects, specimens, models, posters, textbooks, workbooks, programmed instruction guides, newspaper and magazine articles, pamphlets, films, filmstrips, videotapes, tape recordings, records, songs, radio and television programs, slides, transparencies, and exhibits. Pencils, paper, chalk, chalkboards, and so on are in reality instructional aids, but they will not be discussed here.

Aids to learning are used for a variety of purposes, but in general they serve as (1) sensory experiences that provide greater understanding of abstract thoughts and ideas, making them concrete and specific, and (2) important motivational devices.

Bulletin boards are an effective way to present information using cartoons, charts, graphs, maps, posters, and other illustrative materials. Teachers should constantly be alert for potential bulletin board material relating to health and safety; it may appear in newspapers, magazines, pamphlets, and other printed materials. Students can actively participate in locating and preparing suitable material for the bulletin board.

Cartoons relating to a wide range of current problems in child health and safety can be produced by the children or selected from newspapers and magazines. Cartoons often provide the qualities of humor and relevance that can motivate pupils toward improved attitudes and behaviors. Teachers should take care that the humor does not overshadow the message presented.

Charts, graphs, maps, posters, and *data* (Fig. 13-2), for these visual aids are readily available from numerous sources or can be prepared by students, teachers, or both. They should not be too involved and complicated but rather represent one or a few basic ideas or concepts that can be readily perceived and understood by pupils.

Objects, specimens, and *models* may be animate or inanimate. Hamsters may be used in classroom diet studies. On occasion children may bring a pet to class and talk about caring for its health and safety. Specimens, such as lung tissue (smoker and nonsmoker) or animal organs, can provide realism in certain learning situations. Anatomy models—a torso, ear, eye, or brain—can help students to better understand the remarkable interrelationships of body or-

"I don't care if it does run up the light bill . . . brush them!"

FIG. 13-1. *(Copyright 1969 by Consumers Union of United States, Inc., Mount Vernon, NY 10550. Reprinted by permission from Consumer Reports, March. 1969.)*

FIG. 13-2. Posters are usable in health teaching. *(Courtesy Mary Wilbert Smith, Educational Service District #121, Seattle, Wash.)*

gans and systems in maintaining good health.

Textbooks are available and serve as basic reference sources for both pupil and teacher. These aids are discussed in greater detail later in this chapter.

Newspaper items, magazine articles, pamphlets, books, and *other printed material* (Figs. 13-3 and 13-4)—including popular paperbacks and reference books—offer good sources of information for the teacher and students in connection with research projects, class discussion, bulletin board material, and related assignments. Care should be taken to assure that these sources are up to date and scientifically sound.

Poems are generally more effective with younger children. Even with children in the lower grades, the message should be clear and precise, not vague and trite.

Filmstrips, films, videotapes, transparencies, and *slides* are available in many topical areas. Most are commercially produced, though pupils

and teachers can prepare some of their own transparencies, slides, films, and filmstrips. See the section on student- and teacher-prepared instructional aids (p. 384) for additional details.

Tape recordings are generally available in two forms: cassettes and reel-to-reel tapes. The cassette is by far the most popular and easiest to handle for use in schools. Tapes are available with prepared audio, or they can be purchased blank. Prepared tapes often accompany some other material, such as a model or filmstrip. Student- and/or teacher-prepared tapes can add much excitement to health learning. Even very young students can learn to make their own recordings using a cassette. In addition, the audio portions of radio and television programs and films can be recorded for use in the classroom. Resource people can be interviewed using tape recordings for enrichment of classroom studies.

Music, records, and *songs* appeal to children. Music can aid in relaxation, the lyrics of a catchy

FIG. 13-3. Students use magazine materials to learn health concepts. *(Courtesy Mary Wilbert Smith, Educational Service District #121, Seattle, Wash.)*

FIG. 13-4. Duplicated materials aid students in learning about drugs through independent study. *(Courtesy Mary Wilbert Smith, Educational Service District #121, Seattle, Wash.)*

tune can assist in conveying health content, and songs can be a fun way of learning.

Television and *radio*, both at school and in the home, offer many opportunities for timely and worthwhile health education. Specials on television and radio deal with the health and safety problems of children as well as those of adults. Problems are usually accurately presented and analyzed by the networks and many local stations. These two all-pervasive media also provide health news items and public service announcements, the latter usually bringing a message from an official or voluntary health agency or a professional society within the health professions.

Even commercials on television and radio can be used as teaching aids. Students can discuss the questions of the validity and reality of commercials promoting products and services for weight reduction and skin problems, the nutritional value of foods, eye care, toy safety, alcoholic beverages, motor vehicles (including motor bikes and mopeds), and other health-related topics.

Multimedia kits for teaching about specific health topics are now purchased and used by many schools. They generally are made up of all the material aids a teacher would need to teach some specific health concepts or content. A simple kit might include a set of filmstrips, a record or a cassette, and a teacher's guide. More complex kits also include 16-mm films, puppets, games, worksheets, posters, and other "hands-on" items. Good kits are extremely helpful, because all the materials needed to teach the unit are located in one place, which saves the teacher much valuable time.

Exhibits may be the result of a pupil project or they may be bought, rented, or obtained free from commercial sources, health departments, voluntary health agencies, agricultural extension services, military organizations, and professional—medical, dental, or nursing—societies. Exhibits should be timely and attractive, should offer a clear message, and should not be left on display for too long. They may serve in three ways: (1) motivation of students, (2) peer education, and (3) parent education.

Computers (physical machinery called "hardware") are rapidly becoming accepted as classroom teaching aids. A few health-related computer programs ("software") are available for purchase. One example of such a program is "Grab a Byte," a computer program in nutrition for grades 6, 7, and 8, produced by the Washington State Dairy Council and the Seattle Pacific Science Center. There are three separate programs within this packet:

Restaurant: Students enter their own height, weight, and age into the computer. From an accompanying menu, they then choose a variety of foods to create a meal. The computer responds by displaying the nutritional value of the chosen meal based on calories, proteins, vitamins, and so on.

Grab a Grape: Students choose from six nutritional categories to be quizzed at three levels of difficulty. Categories include food facts, weight management, and food and sports, among others.

Nutrition Sleuth: The student becomes "Inspector Good Diet" and is given a clue to solve a nutrition mystery. An incorrect response results in a new clue. The score is displayed as each new nutrition concept is presented.

A major problem with computers in the classroom is nonstandardized equipment. A package programmed for use with computer brand *A* cannot directly be used in computers brand *B*, *C*, or *D*. To overcome this problem, teachers can learn to develop their own programs. Some major computer retail outlets offer free or inexpensive courses to prospective purchasers, and colleges and universities have training available. The possibilities for innovative health teaching through the use of computers that will motivate students is extremely exciting.

HOW SHOULD INSTRUCTIONAL AIDS BE USED?

Teachers should give consideration to certain basic procedures when they use instructional aids if they are to obtain the best results. The following factors must receive consideration: (1)

the selection of proper aids, (2) the availability of items, (3) adequate preparation for use, and (4) evaluation.

Guiding principles

The following suggestions will help guide the teacher in the proper use of instructional aids:

1. The teacher must clearly know how a particular learning aid fits into a specific situation. Material aids are not meant to do the teaching for the teacher. They should be used to provide greater meaning to the lesson.
2. Audiovisual materials should always be previewed by the teacher before use in class.
3. Teachers should have aids readily accessible when the lesson starts. There is nothing more disconcerting for a class than to have to wait for the teacher to locate materials that have been misplaced. When this occurs, continuity and interest in the lesson are often lost.
4. If a number of different material aids are to be used, it may be advisable to use them one at a time in sequence. More than one item can be displayed at a time when it is necessary to show relationships with graphs or charts. When used in a logical sequence, instructional aids should complement each other.
5. Evaluation should be made each time material aids are used. This need not be a cumbersome process. Teacher observations of pupil attention, interest, opinions, and other subjective feedback are often adequate ways of obtaining clues to the effectiveness of a particular learning aid. Questions can be asked to ascertain if students understand the main points represented, if the aids show the relationships to material already introduced, and if the aids helped to achieve the objectives of the lesson.

Selection of instructional aids

The variety of materials available in health instruction and the many uses for these materials require the need for careful selection by the teacher. Each type of aid has a particular function, that is, each aid usually can be used to the best advantage with some particular type of presentation. Some examples of this follow:

1. If an object or its parts are to be named, selected, or manipulated, have the object or a model of it for students to view and use; objects can include items such as actual food, food containers, animal organs, microscopes and slides, bicycles, seat belts, stethoscopes, and sphygmomanometers.
2. If an object is inaccessible, perhaps it can be adequately represented by still pictures. A series of still pictures can capture an event. They can be used in station work or on bulletin boards for students to work with in small groups or independently.
3. Films are appropriate when motion and time-space relationships are important, such as when learning about the circulatory and other body systems, environmental concepts, and consumer health issues. Films are also effective in depicting social interaction and behavioral concepts.

Another important point in the proper selection of any audiovisual aid is its suitability and appropriateness for the age, maturity, family and community background, and experience of the children with whom it is to be used. A teaching aid is most valuable when it meets these criteria. Consequently, if an aid is unsuited to the level of maturity, background, experience, interest, and needs of a particular group, it cannot provide the maximum impact. If an aid is too advanced or difficult for the group, it may be frustrating. If it is below the maturity level of a group, it may stifle interest.

Availability of instructional aids

Teachers must plan well in advance of the need for instructional aids to be assured of availability at the time needed. It may take 6 to 8 weeks or longer to reserve films, cassettes, books, or other audiovisual materials from the health resource center, building library, local community health agency, or other source. Planning generally ensures the availability of the desired teaching aids and allows time for preview and examination before classroom use. In addition, should teachers find an item cannot be obtained on the desired date or dates, they have sufficient time to change their teaching schedule, locate substitute materials, or prepare teacher-made aids if they plan ahead.

Preparation for use of instructional aids

Adequate preparation by both the teacher and the pupils is necessary for instructional aids to be used effectively. One undesirable tendency in the use of instructional aids is to use them without attempting to ensure that the pupils derive the greatest benefit from their use. Films and television have often been used more for entertainment than for their contribution to learning. This does not mean to imply that aids should not be entertaining. It does mean that aids cannot be justified in health education solely on the basis of their entertainment value.

With some visual aids (motion pictures, videotapes, slides, and filmstrips) lesson plans and teacher's guides are supplied. In most cases, though, it is necessary for teachers to adapt these lessons or guides based on their knowledge of the students' needs.

Proper preparation by both teacher and pupils helps to avoid passive receptivity on the part of the children. The teacher should clearly articulate to the students the learning objectives to be derived from using material aids. Thus the learners know what is expected of them, what to examine the material for, and how the experience relates to their study.

A preplanned debriefing should follow the use of most material aids. This can be done orally or in writing, individually or in groups, and lead by either the teacher or student(s). Questions similar to the following can help the students debrief and the teacher assess student understanding and perceptions: "What were some of the important things you learned from this film?" "How do you think the young girl felt when her dog died?" "How do you think the young boy felt when he learned his family was moving to the city?" "If you were going to make a film about this topic, what would you do differently?" "Were there things you didn't understand about the film?"

An important teaching technique is to use the material more than once. For example, a film might be introduced and shown to the students. Following a discussion in which students articulate what they observed, heard, and learned, the same film is shown again. Before the second viewing the teacher can suggest certain key points students should look and listen for to clarify discrepancies expressed during the debriefing, and alert them to detect significant facts that were apparently missed or misunderstood during the first viewing. The second viewing should also be followed by a debriefing session or assignment.

Effective use of instructional aids can improve learning, but aids should not limit the degree of creativity and ingenuity of the teacher nor limit student interaction.

Evaluation of instructional aids

Instructional aids in health education need to be evaluated to determine (1) their value in the educational process, and (2) their contribution to the achievement of the instructional goals.

Objective evaluation of instructional aids is difficult for the classroom teacher because assessments are complex and time consuming, and reliable and valid instruments are not available. However, subjective measurements can serve as indicators of the value of the aids being used. The following are suggestions for general questions to be asked to determine the effectiveness of instructional aids:

How well do the materials used contribute to the students' achievement of the objectives?

Are the materials appealing to the students as evidenced by class interest and attention?

What changes in the materials need to be made to make them more appealing to students and to more effectively achieve the instructional objectives?

Are arrangements for the use of the materials convenient?

Is the content presented accurate?

Are the materials suitable for grade level, maturity, and experience of students?

Are there sexual, racial, or other biases in the material?

Are the costs reasonable?

What is the value of the material in terms of effort and time in preparation and expense?

In some cases, the answers to these questions will be all the teacher needs to decide whether or not to use a particular material aid. Other situations may require a more extensive evaluation. Samples of specific evaluation forms for a variety of learning materials including textbooks, films, resource speakers, and others are given in Chapter 14 and Appendix I.

WHERE CAN TEACHERS FIND INSTRUCTIONAL AIDS?

Instructional aids for teaching health may be found within the school building or district, county or regional educational entities, and organizations outside the school. In schools, the sources include textbooks, libraries/learning resource centers, and individuals. Outside schools, material may be obtained from health film centers, professional journals, popular magazines, state departments, the federal government, state and national organizations, clearinghouses, professional organizations and agencies, and commercial businesses.

Materials found within the school

School textbooks. Textbooks on health and safety are available for all grade levels in the schools. Several commercial publishers offer series of textbooks that range from grades K through 8. Numerous schools throughout the country now provide one or more of the health series to encourage systematic progression of learning, beginning with the primary grades

and progressing through the upper elementary grades.

Although the quality of elementary school health textbooks has improved greatly over the years, they have obvious limitations. First, it is impossible for authors and publishers to keep the contents up to date because the lag between writing, publishing, and delivering a textbook. The amount of health research and information generated annually is staggering, and it is impossible to incorporate this knowledge into the textbook publishing process in a timely manner.

Second, textbook publishers must give major consideration to including only topics that will be acceptable to screening committees in populous states that have statewide textbook adoption lists. Thus topics that might be of great interest to students may be downplayed or omitted for economic reasons. Some publishers now offer supplemental booklets on topics considered important but too controversial to include in the textbook itself.

Finally, the readability of the text will probably be too easy for some students and too difficult for others in the same classroom. Thus some learners may be bored while others are frustrated.

Given these limitations, textbooks can still be a valuable aid in teaching health. They contain much good information in a concise, well-ordered form. A good text can serve as the base for an enriched exploration of health topics, but it should be supplemented by appropriate aids as discussed in this chapter. In addition, it can provide an inexperienced teacher of health education with a secure starting point.

Turner, Randall, and Smith* cited five major advantages to using a good health textbook:

1. It gives an accurate presentation of essential facts.
2. It presents an orderly and comprehensible arrangement of the material.
3. It furnishes a common core of content for the class.

*Turner, C.E., Randall, H.B., and Smith, S.L.: School health and health education, ed. 6, St. Louis, 1970, The C.V. Mosby Co.

4. It contains such teaching and learning aids as references, questions, summaries, reviews, exercises, pictures, maps, and diagrams.
5. It saves time.

TEXTBOOK SERIES FOR ELEMENTARY SCHOOLS. The textbook series are generally accompanied by a teacher's manual either bound with the text or as a separate booklet. Some publishers provide free and inexpensive materials for health education, including charts that outline the concepts to be taught at the various grade levels.

Health and safety textbooks for elementary schools can be obtained from the following sources:

Scott, Foresman & Co.
1900 E. Lake Ave.
Glenview, IL 60025
(312) 729-3000

> 1983 edition of *Choosing Good Health:* volumes available for kindergarten through grade 8.

Laidlaw Brothers
Thatcher & Madison
River Forest, IL 60305
(312) 366-5320

> 1983 edition of *Good Health For Better Living:* volumes available for kindergarten through grade 8 (current program: "Healthful Living"):
> Kindergarten—*Study Prints*
> Grade 1—*Your Health*
> Grade 2—*Being Healthy*
> Grade 3—*Your Health and You*
> Grade 4—*Keeping Healthy*
> Grade 5—*Growing up Healthy*
> Grade 6—*Health for Living*
> Grade 7—*A Healthier You*
> Grade 8—*Your Health and Your Future*

Steck-Vaughn Co.
Box 2028
Austin, TX 78768
(512) 476-6721

> 1983 edition of *Choosing Good Health:* volumes available for kindergarten through grade 8.

Harcourt Brace Jovanovich, Inc.
757 Third Ave.
New York, NY 10017
(212) 888-4433

> 1978 edition of *Health Decisions for Growth:* volumes available for grades 1, 2, and 3. 1983 edition of *Health Decisions for Growth:* volumes available for grades 4, 5, and 6:
> Grade 1—*As You Grow*
> Grade 2—*You Make Choices*
> Grade 3—*At Your Best*
> Grade 4—*You Learn and Change*
> Grade 5—*Balance in Your Life*
> Grade 6—*Toward Your Future*
> 1983 edition of *HBJ Health Program:* volumes available for grades 4 through 8.

Charles E. Merrill Publishing Co.
1300 Alum Creek Dr.
Columbus, OH 43216
(614) 258-8441

> 1983 edition of *Health Focus on You:* volumes available for grades 1 through 8.

Libraries/learning resource centers. The school library is an excellent first place to look for good teaching aids other than textbooks. In many schools, libraries also serve as learning resource centers where a variety of teaching aids such as filmstrips, flat pictures, small kits, and other materials may be found. In some districts, a separate audiovisual center has been established that should be explored for health materials. Teachers should develop a close working relationship with the librarians and learning resource center staff.

Fiction and *nonfiction books* relating to numerous pertinent health topics can be found in the school library. Such books provide a meaningful and appropriate medium for integrating health learning with reading skills. A limited list of health-related library books, categorized by subject area with appropriate grade levels, may be found in Appendix E. Annotations are included to illustrate the possibilities of expanding and individualizing the health instruction program through the use of library books.

Encyclopedias and *almanacs* offer an interesting variety of health information that can serve as a valuable resource for integrating and correlating health studies with language skills, mathematics, and research. A sampling of topics contained in these reference materials includes census data, U.S. health expenditures, statistics about the handicapped, health costs per capita, information on heart disease including warning signs and risk factors, cardiovascular disease statistical summaries (charts and graphs), suicide rates, and data on fires, accidents, agriculture, air pollution, first aid, nutrition, and many other subjects. Also, most almanacs have a chronology of the year's events, which includes many health-related items. Reference books like these can be valuable, quick, and easy sources of information for students and teachers.

Newspapers often carry special articles by health authorities and science writers and frequently include daily news items on health and safety. The content is generally accurate but may at times be sensationalized. Newspaper articles can be used to provide current information for bulletin board displays and to help pupils develop the ability to critically analyze material.

A major advantage of using the various current materials in health education is that, from an early age, children may be taught to become discriminating and careful in their evaluation of reports that may be sensational, unsubstantiated, and inadequately documented.

Individuals. The *school nurse* can be an invaluable help in locating good teaching aids. Most school nurses are extremely interested in health education and very willing to assist the classroom teacher in a supportive and competent manner.

Building principals, district health coordinators, and *curriculum generalists* are additional resource people the teacher can consult to locate appropriate sources of instructional material. Many building principals will also help the teacher find ways to offset the cost of health materials.

One should also check with *other teachers* in the building or district who conduct classes at the same grade level. Most teachers are very willing to share not only materials and sources, but also teaching/learning activities and teaching ideas.

Materials located outside the school environment

Health film centers. There are many films and filmstrips available from a variety of sources outside the school setting. No attempt has been made in this section to identify specific audiovisual aids by title, description, or grade level because distributors continually withdraw and add new ones to keep their lists current. Therefore listed next will be the major central sources of these teaching aids. Teachers should check local units for assistance.

College and university film libraries in the vicinity generally have good films on health and safety. Check with the film librarian or the library nearest to you.

Departments of health at city, county, or state levels usually maintain a health film library. Many of these relate to the health problems of elementary students. Write or call for a film catalogue.

Voluntary health agencies produce and distribute excellent films, usually dealing with those health problems or diseases with which the agency is mainly concerned. Consult your local telephone directory or that of the major city in your state for information on the locations of the leading voluntary agencies. Write or call for a film catalog.

Commercial organizations and firms prepare and distribute films on health and safety. They also provide catalogs of health films that may be found in the school library or obtained by writing directly to the organization.

State departments of education often maintain a film library, usually containing good health films. However, since their interest is in both elementary and secondary schools, it is important to check carefully to determine the grade level for which a particular film is designed.

Professional organizations of local and state medical or dental societies have films suitable for showing to nonprofessional young people. Telephone directories will help in locating these organizations.

In addition to these centralized general sources, there are many commercial film distributors. Building librarians and learning resource specialists receive catalogs and other descriptive pamphlets from distributors and producers on a regular basis. Often, films can either be rented or purchased.

Professional journals. Health education professional journals, found in many college, university, and public libraries, are another source of information on teaching aids. Note that some of the information about aids in these journals is carried in paid advertisements, while other aids are examined by authorities and appear in the materials review sections. Professional journals contain many reports and studies of value in the instruction program. They also include information on children's health problems as well as content information. Some of these journals include the following:

Health Education
The Journal of School Health
Journal of Nutrition Education
American Journal of Public Health
New England Journal of Medicine
Journal of the American Medical Association
Science
Health Values
Scientific American

Popular magazines. Popular magazines frequently provide well-written, authoritative articles on new developments in health. These articles must be carefully evaluated for scientific accuracy.

State departments. Local, county and state health departments often have education sections staffed by individuals willing to help classroom teachers obtain good materials. State departments of education and the state library system may also be tapped for sources of information. Again, the teacher is advised to be specific in making requests.

Federal government. The federal government is valuable as a source of free and inexpensive materials. Some telephone directories contain information on federal bookstores and specific regional federal offices. Assistance in obtaining federal publications can usually be obtained from the home office of one's senator or representative. Inquiries and orders can also be made directly by writing the Superintendent of Documents, U.S. Government Printing Office, Washington, DC 20402.

State and national organizations. Many national public and private organizations with health improvement goals provide suitable materials for teacher and/or student use. In some instances the national organizations have state and/or local affiliates, such as The American Heart Association, The American Cancer Society, and the March of Dimes Birth Defects Foundation. When a teacher is aware of a state or local affiliate, all requests for material should first be sent to that unit. A list of some of the national organizations that provide free and low-cost health education material is found in Appendix F.

Clearinghouses. The growth of interest in health during the past decade is evidenced by the increasing number of clearinghouses of information related to various health topics. This phenomenal interest is illustrated by the fact that the federal government determined the necessity for a clearinghouse for health information clearinghouses! A listing of the various clearinghouses is found in Appendix G.

TEACHER- AND STUDENT-PREPARED INSTRUCTIONAL AIDS

Technological advances have opened the doors for teachers to develop their creativity even further and to instill new excitement and meaning into their health instruction programs. Audio cassettes, videotapes, classroom computers, 35-mm and Polaroid cameras, and super 8-mm cameras with or without sound are some of the equipment that teachers and pupils can easily operate. This equipment also provides an opportunity for cross-grade teaching with older students working on productions with younger students.

Having students role play saying no when offered an alcoholic beverage is a fairly common classroom activity. Recording the role playing on tape or video brings a whole new dimension to the learning process. Often when students role play in front of the class, they are nervous and do not recall what happened. What they say and do cannot be reflected on nor recalled. Use of a recorder enables pupils to see and/or hear how they responded. It provides an excellent opportunity to debrief pupils on the experience by analyzing what actually occurred and to explore other effective options.

Pedestrian, bicycle, and motor vehicle passenger safety practices and procedures are often discussed in elementary health lessons. A teacher- or student-made super 8-mm film of actual safety hazards and positive preventive actions in the students' school and community environments can add realism and new meaning to the study. A "home-made" slide presentation with teacher or student narrative is another creative alternative to the presentation of this information.

Teacher-created slides and other materials can be used in testing. A hazardous situation depicted on the screen can be the focus for the questions, "What problems do you see?" "What would you do in this situation?" and "If you saw a younger child here what would you do or what would you tell him or her?"

Photographs, flat pictures, and slides are among the least expensive instructional materials that can be created. Quality pictures can help learning to be more interesting and effective. An appropriately selected picture will help a student to (1) view more clearly a complex relationship, (2) recall a concrete or specific situation, (3) grasp the appearance of a reality, (4) easily understand an important concept, and (5) come up with questions, which will often lead far beyond the immediate purpose of the photographs.

Whether photographs contribute to learning depends on how the teacher structures the learning situation. As in reading, pupils need to have their attention directed to things they can expect to find in photographs. Students must be helped to see rather than merely left to look. Carefully planned questions must be prepared by the teacher such as the following: "What do you see in this picture?" "What is the baby trying to reach?" "Is this a safe place to be?" "What do you see that makes you think it is safe?" and "What do you see that makes you think this person is lost?"

The teacher is also responsible for structuring the situation to ensure the attainment of specific outcomes. It is possible to use photographs and get responses ranging from a simple recitation of facts to complex and creative thinking. Photographs can be mounted on bulletin boards with names or written descriptions covered by flaps of paper. After a student identifies the picture, he or she lifts the flap to check the answer. Students could identify pictures they have not seen before that illustrate the idea or concept under study. They can describe what they see in the photograph along with the application of their own creative thoughts about the concept.

Flat pictures can either be held up for the entire class to see or mounted on a bulletin board for viewing individually and at greater length by students (Fig. 13-3). They can be placed at a specific class station where students are asked to arrange them in a logical order to show cause-and-effect relationships or changes in sequence. Pictures dealing with the specific topics can be mixed with irrelevant pictures, and students can be challenged to select the pertinent pictures.

Students may be asked to list appropriate questions about a picture or series of pictures. Photographs can also be used to test students' understanding of relationships and major concepts.

These questions can serve in the selection of photographs appropriate for specific classroom instruction:

Is the photograph clear and forceful?

Is the detail clear and large enough for study?

FIG. 13-5. Identification of emotions using "Feelings Wheel." *(Courtesy Mary Wilbert Smith, Educational Service District #121, Seattle, Wash.)*

Is the photograph large enough for group study or should it be used by one individual at a time?

Is the photograph interesting?

Does the photograph have a definite center of interest?

Does the photograph direct attention to the most significant facts rather than to unimportant details?

Is the photograph authentic?

Does the photograph cover information that the student needs?

Does the photograph answer questions or explain or clarify concepts?

A filmstrip can be made without expensive photographic equipment from a roll of 35-mm clear or white movie leader and magic markers or a variety of colored, felt-tipped pens. The leader usually comes in 50-foot rolls and can be purchased at a nominal cost from most photography equipment stores.

A story line, theme, or sequence of events should be developed before the preparation of the filmstrip. Students can then draw or write directly on the leader with the colored markers. Each picture should be about 1 inch by 1 inch in size. A commercially made filmstrip should be available for comparison to ensure that all characters are drawn in the proper direction. (The tops and bottoms of each picture should be adjacent to each other.) The finished product can be shown through a regular 35-mm filmstrip projector.

Films can now be made with relative ease and minimal cost because of technologic advances in the equipment and processing of super 8-mm film. This provides an opportunity for the elementary school health teacher to develop and maintain an inexpensive film library related specifically to the health curriculum.

Some suggestions for teacher and student films include the following:

Identify the purpose and objective of the film.

Limit subject matter to one major idea or concept or a few closely related concepts. The focus should be on the major purpose of the lesson.

Involve subject matter or techniques that cannot be covered in the normal classroom setting in other ways.

Develop a storyboard before filming to ensure a logical sequence of action.

Confine the length of the film to 4 to 6 minutes, although the actual presentation of the film might take longer if the teacher elects to make selective stops during viewing for special emphasis.

Puppets are excellent teaching aids. There are many types of puppets that children and teachers can make out of inexpensive materials and odds and ends. Paper plates mounted on wooden tongue depressors, tongue depressors with facial features drawn directly on them, paper bag puppets, and hand puppets made from old stockings with buttons, yarn, and felt sewn for eyes, mouth, nose, and hair are among the various kinds.

Puppets do not have to be elaborately made for children to love and identify with them. With skillful guidance by the teacher, puppets can be used to help students resolve many situations and problems on the playground, deal with feelings of rejection, learn about ways to treat others, deal with someone who cheats or bullies, learn how to say no to pressure from other children, and learn positive ways to express feelings.

SELECTED PROBLEMS WITH INSTRUCTIONAL AIDS
Eliminating bias in the selection and use of instructional aids

For years, little attention was paid to the hidden messages in many educational materials. Most prominent among these were messages of sexism, ageism, and racism. Although the reasons are complex, girls were generally portrayed as passive and boys as assertive and adventuresome. Boys became doctors, firefighters, scientists, and police officers, while girls became nurses and mothers. With rare exceptions, senior citizens, blacks, native Americans, Asians, Latinos, and those of other cultures and races either did not exist in these materials or were presented in demeaning ways.

Because of a raised consciousness of these matters, there is no longer any need to tolerate the use of sexually or racially biased materials by any teacher except in a study of bias. The following criteria are listed as illustrative of the kind of considerations the teacher should use to detect bias when reviewing material aids for health instruction.*

1. Check the illustrations.
   Look for stereotypes.
   Look for tokenism.
   Who's doing what?
2. Check the storyline.
   What is the main message?
   Are one group's standards projected as the ideal?
   How are problems presented and resolved?
   Could the story be told if the sex roles were reversed?
3. Examine the life-styles presented.
   Are negative value judgments implied?
   Do the life-styles reflect reality?
4. Examine the relationships between people.
   Who has the power?
   Who is portrayed in supporting, subservient roles?
   How are family relationships depicted?
5. Note the "heroes."
   Whose interest is a particular hero really serving?
6. Consider the effects on a child's self-image.
   Are norms established that limit any child's aspirations and self-concept?

---

*Adapted from Guidelines for selecting bias-free textbooks and storybooks, New York, no date given, Council on Interracial Books for Children.

Does the material reinforce or counteract positive associations with the color white and negative associations with the color black?

Who performs all the brave and heroic deeds?

7. Watch for loaded words.

Are there words or phrases that have offensive overtones?

The generic use of the word man was accepted in the past; its use in this way today is outmoded.

Determining readability of written materials

The reading level of a written material indicates the approximate *reading grade level* a student must have attained to be able to read the material successfully. Reading level is an important factor in determining whether written materials are appropriate for the grade levels at which they may be introduced. Within any given elementary school classroom, the wide variance in student reading ability results in pupils being assigned to reading groups according to their skill. Reading specialists sometimes help with this, but the good teacher is able to analyze printed health education materials to determine those items appropriate for students' reading ability in groups or individually.

There are several systems used for determining the readability level of written materials. The Fry Readability Formula (Fig. 13-6) is one of the most widely used instruments for measuring readability. Others include the SMOG, New Hampshire, LORGE, SPACHE, Dale-Chall, and CLOZE. Although readability scores arrived at through any of these procedures must be considered approximations, they are a great asset in analyzing pamphlets, magazine articles, texts, and other written materials.

Sponsored materials

Many groups and individuals offer educational materials for classroom use. Much of this material is good and can be used to supplement, broaden, and enrich the content found in the regular text and reference books. Such material is valuable to the health program in that it can provide students with a variety of points of view on important problems and issues. It also usually represents the special interest of the sponsoring organization; therefore it is referred to as *sponsored material*. The list in Appendix F is illustrative of sources of sponsored material.

The introduction of sponsored materials into the classroom must be done with a certain degree of caution. All materials must be carefully evaluated by the teacher with assistance from other personnel such as the nurse and principal. One of the first things a teacher new to a district should learn is the policy and procedures relating to the use of sponsored materials.

The following questions can serve as general guidelines for deciding whether to use sponsored materials in the classroom:

1. Is the content accurate?
2. Is the material helpful in achieving the goals and objectives set up for a particular lesson, unit, or course?
3. Can the material be used without obligating the school to an individual or group in any way?
4. Is the material free of obtrusive or objectionable advertising?
5. Does the material promote or support the point of view of a special interest group? If so, are classroom materials available to present other points of view?

When in doubt as to whether or not to use sponsored material, teachers should try to view the entire lesson from the perspective of the students. Teachers should determine all the messages the students will receive from the questionable material and the context in which it will be presented. They should also consider the possibilities for modifying the materials. If the content is accurate and important to the lesson but there is an excess of advertising, the advertising should be physically eliminated.

GRAPH FOR ESTIMATING READABILITY — EXTENDED

by Edward Fry, Rutgers University Reading Center, New Brunswick, N.J. 08904

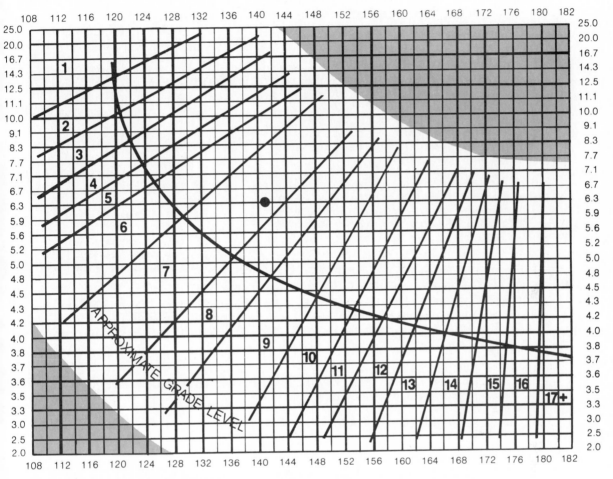

Average number of syllables per 100 words

DIRECTIONS: Randomly select 3 one hundred word passages from a book or an article. Plot average number of syllables and average number of sentences per 100 words on graph to determine the grade level of the material. Choose more passages per book if great variability is observed and conclude that the book has uneven readability. Few books will fall in gray area but when they do grade level scores are invalid.

Count proper nouns, numerals and initializations as words. Count a syllable for each symbol. For example, "1945" is 1 word and 4 syllables and "IRA" is 1 word and 3 syllables.

EXAMPLE:		SYLLABLES	SENTENCES
1st Hundred Words		124	6.6
2nd Hundred Words		141	5.5
3rd Hundred Words		158	6.8
	AVERAGE	141	6.3

READABILITY 7th GRADE (see dot plotted on graph)

For further information and validity data see the *Journal of Reading* December, 1977.

FIG. 13-6. Fry Readability Graph. *(Courtesy Edward Fry, Rutgers University.)*
Continued.

EXPANDED DIRECTIONS FOR WORKING READABILITY GRAPH

1. Randomly select three (3) sample passages and count out exactly 100 words beginning with the beginning of a sentence. Do count proper nouns, initializations, and numerals.

2. Count the number of sentences in the hundred words estimating length of the fraction of the last sentence to the nearest 1/10th.

3. Count the total number of syllables in the 100-word passage. If you don't have a hand counter available, an easy way is to simply put a mark above every syllable over one in each word, then when you get to the end of the passage, count the number of marks and add 100. Small calculators can also be used as counters by pushing numeral "1", then push the "+" sign for each word or syllable when counting.

4. Enter graph with <u>average</u> sentence length and <u>average</u> number of syllables; plot dot where the two lines intersect. Area where dot is plotted will give you the approximate grade level.

5. If a great deal of variability is found in syllable count or sentence count, putting more samples into the average is desirable.

6. A word is defined as a group of symbols with a space on either side; thus, "Joe," "IRA," "1945," and "&" are each one word.

7. A syllable is defined as a phonetic syllable. Generally, there are as many syllables as vowel sounds. For example, "stopped" is one syllable and "wanted" is two syllables. When counting syllables for numerals and initializations, count one syllable for each symbol. For example, "1945" is 4 syllables and "IRA" is 3 syllables, and "&" is 1 syllable.

FOOTNOTE: This "extended graph" does not outmode or render the earlier (1968) version inoperative or inaccurate; it is an extension.

FIG. 13-6, cont'd. Fry Readability Graph. *(Courtesy Edward Fry, Rutgers University.)*

Games for health education

Using games as educational tools is a practice that has been on the increase in recent years. There are many educational games now on the commercial market, and some businesses offer schools free or inexpensive games related to their products. The games most notable among these deal with nutrition. Product-related games must be carefully analyzed by the teacher. Frequently they teach nothing, or they teach misconceptions, about health.

Some games promoted as educational aids in reality promote (directly or indirectly) a particular product or brand line. Many games are not adequately field tested or evaluated. Competitive games may encourage winning the game rather than learning. Teachers should critically evaluate any educational health games before trying them with students.

Before deciding to use any specific game for teaching health, the teacher should give consideration to these questions:

1. Is the game appropriate for the age group of the intended players?
2. What is the primary function of the game? (What is it to do or represent?)
3. How will the game help students reach the health objectives of the particular lesson or unit?
4. Is the emphasis of the game on learning or winning?
5. What kinds of decisions must the players make? (Pure guesses, chance, logical, or evaluative decisions, and so on.)
6. Are the anticipated results worth the class time invested?
7. Does the game directly or subtly promote a special interest or product?
8. What are the potential side effects of the game?

Factors of effective use of television

The teaching effectiveness of instructional television programs designed for classroom use and programs designed for general viewing is well documented by over 20 years of research. A critical factor in what a child will learn from television is the presence of a mentor (teacher or parent) who shares the viewing and discusses what is seen with the child. Among the variables that account for successful learning from television are those listed here.*

Characteristics of effective instructional television programs. Significant gains in student achievement can take place with television programs having these characteristics:

Key concepts are repeated in a variety of ways.

Use is made of animation, novelty, variety, and simple visuals.

The program entertains as well as informs.

A trained communicator is used to present information.

There are opportunities for students to participate in a learning activity, either in response to information presented in the programs or as part of a game presented by the program.

The length of the program is matched to the attention span of the intended audience.

The principles of effective audiovisual presentation are followed.

Characteristics of effective instructional television viewing. Achievement gains from viewing television occur when teachers do the following:

Prepare students to receive information to be presented by the television program

Provide reinforcing discussions and activities following viewing

Provide corrective feedback to students, based on what students reveal they have understood from the program, in follow-up discussions between students and teachers

Provide students with frequent feedback on their achievement as a result of viewing

---

*Adapted from Television in the classroom: what the research says, Tumwater, Wash., 1981, State Superintendent of Public Instruction.

SUMMARY

Properly selected and applied instructional aids combined with skilled teaching bring excitement and fun to health learning. The interest of the general population in health has resulted in an abundance of information and materials about health-related topics. This abundance of instructional aids has increased the importance of wisdom and discretion in selecting and using health materials.

Elementary school teachers of health should know the proper and most effective uses of the various forms of instructional aids, where to find them (both within the school and from outside sources), and how to create their own aids when appropriate. Teachers also need to find access to scientifically valid health information through libraries, colleges and universities, state and federal offices, professional journals, and the mass media.

There are problems associated with many instructional aids. Teachers need to know how to identify and eliminate sexism, racism, and ageism in instructional materials, determine the readability of written materials, and analyze commercial or special-interest messages in sponsored materials.

Identification and selection of instructional aids for health teaching is an important responsibility for the elementary school teacher. The school nurse, librarian, learning resource staff, principal, and district health coordinator or curriculum director are key resource people who can help the teacher in locating, selecting, using, and evaluating instructional materials.

QUESTIONS FOR DISCUSSION

1. What are the two main purposes served by instructional aids?
2. Identify some specific kinds of instructional aids and give examples of how they can be used to enhance health teaching.
3. What are the four major factors to consider when using instructional aids? Elaborate on each factor.
4. Explain the statement, "Subjective measurements can serve as indicators of the value of instructional aids."
5. What are the pros and cons concerning the use of textbooks for health instruction?
6. Identify the different kinds of instructional aids for health teaching that can be found in the school library.
7. What sources of instructional aids for health, besides the school library, are available for teachers?
8. What are sponsored materials for health education? How can they be used? Identify any concerns the teacher should be aware of before using sponsored material.
9. Identify and describe the kinds of inexpensive instructional aids that can be made by teachers and/or students.

SELECTED REFERENCES

Beyrer, M.K., Nolte, A.E., and Solleder, M.K.: A directory of selected references and resources in health instruction, ed. 3, Atlanta, Ga., 1983, U.S. Department of Health and Human Services, Center for Health Promotion and Education.

Children's books about special children, Childhood Education 57:March/April 1981.

Cornacchia, H.J., Smith, D.E., and Bentel, D.J.: Drugs in the classroom: a conceptual model for school programs, ed. 2, St. Louis, 1978, The C.V. Mosby Co.

Dawson, M.E., and Gay, G., editors: Guidelines for avoiding biases and stereotypes in instructional television, Bloomington, Ind., 1978, Agency for Instructional Television.

Educator's guide to free health, physical education, and recreation materials, Randolph, Wis., 1969, Educators Progress Service, Inc.

Elementary school library collection: a guide to books and other media, ed. 13, Greensboro, N.C., 1982, Bro-Dart Foundation.

Elementary teachers guide to free curriculum materials, Randolph, Wis., published annually, Educators Progress Service, Inc.

Eta Sigma Gamma: Selected sources of instructional materials: a national directory of sources of instructional materials in health education, patient education, and safety education, Muncie, Ind., 1980, Eta Sigma Gamma.

Guidelines for selecting bias-free textbooks and storybooks, New York, Council on Interracial Books For Children.

Handbook I: Guidelines for the development of instructional materials selection policies, Olympia, Wash., 1981, Superintendent of Public Instruction.

Handbook II: Textbook selection criteria, Olympia, Wash., 1981, Superintendent of Public Instruction.

Harris, W.H.: Suggested criteria for evaluating health and safety teaching materials, Journal of Health, Physical Education, and Recreation 35:Feb. 1964.

Hopkins, L.B.: Age is one thing we all share, Teacher 95: Dec. 1978.

Hopkins, L.B.: The best of book bonanza, New York, 1979, Holt, Rhinehart & Winston.

Human Interaction Research Institute in collaboration with National Institute of Mental Health: Information resources and how to use them, Rockville, Md., 1975, The National Institute of Mental Health.

Joint Committee of the National Education Association and the Association of American Publishers: Selecting instructional materials for purchase: procedural guidelines, Washington, D.C., 1972, The National Association.

Kemp, J.E.: Planning and producing audiovisual materials, ed. 4, New York, 1980, Harper & Row, Publishers, Inc.

Madison, John P.: Teaching about age and aging, Social Education 44:Nov./Dec. 1980.

Moursund, D.: Teacher's guide to computers in the elementary school, LaGrande, Ore., 1980, International Council for Computers in Education and Eastern Oregon State College.

National Information Center for Educational Media: Computerized up-to-date references on films, Los Angeles, Calif., University of Southern California.

Osborn, B.M., and Sutton, W.: Evaluation of health education materials, Journal of School Health 34:Feb. 1964.

Schloss, P.J., and Milliren, A.P.: Learning aids: teacher made instructional devices, Springfield, Ill., 1975, Charles C Thomas, Publisher.

Television in the classroom: what the research says . . . , Olympia, Wash., 1981, Superintendent of Public Instruction.

Thomas, J.L., editor: Nonprint in the secondary curriculum: readings for reference, Littleton, Colo., 1982, Libraries Unlimited, Inc.

PART SIX

Evaluation

14

EVALUATING THE SCHOOL HEALTH PROGRAM

Evaluation has always been important to teachers. Conscientious teachers want and need to know the effect of their teaching on pupils. These understandings are important so that teachers may continually strive to improve learning. In health education they are especially significant in determining the impact of instructional programs on the lives of students. Hochbaum* wrote, "The task of health education is to equip people intellectually and emotionally to make sound decisions on matters affecting their health, safety, and welfare." The process used to determine the achievement of this task is referred to as evaluation.

School health programs have received little or no evaluation attention. Health education in particular has not received much consideration in this regard. One reason for this neglect has been that authorities have had to concentrate their efforts in gaining acceptance for or in making the public aware of the need for the establishment of instructional programs in schools. Also, the evaluation process is more complex in

health education than in many other educational areas because of the difficulties faced in trying to determine improvement in students' health behavior. Some pupil health attitudes and practices may be immediately observable, whereas others may not be noted for months or years after the instructional program is completed. These delayed changes may be the result of the additive effects of reinforcing information, new life situations, psychological maturation, or changed environment.

This chapter will attempt to provide understandings about evaluation as applied to the total school health program and to offer practical suggestions that teachers may find useful in their classrooms and schools. This coverage is not meant to be all inclusive because of the complexity of the problem and the limited information available. It will include the four major components of the health program—instruction, services, environment, and coordination—with primary emphasis on instruction.

WHAT IS EVALUATION?

Evaluation is a process of determining the worth or value of something relative to a given

---

*Hochbaum, G.M.: Measurement of effectiveness of health education activities, International Journal of Health Education 14:Apr./June 1971.

purpose or objective. The word is used synonymously with such terms as *measurement, assessment,* and *accountability.* Measurement is the part of evaluation that deals with quantitative results. It answers the question "How much?" Is there a health instruction curriculum? Are teaching aids available? Are nurses employed? The more important questions that must be answered include, "How good and of what value is the school health program?" What impact does it have on the lives of elementary school children? Does it help children to live in a healthful manner? Are all students with health problems identified, and are school programs adjusted to their needs? Are teaching materials current and useful?

Evaluation must be concerned with both quantitative (How much?) and qualitative (How good?) information. Quantitative data refer to such information as the test scores of pupils, the number of nurses employed, and the number of meals served in the school lunch program. Qualitative data provide such understandings as the effectiveness of the program on children in terms of school adjustments and correction of health problems, nurse efficiency, nutritional value of meals in the school lunch or breakfast program, and the extent of behavioral change in pupils.

The techniques used to gather information for assessment purposes may provide objective or subjective evidence. Objective data are obtained through such methods as surveys, checklists, inventories, and examinations given before and after programs have started, which are then statistically organized and analyzed. Subjective data are derived from the observations and opinions of teachers and others. Conclusions are drawn from these observations.

Evaluation is both a process and a product. It is not only a means to an end but an end in itself. It must concern itself with the procedures used to achieve the objectives of the program and with the methods used to reach these goals. For example, the teaching/learning activities and the teaching aids used are interrelated with the pupil behaviors sought by the teacher in the instructional program. These activities serve as the means to the end (pupil behaviors). If they are inappropriate or ineffective, they may not adequately contribute to the objective of helping pupils to live in a healthful manner.

Evaluation is a continuous process. It may involve planned and organized efforts using procedures to gather objective evidence, or it may be day-to-day assessment by teachers to obtain subjective information through observations. Evaluation is an integral part of teaching that is in need of emphasis equal to that for the other phases of the health instruction program.

WHY EVALUATION IN SCHOOL HEALTH?

At this point, there is need to review the *reasons for evaluating* the school health program.

First, it is sound practice to continually assess the achievement of objectives in the instructional, services, and environmental aspects of the program to assure that it keeps up with new developments in education and the health services.

Second, there is the responsibility, or accountability, to measure, evaluate, and report on policies, procedures, and learning outcomes to pupils, parents, school health coordinators, and other concerned persons.

Third, evaluation is an essential part of good teaching. While testing and other evaluative techniques may be overdone in some classes, they are part and parcel of the teaching/learning process. Both teacher and pupil can function more efficiently when they are periodically apprised of where they are, where they are going, and how much progress they have made.

Fourth, health services help identify children who are experiencing problems that affect learning, motivation, and discipline. A periodic evaluation of the health services program is essential to ensure that the program is functioning properly and benefiting the maximum number of students on a cost-effective basis.

Fifth, the school environment must be regularly evaluated to be certain controls that allow maximum teaching and learning effectiveness and minimize environment-related stress are maintained. An evaluation of the school environment should include the structure of daily activity as well as the mechanics associated with the physical environment.

The *specific uses of evaluation* in school health instruction include the following:

1. To use as a diagnostic device. Tests can be given at the beginning of a subject or unit of study for this purpose. Both teacher and pupil benefit from knowing what they know (and, perhaps more importantly, what they do not know), how they feel, and what they do with respect to certain health and safety problems.

2. To determine progress toward objectives and to appraise the changes in understandings, attitudes, and practices that result from learning experiences in health education. In this way pupil progress may be directly assessed—though it should be kept in mind that important changes in attitude and behavior often may not occur or show for months or years.

3. To motivate pupils by stimulating their curiosity about specific health issues. The teacher can then observe the way they react to such problems in thought and practice.

4. To identify students who may be in need of special health guidance or counseling.

5. To provide data useful in the continual revision of course and curriculum content. Testing affords an objective approach to curriculum improvement in terms of better meeting the pupil needs.

6. To provide a basis for grading. The results of sound tests will help to provide information for grading and reports of pupils' progress.

7. To provide a basis for meaningful parent education and involvement during parent-teacher conferences. Discussing student progress in health studies lends itself to reinforcing parental responsibility for student health and allows the opportunity for the parent to share observed student health attitudes and practices in the nonschool setting.

8. To provide information useful for program planning. Results of student interest tests

and achievement tests can help determine appropriate grade level placement for content and time allotments in the total curriculum.

9. To improve instruction by providing feedback on teaching methods and instructional aids.

10. To develop good public relations for the health instruction program. Students and parents alike tend to place a higher value on those subjects or courses in which they are tested and assigned a grade. Also, reports of status and progress in specific units of study help to communicate the idea that modern health education is significantly more comprehensive and sophisticated than the old "narrow-gauge" hygiene course that was centered around anatomy and physiology.

WHAT IS TO BE EVALUATED?

The total school health program should be subject to evaluation. This includes the major components of instruction, services, and environment and the coordination of the program. Appendix H contains a good checklist of evaluative criteria for a total program. The suggested evaluation is to a degree both quantitative and qualitative. Teachers should not be threatened by evaluation. If they feel the need for assistance, there is always someone in the school or school district who can help.

This section will deal primarily with evaluation of the elementary health instruction program, since this is the major purpose of the text.

School health services

On the surface, evaluation of the school health services program may seem to be a rather simple matter of marking yes or no on a checklist. Is the service available or is it not? Checklists for evaluating school health services do help and are a legitimate part of any such assessment. However, they reveal nothing about the quality of service actually available. It is not as important for students, teachers, and parents to know how many nurses are employed or contracted for by the district as it is for them to know how often nurses are available to them, and whether the nurses are capable of contributing to the elementary school health program. Since there are no national standards for school health services, one may anticipate a wide divergence in the quantity and quality of programs in local school districts. Appendix H provides one of the better checklists available for evaluating school health services programs.

Checklists for school health services usually include questions relating to health examinations, emergency care, screening tests for vision, hearing, and growth, dental inspections or examinations, immunizations, teacher observation of pupil health, first aid, and follow-up programs. Although a checklist may be useful in describing the scope of services available, it does not help in understanding the teacher's role. Most of the actual services are provided by the nurse or other qualified health professionals. There are, however, four important areas in which teachers have considerable responsibility: (1) observation for health problems, (2) emergency care, (3) follow-up programs, and (4) educational programs that complement some of the health services.

1. *Teacher observation* for student health problems is a major responsibility requiring conscientious effort. Few teachers are actually trained to identify children with possible vision, hearing, or postural problems. Lice and ringworm may be easier to spot, but identifying these problems still requires some training and experience. Problems relating to physical, sexual, and mental abuse are often more difficult to observe, as are those concerning drug and alcohol abuse. The teacher should ask, "If observation for health problems is one of my duties, who trains me, or how am I to gain the necessary skill?"

2. *Emergency care* is a matter all teachers have to face sometime in their career. The situation may involve a simple bruise, a seizure, broken bone, or an appendicitis attack. If the nurse is not in the building all day, is there someone else qualified to handle emergency care? Who? Is there a clearly written emer-

gency care policy and procedure for district personnel? Has it been approved by appropriate medical and emergency care personnel? Is the teacher expected to give immediate care at the emergency site? If so, will the district provide periodic in-service training for teachers in first aid and emergency skills?

3. *Follow-up programs,* in this context, refer to what happens to the child who has had an identifiable health problem. It may include referral, treatment, and reentry into the school program. It is important that the teacher be kept informed as to the status of the child to plan for a smooth reentry to the classroom. The nurse can play a crucial role in this situation by carefully instructing the teacher on what to expect from the child and by providing clues for teacher observation to ensure that any signs of remission are noted and quickly reported. Follow-up programs are extremely difficult without the service of a school nurse.

4. *Educational programs* should relate to many of the health services provided to children. Basic visual, hearing, and growth and weight screenings offer excellent opportunities to teach about sight, sound, and the body. Too often these opportunities are missed and children go from year to year never knowing what their vision test results were or what having 20/20 vision means. Neither do these children realize that someday they must assume full responsibility for their own health checkups. This is another area in which nurse and teacher should collaborate.

A thoughtful review of the school health services program should lead one to conclude that the nurse is the key element for a good program. An evaluative checklist can show on paper that a program exists, but it is usually the nurse who brings life, depth, and quality to the services. In assessing a school health services program the key questions are: How often is the nurse in the building? What is the role of the nurse? How much support does he or she receive? The answers to these three questions will provide a better evaluation of the school health services program than any checklist.

The scope of school health services, including

basic policies and procedures, should be written and made available to all school employees. Teachers must understand their role in relation to student health problems. They should be familiar with what services are available, where and how to make referrals, and the proper procedures to follow.

Healthful school environment

Many health factors of the school environment are relatively easy to evaluate with a checklist that includes some of these questions: Is the water supply inspected regularly? Does the sewage system function properly and meet state standards? Is there an automatic fire alarm system, and is it checked regularly? Is playground equipment in good repair, organized for maximum safety, and regularly checked? Does the classroom lighting meet acceptable standards? Are heat and ventilation systems functioning properly? Appendix H provides an illustrative instrument that may be used to assess the school environment.

There are other factors that have a more subtle effect on the school environment. One example is personal space. Students, especially older children, have need for personal space as well as space for social interaction. Personal space can include a desk for younger students in a self-contained classroom or a locker for older students. It can also include areas such as courtyards where students can find solitude or quiet time during breaks or recess. This factor can have a significant impact on the emotional environment of the school and/or classroom. Noise, color, texture, and odor are other subtle features of a healthy school enviroment that must receive consideration.

The teacher is the most critical environmental factor in the emotional setting of the school. The climate in the classroom that provides security for children, the opportunity for freedom of student expression, and the fair and just treatment of all students are factors that must constantly be assessed by teachers. Sound teacher health behaviors in regard to rest, nutrition, exercise, and personal habits are necessary for optimal

functioning. Teachers may need to prepare a self-inventory for their own personal use.

Coordination

Coordination refers to the interrelation of health instruction, services, and environment. It refers to the consistency with which each of the three components of the health program are performed throughout the district. The degree of coordination of the health program depends to a large extent on the size of the district.

The following are some of the basic criteria to consider when assessing coordination of the school health program:

1. The district has a planned health education program with identified objectives and scope and sequence of instruction for each grade level.
2. Responsibilities are defined for all persons involved in the health program (principals, teachers, school nurses, and others).
3. The district has assigned personnel to provide leadership for the implementation and maintenance of a comprehensive health education program and has provided the necessary resources.

Additional criteria are listed in Appendix H under "Administration."

EVALUATING THE HEALTH INSTRUCTION PROGRAM

The health instruction program can be assessed in terms of the process used and the product, end results, impact on students. Each of these categories can in turn be assessed both quantitatively and qualitatively. *Process evaluation* includes teaching aids and teaching strategies and techniques. It may also cover a variety of other areas such as adequacy of objectives and content in meeting student needs and interests, the curriculum guide, appropriate grade level for topics, and content and teaching aids. *Product evaluation* refers generally to the effect of the program on students in terms of the extent to which the stated knowledges, attitudes, and practice objectives have been achieved.

Should teachers desire to conduct a brief but limited quantitative assessment of the instructional program, Appendix H contains a section that will be useful. This checklist also includes some qualitative assessment.

This section of the text will limit its coverage of instructional program evaluation to those short-term aspects that are feasible for teacher implementation. These aspects include student achievement and progress, instructional aids, and instructional methods.

Techniques used in evaluation

The techniques used in evaluation may also be referred to as instruments, devices, procedures, and strategies. Those that may be appropriate for the teacher to use in the classroom include (1) paper-and-pencil procedures—self-appraisal, peer appraisal, questionnaires, checklists, tests, surveys, anecdotal records, samples of pupils' work (projects, reports), and rating scales—and (2) observations of pupils by teachers and parents.

Teachers who plan to use paper-and-pencil tests should conduct both pretests and posttests. Without pretests to enable the teacher to make a comparison of learning achievements, there is no way to determine whether the knowledges, attitudes, and practices reflected in posttests existed before the instructional program, or whether they can be attributed to the educational activities themselves.

In grades K through 2, paper-and-pencil devices may be used, but they will have to be presented in pictorial form. Also, teachers may have to rely to a greater extent on observations of pupils' behavior and emotional expressions, with the help of parent information received from conferences and other sources.

Evaluating student achievement and progress

How can a teacher know how pupils have been affected by the health instruction program if no effort is made to determine what they have learned? The need for clear and concise cogni-

tive (knowledge), affective (attitudes), and action (practices) domain objectives for accurately assessing pupil achievement must be reemphasized. The taxonomy of objectives by Bloom and others shown in Chapter 9 provides the information that will aid in the preparation of these objectives. When written out in this fashion, goals give clues to the evaluation process.

Measuring health knowledge.   Health knowledges are the easiest of the objectives to measure. However, teachers will need to determine the type and frequency of devices to use depending on the length of the health instruction program and the amount of time available for evaluation. Teachers can select the strategies that are appropriate for their classrooms from those presented next.

TEACHER-PREPARED PAPER-AND-PENCIL PROCEDURES. Paper-and-pencil procedures are the most universal means of collecting evidence related to health knowledges. They may take the form of tests, self-appraisals, or peer appraisals.

TESTS. The two kinds of paper-and-pencil tests most often prepared by teachers are the objective test and the written essay or subjective test. Objective test items may be placed in the two broad categories of *recognition* and *recall*. The recognition type of test item requires that the pupil recognize and select the correct answer, which is shown among other, incorrect answers in the test item. The recall type of test item requires that the pupil supply the correct answer, which has been omitted from the test item.

There are several variations of the recognition test item. Some of these include true-false, multiple choice, and matching. In measuring for health knowledge, it is recommended that the teacher use a variety of recognition test items rather than rely on one type. The purpose of this is to help offset the limitations involved in the various recognition items.

The true-false test item may have little diagnostic value, since a correct response may be merely an indication that the pupil guessed correctly in selecting the answer. When true-false items are used, extreme care should be taken in constructing the false items so they will not leave a fixed false idea with pupils, particularly slow-learning pupils. Teachers should keep the following criteria in mind when developing or reviewing true-false questions:

1. Are statements true or false without additional qualifications?
2. Are statements expressed simply and clearly?
3. Are items relatively short and restricted to one central idea?
4. Are statements ambiguous?
5. Do statements contain determiners? False statements—only, never, all, always, none, every, no; true statements—usually, several, sometimes, constantly, often.

The *multiple-choice item*, when carefully prepared, can be very thought provoking. It is an excellent way of determining whether pupils have achieved the desired health knowledge and information. In the multiple-choice test item, there are usually three to five possible responses. Five responses are preferred, because as the number of possible answers is increased the possibility of guessing the correct answer is reduced. Points to consider when developing or reviewing multiple-choice questions include the following:

1. Are there four or five distractors with only one answer?
2. Are the distractors reasonably plausible?
3. Is there grammatical consistency?
4. Does the introduction contain clues?
5. Are choices of answers brief?
6. Are there ambiguities?

The *matching test item*, when properly constructed, can be useful in measuring achievement and educative growth. Matching test items have the obvious limitation of being the type of items used for the collection of mere factual information. The following four questions can serve as guides in creating or reviewing matching type questions:

1. Are lists of comparative items as homogeneous as possible?
2. Are some items included that cannot be matched?
3. Can questions be easily scored?
4. Are lists of responses relatively short?

The completion test item requires the pupil to supply the correct answer in the form of a recall or fill-in item. This test item places a premium on rote memorization of health facts. A limitation is that the test item may be such that more than one correct answer can be given. For example, in a recall test item such as "Exercise generally shows an increase in _____ development," both "muscular" and "organic" are correct answers. On the other hand, a recall item such as "_____ makes up the greatest part of the body," has only one possible correct answer, which is "water." When there is a possibility of more than one correct answer, the teacher should include each in the test scoring key.

These three points will assist the teacher to develop or select good completion-type items:

1. Make certain that only one response is correct.
2. Do not put in so many blanks that the question loses meaning.
3. Do not permit the syntax of the statement or the length of the blank to give a hint as to the answer.

ESSAY. *The written essay* or *subjective test* of health knowledge, although somewhat lacking in objectivity, helps gain evidence of achievement and educative growth that frequently cannot be measured through the purely objective test. For example, the teacher can formulate questions in such a way as to provide for better problem-solving situations than are usually possible in straight objective tests. The teacher may ask pupils to write a summary of what has been learned through the study of a certain health unit. If this procedure is undertaken, the teacher should analyze the summaries to determine how closely they are related to the objectives of the unit. In this way the teacher should be able to ascertain to a reasonable degree whether pupils have gained insight into the understanding and concepts that formed the basis for the unit objectives. To realize the optimal benefit from essay-type questions, the following points are suggested:

1. Questions should be clearly and carefully constructed.

2. Written instructions for answering should be clear and explicit.

SELF-APPRAISALS. Merely asking pupils to indicate what they have learned by giving them a blank sheet of paper so they can present their anonymous comments frequently provides valuable clues to evaluative information.

PEER APPRAISALS. The technique of having other students assess the learnings of their classmates has advantages if selectively used by teachers. Careful planning is necessary if this technique is to be successful, because pupils need to clearly understand the purpose and the procedure.

ORAL QUESTIONING. When used, oral questioning necessitates that the teacher devise a technique suitable for keeping satisfactory records. Otherwise, there will be no documentary evidence of growth when final evaluations and appraisals are made. Some teachers find it desirable and helpful to keep a log in which results of oral questioning can be quickly recorded.

Oral inquiry may be formal or informal in nature. In an event, questions should be such that the teacher can actually tell whether pupils are accumulating satisfactory health knowledge. Because of this, certain types of questions usually should be avoided. For example, questions that require only a yes or no answer may have little value, because the pupil will have a 50% chance of guessing the correct answer. On the other hand, questions necessitating critical thinking and judgment can be phrased in such a way that the teacher should be able to immediately detect evidence of correct and accurate health knowledge. Perhaps one of the main disadvantages that teachers have found in using the oral questioning technique is that it may be difficult to appraise the achievement of all pupils if classes are large. The chief advantage of this means of measurement is that the teacher may obtain a more valid estimate of the individual's learning, especially for those who experience great difficulty with written tests.

DEMONSTRATIONS. Measurement of health knowledge through demonstrations can be carried out by either teacher demonstrations or pupil demonstrations. When the teacher demonstrates, the pupils are required to identify those things that are demonstrated. When pupils perform a demonstration, they show the health knowledge they have gained as well as their interest in the topic.

The efficacy of this approach to health knowledge measurement is obvious; it tests pupil knowledge in a real and lifelike situation that could be carried over and applied in a practical way, such as helping in the selection of nutritious foods while shopping with the family.

Asking pupils to demonstrate certain procedures that were developed in a health unit is a valid way of measuring health knowledge. The chief disadvantage of this technique is the amount of time required. Measurement of health knowledge through pupil demonstration may provide for a better indication of educative growth in those pupils who do not express themselves well on written tests.

PUPIL PROJECTS. Appraisal of learning in terms of health knowledge need not always take the form of testing. For example, the teacher can evaluate scrapbooks, notebooks, special projects, and other materials prepared by pupils. This can be done for the purpose of determining whether pupils have gained insight into certain health concepts necessary for the satisfactory preparation of these materials.

TEACHER OBSERVATION. One of the best techniques in health appraisal, teacher observation, can also be a primary measure in the assessment of pupils' progress. Teachers know their pupils. They see them day in and day out. They are in a good position to judge pupil learnings. Since parents also observe their children, communication between teachers and parents is most helpful in evaluating pupil progress.

STANDARDIZED TESTS. There are a number of standardized tests used to gather information regarding health knowledges. The standardized test is one that has been previously administered to large number of pupils to establish norms for specific grade levels or combinations of grade levels.

One of the major problems of using standardized tests is that they often lack curricular

STUDENT FIRE SAFETY ATTITUDES

Please circle the numbers to the right that best express your feelings about each of the following statements:

	Strongly agree	Agree	Don't care	Disagree	Strongly disagree
1. The stop, drop, and roll procedure should be used when clothes are on fire.	5	4	3	2	1
2. In smoke-filled rooms people should crawl low to get out.	5	4	3	2	1
3. Fire drills at school are important.	5	4	3	2	1
4. Smoke detectors are needed in homes.	5	4	3	2	1
5. Fire and smoke discovered should be promptly reported to fire departments.	5	4	3	2	1
6. Fire fighters are community protectors.	5	4	3	2	1
7. Home escape plans are necessary in case of fire.	5	4	3	2	1
8. Fire burns may be dangerous to people.	5	4	3	2	1
9. Fire inspection of buildings should take place on occasions.	5	4	3	2	1
10. Improper storage of flammable materials is hazardous.	5	4	3	2	1
11. Matches, flammable substances, and electrical appliances should be used safely.	5	4	3	2	1
12. Lightning may cause fires.	5	4	3	2	1
13. Overloaded electrical circuits are hazardous.	5	4	3	2	1
14. Baby-sitter fire safety plans protect individuals.	5	4	3	2	1
15. Electrical equipment that has been tested for fire and safety hazards should be used.	5	4	3	2	1

FIG. 14-1. Student fire safety attitudes.

validity. Many test items do not relate to the objectives, content, and learning activities of the local school health instruction programs.

Appraising health attitudes. Assessment of pupils' attitudes toward health is difficult, and it is almost impossible to obtain objective information. Attitudes are concerned with one's feelings, emotions, beliefs, and values, which are reflected in behavior. Observations of pupils' actions may provide clues to their feelings and emotions. However, attitudes are elusive and may change with the time of the day or the environment or situation. Some pupils may not wish to reveal their true feelings because of their home situations or other conditions. Therefore pupil replies may be unreliable, and the information received from whatever technique used by teachers is suspect and should be accepted with skepticism. These data should serve only as indicators of student attitudes. The chances of obtaining more reliable information may be increased when attitudes are obtained from an entire class rather than from individual students. Thus procedures should be completed anonymously by students; names should not be required on any paper-and-pencil devices used to assess attitudes.

There are a variety of techniques that classroom teachers may use to assess attitudes. The paper-and-pencil inventory using a Likert-type scale, as shown in Fig. 14-1, is one example. A series of sentence completions on the subject of mental health is another example.

I am cool when I _____.
I am happiest when I _____.
I feel best when people _____.
The thing I want most _____.
I feel important when _____.
I'd like my friends to _____.

Other techniques that have been tried with some degree of success include students' completions of unfinished stories about health and anonymous pupil self-appraisals of their feelings. Sometimes informal pupil conferences and conversations can reflect health attitudes.

Perhaps the simplest and most practical strategy is the use of teacher observations. For example, teachers can observe (1) pupils' eating habits in the school cafeteria with regard to food preferences, (2) students freely asking questions informally before and after class about particular health topics covered, and (3) children's safety behavior on playgrounds, to and from school, and during fire drills.

The unreliability of the evidence from the attitude procedures described does not mean they should not be used. Attitudes are closely related to behaviors, and they must be assessed despite the limitations of procedures that only provide indications of pupils' feelings and emotions. Objective data may be obtained if teachers keep anecdotal records of pupils' emotions and beliefs and periodically analyze them for attitudinal changes. In addition, attitudes can often be validated through parent conversations and other teacher discussions.

Assessing health practices. Health practices may be more difficult to assess than attitudes. Most health behaviors are not observable in the classroom because they take place in the home or in the community. Also, many may not emerge for months or years after pupils have completed their schooling. Therefore most of the information collected may have to be subjective in nature.

The procedures to use for health practices evaluation include paper-and-pencil devices such as questionnaires and checklists, informal conferences and discussions with pupils and parents, and teacher observations. Paper-and-pencil checklists such as the one illustrated for grades 5 through 8 have limitations, because the information received may not be reliable. If students are permitted to complete these forms anonymously, the chances for truthful information are increased.

Drugs I have used the past 12 months

Check the appropriate box below for these drugs.

	NUMBER OF TIMES				
	0	1-2	3-9	10-49	50+
Alcoholic beverages	☐	☐	☐	☐	☐
Tobacco	☐	☐	☐	☐	☐
Marijuana	☐	☐	☐	☐	☐
LSD	☐	☐	☐	☐	☐

	NUMBER OF TIMES				
	0	1-2	3-9	10-49	50+
Amphetamines (meth, speed, bennies, pep pills)	☐	☐	☐	☐	☐
Barbiturates (downers, reds, yellow jackets, blues)	☐	☐	☐	☐	☐
Heroin		☐	☐	☐	☐
Cocaine		☐	☐	☐	☐
Solvents		☐	☐	☐	☐

Informal conferences and discussions with children, parents, and other school personnel may provide indications that pupils are brushing and flossing teeth, eating nutritious foods, and being safe pedestrians.

In assessing health practices, teachers will probably have to rely mainly on their own observations and those of others. Reports may come from nurses, physicians, parents, and school personnel that will provide indications of the extent of behavioral changes or behaviors. Teachers may wish to prepare a parent inventory to be taken home by students before and after a particular health unit. Although this procedure is not completely reliable, it can provide supportive information to teacher observations.

Teacher evaluation of health practices must involve a variety of the strategies presented here to validate the pupil behavior indicators that have been observed.

Evaluating health instruction material aids

Instructional material aids generally refer to such items as textbooks, films, cassettes, slides, still pictures, and other things that are helpful in the teaching process. In those instances when they are used for individual instruction, cassettes and programmed learning materials may in themselves serve as the basic program.

The selection of materials for use in health education should be done on a systemized basis with thoroughness and awareness of need. Materials should not be selected before objectives and content have been determined.

Health teaching items should be evaluated on a regular basis, before and after the selection

process. Educators should use existing devices for evaluation or create their own. The information collected should be kept on file for reference as needed. Fig. 14-2 illustrates a sample audiovisual evaluation form. Appendix I contains a more detailed instrument that teachers may find more useful. These procedures may be modified to meet specific teacher needs. Teachers may also observe student reactions to material aids in terms of interest and motivation to obtain a rapid assessment.

Teaching aids should be free of sexual, racial, ethnic, and other biases. Suggestions and criteria for assessing such matters may be found in Chapter 14 and Appendix I.

Resource speakers are considered a type of instructional aid and should be evaluated. These questions are useful in the assessment process:
1. Was the presentation biased or slanted?
2. Was the presentation appropriate for the age level addressed?
3. Was the presenter well organized?
4. What objectives were met by the presentation?

Students should be asked to respond to the question, "What did you learn from this person?"

Teachers should be cautioned to inform building principals in advance when planning to use an outside resource person. Teachers waive their right of administrative support if problems occur with a resource speaker and the principal was not notified *before the event.*

Evaluating health instruction methods

The instruction methods teachers use in the classroom are fundamental to the successful achievement of the established objectives in health education, as in other subject areas. Therefore teachers must continually assess the procedures they use.

One phase of methods evaluation involves the selection of appropriate teaching procedures before instruction starts. Information found in Chapter 12 provides guideline questions that are helpful.

```
                    AUDIO VISUAL EVALUATION FORM

    Film                Filmstrip                Other

    Title:

    Length:

    Year produced:

    Color      B&W

    Description of content:




    Intended teaching purpose(s):




    Main ideas and/or skills presented:




    Production rating                          Encircle
    Photography                            Good      Bad
    Sound                                  Good      Bad
    Vocabulary                             Good      Bad
    Acting                                 Good      Bad

    Contents rating
    Accurate and authentic                 Yes       No
    Correlated with curriculum             Yes       No
    Presents needed facts                  Yes       No
    Stimulates pupil activity              Yes       No
    Void of racial, ethnic, sex bias       Yes       No

    Types of learning                      Check
    Developing concepts

    Values clarification

    Critical thinking

    Behavior modification

    List particular strengths or weaknesses:
```

FIG. 14-2. Audiovisual evaluation form.

These five rather simple techniques can help in assessing the effectiveness of health instruction methods:

1. Teachers observe pupils' reactions and check their own internal feelings of effectiveness. Experienced teachers know when instruction is going well and when a method or activity is going flat.
2. Teachers ask students to respond orally or in writing to these questions:

    "What did you learn today about *(topic)*?"

    "How did you feel when we *(method/activity)*?"

    "If you were going to teach today's lesson to your friends, how would you do it?"
3. Use a tape recorder to capture the dialogue and tone of the class during the lesson. Analyze the tape.
4. Videotape the lesson if feasible. Analyze the tape.
5. Ask the principal, nurse, coordinator, or another teacher to attend class to evaluate a specific lesson or lessons.

Student grades in health instruction

Pupils and parents alike show great interest in report cards. Pupils generally like to be rated in comparison with their classmates and with their own previous marks. The typical elementary school child expects to get a report on status and progress. Often, the report card provides the parents with their only information about what is taught in the school. The report card can reflect school philosophy and serve as an important medium for communication with the public. Although many elementary schools use the letter system (A-B-C-D-F) for reporting pupil progress and performance, the trend toward more functional and descriptive methods of reporting continues.

Many elementary schools today attempt to assess a pupil's progress in the light of that pupil's capacities and abilities. Such an approach usually means that a pupil is marked as O for outstanding progress, S for satisfactory progress, and U for unsatisfactory progress. The emphasis is on the progress, or educational growth, of each child as an individual. At the elementary school level, progress reports are usually supplemented by parent-teacher conferences. These conferences should bring about a sharing and comparing of knowledge and observation that contributes to a better understanding of the child's performance in school.

The parent-teacher conference should use the report card simply as a point of departure for analyzing the pupil's strong and weak points. Usually, if parents are objective, they can provide the teacher with significant information on a child's health attitudes and practices in and around the home. Skilled teachers make the most of these all-too-brief conferences.

Principles of grading pupils. There is no single best way to assign grades in health instruction at all grade levels. These are some basic principles teachers can use to assure that grading is fair for all students:

1. Grades should reflect *actual class achievement*. Factors such as neatness, spelling, handwriting, and absence do not reflect on achievement in health learning and therefore should not be considered as criteria for grading. However, teachers should encourage and strive for quality of performance.
2. Grades should *not* be used for disciplinary or manipulatory puposes. Such practice detracts from the importance of health learning.
3. Students should be well acquainted with the grading method to be used by the teacher.
4. Pupils should have access to their grade progress throughout the study of health. They should be provided guidance in ways to improve their standing at any time.

Basis for grading. Teachers should collect sufficient data of student achievement to permit valid judgments to be made. It is better to use several kinds of indicators of progress rather than one. Remember, individuals learn in different ways and react to measuring techniques differently. Some students can express themselves and are articulate orally but have little success on written examinations.

Grades should be based on a combination of performances including the following:

Daily recitations and oral presentations
Homework
Written assignments or graphics
Examinations and quizzes
Extra credit opportunities
Pupil self-evaluation

Obviously, some of these activities are too advanced for very young children, but many can be modified to provide for a combination of performances. Primary grade students can do daily recitations and simple oral reports. They can also draw or cut pictures from magazines to illustrate health learnings, and they can be given simple oral examinations.

Problems in grading. Grades in health education should be based on pupil achievements in terms of knowledges gained, projects and activities completed, and general quality of work performed. Health attitudes and practices, however important in terms of objectives, are virtually impossible to use for grading purposes. Doing so can result in external motivation, untruthfulness, and other problems. Also, determining specific student progress is very difficult.

For some pupils, grades become the end purpose of study. These pupils become preoccupied with the process of memorizing the subject matter and consider the grade the end result. They do not apply their knowledge to personal decisions that will positively affect their health.

Teachers can also create problems in grading. Some use grades for disciplinary or motivational purposes when other methods fail. Others lack objective, clearly defined criteria for assigning grades. Some teachers tend to grade students with whom they work well higher than the student's achievement warrants.

Occasionally, personality conflicts between a pupil and teacher can cause the pupil to be penalized when grades are assigned. The problems of discipline and personality conflict must be dealt with as separate issues.

Many of these problems can be avoided if the teacher is organized, has a well-planned grading system that allows for individual differences, and communicates the proper perspective of grades in the educational process to pupils and parents alike.

WHO EVALUATES?

The answer to the question, "Who evaluates?" is based on the answer to the question, "What is to be evaluated?" This chapter deals with evaluating the total school health program. The elementary teacher should not be expected to evaluate the total health program. This is a major undertaking for which the responsibility should be shared by school administrators, board members, district health and/or curriculum specialists, teachers, nurses, parents, and in some instances, health professionals from the community, local university, and state departments of education.

The teacher is the key person in the evaluation of the instructional program in the classroom. Evaluation of the instructional program includes content, methods, materials, and student progress evaluations. Assistance in this evaluation may come from the principal, nurse, librarian, district health and/or curriculum specialist, parents, and students.

Effective evaluation is not easy, but it is necessary and can be rewarding. It can result in a teacher feeling like a significant contributor in the development of student as well as personal health behavior. Positive community public relations can result when teachers demonstrate pride in their school health programs. More importantly, evaluation enables students to receive improved health instruction and helps them learn to make intelligent decisions about life-styles that will affect their health.

SUMMARY

Evaluation is a way to determine the worth or value of something. In school health there is need to determine the effectiveness, in terms of process and product, of the total program and its components. These include instruction, services, environment, and coordination.

The teacher has an important role in evaluation. It is limited in terms of the total program as well as in terms of the services, environment, and coordination aspects. However, the teacher has a major responsibility for determining the impact of the health instruction program on students.

Evaluation of health knowledge objectives can be achieved relatively easily and effectively. However, assessment of health attitudes and practices is more complex and difficult. Teacher observations can be used as indicators of success despite their subjectiveness. They can be organized to provide objective and fairly reliable data.

Grades are valuable in the health instruction program, because they provide student motivation and parent information. They should be based on student achievement. Student attitudes and practices are virtually impossible to grade and therefore should not be a part of the grading system.

QUESTIONS FOR DISCUSSION

1. What is the difference between measurement and evaluation?
2. Why is evaluation important to the school health program?
3. What use can parent-teacher conferences be in assessing pupil learning in health?
4. What are some of the basic points to consider when evaluating instructional aids for health?
5. If you could only evaluate one portion of the school health services, which would you select? Why?
6. What are the most effective kinds of recall and recognition items for a health test? To what extent would you use such items? Why?
7. What are the specific uses of evaluation in health? Which of these do you consider most important? Why?
8. How are behavioral objectives related to the evaluative procedures and techniques a teacher uses?
9. Can a student's health values be realistically and reliably evaluated? How?
10. Why is it important to periodically evaluate teaching methods in health?
11. What is your opinion about grading in elementary health education?
12. Who is responsible for evaluation of health education?

SELECTED REFERENCES

Allen, R.E.: Evaluation of the conceptual approach to teaching health education, Journal of School Health 43:May 1973.

California State Department of Education: Elementary school health education program inventory, Sacramento, Calif., 1962, The Department.

Charles, C.M.: Individualizing instruction, ed. 2, St. Louis, 1980, The C.V. Mosby Co.

Cornely, P.B., and Bigman, S.K.: Some considerations in changing health attitudes, Children 39: Jan. 1963.

Department of Health and Medical Services: Fifty-second annual report, 1976-1977, Denver, 1977, Denver School Press and The Department.

Dalis, G.: Effect of precise objectives upon student achievement in health education, Journal of Experimental Education, Winter 1970.

Foder, J.T., and Dalis, G.T.: Health instruction; theory and application, ed. 3, Philadelphia, 1978, Lea & Febiger.

Green, L.W., and Gordon, N.P.: Productive research design for health education investigations, Health Education, 13:May/June 1982.

Henerson, M.E., Morris, L.L., and Fitz-Gibbon, C.T.: How to measure attitudes, Beverly Hills, Calif., 1978, Sage Publications, Inc.

Hochbaum, G.M.: Behavior modification, School Health Review 2: Sept. 1971.

Hochbaum, G.M.: Measurement of effectiveness of health education activities, International Journal of Health Education 14:April/June 1971.

Howell, K.A., and Martin, J.E.: An evaluation model for school health services, Journal of School Health 48:Sept. 1978.

Kreuter, M.W.: School health evaluation, Health Education 8: March/April 1977.

Kolbe, L.J., and Iverson, D.C.: Research in school health education: a needs assessment, Health Education 11: Jan./Feb. 1980.

Morris, L.L., and Fitz-Gibbon, C.T.: Evaluator's handbook, Beverly Hills, Calif., 1978, Sage Publications, Inc.

National Society for the Study of Education: Educational evaluation; new roles, new means, Chicago, 1969, University of Chicago Press.

Oberteuffer, D., Harrelson, O.A., and Pollock, M.B.: School health education, New York, 1972, Harper & Row, Publishers, Inc.

Pikulski, J.J., and Shanaban, T., editors: Approaches to the informal evaluation of reading, Newark, Delaware, 1982, International Reading Association.

Rosenshine, B.: Evaluation of instruction, Review of Educational Research 40:April 1970.

Sanders, N.M.: Classroom questions: what kinds? New York, 1966, Harper & Row, Publishers, Inc.

Shaw, J.H.: Evaluation in the school health instruction program, American Journal of Public Health 47:May 1957.

Sinclair, R.L.: Elementary school environment survey, Amherst, Mass., 1969, University of Massachusetts.

Sliepcevich, E.M.: School health education study; a summary report, Washington, D.C., 1964, School Health Education Study.

Solleder, M.K.: Evaluation instruments in health education, Washington, D.C., 1969, American Alliance for Health, Physical Education, and Recreation.

Steele, S.M.: Contemporary approaches to program evaluation, Washington, D.C., 1973, Educational Resources Division Capitol Publications, Inc.

Thompson, V.M.: Accountability in school health, Journal of School Health 49:Jan. 1979.

Wilhelms, F.T., editor: Evaluation as feedback and guide, Washington, D.C., 1967, Association for Supervision and Curriculum Development.

Willgoose, C.E.: Providing for change; new directions. In Read, D.A., editor: New directions in health education, New York, 1971, Macmillan, Inc.

Appendixes

A

Communicable disease
summary
for teachers

COLORADO STATE DEPARTMENT OF PUBLIC
HEALTH, COMMUNICABLE DISEASE CONTROL SECTION, 1978*

Many communicable diseases are as contagious before the start of symptoms as afterwards. For this reason parents should be instructed to keep their children at home whenever they appear to be ill, even with a common cold.

Teachers should observe all children as they come into the schoolroom and throughout the day for signs of illness. A child who becomes ill should be isolated from the other children, and the parents notified to remove the child from school.

Teachers should watch for the appearance of a rash or for a child with cold symptoms, including a cough—common symptoms of infectious diseases.

When children are exposed to a communicable disease in the classroom, the parents should be notified so that those children who have not had the disease can be observed for symptoms at the end of the incubation period.

*This communicable disease summary for teachers has been adapted from Colorado State Department of Health Communicable Disease Summary, Communicable Disease Control Section, May 1978.

CHICKENPOX

Chickenpox is a very contagious but not a serious disease. It is caused by a virus. There are few, if any, complications.

What to look for	When cases are occurring in school or community, watch for symptoms of a "cold" or a rash. The rash of chickenpox resembles small blisters and usually appears on body, chest, or upper back 14 to 21 days after exposure. Children may have no sign of rash when they come to school and by midmorning it may begin to appear.
How disease is spread	By contact with case, from 5 days before symptoms appear in the case to 6 days after last vesicles appear. Spread by droplets from the nose and throat. Scabs are not infectious.

How to prevent	No immunization. Child who has chickenpox should be kept away from others until no new "spots" appear (usually 6 to 7 days). Examine household contacts for symptoms before sending to school during incubation period.
Regulations	*Case:* Exclude from school until 2 days after all lesions have crusted and there are no "weeping" vesicles.
	Contact: None.

COMMON COLD

The common cold is easily spread from one person to another. It may be caused by over 100 viruses. Everyone is susceptible to common colds. Complications may occur, and parents should be urged to keep children at home at the first sign of a cold. Many times symptoms of colds are early signs of other childhood illnesses.

What to look for	Common symptoms are runny nose, sneezing, general tired feeling. There is usually no fever unless complications have developed.
How disease is spread	By contact with a person who has a cold. The discharges from the nose and mouth are infectious, and the disease is spread by sneezing or coughing.
How to prevent	No immunizing agent. Avoid people who have colds if possible. Urge parents to keep children with colds at home.
Regulations	None.

DIARRHEAL DISEASES

Diarrhea and/or vomiting may occur as sporadic cases or in epidemics. They are caused by a number of different viruses and bacteria.

How disease is spread	The most common method is probably by person-to-person spread in cases of viruses and by improperly washed hands in case of bacteria. In rare instances, food contaminated with bacteria or virus by an infected person or faulty sanitation may result in food poisoning.
How to prevent	It is probably unlikely that all cases can be prevented with presently available methods. However, by educating children in good personal hygiene the spread of these illnesses can be kept to a minimum. Ill children may not feel well enough to attend school but exclusion is not mandatory.

DIPHTHERIA

Diphtheria is a dangerous disease both during the illness and because of complications. A child should be seen by a doctor immediately if symptoms suggestive of dipththeria occur. It is caused by a bacterium.

What to look for	It begins with a sore, inflamed throat; patches of a grayish membrane may be seen in the throat, and signs of fever will appear. The symptoms rapidly become more severe. A person may develop diphtheria within a few hours to 4 to 5 days after being exposed.
How disease is spread	By contact with a case or with a person who "carries" the germ in the throat but is not sick. The discharges from the nose and throat carry the germs.
How to prevent	All children should be immunized against diphtheria in first year of life. When cases occur in a community, school children should be given booster shots.
Regulations	*Case:* Exclude until released by health department or private doctor.
	Contacts: Household and other intimate contacts—same as case.

DOG BITES

If a child is bitten by a dog or other animal while at school, the parents must be notified. A child with an animal bite should have immediate medical treatment. The school is also responsible for notifying the health department of any dog bite. Most animal bites are provoked, and a person is not exposed to rabies unless the animal has rabies.

How to prevent

1. Immunize all dogs and cats.
2. Report all cases of animal bites to local health department.
3. If there is any delay in getting patient to a physician, wash wound with soap and rinse thoroughly.
4. Treatment as recommended by a physician after bite by rabid animal.
5. Any animal biting a person must be *confined* for a period of *10 days* from the date of the bite. Should the animal become ill or die during the observation period, the doctor should be promptly notified. Never destroy an animal that is being observed for rabies.

GERMAN MEASLES (RUBELLA)

German measles is a very contagious but very mild disease. It is caused by a virus. When a pregnant woman develops it during the first 3 months of her pregnancy, her child may be born with certain defects.

What to look for — It may begin with mild symptoms of a cold, but usually the first symptom is a rash. The rash is fine and faint and appears on the face and chest. Glands are usually swollen along the hairline in the back of the neck and below the ear. These symptoms occur between 8 and 21 days after exposure.

How disease is spread — By contact with a case. The droplets from the nose and throat are infectious, especially before the rash appears.

How to prevent — All children should receive rubella vaccine before school age. A child developing the disease should be kept home until the rash disappears, 2 or 3 days usually.

Regulations — *Case:* Exclude from school until symptoms are gone.
Contacts: None.

HEAD LICE (PEDICULOSIS)

Pediculosis means being infested with head lice. It is common in areas where people live under crowded conditions or where children are in close contact as in school.

What to look for — Itching is the main sign. One does not always see the lice; one sees the eggs that the louse lays on the hair—they look like tiny beads strung along the hair.

How disease is spread — By close contact with infested persons or by using their caps, scarves, or combs.

How to prevent — By the application of an effective insecticide promptly to the head of a case to prevent spread. Children should not be in school so long as they have lice. They can be in school if they are under treatment.

Regulations — None.

IMPETIGO

Impetigo is a contagious skin infection caused by bacteria. It spreads easily if neglected.

What to look for — The first sign of impetigo is the appearance of crusty sores, often around the nose and mouth. The sores start as a small blister that soon breaks open and forms a brownish crust.

How disease is spread	The discharge from the sores of impetigo is infectious. Articles used by person who has the infection (towels, washcloths, etc.) can also carry the germs.
How to prevent	No immunizing agent. When treated, impetigo clears up in 2 or 3 days.
Regulations	*Case:* Exclusion from school is not essential unless a physician suggests it. *Contacts:* None.

EPIDEMIC MENINGITIS

Epidemic meningitis, caused by a bacterium, is a medical emergency. If there is a case in school, parents should be notified so that they may contact their physician.

What to look for	This illness develops suddenly with high fever, intense headache, stiff neck, nausea, or vomiting.
How disease is spread	By direct contact with persons who have this disease. It is also spread through the nose and throat droplets of people who carry the disease but are not sick (carriers).
How to prevent	No specific preventive measure except chemoprophylaxis that may be prescribed by a physician.
Regulations	*Case:* Exclude from school until released by private physician or health department. *Contacts:* None.

MEASLES

Measles is a very contagious disease, especially in the first few days before the rash appears. This disease is dangerous for young children or children ill with some other condition. Complications can b severe. It is caused by a virus.

What to look for	This disease begins with cold symptoms; sneezing, inflamed eyes, a hard, dry cough. The fever is high, and a rash develops after several days of fever—blotchy, dusky red in color. Symptoms develop 7 to 14 days after exposure.
How disease is spread	By contact with a person who has it. Discharges from the nose and throat are infectious, especially early in the illness before symptoms appear.
How to prevent	By vaccination with live measles vaccine, preferably at 1 year of age. Children in the family of a case who have not had measles or vaccine should be observed closely for symptoms of illness during the second week after exposure.
Regulations	*Case:* Exclude from school for 4 days following appearance of rash. *Contacts:* None.

HEPATITIS A (FORMERLY INFECTIOUS HEPATITIS)

Hepatitis A is a disease caused by a virus that produces inflammation of the liver. Often occurs in epidemics in schools and among members of households of cases.

What to look for	Early signs of this disease are nausea, possibly vomiting, extreme fatigue, and often pain in the upper abdomen. Following these symptoms some cases develop jaundice—a yellow color in the skin and whites of the eyes. Many cases excrete dark (coffee-colored) urine and light (clay-colored) stools. Symptoms develop 15 to 50 days following exposure.
How disease is spread	By person-to-person contact. The virus causing hepatitis is found in the human bowel and spread by dirty hands to the mouth. It can be spread by water contaminated with human excretions.

How to prevent	Gamma globulin may be given to the members of the family of a case. This serum is too limited to give in mass programs. Careful handwashing, after using the toilet and before meals, will help control the spread.
Regulations	*Case:* Exclude from school for 1 week after onset of jaundice or until symptoms are gone. *Contacts:* None.

MUMPS

Mumps, caused by a virus, is highly contagious but so mild that one third of all cases are unrecognized. Mumps is usually not dangerous except in teenagers or adults.

What to look for	In a young child, the first sign is a swelling under the ear lobe. Symptoms appear 14 to 21 days after exposure, commonly 18 days.
How disease is spread	By contact with a person who has it. Droplets from the nose and mouth are infectious from 2 days before the swelling appears until the swelling has subsided.
How to prevent	A live attenuated virus is available and may be given in combination with measles and rubella vaccine at 15 months of age.
Regulations	*Case:* Exclude from school until the swelling is gone. *Contacts:* None.

PINK EYE (CONJUNCTIVITIS)

Conjunctivitis is not a single disease like mumps or measles. It is an eye infection and can be caused by a number of germs. Children under 5 years of age are most often infected.

What to look for	The whites of the eyes are reddened and drain matter. Sometimes the lids are swollen and stuck together. Usually develops 24 to 72 hours after exposure.
How disease is spread	By direct contact or contact with articles used by an infected person (towels, washcloths, and so on).
How to prevent	No immunizing agent. A child should not be in school during the acute stage.
Regulations.	None.

POLIOMYELITIS

Poliomyelitis, caused by a virus, like many other illnesses, causes headache and pain in the back. However, in polio, this pain is often followed by paralysis.

What to look for	Headache or stiffness of the neck or back. A child with these symptoms should see a doctor.
How disease is spread	This is not clearly understood. The virus is present in the throat secretions for about 1 week and 4 to 6 weeks in the stools of cases. No way is known to prevent the virus from spreading.
How to prevent	By immunization. Everyone should be immunized beginning at 6 weeks to 2 months of age. Schools should urge that all children be immunized before entry into school.
Regulations	*Case:* Exclude case from school until released by health department or physician. *Contacts:* None.

RINGWORM

Ringworm is a fungal skin infection that appears as a circular dry spot on the skin or as bald spots on the scalp that contain short, whiskery-like hairs.

What to look for	Dry, circular patches on the skin and bare spots on the scalp.
How disease is spread	By direct contact with children or animals who have it. By the use of caps, combs, towels of infected persons.
How to prevent	Cases must be under treatment, including wearing a cap if the ringworm is on the scalp. When ringworm is present in a family or in school, children should be examined frequently for signs so that treatment can be started early. Domestic animals affected with the fungus, both large and small, should be isolated and not handled until a cure has been effective.
Regulations	*Case:* None if case is under treatment and wears protective cap. *Contacts:* None.

SCABIES

In scabies, the skin is infested by a tiny burrowing itch mite.

What to look for	Evidence of scratching. The mite burrows under the skin between the fingers, bend of elbow, or wherever skin touches skin. The small lesions resemble pinholes occurring along a line.
How disease is spread	By direct contact with an infested person—handshaking, contact with clothing or articles used by such a person.
How to prevent	Cases must be treated. All infested members of the family of a case should be treated at the same time.
Regulations	*Case:* Exclude from school until symptoms are gone. *Contacts:* None.

SEXUALLY TRANSMITTED DISEASE

The two most common sexually transmitted diseases are syphilis, caused by a spirochete, and gonorrhea, caused by a bacterium. Both are spread by sexual contact.

Syphilis (clinical stages)	1. Primary stage is manifested by a sore of varying size occurring on skin or mucous membranes approximately 10 days to 10 weeks following exposure. Persons are capable of spreading the disease at this stage. Occasionally, persons have syphilis without being aware of the sore. 2. The secondary stage is manifested by generalized rash within a month or two after primary syphilis if it has not been adequately treated or has gone unnoticed. Persons are infective at this time. 3. The late stages, noninfectious, result in severe damage to heart, blood vessels, brain, and spinal cord. *Treatment:* A person with any possibility of having syphilis or having been exposed should consult a physician.
Gonorrhea	1. In males, it causes a purulent urethral discharge often manifested by burning urination 2 to 9 days after exposure. 2. In females, it causes a discharge from urethra or vagina or may cause infection in the fallopian tubes or ovaries, producing fever and abdominal pain. *Treatment:* A physician should be consulted if any of these symptoms occur or exposure to possible infected person is known.

STREPTOCOCCAL INFECTIONS (INCLUDING SCARLET FEVER)

The streptococci are bacteria. Slight attacks of strep throat are just as contagious as severe ones. Scarlet fever and strep throat are the same disease except for the rash. Children should not be in school with a sore throat and should be treated.

What to look for	Strep infections begin suddenly. Headache, fever, sore throat are common. The glands of the neck are swollen. Scarlet fever rash may appear within 24 hours—fine, granular to the touch. Symptoms develop 1 to 5 days after exposure.
How disease is spread	By contact with case or carrier. Discharges from the nose and throat are infectious. Strep infections often spread through the mild, unrecognized case.
How to prevent	Children should not be in school with a sore throat. A physician should be consulted concerning evaluation and treatment of a child with sore throat and to consider treatment of other family members in order to limit spread.
Regulations	*Case:* Exclude from school 48 hours or until symptoms are gone if under treatment. If not under treatment exclude until symptoms are gone—not less than 7 days. *Contacts:* None.

TUBERCULOSIS

Tuberculosis is usually a long-term disease and usually is a disease of the lungs. It is caused by a bacterium. It may involve bones or other organs. Primary tuberculosis, which is the kind most often found in children, usually shows no symptoms and is not infectious. When a child is found to have tuberculosis, it is rare that it is in a stage where the child could expose other children.

What to look for	There is no way to observe children for tuberculosis. Once in a while a child will show a low fever and be tired and listless because of tuberculosis, but these symptoms may be caused by many things. Such a child should be examined by a physician, though not because the child may be a threat to others.
How disease is spread	For all practical purposes, tuberculosis is an air-borne disease spread by inhalation of droplets resulting from coughing, sneezing, or talking by persons with active tuberculosis. Children become infected by exposure to an active case, most often a parent, grandparent, or teacher.
How to prevent	There is no practical immunization. The best prevention is through locating infectious cases, usually adults, and keeping these away from others until treatment with specific antibodies makes them noninfectious. Persons with positive skin test, especially a child, may be advised by a physician to take antituberculous medication. Of special value in preventing TB are skin testing programs. A child with a positive skin test has TB germs in the body and may point the way to an active case and should be seen by a physician for evaluation as to whether specific antituberculous medication is indicated. General good health habits, adequate rest, good nutrition, and medical care for illness are important.
Regulations	*Case:* Doctor determines whether child may attend school. When a child is kept out of school because of tuberculosis, it is usually not because of danger to others. *Contacts:* None. May attend school. NOTE: A positive tuberculosis skin test alone does not indicate that a child is infectious. It does indicate that the child has been infected, at some time in his life, with tubercle bacilli and should be examined at regular 1- to 2-year intervals for evidence of active tuberculosis. If it is a young child, the family should be checked to see if there is an active case.

WHOOPING COUGH (PERTUSSIS)

Whooping cough is most dangerous in infancy. It is especially infectious during the first or second week, before the whoop occurs. Complications can be severe. It is caused by bacteria.

What to look for	Usually not possible to recognize until characteristic whoop appears. Cough is only constant symptom and may be caused by many diseases other than whooping cough. Symptoms appear 5 to 21 days following exposure.
How disease is spread	By contact with a case. Discharges of the nose and throat probably most infectious before whoop appears.
How to prevent	By immunization with whooping cough vaccine. Since these shots are not recommended after 5 years of age, all children should be immunized for pertussis (as well as diphtheria and tetanus toxoid) in first year of life.
Regulations	*Case:* Exclude from school 4 weeks after the onset of illness or until the cough has stopped, whichever period is shorter. *Contacts:* None.

B

Immunization requirements
for school enrollment
1975-1976

Immunizations required for specific diseases*

	Smallpox	Tetanus	Diphtheria	Whooping cough	Polio	Measles	German measles	Mumps	Tuberculin test	Other
Alabama	†	X	X	X	X	X	X		X	
Alaska		X	X	X	X	X	X		X	
Arizona		†	†	†	†	†	†		†	
Arkansas		X	X	X	X	X	X			
California		X	X	X	X	X	X	X		
Colorado		X	X	X	X	X	X			
Connecticut	‡	X	X	X	§	§	X			
Delaware				X	X	X	X			
Florida		X	X		X	X	X			
Georgia		X	X	X	X	X	X			
Hawaii			X		X	X	X		X	
Idaho										
Illinois			X	X	X	X	X	X		
Indiana‖										
Iowa										
Kansas		X	X	X	X	X	X		X	
Kentucky		X	X	X	X	X			X	
Louisiana			X	X	X	X	X			
Maine										
Maryland		X	X	X	X	X	X			
Massachusetts		X	X	X	X	X				
Michigan		X	X	X	X	X			X	
Minnesota						X	X			
Mississippi	†	†	†	†	†	†	†	†	†	
Missouri			X		X	X	X			

*Adapted from Garcia, E.M.: Immunization requirements for school enrollment by states, 1975-76, unpublished report, Las Cruces, N.M., 1976, New Mexico State University.
†Optional.
‡Varies within the system and/or states.
§May require.

Continued.

423

Immunizations required for specific diseases—cont'd

	Smallpox	Tetanus	Diphtheria	Whooping cough	Polio	Measles	German measles	Mumps	Tuberculin test	Other
Montana§		X	X	X	X	X	X			
Nebraska										
Nevada			X	X	X	X	X			¶
New Hampshire		X	X	X	X	X	X	†	X	
New Jersey	X		X		X	X			X	
New Mexico										
New York			X		X	X	X			
North Carolina	X	X	X	X	X	X				
North Dakota		X	X	X	X	X	X	X		
Ohio	X	X	X	X	X	X	X			
Oklahoma		X	X	X	X	X	X		X	
Oregon				X	X	X				
Pennsylvania		X	X		X	X	X		‖	
Rhode Island		X	X		X	X	X			
South Carolina		X	X	X	X		X			
South Dakota		X	X	X	X	X	X		X	
Tennessee		X	X	X	X	X	X		X	
Texas		X	X		X	X	X			
Utah			X	X	X	X	X			
Vermont										
Virginia		X	X	X	X	X	X			
Washington		X	X		X	X	X			
West Virginia		X	X	X	X	X	X		X	
Wisconsin		X	X	X	X	X	X			
Wyoming		‡								

†Optional.
‡Varies within the system and/or states.
§May require.
‖Not required for admission, but on original entry.
¶D.T. boosters.

C

Education for health in the school community setting

A POSITION PAPER*

The school is a community in which most individuals spend at least 12 years of their lives, and more if they have the advantages of early childhood programs, college education, and continuing education for adults. The health of our school-age youth will determine to a great extent the quality of life each will have during the growing and developing years and on throughout the life cycle. Their capacity to function as health-educated adults will in turn help each to realize the fullest potential for self, family, and the various communities of which each individual will be a part.

The American Public Health Association believes that health education should be a continuing process, from conception to death, and that such education must be comprehensive, coordinated, and integrated in all community planning for health.

The school, as a social structure, provides an

educational setting in which the total health of the child during the impressionable years is of priority concern. No other community setting even approximates the magnitude of the grades K to 12 school educational enterprise, with an enrollment in 1973-1974 of 45.5 million in nearly 17,000 school districts comprising more than 115,000 schools with some 2.1 million teachers. This is to say nothing of the administrative, supervisory, and service manpower required to maintain these institutions. In addition, more than 40% of children aged 3 to 5 are enrolled in early childhood education programs. Thus it seems that the school should be regarded as a social unit providing a focal point to which health planning for all other community settings should relate.

Schools provide an environment conducive to developing skills and competencies that will help the individual confront and examine a complexity of social and cultural forces, persuasive influences, and ever-expanding options as these affect health behavior. Today's health problems do not lend themselves to yesterday's solutions. Specificity of cause is multiple rather than singular. The individual must assume in-

---

*Adapted from Governing Council of the American Public Health Association: Education for health in the school community setting; a position paper, New Orleans, Oct. 23, 1974, The Council. A "position paper" is defined as a major exposition of the Association's viewpoint on broad issues affecting the public's health.

creasing responsibility for solutions to major public health problems and consequently must be educated to do so.

Education for and about health is not synonymous with information. Education is concerned with behavior—a composite of what an individual knows, senses, and values, and of what one does and practices. Factual data are but temporary assumptions to be used and cast aside as new information emerges. Health facts unrenewed can become a liability rather than an asset. The health-educated citizen is one who possesses resources and abilities that will last throughout a lifetime, such as critical thinking, problem-solving, valuing, self-discipline, and self-direction, and that lead to a sense of responsibility for community and world concerns.

The school curriculum offers an opportunity to view health issues in an integrated context. It is designed to help the learner gain insights about the personal, social, environmental, political, and cultural implications of each issue. Planning for health care delivery, for example, is not simply a matter of providing for manpower, services, and facilities. These things must be considered in concert with housing, employment, transportation, cultural beliefs and values, and the rights and dignity of the persons involved. Nor will nutritional practices be improved substantially by programs based on groupings, labeling, or issuing stamps, because food practices and eating patterns are equally influenced by how, when, where, why, and with whom one eats.

APHA is concerned about the traditional crisis approach to health care. The expense involved in treatment, rehabilitation, recuperation, and restoration to health has sent medical costs soaring. More facilities, services, and manpower to staff the facilities and to provide the services appear to be the nation's leading priorities. The alternative is a redirection of the nation's health goals toward a primary preventive—and constructive—approach to health, through education for every individual.

Because of vested interests, political pressures, mass media sensationalism, and health agency structures with categorical interests, health education programs in schools are compelled to deal with a multitude of separate health issues, with only a few of these given priority at any given time. Too frequently, programs developed to deal with crucial issues are eliminated although the problems remain, because another crisis emerges calling for more new crash programs. A revolving critical issue syndrome has been the result, with the same problems considered crucial a decade or more ago emerging once again. Focusing on selected categorical issues has potential value if time, energy, personnel, and money are available to sustain the emphasis and expand such efforts into an integrated and viable health education framework. A broad concept of healthful living that has consideration for psychosocial dimensions should be the basis for health education.

APHA is encouraged by recent developments in an increasing number of states that attest to recognition of the significance of a comprehensive health education program in grades K to 12. Also encouraging are the exemplary programs being established in many school districts and the expressed intention of the federal government to implement an action plan for "better health through education."

Therefore the American Public Health Association supports the concept of a national commitment to a comprehensive, sequential program of health education for all students in the nation's schools, kindergarten through the twelfth grade. The Association will exert leadership through its sections and affiliates to assure the following for health education:

1. Time in the curriculum commensurate with other subject areas.
2. Professionally qualified teachers and supervisors of health eduation.
3. Innovative instructional materials and appropriate teaching facilities.
4. Increased financial support at the local, state, and national levels to upgrade the quantity and quality of health education.
5. A teaching/learning environment in which opportunities for safe and optimal living exist, and one in which a well-organized and complete health service is functioning.

D

Sources of selected elementary health education programs available in schools*

Actions for Health
Charles E. Lewis, M.D.
Professor of Medicine
Department of Medicine
School of Medicine
University of California
Los Angeles, CA 90024
(213) 825-6709

APPLE (All-inclusive Planning Program for Longevity Education)
Dr. Ken Gunter
Project Director
Pickens County Board of Education
Carrollton, AL 35447
(205) 367-8102

Assisting Adolescents in Personal Decision Making through Health Education
Milton Schmidt
Director, Instructional Services
Cherry Creek School District #5
Holly Ridge Center
3301 South Monaco Boulevard
Denver, CO 80222
(303) 757-6201

Beaver Dam School Health Education
Dick Fitzpatrick
Director of HPE & Athletics
500 Bould Street
Beaver Dam, WI 53916
(414) 885-9241

Beverly Public Schools Health Education Curriculum
Thomas J. Durkin, Ed.D.
Health Resource Specialist
Beverly Public Schools
186 Cabot Street
Beverly, MA 10915
(617) 927-5651

Blast Off to Health
Judith Miller
Project Director
Hibbing Senior High School
Hibbing, MN 55746
(218) 263-4850

Brockton School Health Education Program
Vincent Ricardi
Coordinator, Health Education and Services
Brockton Public Schools
43 Crescent Street
Brockton, MA 02401
(617) 580-7575

---

*Adapted from U.S. Department of Health and Human Services, Centers for Disease Control, Center for Health Promotion and Education: A compendium of health education programs available for use in schools, Atlanta, 1982.

Buncome County/Asheville City Schools Health Education Program
Doug Jones
Health Education Coordinator
Buncome County Schools/Ashville City Schools
391 Hendersonville Road
Asheville, ND 28803
(704) 274-9317

Caspar Alcohol Education Program
Lena DiCicco
Director
Caspar Alcohol Education
226 Highland Avenue
Somerville, MA 02143
(617) 623-2080

Chicago Heart Health Curriculum Program
Albert Sunseri, Ph.D.
Co-Investigator, Chicago Heart Health
    Curriculum Program
Chicago Heart Association
20 North Wacker Drive
Chicago, IL 60606
(312) 346-4675

Claremont School District Health Education Program
Judith Maculiewicz
Supervisory Union #6
Claremont, NH 03743

Cleveland County School Health Education Program
James H. Hines, Jr.
Health Education Coordinator
Cleveland County Schools
130 South Post Road
Shelby, NC 28150
(704) 487-8581

Comprehensive Health Instruction
Harry B. Kiefer
Project Director
207 East Fifth Street
Fulton, MO 65251
(314) 642-8733

Conceptual Approach to Functional Health Education
Robert Turnage
Coordinator of Health, Safety, and Physical
    Education
Meridian Public Schools
P.O. Box 31
Meridian, MS 39301
(601) 483-6271

DARTE: Drug Abuse Reduction through Education
Kenneth Kaminsky
Director, DARTE
33500 Van Borm Road
Wayne MI 48184
(313) 326-9300

Durango Health Education Program
Mary Ruth Bowman, RN, BS
School Nurse/Health Education Coordinator
Durango High School
Box 181
Durango, CO 81301
(303) 247-3827

An Early Start to Good Health
Jerry Maburn
American Cancer Society
777 Third Avenue
New York, NY 10017
(212) 371-2900

Epilepsy School Alert
Ann Scherer
Director, Public Information & Education
Epilepsy Foundation of America
4351 Garden City Drive
Landover, MD 20785
(301) 638-5229

The Eyes Have it
Lydia Maguire
Director of Public Relations
National Society to Prevent Blindness
79 Madison Avenue
New York, NY 10016
(212) 684-3505

**Fairbanks North Star Borough School
District Health Curriculum**
William T. Schecter
Fire Chief
University of Alaska Fire Department
Fairbanks, AK 99701
(907) 479-7069

**Family Life Sex Education Comprehensive
Curriculum Guide**
Sara Traphagen
Planned Parenthood Association of
Humboldt County
2316 Harrison Ave
Eureka, CA 95501
(707) 442-2961

Food: Your Choice
Richard J. Walther, M.P.H.
Program Consultant
National Dairy Council
6300 North River Road
Rosemont, IL 60018
(312) 696-1020

Getting to Know Me
Rick Kearns
Consultant, Health Education
State Department of Education
Len B. Jordan Building
Boise, ID 83720
(208) 384-2281

**Hazelwood School District Comprehensive
School Health Education Program**
Roy Tanner
Physical Education, Health, & Safety Consultant
Hazelwood School District
15955 New Halls Ferry Road
Florissant, MO 63031
(314) 921-4450

Health Activities Project
Dr. Robert C. Knott
Co-Director, HAP
Lawrence Hall of Science
University of California
Berkeley, CA 94720
(415) 642-3579

Health & Family Life Education Program
George C. Chamis, Ph.D.
Coordinator, Health & Family Life Education
Flint Community Schools
806 West 6th Avenue
Flint, MI 48503
(313) 762-1377

Health Course of Study
Richard J. Webster
Consultant of Health & PE
Rochester Public Schools
Coffman Building
Rochester, MN 55901
(507) 285-8558

**Health Education Curriculum United Way
Health Foundation**
Margaret Kirkpatrick
Director, United Way Health Foundation
618 Second Street, N.W.
Canton, OH 44703
(216) 455-0378

**Health Skills for Life: Health Education
Project (H.E.P.)**
James A. Terhune
Health Education Project
Eugene 4-J School District
200 N. Monroe
Eugene, OR 97402
(503) 687-3561

**"Here's Looking at You Two" Alcohol Education
Project**
Clay Roberts
9131 California Ave. S.W.
Seattle, WA 98136
(206) 932-8409

I Do Declare: I Am Aware
Horace W. Moore
Director, Youth Services
American Red Cross
17th and D Streets, N.W.
Washington, DC 20006
(202) 857-3604

Inside-Out
Bob Fox
Associate Executive Director
Agency for Instructional Television
Box A
Bloomington, IN 47402
(812) 339-2203

Jamestown Elementary Nutrition Curriculum
Kathryn Richards
Project Director
PO Box 269
Jamestown, ND 58401

**Jefferson County Schools Human Sexuality
  Strand of Health Education Program**
Don Shaw
Coordinator of Health
Jefferson County Schools
1209 Quail
Lakewood, CO 80215
(303) 231-2387

Keene Elementary Health Guide
Jane Steiner
Health Coordinator
34 West Street
Keene, NH 03431
(603) 352-1911

Know Your Body
Betty Jean Carter
Director, Child Health Education
American Health Foundation
320 East 43rd Street
New York, NY 10017
(212) 953-1900

Kokomo Health Crisis Education Project
Bill Keaffaber
Project Coordinator
Health Crisis Education Project
100 West Lincoln Road
Kokomo, IN 46901
(317) 453-5400

Learn Not to Burn
National Fire Protection Association
Batterymarch Park
Quincy, MA 02269

Lincoln School Health Education Program
Dean A. Austin
Consultant for H & PE
Lincoln Public Schools
P.O. Box 82889
Lincoln, NE 68501
(402) 473-0263

Long Beach Health Education Program
Sandra French
Consultant, Long Beach United School District
710 Locust Avenue
Long Beach, CA 90813
(213) 436-9931

The Magic of Sight
Lydia Maguire
National Society to Prevent Blindness
79 Madison Avenue
New York, NY
(212) 684-3505

Marshalltown School Health Education Program
Opal Fagle, R.N.
Director, Health Services and Health Education
Marshalltown Community School District
317 Columbus Drive
Marshalltown, IA 50518
(515) 752-6767

Me/Me Drug Prevention Education Program
Artie Kearney, Ph.D.
Me/Me Incorporated
400 South Linwood Avenue
Appleton, WI 54911
(414) 735-0114

Multidisciplinary Health Education Project
Annette Jacobson
Consultant Grants Pass School District
223 S,E, "M" Street
Grants Pass, OR 97526
(501) 479-2628

**My Body is Mine, My Emotions are Mine, My
  Environment is Mine/All These are my
  Responsibility to Understand and Care for**
Ginger Roessl
Nurse
904 Talbot Avenue
Albany, CA 94705
(415) 526-6441

**North Clackamas School District Health
  Education Program**
Megan Walth
Curriculum Coordinator
North Clackamas School District #12
2302 S.E. Willard Street
Milwaukie, OR 97222
(503) 653-3828

**Nutrition Density Nutrition Education
  Curriculum**
Douglas B. Wood
Utah State University Foundation
UMC 93
Logan, UT 84322
(801) 750-2603

Nutrition Education Systems: Big Ideas
Marguerite Stetson
Nutrition Specialist, Cooperative Extension
  Service
University of Alaska
Fairbanks, AK 99701
(907) 479-7254

Ocean Township Health Education
John Nacarlo
Health Instructor
Ocean Township School
Dow Avenue
Ocean, NJ 07755
(201) 531-6600, ext. 350

Ombudsman: A Classroom Community
Bob Gidurz
Dissemination Coordinator
Charlotte Drug Education
1416 E. Morehead Street
Charlotte, NC 28204
(704) 374-3211

An Option to See
Lydia Maguire
Director of Public Relations
National Society to Prevent Blindness
79 Madison Avenue
New York, NY 10016
(212) 684-3505

**Peabody Comprehensive Health/Science
  Curriculum**
Edgar N. Johnson, Ed.D.
Educational Director of Health
School Department
210 Washington Street
Peabody, MA 10960
(617) 531-1600, ext. 129

Primary Grades Health Curriculum Project
Roger Schmidt
American Lung Association
1740 Broadway
New York, NY 10019
(212) 245-8000

Project HEED
Carol Skerry Ashford
Health Coordinator
Project HEED
Cabarrus County Schools
PO Box 388
Concord, NC 28025
(704) 786-6191

Project Prevention
Howard Gonser
Project Director
Chenowith School District No. 9
3632 West 10th Street
The Dalles, OR 97058
(214) 750-6363

Putting Your Heart into the Curriculum
Arleta Estes
American Heart Association
7320 Greenville
Dallas, TX 75231
(214) 750-6363

Racine School Health Education Project
Grace C. Piskula
Director, Health/Safety/Physical Education
Racine Unified Schools
2220 Northwestern Avenue
Racine, WI 53404
(414) 631-7071

Ridgewood Health Education Program
David B. Marsh
Director of Health & Physical Ed
Ridgewood Public Schools
49 Cottage Place
Ridgewood, NY 07451
(201) 444-9600

RIPPLES
Bob Fox
Associate Executive Director
Agency for Instructional Television
Box A
Bloomington, IN 47402
(812) 339-2203

School Health Awareness Project
Donna Davis, M.P.H.
Project Coordinator
Cumberland County Health Department
790 E. Commerce Street
Bridgeton, NJ 08302
(609) 451-8000, ext. 371

School Health Curriculum Project
Roy L. Davis
Center for Health Promotion & Education
Centers for Disease Control
Atlanta, GA 30333
(404) 329-3115

The School Health Education Program
Dr. Valorie E. Nybo
Director, School Health Education Program
Maine Lung Association
128 Seall Street
Augusta, ME 04330
(207) 622-6394

Seekonk School Health Education Program
Robert Frazer
Supervisor of Health Education
Seekonk High School
Seekonk, MA 02771
(617) 336-7273

Self-Incorporated
Bob Fox
Agency for Instructional Television
Box A
Bloomington, IN 47402
(812) 339-2203

Seymour Safely Vision Education Program
Reynold W. Malmer, APR
Director, Communications Division
American Optometric Association
243 North Lindbergh Boulevard
St. Louis, MO 63141
(314) 991-4100

Skills for Living
Mary Bronson Merki
Instructional Facilitator—Health
Dallas Independent School District
3700 Ross Avenue, Box 152
Dallas, TX 75204
(214) 838-1450

The Sunflower Project
Donna Osness, Ed.D.
Director of Health Education & Health Services
Mohawk Instructional Center
6649 Lamar
Shawnee Mission, KS 66202
(913) 384-6800, ext. 226

Super Heart: A Heart Disease Intervention Program for Young Children
Lucy Strobel
Director, Project Super Heart
Institute for Experimentation in Teacher Education
SUNY—College at Cortland
Cortland, NY 13045
(607) 753-4705

Syosset Health Education/Family Life Education and Human Sexuality
Wilson Gerhart
Asst. Supt. for Elementary Education
Syosset Central Schools
Pell Avenue
Syosset, NY 11791
(516) 921-5500, ext. 204

3R'S and HBP
Sandra Owen
School Program Coordinator
American Heart Association, Georgia Affiliate
Box 13589
Atlanta, GA 30324
(404) 261-2260

E

A sample of health education fiction and nonfiction books

Annotations of the library books contained in this list are taken from a variety of sources; however, the main source was *The Elementary School Library Collection, 13th edition.* * These titles are related to specific areas that could be included in an elementary school health education program. This list is meant to be illustrative, not exhaustive.

The list has been organized by topic areas, with books listed alphabetically by authors. Approximations of reading levels are included by the following code: P, Primary; I, intermediate; and U, upper.

---

*Winkel, L., and others, editors: The elementary school library collection, a guide to books and other media, ed. 13, Williamsport, Pa., 1981, Bro-Dart Foundation.

AGING

BUCKLEY, HELEN E., Grandmother and I, Lothrop, Lee & Shepard, 1961. (P)

A little girl explains that there are times when grandmother's lap is better than that of anyone else. Fiction.

BUCKLEY, HELEN E., Grandfather and I, Lothrop, Lee & Shepard, 1959. (P)

Grandfather is never in a hurry, and a small boy enjoys walking, stopping, and looking when they go out together. Fiction.

BORACK, BARBARA, Grandpa, Harper & Row, 1967. (P)

Marilyn tells of a wonderful visit with her grandparents. She and grandpa have great fun doing little special things. Every morning grandpa hides, but Marilyn finds him, "because he hides in the same place every time." Fiction.

GAUCH, PATRICIA, Grandpa and Me, Coward, 1972. (I)

Beautifully illustrated portrayal of grandfather and grandson in a vacation setting. Older man is strong, active, and caring. Fiction.

GOFFSTEIN, M.B., Fish for Supper, Dial, 1976. (P)

Independent older woman catches, cleans, and cooks her own fish in this simple, well-illustrated book for very young children. Fiction.

HEIN, LUCILLE, My Very Special Friend, Judson, 1974. (I-U)

Sensitive relationship between a young girl and her elderly, yet active and creative, great-grandmother. Fiction.

KIRK, BARBARA, Grandpa, Me and Our House in the Tree, Macmillan, 1978. (I)

After there is a debilitating illness, grandfather and grandson must restructure their formerly physically active relationship. Sensitive portrayal of the needs of both. Fiction.

LASKY, KATHRYN, I Have Four Names for My Grandfather, Little, Brown & Co., (P)

Grandfather and grandson are photographed in both active and passive situations. Especially good presentation of communication across generations. Nonfiction.

MATHIS, SHARON BELL, Hundred Penny Box, Viking, 1975 (Newberry Honor Book). (I)

When Michael's 100-year-old, Great-Great-Aunt Dew comes to live with them, she brings along an old, beat-up box, with as many pennies as her age in it. He loves to hear the tales she tells about the year she got each penny, while he counts out the pennies. A warm story of the love between old age and youth. Fiction.

MATHIS, SHARON BELL, Hundred Penny Box (phonodisc), Newberry Award Records/Random House School Division, 1977, 2s 12-inch, 33 rpm. Also available as cassette. Includes teacher's guide. (I)

Adapted from the Newberry Honor Book of the same title, this rendition is set against a background of song and provides an extra dimension of real interest for the book. Guide provides discussion on "Aging in the United States" and other data helpful for the teacher. Fiction.

MAXER, NORMA FOX, Figure of Speech, Delacorte, 1973. (I)

Thirteen-year-old Jenny has always found it difficult to relate to anyone in her family except Grandpa. But her parents refer to the 83-year-old man as "failing," and she overhears them say that "everyone passes away," and "his time is coming." That night they find that Grandpa has pinned a note to the bulletin board saying, "I ain't going to pass away. I'm goin' to die. My time ain't going to come. I'll be dead." Jenny and Grandpa share together his attempt to salvage the last shreds of his dignity in a touching and also realistic tale. Fiction.

SKORPEN, LIESEL, Mandy's Grandmother, Dial, 1975. (P)

Unconventional Mandy meets conventional grandmother. Each comes to appreciate the other, and they develop a warm and loving relationship. Fiction.

WHITMAN, SALLY, A Special Trade, Harper & Row, 1978. (I-U)

At first an elderly man and a young girl are presented with the man as the initiator—caring, helping, teaching. After there is a serious illness, roles change, but the relationship remains strong and mutual. Fiction.

WILLIAMS, BARBARA, Kevin's Grandma, Dutton, 1975. (P)

Two boys compare grandmothers. One is conventional, yet interesting and self-sufficient. The other is outrageous, delightfully eccentric, and not quite believable. Fiction.

ALCOHOL

FORRAI, MARIA S., Look at Alcoholism, Larner, 1977 (Larner Awareness series). (I-U)

The graphic photographs clearly depict the problems of alcohol abuse to any student regardless of reading level. The accompanying minimal text will encourage classroom discussion. Nonfiction.

MAZER, HARRY, War on Villa Street, Delacorte, 1978. (I-U)

Willis Pierce is an eighth-grade boy with an alcoholic father and an overworked mother. A lonely and unhappy boy, repeated threats and beatings by a bully and his gang only increase his frustration. But Willis, while sensitive, is not a quitter. Tutoring a sixteen-year-old retarded boy in athletic skills while daring to compete in track himself, he gains in confidence. This memorable portrait of adolescence is very popular with young readers. Fiction.

NEVEILLE, EMILY CHENEY, Garden of Broken Glass, Delacorte, 1975. (I-U)

Brian, his sister, and their mother who drinks to the point of alcoholism; fat Martha, Dwayne, and his parents who force him to keep a straight and narrow path . . . these are the friends whose life in a black ghetto is described by a Newberry Prize Winner with perception and understanding. Fiction.

SEIXAS, JUDITH S., Alcohol—What It Is, What It Does, Greenwillow, 1977 (Greenwillow read-along books). (I)

Through bright cartoon illustrations, facts about alcohol; what it is, where it can be found, and its effects on the mind and body are introduced. Straightforward information with no sermonizing in an easy-to-read format. Nonfiction.

SEIXAS, JUDITH S., Living With a Parent Who Drinks too Much, Greenwillow, 1979. (I-U)

Explains what it is like to live with a parent who drinks too much by describing alcoholism, behavior of alcoholics, and problems the family faces. Suggests ways to cope with medical emergencies for the alcoholic and counseling help for the child. Nonfiction.

SILVERSTEIN, ALVIN, and SILVERSTEIN, VIRGINIA B., Alcoholism, Lippincott, 1975. (U)

After learning the medical and historical facts about drinking, the authors hope readers will be able to make an intelligent decision about drinking. In a clear, concise text these reknowned authors discuss all major aspects of alcohol use and abuse, causes and treament of alcoholism, teenage drinking, and living with an alcoholic parent. Nonfiction.

TOLZ, MARY, Edge of Next Year, Harper & Row, 1974. (I)

A previously happy family is broken up when the mother is killed in an automobile accident. Thirteen-year-old Orin has to take responsibility for running the house and watching over Victor after school is out. Victor loses himself in building a vivarium in the attic, while the father takes to drink. Within less than a year, the family faces catastrophe. The complex feelings of a boy who has to face severe loss are subtly explored by a skilled writer in this story of death and alcoholism. Fiction.

ANATOMY AND PHYSIOLOGY

ALLISON, LINDA, Blood and Guts; a Working Guide to Your Own Insides, Little, Brown & Co., 1976. (I)

A refreshing and fun look at the parts of the human body. They are all described in text and stories, and there are experiments and projects explained to discover how our parts function. Many humorous cartoons illustrate the experiments and descriptions. A real up-tempo book that will appeal to many students. Nonfiction.

BRANDRETH, BYLES, This Is Your Body, Sterling, 1979. (U)

Approaches the study of structure and function of the body in an entertaining, yet accurate, manner. The 26 chapters are alphabetically arranged, offering one or more projects to be completed by an individual. Can be used by single student or as support material in health or anatomy class. Nonfiction.

BRENNER, BARBARA, Bodies, Dutton, 1973. (P)

Everyone has a body and here in vital, vibrant photos showing bodies of many shapes and sizes you can see how one works and what it can do. Nonfiction.

CURTIS, DR. ROBERT H., Medical Talk for Beginners, Messner, 1976. (U)

When new vocabulary pops up, steer older readers to this book. It is an attractively designed dictionary of medical terms from abdomen to x-ray. Nonfiction.

GLEMAN, RIATA GOLDEN, and BUXBAUM, SUSAN KOVACS, Ouch! All About Cuts and Hurts, Harcourt, 1977. (P-I)

The volume is organized alphabetically and is a simple introduction to what happens to the body when common injuries occur, such as black-and-blue marks, bumps, cuts, nosebleeds, stitches, and scars, and how the body reacts to repair such damage. Nonfiction

GOLDSMITH, ILSE, Anatomy for Children, Sterling, 1964. (I)

Explains the structure and function of cells, limbs, and organs of the human body, and the complex systems of respiration, circulation, digestion, glands, nerves, and reproduction. An interesting feature is the summary of facts at each chapter's end. Nonfiction.

GROSS, RUTH BELOV, Book About Your Skeleton, Hastings House. In Canada, Sounders of Toronto, 1979 (A Science starter book). (P)

This lucid explanation of the bone structure of the body includes the various functions of bones and the skeleton. Two complete skeletons are shown at the end, labeled with common and scientific names. Nonfiction.

KAUFMAN, JOE, How We Are Born, How We Grow, How Our Bodies Work . . . and How We Learn, Webster, 1975. (I-U)

Contains a treasure lode of information for children of all ages. An attractive, oversized volume designed to give girls and boys a true understanding of their bodies, it answers many questions children might pose. For example: What makes you yawn when you are sleepy? Where do tears come from? Why does your body shiver when you are cold? Colorful illustrations help illuminate human processes such as birth, sight, digestion, dreaming, learning, and memory. Younger students will glean a great deal just by thumbing through the pages; older students can use the text for reference. Nonfiction.

KLEIN, AARON E., You and Your Body; a Book of Experiments to Perform on Yourself, Doubleday, 1977. (I)

A different approach to the study of human physiology through a series of quick and easy experiments that do not require any complicated equipment. The directions are clear and concise, and the experiments can be performed by individuals, small groups, or an entire class. Nonfiction.

McGUIRE, LESLIE, Susan Perl's Human Body Book, Platt & Munk, 1977. (A Cricket book). (P-I)

Simple, direct answers for a multiplicity of questions about the human body, such as What holds the body up? and What happens to food after it is eaten? are complimented by delightful, whimsical pictures. A different book to share with younger children. Nonfiction.

SHOWERS, PAUL, A Drop of Blood, Crowell, 1967. (P)

Explains what blood is, how it works for our bodies, and why it is important to us. Nonfiction.

SHOWERS, PAUL, Your Skin and Mine, Crowell, 1967. (P)

This book encourages readers to make and examine fingerprints. It is also available in Spanish, as Tu Piel y la Mia. Nonfiction.

SILVERSTEIN, ALVIN, and SILVERSTEIN, VIRGINIA B., Skeletal System; Frameworks for Life, Prentice-Hall, 1972. (U)

Analyzes the structure and function of the human skeletal system and compares it with that of other animals. Excellent and informative text includes terminology and definitions for intermediate readers. Can be used for classroom projects, individual study, enjoyable reading by those who wish to know more about the human body. Nonfiction.

THOMPSON, STEPHANIE, Know Your Human Body, Rand McNally, 1977. (I-U)

Each chapter consists of only two pages but explains in detail every aspect of the human body, using large, clear diagrams. A quiz with the answers and a page of suggested projects are also included. Nonfiction.

TULLY, MARIANE, Facts About the Human Body, Watts, 1977. (I-U)

Unusual information is offered in this question-and-answer book about various parts of the human body. Authors have used actual questions from students and have responded with direct answers. Unfamiliar words printed in boldface type are all found in the glossary in the back of the book. Nonfiction.

DEATH

CARRICK, CAROL, Accident, Clarion, 1976. (P-I)

Christopher and his dog Badger walk along the road to meet his father and mother, but when a truck comes along, Badger starts to cross the road and is killed. Christopher is grief stricken, and it is only when he and his father search for a stone marker for Badger's grave that he can express his grief. Fiction.

MANN, PEGGY, There Are Two Kinds of Terrible, Doubleday, 1977. (P)

Robbie breaks his arm on the last day of school and has to spend summer with a big cast on it. He thinks that is terrible, but then he discovers that there are two kinds of terrible—regular terrible that can happen to anyone and you can get over—and real terrible that has no end. . . . A story of the death of a loved one written with great insight and emotion. Fiction.

DENTAL HEALTH

DE GROAT, DIANE, Alligator's Toothache, Crown, 1977. (P)

Alligator's predicament—a toothache and fear of the dentist—is eventually resolved through trickery and is eloquently portrayed through the three-color pen-and-ink drawings in this wordless book. Fiction.

DOSS, HELEN, All the Better to Bite With, Messner, 1976. (I)

Here is a guided tour of our teeth and mouth, introduced by a discussion of different animal teeth. Parts of the mouth and teeth, causes and prevention of tooth and gum disease, dentist office procedures, and intelligent choice of foods are all discussed in a clear text accompanied by black and white photographs and diagrams. Nonfiction.

HAMMOND, WINIFRED G., Riddle of Teeth, Coward-McCann, 1971. (I)

Most chapters of this factual book about teeth contain interesting projects for readers to try at home or in school with classmates. The author is very specific in her discussion of formation of teeth, the different kinds of teeth and how they work, the causes of caries and other dental diseases, and the fight to control and prevent the loss of teeth. Children who are preparing for orthodontia can learn much from this book, and it can be used in health classes, by dentists, and for general reading about the care and protection of the teeth and mouth. Nonfiction.

KESSLER, ETHEL, Our Tooth Story; a Tale of Twenty Teeth, Dodd-Mead, 1972. (P)

Cartoonlike illustrations add to the children's story of their visits to the dentist. There is emphasis on the importance of regular checkups, the fundamentals of caring for the teeth by brushing and good diet, and the ways in which the establishment of good dental habits help protect the teeth. Nonfiction.

McPHAIL, DAVID, Bear's Toothache, Little, Brown & Co., 1972 (An Atlantic Monthly Press book). (P)

A small boy's sleep is disturbed by the howling of a big bear with a toothache. After inviting the bear in, the boy tries to cure the ache by pulling the tooth. Tugging on the tooth fails, eating steak and all else in the refrigerator doesn't work, but eventually the tooth does come out. The happy bear goes on his way, and the little boy sleeps with an enormous tooth under his pillow. Fiction.

POMERANTZ, CHARLOTTE. Mango Tooth, Greenwillow, 1977. (P)

Posy is starting to lose her baby teeth. The first one is loosened by a mango pit, and it earns her a dime. Then go the "chicken bone tooth" and the "Turkish tootsie tooth," each providing another dime. But clever Posy nets two dimes on the fourth tooth, an "elephant tooth." Not many people can loosen a tooth on an elephant. Fiction.

ROSS, PAT, Molly and the Slow Teeth, Lee & Shepard, 1980. (P)

Molly is an unhappy second grader, because while all her classmates are losing their baby teeth and getting rewards from the Tooth Fairy, she doesn't even have a loose tooth. She tries to fool the Tooth Fairy with a small white pebble, but that doesn't work. Only weeks and weeks of waiting and a hard apple finally put a gaping smile on Molly's face and her name on the class tooth chart. Fiction.

SHOWERS, PAUL, How Many Teeth? Crowell, 1962 (A Let's-read-and-find-out science book). (P)

The loss of a front tooth is common to all children and is one of childhood's great experiences. The subject is treated with respect, but the tooth loss has a light touch, with a happy, now-we-are-growing-up significance. Other facts about the teeth are informally presented. Easy-to-read with illustrations. Nonfiction.

WILLIAMS, BARBARA, Albert's Toothache, Dutton, 1974. (P)

No one in the family believes Albert when he complains of a toothache. Father Turtle says it's impossible, since turtles don't have teeth. Nevertheless Albert refuses his favorite food, won't play ball, and stays in bed all day, until Grandmother comes to visit. She believes Albert and knows just how to cure his toothache. Also available in Spanish, as *El Dolor de Muelas de Alberto*. Fiction.

DISEASES AND HEALTH PROBLEMS

COOER, ELANOR, Sadako and the Thousand Paper Cranes, Putnam, 1977. (I)

Sadako was 2 when the atom bomb was dropped on her hometown of Hiroshima. Now, at age 12, she has developed leukemia, and she and her supportive family must fight her disease. Fiction.

COHEN, DANIEL, Vaccination and You, Messner, 1969. (U)

The story of vaccination or immunization against disease, from the time of Edward Jenner and vaccination against smallpox, Pasteur's study of germs under microscope, and Koch's isolation of bacteria to Ehrlich's conquest of diptheria, Salk and Sabin's efforts against polio, and Drs. Hilleman and Ender's work on a vaccine for measles. Nonfiction.

DONAHUE, PARNELL, and CAPELLAOR, HELEN, Germs Make Me Sick: a Health Handbook for Kids, Knopf, 1975. (U)

Describes a wide variety of diseases and their treatment, and offers a brief discussion of germs in general. Included are diseases of the gastrointestinal tract (food poisoning, stomach sickness), the respiratory tract (colds, sore throats, sinusitis), germs on the skin (warts, acne, athlete's foot), and viral exanthems (measles, chickenpox). A separate chapter discusses "Some Diseases You Probably Won't Get," such as meningitis, rabies, and rheumatic fever. The final chapter tells about "Getting Well and Staying There." A glossary and index are appended. Nonfiction.

REY, MARGARET, and REY, H.A., Curious George Goes to the Hospital, Houghton Mifflin, 1966. (P)

If a trip to the hospital—as a visitor or patient—is scheduled for your students, this selection for younger readers will help smooth the way. The all-time favorite chimp swallows a piece of a jigsaw puzzle and is hospitalized after an x-ray reveals the cause of his discomfort. Fiction.

SAMPSON, FAY, Watch on Patterick Fell, Greenwillow, 1980. (U)

Patterick Fell is an English plant that stores nuclear waste from around the world. Teenage Roger's father is the director and his mother a distinguished coworker, and Roger has never questioned the plant's validity until the protests mount, and his younger sister joins them. When an explosion nearly levels the plant, the family rethinks its commitment. A very timely book, but some British attitudes and idioms may need explanation. Fiction.

SHARMAT, MARJORIE WEINMAN, I Want Mama, Harper & Row, 1974. (P)

Tenderly describes a young girl's concern over her mother going to the hospital. Fiction.

SILVERSTEIN, VIRGINIA B., and SILVERSTEIN, DR. ALVIN, Itch, Sniffle and Sneeze: All About Asthma, Hay Fever and Other Allergies, Four Winds, 1978. (P-I)

If any of your children sneeze every August, get those annoying itchy bumps on their skin when they eat chocolate, or have trouble breathing when they play with a puppy, this book should be passed on to them. The text succinctly tells what allergies are, how the body reacts to them, things people are allergic to, and how to cope with allergies. Nonfiction.

WINN, MARIE, The Sick Book: Questions and Answers About Hiccups and Mumps, Sneezes and Bumps, and Other Things That Go Wrong With Us, Four Winds, 1976. (P-I)

This is an informative volume about common childhood illnesses. Presented in a lively question-and-answer format, the various sections deal with colds and the flu, allergies, chickenpox, mumps, measles, skin troubles, and broken bones. Each ailment is presented so that readers will understand what happens when they are sick. A special section at the end of the book explains how our bodies work when they are healthy. Nonfiction.

DRUGS

HYDE, MARGERT O., Know About Drugs, ed. 2, McGraw-Hill, 1979. (I-U)

Along with the basic information about all drugs, the authors include facts about the use and abuse of drugs, marijuana, alcohol, coca and cocaine, cigarettes, PCP (angel dust), inert inhalants, heroin, barbiturates, methaqualone, and a wide variety of tranquilizers, amphetamines, and LSD and other hallucinogens. Knowing the facts should enable the student to make his or her own decisions as to whether drugs heal or provide pleasure or trouble. Nonfiction.

MARR, JOHN S., Good Drug and the Bad Drug, Evans, 1970. (I)

A city doctor has written in simple terms the course of two complete trips of drugs through the body. By means of illustrations, the good drug is shown as it travels toward the infected area in an effort to effect a cure. Having established certain basic concepts, the doctor then describes the harmful effects of a bad drug. A book that lends itself to class discussion. Nonfiction.

MOREY, WALT, Lemon Meringue Dog, Dutton. In Canada, Clarke, Irwin, 1980. (U)

Chris, age 20, is the junior member of a new Coast Guard narcotic squad that uses dogs to uncover drugs. On their first assignment on a ship, his dog Mike is curiously diverted by a surprise cache of his favorite lemon meringue pies, ruining the drug bust. Demoted, Chris buys Mike, and moonlighting as a night watchman he redeems them both by uncovering a huge and dangerous drug ring. A good action story with a low reading level. Fiction.

SHREVE, SUSAN, Nightmares of Geranium Street, Knopf, 1977. (P)

Elizabeth's family has chosen to stay on in their long-time home in a deteriorating area of Germantown, Pennsylvania. She has become the "Rex" of a club of children. When Amanda comes to live with her Aunt Tess the club—the Nightmares—become very curious about what happens in their house. Slowly it becomes evident that Tess is involved in a drug ring, as the children observe and become involved in disclosing. They never actually take drugs themselves—partly because of the strict discipline in Elizabeth's own family. An interesting and valuable picture of inner-city life from a true child's point of view. Fiction.

TOBIAS, ANN, Pot, What It Is, What It Does, Greenwillow, 1979 (Greenwillow read-alone books). (I-U)

This overview of marijuana—its history, how it affects the body and the mind, and the laws concerning its use—leaves the reader to decide whether or not to use it. Nonfiction.

FAMILY

BLAINE, MARGE, Terrible Thing That Happened at Our House, Four Winds, 1975. (P-I)

Two young children dislike the changes in their family life when Mother goes back to work. Everyone has to rush around in the morning, they have to eat in the noisy, smelly school lunchroom, no one has time to listen, and there's no time for stories, games, or trips to the gas station. Things are just too topsy-turvy. Fiction.

BRANDENBERG, FRANZ, Nice New Neighbors, Greenwillow, 1977. (P)

When Mr. and Mrs. Fieldmouse and their six children move to a new home, the neighborhood children are unfriendly. The resourceful mouse children invent their own play and suddenly they are very popular. All the neighbor children beg to join in. Fiction.

BURNINGHAM, JOHN, Baby, Crowell, 1975. (P)

In few words a young boy tells about the new baby at his home. Fiction.

BURNINGHAM, JOHN, Snow, Crowell, 1975. (P)

It snows one day, and a little boy tells of all the fun he and his mother have playing in the snow. Fiction.

HAZEN, BARBARA SHOOK, Tight Times, Viking. In Canada, Penguin Books Canada, Ltd., 1979. (P)

A youngster doesn't understand why something called "tight times" keeps him getting a dog and causes Mommy to go to work and Daddy to lose his job. But in spite of all their problems, when the child brings home a starved kitten Mommy and Daddy say the new pet can stay. Fiction.

LIVINGSTON, CAROLE, Why Was I Adopted? Lyle Stuart, 1978. (I-U)

Presents facts of adoption in clever and appealing text and illustrations. Focuses on reasons for and ways of being adopted and how special adopted children are to parents. Concludes with questions children frequently ask. Nonfiction.

McCORD, JEAN, Turkeylegs Thompson, Atheneum. In Canada, McClelland & Stewart, 1979. (I-U)

Even pugnacious Turkeylegs (really 12-year-old Betty Ann) has a breaking point. Virtually without friends, she helps her single-parent mother care for her whiny little brother and her enchanting little sister. But buffeted by a pervert exposing himself to her, her little sister's death, and her alcoholic father's return home, she runs away to the hills she loves, but returns home to face her grief and confusion when her young friend Charlie meets her and counsels patience. A bleak, sometimes painful story, with a very believable main character. Fiction.

NAYLOR, PHYLLIS REYNOLDS, Getting Along in Your Family, Abingdon, 1976. (I-U)

Explores family life and related problems—fighting, sharing tasks, being loyal, showing love, and coping with mental disturbances, alcoholism, and divorce. Will help children understand their brothers, sisters, and parents. Nonfiction.

NEUFELD, JOHN, Edgar Allan: a Novel, Phillips, 1968. (I-U)

Michael Ficket, 12 years old, tells the story of the events—and motivations behind them—that occurred in his family when his parents adopted a little black boy, Edgar Allan. Edgar Allan's arrival means a testing of everything in which Michael believes, including his father's actions and motives. Divided loyalties finally make the family realize that good intentions are not enough. Fiction.

NOLAN, MADEENA SPRAY, My Daddy Don't Go to Work, Carolrhoda Books, 1978. (P)

A young black girl tells about her daddy who goes out every day looking for a job but just can't find a place that needs him. Although her daddy is discouraged, the little girl likes having him home to play ball with her and listen to her after school. Fiction.

PURSELL, MARGARET SANFORD, Look at Adoption, Lerner, 1977. (I-U)

Straightforward discussion of adoption, including reasons children are available and steps necessary for adoption. Nonfiction.

RAYNOR, DORKA, This Is My Father and Me, Whitman, 1973. (P-I)

Photographic essay on the relationship between father and child in many different countries. Nonfiction.

RICHARDS, ARLENE KRAMER, How to Get It Together When Your Parents Are Coming Apart, McKay, 1976. (I-U)

Through many representative stories of adolescents, this guide offers suggestions to young people for coping with divorce. Divided into three parts (marriage trouble, during the divorce, and after the divorce), the emphasis is to assuage guilt feelings on the part of the children and to provide specific addresses for finding outside help. Nonfiction.

STEIN, SARA, Adopted One: an Open Family Book for Parents and Children Together, Walker. In Canada, Beaverbooks, Ltd., 1979. (U)

Dual text for adult and child readers tells how Joshua feels about being adopted and gives parental guidance in understanding his needs for information about adoption. Black and white photographs on each page effectively express emotion. Nonfiction.

STOLZ, MARY, Go and Catch a Flying Fish, Harper & Row. In Canada, Fizhenry & Whiteside, 1979 (An Ursual Nordstrom book). (P-I)

The seemingly idyllic life of the Reddick family centers on the sea, sun, and sand of Florida's Gulf Coast. Although the three children—13-year-old Taylor and her younger brothers, aged 10 and 4—are aware that something is wrong, no one, not even her husband, Tony, is prepared for Junie's abrupt departure for "time on her own." Fiction.

TATE, ELEANORA E., Just an Overnight Guest, Dial, 1980. (I-U)

Margie is a 9-year-old black girl living with her family in a Mississippi River town. When her mother introduces Ethel, who is half white, into their warm, stable home, Margie is confused and jealous. Her father gently explains that Ethel is her cousin, her uncle Jake's child, and will be more than just an overnight guest. Some frank language makes this less suitable for younger readers. Fiction.

TAX, MEREDITH, Families, Little, Brown & Co., 1981. (P)

Positive and humorous description of different kinds of families as told by 6-year-old Angie. Includes animals (lions, dogs, chickens, ants) and people (parents, single parent, stepparents, grandparents, two women). Nonfiction.

HANDICAPS

ADAMS, BARBARA, Like It Is: Facts and Feelings About Handicaps From Kids Who Know, Walker, 1979. (I)

Six kids with handicaps tell what it's like to live in their unique worlds. The reader learns how handicapped people wish to be treated and what one can do to help. Nonfiction.

BRIGHTMAN, ALAN, Like Me, Little, Brown & Co., 1976. (P)

Rhyming text and beautiful photographs explain the concept of mental retardation for the younger reader. Nonfiction.

CHARLIP, REMY, and CHARLIP, MARY BETH, Handtalk: an ABC of Finger Spelling and Sign Language, Four Winds, 1980 (reprint of edition published by Parents' Magazine Press, 1974). (P)

All ages will enjoy learning about the ways people can talk without using their voices: finger spelling (making words letter by letter with the fingers) and signing (using the hands to convey a picture for a word or idea). Full-color pictures show children how it's done. Nonfiction.

CLIFTON, LUCILLE, My Friend Jacob, Dutton, 1980. (P)

Sam and Jacob are neighbors and the very best of friends. Though 17-year-old Jacob is mentally retarded, 8-year-old Sam learns they can love and help each other. Fiction.

DAVIDSON, MARGARET, Helen Keller, Hastings, 1970. (I)

This biography concentrates on Helen Keller's childhood and how, with Annie Sullivan's help, she overcame her handicaps. Helen Keller was blind and deaf. Nonfiction.

GRIESE, ARNOLD A., At the Mouth of the Luckiest River, Crowell, 1973. (I)

A convincing tale of Talek, an Alaskan Indian boy who becomes a leader among his people despite being crippled. Set in the 19th century. Fiction.

HERMES, PATRICIA, What If They Knew? Harcourt, 1980. (I)

Jeremy is an epileptic who learns that real friends don't care if you're different in some ways. Fiction.

JONES, RON, The Acorn People, Abingdon, 1976. (I)

Teachers may wish to read aloud some parts of this story of five severely handicapped children in a Boy Scout camp with an unprepared counselor. Older children will learn about courage through their own reading. Fiction.

KAMIEN, JANET, What If You Couldn't . . . ? A Book About Special Needs, Scribner's, 1979. (I)

An informational book about handicaps that includes "experiments" that will help children to understand the everyday problems that confront the handicapped. Nonfiction.

LASKER, JOE, He's My Brother, Whitman, 1974. (P)

Jamie is not retarded, but he is a slow learner who often becomes frustrated at school. The other children make fun of him and tease him. There are many things he can't do well, but Jamie is kind and gentle to animals, babies, and young children. He draws well and is also very good on the drums. His parents are patient and understanding. His brother and sister are good to him and make up stories to tell him they love him. Nonfiction.

LEVINE, EDNA S., Lisa and Her Soundless World, Human Science Press, 1974. (I)

Eight-year-old Lisa is deaf and attends special schools to learn to use sign language and to lip read, as well as to improve her speech. Fiction.

MACLACHLAN, PATRICIA, Through Grandpa's Eyes, Harper & Row, 1980. (P)

John loves to visit his blind Grandpa who teaches him how to "see" through touch, sound, and smell. A tender story with poetic illustrations. Fiction.

MILLER, EDNA, Mousekin's Close Call, Prentice-Hall, 1978. (P)

Mousekin watches some other animals protect themselves and their young by pretending to be handicapped. There's no pretending when Mousekin is caught by a weasel, but a startled one-legged sparrow comes to the rescue and proves that the handicapped are achievers too. Fiction.

PETERSEN, PALLE, Sally Can't See, Crowell, 1977 (A John Day Book). (P)

The life of a blind child and how she learns and plays is described in a brief text illustrated with color photographs. Nonfiction.

PETERSON, JEANNE WHITEHOUSE, I Have A Sister—My Sister is Deaf, Harper & Row, 1977. (P)

Soft black-and-white drawings depict the daily life in a loving home where one child is deaf. Fiction.

PHELAN, TERRY WOLFE, The S. D. Valentine, Four Winds, 1979. (I)

Children identify with the young people who learn how to relate to Connie, the new girl in class who must use a wheelchair. Fiction.

ROBINET, HARRIETTE GILLEM, Ride the Red Cycle, Houghton Mifflin. (I)

Gutsy, crippled Jerome is determined to learn to ride his tricycle, and with the help of his family, he does. Fiction.

SAVITZ, HARRIET MAY, Run, Don't Walk, Watts, 1979. (I)

Two teenagers confined to wheelchairs take some positive actions to prevent being discriminated against because of their handicaps. Fiction.

SIEGEL, DOROTHY SCHAINMAN, Winners: Eight Special Young People, Messner, 1978. (I-U)

Biographical sketches of eight courageous young people, each with a different handicap. These children have not permitted their problems to curtail their activities more than is absolutely necessary. Nonfiction.

SLEPIAN, JAN, The Alfred Summer, Macmillan, 1980. (I-U)

Lester could care less that Alfred is slightly retarded. After all, Alfred doesn't mind about Lester's cerebral palsy. Together with two other friends, they are a memorable quartet. Fiction.

SMITH, DORIS BUCHANAN, Kelly's Creek, Crowell, 1975. (I)

Young Kelly suffers from perceptual learning problems and must find his own way to live with his handicap and achieve self-respect. Fiction.

SMITH, LUCIA B., A Special Kind of Sister, Holt, 1979. (P)

Seven-year-old Sarah talks about her feelings for her retarded younger brother Andy. Fiction.

SPENCE, ELEANOR, The Devil Hole, Lothrop, 1977. (I)

The more sophisticated reader will enjoy this moving novel of an Australian family's struggles when their fourth child is born autistic. Fiction.

SULLIVAN, MARY BETH, BRIGHTMAN, ALAN J., and BLATT, JOSEPH, Feeling Free, Addison-Wesley, 1979.

In this spin-off of the television series by the same name, handicapped children talk about their disabilities. A great aid to mainstreaming, the book is directed toward children and adults who are unprepared to interact with the handicapped. Nonfiction.

WHITE, PAUL, Janet at School, Crowell, 1978, (A John Day Book). (P)

Janet has spina bifida and cannot move or feel her legs. As children learn about her daily life in this straightforward, caring account, they will grasp the difficulties people with this disease must overcome. Nonfiction.

WOLF, BERNARD, Don't Feel Sorry for Paul, Lippincott, 1974. (I)

Born with his hands and feet incompletely formed, Paul is encouraged to be independent all his life. This book shows his progress. Nonfiction.

WOLF, BERNARD, Anna's Silent World, Lippincott, 1977. (P)

Abundant black-and-white photographs show Anna at home, in school, at dancing class, and at the New York League for the Hard of Hearing. Hearing aids and the process of learning to speak are explained. Nonfiction.

MENTAL AND EMOTIONAL PROBLEMS

BONSAIL, CROSBY, Who's Afraid of the Dark? Harper & Row. In Canada, Fitzhenry & Whiteside, 1980. (P)

A little boy tries to teach his dog Stella to be unafraid of the dark and the night noises, but the readers know it's really the boy who's scared. Fiction.

BURNINGHAM, JOHN, Friend, Crowell, 1976. (P)

A little boy has a best friend named Arthur. The two children always play together, but sometimes they fuss and don't like each other, and Arthur goes home. Fiction.

DIXON, PAIGE, Walk My Way, Atheneum. In Canada, McClelland & Stewart, 1980. (I-U)

Fourteen-year-old Kitty is 5 feet 11 inches tall, and clumsy. Her brutal father mistreats her, and she decides to go and live with her mother's friend who raised her. On the 50-mile trip through the woods to the coast of Maine, she meets a lost dog and an ill old man and his grandson. Through helping them, Kitty also learns how to help herself. Fiction.

GREENE, LAURA, I Am Somebody, Childrens Press. In Canada, Regensteiner, 1980. (P-I)

Story is told in the first person by a not-so-good ball player. Nathan deals with the frustration of not being chosen first, being tagged out at base, and missing an important catch. There is no miraculous ending. Nathan has a collection of feathers that he shares with a friend. He loves to play baseball, but he is better at collecting. Nonfiction.

HALL, MALCOLM, Friends of Charlie Ant Bear, Coward-McCann. In Canada, Academic, 1980. (P)

Charlie Ant Bear is jealous of his best friend Wild Bob Ding, who is liked by everyone in town because of his funny practical jokes. Gloomy Charlie buys a joke book thinking that he too can become popular. All his jokes and tricks backfire, and Charlie is feeling worse than ever, until he and Bob try one final trick that tops them all. Fiction.

HAZEN, BARBARA SHOOK, Me I See, Abingdon, 1978. (P)

Through rhymed verse and full-page illustrations, a little girl discovers the different parts of her body and how she is different from anyone else. Nonfiction.

KAVANAUGH, DORRIET, Listen to Us. The Children's Express report, edited by Dorriet Kavanaugh; produced by Children's Express and Robert Clampitt, Workman, 1978. (U)

Compilation of writings and interviews of children ages 5 to 17 on family, divorce, school, sex, handicaps, friendship, drugs, television, money, religion, discrimination, emotions, and much, much more. Readers will find that they are not alone in their growth and development, which will build increased self-confidence. Nonfiction.

LEVOY, MYRON, Alan and Naomi, Harper & Row, 1977. (I-U)

Naomi is a French Jewish girl, traumatized by Nazi brutality, who comes to live in a New York City apartment building with her mother. A neighbor boy, Alan Silverman, is asked by his parents to befriend her and help her return to reality. Though this means giving up his only sport, stickball, in which he is beginning to wear down accusing taunts of "sissy," Alan complies with his parents' wishes and establishes a special friendship with Naomi. Fiction.

THOMAS, MARLO, Free to Be . . . You and Me, McGraw-Hill, 1974. (U)

A collection of songs, poems, stories, and pictures by well-known composers, writers, and artists, with an overall theme that debunks old sexual and racial stereotypes and emphasizes the idea that anyone is free to be who they are and who they want to be. Several short stories have been added to the material on the record of the same title. Nonfiction.

NUTRITION

BERGER, MELVIN, New Food Book; Nutrition, Diet, Consumer Tips and Foods of the Future, Crowell. In Canada, Fitzhenry & Whiteseid Ltd., 1978. (U)

A collection of valuable food information including nutrition, diet, consumer education, experiments designed for elementary students, food production and processing, the present food crisis and its causes and possible solutions, and up-to-date information concerning cholesterol. Nonfiction.

BORGHESE, ANITA, Down to Earth Cookbook, Revised edition, Scribner's, 1980. (U)

Introduction to natural cooking for intermediate graders. Contains explanations of terms, utensils, and ingredients, gives clear directions for all recipes, and introduces the user to unfamiliar foods. Pleasant illustrations enhance the text. Nonfiction.

COBB, VICKI, More Science Experiments You Can Eat, Lippincott, 1979. (U)

Describes food experiments that investigate, spoilage, dehydration, ripening, acidity, flavorings, and extracts. In discussing additives, the author relies on the Food and Drug Administration's questionable Generally Regarded As Safe (GRAS) list. Nonfiction.

JONES, HETTIE, How to Eat Your ABC's; a Book About Vitamins, Four Winds, 1976. (I-U)

An attractive, neat format and an informal text will be appealing to many middle graders. The history of vitamin research and the roles each vitamin plays and where to get it are included. Nutrition is stressed in problem-solving menu ideas, food charts, and a few easy and yummy recipes. An important topic today in our world of junk food. This book will be of use in nutrition and food units. Nonfiction.

PERL, LILA, Eating the Vegetarian Way: Good Food From the Earth, Morrow, 1980. (U)

An in-depth discussion as to what vegetarianism is and why it has become a new trend in American eating patterns. Final chapter is devoted to recipes that would appeal to boys and girls. Nonfiction.

U.S. DEPARTMENT OF AGRICULTURE, What's to Eat? and Other Questions Kids Ask About Food, foreword by Bob Bergland. Superintendent of Documents (U.S. Government Printing Office 001-000-04041-3), 1979. (I)

Useful for both teachers and students, this colorful book is full of facts on nutrition and includes recipes, games about food and health, and activities for consumer education. Nonfiction.

SAFETY

ELGIN, KATHLEEN, Fall Down, Break a Bone, Skin Your Knee Book, Walker, 1974. (U)

Major and minor wounds and injuries, including fractures, burns, bruises, warts, sprains, and sunburns, are discussed in text with accompanying drawings. First-aid suggestions are given. Useful for study of human body. Nonfiction.

KESSLER, LEONARD, Tale of Two Bicycles, Safety on Your Bike, Lothrop, Lee & Shepard, 1971. (P)

Humorous text and illustrations on the serious subject of bicycle safety. Freddy and Tommy both receive identical bikes for their birthdays, but from the very first, Tommy does not like his gift; he disregards all safety rules, hurts himself repeatedly, endangers others with his bad bicycle manners, and ends up demolishing his bike. Ends with safety tips for bike riders. Good addition to a primary collection. Fiction.

KESSLER, LEONARD, Who Tossed That Bat? Safety on the Ballfield and Playground, Lothrop, Lee & Shepard, 1973. (P)

Advice in verse form on safety as a participant and observer on the ballfield and playground. A delightful way for beginning readers to be reminded of sports and playground safety rules. Nonfiction.

SEXUALITY

BURN, HELEN JEAN, Better Than the Birds, Smarter Than the Bees; No-Nonsense Answers to Honest Questions About Sex and Growing Up, Abingdon, 1969. (U)

Frank answers are given to honest questions about sex and growing up asked by adolescents. Compiled by one of the members of the Planned Parenthood Association's speaker's bureau, the book provides simple yet complete and satisfying answers to questions relating to the psychologic angle of sex, the physiologic differences between boys and girls, the "marriage bit," and the "no-no's." The bibliography includes selected references on aspects of sex education, films for use in sex education, and selected fiction on sexual problems. Nonfiction.

MAY, JULIAN, New Baby Comes, Creative Education, 1970. (P)

By means of illustrations and simple text, the growth of a baby is followed until its birth in a hospital and the beginning of its life as a new member of the family. Despite the low reading level, a practical book for the older child. Nonfiction.

SHEFFIELD, MARGARET, Where Do Babies Come From? Knopf, 1973. (I)

A first sex education book that has the answer to what children really want to know. All of the facts are included in the text using correct terminology. The direct illustrations are soft colored paintings. The book gracefully creates a mood of reverence for life in representing human reproduction. Adopted from a BBC award-winning program. Nonfiction.

SMOKING

MARR, JOHN S., Breath of Air and Breath of Smoke, Evans, 1971. (I-U)

The first part of the book contains a detailed description of the respiratory system with many illustrations. Then the processes of inhalation and exhalation are carefully explained again with illustrations. Without critique, the author describes the effect that smoking has on the body. Three-color illustrations are used on every page to enhance the interesting text. Nonfiction.

SONNETT, SHERRY, Smoking, Watts, 1977. (U)

The history of tobacco and smoking, how it affects people physically, and the diseases it promotes are clearly explained in this slim book. A good book for student reports and classroom units on cancer and health. Nonfiction.

F

Sources of free and low-cost sponsored instructional aids for health teaching

Since some organizations move, change policy, or go out of business each year, it is virtually impossible to prepare a list of sources of free and inexpensive materials that will not require revision periodically. Teachers can keep up-to-date on such changes by conferring with the librarian or by requesting that their letters of inquiry be forwarded. Teacher's manuals that accompany many health textbooks furnish the teacher with accurate and selective lists of printed materials, films and filmstrips, and their sources.

The national organizations with asterisks have state or regional affiliates or offices. When this is known, the teacher should first request materials or information from the nearest unit.

Abbott Laboratories
Abbott Park, D-383
North Chicago, IL 60064

Aetna Life and Casualty Companies
Public Relations and Advertising
151 Farmington Avenue DA06
Hartford, CT 06115

Al-Anon Family Group Headquarters*
PO Box 182
Madison Square Station
New York, NY 10159

Allstate
Corporate Relations Department
Allstate Plaza
Northbrook, IL 60062

American Alliance for Health, Physical Education,
    Recreation, and Dance
1900 Association Drive
Reston, VA 22091

American Automobile Association*
Traffic Safety Department
8111 Gatehouse Road
Falls Church, VA 22047

American Cancer Society, Inc.*
4 West 35th Street
New York, NY 10001

American Chiropractic Association*
1916 Wilson Blvd.
Arlington, VA 22201

American Dental Association
Bureau of Health Education and
    Audiovisual Services
211 Chicago Avenue
Chicago, IL 60611

American Diabetes Association*
2 Park Avenue
New York, NY 10016

American Dry Milk Institute, Inc.
130 North Franklin Street
Chicago, IL 60606

American Foundation for the Blind
15 West 16th Street
New York, NY 10011

American Institute of Baking
Communications Department
1213 Bakers Way
Manhattan, KS 66502

American Institute of Family Relations
5287 Sunset Blvd.
Los Angeles, CA 90027

American Lung Association*
1740 Broadway
New York, NY 10019

American Medical Association*
Department of Health Education
535 North Dearborn Street
Chicago, IL 60610

American Optometric Association
Department of Public Information
243 N. Lindbergh Blvd.
St. Louis, MO 63141

American Osteopathic Association
212 East Ohio Street
Chicago, IL 60611

American Podiatry Association
20 Chevy Chase Circle N.W.
Washington, DC 20015

American National Red Cross*
17th and D Streets N.W.
Washington, DC 20006

American School Health Association
PO Box 708
Kent, OH 44240

American Social Health Association
260 Sheridan Ave., Suite 307
Palo Alto, CA 94306

American Veterinary Medical Association
930 North Meacham Road
Schaumburg, IL 60196

Better Vision Institute, Inc.
230 Park Ave.
New York, NY 10169

Channing L. Bete Co., Inc.
200 State Road
South Deerfield, MA 01373

Consumer Information Center
Pueblo, CO 81009

Consumer Nutrition Center
Human Nutrition Information Service
U.S. Department of Agriculture
Hyattsville, MD 20782

Distilled Spirits Council of the United States
1300 Pennsylvania Building
Washington, DC 20004

Environmental Protection Agency
401 M St. S.W.
Washington, DC 20460

Epilepsy Foundation of America
4351 Garden City Drive
Landover, MD 20785

FDA/Consumer Communications (HFE-88)
5600 Fishers Lane
Rockville, MD 20857

General Mills, Inc.
Publications & Editorial Department
9200 Wayzata Blvd.
Minneapolis, MN 55426

The Gillette Company
Personal Care Division
Box 61
Boston, MA 02199

The Gillette Company
Prudential Building—24th Floor
Boston, MA 02199

The Hogg Foundation for Mental Health
University of Texas–Austin
PO Box 7998, University Station
Austin, TX 78712

Institute of Makers of Explosives
1575 Eye St. N.W., Suite 550
Washington, DC 20005

Kellogg Co.
235 Porter St.
Battle Creek, MI 49017

Kemper Insurance Companies
Long Grove, IL 60049

The Life Cycle Center
Kimberly-Clark Corporation
PO Box 9474
St. Paul, MN 55194

Lead Industries Association
292 Madison Ave.
New York, NY 10017

Lever Brothers Company, Inc.
Lever House
390 Park Avenue
New York, NY 10022

March of Dimes*
1275 Mamaraneck Ave.
White Plains, NY 10605

Mental Health Materials Center
30 E. 29th St.
New York, NY 10016

Metropolitan Life Insurance Company
Health and Safety Education Division
One Madison Avenue
New York, NY 10010

Muscular Dystrophy Association
810 Seventh Avenue
New York, NY 10019

National Association for Hearing and Speech Action
  (NAHSA)
10801 Rockville Pike
Rockville, MD 20852

National Clearinghouse for Drug Abuse
  Information
PO Box 416
Kensington, MD 20975

National Council on Alcoholism
733 Third Ave.
New York, NY 10017

National Council on Family Relations
1219 University Ave. S.E.
Minneapolis, MN 55414

National Dairy Council*
6300 North River Rd.
Rosemont, IL 60018

National Fire Protection Association
Batterymarch Park
Quincy, MA 02269

National Health Council, Inc.
70 West 40th Street
New York, NY 10018

National Heart, Lung, and Blood Institute
Information Office
National Institutes of Health
Bethesda, MD 20205

National Institute on Drug Abuse
  Clearinghouse
Public Inquiries
5600 Fishers Lane
Rockville, MD 20857

National Kidney Foundation
Two Park Ave.
New York, NY 10016

National Institute of Mental Health
Public Inquiries
5600 Fishers Lane
Rockville, MD 20857

National Livestock and Meat Board*
Nutritional Department
444 N. Michigan Ave.
Chicago, IL 60611

National Mental Health Association
1800 N. Kent Street
Rosslyn, VA 22209

National Multiple Sclerosis Society*
205 East 42nd Street
New York, NY 10017

National Safety Council
444 N. Michigan
Chicago, IL 60611

NIAAA National Clearinghouse for Alcohol
  Information
PO Box 2345
Rockville, MD 20852

Office on Smoking and Health
5600 Fishers Lane
Rm 1-10
Park Building
Rockville, MD 20857

Ortho Pharmaceuticals
Raritan, NJ 08869

Personal Products Company
c/o Karol Media
PO Box 2000
South Hackensack, NJ 07606

Pet Milk Co.
Director of Home Economics
400 S. Fourth Street
St. Louis, MO 63102

Pharmaceutical Manufacturers' Association
Department NW-601
1155 15th Street N.W.
Washington, DC 20005

Planned Parenthood Federation of America, Inc.*
Publications Department
810 Seventh Avenue
New York, NY 10019

President's Council on Physical Fitness
  and Sports
400 Sixth Street S.W.
Washington, DC 20202

Proprietary Association
1700 Pennsylvania Ave. N.W.
Washington, DC 20006
Attention: Mary B. Alterman, Librarian

Prudential Insurance Company of America
Public Relations and Advertising
Box 36
Newark, NJ 07101

Public Affairs Committee
381 Park Avenue South
New York, NY 10016

Public Health Service
Public Inquiries Branch
U.S. Department of Health and Human Services
Washington, DC 20025

Ralston Purina Company
Corporate Consumer Services—Public Relations
Checkerboard Square
St. Louis, MO 63164

Rutgers Center of Alcohol Studies
Smithers Hall
New Brunswick, NJ 08903

Schering Corporation
Kenilworth, NJ 07033

Sex Information and Education Council of the
  United States
80 Fifth Ave., Suite 801
New York, NY 10011

Smith Kline & French Laboratories
1900 Market Street, Suite #410
PO Box 7929
Philadelphia, PA 19101

State Farm Insurance Companies
Public Relations Department
One State Farm Plaza
Bloomington, IL 61761

Sunkist Growers
14130 Riverside Dr.
Sherman Oaks, CA 91423

Superintendent of Documents
U.S. Government Printing Office
Washington, DC 20402

The Travelers Film Library
One Tower Square
Hartford, CT 06115

United Cerebral Palsy Association, Inc.
66 E. 34th
New York, NY 10016

Wheat Flour Institute
600 Maryland Ave.
Suite 305 W
Washington, DC 20024

G

Selected federal health information clearinghouses and information centers

AGING

National Clearinghouse on Aging
330 Independence Avenue S.W.
Washington, DC 20201
(202) 245-2158

Provides access to information and referral services that assist the older American in obtaining services. Distributes Administration on Aging publications.

ALCOHOL

National Clearinghouse for Alcohol Information (NCALI)
PO Box 2345
Rockville, MD 20852
(301) 468-2600

Gathers and disseminates current knowledge on alcohol-related subjects.

ARTHRITIS

Arthritis Information Clearinghouse
PO Box 34427
Bethesda, MD 20817
(301) 881-9411

Identifies materials concerned with arthritis and related musculoskeletal diseases and serves as an information exchange for individuals and organizations involved in public, professional, and patient education. Refers personal requests from patients to the Arthritis Foundation.

BLIND AND PHYSICALLY HANDICAPPED

National Library Service for the Blind and Physically Handicapped
Library of Congress
1291 Taylor Street N.W.
Washington, DC 20542
(202) 287-5100; (800) 424-8567

Works through local and regional libraries to provide free library service to persons unable to read or use standard printed materials because of visual or physical impairment. Provides information on blindness and physical handicaps on request. A list of participating libraries is available.

CANCER

Cancer Information Clearinghouse
National Cancer Institute
Office of Cancer Communications
9000 Rockville Pike, Building 31, Room 10A18
Bethesda, MD 20205
(202) 842-7614

Collects information on public, patient, and professional cancer education materials and disseminates it to organizations and health care professionals.

Office of Cancer Communication
National Cancer Institute
Cancer Information Service
Bethesda, MD 20205
(301) 496-5583; (800) 638-6694
> Answers requests for cancer information from patients and the general public. The National Cancer Institute sponsors a toll-free telephone number to supply cancer information to the general public.

CHILD ABUSE

Clearinghouse on Child Abuse and
Neglect Information
PO Box 1182
Washington, DC 20013
(202) 755-0590
> Collects, processes, and disseminates information on child abuse and neglect.

CONSUMER EDUCATION

Consumer Education Resource Network (CERN)
1555 Wilson Blvd., Suite 600
Rosslyn, VA 22209
(703) 522-4616; (800) 336-0222
> Provides reference and referral services to consumer educators, serves as a depository of information and materials, and conducts training and technical assistance programs.

CONSUMER INFORMATION

Consumer Information Center
Pueblo, CO 81009
(202) 566-1794
> Distributes consumer publications on topics such as children, food and nutrition, health, exercise, and weight control. The Consumer Information Catalog is available free from the Center and must be used to identify publications requested.

DIABETES

National Diabetes Information Clearinghouse
Box: NDIC
Bethesda, MD 20205
(202) 842-7630
> Collects and disseminates information on patient education materials and coordinates the development of materials and programs for diabetes education.

DIGESTIVE DISEASES

National Digestive Diseases Education
and Information Clearinghouse
1555 Wilson Blvd., Suite 600
Rosslyn, VA 22209
(703) 522-0870
> Provides information on digestive diseases to health professionals and consumers.

DRUG ABUSE

National Clearinghouse for
Drug Abuse Information
PO Box 416
Kensington, MD 20795
(301) 443-6500
> Collects and disseminates information on drug abuse. Produces informational materials on drugs, drug abuse, and prevention.

ENVIRONMENTAL PROTECTION

Environmental Protection Agency (EPA)
Public Information Center
EPA PM-215
401 M Street S.W.
Washington, DC 20460
(202) 755-0707
> Public information materials on such topics as hazardous wastes, the school asbestos project, air and water pollution, pesticides, and drinking water are available. Offers information on the agency and its programs and activities.

FAMILY PLANNING

National Clearinghouse for
Family Planning Information
PO Box 2225
Rockville, MD 20852
(301) 881-9400
> Collects family planning materials, makes referrals to other information centers, and distributes and produces materials. Primary audience is federally funded family planning clinics.

FOOD AND DRUGS

Food and Drug Administration (FDA)
Office for Consumer Communications
5600 Fishers Lane, Room 15B-32 (HFE-88)
Rockville, MD 20857
(301) 443-3170
> Answers consumer inquiries for the FDA and serves as a clearinghouse for its consumer publications.

FOOD AND NUTRITION

Food and Nutrition Information Center (FNIC)
National Agricultural Library Building, Room 304
Beltsville, MD 20705
(301) 344-3719
> Serves the information needs of persons interested in human nutrition, food service management, and food technology. Acquires and lends books, journal articles, and audiovisual materials dealing with these areas of concern.

GENETIC DISEASES

National Clearinghouse for
  Human Genetic Diseases
805 15th Street N.W., Suite 500
Washington, DC 20005
(202) 842-7617

Provides information on human genetics and genetic diseases for both patients and health care workers. Reviews existing curricular materials on genetic education.

HANDICAPPED

Clearinghouse on the Handicapped
Switzer Building, 330 C Street S.W.
Washington, DC 20202
(202) 245-0080

Responds to inquiries from handicapped individuals and serves as a resource to organizations that supply information to, and about, handicapped individuals.

HEALTH INDEXES

Clearinghouse on Health Indexes
National Center for Health Statistics
Division of Analysis
3700 East-West Highway
Hyattsville, MD 20782
(301) 436-7035

Provides informational assistance in the development of health measures for health researchers, administrators, and planners.

HEALTH INFORMATION

National Health Information Clearinghouse (NHIC)
PO Box 1133
Washington, DC 20013-1133
(703) 522-2590 (in VA); (800) 336-4797

Helps the public locate health information through identification of health information resources and an inquiry and referral system. Health questions are referred to appropriate health resources that, in turn, respond directly to inquirers.

HEALTH PROMOTION AND EDUCATION

Center for Health Promotion and Education (CHPE)
1300 Clifton Road, Building 14
Atlanta, GA 30333
(404) 329-3235

Provides leadership and program direction for the prevention of disease, disability, premature death, and undesirable and unnecessary health problems through health education. Formerly called the Bureau of Health Education.

HIGH BLOOD PRESSURE

High Blood Pressure Information Center
120/80 National Institutes of Health
Bethesda, MD 20205
(703) 558-4827

Provides information on the detection, diagnosis, and management of high blood pressure to consumers and health professionals.

HIGHWAY SAFETY

National Highway Traffic Safety
  Administration (NHTSA)
U.S. Department of Transportation
Washington, DC 20590
(202) 426-0123; (800) 424-9393

Works to reduce highway traffic deaths and injuries. Publishes a variety of safety information brochures, conducts public information campaigns on vehicle defects and drunken driving, and maintains a toll-free hotline for consumer complaints on auto safety.

INJURIES

National Injury Information Clearinghouse
5401 Westbard Avenue, Room 525
Washington, DC 20207
(301) 492-6424

Collects and disseminates injury data and information relating to the causes and prevention of death, injury, and illness associated with consumer products. Requests of a general nature are referred to the Consumer Product Safety Commission's Communications Office.

MENTAL HEALTH

National Clearinghouse for
  Mental Health Information
Public Inquiries Section
5600 Fishers Lane, Room 11A-21
Rockville, MD 20857
(301) 443-4513

Acquires and abstracts the world's mental health literature, answers inquiries from the public, and provides computer searches for the scientific and academic communities.

PHYSICAL FITNESS

President's Council on
  Physical Fitness and Sports
Washington, DC 20201
(202) 755-7478

Conducts a public service advertising program and cooperates with governmental and private groups to promote the development of physical fitness leadership, facilities, and programs. Produces informational materials on exercise, school physical education programs, sports, and physical fitness for youth, adults, and the elderly.

POISON CONTROL

Division of Poison Control
Food and Drug Administration
5600 Fishers Lane
Rockville, MD 20857
(301) 443-6261

Works with the national network of 600 poison control centers to reduce the incidence and severity of acute poisoning. Directs toxic emergency calls to a local poison control center.

PRODUCT SAFETY

Consumer Product Safety Commission (CPSC)
Washington, DC 20207
(800) 638-8326 (in the District of Columbia;
(800) 492-8363 (in Maryland);
(800) 638-8333 (in Alaska, Hawaii, the Virgin Islands, and Puerto Rico)
(301) 492-6800 (in all other states)

Evaluates the safety of products sold to the public. Provides printed materials on different aspects of consumer product safety on request. Does not answer questions from consumers on drugs, prescriptions, warranties, advertising, repairs, or maintenance.

RAPE

National Rape Information Clearinghouse
5600 Fishers Lane, Room 15-99
Rockville, MD 20857
(301) 443-1910

Maintains a listing of rape prevention and treatment resources to help people locate services available in their community and to facilitate networking among those working in the field of sexual assault. Has very little information for inquiries from the general public and prefers to refer them to local resources.

REHABILITATION

National Rehabilitation
   Information Center (NARIC)
4407 Eighth Street N.E.
Washington, DC 20017-2299
(202) 635-5822

Supplies publications and audiovisual materials on rehabilitation and assists in locating information on dates, places, names, addresses, or statistics. The collection includes materials relevant to the rehabilitation of all disability groups.

SMOKING

Office on Smoking and Health
Technical Information Center
5600 Fishers Lane, Room 158
Rockville, MD 20857
(301) 443-1690

Offers bibliographic and reference service to researchers and others and publishes and distributes a number of titles in the field of smoking.

SUDDEN INFANT DEATH SYNDROME (SIDS)

Sudden Infant Death Syndrome Clearinghouse
1555 Wilson Blvd., Suite 600
Rosslyn, VA 22209
(703) 522-0870

Provides information on SIDS to health professionals and consumers.

H

Criteria for evaluating the elementary school health program

CALIFORNIA STATE DEPARTMENT OF EDUCATION*

Criteria for Evaluating the Elementary School Health Program provides school personnel with a tool to use in making an evaluation of the school health program. The results of such an evaluation reveal the strengths and weaknesses of the program. Where weaknesses are revealed, the school health committee may act to bring all the available forces into action for the express purpose of securing strength in the program where weaknesses exist and for planning ways all other phases of the program may be kept strong.

The criteria are organized into four divisions: I—Administration, II—Health instruction, III—Health services, and IV—Healthful school environment. The criteria are expressed in terms of desirable practices presented in the left column. The evaluation should be made by a representative group of the faculty, including administrators, teachers, and health service personnel. The results should express judgments approved by the evaluation committee as a whole.

Provision is made for the quality of each *provision* or *practice* stated in the criteria to be judged on a four-point scale: *excellent, good, fair,* or *poor.* If the provision is not made, the practice is not followed; or if the quality is fair or poor, there is space for listing changes needed. At the top of each section, space is provided for recording recommended steps to be taken in relation to the changes needed. Care should be taken to make recommendations that will not have an adverse effect on provisions or practices already judged excellent or good.

---

*Adapted from Criteria for evaluating the elementary school health program, Sacramento, Calif., 1977, California State Department of Education.

SUGGESTED PROCEDURE FOR USING THE CRITERIA FOR EVALUATING THE ELEMENTARY SCHOOL HEALTH PROGRAM

1. Determine the membership of study group to evaluate the program.
2. Determine the need for consultant help.
3. Study thoroughly the criteria and the provisions for making the desired evaluations.
4. Determine whether the program meets each criterion.
5. If the criterion is met, determine the quality of the provision or practice according to the following scale: *excellent*—near perfection; *good*—satisfactory; *fair*—slightly less than satisfactory; *poor*—unsatisfactory.
6. If the criterion is not met—that is, the provision not made or the practice not followed—indicate by a check in the appropriate column.
7. Compile a list of the changes needed and determine how the changes can be secured to best advantage.
8. Set up a priority for accomplishing the changes.
9. Develop recommendations for making the needed changes and record in appropriate space at the top of each section.
10. Submit the recommendations to the administration for action.

Criteria for evaluating the elementary school health program

Criteria	Quality of provision or practice					Changes needed
	Excellent (near perfection)	Good (satisfactory)	Fair (slightly less than satisfactory)	Poor (unsatisfactory)	Provision not made or practice not followed	
I. Administration						
A. The policies of the district's governing board provide for a school health program designed to help all pupils achieve the degree of health their potentialities permit through health instruction, health services, a healthful school environment—essentials of the program.	RECOMMENDED STEPS TO BE TAKEN:					
B. A written statement of the school district's point of view regarding the kind and quality of the school health program is available.	RECOMMENDED STEPS TO BE TAKEN:					
C. Responsibility for planning, developing, and administering the district's school health program is delegated by the governing board of the district to the district superintendent of schools. 1. A health committee with a membership that includes school personnel, representatives of community health services, and representatives of the other important segments of the community is assigned advisory responsibilities for the district's school health program.	RECOMMENDED STEPS TO BE TAKEN:					
D. The principal of the school has outlined the practices that are employed in operating the school health program. 1. A health council or committee with a membership that includes an administrator, teachers, health personnel, and, when possible, counselors, custodians, and school lunch personnel is assigned advisory responsibilities for the school health program.	RECOMMENDED STEPS TO BE TAKEN:					
E. Clerical help, equipment, and supplies, in keeping with the pupil population, are provided for the health services program.	RECOMMENDED STEPS TO BE TAKEN:					
F. Health personnel are adequate in number and specialization to provide needed services. 1. School nurses are available in a ratio of 1 nurse for each 1,000 to 1,400 pupils. (Distances traveled to visit homes and types of terrain should be considered in determining the desired ratio.) 2. Physicians are available for consultation and advice. 3. Dentists are available for consultation and advice.	RECOMMENDED STEPS TO BE TAKEN:					

Continued.

Criteria for evaluating the elementary school health program—cont'd

Criteria	Quality of provision or practice					Changes needed
	Excellent (near perfection)	Good (satisfactory)	Fair (slightly less than satisfactory)	Poor (unsatisfactory)	Provision not made or practice not followed	
G. The professional library and the school library are well supplied with health materials.	RECOMMENDED STEPS TO BE TAKEN:					
H. Each classroom is supplied with the materials needed for use in health instruction.	RECOMMENDED STEPS TO BE TAKEN:					
1. The classrooms for each grade are supplied with the basic textbooks in health.						
2. Each classroom is supplied with health materials, in addition to adopted textbooks, that cover each phase of health.						
3. The scope of the materials in each classroom is sufficient to provide for all the pupils, from the slowest to the fastest learner.						
I. The in-service education program for school personnel provides for health instruction to have the same emphasis as other areas of instruction.	RECOMMENDED STEPS TO BE TAKEN:					
J. The in-service education program for school personnel provides for study of the school health services.	RECOMMENDED STEPS TO BE TAKEN:					
II. Health instruction	RECOMMENDED STEPS TO BE TAKEN:					
A. A course of study for health, a course of study and a teacher's guide, or a combination of study and teacher's guide is provided by the school district or the office of the county superintendent of schools for use in the school.						
B. The course of study contains statements of the purposes of health instruction and the objectives to be sought; an outline of the contents that shows both scope and sequence; units of instruction, lists of materials and sources of materials, and recommended means and procedures for evaluating pupils' progress.	RECOMMENDED STEPS TO BE TAKEN:					
1. The scope of the content for the total program includes the following areas:						
a. Consumer health						
b. Mental-emotional health						
c. Drug use and misuse						
d. Family health (including human sexuality, masculine and feminine qualities, marriage, and family planning)						

f. Nutrition
g. Exercise, rest, and posture
h. Diseases and disorders
i. Environmental health hazards (including pollution, radiation hazards, accidents, and first aid)
j. Community health resources

2. The basic program of health instruction is developed through the use of units devoted primarily to health.

3. Health instruction is enriched by making it a correlated phase of units in other subjects, such as science, social studies, and homemaking.

4. Pupils' interests and needs are used as motivation for learning.

5. Health instruction is adapted to the pupils' abilities by employing a variety of methods.

6. Instruction is enriched through the use of the up-to-date information that is made available by official and voluntary health agencies and professional associations.

7. Instruction is enriched by the use of up-to-date audiovisual materials, such as films and film strips, charts and pictures, and radio and television programs.

III. Health services

A. A health services guide is provided by the school district or by the office of the county superintendent of schools.

RECOMMENDED STEPS TO BE TAKEN:

B. A health services committee, preferably a subcommittee of the health council or committee, has advisory responsibility for health services.

RECOMMENDED STEPS TO BE TAKEN:

C. Health services are provided in accordance with the provisions of the guide, provided, however, that the advice of the health services committee is an important consideration in decisions regarding adaptations required to meet special needs of individuals and of the school population.

RECOMMENDED STEPS TO BE TAKEN:

D. The school health services are of sufficient scope to provide school personnel the information and assistance needed to determine status of, protect, and promote the health of pupils.

RECOMMENDED STEPS TO BE TAKEN:

1. Guidance and assistance are provided in securing an appraisal of each pupil's health status.

2. School personnel, pupils, and parents are counseled regarding the results of health appraisals and ways to protect and promote one's health.

3. Procedures designed to help prevent and control disease are established.

4. First aid for the injured and emergency care for cases of sudden illness are provided.

5. School health services are coordinated with those provided by professional health agencies in the community.

Continued.

Criteria for evaluating the elementary school health program—cont'd

Criteria	Quality of provision or practice					Changes needed
	Excellent (near perfection)	Good (satisfactory)	Fair (slightly less than satisfactory)	Poor (unsatisfactory)	Provision not made or practice not followed	
III. Health services—cont'd						
E. School health personnel encourage and guide teacher observation of pupils' health characteristics and accept referrals of pupils whose characteristics are unlike those of the well child.	RECOMMENDED STEPS TO BE TAKEN:					
F. School personnel inform and advise parents regarding medical examinations their children should have and assist in making provision for the medical examinations as necessary.	RECOMMENDED STEPS TO BE TAKEN:					
1. Parents are advised to have medical examinations for their children before school entrance.						
2. Provision is made for pupils to have medical examinations as required by existing conditions. (Preferably this provision is made in cooperation with the local medical society.)						
3. Procedures are established for the cumulative health record to follow the pupil from grade to grade and school to school.						
G. School personnel inform parents of the importance of eye examinations for children before school entrance, maintain a vision screening program, and inform and advise parents regarding eye conditions of their children that require the attention of a specialist.	RECOMMENDED STEPS TO BE TAKEN:					
H. School health personnel provide for all pupils to have group hearing tests at regular intervals, individual tests for pupils discovered with hearing difficulties; inform and advise parents regarding their children's need for examinations by ear specialists; and recommend classroom adjustments for children with hearing difficulties.	RECOMMENDED STEPS TO BE TAKEN:					
I. Health services provide for parents to be informed regarding their children's need for regular dental examinations beginning before the children's entrance to school, and for parents of children who have defective dental conditions to be informed regarding the undesirable effects of the conditions and advised regarding essential treatment.	RECOMMENDED STEPS TO BE TAKEN:					

tions in growth patterns that merit special attention.

K. Follow-up procedures are taken as necessary—begin when pupils with health difficulties are identified and conclude when the health difficulties have been corrected or their effects minimized.

RECOMMENDED STEPS TO BE TAKEN:

L. Health counseling and guidance is provided.

RECOMMENDED STEPS TO BE TAKEN:

M. Provisions are made for supplying teachers with health information concerning handicapped pupils and for recommending cases for whom-home teaching may be necessary.

RECOMMENDED STEPS TO BE TAKEN:

N. The health services program includes provisions for the prevention and control of communicable diseases.

1. Parents of preschool children are advised by the school to protect their children as early as possible against communicable diseases for which immunization is available.

2. School personnel cooperate with representatives of the local health department in planning community immunization programs available to pupils.

3. The school cooperates with local health agencies in conducting a tuberculosis case-finding program for pupils and school personnel.

RECOMMENDED STEPS TO BE TAKEN:

O. The health services program provides emergency service for injury and sudden illness and for disasters.

1. Updated written policies and procedures for first aid and emergency care are provided to all school personnel.

2. The policies and procedures pertaining to first aid and emergency care are approved by the local medical society or the health department.

3. Phone numbers of parents and of physicians to call in emergencies are on file for each pupil.

4. Parents are notified immediately in instances of serious injury or illness.

5. Teachers are prepared to render first aid.

6. First-aid kits are available in each classroom and in the principal's office.

RECOMMENDED STEPS TO BE TAKEN:

IV. Healthful school environment

A. The school environment is protected by employing personnel whose health is good, requiring all personnel to have regular health examinations, and providing measures that encourage good health practices.

RECOMMENDED STEPS TO BE TAKEN:

Continued.

Criteria for evaluating the elementary school health program—cont'd

Criteria	Quality of provision or practice					Changes needed
	Excellent (near perfection)	Good (satisfactory)	Fair (slightly less than satisfactory)	Poor (unsatisfactory)	Provision not made or practice not followed	
IV. Healthful school environment—cont'd						
B. A wholesome emotional climate prevails and essential provisions are made for its maintenance.	RECOMMENDED STEPS TO BE TAKEN:					
1. The morale of teachers is at a high level.						
2. The following provisions are made for the maintenance of staff morale at a high level:						
a. Leaves of absence without pay are granted for specified purposes.						
b. Sabbatical leaves for study or travel are granted certificated personnel in accordance with written policies of the district.						
c. Communication is maintained between the administration and teaching personnel.						
d. A teamwork approach is used in the prevention and solving of staff problems.						
3. The following provisions are employed to create classroom environments that are conducive to learning:						
a. The teachers adapt learning experiences to each child's developmental pattern of growth and needs.						
b. The daily program provides for a balance of quiet and active experiences.						
c. Opportunities are provided for each child to release tension by participating in various types of esthetic and physical activities.						
d. Teachers discuss required behavior standards with pupils.						
e. Pupils share responsibility for securing desired classroom behavior.						
f. Discipline and grading procedures are fair and consistent.						
g. The teacher-pupil ratio permits the individualization of instruction to the extent required for maximal learning.						
4. Pupils are given the following types of opportunities to develop as self-directing individuals:						
a. To share responsibility for solving social problems in the						

to assume leadership responsibility, and to participate in classroom and student government activities.

c. To plan and organize school activities under teacher supervision.

5. Teachers are helped by the principal and special school personnel—the school psychologist, counselors, curriculum consultants, and others to solve problems that arise in their classes.

6. School personnel and parents are encouraged in the following ways to work cooperatively in solving the problems that are causing pupils to make less than maximum use of their abilities.

C. The school food services are conducted so that each pupil has opportunity to have a wholesome and nutritionally adequate lunch in an environment that is pleasant and sanitary; and pupils are helped to learn the importance of good eating habits, eating well-balanced meals, using good table manners.

1. A Type A lunch, a lunch that meets the nutritional standards of the Type A lunch, or both are served daily.

2. Lunchroom and kitchen facilities are periodically inspected by sanitarians from the local health department.

RECOMMENDED STEPS TO BE TAKEN:

D. The health service unit provides the required space for each type of activity conducted in the unit and is properly equipped with built-in facilities.

RECOMMENDED STEPS TO BE TAKEN:

E. The school site meets the standards established for schools as set forth in the California Administrative Code, Title 5.

1. The size of the elementary school site meets the recommendations set forth in Title 5 of the California Administrative Code. (Five net usable acres plus one additional acre for each 100 pupils of predicted ultimate enrollment, plus one additional acre for each 100 or major fraction of the number of seventh- and eighth-grade pupils for the predicted ultimate maximum enrollment.)

2. The school is centrally located in the geographic area served.

3. The area in which the school is located is relatively free of disturbing noises, noxious odors, and other distractions.

4. Water drains rapidly from outdoor areas.

RECOMMENDED STEPS TO BE TAKEN:

F. A planned procedure is followed to detect and correct possible unsafe conditions of buildings, grounds, and equipment.

RECOMMENDED STEPS TO BE TAKEN:

Continued.

Criteria for evaluating the elementary school health program—cont'd

Criteria	Quality of provision or practice					Changes needed
	Excellent (near perfection)	Good (satisfactory)	Fair (slightly less than satisfactory)	Poor (unsatisfactory)	Provision not made or practice not followed	
IV. Healthful school environment—cont'd	RECOMMENDED STEPS TO BE TAKEN:					
G. The buildings and play areas are designed to provide for the successful operation of the school program and kept in good condition.						
1. All doors providing exit from buildings are equipped with panic bars.						
2. Ceilings and walls of classrooms and inside corridors are constructed with sound-absorbing materials.						
3. Areas or rooms in which noise-producing activities, such as band practice and playing games, take place are located at points where noises are likely to be least disturbing to classes held in other areas.						
4. The enrollments in classes assigned to rooms are not in excess of the number of pupils for which the rooms were originally planned.						
H. Essential provisions have been made to secure in each classroom the conditions needed for eye comfort.	RECOMMENDED STEPS TO BE TAKEN:					
1. The lighting in classrooms is soft, even, properly distributed, and sufficiently bright for eye comfort.						
2. The colors of the walls, ceilings, and chalkboards are conducive to eye comfort.						
I. The classrooms and the library are heated or cooled and ventilated as required to provide good working conditions for teachers and pupils.	RECOMMENDED STEPS TO BE TAKEN:					
J. Drinking fountains in the building and on the school grounds are sufficient in number, of desirable design, of proper height, conveniently located, and cleaned daily.	RECOMMENDED STEPS TO BE TAKEN:					
1. An adequate number of drinking fountains are available (one for each 75 pupils and at least one on each floor of a multi-						

		RECOMMENDED STEPS TO BE TAKEN:		

2. The water supply is regularly inspected by health department personnel.

K. The handwashing and toilet facilities are sufficient in number and kept clean.
1. The toilet rooms are readily accessible from classrooms and play areas.
2. Each toilet room contains at least 1 wash basin equipped with hot and cold running water for every 50 pupils using the room.
3. An adequate number of toilets for girls are available (1 for each 30 girls).
4. An adequate number of toilets and urinals are available for boys (1 toilet for each 60 boys), 1 urinal for each 30 boys).
5. A supply of liquid or powdered soap is available near each wash basin.
6. The supply of toilet paper and hand towels is replenished each day at specified intervals.

		RECOMMENDED STEPS TO BE TAKEN:		

L. Fire prevention equipment is conveniently located and inspected at regular intervals.
1. All school personnel know the location of fire signal switches in the school and of fire alarm boxes near the school.
2. Fire extinguishers are of a type approved by the local fire department and are inspected at regular intervals by fire officials.

		RECOMMENDED STEPS TO BE TAKEN:		

M. The procedures to be followed in the case of various types of disasters are known by all school personnel and pupils.
1. Written procedures to be followed in times of disaster are displayed in prominent places throughout the school.
2. School personnel and pupils have practices and know the procedure to be followed in case of a fire, an earthquake, or other disaster.
3. Fire drills are held monthly.
4. Drills for disasters other than might be caused by fire are held at specified intervals throughout the school year.

I

General criteria for evaluating health instructional materials and comparative text analysis

GENERAL CRITERIA FOR EVALUATING HEALTH INSTRUCTIONAL MATERIALS*

The following criteria are to help you evaluate health instructional materials. Indicate your judgment by circling the appropriate number. Each item must be rated. A separate evaluating sheet is necessary for each set of materials considered for recommendation.

NOTE: Comments that would add to this evaluation would be appreciated. Please use last page.

EVALUATED BY _____ DATE _____
COMMITTEE _____ SCHOOL _____
Data for materials evaluated:

Author _____
Title _____
Publisher or producer _____
Copyright date _____ Type of material _____
Grade level of material being evaluated _____
Is this material part of a series? Yes ☐ Series grade level _____
No ☐

Title of series _____
Cost per item _____

---

*Modified from: Handbook I: Guidelines for the development of instructional materials selection policies, Olympia, Wash., State Office of Public Education.

SUMMARY OF EVALUATION

	High ----------------------------- Low					M*	NA†
I. Text format	5	4	3	2	1	0	0
II. Audiovisual format considerations	5	4	3	2	1	0	0
III. Organization and overall content	5	4	3	2	1	0	0
IV. Bias content	5	4	3	2	1	0	0
V. Teacher's guide	5	4	3	2	1	0	0
VI. Additional support materials	5	4	3	2	1	0	0
VII. Purchase priority	5	4	3	2	1		

I. TEXT FORMAT

	High ----------------------------- Low					M*	NA†
1. General appearance	5	4	3	2	1	0	0
2. Size and color practical for classroom use	5	4	3	2	1	0	0
3. Binding: durability and flexibility	5	4	3	2	1	0	0
4. Quality of paper	5	4	3	2	1	0	0
5. Readability of type	5	4	3	2	1	0	0
6. Appeal of page layouts	5	4	3	2	1	0	0
7. Usefulness of chapter headings	5	4	3	2	1	0	0
8. Appropriateness of illustrations	5	4	3	2	1	0	0
9. Usefulness of references, index, bibliography, appendix	5	4	3	2	1	0	0
10. Consistency of format	5	4	3	2	1	0	0

II. AUDIOVISUAL FORMAT AND CONSIDERATIONS

	High ----------------------------- Low					M*	NA†
1. Sound quality	5	4	3	2	1	0	0
2. Picture quality	5	4	3	2	1	0	0
3. Emotional impact	5	4	3	2	1	0	0
4. Other qualities: vitality, style, imagination	5	4	3	2	1	0	0
5. Authoritative and well-researched, free of propaganda	5	4	3	2	1	0	0
6. Length suitable to audience and content	5	4	3	2	1	0	0
7. Durability	5	4	3	2	1	0	0
8. Usefulness in more than one subject area: write areas here _____	5	4	3	2	1	0	0

III. ORGANIZATION AND OVERALL CONTENT: COVERAGE OF HEALTH AREAS (How comprehensive is the coverage?)

	High ----------------------------- Low					M*	NA†
1. Anatomy and physiology	5	4	3	2	1	0	0
2. Community health (e.g., noise, chemical, water pollution control; community resources)	5	4	3	2	1	0	0

*Missing; material should have had item but does not.
†Not applicable.

Continued.

SUMMARY OF EVALUATION—cont'd

	High				Low	M*	NA†
3. Consumer health (e.g., evaluating health products, use of medicines, components of health examinations, health care delivery system)	5	4	3	2	1	0	0
4. Disease prevention (e.g., life-style and disease, emotional illness, cancer, cardiovascular disorders, immunizations, diseases of interest to ethnic groups; oral health)	5	4	3	2	1	0	0
5. Adult life-style (e.g., changing roles; decisions about sex, marriage, and family; careers)	5	4	3	2	1	0	0
6. Fitness (e.g., benefits of fitness, fitness regimen, grooming and self-concept, fatigue, balanced diets, obesity, ethnic foods)	5	4	3	2	1	0	0
7. Growth and development (e.g., reproduction process, prenatal concerns, tools of inheritance, birth defects, genetic counseling, effects of drugs and nutrition on developing embryo and fetus)	5	4	3	2	1	0	0
8. Mental health (e.g., coping skills, stress, human needs and emotions, self-concept, mental illness, psychologic growth and development, stereotyping)	5	4	3	2	1	0	0
9. Safety and first aid	5	4	3	2	1	0	0
10. Smoking, drugs, and alcohol (psychoactive drugs, medical use prescription and over-the-counter drugs)	5	4	3	2	1	0	0
11. Nutrition (e.g., basic necessities; balance; metabolism; changing needs; facts, fads, and fallacies; preparation)	5	4	3	2	1	0	0

IV. BIAS CONTENT

	High				Low	M*	NA†
1. Presents more than one viewpoint of controversial issues	5	4	3	2	1	0	0
2. Presents accurate facts when generalizations are made	5	4	3	2	1	0	0
3. Includes all socioeconomic levels and settings and all ethnic groups	5	4	3	2	1	0	0
4. Gives balanced treatment of the past and present	5	4	3	2	1	0	0
5. Promotes the diverse character of our nation by:							
(a) Presenting the positive nature of cultural differences	5	4	3	2	1	0	0

	High				Low	M*	NA†
(b) Using languages and models that treat all human beings with respect, dignity, and seriousness	5	4	3	2	1	0	0
(c) Including characters that help students identify positively with their heritage and culture	5	4	3	2	1	0	0
(d) Portraying families realistically (one parent, two parents, several generations)	5	4	3	2	1	0	0
(e) Portraying the handicapped realistically	5	4	3	2	1	0	0
6. Includes minorities and women by:	5	4	3	2	1	0	0
(a) Presenting their roles positively but realistically	5	4	3	2	1	0	0
(b) Having their contributions, inventions, or discoveries appear alongside those of white men	5	4	3	2	1	0	0
(c) Depicting them in a variety of occupations and at all levels in a profession	5	4	3	2	1	0	0
(d) Having their work included in materials	5	4	3	2	1	0	0
(e) Presenting information from their perspective	5	4	3	2	1	0	0
(f) Having appropriate illustrations	5	4	3	2	1	0	0

V. TEACHER'S GUIDE FOR TEXTS OR AUDIOVISUAL MATERIALS

	High				Low	M*	NA†
1. Easy to use	5	4	3	2	1	0	0
2. Answers provided	5	4	3	2	1	0	0
3. Background information	5	4	3	2	1	0	0
4. Teaching strategies	5	4	3	2	1	0	0
5. Ideas for motivation, follow-up, extension	5	4	3	2	1	0	0
6. Guidelines for evaluation	5	4	3	2	1	0	0
7. Inclusion of script	5	4	3	2	1	0	0
8. Bibliography	5	4	3	2	1	0	0

VI. ADDITIONAL SUPPORT MATERIALS THAT ACCOMPANY TEXT

Please list the materials, (e.g., workbooks, tests, and use separate form for each one listed   _____

_____

_____

USE THIS SPACE FOR COMMENTS:

COMPARATIVE TEXT ANALYSIS

The following form, entitled "Comparative Text Analysis," is included as an aid for those who may have the opportunity to review numerous texts in the process of selecting one for local adoption. It can also be used to build a case for replacing old health textbooks. Although the format is designed for facilitating comparison of texts, the items are appropriate for evaluating a single text.

Using the following rating scale, evaluate the material in each area identified.

High------------------------Low	Missing	Not Applicable
4 3 2 1	0	NA

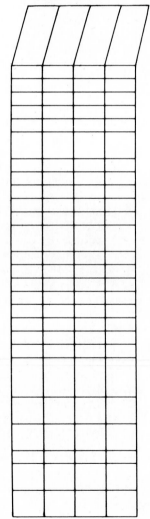

Fill in *title*, *publisher*, and *copyright date* for each text.

A. *TECHNICAL QUALITY*
  1. General appearance
  2. Readability of type
  3. Quality of paper and binding
  4. Appropriateness of illustrations
  5. Format and general organization

B. *EFFECTIVENESS OF MATERIAL*
  1. Adapts to individual needs and/or interests
  2. Has appropriate sequential development
  3. Provides varied teaching and learning strategies
  4. Provides for measuring student achievement
  5. Provides management system for tracking student progress
  6. Provides clearly organized teacher edition

C. *CONTENT*
  1. Consistent with district, program, and course goals
  2. Reflects respect for personal worth
  3. Aids in building positive attitudes and understandings
  4. Depicts cultural diversity
  5. Deals effectively with issues and problems
  6. Offers accurate and/or realistic treatment of subject
  7. Incorporates balanced viewpoints
  8. Makes provision for distinguishing between fact and opinion
  9. Stimulates critical thinking

D. *CRITERIA FOR SEX BIAS*
  1. Material divides qualities such as leadership, imagination, intelligence, and courage approximately evenly between male and female characters.
  2. Females and males are equally represented as central characters in story and illustrative materials.
  3. Both men and women are shown performing similar work in related fields.
  4. Males and females are shown working together.
  5. People are referred to by their own names and roles as often as they are referred to as someone's spouse, parent, or sibling.
  6. Stereotyping language such as "women chatting"/"men discussing" is avoided.

7. Biographic or historic materials include a variety of male and female contributions to society.
8. Both males and females are given credit for discoveries and contributions to social, artistic, and scientific fields.
9. Groups that may include both males and females are referred to in "neutral" language such as "people, mail carriers, fire fighters, or legislators."

E. *CRITERIA FOR RACIAL/ETHNIC BIAS*
   1. Materials contain racial/ethnic balance in main characters and in illustrations.
   2. Oversimplifications and generalizations about racial groups are avoided in illustrations and in text material.
   3. Minority characters are shown in a variety of life-styles in active, decision-making, and leadership roles.
   4. The vocabulary of racism is avoided.
   5. Minority characters are given credit for discoveries and contributions to social, artistic, and scientific fields.

Using the following rating scale, evaluate the material in each area identified.

High------------------------*Low*				*Missing*	*Not Applicable*
4	3	2	1	0	NA

SUMMARY INFORMATION

List total points for each area by Publisher and Title.
A. TECHNICAL QUALITY
B. EFFECTIVENESS OF MATERIAL
C. CONTENT
D. SEX BIAS
E. RACIAL/ETHNIC BIAS

Grand total scores

Additional rationale for selection of these materials: _____

_____

_____

INDEX